Words on Words

Quotations About Language and Languages

David Crystal and Hilary Crystal

The University of Chicago Press

The University of Chicago Press, Chicago 60637
Penguin Books Ltd, London UB7 0DA, England

08 07 06 05 04 03 02 01 00   1 2 3 4 5

Library of Congress Cataloging-in-Publication Data

Crystal, David, 1941–
    Words on words : quotations about language and languages / David
Crystal and Hilary Crystal.
        p. cm.
    Includes bibliographical references and index.
    ISBN 0-226-12201-8 (alk. paper)
    1. Language and languages—Quotations, maxims, etc.   I. Crystal,
Hilary.   II. Title.

    P106.C765 2000
    400—dc21   00-039221

This book is printed on acid-free paper.

Contents

Introduction

There have been books of quotations on music, politics, science, pop songs, and many other subjects, with such fascinating titles as *Read My Lips* and *Rave On* – but not (until now) on language. As is often the case, the motivation for the book came from a simple question. Our student son, wanting to use a half-remembered quotation for a university essay on language, had asked us what it was exactly, and who had said it. Something about 'a language being a dialect with an army', he said. Yes, we half-remembered the quotation too, but could not recall who had said it. It took half an hour of trawling through our library to find a source and to discover, in the process, that the quotation was not quite right (see 10:33). We reflected on the cumulative time we must have spent hunting down quotations in the past. We then looked at the frequency with which quotations about language actually appear in publications about language – especially as epigraphs at the opening of a chapter or the front of a book, as a taking-off point for an article, or as the focus of an examination question. Rare indeed is it to find an author who does not at some point stand on the linguistic shoulders (or hide behind the back) of another. We can only guess at the time and frustration experienced within the language professions as a whole, as their members engage in the task of quotation-hunting – either tracking down something one already (half) knows, or finding something freshly appropriate to what one is writing. It is also possible to estimate the extent to which this poses a problem, for about a fifth of the language quotations which we found in general anthologies turned out to be inaccurate when checked against their sources.

But it is not only professional linguists who use quotations about language. Language is one of those topics with enormous popular appeal – for it is the stock-in-trade of orators, media personalities, and writers of all kinds. An apt quotation about pronunciation, slang, or style is likely to enhance many a lay opinion, whether the context be a school essay, a radio quiz show, a political speech, a novel, or a letter to the press complaining about a point of usage. When we encounter language quotations (as these pages demonstrate) from such different worlds as Plato and Winnie-the-Pooh, Shakespeare and James Bond, it is evident that we are dealing here with a domain whose interest and relevance is universal – far greater, at any rate, than the topics which are already well served by quotation collections. Indeed, insightful comments about language are found in every walk of life. The problem with this book has, accordingly, been not how to fill it, but how to stop. Every (literary) author we have looked at has provided us with material. And we have, of course, read only a tiny fraction of what could be read, and listened to an even tinier fraction of what exists in sound archives.

Sources

Where have the quotations in this book come from, in fact? From many different sources. We do not believe in reinventing the wheel. We therefore began by reading all the standard anthologies of quotations, to see what they had already picked up on the language topic (not a great deal). We then chose certain key authors and worked systematically through them – if 'work' is the right word for having an excuse to read or re-read all of Shakespeare, Dickens, Wordsworth, Twain, and others. Several authors are known for their observations on language, such as Johnson, Emerson, Hazlitt, Butler, Wilde, Castiglione, and Montaigne, and their essays received special attention. One source led to another, because often observations about language, at a given time, were made in response to others – the nineteenth-century arguments about the origins of language are a case in point, bringing together a cluster of famous names, such as Darwin, Müller, and Whitney, as well as some famous extracts (such as the Psammetichus origins of language experiment) which, because of their standing in the history of linguistic thought, demand more space than the average quotation. Some sources were read with high expectations, but yielded next to nothing – such as Pepys' *Diary*. Others were unexpectedly fruitful, such as the works of Laurence Sterne.

We would of course like to have read everything, and people who are unable to find a favourite quotation of theirs within these pages must remember that we were working within a space constraint of 150,000 words and a time-frame of just over a year, from conception to publisher's deadline. We are under no illusions, then, that this book is anything more than a first bite at the language-quotations apple. In particular, we are conscious of the way we have inevitably focused on English-language authors. Parallel books could be compiled using the literature of any language, and we hope they will appear. In the meantime, although we have included items by authors of some forty nationalities, it is obvious that there will be a vast amount more in the leading authors of other cultures, and we acknowledge this limitation.

Readers aware of the first author's background in linguistics will be surprised to find relatively few quotations from professional linguists here. The reason is not for want of searching. On the whole, linguists are remarkably unquoteworthy. There are of course quotations aplenty in the specialist linguistics literature, but these quotations are there to help make a professional case; they are typically technical, make sense only in context, and offer nothing by way of dramatic or memorable expression. A search through hundreds of pages of the main linguistic authors produced nothing especially memorable, by way of a quotation.[1] Textbooks, monographs, popular introductions, and the like, provide very little, sometimes nothing at all. That is why we have nothing, for example, from such famous names as the phonetician Daniel Jones, or from Roman Jakobson. The samples of their work which were chosen proved fruitless. Conscious of what professional linguists would say if there were no linguistics personalities here at all, we have done our best with Saussure, Chomsky, Bloomfield, and some other major names, extracting some of their observations which have been

1. This is not something we recommend a professional to do very often. Re-reading the books one read as an undergraduate, forty years on, brings to light an uncomfortable number of ideas that one had always thought of as one's own! Equally discomfiting is one's inability to understand one's own, often extensive, marginalia.

so widely repeated over the years that they perhaps deserve the status of general quotations. The same point applies to, for example, the observation from Sir William Jones about Sanskrit, that of Benjamin Lee Whorf about language and thought, and a few other cases. Just occasionally, we have encountered a linguist who evidently delighted in the art of the well-turned phrase – Edward Sapir and Otto Jespersen are prime examples. But, on the whole, we were disappointed in our search through the standard texts.

Criteria

All of this raises the question, 'What counts as a quotation?' We used several criteria. First, in view of the general nature of the readership of this book, the subject matter had to be of a correspondingly general kind – an observation about the nature of language as a whole, or about one of its widely recognized branches or topics, such as speaking, reading, usage, eloquence, slang, and grammar. Secondly, we were looking for memorability, in the sense that an extract had already achieved some currency within the English-language community – a kind of linguistic equivalent of 'To be or not to be'. (There were very few of these.) Thirdly, we looked for relevant items which have actually been used as quotations in the press, in textbooks, and elsewhere. Fourthly, we looked for succinctness and autonomy of expression. An ideal quotation, for us, would be a single sentence long, making a point which stands alone without need of any further context. There are actually very few of these, too, other than proverbial expressions – as illustrated by our regular use of square brackets at the beginning of a quotation to give the context for what follows. Fifthly, we looked for observations which relied on vivid or unusual metaphors, similes, and other figurative expressions. There were plenty of these, especially in the literary domain. On occasion, we found fine imaginative treatments of a topic which extended over several sentences, and we have included these as wholes – the boundary between a quotation and an anecdote is often difficult to draw. Sixthly – a negative criterion – we tried to avoid banal observations of the 'language is complicated' type. And lastly, we found we had a penchant for ironic, satirical, humorous, or playful observations about language, and there turned out to be quite a large number of these.

Using these criteria, one quickly develops an eye for a potential quotation (with a single exception).[1] The vast majority, accordingly, are personal choices, not previously selected (as far as we are aware) in any other book. Grouped into themes, we think they make an interesting selection – indeed, we have sometimes found the unexpected juxtapositions of opinions quite fascinating, and a potential source of many a possible article on the history of ideas. At times, we have included an item simply because it identifies a little-known work on the subject, which we think people interested in language ought to know about. For example, we had never read before Christopher Morley's article 'What Men Live By': it is a little gem of linguistic humour, and (in the spirit of the collector) we think everybody ought to know it (see 26:89–91). There have been many other occasions when we came across an observation about language expressed with great insight in a completely unexpected place. To draw attention to such sources should be one of the aims of a quotations anthology.

1. The exception is the writing of the first author, where he found it impossible to make a judgement about whether anything he had written was quoteworthy. We have therefore included extracts from his work (using the above criteria) only in those cases where we found others had quoted him. There are very few of these. So it goes.

Organization

We have used a semantic (rather than an authorial or alphabetical) approach in this book, identifying sixty-five themes, grouped into seven topics, and allocating quotations accordingly. Several quotations can be assigned to more than one theme, so cross-references identifying further relevant items are given at the end of each thematic section. Within themes, quotations are ordered alphabetically by author, and then (if more than one quotation appears from a single author) by date. Sequences of proverbs within a theme are ordered alphabetically on the basis of the most relevant keyword (for example, a proverb about *speech* will appear before one about *words*). Cross-references between individual quotations are occasionally added, when we have noticed a close connection between them.

After each quotation we give its source, beginning with the author's name (where this is relevant), the date of the quotation (where known), and the location. Within each quotation, we try to provide continuous extracts, using ellipsis dots only to avoid unnecessary discourse-connecting words such as 'thus' or 'however', or to eliminate an authorial parenthesis or amplification. Quite often we give some relevant context for a quotation, placed before it within square brackets. This is especially useful when the quotation is from a play or novel, where we need to identify the speaker (and often, addressee). The topic to which a quotation relates also sometimes needs to be explained, and as far as possible we do this using a paraphrase of the author's own words.

Because most of the quotations are not immediately recognizable, in the way that 'To be or not to be' is, there are implications for the design of the index. An index of first lines, or famous metaphors, or key words in context, is not the way to handle the material in this book. Of course, if a quotation *is* well known, then it must be handled accordingly: thus, 'all grammars leak' is indexed as a whole (as well as under *grammars* and *leak*). But most of the items are not like this. As a result, the general index looks much more like a conventional book index, with important concepts selected and grouped so that people who want to find quotations relevant to a particular topic (other than those evident from the sectional grouping into general themes) will be able to do so. Some quite interesting groups of sub-headings emerge in this way. This approach also proves to be the most useful when trying to track down a quotation which has been translated into English, and where the actual words used in the translation can only represent (rather than uniquely identify) the words found in the original.

The general index is, accordingly, much larger than the indexes usually found in books of quotations. It has been designed with two different aims in mind. First, and most obviously, it is to help people find a quotation that they already know (although they are unclear about its source or author) or – far more important – that they *think* they know. If our own experience is typical, people regularly half-remember quotations. The problem for the indexer is that there is no way of predicting which half of the quotation will be recalled. All the key words and phrases in a quotation therefore have to be seen as potential access points, and the index must include them all. Secondly, the general index has to help people find a set of quotations which they do not know already but which they are looking for in order to meet a particular need (in a speech, article, lecture . . .). Here, the thematic divisions of the book are an important resource – but the sixty-five divisions we have recognized do not go far enough to meet the needs of people who want to know whether there are any language quotations about Hebrew, heaven, or horses, or whether words have ever been compared to bees, birds, or boats. An in-depth alphabetical index (arranged word by word) is the most convenient way of aiding their search.

There is a separate index of authors, arranged letter-by-letter, and giving their dates, nationalities, and professions. The dates are to enable readers to see the period within which an author was writing: for example, observations about English as an emerging world language vary in their impact, depending on the century in which they are being uttered. The nationalities and professions add an important contextual dimension. *What* is said is often not as important as *who* said it. Essentially the same observation can take on very different implications if it comes from a poet, a professional linguist, or a film star – or, to continue the above example, whether a claim about world English is being made by an English or a French speaker. After each author, there is a listing of all the quotations from that person in the book. There is also a separate index of sources.

Envoi

Any second edition of a book of quotations is likely to be much better than the first, because it benefits from readers who take the trouble to tell the editors about their personal favourites omitted from the collection. If this book does ever achieve a new edition, we are in no doubt that this will happen, and we very much welcome proposals for inclusion, in anticipation.

David Crystal
Hilary Crystal
Holyhead, May 1999

Language

1 *The Nature of Language*

The nature and functions of language

1:1 Colours speak all Languages, but Words are understood only by such a People or Nation. For this reason, tho' Mens Necessities quickly put them on finding out Speech, Writing is probably of a later Invention than Painting.

Joseph Addison, 27 June 1712, 'Secondary Pleasures of the Imagination: Consideration Limited to Literature', *The Spectator*, no. 416

1:2 Language is only in part an individual instrument. It is in the main a community instrument used for community purposes. As such it tends to launch out on a career of its own, to which individuals contribute very much as the coral insect contributes to the growth of a coral reef or island.

L. S. Amery, November 1949, *Thought and Language*, Presidential Address to the English Association, p. 7

1:3 Language has been the master tool which man, in his endless adventure after knowledge and power, has shaped for himself, and which, in its turn, has shaped the human mind as we know it. It has continuously extended and conserved the store of knowledge upon which mankind has drawn. It has furnished the starting-point of all our science. It has been the instrument of social cohesion and of moral law, and through it human society has developed and found itself. Language, indeed, has been the soul of mankind.

L. S. Amery, November 1949, *Thought and Language*, Presidential Address to the English Association, p. 19

1:4 [Mrs Flowers, on Marguerite's reluctance to talk in class] 'Now no one is going to make you talk – possibly no one can. But bear in mind,

language is man's way of communicating with his fellow man and it is language alone which separates him from the lower animals.' That was a totally new idea to me, and I would need time to think about it. 'Your grandmother says you read a lot. Every chance you get. That's good but not enough. Words mean more than what is set down on paper. It takes the human voice to infuse them with the shades of deeper meaning.' I memorized the part about the human voice infusing words. It seemed so valid and poetic.

Maya Angelou, 1969, *I Know Why the Caged Bird Sings*, Ch. 15

1:5 Any refusal of language is a death.

Roland Barthes, 1957, '*Le myth, aujourd'hui*', in *Mythologies* (trans.)

1:6 Language is a skin; I rub my language against another language.

Roland Barthes, 1977, '*Déclaration*', in *Fragments d'un discours amoureux* (trans.)

1:7 It cannot be denied that words are of excellent use, in that by their means all that stock of knowledge which has been purchased by the joint labours of inquisitive men in all ages and nations, may be drawn into the view and made the possession of one single person. But at the same time it must be owned that most parts of knowledge have been strangely perplexed and darkened by the abuse of words, and general ways of speech wherein they are delivered, that it may almost be made a question whether language has contributed more to the hindrance or advancement of the sciences.

George Berkeley, 1710, *Principles of Human Knowledge*, Introduction

1:8 Deep waters, such are the words of man: a swelling torrent, a fountain of life.
The Bible, Proverbs 18:4 (Jerusalem Bible)

1:9 [book title] A mouthful of air.
Anthony Burgess, 1992, *A Mouthful of Air: Language and Languages, especially English*

1:10 [Erewhonian belief] Reason betrays men into the drawing of hard and fast lines, and to the defining by language – language being like the sun, which rears and then scorches.
Samuel Butler (1835–1902), 1872, *Erewhon*, Ch. 21

1:11 The essence of language lies in the intentional conveyance of ideas from one living being to another through the instrumentality of arbitrary tokens or symbols agreed upon and understood by both as being associated with the particular ideas in question.
Samuel Butler (1835–1902), 1890, lecture in London on *Thought and Language*

1:12 [on Nigel, having said 'I love you' to Frederica] He has learned what a surprising number of men never learn, the strategic importance of those words. He is not a verbal animal. Much of what he says, Frederica has noticed without yet thinking about it, is dictated by the glaze of language that slides over and obscures the surface of the world he moves in, a language that is quite sure what certain things are, a man, a woman, a girl, a mother, a duty. Language in this world is for keeping things safe in their places.
A. S. Byatt, 1996, *Babel Tower*, Ch. 2

1:13 It is said that life and death are under the power of language.
Hélène Cixous, 1969, *Dedans* (trans.)

1:14 Language is a poor thing. You fill your lungs with wind and shake a little slit in your throat, and make mouths, and that shakes the air; and the air shakes a pair of little drums in my head – a very complicated arrangement, with lots of bones behind – and my brain seizes your meaning in the rough. What a roundabout way, and what a waste of time.
George du Maurier, 1891, *Petter Ibbetson*

1:15 [Ladislaw, contrasting painting with language] Language gives a fuller image, which is all the better for being vague. After all, the true seeing is within; and painting stares at you with an insistent imperfection.
George Eliot, 1871–2, *Middlemarch*, II, Ch. 19

1:16 The etymologist finds the deadest word to have been once a brilliant picture. Language is fossil poetry.
Ralph Waldo Emerson, 1844, 'The Poet', in *Essays: Second Series*

1:17 The poet is the Namer, or Language-maker, naming things sometimes after their appearance, sometimes after their essence, and giving to every one its own name and not another's, thereby rejoicing the intellect, which delights in detachment or boundary. The poets made all the words, and therefore language is the archives of history.
Ralph Waldo Emerson, 1844, 'The Poet', in *Essays: Second Series*

1:18 We infer the spirit of the nation in great measure from the language, which is a sort of monument to which each forcible individual in a course of many hundred years has contributed a stone. And, universally, a good example of this social force is the veracity of language, which cannot be debauched. In any controversy concerning morals, an appeal may be made with safety to the sentiments which the language of the people expresses. Proverbs, words and grammar-inflections convey the public sense with more purity and precision than the wisest individual.
Ralph Waldo Emerson, 1844, 'Nominalist and Realist', in *Essays: Second Series*

1:19 Language is a city to the building of which every human being brought a stone; yet he is no more to be credited with the grand result than the acaleph which adds a cell to the coral reef which is the basis of the continent.
Ralph Waldo Emerson, 1875, 'Quotation and Originality', in *Letters and Social Aims*

1:20 Reading makes a full man, meditation a profound man, discourse a clear man.
Benjamin Franklin, 1732–57, *Poor Richard's Almanack* [cf. 20:4]

1:21 Language was all that I could do, but it never, I felt, came close to a dance or a song or a gliding through water. Language could serve as a weapon, a shield and a disguise, it had many strengths. It could bully, cajole, deceive, wheedle and intimidate. Sometimes it could even delight, amuse, charm, seduce and endear, but always as a solo turn, never a dance.
Stephen Fry, 1997, 'Joining in', Sect. 3, in *Moab Is My Washpot*

1:22 The war is language, / language abused / for Advertisement / language used / like magic for power on the planet / Black Magic language / formulas for reality.

Allen Ginsberg, 1972, 'Wichita Vortex Sutra', in A. De Loach (ed.), *The East-Side Scene: American Poetry 1960–65*

1:23 There's a cool web of language winds us in, / Retreat from too much joy or too much fear.

Robert Graves, 1927, 'The Cool Web'

1:24 Language, – human language, – after all is but little better than the croak and cackle of fowls, and other utterances of brute nature, – sometimes not so adequate.

Nathaniel Hawthorne, 14 July 1850, *American Notebooks*

1:25 Language . . . makes progress possible.

S. I. Hayakawa, 1939, *Language in Thought and Action*, Ch. 1

1:26 Language is the house of Being.

Martin Heidegger, 1947, *Letter on Humanism* (trans. P. D. Hertz)

1:27 Man is man only because he is granted the promise of language, because he is needful to language, that he may speak it.

Martin Heidegger, 1959, 'The Nature of Language', in *On the Way to Language* (trans. P. D. Hertz)

1:28 [the guiding keyword for the nature of language] The being of language: the language of being.

Martin Heidegger, 1959, 'The Nature of Language', in *On the Way to Language* (trans. P. D. Hertz)

1:29 Speciall uses of Speech are these; First, to Register, what by cogitation, wee find to be the cause of any thing, present or past; and what we find things present or past may produce, or effect: which in summe, is acquiring of Arts. Secondly, to shew to others that knowledge which we have attained; which is, to Counsell, and Teach one another. Thirdly, to make known to others our wills, and purposes, that we may have the mutuall help of one another. Fourthly, to please and delight our selves, and others, by playing with our words, for pleasure or ornament, innocently.

Thomas Hobbes, 1651, 'Of Speech', in *Leviathan*, I, Ch. 4

1:30 [identifying the four 'abuses of language'] First, when men register their thoughts wrong, by the inconstancy of the signification of their words; by which they register for their conceptions, that which they never conceived; and so deceive themselves. Secondly, when they use words metaphorically; that is, in other sense than that they are ordained for; and thereby deceive others. Thirdly, when by words they declare that to be their will, which is not. Fourthly, when they use them to grieve one another.

Thomas Hobbes, 1651, 'Of Speech', in *Leviathan*, I, Ch. 4

1:31 *Language*, the most valuable single possession of the human race.

Charles F. Hockett, 1958, *A Course in Modern Linguistics*, Ch. 1

1:32 Man does not live on bread alone: his other necessity is communication.

Charles F. Hockett, 1958, *A Course in Modern Linguistics*, Ch. 64 [cf. 57:10]

1:33 It really is intolerable that we can say only one thing at a time; for social behavior displays many features at the same time, and so in taking them up one by one we necessarily do outrage to its rich, dark, organic unity.

George C. Homans, 1961, *Social Behavior: Its Elementary Forms*

1:34 Since the *natural disposition* to language is universal in man, and everyone must possess the key to the understanding of all languages, it follows automatically that the *form* of all languages must be essentially the *same*, and always achieve the universal purpose. The *difference* can lie only in the means, and only within the limits permitted by attainment of the goal.

Wilhelm von Humboldt, 1836, *On Language: the Diversity of Human Language-structure and its Influence on the Mental Development of Mankind* (trans. P. Heath), p. 214

1:35 We shall never approach a complete understanding of the nature of language, so long as we confine our attention to its intellectual function as a means of communicating thought.

Otto Jespersen, 1946, 'Speech and Language', in *Mankind, Nation and Individual*, Ch. 1

1:36 *Language* most shewes a man: speake that I may see thee. It springs out of the most retired, and inmost parts of us, and is the Image of the Parent of it, the mind.

Ben Jonson, 1640 (published posthumously), *Timber: or, Discoveries made upon Men and Matter* [cf. 17:31]

1:37 My language is the universal whore whom I have to make into a virgin.

Karl Kraus, quoted in W. H. Auden, *The Dyer's Hand*, 'Prologue: Writing'

1:38 Language is a form of human reason, which has its reasons which are unknown to man.

Claude Lévi-Strauss, 1962, *La Pensée sauvage* (trans.), Ch. 9

1:39 Language exists to communicate whatever it can communicate.

C. S. Lewis, 1960, *Studies in Words*, Ch. 12

1:40 God having designed Man for a sociable Creature, made him not only with an inclination, and under necessity to have fellowship with those of his own kind; but furnished him also with Language, which was to be the great Instrument, and common Tye of Society.

John Locke, 1690, 'Of Words or Language in General', in *An Essay Concerning Humane Understanding*, III, Ch. 1, Sect. 1

1:41 The mastery over reality, both technical and social, grows side by side with the knowledge of how to use words.

Bronislaw Malinowski, 1935, 'The Language of Magic and Gardening', in *Coral Gardens and their Magic*, II, Div. 5

1:42 For whatever is truly wonderous and fearful in man, never yet was put into words or books.

Herman Melville, 1851, *Moby Dick*, Ch. 110

1:43 For the account of our tung, both in pen and speche, no man will dout thereof, who is able to iudge what those thinges be, which make anie tung to be of account, which things I take to be thré, the autoritie of the peple which speak it, the matter & argument, wherein the speche dealeth, the manifold vse, for which the speche serueth. For which all thré, our tung nedeth not to giue place, to anie of her peres [*peers*].

Richard Mulcaster, 1582, *The First Part of the Elementarie*, Ch. 13

1:44 A good simulation, be it religious myth or scientific theory, gives us a sense of mastery over experience. To represent something symbolically, as we do when we speak or write, is somehow to capture it, thus making it one's own.

Heinz R. Pagels, 1988, *The Dreams of Reason*

1:45 Language, as commonly apprehended, is a human invention, designed to meet a human need, a fact so excruciatingly obvious that you'd think that no one could forget it – yet some philologists do forget it.

Eric Partridge, 1963, *The Gentle Art of Lexicography*, Ch. 2

1:46 One goes to the potter for pots, but not to the grammarian for words. Language is already there among the people.

Patanjali, 2nd century BC, *Mahabhasya* (trans.)

1:47 The tongue weaves for clothes; the pen tills for food.

Proverbial (Chinese)

1:48 Only where there is language is there world.

Adrienne Rich, 1969, 'The Demon Lover', in *Leaflets*

1:49 Language . . . is the instrument of all our distinctively human development, of everything in which we go beyond the other animals.

I. A. Richards, 1936, *The Philosophy of Rhetoric*, p. 131

1:50 Philosophy is a battle against the bewitchment of our intelligence by means of language.

Antoine de Saint-Exupéry, attributed, mid 20th century (trans.) [but see also 2:148]

1:51 Language is a purely human and non-instinctive method of communicating ideas, emotions, and desires by means of a system of voluntarily produced symbols. These symbols are, in the first instance, auditory and they are produced by the so-called 'organs of speech'.

Edward Sapir, 1921, *Language*, Ch. 1

1:52 Language is probably the most self-contained, the most massively resistant of all social phenomena. It is easier to kill it off than to disintegrate its individual form.

Edward Sapir, 1921, *Language*, Ch. 9

1:53 Language is the most massive and inclusive art we know, a mountainous and anonymous work of unconscious generations.

Edward Sapir, 1921, *Language*, Ch. 10

1:54 Language is itself the collective art of expression, a summary of thousands upon thousands of individual intuitions.

Edward Sapir, 1921, *Language*, Ch. 11

1:55 Language is a great force of socialization, probably the greatest that exists.

Edward Sapir, 1933, 'Language', in *Encyclopedia of the Social Sciences*, IX

1:56 I distrust the incommunicable: it is the source of all violence.

Jean-Paul Sartre, July 1947, '*Qu'est-ce que la littérature?* [What is literature?]', in *Les Temps Modernes* (trans.)

1:57 Language is a social fact.

Ferdinand de Saussure, 1916, *Course in General Linguistics* (trans. W. Baskin), Introduction, Ch. 2

1:58 Language is a system of signs that express ideas.

Ferdinand de Saussure, 1916, *Course in General Linguistics* (trans. W. Baskin), Introduction, Ch. 3

1:59 Language is comparable to a symphony in that what the symphony actually is stands completely apart from how it is performed.

Ferdinand de Saussure, 1916, *Course in General Linguistics* (trans. W. Baskin), Introduction, Ch. 4

1:60 Language exists in the form of a sum of impressions deposited in the brain of each member of a community, almost like a dictionary of which identical copies have been distributed to each individual.

Ferdinand de Saussure, 1916, *Course in General Linguistics* (trans. W. Baskin), Introduction, Ch. 4

1:61 A game of chess is like an artificial realization of what language offers in a natural form.

Ferdinand de Saussure, 1916, *Course in General Linguistics* (trans. W. Baskin), I, Ch. 3

1:62 Syllables govern the World.

John Selden, 1689, 'CIX – Power. State', in *Table-Talk*

1:63 We live inside the act of discourse.

George Steiner, 1967, 'The Retreat from the Word', in *Language and Silence*

1:64 Language seeks vengeance on those who cripple it.

George Steiner, 1967, 'The Retreat from the Word', in *Language and Silence*

1:65 Everything forgets. But not a language. When it has been injected with falsehood, only the most drastic truth can cleanse it. Instead, the post-war history of the German language has been one of dissimulation and deliberate forgetting.

George Steiner, 1967, 'The Hollow Miracle', in *Language and Silence*

1:66 Languages code immemorial reflexes and twists of feeling, remembrances of action that transcend individual recall, contours of communal experience as subtly decisive as the

contours of sky and land in which a civilization ripens. An outsider can master a language as a rider masters his mount; he rarely becomes as one with its undefined, subterranean motion.

George Steiner, 1967, 'K', in *Language and Silence*

1:67 Eros and language mesh at every point. Intercourse and discourse, copula and copulation, are sub-classes of the dominant fact of communication.

George Steiner, 1975, *After Babel*, Ch. 1

1:68 Language is the main instrument of man's refusal to accept the world as it is.

George Steiner, 1975, *After Babel*, Ch. 3

1:69 [on some approaches to language] The idea that language itself is the great philosophical mystery, and that it has some sort of life of its own, that we are its creatures, is brought in to reinforce ... conclusions about the role of metaphor, contradiction, paradox, and ambiguity that ... deriv[e] from the ramification of the Hegelian notion of the dialectic. Language, eight-armed, problematic, demiurgic, infinitely entrailed, must be honoured. Its riddling, jokey, mischievous, metaphoric, flawed, lapsible, parapraxic life must not be repressed, but tolerated, pleasured, submitted to, enjoyed, and so revealed for what it is.

Galen Strawson, March 1982, *Quarto*

1:70 Every language has the right to be regarded as an actual, existing organism, not merely as the representative of earlier stages.

Henry Sweet, 1876, 'Words, Logic and Grammar', in *Transactions of the Philological Society*

1:71 Man invented language to satisfy his deep need to complain.

Lily Tomlin, quoted in Steven Pinker, 1994, *The Language Instinct*, Ch. 2

1:72 I found it impossible to make many steps in the search after truth and the nature of human understanding, of good and evil, of right and wrong, without well considering the nature of language, which appeared to me to be inseparably connected with them.

John Horne Tooke, 1786, *The Diversions of Purley*, p. 7

1:73 Language contains so faithful a record of the good and of the evil which in time past have been working in the minds and hearts of men, we shall not err, if we regard it as a moral barometer indicating and permanently marking the rise or fall of a nation's life.

Richard Chenevix Trench, 1851, 'On the Morality in Words', in *On the Study of Words*, Lecture 3

1:74 Language is the expression of ideas; and if the people of our country cannot preserve an identity of ideas, they cannot retain an identity of language.

Noah Webster, 1828, *American Dictionary of the English Language*, Preface

1:75 Each word may be not unfitly compared to an invention; it has its own place, mode, and circumstances of devisal, its preparation in the previous habits of speech, its influence in determining the after-progress of speech-development; but every language in the gross is an institution, on which scores or hundreds of generations and unnumbered thousands of individual workers have labored.

William Dwight Whitney, 1875, 'Nature and Origin of Language', in *The Life and Growth of Language*, Ch. 14

1:76 [on the need for expression through the medium of colour] Some artists feel their passion too intense to be expressed in the simplicity of language, and find in crimson and gold a mode of speech more congenial because not quite so translucent.

Oscar Wilde, 1877–8, in Richard Ellmann, *Oscar Wilde* (1987), Ch. 4

1:77 The limits of my language mean the limits of my world.

Ludwig Wittgenstein, 1921, *Tractatus Logico-Philosophicus* (trans.), p. 148

1:78 I shall in the future again and again draw your attention to what I shall call language games. These are ways of using signs simpler than those in which we use the signs of our highly complicated everyday language. Language games are the forms of language with which a child begins to make use of words. The study of language games is the study of primitive forms of language or primitive languages.

Ludwig Wittgenstein, 1933–4, *The Blue Book*, in *The Blue and Brown Books* (1965), p. 17

1:79 For remember that in general we don't use language according to strict rules – it hasn't been taught us by means of strict rules, either. *We*, in our discussions on the other hand, constantly compare language with a calculus proceeding according to exact rules.

This is a very one-sided way of looking at language.

Ludwig Wittgenstein, 1933–4, *The Blue Book*, in *The Blue and Brown Books* (1965), p. 25

See also: 3:27, 10:7, 17:13–14, 17:16, 17:31

2 *Language in Thinking and Thought*

Thinking and reasoning in relation to speech and language

2:1 No one means all he says, and yet very few say all they mean, for words are slippery and thought is viscous.
Henry Adams, 1907, 'The Grammar of Science', in *The Education of Henry Adams*, Ch. 31

2:2 When our Thoughts are great and just, they are often obscured by the sounding Phrases, hard Metaphors, and forced Expressions in which they are cloathed.
Joseph Addison, 14 April 1711, 'English Tragedy: Style, Language and Verse', *The Spectator*, no. 39

2:3 The word, or thought – for the word *is* the whole thought – is then just the instrument of our particular purpose, be it to convey or gain information or to result in action. We use it, as the tennis player uses his racket, as a necessary link between purpose and result.
L. S. Amery, November 1949, *Thought and Language*, Presidential Address to the English Association, p. 7

2:4 Words spoken are symbols or signs of affections or impressions of the soul; written words are the signs of words spoken. As writing, so also is speech not the same for all races of men. But the mental affections themselves, of which these words are primarily signs, are the same for the whole of mankind, as are also the objects of which these affections are representations or likenesses, images, copies.
Aristotle, 4th century BC, *De interpretatione* (trans. H. P. Cook), I

2:5 [reflecting on the laws of numbers and dimensions held in memory] I have heard the sounds of the words by which their meaning is expressed when they are discussed, but the words are one thing and the principles another. The words may sometimes be spoken in Latin and at other times in Greek, but the principles are neither Greek nor Latin. They are not language at all.
St Augustine, 397–8, *Confessions* (trans. R. S. Pine-Coffin), X, Sect. 12

2:6 Never speak more clearly than you think.
Howard Henry Baker, junior, 6 September 1987, *New York Times*

2:7 Thought itself needs words. It runs on them like a long wire. And if it loses the habit of words, little by little it becomes shapeless, somber.
Ugo Betti, 1946, *Crime on Goat Island* (trans.), I. iv

2:8 Thoughts hardly to be packed / Into a narrow act, / Fancies that broke through language and escaped.
Robert Browning, 1864, 'Rabbi Ben Ezra', stanza 25

2:9 Wordiness and intellection – / The more with them, the further astray we go; / Away therefore with wordiness and intellection, / And there is no place where we cannot pass freely.
Buddhist Scriptures, c.600, 'On Believing in Mind', in *Seng-ts'an* (trans. E. Conze, 1959), II, Ch. 3, Sect. 5

2:10 It is extremely natural for us to desire to see such our thoughts put into the dress of words, without which indeed we can scarce have a clear and distinct idea of them our selves.
Eustace Budgell, 1711–12, *The Spectator*, no. 379

2:11 Words are but pictures, true or false, design'd / To draw the lines and features of the mind; / The characters and artificial draughts /

T'express the inward images of thoughts; / And artists say a picture may be good, / Although the moral be not understood; / Whence some infer they may admire a style, / Though all the rest be e'er so mean and vile; / Applaud th' outsides of words, but never mind / With what fantastic tawdry they are lin'd.

Samuel Butler (1612–80), 1670s, 'Satire upon the Imperfection and Abuse of Human Learning', fragments of an intended second part

2:12 Thought is no more identical with language than feeling is identical with the nervous system.

Samuel Butler (1835–1902), 1890, lecture in London on 'Thought and Language'

2:13 Words are organised thoughts, as living forms are organised actions.

Samuel Butler (1835–1902), *The Note-Books of Samuel Butler* (1912)

2:14 The mere fact that a thought or idea can be expressed articulately in words involves that it is still open to question; and the mere fact that a difficulty can be definitely conceived involves that it is open to solution.

Samuel Butler (1835–1902), *The Note-Books of Samuel Butler* (1912)

2:15 Words impede and either kill, or are killed by, perfect thought; but they are, as a scaffolding, useful, if not indispensable, for the building up of imperfect thought and helping to perfect it.

Samuel Butler (1835–1902), *The Note-Books of Samuel Butler* (1912)

2:16 [Professor Teufelsdröckh] Language is called the Garment of Thought: however, it should rather be, Language is the Flesh-Garment, the Body, of thought. . . . Metaphors are her stuff: examine Language; what, if you except some few primitive elements (of natural sound), what is it all but Metaphors, recognised as such, or no longer recognised; still fluid and florid, or now solid-grown and colourless? If those same primitive elements are the osseous fixtures in the Flesh-Garment, Language, – then are Metaphors its muscles and tissues and living integuments.

Thomas Carlyle, 1833, *Sartor Resartus*, I, Ch. 11

2:17 Speech is too often not . . . the art of concealing Thought; but of quite stifling and suspending Thought, so that there is none to conceal:

Thomas Carlyle, 1833, *Sartor Resartus*, III, Ch. 3 [cf. 2:139]

2:18 'Then you should say what you mean,' the March Hare went on. 'I do,' Alice hastily replied; 'at least, – at least I mean what I say – that's the same thing, you know.' 'Not the same thing a bit!' said the Hatter. 'Why, you might just as well say that "I see what I eat" is the same thing as "I eat what I see!"'

Lewis Carroll, 1865, *Alice's Adventures in Wonderland*, Ch. 7 [cf. 2:69]

2:19 The carl [churl] spak oo [one] thing, but he thoghte another.

Geoffrey Chaucer, 1390s, 'The Friar's Tale', 270, in *The Canterbury Tales*

2:20 Pedagogy is the queen of all the arts, but in teaching we unavoidably must use an enormous number of words as go-betweens, which creates confusion, because those who listen must transform the words into concepts and ideas.

Comenius, 17th century, quoted as an epigraph in Leo Braudy, 'Succeeding in Language', in L. Michaels and C. Ricks (eds), *The State of the Language* (1980), (trans.)

2:21 I see grammar as the first part of the art of thinking.

Étienne de Condillac, 1775, '*Grammaire*', in *Cours d'études pour l'instruction du Prince de Parme* (trans. F. Philip and H. Lane), II, Introduction

2:22 We judge and reason with words, just as we calculate with numerals; and languages are for ordinary people what algebra is for geometricians.

Étienne de Condillac, 1775, '*Grammaire*', in *Cours d'études pour l'instruction du Prince de Parme* (trans. F. Philip and H. Lane), II

2:23 If we clearly consider what our intention is when we speak, we shall find that it is nothing else but to unfold to others the thoughts of our own mind.

Dante, *c*.1304, *De vulgari eloquentia* (trans. A. G. Ferrers Howell), I, Ch. 2

2:24 Since language is as necessary an instrument of our thought as a horse is of a knight, and since the best horses are suited to the best knights, . . . the best language will be suited to the best thoughts.

Dante, *c*.1304, *De vulgari eloquentia* (trans. A. G. Ferrers Howell), II, Ch. 1

2:25 [on being asked if his stammer was a problem) No, Sir, because I have time to think before I speak, and don't ask impertinent questions.
Erasmus Darwin, late 18th century, quoted by Francis Darwin in 'Reminiscences of My Father's Everyday Life', in his edition of Charles Darwin's *Autobiography* (1877)

2:26 Democratic nations are passionately addicted to generic terms or abstract expressions because these modes of speech enlarge thought and assist the operations of the mind by enabling it to include many objects in a small compass. ... These abstract terms which abound in democratic languages, and which are used on every occasion without attaching them to any particular fact, enlarge and obscure the thoughts they are intended to convey; they render the mode of speech more succinct and the idea contained in it less clear. But with regard to language, democratic nations prefer obscurity to labour.
Alexis de Tocqueville, 1835–40, *De la Démocratie en Amérique [Democracy in America]* (trans.), Ch. 16

2:27 [to Browning, who had observed Disraeli giving two contradictory opinions in one evening about some works of art, and dared to enquire why] It is only you poets who think there is any connexion between what we say and what we think.
Benjamin Disraeli, 1832, attributed by Robert Browning: in Edward Lyttelton, *The Claim of our Mother Tongue*, The English Association Pamphlet 87 (March 1934), p. 11

2:28 [Idios, responding to Allophanes' criticisms of his being absent from court] To know and feele all this, and not to have / Words to expresse it, makes a man a grave / Of his owne thoughts.
John Donne, 1613, *Epithalamions*, 'Ecclogue', 96

2:29 [on wit] A propriety of thoughts and words; or, in other terms, thoughts and words elegantly adapted to the subject.
John Dryden, 1677, 'The Author's Apology for Heroick Poetry and Heroick Licence', preface to *The State of Innocence and Fall of Man* [cf. 27:2]

2:30 Thought, if it be translated truly, cannot be lost in another Language; but the words that convey it to our apprehension (which are the Image and Ornament of that thought) may be so ill chosen as to make it appear in an unhandsome dress, and rob it of its native Lustre.
John Dryden, 1683, *Preface concerning Ovid's Epistles*

2:31 Miditation is a gift con-fined to unknown philosophers an' cows. Others don't begin to think till they begin to talk or write.
Finley Peter Dunne, 1900, 'Casual Observations', in *Mr Dooley's Philosophy*

2:32 The words or the language, as they are written or spoken, do not seem to play any role in my mechanism of thought.
Albert Einstein, 1945, quoted in Arthur Koestler, *The Act of Creation*, Ch. 7

2:33 The mere fact of naming an object tends to give definiteness to our conception of it – we have then a sign that at once calls up in our minds the distinctive qualities which mark out for us that particular object from all others.
George Eliot, in Gordon S. Haight (ed.), *The George Eliot Letters* (1954), II, p. 251

2:34 The moment our discourse rises above the ground line of familiar facts, and is inflamed with passion or exalted by thought, it clothes itself in images.
Ralph Waldo Emerson, 1836, 'Language', in *Nature*, Ch. 4

2:35 I wish to say what I think and feel today, with the proviso that tomorrow perhaps I shall contradict it all.
Ralph Waldo Emerson, 1839, *Journals*

2:36 First learn the meaning of what you say, and then speak.
Epictetus, 2nd century, *Discourses* (trans. T. W. Higginson), III, 23

2:37 The most beautiful works are those where there is least content; the closer the expression is to the thought, the more indistinguishable the word from the content, the more beautiful is the work. I believe the future of art lies in this direction.
Gustave Flaubert, 16 January 1852, letter to Louise Colet, in M. Nadeau (ed.), *Les Oeuvres* (trans., 1964)

2:38 Think before you speak is criticism's motto; speak before you think creation's.
E. M. Forster, 1951, 'Raison d'être of Criticism', in *Two Cheers for Democracy*

2:39 To one who has enjoyed the full life of any scene, of any hour, what thoughts can be recorded about it seem like the commas and semicolons in the paragraph – mere stops.

Margaret Fuller, 1844, *Summer on the Lakes*, p. 1

2:40 One's complete sentences are attempts, as often as not, to complete an incomplete self with words.

William H. Gass, 1977, interview in *Paris Review* (Summer)

2:41 In much of your talking, thinking is half murdered. / For thought is a bird of space, that in a cage of words may indeed unfold its wings but cannot fly.

Kahlil Gibran, 1923, 'On Talking', in *The Prophet*

2:42 He who best knows how to conceal his necessity and desires is the most likely person to find redress, . . . the true use of speech is not so much to express our wants, as to conceal them.

Oliver Goldsmith, 20 October 1759, 'On the Use of Language', in *The Bee*, no. 3

2:43 Thoughts, that breathe, and words, that burn.

Thomas Gray, 1757, *The Progress of Poesy*, 110

2:44 Thought flies and words go on foot. Therein lies all the drama of a writer.

Julien Green, 4 May 1943, *Journal*

2:45 Words are the fortresses of thought.

William Hamilton, quoted by Samuel Butler (1835–1902) in a lecture on 'Thought and Language' (1890)

2:46 [of tunnelling through a sandbank] Language is to the mind precisely what the arch is to the tunnel. The power of thinking and the power of excavation are not dependent on the words in the one case or on the mason-work in the other; but without these subsidiaries neither could be carried on beyond its rudimentary commencement.

William Hamilton, quoted by Samuel Butler (1835–1902) in a lecture on 'Thought and Language' (1890)

2:47 The worst thing is that we live in a contaminated moral environment. We fell morally ill because we became used to saying something different from what we thought.

Vaclav Havel, 1 January 1990, first speech as President of Czechoslovakia (trans.)

2:48 Language, if it throws a veil over our ideas, adds a softness and refinement to them, like that

which the atmosphere gives to naked objects.

William Hazlitt, 1817, 'On Classical Education', in *The Round Table*

2:49 To think justly, we must understand what others mean: to know the value of our thoughts, we must try their effect on other minds.

William Hazlitt, 1826, 'On People of Sense', in *The Plain Speaker*

2:50 Man acts as if he were the shaper and master of language, while it is language which remains the mistress of man.

Martin Heidegger, 1954, quoted as an epigraph in George Steiner, *After Babel* (trans.)

2:51 If no thought / your mind does visit, / make your speech / not too explicit.

Piet Hein, 1966, 'The Case for Obscurity', in *Grooks*

2:52 Words are the tools of thought, and you will often find that you are thinking badly because you are using the wrong tools, trying to bore a hole with a screw-driver, or draw a cork with a coal-hammer.

A. P. Herbert, 1935, 'Invitation to the War', in *What a Word!*

2:53 The generall use of Speech, is to transferre our Mentall Discourse, into Verbal; or the Trayne of our Thoughts, into a Trayne of Words.

Thomas Hobbes, 1651, 'Of Speech', in *Leviathan*, I, Ch. 4

2:54 [of talking] It shapes our thoughts for us; – the waves of conversation roll them as the surf rolls the pebbles on the shore.

Oliver Wendell Holmes, senior, 1858, *The Autocrat of the Breakfast Table*, Ch. 2

2:55 I rough out my thoughts in talk as an artist models in clay. Spoken language is so plastic, – you can pat and coax, and spread and shave, and rub out, and fill up, and stick on so easily, when you work that soft material, that there is nothing like it for modelling.

Oliver Wendell Holmes, senior, 1858, *The Autocrat of the Breakfast Table*, Ch. 2

2:56 One has to dismount from an idea, and get into the saddle again, at every parenthesis.

Oliver Wendell Holmes, senior, 1858, *The Autocrat of the Breakfast Table*, Ch. 8

2:57 The very aim and end of our institutions

is just this: that we may think what we like and say what we think.

Oliver Wendell Holmes, senior, 1860, *The Professor at the Breakfast Table*, Ch. 5

2:58 We must think things not words, or at least we must constantly translate our words into the facts for which they stand, if we are to keep the real and the true.

Oliver Wendell Holmes, junior, 17 January 1889, address to the New York State Bar Association

2:59 A moment's thinking, is an hour in words.

Thomas Hood, 1827, 'Hero and Leander', stanza 41

2:60 Language is the formative organ of thought.

Wilhelm von Humboldt, 1836, *On Language: the Diversity of Human Language-structure and its Influence on the Mental Development of Mankind* (trans. P. Heath), p. 54

2:61 He that thinks with more extent than another, will want words of larger meaning.

Samuel Johnson, 1758, *The Idler*, no. 70

2:62 This is one of the disadvantages of wine, it makes a man mistake words for thoughts.

Samuel Johnson, 1778, in James Boswell, *The Life of Samuel Johnson* (1791), Ch. 47

2:63 Language is the dress of thought.

Samuel Johnson, 1779–81, 'Cowley', in *Lives of the English Poets*

2:64 Questions show the mind's range, and answers its subtlety.

Joseph Joubert, 1842, *Pensées* (trans.), Sect. 3, Part 21

2:65 Yet the sweet converse of an innocent mind, / Whose words are images of thoughts refined, / Is my soul's pleasure.

John Keats, 1817, 'O Solitude! if I must with thee dwell'

2:66 If I cannot speak your language, that is no reason that I cannot think some of your thoughts.

Rudyard Kipling, March 1927, 'The Spirit of the Latin' (speech to the Brazilian Academy of Letters), in *A Book of Words*

2:67 Language itself is never completely explicit. Words have suggestive, evocative powers; but at the same time they are merely stepping stones for thought.

Arthur Koestler, 1964, 'Originality, Emphasis, Economy', in *The Act of Creation*, Ch. 3

2:68 Words are a blessing which can turn into a curse. They crystallize thought; they give articulation and precision to vague images and hazy intuitions. But a crystal is no longer a fluid.

Arthur Koestler, 1964, 'The Snares of Language', in *The Act of Creation*, Ch. 7

2:69 The counterpart to the little girl's [Alice's] predicament is the little boy's who said: 'I see what I mean but I don't know how to say it.'

Arthur Koestler, 1964, 'The Snares of Language', in *The Act of Creation*, Ch. 7 [cf. 2:18]

2:70 Language can become a screen which stands between the thinker and reality. This is the reason why true creativity often starts where language ends.

Arthur Koestler, 1964, 'The Snares of Language', in *The Act of Creation*, Ch. 7

2:71 There are some who speak one moment before they think.

Jean de La Bruyère, 1688, '*De la société et la conversation*', in *Les Caractères* (trans.), no. 15

2:72 It remains for us to examine the spiritual element of speech which constitutes one of the greatest advantages which man has over all the other animals, and which is one of the greatest proofs of man's reason. This is the use which we make of it for signifying our thoughts, and this marvellous invention of composing from twenty-five or thirty sounds an infinite variety of words, which although not having any resemblance in themselves to that which passes through our minds, nevertheless do not fail to reveal to others all of the secrets of the mind, and to make intelligible to others who cannot penetrate into the mind all that we conceive and all of the diverse movements of our souls.

Claude Lancelot and Antoine Arnauld, 1660, *Grammaire générale et raisonnée* [the Port-Royal Grammar] (trans. J. Rieux and B. E. Rollin), II, Ch. 1

2:73 Ideas are enclosed and almost bound in words like precious stones in a ring.

Giacomo Leopardi, 27 July 1822, *Zibaldone* (trans. G. Steiner)

2:74 A period is to let the writer know he has finished his thought and he should stop there if he will only take the hint.

Art Linkletter, 1965, *A Child's Garden of Misinformation*, Ch. 3

2:75 Words, in their primary or immediate signification, stand for nothing but the ideas in the mind of him who uses them.

John Locke, 1690, 'Of Words or Language in General', in *An Essay Concerning Humane Understanding*, III, Ch. 2, Sect. 2

2:76 Wisely the Hebrews admit no / Present tense in their language; / While we are speaking the word, / it is already the Past.

Henry Wadsworth Longfellow, 1882, 'Elegiac Verse' no. 12, in *In the Harbour*

2:77 For words finely used are in truth the very light of thought.

Longinus (traditional attribution; in fact by an earlier, unknown author), 1st century BC, *On the Sublime* (trans. T. S. Dorsch), Ch. 30

2:78 The only living language is the language in which we think and have our being.

Antonio Machado, 1943, *Juan de Mairena* (trans. Ben Belitt), p. 30

2:79 The main function of language is not to express thought, not to duplicate mental processes, but rather to play an active pragmatic part in human behaviour.

Bronislaw Malinowski, 1935, 'The Language of Magic and Gardening', in *Coral Gardens and their Magic*, II, Part 4, Div. 1

2:80 Syntax and vocabulary are overwhelming constraints – the rules that run us. Language is using *us* to talk – we think we're using the language, but language is doing the thinking, we're its slavish agents.

Harry Mathews, 26 May 1988, interview in *City Limits*

2:81 I sometimes hear people who apologize for not being able to say what they mean, maintaining that their heads are so full of fine things that they cannot deliver them for want of eloquence. That is moonshine. ... They themselves do not yet know what they mean. Just watch them giving a little stammer as they are about to deliver their brain-child: you can tell that they have labouring-pains not at childbirth but during conception!

Michel de Montaigne, 1572–80, 'On Educating Children', in *The Complete Essays* (trans. M. A. Screech, 1987), I, no. 26

2:82 Labels are devices for saving talkative persons the trouble of thinking.

John Morley, 1871, 'Carlyle', in *Critical Miscellanies*

2:83 Words without thought are dead sounds; thoughts without words are nothing. To think

is to speak low; to speak is to think aloud. The word is the thought incarnate.

Max Müller, 1861, 'The Theoretical Stage, and the Origin of Language', in *Lectures on the Science of Language*, p. 9

2:84 Though the faculty of language may be congenital, all languages are traditional. The words in which we think are channels of thought which we have not dug ourselves, but which we found ready-made for us.

Max Müller, 1873, 'Lectures on Mr Darwin's Philosophy of Language', in *Fraser's Magazine*, nos. 7–8

2:85 Language . . . is not outside the mind, but is *the* outside of the mind.

Max Müller, 1873, 'Lectures on Mr Darwin's Philosophy of Language', in *Fraser's Magazine*, nos. 7–8

2:86 Language is the autobiography of the human mind.

Max Müller, quoted in N. Chaudhuri, *Scholar Extraordinary* (1974)

2:87 [in answer to the question, 'What language do you think in?'] I don't think in any language. I think in images. I don't believe that people think in languages. They don't move their lips when they think. It is only a certain type of illiterate person who moves his lips as he reads or ruminates. No, I think in images, and now and then a Russian phrase or an English phrase will form with the foam of the brainwave, but that's about all.

Vladimir Nabokov, July 1962, interview in *Strong Opinions* (1974), p. 14

2:88 When people cease to complain, they cease to think.

Napoleon I, 1804–15, *Maxims* (trans.)

2:89 Some wise men said that words were given to us to conceal our thoughts, / But if a person has nothing but truthful words why their thoughts haven't even the protection of a pair of panties or shoughts, / And a naked thought is ineffectual as well as improper, / And hasn't a chance in the presence of a glib chinchilla-clad whopper.

Ogden Nash, 1940, 'Golly, How Truth will Out!', in *The Face is Familiar* [cf. 2:139]

2:90 Most thinkers write badly, because they

communicate not only their thoughts, but also the thinking of them.

Friedrich Nietzsche, 1878, *Human, All Too Human* (trans. H. Zimmern), p. 188

2:91 Words . . . 'mean' nothing by themselves. . . . It is only when a thinker makes use of them that they stand for anything, or, in one sense, have 'meaning'. They are instruments.

C. K. Ogden and I. A. Richards, 1923, *The Meaning of Meaning*, Ch. 1

2:92 By speaking, by thinking, we undertake to clarify things, and that forces us to exacerbate them, dislocate them, schematize them. Every concept is in itself an exaggeration.

José Ortega y Gasset, December 1949, 'In Search of Goethe from Within, Letter to a German', in *Partisan Review* (trans. W. R. Trask)

2:93 A man may take to drink because he feels himself to be a failure, and then fail all the more completely because he drinks. It is rather the same thing that is happening to the English language. It becomes ugly and inaccurate because our thoughts are foolish, but the slovenliness of our language makes it easier for us to have foolish thoughts. The point is that the process is reversible.

George Orwell, 1946, 'Politics and the English Language', *Horizon*, no. 13

2:94 Newspeak was the official language of Oceania.

George Orwell, 1949, *Nineteen Eighty-Four*, I, Ch. 1, note 1

2:95 [Syme] Don't you see that the whole aim of Newspeak is to narrow the range of thought? In the end we shall make thoughtcrime literally impossible, because there will be no words in which to express it.

George Orwell, 1949, *Nineteen Eighty-Four*, I, Ch. 5

2:96 People can be forgiven for overrating language. Words make noise, or sit on a page, for all to hear and see. Thoughts are trapped inside the head of the thinker. To know what someone else is thinking, or to talk to each other about the nature of thinking, we have to use – what else, words! It is no wonder that many commentators have trouble even conceiving of thought without words – or is it that they just don't have the language to talk about it?

Steven Pinker, 1994, *The Language Instinct*, Ch. 3

2:97 True Wit is Nature to advantage dress'd, / What oft was thought, but ne'er so well express'd.

Alexander Pope, 1711, 'An Essay on Criticism', 297

2:98 Expression is the dress of thought, and still / Appears more decent, as more suitable; / A vile conceit in pompous words express'd, / Is like a clown in regal purple dress'd: / For diff'rent styles with diff'rent subjects sort, / As several garbs with country, town, and court.

Alexander Pope, 1711, 'An Essay on Criticism', 318

2:99 There is nothing like desire for preventing the things one says from bearing any resemblance to what one has in one's mind.

Marcel Proust, 1921, *Le Côté de Guermantes* (trans.), II

2:100 One may think that dares not speak.

Proverbial

2:101 Speech is the picture of the mind.

Proverbial

2:102 A slip of the tongue is no fault of the mind.

Proverbial (Irish)

2:103 Books do not exhaust words, nor words thoughts.

Proverbial (Chinese)

2:104 The point is the seeing – the grace / beyond recognition, the ways / of the bird rising, unnamed, unknown, / beyond the range of language, beyond its noun.

Alastair Reid, 1978, 'Growing, Flying, Happening', in *Weathering*

2:105 Words are the small change of thought.

Jules Renard, November 1888, *Journal* (trans. L. Bogan and E. Roget)

2:106 In France particularly, words reign over ideas.

George Sand, 1832, *Indiana* (trans.), I, Ch. 2

2:107 In this world we must either institute conventional forms of expression or else pretend that we have nothing to express; the choice lies between a mask and a fig-leaf.

George Santayana, 1922, 'Carnival', in *Soliloquies in England*

2:108 Language is primarily a pre-rational function. It humbly works up to the thought that is latent in, that may eventually be read into, its classifications and its forms; it is not, as is generally but naïvely assumed, the final label put upon the finished thought.

Edward Sapir, 1921, *Language*, Ch. 1

2:109 Culture may be defined as *what* a society does and thinks. Language is a particular *how* of thought.

Edward Sapir, 1921, *Language*, Ch. 10

2:110 Languages are more to us than systems of thought transference. They are invisible garments that drape themselves about our spirit and give a predetermined form to all its symbolic expression.

Edward Sapir, 1921, *Language*, Ch. 11

2:111 The Universe lay spread at my feet and each thing was humbly begging for a name, and giving it one was like both creating it and taking it. Without this fundamental illusion, I should never have written.

Jean-Paul Sartre, 1964, 'Reading', in *Words* (trans. I. Clephane), I

2:112 Just at the age 'twixt boy and youth, / When thought is speech, and speech is truth.

Walter Scott, 1808, *Marmion*, Canto 3, Introduction

2:113 When things have taken hold of the mind, the words come crowding forth.

Lucius Annaeus Seneca, 1st century, *Controversiae*, III

2:114 [Rosalind, to Celia] Do you not know that I am a woman? When I think, I must speak.

William Shakespeare, 1600, *As You Like It*, III. ii. 244

2:115 [Claudius] My words fly up, my thoughts remain below: / Words without thoughts never to heaven go.

William Shakespeare, 1600–1601, *Hamlet*, III. iii. 97

2:116 [Horatio, of Ophelia] Her speech is nothing, / Yet the unshaped use of it doth move / The hearers to collection. They aim at it, / And botch the words up fit to their own thoughts, / Which, as her winks and nods and gestures yield them, / Indeed would make one think there might be thought, / Though nothing sure, yet much unhappily.

William Shakespeare, 1600–1601, *Hamlet*, IV. v. 7

2:117 [Angelo] When I would pray and think, I think and pray / To several subjects; heaven hath my empty words, / Whilst my invention, hearing not my tongue, / Anchors on Isabel; God in my mouth, / As if I did but only chew his name, / And in my heart the strong and swelling evil / Of my conception.

William Shakespeare, 1604, *Measure for Measure*, II. iv. 1

2:118 [Menenius] What I think, I utter, and spend my malice in my breath.

William Shakespeare, 1608, *Coriolanus*, II. i. 52

2:119 I think good thoughts whilst others write good words. / . . . Then others for the breath of words respect, / Me for my dumb thoughts, speaking in effect.

William Shakespeare, Sonnet 85, published in 1609

2:120 [Asia, of Prometheus] He gave man speech, and speech created thought, / Which is the measure of the universe.

Percy Bysshe Shelley, 1820, *Prometheus Unbound*, II. iv

2:121 [Earth] Language is a perpetual Orphic song, / Which rules with daedal harmony a throng / Of thoughts and forms, which else senseless and shapeless were.

Percy Bysshe Shelley, 1820, *Prometheus Unbound*, IV

2:122 A single word even may be a spark of inextinguishable thought.

Percy Bysshe Shelley, 1821, *A Defence of Poetry*

2:123 SIR LUCIUS O'TRIGGER: For give me leave to tell you, a man may think an untruth as well as speak one.

CAPTAIN ABSOLUTE: Very true, sir; but if a man never utters his thoughts, I should think they might stand a chance of escaping controversy.

Richard Sheridan, 1775, *The Rivals*, IV. iii

2:124 A word is the carving and colouring of a thought, and gives it permanence.

Osbert Sitwell, 1949, *Laughter in the Next Room*, Ch. 7

2:125 How often misused words generate misleading thoughts.

Herbert Spencer, 1879, *The Principles of Ethics*, I, Part 2, Ch. 8

2:126 My brothers and sister and I were brought up in an atmosphere which I would describe as 'Puritan decadence'. Puritanism names the behaviour which is condemned; Puritan decadence regards the name itself as indecent, and pretends that the object behind that name does not exist until it is named.

Stephen Spender, 1951, *World within World*, p. 314

2:127 Only idealists can speak of thinking without language.
Josef Stalin, 'On Linguistics' (trans. 1982), *Nature*, no. 299

2:128 Language is a finite instrument crudely applied to an infinity of ideas.
Tom Stoppard, 1972, *Jumpers*, p. 63

2:129 Language may be defined as the expresssion of thought by means of speech-sounds.
Henry Sweet, 1900, *The History of Language*, Ch. 1

2:130 For no thought of man made Gods to love or honour / Ere the song within the silent soul began, / Nor might earth in dream or deed take heaven upon her / Till the word was clothed with speech by lips of man.
Algernon Charles Swinburne, 1866, *The Last Oracle*

2:131 Speech was given to man to disguise his thoughts.
Charles-Maurice de Talleyrand, attributed, early 19th century (trans.)

2:132 I sometimes hold it half a sin / To put in words the grief I feel; / For words, like Nature, half reveal / And half conceal the Soul within.
Alfred, Lord Tennyson, 1850, *In Memoriam A. H. H.*, Canto 5

2:133 When each by turns was guide to each, / And Fancy light from Fancy caught, / And Thought leapt out to wed with Thought / Ere Thought could wed itself with Speech.
Alfred, Lord Tennyson, 1850, *In Memoriam A. H. H.*, Canto 23

2:134 My words are only words, and moved / Upon the topmost froth of thought.
Alfred, Lord Tennyson, 1850, *In Memoriam A. H. H.*, Canto 51

2:135 One inconvenience I sometimes experienced in so small a house, the difficulty of getting to a sufficient distance from my guest when we began to utter the big thoughts in big words. You want room for your thoughts to get into sailing trim and run a course or two before they make their port. The bullet of your thought must have overcome its lateral and ricochet motion and fallen into its last and steady course before it reaches the ear of the hearer, else it may plough out again through the side of his head. Also, our sentences wanted room to unfold and form their columns in the interval.
Henry Thoreau, 1854, 'Visitors', in *Walden*

2:136 Language is as truly on one side the limit and restraint of thought, as on the other side that which feeds and unfolds thought.
Richard Chenevix Trench, 1851, 'Introductory Lecture', in *On the Study of Words*

2:137 Language is the amber in which a thousand precious and subtle thoughts have been safely embedded and preserved.
Richard Chenevix Trench, 1851, 'Introductory Lecture', in *On the Study of Words*

2:138 An idea does not pass from one language to another without change.
Miguel de Unamuno, 1913, *The Tragic Sense of Life* (trans. J. E. C. Flitch), Preface

2:139 People use thought only to justify their wrong-doings, and words only to conceal their thoughts.
Voltaire, 1763, 'Le Chapon et la poularde', in *Dialogues* (trans.) [cf. 2:17, 2:89]

2:140 Philosophy *begins* with distrusting language – that medium that pervades, and warps, our very thought.
Friedrich Waismann, 1952, 'Analytic-Synthetic V', in *Analysis*, no. 13

2:141 The little girl had the making of a poet in her who, being told to be sure of her meaning before she spoke, said, 'How can I know what I think till I see what I say?'
Graham Wallas, 1926, in May Wallas (ed.), *The Art of Thought* (1945), Ch. 4 [cf. 49:8]

2:142 It does not matter what men say in words, so long as their activities are controlled by settled instincts. The words may ultimately destroy the instincts. But until this has occurred, words do not count.
A. N. Whitehead, 1925, *Science and the Modern World*, Ch. 1

2:143 Language, then, is the spoken means whereby thought is communicated, and it is only that. Language is not thought, nor is thought language; nor is there a mysterious and indissoluble connection between the two, as there is between soul and body, so that the one cannot exist and manifest itself without the other. There can hardly be a greater and more pernicious error, in linguistics or in metaphysics, than the doctrine that language and thought are identical.
William Dwight Whitney, 1867, *Language and the Study of Language*

2:144 We dissect nature along lines laid down by our native languages. The categories and types that we isolate from the world of phenomena we do not find there because they stare every observer in the face; on the contrary, the world is presented in a kaleidoscopic flux of impression which has to be organized by our minds – and this means largely by the linguistic systems in our minds. We cut nature up, organize it into concepts, and ascribe significances as we do, largely because we are parties to an agreement to organize it in this way – an agreement that holds throughout our speech community and is codified in the patterns of our language.
Benjamin Lee Whorf, 1940, 'Science and Linguistics'

2:145 Thought and language are to the artist instruments of an art.
Oscar Wilde, 1890, *The Picture of Dorian Gray*, Preface

2:146 It is only by language that we rise above them [the lower animals] – by language, which is the parent, not the child, of thought.
Oscar Wilde, 1891, 'The Critic as Artist', in *Intentions*

2:147 [Lord Goring to Sir Robert Chiltern] I am always saying what I shouldn't say. In fact, I usually say what I really think. A great mistake nowadays. It makes one so liable to be misunderstood.
Oscar Wilde, 1895, *An Ideal Husband*, II

2:148 Philosophy is a battle against the bewitchment of our intelligence by means of language.
Ludwig Wittgenstein, 1953, *Philosophical Investigations* (trans.), I, Sect. 109 [but see also 1:50]

2:149 Lively thoughts / Give birth, full often, to unguarded words.
William Wordsworth, 1795–1814, *The Excursion*, III, 493

2:150 Think like a wise man but express yourself like the common people.
W. B. Yeats, 21 December 1935, *Letters on Poetry from W. B. Yeats to Dorothy Wellesley* (1940)

2:151 Where Nature's end of language is declin'd, / And men talk only to conceal the mind.
Edward Young, 1725, 'Satire 2', in *The Love of Fame, the Universal Passion*, 207

2:152 Speech, thought's canal! speech, thought's criterion, too! / Thought in the mine, may come forth gold or dross; / When coin'd in words, we know its *real* worth.
Edward Young, 1742–6, *The Complaint: or, Night-Thoughts on Life, Death and Immortality*, 'Night II', 469

See also: 5:71, 8:3, 8:62, 19:15, 20:5, 20:16, 21:25, 21:40, 26:129, 27:2, 27:25, 27:36, 29:13, 29:52, 36:25, 36:89, 38:23, 47:15, 47:44, 51:51, 54:34

3 *Language Myths and Origins*

The origins and early history of speech and language

3:1 Nature, as we say, does nothing without some purpose; and for the purpose of making man a political animal she has endowed him alone among the animals with the power of reasoned speech.

Aristotle, 4th century BC, *Politics* (trans. T. A. Sinclair), I, Ch. 2

3:2 In origin all language is concrete or metaphorical. In order to use language to express abstractions, we have to ignore its original concrete and metaphorical meanings.

W. H. Auden, 1948, 'Notes on the Comic', in *The Dyer's Hand and other essays*

3:3 Speechless Evil / Borrowed the language of Good / And reduced it to noise.

W. H. Auden, 1964, postscript to 'The Cave of Making', in *Thanksgiving for a Habitat*

3:4 Every created thing has ways of pronouncing its ownhood.

W. H. Auden, 1969, 'Natural Linguistics'

3:5 If it were possible to talk to the unborn, one could never explain to them how it feels to be alive, for life is washed in the speechless real.

Jacques Barzun, 1959, *The House of Intellect*

3:6 A word, a phrase –: from cyphers rise / Life recognized, a sudden sense, / The sun stands still, mute are the skies, / And all compacts it, stark and dense.

Gottfried Benn, 1941, 'A Word', in *Primal Vision* (trans. R. Exner)

3:7 So out of the ground the Lord God formed every beast of the field and every bird of the air, and brought them to the man to see what he would call them; and whatever the man called every living creature, that was its name.

The Bible, Genesis 2:19 (Revised Standard Version)

3:8 Throughout the earth men spoke the same language, with the same vocabulary.

The Bible, Genesis 11:1 (Jerusalem Bible)

3:9 Now Yahweh came down to see the town and the tower that the sons of man had built. 'So they are all a single people with a single language!' said Yahweh. 'This is but the start of their undertakings! There will be nothing too hard for them to do. Come, let us go down and confuse their language on the spot so that they can no longer understand one another.' Yahweh scattered them thence over the whole face of the earth, and they stopped building the town. It was named Babel therefore, because there Yahweh confused the language of the whole earth. [Authorized Version: because the Lord did there confound the language of all the earth.]

The Bible, Genesis 11:5 (Jerusalem Bible)

3:10 Language does not leave fossils, at least not until it has become written.

Richard Brautigan, 1967, 'Prelude to the Mayonnaise Chapter', in *Trout Fishing in America*

3:11 [on the evolution of language] Bodily gesture has a very limited range: stones, trees, whole forests may get in the way of it; darkness will render it quite useless. Speech is a kind of light in darkness.

Anthony Burgess, 1992, *A Mouthful of Air*, I, Ch. 1

3:12 [of Igdrasil, the Tree of Existence] It is the past, the present, and the future; what was done, what is doing, what will be done; 'the infinite conjugation of the verb *To do*.' Considering how human things circulate, each inextricably in communion with all, – how the word I speak to you to-day is borrowed, not from Ulfila the Moesogoth only, but from all men since the first man began to speak, – I find no similitude so true as this of a Tree.

Thomas Carlyle, 1840, 'The Hero as Divinity', in *On Heroes, Hero-Worship, and the Heroic in History*, Lecture 1

3:13 To man alone of all existing beings was speech given, because for him alone was it necessary.

Dante, c.1304, *De vulgari eloquentia* (trans. A. G. Ferrers Howell), I, Ch. 2

3:14 Hebrew was the language which the lips of the first speaker formed.

Dante, c.1304, *De vulgari eloquentia* (trans. A. G. Ferrers Howell), I, Ch. 6

3:15 Language is an art, like brewing or baking; but writing would have been a much more appropriate simile. It certainly is not a true instinct, as every language has to be learnt. It differs, however, widely from all ordinary arts, for man has an instinctive tendency to speak . . . whilst no child has an instinctive tendency to brew, bake, or write.

Charles Darwin, 1871, 'Mental Powers', in *The Descent of Man*, Ch. 2

3:16 The survival or preservation of certain favoured words in the struggle for existence is natural selection.

Charles Darwin, 1871, 'Mental Powers', in *The Descent of Man*, Ch. 2

3:17 A language of power and compass cannot arise except amongst cities and the habits of luxurious people.

Thomas De Quincey, April 1839, 'The English Language', *Blackwood's Magazine*

3:18 As we go back in history, language becomes more picturesque, until its infancy, when it is all poetry.

Ralph Waldo Emerson, 1836, 'Language', in *Nature*, Ch. 4

3:19 [of man] The phonetic animal *par excellence*.

J. R. Firth, 1930, *Speech*, Ch. 1

3:20 Voice developed in the trees, gesture on the ground.

J. R. Firth, 1930, *Speech*, Ch. 1

3:21 [denying the notion of primitiveness in language] All languages are equally primitive.

J. R. Firth, 1937, *The Tongues of Men*, Ch. 2

3:22 Speech and drawing are nine-tenths of humanity.

J. R. Firth, 1937, *The Tongues of Men*, Ch. 4

3:23 [The Egyptian king] Psammetichus, finding that mere inquiry failed to reveal which was the original race of mankind, devised an ingenious method of determining the matter. He took at random, from an ordinary family, two newly born infants and gave them to a shepherd to be brought up amongst his flocks, under strict orders that no one should utter a word in their presence. They were to be kept by themselves in a lonely cottage, and the shepherd was to bring in goats from time to time, to see that the babies had enough milk to drink, and to look after them in any other way that was necessary. All these arrangements were made by Psammetichus because he wished to find out what word the children would first utter, once they had grown out of their meaningless baby-talk. The plan succeeded: two years later the shepherd, who during that time had done everything he had been told to do, happened one day to open the door of the cottage and go in, when both children, running up to him with hands outstretched, pronounced the word 'becos'. The first time the shepherd made no mention of it; but later, when he found that every time he visited the children to attend to their needs the same word was constantly repeated by them, he informed his master. Psammetichus ordered the children to be brought to him, and when he himself heard them say 'becos' he determined to find out to what language the word belonged. His inquiries revealed that it was the Phrygian for 'bread', and in consideration of this the Egyptians yielded their claims and admitted the superior antiquity of the Phrygians. That this was what really happened I myself learnt from the priests of Hephaestus at Memphis, though the Greeks have various improbable versions of the story, such as that Psammetichus had the children brought up by women whose tongues he had cut out. The version of the priests, however, is the one I have given.

Herodotus, 5th century BC, in *The Histories* (trans. Aubrey de Sélincourt, 1996), II, Ch. 2

3:24 The most noble and profitable invention of all other, was that of SPEECH, consisting of *Names* or *Appellations*, and their Connexion; whereby men register their Thoughts; recall them when they are past; and also declare them one to another for mutuall utility and conversation; without which, there had been amongst men, neither Common-wealth, nor Society, nor Contract, nor Peace, no more than amongst Lyons, Bears, and Wolves.

Thomas Hobbes, 1651, 'Of Speech', in *Leviathan*, I, Ch. 4

3:25 Words well up freely from the breast, without necessity or intent, and there may well have been no wandering horde in any desert that did not already have its own songs. For man, as a species, is a singing creature, though the notes, in his case, are also coupled with thought.

Wilhelm von Humboldt, 1836, *On Language: the Diversity of Human Language-structure and Its Influence on the Mental Development of Mankind* (trans. P. Heath), p. 60

3:26 [on the origins of language] It must have come by inspiration. A thousand, nay, a million of children could not invent a language. . . . inspiration seems to me to be necessary to give man the faculty of speech; to inform him that he may have speech; which I think he could no more find out without inspiration than cows or hogs would think of such a faculty.

Samuel Johnson, 1783, in James Boswell, *The Life of Samuel Johnson* (1791), Ch. 56

3:27 Language may have created man, rather than man language.

Jacques Monod, 3 November 1967, inaugural lecture, Collège de France (trans.)

3:28 As for the power of speech, it is certain that, if it is not natural, then it cannot be necessary. And yet I believe (though it would be difficult to assay it) that if a child, before learning to talk, were brought up in total solitude, then he would have some sort of speech to express his concepts; it is simply not believable that Nature has refused to us men a faculty granted to most other animals; we can see they have means of complaining, rejoicing, calling on each other for help or inviting each other to love; they do so by meaningful utterances; if that is not talking, what is it?

Michel de Montaigne, 1572–80, 'An Apology for Raymond Sebond', in *The Complete Essays* (trans. M. A. Screech, 1987), II, no. 12

3:29 The onomatopoeic theory goes very smoothly as long as it deals with cackling hens and quacking ducks; but round that poultry-yard there is a high wall, and we soon find that it is behind that wall that language really begins.

Max Müller, quoted in Otto Jespersen, *Language: its Nature, Development and Origin* (1922), p. 29

3:30 'I always thought the Tower of Babel such a sinister myth,' said Freddie. 'Who could love a God who deliberately confused mankind in that mean way?' 'One could respect him,' said Clifford. 'He knew his business.'

Iris Murdoch, 1975, 'Thursday' (second week), in *A Word Child*

3:31 Echo still had a body then, she was not just a voice: but although she was always chattering, her power of speech was no different from what it is now. All she could do was to repeat the last words of the many phrases that she heard. Juno had brought this about because often, when she could have caught the nymphs lying with her Jupiter on the mountainside, Echo, knowing well what she did, used to detain the goddess with an endless flow of talk, until the nymphs could flee. When Juno realized what was happening, she said : 'I shall curtail the powers of that tongue which has tricked me: you will have only the briefest possible use of your voice.' And in fact she carried out her threats. Echo still repeats the last words spoken, and gives back the sounds she has heard.

Ovid, 1st century, *Metamorphoses* (trans.), III, c.350

3:32 [book title] The language instinct.

Steven Pinker, 1994, *The Language Instinct: The New Science of Language and Mind*

3:33 Since Man from beast by Words is known, / Words are Man's province, Words we teach alone.

Alexander Pope, 1742, *The Dunciad*, IV, 149

3:34 In whatever language it may be written, every line, every word is welcome that bears the impress of the early days of mankind.

Proverbial (German)

3:35 One must let people talk, since fish can't.

Proverbial (Polish)

3:36 Words are the daughters of Earth, and things are the sons of Heaven.

Proverbial (Indian) [cf. 27:25]

3:37 The language which has the most ingenious grammar is the most unmixed, the most original, oldest and nearest to the source; for the grammatical inflections and endings are constantly lost with the formation of a new language, and it requires a very long time and intercourse with other people to develop and rearrange itself anew.

Rasmus Rask, 1818, 'An Investigation Concerning the Source of the Old Northern or Icelandic Language' (trans. W. P. Lehmann)

3:38 [of the role of interjections, in the origins of language] They are never more, at best, than a decorative edging to the ample, complex fabric.

Edward Sapir, 1921, *Language*, Ch. 1

3:39 The gift of speech and a well ordered language are characteristic of every known group of human beings. No tribe has ever been found which is without language and all statements to the contrary may be dismissed as mere folklore.

Edward Sapir, 1933, 'Language', in *Encyclopedia of the Social Sciences*, IX

3:40 Man's word is God in man.

Alfred, Lord Tennyson, 1869, 'The Coming of Arthur', in *The Idylls of the King*, I, 132

3:41 Word by word / The tower of speech grew. / He looked at it from the air / He reclined on. One word more and / It would be on a level with him; vocabulary / Would have triumphed . . . He leaned / Over and looked at the dictionary / They used. There was the blank still / By his name . . .

R. S. Thomas, 1978, 'The Gap', in *Frequencies*

3:42 The dominion of speech is erected upon the downfall of interjections.

John Horne Tooke, 1786, *The Diversions of Purley*, p. 32

3:43 What a good thing Adam had. When he said a good thing he knew nobody had said it before.

Mark Twain, *Notebooks* (1935)

3:44 Prajapati, the Creator of all, rested in life-giving meditation over the worlds of his creation; and from them came the three *Vedas*. He rested in meditation and from these came the three sounds: BHUR, BHUVAS, SVAR, earth, air, and sky. He rested in meditation and from the three sounds came the sound OM. Even as all leaves come from a stem, all words come from the sound OM.

Chandogya Upanishad, c.8th century BC, II, Ch. 23, Sect. 2, in *The Upanishads* (trans. Juan Mascaró, 1965)

3:45 I am not like a lady at the court of Versailles, who said: 'What a great shame that the bother at the tower of Babel should have got language all mixed up; but for that, everyone would always have spoken French.'

Voltaire, 26 May 1767, 'Letter to Catherine the Great' (trans.)

3:46 A fair realization of the incredible degree of the diversity of linguistic system that ranges over the globe leaves one with an inescapable feeling that the human spirit is inconceivably old; that the few thousand years of history covered by our written records are no more than the thickness of a pencil mark on the scale that measures our past experience on this planet.

Benjamin Lee Whorf, 1940, 'Science and Linguistics'

See also: 2:120, 45:56, 59:43

4 *Body Language*

Facial expressions, gestures, and other forms of non-verbal communication

4:1 [of clothes] They are, after all, a language; they do not so much say things about as, they are what is said.

Iain Banks, 1986, *The Bridge*, Ch. 2

4:2 When the lady drank to the gentleman only with her eyes, and he pledged with his, was there no conversation because there was neither noun nor verb? Eyes are verbs, and glasses of wine are good nouns enough as between those who understand one another. Whether the ideas underlying them are expressed and conveyed by eyeage or by tonguage is a detail that matters nothing.

Samuel Butler (1835–1902), 1890, lecture in London on 'Thought and Language'

4:3 'Tis pleasing to be schooled in a strange tongue / By female lips and eyes, that is, I mean, / When both the teacher and the taught are young, / As was the case at least where I have been. / They smile so when one's right, and when one's wrong / They smile still more, and then there intervene / Pressure of hands, perhaps even a chaste kiss. / I learned the little that I know by this.

Lord Byron, 1819–24, *Don Juan*, Canto 2, stanza 164

4:4 The expression of a man's face is commonly a help to his thoughts, or glossary on his speech; but the countenance of Newman Noggs, in his ordinary moods, was a problem which no stretch of the ingenuity could solve.

Charles Dickens, 1838–9, *Nicholas Nickleby*, Ch. 3

4:5 [Fanny Squeers, reacting to her maid's remarks about Miss Price's appearance] 'How you talk!' 'Talk, miss! It's enough to make a Tom cat talk French grammar, only to see how she tosses her head.'

Charles Dickens, 1838–9, *Nicholas Nickleby*, Ch. 12

4:6 All over Italy, a peculiar shake of the right hand from the wrist, with the forefinger stretched out, expresses a negative – the only negative beggars will ever understand. But, in Naples, those five fingers are a copious language.

Charles Dickens, 1844, 'A Rapid Diorama', in *Pictures From Italy*

4:7 [of Lady Dedlock's portrait] 'That's very like Lady Dedlock,' says Mr Guppy. 'It's a speaking likeness.' 'I wish it was,' growls Tony, without changing his position. 'I should have some fashionable conversation here, then.'

Charles Dickens, 1852–3, *Bleak House*, Ch. 32

4:8 [of Mr Kenge, on the legal system] Gently moving his right hand as if it were a silver trowel, with which to spread the cement of his words on the structure of the system, and consolidate it for a thousand ages.

Charles Dickens, 1852–3, *Bleak House*, Ch. 62

4:9 [Silas Wegg, of Mr Venus] 'Comrade, what a speaking countenance is yours!' Mr. Venus involuntarily smoothed his countenance, and looked at his hand, as if to see whether any of its speaking properties came off.

Charles Dickens, 1864–5, *Our Mutual Friend*, III, Ch. 7

4:10 Have we not kept our guards, like spie on spie? / Had correspondence whilst the foe stood by? ... / Shadow'd with negligence our most respects? / Varied our language through all dialects, / Of becks, winks, looks, and often under-boards / Spoak dialogues with our feet far from our words?

John Donne, 1590s, 'Elegy no. 12: His Parting from Her', 45

4:11 The eyes of men converse as much as their tongues, with the advantage, that the ocular dialect needs no dictionary, but is understood all the world over.

Ralph Waldo Emerson, 1860, 'Behavior', in *The Conduct of Life*

4:12 When the eyes say one thing, and the tongue another, a practised man relies on the language of the first.

Ralph Waldo Emerson, 1860, 'Behavior', in *The Conduct of Life*

4:13 Face of a traitor! / When the mouth says yes, the look says maybe.

Victor Hugo, 1838, *Ruy Blas* (trans.), I. ii

4:14 For him who has eyes to see and ears to hear no mortal can hide his secret; he whose lips are silent chatters with his fingertips and betrays himself through all his pores.

Harold D. Lasswell, 1930, *Psychopathology and Politics*, Preface

4:15 Not spoken in language, but in looks / More legible than printed books.

Henry Wadsworth Longfellow, 1874, *The Hanging of the Crane*, Sect. 3

4:16 A kiss can be a comma, a question mark or an exclamation point. That's basic spelling that every woman ought to know.

Mistinguett, December 1955, *Theatre Arts*

4:17 Gestures and movements animate words, especially in the case of those who gesticulate brusquely as I do and who get excited. Our bearing, our facial expressions, our voice, our dress and the way we stand can lend value to things which in themselves are hardly worth more than chatter.

Michel de Montaigne, 1572–80, 'On Presumption', in *The Complete Essays* (trans. M. A. Screech, 1987), II, no. 17

4:18 There are so many kinds of walking. I walked a special kind of metaphysical sad London walking, which I had walked before, only I performed it now with an almost ritualistic intensity. In Russian there is no general word for 'go'. Going has to be specified as walking or riding, then as habitual or non-habitual walking or riding, then as perfective or imper-

fective habitual or non-habitual walking or riding, all involving different verbs. The sort of walking which I indulged in on that Sunday deserved a special word to celebrate its conceptual peculiarity.

Iris Murdoch, 1975, 'Monday' (second week), in *A Word Child*

4:19 Words, whenever they cannot directly ally themselves with and support themselves upon gestures, are at present a very imperfect means of communication.

C. K. Ogden and I. A. Richards, 1923, *The Meaning of Meaning*, Ch. 1

4:20 The eyes have one language everywhere.

Proverbial

4:21 One may know your meaning by your gaping.

Proverbial

4:22 A kiss, when all is said, what is it? / An oath that's given closer than before; / A promise more precise; the sealing of / Confessions that till then were barely breathed; / A rosy dot placed on the i in loving.

Edmond Rostand, 1897, *Cyrano de Bergerac* (trans. C. Renauld), III. x

4:23 [Falstaff, after being recognized, because of his size, by a rebel knight] I have a whole school of tongues in this belly of mine, and not a tongue of them all speaks any other word but my name.

William Shakespeare, 1597, *Henry IV, Part 2*, IV. ii. 18

4:24 [Ulysses, of Cressida] There's language in her eye, her cheek, her lip; / Nay, her foot speaks.

William Shakespeare, 1602, *Troilus and Cressida*, IV. vi. 56

4:25 [First Gentleman, reporting on the meeting between the King and Camillo] They seemed almost, with staring on one another, to tear the cases of their eyes. There was speech in their dumbness, language in their very gesture.

William Shakespeare, 1609–10, *The Winter's Tale*, V. ii. 11

4:26 PUFF [explaining to Sneer what an actor's shake of the head meant]: Why, by that shake of the head, he gave you to understand that even though they had more justice in their cause, and wisdom in their measures – yet, if there was not a greater spirit shown on the part of the people, the country would at last fall a sacrifice to the hostile ambition of the Spanish monarchy.

SNEER: The devil! did he mean all that by shaking his head?

PUFF: Every word of it – if he shook his head as I taught him.

Richard Sheridan, 1779, *The Critic*, I. ii

4:27 [on shaking hands] There is the *high-official*, – the body erect, and a rapid, short shake, near the chin. There is the *mortmain*, – the flat hand introduced into your palm, and hardly conscious of its contiguity. The *digital*, – one finger held out, much used by the high clergy. There is the *shakus rusticus*, – where your hand is seized in an iron grasp, betokening rude health, warm heart, and distance from the Metropolis; but producing a strong sense of relief on your part when you find your hand released and your fingers unbroken. The next to this is the *retentive shake*, – one which, beginning with vigour, pauses as it were to take breath, but without relinquishing its prey, and before you are aware begins again, till you feel anxious as to the result, and have no shake left in you.

Sydney Smith, 1855, in Lady Holland, *A Memoir of the Reverend Sydney Smith*

4:28 He stood before them with his body swayed, and bent forwards just so far, as to make an angle of 85 degrees and a half upon the plain of the horizon; – which sound orators, to whom I address this, know very well, to be the true persuasive angle of incidence.

Laurence Sterne, 1760, *The Life and Opinions of Tristram Shandy, Gentleman*, II, Ch. 17

4:29 There are certain combined looks of simple subtlety, where whim, and sense, and seriousness, and nonsense, are so blended, that all the languages of Babel set loose together could not express them: they are communicated and caught so instantaneously, that you can scarce say which party is the infector.

Laurence Sterne, 1768, 'The Gloves', in *A Sentimental Journey*

4:30 [on exchanging bows] There is not a secret so aiding to the progress of sociality, as to get master of this *short hand*, and be quick in rendering the several turns of looks and limbs, with all their inflections and delineations, into plain words. For my own part, by long habitude, I do it so mechanically, that when I walk the streets of London, I go translating all the way; and have more than once stood behind in the circle, where not three words have been said, and have brought off twenty different dialogues with me, which I could have fairly wrote down and sworn to.

Laurence Sterne, 1768, 'The Translation', in *A Sentimental Journey*

4:31 Nor do they trust their tongue alone, / But speak a language of their own; / Can read a nod, a shrug, a look, / Far better than a printed book; / Convey as libel in a frown, / And wink a reputation down.

Jonathan Swift, 1729, 'The Journal of a Modern Lady', 188

4:32 A man who wishes to impose his opinions on others is unsure of their value. He has to uphold them by all possible means. He adopts a special tone of voice, thumps the table, smiles on some and browbeats others. In short, he borrows from his body the wherewithal to bolster up his mind.

Paul Valéry, 1942, 'N', in *Bad Thoughts and Not So Bad* (trans. S. Gilbert)

See also: 15·38, 18·34, 25·53, 26·49

5 *Meaning and Sense*

The nature of meaning, definition, sense, and nonsense

5:1 Our use of words is generally inaccurate and seldom completely correct, but our meaning is recognized none the less.

St Augustine, 397–8, *Confessions* (trans. R. S. Pine-Coffin), XI, Sect. 20

5:2 A word never – well, hardly ever – shakes off its etymology and its formation. In spite of all changes in and extensions of and additions to its meanings, and indeed rather pervading and governing these, there will still persist the old idea.

J. L. Austin, 1961, 'A Plea for Excuses', in *Philosophical Papers*, Ch. 6

5:3 The criterion which we use to test the genuineness of apparent statements of fact is the criterion of verifiability. We say that a sentence is factually significant to any given person, if, and only if, he knows how to verify the proposition which it purports to express – that is, if he knows what observations would lead him, under certain conditions, to accept the proposition as being true, or reject it as being false.

A. J. Ayer, 1936, *Language, Truth and Logic*, Ch. 1

5:4 The propositions of philosophy are not factual, but linguistic in character – that is, they do not describe the behaviour of physical, or even mental, objects; they express definitions, or the formal consequences of definitions.

A. J. Ayer, 1936, *Language, Truth and Logic*, Ch. 2

5:5 Sentences which simply express moral judgements do not say anything. They are pure expressions of feeling and as such do not come under the category of truth and falsehood.

A. J. Ayer, 1936, *Language, Truth and Logic*, Ch. 6

5:6 Information is any difference that makes a difference.

Gregory Bateson, September 1984, *Scientific American*, p. 41

5:7 Error is never so difficult to be destroyed as when it has its root in Language.

Jeremy Bentham, quoted as an epigraph in C. K. Ogden and I. A. Richards, *The Meaning of Meaning* (1923)

5:8 Meaning . . . will prove to be more like a handclasp than like a crystal.

Max Black, 1968, *The Labyrinth of Language*, Ch. 7

5:9 We have defined the *meaning* of a linguistic form as the situation in which the speaker utters it and the response which it calls forth in the hearer.

Leonard Bloomfield, 1933, *Language*, Ch. 9

5:10 Definitions . . . are like steps cut in a steep slope of ice, or shells thrown on to a greasy pavement; they give us foothold, and enable us to advance, but when we are at our journey's end we want them no longer.

Samuel Butler (1835–1902), 1890, lecture in London on 'Thought and Language'

5:11 A definition is the enclosing a wilderness of idea within a wall of words.

Samuel Butler (1835–1902), *The Note-Books of Samuel Butler* (1912)

5:12 Definitions are a kind of scratching and generally leave a sore place more sore than it was before.

Samuel Butler (1835–1902), *The Note-Books of Samuel Butler* (1912)

5:13 [Gerard Wijnnobel's reflections on his father's and grandfather's speculations about language] The lesson he drew . . . was that it is possible for human beings to *spend the whole of their lives on nonsense*. And not only that, but perhaps also there was a trap, a quirk, a temptation *in the nature of language itself* that led people, that induced them to spend the whole of their lives on nonsense.

A. S. Byatt, 1996, *Babel Tower*, Ch. 6

5:14 I do believe, / Though I have found them not, that there may be / Words which are things.

Lord Byron, 1816, *Childe Harold's Pilgrimage*, Canto 3, stanza 114

5:15 [Doge, to Benintende] True *words* are *things*, / And dying men's are things which long outlive, / And oftentimes avenge them.

Lord Byron, 1820, *Marino Faliero, Doge of Venice*, V. i

5:16 Meaning, however, is no great matter.

C. S. Calverley, 'Lovers, and a Reflection', in *Complete Works* (1901)

5:17 The declared meaning of a spoken sentence is only its overcoat, and the real meaning lies underneath its scarves and buttons.

Peter Carey, 1988, *Oscar and Lucinda*, Ch. 43

5:18 [on Adam Smith's thoughts about the origins of adjectives] We cannot annihilate a man for etymologies like that!

Thomas Carlyle, 1840, 'The Hero as Divinity', *On Heroes, Hero-Worship, and the Heroic In History*, Lecture 1

5:19 [The Duchess] Take care of the sense, and the sounds will take care of themselves.

Lewis Carroll, 1865, *Alice's Adventures In Wonderland*, Ch. 9

5:20 'When I use a word,' Humpty Dumpty said, in rather a scornful tone, 'it means just what I choose it to mean – neither more nor less.' 'The question is,' said Alice, 'whether you *can* make a word mean so many different things.' 'The question is,' said Humpty Dumpty, 'which is to be master – that's all.'

Lewis Carroll, 1872, *Through the Looking Glass*, Ch. 6

5:21 [Humpty Dumpty] 'Impenetrability! That's what *I* say!' 'Would you tell me, please,' said Alice, 'what that means?' 'Now you talk like a reasonable child,' said Humpty Dumpty, looking very much pleased. 'I meant by "impenetrability" that we've had enough of that subject, and it would be just as well if you'd mention what you mean to do next, as I suppose you don't mean to stop here all the rest of your life.' 'That's a great deal to make one word mean,' Alice said in a thoughtful tone. 'When I make a word do a lot of work like that,' said Humpty Dumpty, 'I always pay it extra.' 'Oh!' said Alice. She was too much puzzled to make any other remark. 'Ah, you should see 'em come round me of a Saturday night,' Humpty Dumpty went on, wagging his head gravely from side to side, 'for to get their wages, you know.'

Lewis Carroll, 1872, *Through the Looking Glass*, Ch. 6

5:22 'I'm sure I didn't mean – ' Alice was beginning, but the Red Queen interrupted her impatiently. 'That's just what I complain of! You *should* have meant! What do you suppose is the use of a child without any meaning? Even a joke should have some meaning – and a child's more important than a joke, I hope.'

Lewis Carroll, 1872, *Through the Looking Glass*, Ch. 9

5:23 [Count Lodovico, on those who use antique words for their own sake] To divorce sense from words is like divorcing the soul from the body: in neither case can this be done without causing destruction.

Baldesar Castiglione, 1528, *The Book of the Courtier* (trans. G. Bull, Penguin 1967), I, p. 76

5:24 The basic tool for the manipulation of reality is the manipulation of words. If you can control the meaning of words, you can control the people who must use the words.

Philip K. Dick, 1986, 'How to Build a Universe That Doesn't Fall Apart Two Days Later', in *I Hope I Shall Arrive Soon*

5:25 Signs are small measurable things, but interpretations are illimitable, and in girls of sweet, ardent nature, every sign is apt to conjure up wonder, hope, belief, vast as a sky, and coloured by a diffused thimbleful of matter in the shape of knowledge.

George Eliot, 1871–2, *Middlemarch*, I, Ch. 3

5:26 That was a way of putting it – not very satisfactory: / A periphrastic study in a worn-out poetical fashion, / Leaving one still with the intolerable wrestle / With words and meanings.

T. S. Eliot, 1944, 'East Coker', Part 2, in *Four Quartets*

5:27 Every word was once a poem. Every new relation is a new word.

Ralph Waldo Emerson, 1844, 'The Poet', in *Essays: Second Series*

5:28 All the facts in Nature are nouns of the intellect, and make the grammar of the eternal language. Every word has a double, treble, or centuple use and meaning.

Ralph Waldo Emerson, 1860, 'Beauty', in *The Conduct of Life*

5:29 The very truths which concern us most can only be half spoken, but with attention we can grasp the whole meaning.

Baltasar Gracián, 1647, *The Art of Worldly Wisdom* (trans. J. Jacobs), p. 146

5:30 The meanings of words are NOT in the words; they are in US.

S. I. Hayakawa, 1939, *Language in Thought and Action*, Ch. 18

5:31 When you see whence a name has arisen, you will understand its force the soonest.

St Isidore of Seville, 7th century, *Origines*, I, 29

5:32 It all depends what you mean by . . .

C. E. M. Joad, 1940s, 'The Brains Trust', BBC radio

5:33 WALKER: 'Do you think, sir, that there are any perfect synonymes in any language?'
　　JOHNSON: 'Originally there were not; but by using words negligently, or in poetry, one word comes to be confounded with another.'

Samuel Johnson, 1783, in James Boswell, *The Life of Samuel Johnson* (1791), Ch. 56

5:34 In all speech, words and sense, are as the body, and the soule. The sense is as the life and soule of Language, without which all words are dead.

Ben Jonson, 1640 (published posthumously), *Timber: or, Discoveries made upon Men and Matter*

5:35 Thus we may conceive how *Words*, which were by Nature so well adapted to that purpose, come to be made use of by Men, as *the Signs* of their *Ideas*; not by any natural connection, that there is between particular articulate Sounds, and certain *Ideas*, for then there would be but one Language amongst all Men; but by a voluntary Imposition, whereby such a Word is made arbitrarily the Mark of such an *Idea*. The use then of Words, is to be sensible Marks of *Ideas*; and the *Ideas* they stand for, are their proper and immediate Signification.

John Locke, 1690, 'Of Words or Language in General', in *An Essay Concerning Human Understanding*, III, Ch. 2, Sect. 1

5:36 We should have a great many fewer disputes in the world if words were taken for what they are, the signs of our ideas only, and not for things themselves.

John Locke, 1690, 'Of Words or Language in General', in *An Essay Concerning Humane Understanding*, III, Ch. 10

5:37 Words are part of action and they are equivalents to actions.

Bronislaw Malinowski, 1935, 'The Language of Magic and Gardening', in *Coral Gardens and their Magic*, II, Part 4, Div. 1

5:38 In all communities, certain words are accepted as potentially creative of acts. You utter a vow or you forge a signature and you may find yourself bound for life to a monastery, a woman or a prison.

Bronislaw Malinowski, 1935, 'The Language of Magic and Gardening', in *Coral Gardens and their Magic*, II, Part 4, Div. 5

5:39 [Simonides] How a good meaning / May be corrupted by a misconstruction.

Thomas Middleton (with William Rowley and Philip Massinger), c.1618, *The Old Law*, I. i

5:40 [Clifford] What you can't say you can't say and you can't whistle it either, as my old philosophy tutor used to observe.

Iris Murdoch, 1975, 'Monday' (first week), in *A Word Child*

5:41 Nothing is more common than for men to think that because they are familiar with words, they understand the ideas they stand for.

John Henry Newman, quoted as an epigraph in Max Black (ed.), *The Importance of Language* (1962)

5:42 The meaning of meaning.

C. K. Ogden and I. A. Richards, 1923, book title

5:43 What is above all needed is to let the meaning choose the word, and not the other way about. In prose, the worst thing one can do with words is to surrender to them.

George Orwell, 1946, 'Politics and the English Language', *Horizon*, no. 13

5:44 Meanings receive their dignity from words instead of giving it to them.

Blaise Pascal, c.1654–62, *Pensées* (trans. W. F. Trotter), no. 50

5:45 Everything's been said, no doubt. If words hadn't changed meaning, and meaning, words.

Jean Paulhan, 1944, *Clef de la poésie* (trans.)

5:46 Does not the eternal sorrow of life consist

in the fact that human beings cannot understand one another, that one person cannot enter into the internal state of another?

Ivan Pavlov, 1928, *Lectures on Conditioned Reflexes*, I, p. 50

5:47 [Hermogenes] Cratylus . . . says that everything has a right name of its own, which comes by nature, and that a name is not just whatever people call a thing by agreement, just a piece of their own voice applied to the thing, but that there is a kind of inherent correctness in names, which is the same for all men.

Plato, 4th century BC, *Cratylus* (trans. H. N. Fowler), 383

5:48 [Hermogenes] I . . . cannot come to the conclusion that there is any correctness of names other than convention and agreement. For it seems to me that whatever name you give to a thing is its right name; and if you give up that name and change it for another, the later name is no less correct than the earlier, just as we change the names of our servants; for I think no name belongs to any particular thing by nature, but only by the habit and custom of those who employ it and who established the usage.

Plato, 4th century BC, *Cratylus* (trans. H. N. Fowler), 384

5:49 'Tis hard to say, if greater want of skill / Appear in writing or in judging ill; / But, of the two, less dang'rous is th' offence / To tire our patience, than mislead our sense.

Alexander Pope, 1711, 'An Essay on Criticism', 1

5:50 Any general statement is like a cheque drawn on a bank. Its value depends on what is there to meet it.

Ezra Pound, 1934, *The ABC of Reading*, Ch. 1

5:51 Every definition is dangerous.

Proverbial (Latin)

5:52 That's not good language that all understand not.

Proverbial

5:53 Names are not the pledge for things, but things for names.

Proverbial (Romanian)

5:54 One's nonsense makes great company for one.

Proverbial (Irish)

5:55 Pending a satisfactory explanation of the notion meaning, linguists . . . are in the situation of not knowing what they are talking about.

William Van Orman Quine, 1953, *From a Logical Point of View*, p. 47

5:56 To define an expression is, paradoxically speaking, to explain how to get along without it. To define is to eliminate.

William Van Orman Quine, 1987, 'Definition', in *Quiddities*

5:57 You must take care, not that your work can be understood, but that it can by no means be misunderstood.

Quintilian, 1st century, *Institutio Oratoria* (trans. F. Hall), VIII, Ch. 2

5:58 Be sure that you go to the author to get at *his* meaning, not to find yours.

John Ruskin, 1865, 'Of Kings' Treasuries', in *Sesame and Lilies*, p. 24

5:59 The linguistic philosophy, which cares only about language, and not about the world, is like the boy who preferred the clock without the pendulum because, although it no longer told the time, it went more easily than before and at a more exhilarating pace.

Bertrand Russell, 1959, foreword to Ernest Gellner, *Words and Things*

5:60 Meanings are not things, not even very queer things.

Gilbert Ryle, 1957, 'The Theory of Meaning', in C. A. Mace (ed.), *British Philosophy in the Mid-Century*

5:61 To grasp the meaning of the world of today we use a language created to express the world of yesterday. The life of the past seems to us nearer our true natures, but only for the reason that it is nearer our language.

Antoine de Saint-Exupéry, 1939, *Wind, Sand, and Stars* (trans. L. Galantière), Ch. 3

5:62 I confused things with their names: that is belief.

Jean-Paul Sartre, 1964, 'Writing', in *Words* (trans. I. Clephane), II

5:63 The meaning of a proposition is the method of its verification.

Moritz Schlick, 1936, *Philosophical Review*, no. 45

5:64 Say what you will against *Tradition*; we

know the Signification of Words by nothing but Tradition.

John Selden, 1689, 'CXXXVIII – Tradition', in *Table-Talk*

5:65 [The General] When a man talks rot, that's epigram: when he talks sense, then I agree with him.

George Bernard Shaw, 1908, *Getting Married*, I

5:66 When I do not understand, I like to say nothing.

Sophocles, 5th century BC, *Oedipus Tyrannus*, 569

5:67 For by the word *Nose*, throughout all this long chapter of noses, and in every other part of my work, where the word *Nose* occurs, – I declare, by that word I mean a Nose, and nothing more, or less.

Laurence Sterne, 1761, *The Life and Opinions of Tristram Shandy, Gentleman*, III, Ch. 31

5:68 Nature had been prodigal in her gifts to my father beyond measure, and had sown the seeds of verbal criticism as deep within him, as she had done the seeds of all other knowledge, – so that he had got out his penknife, and was trying experiments upon the sentence, to see if he could not scratch some better sense into it.

Laurence Sterne, 1761, *The Life and Opinions of Tristram Shandy, Gentleman*, III, Ch. 37

5:69 [Guildenstern] A man talking sense to himself is no madder than a man talking nonsense not to himself.

Tom Stoppard, 1967, *Rosencrantz and Guildenstern Are Dead*, II

5:70 [Stone] Hell's bells. Don't you understand English? When I say to you, 'Tell me what you mean,' you can only reply, 'I would wish to say so and so.' 'Never mind what you wish to say,' I reply. 'Tell me what you mean.'

Tom Stoppard, 1977, *Professional Foul*

5:71 [the Laputian proposal for doing without language] Since words are only names for things, it would be more convenient for all men to carry about them such things as were necessary to express the particular business they are to discourse on.

Jonathan Swift, 1726, 'A Voyage to Laputa', *Gulliver's Travels*, III, Ch. 5

5:72 [of English] Ours is a precarious language, as every writer knows, in which the merest shadow line often separates affirmation from

negation, sense from nonsense, and one sex from another.

James Thurber, 1961, 'Such a Phrase as Drifts through Dreams', in *Lanterns and Lances*

5:73 Names thus so often surviving things, we have no right to turn an etymology into an argument.

Richard Chenevix Trench, 1851, 'On the History in Words', in *On the Study of Words*, Lecture 4

5:74 But while it is quite true that words will often ride very slackly at anchor on their etymologies, will be borne hither and thither by the shifting tides and currents of usage, yet are they for the most part still holden by them. Very few have broken away and drifted from their moorings altogether.

Richard Chenevix Trench, 1851, 'On the Distinction of Words', in *On the Study of Words*, Lecture 6

5:75 We may speak better of the edges of language rather than of its limits. We can go so far out on the platform of language, but if we try to go further, we fall off into a misuse of words, into nonsensical jabbering, into the void where the rules give out.

Paul van Buren, 1972, *The Edges of Language*, Ch. 5

5:76 When one man speaks to another man who doesn't understand him, and when the man who's speaking no longer understands, it's metaphysics.

Voltaire, 1759, *Candide* (trans.)

5:77 After people have repeated a phrase a great number of times, they begin to realize it has meaning and may even be true.

H. G. Wells, 1946, *The Happy Turning*, p. 3

5:78 It is more important that a proposition be interesting than that it be true.

A. N. Whitehead, 1933, *Adventures of Ideas*, IV, Ch. 16

5:79 I like hearing myself talk. It is one of my greatest pleasures. I often have long conversations all by myself, and I am so clever that sometimes I don't understand a single word of what I am saying.

Oscar Wilde, c.1891, in Richard Ellmann, *Oscar Wilde* (1987), Ch. 13

5:80 DUCHESS OF BERWICK: Do, as a concession to my poor wits, Lord Darlington, just explain to me what you really mean.

LORD DARLINGTON: I think I had better not,

Duchess. Nowadays to be intelligible is to be found out.

Oscar Wilde, 1892, *Lady Windermere's Fan*, I

5:81 What can be said at all can be said clearly; and whereof one cannot speak thereof one must be silent.

Ludwig Wittgenstein, 1921, *Tractatus Logico-Philosophicus* (trans.), Preface

5:82 But if we had to name anything which is the life of the sign, we should have to say that it was its *use*.

Ludwig Wittgenstein, 1933–4, *The Blue Book*, in *The Blue and Brown Books* (1965), p. 4

5:83 Philosophers very often talk about investigating, analysing, the meaning of words. But let's not forget that a word hasn't got a meaning given to it, as it were, by a power independent of us, so that there could be a kind of scientific investigation into what the word *really* means. A word has the meaning someone has given to it.

Ludwig Wittgenstein, 1933–4, *The Blue Book*, in *The Blue and Brown Books* (1965), p. 28

5:84 Language is a labyrinth of paths. You approach from *one* side and know your way about; you approach the same place from another side and no longer know your way about.

Ludwig Wittgenstein, 1953, *Philosophical Investigations* (trans.), I, Sect. 203

5:85 If there were a verb meaning 'to believe falsely', it would not have any significant first person, present indicative.

Ludwig Wittgenstein, 1953, *Philosophical Investigations* (trans.), II, Sect. 10

5:86 [on a book which has used etymology to distinguish between the meanings of the words 'fancy' and 'imagination'] Is not this as if a man should undertake to supply an account of a building, and be so intent upon what he had discovered of the foundation, as to conclude his task without once looking up at the super-structure? Here . . . the judicious Author's mind is enthralled by Etymology; he takes up the original word as his guide and escort, and too often does not perceive how soon he becomes its prisoner, without liberty to tread in any path but that to which it confines him.

William Wordsworth, 1815 edition of the *Lyrical Ballads*, Preface

See also: 2:18, 2:91, 2:141, 16:64, 23:22, 27:18, 37:28, 37:83, 39:12, 46:5, 46:14, 58:8, 63:9

6 *Words or Deeds*

The choice between talk and action, language and living

6:1 Words may be deeds.
Aesop, ?6th century BC, 'The Trumpeter Taken Prisoner', in *Fables* (trans.)

6:2 A man of words and not of deeds / Is like a garden full of weeds.
Anonymous, *Mother Goose* nursery rhymes

6:3 The human tongue is a furnace in which the temper of our souls is daily tried.
St Augustine, 397–8, *Confessions* (trans. R. S. Pine-Coffin), X, Sect. 36

6:4 Social institutions are what they do, not necessarily what we say they do. It is the verb that matters, not the noun.
Aneurin Bevan, 1952, *In Place of Fear*

6:5 Not by words is a slave corrected: even if he understands he will take no notice.
The Bible, Proverbs 29:19 (Jerusalem Bible)

6:6 [Bellair] What signifies a few foolish angry words? they don't break bones nor give black eyes.
George Villiers, 2nd Duke of Buckingham, *The Militant Couple*, in *Dramatick Works* (1715), II

6:7 Beneath the rule of men entirely great / The pen is mightier than the sword.
Edward Bulwer-Lytton, 1839, *Richelieu*, II. ii. 307 [cf. 40:41]

6:8 Talking jaw-jaw is always better than war-war.
Winston Churchill, 26 June 1954, speech at the White House, reported in the *New York Times* (27 June)

6:9 Men's words are ever bolder than their deeds.
Samuel Taylor Coleridge, 1800, *The Piccolomini*, I. iv

6:10 Tzu-kung asked about the true gentleman. The Master said, He does not preach what he practises till he has practised what he preaches.
Confucius, 5th century BC, *The Analects* (trans. A. Waley), II, Sect. 13

6:11 The Master said, A gentleman covets the reputation of being slow in word but prompt in deed.
Confucius, 5th century BC, *The Analects* (trans. A. Waley), IV, Sect. 24

6:12 The Master said, Do not be too ready to speak of it [goodness], lest the doing of it should prove to be beyond your powers.
Confucius, 5th century BC, *The Analects* (trans. A. Waley), XIV, Sect. 21

6:13 The Master said, A gentleman is ashamed to let his words outrun his deeds.
Confucius, 5th century BC, *The Analects* (trans. A. Waley), XIV, Sect. 29

6:14 Words, as is well known, are the great foes of reality.
Joseph Conrad, 1911, *Under Western Eyes*, Prologue

6:15 Though language forms the preacher, / 'Tis 'good works' make the man.
Eliza Cook, 1870, 'Good Works'

6:16 [motto of Sir James Brooke] Deeds, not words.
Maria Edgeworth, 1812, *The Absentee*, Ch. 9

6:17 Words and deeds are quite indifferent modes of the divine energy. Words are also actions, and actions are a kind of words.
Ralph Waldo Emerson, 1844, 'The Poet', in *Essays: Second Series*

6:18 Action can give us the feeling of being useful, but only words can give us a sense of weight and purpose.
Eric Hoffer, 1954, *The Passionate State of Mind*, p. 98

6:19 Democracy will not be salvaged by men who talk fluently, debate forcefully and quote aptly.
Lancelot Hogben, 1938, *Science for the Citizen*, Epilogue

6:20 [referring to Italian saying] Deeds are men, and words are but women.
James Howell, 1645, *Epistolae Ho-Elianae: Familiar Letters*, I, no. 5, 31 [cf. 6:54]

6:21 Words have users, but as well, users have words. And it is the users that establish the world's realities.
LeRoi Jones, 1966, 'Expressive Language', in *Home*

6:22 Lofty words cannot construct an alliance or maintain it; only concrete deeds can do that.
John F. Kennedy, 25 June 1963, address in Frankfurt, West Germany

6:23 Where words prevail not, violence pre-vails; / But gold doth more than either of them both.
Thomas Kyd, c.1589, *The Spanish Tragedy*, II. i

6:24 Words have an ancestor and affairs have a sovereign.
Lao Tzu, 6th century BC, *Tao Te Ching* (trans. D. C. Lau, 1963), II, Ch. 70

6:25 Woord is but wynd; leff woord and tak the dede. [Word is but wind; leave word and take the deed.]
John Lydgate (completed by Benedict Burgh), 15th century, *Secrees [Secrets] of Old Philosoffres*, 1,224

6:26 [Cleremond, to Montross] Oh that thou hadst like others been all words, / And noe performance.
Philip Massinger, 1624, *The Parliament of Love*, IV. ii

6:27 I live on good soup, not on fine language.
Molière, 1672, *Les Femmes savantes* (trans.), II. vii

6:28 [on education] Its end has not been to make us good and wise but learned. And it has succeeded. It has not taught us to seek virtue and to embrace wisdom: it has impressed upon us their derivation and their etymology. We know how to decline the Latin word for virtue: we do not know how to love virtue. Though we do not know what wisdom is in practice or from experience we do know the jargon off by heart.
Michel de Montaigne, 1572–80, 'On Presumption', in *The Complete Essays* (trans. M. A. Screech, 1987), II, no. 17

6:29 Words are beautiful things, but muskets and machine guns are even more beautiful.
Benito Mussolini, c.1932, in Denis Mack-Smith, *Mussolini's Roman Empire* (1976)

6:30 A people which is able to say everything becomes able to do everything.
Napoleon I, 1804–15, *Maxims* (trans.)

6:31 Where hands are required words and letters are useless.
Proverbial (German)

6:32 Say well, and do well, end with one letter. / Say well is good, but do well is better.
Proverbial

6:33 Saying and doing are two things.
Proverbial

6:34 Signposts only show the road, they don't go along it.
Proverbial (Swiss-German)

6:35 Who speaks of it commits it not.
Proverbial (Italian)

6:36 He who speaks well fights well.
Proverbial

6:37 Speaking much and doing little willingly inhabit the same house.
Proverbial (Croatian)

6:38 Talk does not cook rice.
Proverbial (Chinese and Hausa)

6:39 The greatest talkers are always the least doers.
Proverbial (Spanish)

6:40 Where gold speaks, every tongue is silenced.
Proverbial (Latin and Italian)

6:41 A long tongue has a short hand.
Proverbial

6:42 A good word does much, but doesn't fill the fasting.
Proverbial (Norwegian)

6:43 From word to deed as from leaf to root.
Proverbial (Serbian)

6:44 Deeds are fruits, words are but leaves.
Proverbial

6:45 Good words without deeds are rushes and reeds.
Proverbial

6:46 Many words will not fill a bushel.
Proverbial

6:47 Words are but sands; 'tis money buys lands.
Proverbial (Italian)

6:48 Fair words butter no parsnips.
Proverbial [cf. 6:59]

6:49 Good words fill not a sack.
Proverbial (Italian)

6:50 Words of gold are often followed by deeds of lead.
Proverbial (Dutch)

6:51 Good words make us laugh; good deeds make us silent.
Proverbial (French)

6:52 Words do not make flour.
Proverbial (Italian)

6:53 Words and deeds are not weighed in the same balance.
Proverbial (Italian)

6:54 Words are feminine; deeds are masculine.
Proverbial (Italian) [cf. 6:20]

6:55 Words won't make the wheels of a mill go round.
Proverbial (Albanian)

6:56 He often is a lion with words who has a hare's heart in his breast.
Proverbial (Latin)

6:57 Words will not fill your purse.
Proverbial (Polish)

6:58 Words shake but examples attract.
Proverbial (Serbian and Croatian)

6:59 Fair words butter no cabbage.
Proverbial (Serbian and Croatian) [cf. 6:48]

6:60 Words make the purchase but the pence pay.
Proverbial (Swedish)

6:61 Words are good, but hens lay eggs.
Proverbial (German)

6:62 Words are dwarfs, but examples are giants.
Proverbial (Swiss-German)

6:63 Words are mere bubbles of water, but deeds are drops of gold.
Proverbial (Chinese and Tibetan)

6:64 Words are easy, friendship hard.
Proverbial (Lugandan)

6:65 Words are silver, the response is gold.
Proverbial (Swahili)

6:66 The best words give no food.
Proverbial (Wolof)

6:67 Words don't season soup.
Proverbial (Brazilian)

6:68 Write a nibful more, eat a mouthful less.
Proverbial (Marathi)

6:69 Trust the man who hesitates in his speech and is quick and steady in action, but beware of long arguments and long beards.
George Santayana, 1922, 'The British Character', in *Soliloquies in England*

6:70 'Actions speak louder than words' may be an excellent maxim from the pragmatic point of view but betrays little insight into the nature of speech.
Edward Sapir, 1933, 'Language', in *Encyclopedia of the Social Sciences*, IX

6:71 [Valentine, to the Duke] Win her with gifts if she respects not words. / Dumb jewels often in their silent kind / More than quick words do move a woman's mind.
William Shakespeare, 1590–1, *The Two Gentlemen of Verona*, III. i. 89

6:72 [Murderer, to Richard] Tut, tut, my lord, we will not stand to prate. Talkers are no good doers. Be assured, / We go to use our hands, and not our tongues.
William Shakespeare, 1592–3, *Richard III*, I. iii. 348

6:73 [Luciana] Shame hath a bastard fame, well

managed; / Ill deeds is doubled with an evil word.

William Shakespeare, 1594, *The Comedy of Errors*, III. ii. 20

6:74 [King John, of the French] And now instead of bullets wrapped in fire / To make a shaking fever in your walls, / They shoot but calm words folded up in smoke / To make a faithless error in your ears.

William Shakespeare, 1595–6, *King John*, II. i. 227

6:75 BRUTUS: Words before blows: is it so, countrymen?

OCTAVIUS: Not that we love words better, as you do.

BRUTUS: Good words are better than bad strokes, Octavius.

ANTONY: In your bad strokes, Brutus, you give good words.

William Shakespeare, 1599, *Julius Caesar*, V. i. 29

6:76 [Claudius] The harlot's cheek, beautied with plast'ring art, / Is not more ugly to the thing that helps it / Than is my deed to my most painted word.

William Shakespeare, 1600–1601, *Hamlet*, III. i. 53

6:77 TROILUS [to Cressida]: You have bereft me of all words, lady.

PANDARUS: Words pay no debts; give her deeds.

William Shakespeare, 1602, *Troilus and Cressida*, III. ii. 53

6:78 [Troilus, after reading a letter] Words, words, mere words, no matter from the heart.

William Shakespeare, 1602, *Troilus and Cressida*, V. iii. 111

6:79 [Mrs Brown] I'm sure I likes young people to be edicated; but it ain't bringin' 'em up proper to teach 'em nothin' but 'ritin' and readin', as only leads to scribblin' when they did ought to be doin' of their work, or readin' rubbishy books when they did ought to be mendin' of their stockins.

Arthur Sketchley, 1876, *Mrs Brown on Spelling Bees*, p. 4

6:80 I see / that everywhere among the race of men / it is the tongue that wins and not the deed.

Sophocles, 5th century BC, *Philoctetes* (trans. D. Grene)

6:81 Such distance is between high words and deeds! / In proof, the greatest vaunter seldom speeds.

Robert Southwell, 1595, *St Peter's Complaint*

6:82 [on being asked what she found to talk about with her new lover, a hussar] Speech happens not to be his language.

Mme de Staël, attributed, early 19th century (trans.)

6:83 'I am ashamed of my emptiness,' said the Word to the Work. / 'I know how poor I am when I see you,' said the Work to the Word.

Rabindranath Tagore, 1916, *Stray Birds* (trans.), p. 138

6:84 There should be less talk; a preaching point is not a meeting point. What do you do then? Take a broom and clean someone's house. That says enough.

Mother Teresa, 1975, 'Carriers of Christ's Love', in *A Gift for God*

6:85 [Lady Windermere] Actions are the first tragedy in life, words are the second. Words are perhaps the worst. Words are merciless.

Oscar Wilde, 1892, *Lady Windermere's Fan*, IV

See also: 8:7, 17:49, 25:97, 37:82, 53:39, 57:38, 58:6

7 Ever-changing Language

Continuity and change in language over time; loan words and neologisms

7:1 There is one evil that concerns literature which should never be passed over in silence but be continually publicly attacked, and that is corruption of the language, for writers cannot invent their own language and are dependent upon the language they inherit so that, if it be corrupt, they must be corrupted.

W. H. Auden, 1948, 'Prologue: Reading', in *The Dyer's Hand and other essays*

7:2 I am convinced that French, the language which I employ, is comparatively poor in resources. What is to be done in such a case? I must borrow, or steal. I do both, since these borrowings are not subject to an order for restitution, and the theft of words is not a punishable offence.

Jean-Anthelme Brillat-Savarin, 1825, *The Physiology of Taste* (trans.), Preface

7:3 No Languages have been so straitly lock'd up as not to admit of commixture.

Sir Thomas Browne, before 1682, 'Of Languages, and Particularly of the Saxon Tongue', *Certain Miscellany Tracts*, VIII

7:4 One cannot but be impressed by the amazing hospitality of the English language.

Robert Burchfield, 1985, *The English Language*, Ch. 3

7:5 There are no constitutional processes leading to declarations of linguistic independence as there are in politics. No flags are run up as signs or symbols of linguistic sovereignty. There are no governor-generals of language, and no linguistic Boston Tea Parties. Languages break free without ceremony, almost unnoticed by the speakers themselves.

Robert Burchfield, 1985, *The English Language*, Ch. 10

7:6 The English language is like a fleet of juggernaut trucks that goes on regardless. No form of linguistic engineering and no amount of linguistic legislation will prevent the cycles of change that lie ahead.

Robert Burchfield, 1985, *The English Language*, Ch. 10

7:7 No man, however learned or powerful, can exert control over a language, despite the 'Newspeak' of George Orwell's *Nineteen Eighty-Four*. Languages change, and we cannot stop them changing, nor can we determine the modes in which they shall change. It is not even possible to legislate for a language, to say what is right and what is wrong. . . . If it is wrong to say 'you was', then the educated men of the eighteenth century were wrong. If it is sluttish to drop one's aitches, then Queen Elizabeth I was a slut.

Anthony Burgess, 1992, *A Mouthful of Air*, I, Ch. 1

7:8 For Hebrew roots, although they're found / To flourish most in barren ground, / He had such plenty as suffic'd / To make some think him circumcis'd.

Samuel Butler (1612–80), 1663, *Hudibras*, I, Canto 1, 59

7:9 [of Hudibras's speech] 'Twas English cut on Greek and Latin, / Like fustian heretofore on satin.

Samuel Butler (1612–80), 1663, *Hudibras*, I, Canto 1, 97

7:10 [of Hudibras] For he could coin or counterfeit / New words, with little or no wit; / Words so debas'd and hard, no stone / Was hard enough to touch them on; / And when with hasty noise he spoke 'em; / The ignorant for current took 'em.

Samuel Butler (1612–80), 1663, *Hudibras*, I, Canto 1, 109

7:11 Then fear not, if 'tis needful, to produce / Some term unknown, or obsolete in use, / (As Pitt has furnish'd us a word or two, / Which lexicographers declined to do;) / So you indeed, with care, – (but be content / To take this license rarely) – may invent. / New words find credit in these latter days, / If neatly grafted on a Gallic phrase.

Lord Byron, 1811, *Hints From Horace*, 73

7:12 As forests shed their foliage by degrees, / So fade expressions which in season please; / And we and ours, alas! are due to fate, / And works and words but dwindle to a date.

Lord Byron, 1811, *Hints From Horace*, 89

7:13 The alteration and innovation in our tongue as in all others, hath beene brought in by entrance of Strangers, as *Danes*, *Normans*, and others which have swarmed hither, by traffickc, for new words as well as for new wares, have alwaies come in by the tyranne *Time*, which altereth all vnder heaven, by *Vse*, which sway-eth most, and hath an absolute command in words, and by *Pregnant wits*.

William Camden, 1605, 'The Languages', in *Remaines Concerning Britain*

7:14 Whereas our tongue is mixed, it is no dis-grace, whenas all the tongues of *Europe* doe par-ticipate interchangeably the one of the other, and in the learned tongues, there hath been like borrowing one from another.

William Camden, 1605, 'The Languages', in *Remaines Concerning Britain*

7:15 Intercourse between different peoples has always carried new words from one place to another, just like articles of trade, after which they either take root or disappear, depending on whether they are admitted or rejected by usage.

Baldesar Castiglione, 1528, *The Book of the Courtier* (trans. G. Bull, Penguin 1967), Dedication, p. 34

7:16 Just as to try to coin completely new words or to preserve old ones, regardless of usage, is silly and presumptuous, so also, as well as being difficult, it is surely almost impious, equally regardless of usage to try to destroy and, as it were, bury alive, those which have already survived many centuries and under the protec-

tion of usage have defended themselves against the envy of time and maintained their dignity and splendour despite all the changes, caused by war and upheaval in Italy, of language, build-ings, dress and customs.

Baldesar Castiglione, 1528, *The Book of the Courtier* (trans. G. Bull, Penguin 1967), Dedication, p. 34

7:17 [Count Lodovico] Just as the seasons of the year divest the earth of its flowers and fruits, and then adorn it again with others, so time causes those first words to decline and then usage gives life to others, endowing them with grace and dignity until, gradually worn away by the envious depredations of time, they also go to their death; for, at the last, we and all our possessions are mortal.

Baldesar Castiglione, 1528, *The Book of the Courtier* (trans. G. Bull, Penguin 1967), I, p. 80

7:18 And certaynly our langage now vsed vary-eth ferre [far] from that. whiche was vsed and spoken whan I was borne / For we englysshe men / ben [are] borne vnder the domynacyon of the mone. whiche is neuer stedfaste / but euer wauerynge / wexynge one season / and waneth & dyscreaseth another season / And that comyn [common] englisshe that is spoken in one shyre varyeth from a nother.

William Caxton, c.1490, prologue to Virgil's *Booke of Eneydos* [original punctuation retained]

7:19 And one of theym [merchants] named sheffelde a mercer cam into an hows and axed [asked] for mete [food]. and specyally he axyd after eggys And the good wyf answerde . that she coude speke no frenshe. And the merchaunt was angry, for he also coude speke no frenshe, but wolde haue hadde egges / and she vnder-stode hym not / And thenne at laste a nother sayd that he wolde haue eyren / then the good wyf sayd that she vnderstod hym wel / Loo what sholde a man in thyse dayes now wryte . egges or eyren / certaynly it is harde to playse euery man / by cause of dyuersite & chaunge of langage.

William Caxton, c.1490, prologue to Virgil's *Booke of Eneydos* [original punctuation retained]

7:20 And som honest and grete clerkes haue ben wyth me and desired me to wryte the moste curyous termes that I coude fynde / and thus bytwene playn rude / & curyous I stande abasshed. but in my Iudgemente / the comyn termes that be dayli vsed ben [are] lyghter to be vnderstonde than the olde and auncyent englysshe.

William Caxton, c.1490, prologue to Virgil's *Booke of Eneydos* [original punctuation retained]

7:21 BERGANZA: There are some Spanish writers who now and then insert bits of Latin phrases into the conversation, giving the impression to those who do not understand that they are great Latinists, when they scarcely know how to decline a noun or conjugate a verb.

SCIPIO: I consider them to be less harmful than those who really do know Latin, of whom there are some who are so lacking in sense that when they are talking to a cobbler or a tailor they throw in Latin phrases like water.

Miguel de Cervantes, 1613, 'The Dogs' Colloquy', in *Exemplary Stories* (trans. C. A. Jones)

7:22 Ye knowe ek [also] that in forme of speche is chaunge / Withinne a thousand yeer, and wordes tho / That hadden pris, now wonder nyce and straunge / Us thinketh hem, and yet thei spake hem so.

Geoffrey Chaucer, c.1385, *Troilus and Criseyde*, II, 22

7:23 And for ther is so gret diversite / In Englissh and in writyng of oure tonge; / And red [read] wherso thow be, or elles songe, / That thow be understonde, God I beseche!

Geoffrey Chaucer, c.1385, *Troilus and Criseyde*, V, 1,786

7:24 I am of this opinion that our own tung shold be written cleane and pure, unmixt and unmangeled with borowing of other tunges, wherin if we take not heed by tijm, ever borowing and never payeng, she shall be fain to keep her house as bankrupt.

John Cheke, 1561, letter to Sir Thomas Hoby, in preface to Hoby's translation of *The Courtier*

7:25 Words are taken alive from a defunct language.

Hélène Cixous, 1976, *La* (trans.)

7:26 Their talk was endless, compulsive, and indulgent, sometimes sounding like the remains of the English language after having been hashed over by nuclear war survivors for a few hundred years.

Douglas Coupland, 1991, 'It Can't Last', in *Generation X*

7:27 And who, in time, knows whither we may vent / The treasure of our tongue, to what strange shores / This gain of our best glory shall be sent, / T'enrich unknowing nations with our stores? / What worlds in th'yet unformed Occident / May come refined with th'accents that are ours?

Samuel Daniel, 1599, *Musophilus*, I, 957

7:28 I cannot but think that the using and introducing foreign terms of art or foreign words into speech while our language labours under no penury or scarcity of words is an intolerable grievance.

Daniel Defoe, 10 October 1708, *The Review*

7:29 In aristocracies language must naturally partake of that state of repose in which everything else remains. Few new words are coined because few new things are made. . . . The constant agitation that prevails in a democratic community tends unceasingly, on the contrary, to change the character of the language. Besides, democratic nations love change for its own sake, and this is seen as much in their language as in their politics. Even when they have no need to change words, they sometimes have the desire.

Alexis de Tocqueville, 1835–40, *De la Démocratie en Amérique [Democracy in America]* (trans.), Ch. 16

7:30 [of new words and phrases] 'Tis obvious that we have admitted many: some of which we wanted, and therefore our Language is the richer for them: as it would be by importation of Bullion: others are rather Ornamental than Necessary; yet by their admission, the Language is become more courtly: and our thoughts are better drest.

John Dryden, 1672, 'Defence of the Epilogue', appended to *The Conquest of Granada*

7:31 We meet daily with those Fopps, who value themselves on their Travelling, and pretend they cannot express their meaning in *English*, because they would put off to us some *French* Phrase of the last Edition: without considering that, for ought they know, we have a better of our own.

John Dryden, 1672, 'Defence of the Epilogue', appended to *The Conquest of Granada*

7:32 I trade both with the living and the dead, for the enrichment of our native tongue. We have enough in England to supply our necessity, but if we will have things of magnificence and splendour, we must get them by commerce.

John Dryden, 1697, dedication to his translation of *The Aeneid*

7:33 For last year's words belong to last year's

language / And next year's words await another voice.

T. S. Eliot, 1944, 'Little Gidding', Part 2, in *Four Quartets*

7:34 Poetry should help, not only to refine the language of the time, but to prevent it from changing too rapidly.

T. S. Eliot, 1947, 'Milton'

7:35 Our language, or any civilized language, is like the phoenix: it springs anew from its own ashes.

T. S. Eliot, quoted in prefatory note to L. Michaels and C. Ricks (eds), *The State of the Language* (1980)

7:36 [on creating new words] We lack a term; we feel the need of one. Choose a pleasant sound, with no trace of ambiguity about it, which adapts itself to our language, and which is an easy way of making our speech more concise. Each individual first of all sees an opportunity for it; four or five people risk using it unassumingly in informal conversation; others repeat it because of its taste of novelty; and there it is in fashion. In this way a footpath newly begun across a field soon becomes the most well-trodden, when the old road is found to be uneven and not so short.

François Fénelon, 1714, 'Letter to the French Academy' (trans.)

7:37 Our language is at best; and it will fail, / As th'inundation of French words prevail. / Let Waller be our standard: all beyond, / Tho' spoke at court, is foppery and fond.

Robert Gould, 1687, prefixed to Edward Fairfax's *Godfrey of Bulloigne*

7:38 Heedless that new discoveries, inventions, and speculations, converse with foreign nations and their literary productions, and various other causes tending to modify human speech, have always been working changes in English, our linguistic conservatives unconsciously demand, for the realisation of their insensate chimera of fixity, that the course of nature should be suspended, and, withal, that the mind of man should be reduced to complete stagnation.

Fitzedward Hall, 1880, 'English Rational and Irrational', *The Nineteenth Century*, XLIII

7:39 It has always been accepted, and always will be, that words stamped with the mint-mark of the day should be brought into currency. As the woods change their foliage with the decline of each year, and the earliest leaves fall, so words die out with old age; and the newly born ones thrive and prosper just like human beings in the vigour of youth.

Horace, 19–18 BC, *Ars Poetica* (trans. D. S. Dorsch), 58

7:40 Living languages are in a continuous state of change. Only dead languages stay still, which is why Latin and Ancient Greek are the best languages for grammarians. They can legislate for dead languages, without finding that the languages have moved on while they were writing, and made their rules about correctness and incorrectness obsolete.

Philip Howard, 1978, contribution to 'Language: U and non-U, double-U, E and non-E', in Richard Buckle (ed.), *U and Non-U Revisited*, p. 45

7:41 French is not a *static* language and will never become static.

Victor Hugo, 1827, *Cromwell* (trans.), Preface

7:42 There can never be a moment of true standstill in language, just as little as in the ceaselessly flaming thought of men.

Wilhelm von Humboldt, 1836, 'On the Structural Variety of Human Language and its Influence on the Intellectual Development of Mankind' (trans. W. P. Lehmann), Ch. 19

7:43 It has been my endeavour in this work to represent English Grammar not as a set of stiff dogmatic precepts, according to which some things are correct and others absolutely wrong, but as something living and developing under continual fluctuations and undulations, something that is founded on the past and prepares the way for the future, something that is not always consistent or perfect, but progressing and perfectible – in one word, human.

Otto Jespersen, 1909, *A Modern English Grammar*, Preface, I

7:44 When we see men grow old and die at a certain time one after another, from century to century, we laugh at the elixir that promises to prolong life to a thousand years; and with equal justice may the lexicographer be derided, who being able to produce no example of a nation that has preserved their words and phrases from mutability, shall imagine that his dictionary can embalm his language, and secure it from corruption and decay, that it is in his power to change sublunary nature, and clear the world at once from folly, vanity, and affectation.

Samuel Johnson, 1755, *A Dictionary of the English Language*, Preface

7:45 Total and sudden transformations of a language seldom happen; conquests and migrations are now very rare: but there are other causes of change, which, though slow in their operation, and invisible in their progress, are perhaps as much superiour to human resistance, as the revolutions of the sky, or intumescence of the tide.

Samuel Johnson, 1755, *A Dictionary of the English Language*, Preface

7:46 A man coynes not a new word without some perill, and lesse fruit; for if it happen to be received, the praise is but moderate; if refus'd, the scorne is assur'd.

Ben Jonson, 1640 (published posthumously), *Timber: or, Discoveries made upon Men and Matter*

7:47 Words borrow'd of Antiquity, doe lend a kind of Majesty to style, and are not without their delight sometimes. For they have the Authority of yeares, and out of their intermission doe win to themselves a kind of grace-like newnesse. But the eldest of the present, and newest of the past Language is the best.

Ben Jonson, 1640 (published posthumously), *Timber: or, Discoveries made upon Men and Matter*

7:48 What each generation forgets is that while the words which it uses to describe ideas are always changing, the ideas themselves do not change so quickly, nor are those ideas in any sense new. If we pay no attention to words whatever, we may become like the isolated gentleman who invents a new perpetual-motion machine on old lines in ignorance of all previous plans, and then is surprised that it doesn't work. If we confine our attention entirely to the slang of the day – that is to say, if we devote ourselves exclusively to modern literature – we get to think the world is progressing when it is only repeating itself.

Rudyard Kipling, May 1912, 'The Uses of Reading' (speech at Wellington College), in *A Book of Words*

7:49 [on warning that neologisms are never used in the way their creators expect] Smart little writers pick up words briskly; but only as a jackdaw picks up beads and glass.

C. S. Lewis, 1960, *Studies in Words*, Ch. 9

7:50 What enriches a language is its being handled and exploited by beautiful minds – not so much by making innovations as by expanding it through more vigorous and varied applications, by extending it and deploying it. It is not words that they contribute: what they do is enrich their words, deepen their meanings and tie down their usage; they teach it unaccustomed rhythms, prudently though and with ingenuity.

Michel de Montaigne, 1572–80, 'On some Lines of Virgil', in *The Complete Essays* (trans. M. A. Screech, 1987), III, no. 5

7:51 [on French] In our own language there is plenty of cloth but a little want of tailoring. There is no limit to what could be done with the help of our hunting and military idioms, which form a fruitful field for borrowing; locutions are like seedlings: transplanting makes them better and stronger.

Michel de Montaigne, 1572–80, 'On some Lines of Virgil', in *The Complete Essays* (trans. M. A. Screech, 1987), III, no. 5

7:52 [on French] It goes flowing through our fingers every day, and during my lifetime half of it has changed. We say that it is perfect now: each age says that of its own. I do not think it has reached perfection while it is still running away and changing form. It is up to good and useful writings to buckle French on to themselves, and its reputation will follow the fortunes of our State.

Michel de Montaigne, 1572–80, 'On Vanity', in *The Complete Essays* (trans. M. A. Screech, 1987), III, no. 9

7:53 As for the antiquitie of our speche, whether it be measured by the ancient *Almane* [German], whence it cummeth originallie, or euen but by the latest terms which it boroweth daielie from foren tungs, either of pure necessitie in new matters, or of mere brauerie, to garnish it self withall it cannot be young.

Richard Mulcaster, 1582, *The First Part of the Elementarie*, Ch. 13

7:54 The introduction of foreign and learned words, unless where necessity requires them, should never be admitted into our composition. Barren languages may need such assistance, but ours is not one of these.

Lindley Murray, 1795, *English Grammar*, Appendix, Ch. 1

7:55 War is a powerful excitant, perhaps the most rapidly effectual excitant, of language.

Eric Partridge, January 1947, 'Thanks to the War . . .', *Quarterly Review*

7:56 War, decimator of nations and desolation of women, has ever been an augmentor of vocabulary.

Eric Partridge, 1948, 'War as a Word-maker', in *Words at War: Words at Peace*

7:57 Some by old words to fame have made pretence, / Ancients in phrase, mere moderns in their sense; / Such labour'd nothings, in so strange a style, / Amaze th' unlearn'd, and make the learned smile.

Alexander Pope, 1711, 'An Essay on Criticism', 324

7:58 In words, as fashions, the same rule will hold; / Alike fantastic, if too new, or old: / Be not the first by whom the new are try'd, / Nor yet the last to lay the old aside.

Alexander Pope, 1711, 'An Essay on Criticism', 333

7:59 [of the practices of poor poets] Mark where a bold expressive phrase appears, / Bright thro' the rubbish of some hundred years; / Command old words that long have slept, to wake, / Words, that wise Bacon, or brave Raleigh spake; / Or bid the new be English, ages hence, / (For Use will farther what's begot by Sense) / Pour the full tide of Eloquence along, / Serenely pure, and yet divinely strong, / Rich with the treasures of each foreign tongue.

Alexander Pope, 1737, 'The Second Epistle of The Second Book of Horace', *Imitations of Horace*, 165

7:60 Words must die, but man must live.

Proverbial (Jamaican and Trinidadian Creole)

7:61 Language moves down time in a current of its own making.

Edward Sapir, 1921, *Language*, Ch. 7

7:62 So now they have made our English tongue a gallimaufry or hodgepodge of all other speeches.

Edmund Spenser, 1579, letter to Gabriel Harvey, in *The Shepherd's Calendar*

7:63 'Tis manifest, that all new affected Modes of Speech, whether borrowed from the Court, the Town, or the Theatre, are the first perishing Parts in any Language.

Jonathan Swift, 27 September 1710, 'The Continual Corruption of our English Tongue', Letter to Isaac Bickerstaff in *The Tatler*

7:64 But the *English* Tongue is not arrived to such a Degree of Perfection, as to make us apprehend any Thoughts of its Decay; and if it were once refined to a certain Standard, perhaps there might be Ways found to fix it for ever; or at least till we are invaded and made a Conquest by some other State.

Jonathan Swift, 1712, 'A Proposal for Correcting, Improving and Ascertaining the English Tongue'

7:65 I have never known this great Town without one or more *Dunces* of Figure [importance], who had Credit enough to give Rise to some new Word, and propagate it in most Conversations, though it had neither Humor, nor Significancy.

Jonathan Swift, 1712, 'A Proposal for Correcting, Improving and Ascertaining the English Tongue'

7:66 But what I have most at Heart is, that some Method should be thought on for *ascertaining* and *fixing* our Language for ever, after such Alterations are made in it as shall be thought requisite. For I am of Opinion, that it is better a Language should not be wholly perfect, than that it should be perpetually changing.

Jonathan Swift, 1712, 'A Proposal for Correcting, Improving and Ascertaining the English Tongue'

7:67 The language of this country being always upon the flux, the Struldbrugs of one age do not understand those of another, neither are they able after two hundred years to hold any conversation (farther than by a few general words) with their neighbours the mortals; and thus they lie under the disadvantage of living like foreigners in their own country.

Jonathan Swift, 1726, 'A Voyage to Laputa', *Gulliver's Travels*, III, Ch. 10

7:68 When old words die out on the tongue, new melodies break forth from the heart; and where the old tracks are lost, new country is revealed with its wonders.

Rabindranath Tagore, 1912, *Gitanjali* (trans.), p. 37

7:69 [on trying to stop new words entering a language] The French Academy, numbering all or nearly all the most distinguished writers of France, once sought to exercise such a domination over their own language, and might have hoped to succeed, if success had been possible for any. But the language heeded their decrees as little as the advancing tide heeded those of Canute.

Richard Chenevix Trench, 1851, 'On the Rise of New Words', in *On the Study of Words*, Lecture 5

7:70 But who can hope his lines shou'd long / Last, in a daily changing tongue? / While they are new, Envy prevails, / And as that dies, our language fails. ... Poets that Lasting Marble seek / Must carve in Latin, or in Greek; / We

write in Sand. Our language grows, / And, like the tide, our work o'erflows.
Edmund Waller, 1645, 'Of English Verse'

7:71 Numerous local causes, such as a new country, new associations of people, new combinations of ideas in arts and science, and some intercourse with tribes wholly unknown in Europe, will introduce new words into the American tongue. These causes will produce, in a course of time, a language in North America, as different from the future language of England, as the Modern Dutch, Danish and Swedish are from the German, or from one another.
Noah Webster, 1817, 'Letter to Pickering'

7:72 Stability in language is synonymous with *rigor mortis*.
Ernest Weekley, 1929, 'The English Language', p. 9

7:73 Among all other lessons this should first be learned, that wee never affect any straunge ynkehorne [inkhorn] termes, but to speake as is commonly received: neither seeking to be over fine, nor yet living over-carelesse, using our speeche as most men doe, and ordering our wittes as the fewest have done. Some seeke so far for outlandish English, that they forget altogether their mothers language. And I dare sweare this, if some of their mothers were alive, thei were not able to tell what they say: and yet these fine English clerkes will say, they speake in their mother tongue, if a man should charge them for counterfeiting the Kings English.
Thomas Wilson, 1553, 'Plainnesse, What it is', in *The Arte of Rhetorique*

7:74 We must be free or die, who speak the tongue / That Shakespeare spake.
William Wordsworth, 1802, 'It is not to be thought of '

See also: 8:11, 8:18, 8:36, 8:42, 8:46, 8:59, 8:65, 10:2, 10:31, 13:8, 28:13, 38:12, 42:8, 47:4, 51:24

8 *Arguing About Usage*

Issues of usage and correctness in language

8:1 'Whom are you?' he asked, for he had attended business college.

George Ade, 16 March 1898, 'The Steel Box', *Chicago Record*

8:2 [of the phrase 'the Queen's English'] This land's great highway of thought and speech.

Henry Alford, 1864, *The Queen's English*, p. 2

8:3 [after a conversation with a new acquaintance, whose wife then calls out to him, 'Sammy, love!'] A man may as well suck his thumb all his life, as talk, or allow to be talked to him, such drivelling nonsense. . . . Never let the world look through these chinks into the boudoir.

Henry Alford, 1864, *The Queen's English*, p. 262

8:4 As I left I would hear the beginning of an intimate conversation. Momma persistently using the wrong verb, or none at all. 'Brother and Sister Wilcox is sho'ly the meanest —' 'Is,' Momma? 'Is'? Oh, please, not 'is,' Momma, for two or more. But they talked, and from the side of the building where I waited for the ground to open up and swallow me, I heard the soft-voiced Mrs Flowers and the textured voice of my grandmother merging and melting.

Maya Angelou, 1969, *I Know Why the Caged Bird Sings*, Ch. 15

8:5 I beg leave to propose a plan for perfecting the English language in America, thro' every future period of its existence; viz. That a society, for this purpose should be formed, consisting of members in each university and seminary, who shall be stiled, *Fellows of the American Society of Language*: That the society, when established, from time to time elect new members, & thereby be made perpetual. And that the society annu-

ally publish some observations upon the language and from year to year, correct, enrich and refine it, until perfection stops their progress and ends their labour.

Anonymous communication from 'An American', January 1774, *Royal American Magazine*, possibly from John (later, President) Adams

8:6 [on the various plural forms of *rhinoceros*] The moral that I draw from these is / The plural's what one damn well pleases.

Anonymous, 'Hints on Pronunciation for Foreigners', in *The Faber Book of Useful Verse* (1981), p. 149

8:7 O Lord my God, be patient, as you always are, with the men of this world as you watch them and see how strictly they obey the rules of grammar which have been handed down to them, and yet ignore the eternal rules of everlasting salvation which they have received from you. A man who has learnt the traditional rules of pronunciation, or teaches them to others, gives greater scandal if he breaks them by dropping the aitch from 'human being' than if he breaks your rules and hates another human, his fellow man.

St Augustine, 397–8, *Confessions* (trans. R. S. Pine-Coffin), I, Sect. 18

8:8 I'm sick of cautious lyricism / of well-behaved lyricism / of a civil servant lyricism complete with time card office hours set procedures and expressions of esteem for Mr Boss, Sir. / I'm sick of the lyricism that has to stop in midstream to look up the precise meaning of a word. / Down with purists!

Manuel Bandeira, 1930, 'Poética', in *Libertinagem* (trans. as *Poetics*, 1989)

8:9 Heedless of grammar, they all cried 'That's him!'

R. H. Barham, 1840, 'The Jackdaw of Rheims', in *The Ingoldsby Legends*, First Series

8:10 In certain respects the English language is in its present condition inferior to some of its rivals as a convenient carrier of thought; and it would be a disgrace to us if we made no effort to bring it up to the mark.

Robert Bridges, 1925, 'The Society's Work', Society for Pure English, Tract 21

8:11 [on those who imitate French manners] T' adorn their English with French scraps, / And give their very language claps; / To jernie rightly, and renounce / I' th' pure and most approv'd-of tones, / And, while they idly think t'enrich, / Adulterate their native speech: / For though to smatter ends of Greek / Or Latin be the rhetoric / Of pedants counted, and vain-glorious, / To smatter French is meritorious; / And to forget their mother tongue, / Or purposely to speak it wrong, / A hopeful sign of parts and wit, / And that they' improve and benefit.

Samuel Butler (1612–80), 1670s, 'Satire upon our Ridiculous Imitation of the French'

8:12 [on the pedant] Kept tutors of all sorts, and virtuosos, / To read all authors to him, with their glosses, / And made his lacquies, when he walk'd, bear folios / Of dictionaries, lexicons, and scholias, / To be read to him every way the wind / Should chance to sit, before him or behind; / Had read out all th' imaginary duels / That had been fought by consonants and vowels; / Had crackt his skull to find out proper places / To lay up all memoirs of things in cases; / And practis'd all the tricks upon the charts, / To play with packs of sciences and arts, / That serve t' improve a feeble gamester's study, / That ventures at grammatic beast or noddy.

Samuel Butler (1612–80), 1670s, 'Satire upon the Imperfection and Abuse of Human Learning', fragments of an intended second part

8:13 Yet it is better to drop thy friends, O my daughter, than to drop thy 'H.s'.

C. S. Calverley, 'Of Friendship', in *Complete Works* (1901)

8:14 Language is purely a species of fashion . . . It is not the business of grammar, as some critics seem preposterously to imagine, to give law to the fashions which regulate our speech. On the contrary, from its conformity to these, and from

that alone, it derives all its authority and value.

George Campbell, 1776, *The Philosophy of Rhetoric*, I, p. 340

8:15 The power and correct rules of good speech consist more in usage than in anything else and it is always wrong to employ words which are not current.

Baldesar Castiglione, 1528, *The Book of the Courtier* (trans. G. Bull, Penguin 1967), Dedication, p. 33

8:16 [Federico] This matter of contemporary usage, on which you put so much stress, seems to me highly dangerous and very often wrong. If some solecism or other is adopted by many ignorant people, this, in my opinion, hardly means that it should be accepted as a rule and followed by others.

Baldesar Castiglione, 1528, *The Book of the Courtier* (trans. G. Bull, Penguin 1967), I, p. 73

8:17 [Count Lodovico] Good usage in speech, so I believe, is established by men of discernment, who through learning and experience have acquired sound judgement, which enables them to agree among themselves and consent to accept those words which commend themselves to them; and these they recognize by means of a certain instinctive judgement and not by any formula or rule.

Baldesar Castiglione, 1528, *The Book of the Courtier* (trans. G. Bull, Penguin 1967), I, p. 80

8:18 [Don Quixote, explaining his use of an obscure word to Sancho] If some people do not understand these terms it is of little consequence, for they will come into use in time, and then they will be generally understood; for that is the way to enrich the language, which depends upon custom and the common people.

Miguel de Cervantes, 1605, *The Adventures of Don Quixote* (trans. J. M. Cohen), II, Ch. 43

8:19 Would you convey my compliments to the purist who reads your proofs and tell him or her that I write in a sort of broken-down patois which is something like the way a Swiss waiter talks, and that when I split an infinitive, God damn it, I split it so it will stay split.

Raymond Chandler, 18 January 1947, letter to Edward Weeks (editor of the *Atlantic Monthly*)

8:20 I had long lamented that we had no lawful standard of our language set up, for those to repair to, who might chuse to speak and write it grammatically and correctly: and I have as long wished that either some one person of distinguished abilities would undertake the work singly, or that a certain number of gentlemen would form themselves, or be formed by the government, into a society for that purpose.

Lord Chesterfield, 28 November 1754, letter to *The World*

8:21 [on the need for a dictator, to bring order to English] I give my vote for Mr Johnson to fill that great and arduous post. And I hereby declare that I make a total surrender of all my rights and privileges in the English language, as a freeborn British subject, to the said Mr Johnson, during the term of his dictatorship. Nay more; I will not only obey him, like an old Roman, as my dictator, but, like a modern Roman, I will implicitly believe in him as my pope, and hold him to be infallible while in the chair; but no longer.

Lord Chesterfield, 28 November 1754, letter to *The World*

8:22 I regret to see that vile and barbarous vocable *talented*, stealing out of the newspapers into the leading reviews and most respectable publications of the day. Why not *shillinged, farthinged, tenpenced*, &c.? The formation of a participle passive from a noun, is a licence that nothing but a very peculiar felicity can excuse. If mere convenience is to justify such attempts upon the idiom, you cannot stop till the language becomes, in the proper sense of the word, corrupt. Most of these pieces of slang come from America.

Samuel Taylor Coleridge, 8 July 1832, in Henry Nelson Coleridge (ed.), *Specimens of the Table-Talk of the late Samuel Taylor Coleridge* (1835)

8:23 We must use words as they are used or stand aside from life.

Ivy Compton-Burnett, 1955, *Mother and Son*, Ch. 9

8:24 [on his proposal for an English Academy] The Work of this Society shou'd be to encourage Polite Learning, to polish and refine the *English* Tongue, and advance the so much neglected Faculty of Correct Language, to establish Purity and Propriety of Stile, and to purge it from all the Irregular Additions that Ignorance and Affectation have introduc'd; and all those Innovations in Speech, if I may call them such, which some Dogmatic Writers have the Confidence to foster upon their Native Language, as

if their Authority were sufficient to make their own Fancy legitimate.

Daniel Defoe, 1697, 'Of Academies', in *An Essay upon Projects*

8:25 Into this Society [an English Academy] should be admitted none . . . whose *English* has been far from Polite, full of Stiffness and Affectation, hard Words, and long unusual Coupling of *Syllables* and Sentences, which sound harsh and untuneable to the ear, and shock the Reader, both in Expression and Understanding.

In short, there should be room in this Society for neither *Clergyman, Physician*, or *Lawyer*.

Daniel Defoe, 1697, 'Of Academies', in *An Essay upon Projects*

8:26 The Voice of this Society [an English Academy] should be sufficient Authority for the Usage of Words, and sufficient also to expose the Innovations of other mens Fancies; they shou'd preside with a sort of Judicature over the Learning of the Age, and have liberty to Correct and Censure the Exorbitance of Writers, especially of Translators. The Reputation of this Society wou'd be enough to make them the allow'd Judges of Stile and Language; and no Author wou'd have the Impudence to Coin without their Authority. *Custom*, which is now our best Authority for Words, wou'd always have its Original here, and not be allow'd without it. There shou'd be no more occasion to search for Derivations and Constructions, and 'twou'd be as Criminal then to *Coin Words*, as *Money*.

Daniel Defoe, 1697, 'Of Academies', in *An Essay upon Projects*

8:27 'Tis true, Custom is allow'd to be our best Authority for Words, and 'tis fit it should be so; but Reason must be the Judge of Sense in Language, and Custom can never prevail over it. *Words*, indeed, like Ceremonies in Religion, may be submitted to the Magistrate; but *Sense*, like the Essentials, is positive, unalterable, and cannot be submitted to any Jurisdiction; 'tis a Law to it self, 'tis ever the same, even an Act of Parliament cannot alter it.

Daniel Defoe, 1697, 'Of Academies', in *An Essay upon Projects*

8:28 Our Language is both Copious, Significant, and Majestical, and might be reduc'd into a more harmonious sound. But, for want of Publick Encouragement, in this *Iron Age*, we are so far from making any progress in the improvement of our Tongue, that in few years, we shall Speak and Write as Barbarously as our Neighbours.

John Dryden, 1693, 'The Dedication to Examen Poeticum'

8:29 In language, the ignorant have prescribed laws to the learned.

Richard Duppa, 1830, *Maxims*, no. 252

8:30 And don't confound the language of the nation / With long-tailed words in *osity* and *ation*.

John Hookham Frere, 1817–18, *The Monks and the Giants*, Canto 1, 6

8:31 There can be no 'correctness' apart from usage.

C. C. Fries, 1940, *An American English Grammar*, Ch. 1, Sect. 4

8:32 Peremptory and unreasoned pronouncements as to what is bad English are not the least of the minor pests which vex our enlightened age; and the bulk of them, as the better-informed are well aware, may be traced to persons who have given only very slight attention to verbal criticism ... those would-be philologists who collect waifs and strays of antipathies and prejudices, amplify the worthless hoard by their own whimseys, and, to the augmentation of vulgar error, digest the whole into essays and volumes.

Fitzedward Hall, 1880, 'English Rational and Irrational', *The Nineteenth Century*, no. 43

8:33 [of usage purists] Pronouncing, as they do, arbitrarily, or from a predilection for the obsolete, as to what is right and what is wrong, they ought, certainly, to produce credentials from heaven, or from some other exalted quarter, conclusive that their autocratism is authentic.

Fitzedward Hall, 1880, 'English Rational and Irrational', *The Nineteenth Century*, no. 43 .

8:34 The doings of American philologasters [would-be philologists] are, in truth, a curious study.

Fitzedward Hall, 1880, 'English Rational and Irrational', *The Nineteenth Century*, no. 43

8:35 Purism, whether in grammar or in vocabulary, almost always means ignorance. Language was made before grammar, not grammar before language.

Thomas Hardy, 1904, in William Archer, *Real Conversations*

8:36 *Multa renascentur quae iam cecidere, cadentque / Quae nunc sunt in honore vocabula, si volet usus, / Quem penes arbitrium est et ius et norma loquendi.* Many a word long disused will revive, and many now high in esteem will fade, if Custom wills it, in whose power lie the arbitrament, the rule, and the standard of language.

Horace, 19–18 BC, *Ars Poetica* (trans. E. H. Blakeney), 70

8:37 [on political correctness] We want to create a sort of linguistic Lourdes, where evil and misfortune are dispelled by a dip in the waters of euphemism.

Robert Hughes, 1993, *Culture of Complaint*

8:38 The individual in his use of the language has constantly to improvise.

Otto Jespersen, 1946, 'Standards of Correctness', in *Mankind, Nation and Individual*, Ch. 5

8:39 I have laboured to refine our language to grammatical purity, and to clear it from colloquial barbarisms, licentious idioms, and irregular combinations.

Samuel Johnson, 14 March 1752, *The Rambler*, no. 208

8:40 Every language has its anomalies, which, though inconvenient, and in themselves once unnecessary, must be tolerated among the imperfections of human things, and which require only to be registered, that they may not be increased, and ascertained, that they may not be confounded: but every language has likewise its improprieties and absurdities, which it is the duty of the lexicographer to correct or proscribe.

Samuel Johnson, 1755, *A Dictionary of the English Language*, Preface

8:41 To insist always that there should be one word to express a thing in English, because there is one in another language, is to change the language.

Samuel Johnson, 1778, in James Boswell, *The Life of Samuel Johnson* (1791), Ch. 47

8:42 *Custome* [usage] is the most certaine Mistresse of Language, as the publicke stampe makes the current money. But wee must not be too frequent with the mint, every day coyning.

Ben Jonson, 1640 (published posthumously), *Timber: or, Discoveries made upon Men and Matter*

8:43 Next in criminality to him who violates

the laws of his country, is he who violates the language.

Walter Savage Landor, 1824–53, 'Archdeacon Hare and Walter Landor', in *Imaginary Conversations*

8:44 The English language as it is spoken by the politest part of the nation, and as it stands in the writings of our most approved authors, oftentimes offends against every part of grammar.

Robert Lowth, 1762, *A Short Introduction to English Grammar*, Preface [cf. 8:64]

8:45 People should not be sharply corrected for bad grammar, provincialisms, or mispronunciation; it is better to suggest the proper expression by tactfully introducing it oneself in, say, one's reply to a question or one's acquiescence in their sentiments, or into a friendly discussion of the topic itself (not of the diction), or by some other suitable form of reminder.

Marcus Aurelius, 2nd century, *Meditations* (trans. M. Staniforth, 1964, Penguin), I, Sect. 10

8:46 The notion that anything is gained by fixing a language in a groove is cherished only by pedants.

H. L. Mencken, 1919, *The American Language* (4th edition 1947), Ch. 12, Sect. 2

8:47 [on those who are able to speak clearly, whatever their dialect background] 'But he does not know what an ablative is, a conjunctive, a substantive: he knows no grammar!' Neither does his footman or a Petit-Pont fishwife yet they will talk you to death if you let them and will probably no more stumble over the rules of their own dialect than the finest Master of Arts in France.

Michel de Montaigne, 1572–80, 'On Educating Children', in *The Complete Essays* (trans. M. A. Screech, 1987), I, no. 26

8:48 Those who want to fight usage with grammar are silly.

Michel de Montaigne, 1572–80, 'On some Lines of Virgil', in *The Complete Essays* (trans. M. A. Screech, 1987), III, no. 5

8:49 In the nice-minded Department of Prunes and Prisms, / It's I for you / And euphemisms.

Ogden Nash, 1962, 'Laments for a Dying Language – III', in *Everyone but Thee and Me*

8:50 *Sphinxed* about (to put into / One word many feelings – / God forgive me / The sin against grammar!)

Friedrich Nietzsche, 1883–5, 'Amongst the

Daughters of the Desert', in *Thus Spake Zarathustra* (trans. A. Tille), IV

8:51 Language if it is to be used must be a *ready* instrument. The handiness and ease of a phrase is always more important in deciding whether it will be extensively used than its accuracy.

C. K. Ogden and I. A. Richards, 1923, *The Meaning of Meaning*, Ch. 1

8:52 [rules to stop the decline of English] 1 Never use a metaphor, simile or other figure of speech which you are used to seeing in print. 2 Never use a long word where a short one will do. 3 If it is possible to cut a word out, always cut it out. 4 Never use the passive where you can use the active. 5 Never use a foreign phrase, a scientific word or a jargon word if you can think of an everyday English equivalent. 6 Break any of these rules sooner than say anything outright barbarous.

George Orwell, 1946, 'Politics and the English Language', *Horizon*, no. 13

8:53 'Tis true, on Words is still our whole debate, / Disputes of *Me* or *Te*, of *aut* or *at*, / To sound or sink in *cano*, O or A, / Or give up Cicero to C or K.

Alexander Pope, 1742, *The Dunciad*, IV, 219–22

8:54 It must be allowed, that the custom of speaking is the original and only just standard of any language. We see, in all grammars, that this is sufficient to establish a rule, even contrary to the strongest analogies of the language with itself.

Joseph Priestley, 1761, *Rudiments of English Grammar*

8:55 A language can never be properly fixed, till all the varieties with which it is used, have been held forth to public view, and the general preference of certain forms have been declared, by the general practice afterwards.

Joseph Priestley, 1761, *Rudiments of English Grammar*

8:56 We must make up our minds what we mean by usage. If it be defined merely as the practice of the majority, we shall have a very dangerous rule affecting not merely style but life as well, a far more serious matter. For where is so much good to be found that what is right should please the majority?

Quintilian, 1st century, *Institutio Oratoria* (trans. H. E. Butler), I, Ch. 6

8:57 If Quebec's language laws tighten just one more notch, I may have to write my novels in words half the size of French [referring to

Quebec legislation requiring the size of French lettering on public signs to be larger than English], so as not to antagonize our linguistic vigilantes.

Mordecai Richler, 1997, in the *New York Times Book Review*

8:58 [Holofernes, of Armado] He draweth out the thread of his verbosity finer than the staple of his argument. I abhor such fanatical phantasims, such insociable and point-device companions, such rackers of orthography as to speak 'dout', *sine* 'b', when he should say 'doubt'; 'det' when he should pronounce 'debt' – 'd, e, b, t', not 'd, e, t'. He clepeth a calf 'cauf', half 'hauf', neighbour *vocatur* 'nebour' – 'neigh' abbreviated 'ne'. This is abhominable – which he would call 'abominable'. It insinuateth me of *insanire – ne intelligis, domine? –* to make frantic, lunatic.

William Shakespeare, 1593–4, *Love's Labour's Lost*, V. i. 17

8:59 These two Evils, Ignorance and Want of Taste, have produced a Third; I mean the continual Corruption of our *English* Tongue, which, without some timely Remedy, will suffer more by the false Refinements of Twenty Years past than it hath been improved in the foregoing Hundred.

Jonathan Swift, 27 September 1710, 'The Continual Corruption of our English Tongue', letter to Isaac Bickerstaff in *The Tatler*

8:60 [on monosyllabic abbreviations, such as *pozz* 'positive'] Thus we cram one Syllable, and cut off the rest, as the Owl fattened her Mice after she had bit off their Legs, to prevent them from running away; and if ours be the same Reason for maiming our Words, it will certainly answer the End; for I am sure no other Nation will desire to borrow them.

Jonathan Swift, 27 September 1710, 'The Continual Corruption of our English Tongue', letter to Isaac Bickerstaff in *The Tatler*

8:61 [to Isaac Bickerstaff] Make Use of your Authority as Censor, and by an Annual *Index Expurgatorium* expunge all Words and Phrases that are offensive to good Sense, and condemn those barbarous Mutilations of vowels and syllables.

Jonathan Swift, 27 September 1710, 'The Continual Corruption of our English Tongue', letter to Isaac Bickerstaff in *The Tatler*

8:62 [attacking those who abbreviate words] The usual Pretence is, That they spell as they speak: A noble Standard for Language! To depend upon the Caprice of every Coxcomb, who because Words are the Cloathing of our Thoughts, cuts them out and shapes them as he pleases, and changes them of[te]ner than his Dress.

Jonathan Swift, 27 September 1710, 'The Continual Corruption of our English Tongue', letter to Isaac Bickerstaff in *The Tatler*

8:63 Nothing would be of greater Use towards the Improvement of Knowledge and Politeness, than some effectual Method for *Correcting, Enlarging* and *Ascertaining* our Language.

Jonathan Swift, 1712, 'A Proposal for Correcting, Improving and Ascertaining the English Tongue'

8:64 [to Robert, Earl of Oxford] My LORD; I do here, in the Name of all the Learned and Polite Persons of the Nation, complain to Your LORDSHIP, as *First Minister*, that our Language is extremely imperfect; that its daily Improvements are by no means in proportion to its daily Corruptions; that the Pretenders to polish and refine it, have chiefly multiplied Abuses and Absurdities; and, that in many Instances, it offends against every Part of Grammar.

Jonathan Swift, 1712, 'A Proposal for Correcting, Improving and Ascertaining the English Tongue' [cf. 8:44]

8:65 There must be 'reducing agents' in a language: people who keep the inward flow of words to manageable proportions, and who throw out useless old junk. In France they have an academy for the purpose, and here we have a stalwart band of etymologists who strive in a dedicated spirit to keep our language graceful, vigorous and practical. All power to their elbows, pens and tongues, but I believe that their good work for human speech counts for very little beside the powerful and wholly irrational movements of fashion.

Christopher Sykes, 1956, 'What U-future?', in Nancy Mitford (ed.), *Noblesse Oblige*, p. 99

8:66 Those who give us advice in the matter of speaking, some saying to follow usage and others saying to follow theory, are not so much at variance, because usage and regularity are more closely connected with each other than those advisers think. For Regularity is sprung from a certain usage in speech, and from this usage likewise is sprung Anomaly. Therefore, since usage consists of unlike and like words and their derivative forms, neither Anomaly nor Regularity is to be cast aside, unless man is not of soul because he is of body and of soul.

Marcus Terentius Varro, 2nd century, *De lingua latina* (trans. R. G. Kent), IX

8:67 It is in vain to set up a language police to stem living developments. (I have always suspected that correctness is the last refuge of those who have nothing to say.)

Friedrich Waismann, 1952, 'Analytic-Synthetic V', in *Analysis*, no. 13

8:68 Everyone has always regarded any usage but his own as either barbarous or pedantic.

Evelyn Waugh, 1956, 'An Open Letter to the Honble Mrs. Peter Rodd (Nancy Mitford) on a Very Serious Subject', in Nancy Mitford (ed.), *Noblesse Oblige*, p. 77

8:69 English usage is sometimes more than mere taste, judgement, and education – sometimes it's sheer luck, like getting across a street.

E. B. White, 1954, 'Shop Talk', in *The Second Tree from the Corner*

8:70 Authority of general usage, or even of the usage of great writers, is not absolute in language. There is a misuse of words which can be justified by no authority, however great, and *by no usage however general*.

Richard Grant White, 1870, *Words and their Uses, Past and Present*, p. 14

See also: 5:23, 7:7, 7:15–16, 7:21, 7:69, 9:2, 12:24, 13:36, 14:1, 23:5, 24:11, 37:26, 38:26, 52:23

9 *The Language of Youth and Age*

Child language, and the changes between youth and old age

9:1 [on hearing her father speak Pig Latin] I thought my brother and his friends had created Pig Latin. Hearing my father speak it didn't startle me so much as it angered. It was simply another case of the trickiness of adults where children were concerned. Another case in point of the Grownups' Betrayal.

Maya Angelou, 1969, *I Know Why the Caged Bird Sings*, Ch. 9

9:2 I must not speak a useless word, / For children must be seen, not heard. / I must not talk about my food, / Nor fret, if I don't think it good. / I must not say 'the bread is old', / 'the tea is hot' – 'the coffee cold'. / I must not cry for this, or that, / Nor murmur if my meat be fat. / My mouth with food I mustn't crowd, / Nor while I'm eating speak aloud. / Must turn my head to cough, or sneeze, / And when I ask, say 'If you please'.

Anonymous, 'Table Rules for Little Folk', in *The Faber Book of Useful Verse* (1981), p. 83

9:3 [on English] A dreadful language? Man Alive, / I'd mastered it when I was five!

Anonymous, 'Hints on Pronunciation for Foreigners', in *The Faber Book of Useful Verse* (1981), p. 144

9:4 In formal poetry, the role played by the language itself is so great that it demands of the poet that he be as intimate with it as with his own flesh and blood and love it with a single-minded passion. A child who has associated standard English with Mother and dialect with Father has ambivalent feelings about both which can hardly fail to cause trouble for him in later life if he should try to write formal poetry.

W. H. Auden, 1948, 'D. H. Lawrence', in *The Dyer's Hand and other essays*

9:5 [on recalling how he learned to speak] I noticed that people would name some object and then turn towards whatever it was that they had named. I watched them and understood that the sound they made when they wanted to indicate that particular thing was the name which they gave to it, and their actions clearly showed what they meant, for there is a kind of universal language, consisting of expressions of the face and eyes, gestures and tones of voice, which can show whether a person means to ask for something and get it, or refuse it and have nothing to do with it. So, by hearing words arranged in various phrases and constantly repeated, I gradually pieced together what they stood for, and when my tongue had mastered the pronunciation, I began to express my wishes by means of them.

St Augustine, 397–8, *Confessions* (trans. R. S. Pine-Coffin), I, Sect. 8

9:6 Certainly custom is most perfect when it beginneth in young years: this we call education, which is in effect but an early custom. So we see, in languages the tongue is more pliant to all expressions and sounds, the joints are more supple to all feats of activity and motions, in youth than afterwards. For it is true that late learners cannot so well take the ply [are not as pliant], except it be in some minds that have not suffered themselves to fix, but have kept themselves open and prepared to receive continual amendment, which is exceeding rare.

Francis Bacon, 1612/25, 'Of Custom and Education', in *Essays*

9:7 The old repeat themselves and the young have nothing to say. The boredom is mutual.

Jacques Bainville, 1937, 'Charme de la conversation', in *Lectures* (trans.)

9:8 Do not underrate the talk of old men; after all, they themselves learned it from their fathers; from them you will learn how to think, and the art of the timely answer.

The Bible, Ecclesiasticus 8:9 (Jerusalem Bible)

9:9 Though children without study, pains, or thought, / Are languages and vulgar notions taught, / Improve their nat'ral talents without care, / And apprehend before they are aware, / Yet as all strangers never leave the tones / They have been us'd of children to pronounce, / So most men's reason never can outgrow / The discipline it first receiv'd to know, / But renders words they first began to con, / The end of all that's after to be known, / And sets the help of education back, / Worse than, without it, man could ever lack.

Samuel Butler (1612–80), 1670s, 'Satire upon the Imperfection and Abuse of Human Learning', I

9:10 [of Ernest] He was, however, very late in being able to sound a hard 'c' or 'k', and, instead of saying 'Come', he said 'Tum, tum, tum'.

'Ernest,' said Theobald, from the arm-chair in front of the fire, where he was sitting with his hands folded before him, 'don't you think it would be very nice if you were to say 'come' like other people, instead of 'tum'?'

'I do say tum' replied Ernest, meaning that he had said 'come'.

Samuel Butler (1835–1902), 1903, *The Way Of All Flesh*, Ch. 22

9:11 [John Ottokar, on being a twin] We grew up speaking a kind of private language – almost a silent language – of signs and gestures. We closed everyone out. No one could reach us. We were like a child and a mirror that spoke to itself.

A. S. Byatt, 1996, *Babel Tower*, Ch. 9

9:12 'Tis sweet to be awakened by the lark / Or lulled by falling waters; sweet the hum / Of bees, the voice of girls, the song of birds, / The lisp of children and their earliest words.

Lord Byron, 1819–24, *Don Juan*, Canto 1, stanza 123

9:13 'But why do you say "Dindledums", Bruno? *Dandelions* is the right word.' 'It's because he jumps about so,' Sylvie said, laughing. 'Yes, that's it,' Bruno assented. 'Sylvie tells me the words, and then, when I jump about, they get shooken up in my head – till they're all froth!'

Lewis Carroll, 1889, *Sylvie and Bruno*, Ch. 21

9:14 I have few words. My father, who had all of them, left so suddenly that he did not have the time to give them to me.

Hélène Cixous, 1969, *Dedans* (trans.)

9:15 Amenities of conversation sometimes very curious, especially where society of children is involved. Have sometimes wondered at what stage of development the idea of continuity in talk begins to seem desirable – but here, again, disquieting reflection follows that perhaps this stage is never reached at all.

E. M. Delafield, 1930, *The Diary of a Provincial Lady*, 10 August

9:16 [John Willet, to Joe, who has spoken out of turn] 'Silence, sir!' returned his father, 'what do you mean by talking, when you see people that are more than two or three times your age, sitting still and silent and not dreaming of saying a word?'

'Why that's the proper time for me to talk, isn't it?' said Joe rebelliously.

'The proper time, sir!' retorted his father, 'the proper time's no time.'

Charles Dickens, 1867–8, *Barnaby Rudge*, Ch. 1

9:17 [John Willet, to his son Joe] When I was your age I never talked, I never wanted to talk. I listened and improved myself, that's what *I* did.

Charles Dickens, 1867–8, *Barnaby Rudge*, Ch. 1

9:18 'Tommy,' says I, 'spell cat,' I says. 'Go to th' divvle,' says th' cheerub. 'Very smartly answered,' says Mary Ellen. 'Ye shud not ask thim to spell,' she says. 'They don't larn that till they get to colledge,' she says, 'an'' she says, 'sometimes not even thin,' she says.

Finley Peter Dunne, 1900, 'The Education of the Young', in *Mr Dooley's Philosophy*

9:19 [Mrs Garth, to young Ben] Job has only to speak about very plain things. How do you think you would write or speak about anything more difficult, if you knew no more of grammar than he does? You would use wrong words, and put words in the wrong places, and instead of making people understand you, they would turn away from you as a tiresome person. What would you do then?'

'I shouldn't care, I should leave off,' said Ben, with a sense that this was an agreeable issue where grammar was concerned.

George Eliot, 1871–2, *Middlemarch*, Ch. 24

9:20 [Stephen, listening to adult conversation] Words which he did not understand he said over and over to himself till he had learnt them by heart: and through them he had glimpses of the real world about them.

James Joyce, 1916, *Portrait of the Artist as a Young Man*, Ch. 2

9:21 There is frequently more to be learned from the unexpected questions of a child than the discourses of men, who talk in a road, according to the notions they have borrowed and the prejudices of their education.

John Locke, 1693, *Some Thoughts Concerning Education*, Sect. 120

9:22 [Mrs Waddy] Before that child your 'h's' must be like the panting of an engine – to please his father. He'd stop me carrying the dinner-tray or meat-dish hot, and I'm to repeat what I said, to make sure the child haven't heard anything ungrammatical. . . . It's just as you, John, when you sow your seed you think of your harvest. So don't take ill of me, John; I beg of you be careful of your English. Turn it over as you're about to speak.

George Meredith, 1871, *The Adventures of Harry Richmond*, Ch. 3

9:23 [of infants] And they can't talk straight / Any more than they can walk straight; / Their pronunciation is awful / And their grammar is flawful, / And in adults it's drunken and maudlin and deplorable, / But in infants it's tunnin' and adorable.

Ogden Nash, 1936, 'It Must be the Milk', in *The Bad Parents' Garden of Verse*

9:24 The pidgin talk the youthful use / Bypasses conversation. / I can't believe the code they choose / Is a means of communication. / Oh, to be with people over sixty / Despite their tendency to prolixty!

Ogden Nash, 1952, 'You can be a Republican, I'm a Gerontocrat', in *The Private Dining Room*

9:25 I'm seven, and I'm dead bright, / But words give me a fright. / Words are bullies. / Sneaky

things. They lie. / Sometimes trying to understand them / Makes me cry.

Brian Patten, 1987, 'Words', in *First International Symposium: Specific Speech and Language Disorders in Children*

9:26 [of a newborn baby] And now you try / Your handful of notes; / The clear vowels rise like balloons.

Sylvia Plath, 1965, 'Morning Song', in *Ariel*

9:27 Children pick up words as pigeons peas / And utter them again as God shall please.

Proverbial

9:28 [of children] Speak when you are spoken to; come when you are called.

Proverbial

9:29 A child learns quicker to talk than to be silent.

Proverbial (Norwegian)

9:30 A bearded mouth [an old man] speaks no untruth.

Proverbial (Pedi)

9:31 Above all see that the child's nurse speaks correctly. The ideal, according to Chrysippus, would be that she should be a philosopher: failing that he desired that the best should be chosen, as far as possible. No doubt the most important point is that they should be of good character: but they should speak correctly as well. It is the nurse that the child first hears, and her words that he will first attempt to imitate. And we are by nature most tenacious of childish impressions, just as the flavour first absorbed by vessels persists, and the colour imparted by dyes to the primitive whiteness of wool is indelible.

Quintilian, 1st century, *Institutio Oratoria* (trans. H. E. Butler), I, Ch. 1

9:32 [on the way adults talked to him as a ten-year-old] The worst of it was that I suspected the grown-ups of play-acting. The words they spoke to me were like sweets; but they talked to each other in a very different way.

Jean-Paul Sartre, 1964, 'Reading', in *Words* (trans. I. Clephane), I

9:33 A child should always say what's true, / And speak when he is spoken to.

Robert Louis Stevenson, 1885, 'Whole Duty of Children', in *A Child's Garden of Verses*

9:34 [Althæa, of her baby son] Yet was he then

but a span long, and moaned / With inarticulate mouth inseparate words.

Algernon Charles Swinburne, 1865, *Atalanta in Calydon*

9:35 [of the original compositions recited by the girls in Tom Sawyer's school] A prevalent feature in these compositions was a nursed and petted melancholy; another was a wasteful and opulent gush of 'fine language'; another was a tendency to lug in by the ears particularly prized words and phrases until they were worn entirely out; and a peculiarity that conspicuously marked and marred them was the inveterate and intolerable sermon that wagged its crippled tail at the end of each and every one of them.

Mark Twain, 1876, *The Adventures of Tom Sawyer*, Ch. 22

9:36 If men do not keep on speaking terms with children, they cease to be men, and become merely machines for eating and for earning money.

John Updike, 1965, 'A Foreword for Younger Readers', in *Assorted Prose*

9:37 A child, when it begins to speak, learns what it is that it knows.

John Hall Wheelock, 1963, 'A True Poem is a Way of Knowing', in *What is Poetry?*

9:38 [of the aged Grandsire] While thoughts press on, and feelings overflow, / And quick words round him fall like flakes of snow.

William Wordsworth, 1833, 'The Warning'

See also: 12:47, 22:10, 22:12, 22:14, 23:3, 23:50, 28:2, 38:5, 41:26, 63:4–5

Languages

10 *Language Diversity*

The world's languages; language identity, endangerment, maintenance, and death

10:1 English is destined to be in the next and succeeding centuries more generally the language of the world than Latin was in the last or French is in the present age. The reason of this is obvious, because the increasing population in America, and their universal connection and correspondence with all nations will, aided by the influence of England in the world, whether great or small, force their language into general use, in spite of all the obstacles that may be thrown in their way, if any such there should be.
John Adams, 5 September 1780, letter to Congress

10:2 If we should be worrying about anything to do with the future of English, it should be not that the various strands will drift apart but that they will grow indistinguishable. And what a sad, sad loss that would be.
Bill Bryson, 1990, *Mother Tongue: the English Language*, Ch. 16

10:3 When a language dies, so much is lost. Especially in languages which have never been written down, or which have been written down only recently, language is the repository of the history of a people. It is their identity.
David Crystal, 1997, *English as a Global Language*, Ch. 1

10:4 [speculating on a future world in which English is taught to everyone] If this is part of a rich multilingual experience for our future newborns, this can only be a good thing. If it is by then the only language left to be learned, it will have been the greatest intellectual disaster that the planet has ever known.
David Crystal, 1997, *English as a Global Language*, Ch. 5

10:5 A language, like a species, when once extinct, never, as Sir C. Lyell remarks, reappears. The same language never has two birth-places.
Charles Darwin, 1871, 'Mental Powers', in *The Descent of Man*, Ch. 2

10:6 Every language, every language at least in a state of culture and development, has its own separate and incommunicable qualities of superiority.
Thomas De Quincey, April 1839, 'The English Language', in *Blackwood's Magazine*

10:7 A language is the emblem of its speakers.
R. M. W. Dixon, 1997, *The Rise and Fall of Languages*, Ch. 9, Sect. 3

10:8 [following a long list of glosses on the letters U.S.A.] But mostly U.S.A. is the speech of the people.
John Dos Passos, 1938, *U.S.A.*, Prologue

10:9 The noises of the human race are indeed a chattering Babel, a confusion of tongues. Such abounding diversity is at once a challenge to those minds which seek ordered simplicity in the world, and at the same time a collectors' paradise.
J. R. Firth, 1936, 'Alphabets and Phonology in India and Burma', in *Bulletin of the School of Oriental Studies*, no. 8

10:10 Citizens of a multiform Earth, Europeans cannot but listen to the polyphonic cry of human languages. To pay attention to the others who speak their own language is the first step in order to establish a solidarity more concrete than many propaganda discourses.
Claude Hagège, 1992, *Le Souffle de la langue*, in

Umberto Eco, *The Search for the Perfect Language* (trans. 1995), Ch. 17

10:11 Every language is a temple, in which the soul of those who speak it is enshrined.
Oliver Wendell Holmes, senior, 1860, *The Professor at the Breakfast Table*, Ch. 2

10:12 Each language constitutes a certain model of the universe, a semiotic system of understanding the world, and if we have 4,000 different ways to describe the world, this makes us rich. We should be concerned about preserving languages just as we are about ecology.
Vjaceslav Ivanov, 1992, 'Reconstructing the Past', *Intercom*, no. 15, issue 1

10:13 My zeal for languages may seem, perhaps, rather overheated, even to those by whom I desire to be well esteemed. To those who have nothing in their thoughts but trade or policy, present power or present money, I should not think it necessary to defend my opinions; but with men of letters I would not unwillingly compound, by wishing the continuance of every language, however narrow in its extent, or however incommodious for common purposes, till it is reposited in some version of a known book, that it may be always hereafter examined and compared with other languages, and then permitting its disuse.
Samuel Johnson, 13 August 1766, letter to William Drummond, in James Boswell, *The Life of Samuel Johnson* (1791), Ch. 18

10:14 There is no tracing the connection of ancient nations, but by language; and therefore I am always sorry when any language is lost, because languages are the pedigree of nations.
Samuel Johnson, 18 September 1773, in James Boswell, *The Journal of a Tour to the Hebrides*

10:15 [of the people of the Western Isles] Of what they had before the late conquest of their country, there remain only their language and their poverty. Their language is attacked on every side. Schools are erected, in which English only is taught, and there were lately some who thought it reasonable to refuse them a version of the holy scriptures, that they might have no monument of their mother-tongue.
Samuel Johnson, 1773, 'Coriatachan in Sky', in *A Journey to the Western Islands of Scotland*

10:16 In an unwritten speech, nothing that is not very short is transmitted from one generation to another. Few have opportunities of hearing a long composition often enough to learn

it, or have inclination to repeat it so often as is necessary to retain it; and what is once forgotten is lost for ever.
Samuel Johnson, 1773, 'Ostig in Sky', in *A Journey to the Western Islands of Scotland*

10:17 My culture and my language have the right to exist, and no one has the authority to dismiss that.
James Kelman, 11 October 1994, speech at Booker Prize ceremony

10:18 We are vessels of speech, we are the repositories which harbour secrets many centuries old ... We are the memory of mankind; by the spoken word we bring to life the deeds and exploits of kings for younger generations.
Mamadou Kouyaté (West African griot), quoted in V. Edwards and T. J. Sienkewicz, *Oral Cultures Past and Present* (1990), Ch. 1

10:19 The English language no longer belongs to the English. It's an export reject.
George Lamming, 1958, in a BBC radio programme, *Third World*

10:20 Nations are not born, but made. And they are made, ineluctably, in language.
Christopher Looby, 1996, *Voicing America*, Ch. 1

10:21 Because of its history and uses, English remains at one and the same time an emollient which makes diplomatic, commercial, and other contacts easier for everybody everywhere and an irritant which distresses those who are afraid for the vigour, autonomy, purity, and even survival of other languages – including in many instances their own.
Tom McArthur, 1998, *The English Languages*, Ch. 2

10:22 A nation is the universality of citizens speaking the same tongue.
Giuseppe Mazzini, 1832, *La Giovine Italia [Young Italy]* (trans.)

10:23 I have crossed an ocean / I have lost my tongue / from the root of the old one / a new one has sprung.
Grace Nichols, 1983, *i is a long memoried woman*

10:24 [Officer] Now hear this. You are mountain people. You hear me? Your language is dead. It is forbidden. It is not permitted to speak your mountain language in this place. You cannot speak your language to your men. It is not permitted. Do you understand? You may not speak it. It is outlawed. You may speak only the language of the capital. That is the only language permitted in this place. You will be badly punished if you attempt to speak your mountain language in this place. This is a military decree. It is the law. Your language is forbidden. It is dead. No one is allowed to speak your language. Your language no longer exists.

Harold Pinter, 1988, *Mountain Language*, I

10:25 The English and the Scotch, had the kingdoms continued separate, might have been distinct languages, having two different standards of writing.

Joseph Priestley, 1762, *Theory of Language and Universal Grammar*, p. 129

10:26 A nation without a language is a nation without a heart.

Proverbial (Welsh)

10:27 As long as the language lives the nation is not dead.

Proverbial (Czech)

10:28 Our language is one great salad.

Proverbial (Romanian)

10:29 [of English in the 20th century] A language – *the* language – on which the sun does not set, whose users never sleep.

Randolph Quirk, 1984, 'The English Language in a Global Context', in R. Quirk and H. G. Widdowson (eds), *English in the World* (1985), p. 1

10:30 We have room in this country but for one flag, the Stars and Stripes. We have room for but one loyalty, loyalty to the United States.

We have room for but one language, the English language.

Theodore Roosevelt, 3 January 1919, message to the American Defense Society

10:31 A number of dead languages are among the obvious splendours of human intelligence. Many a linguistic mastodon is a more finely articulated, more 'advanced' piece of life than its descendants.

George Steiner, 1975, *After Babel*, Ch. 2

10:32 Let us then seize the present moment, and establish a *national language*, as well as a national government.

Noah Webster, 1789, 'An Essay on the Necessity, Advantages and Practicability of Reforming the Mode of Spelling, and of Rendering the Orthography of Words Consistent to the Pronunciation', *Dissertations on the English Language*, Appendix

10:33 A language is a dialect that has an army and a navy.

Max Weinreich, 1973, *History of the Yiddish Language*

10:34 Mark! how all things swerve / From their known course, or vanish like a dream; / Another language spreads from coast to coast; / Only perchance some melancholy Stream / And some indignant Hills old names preserve, / When laws, and creeds, and people all are lost!

William Wordsworth, 1821, 'Monastery of Old Bangor'

See also: 12:27, 13:27, 62:47

11 *Languages Observed*

The supposed qualities of different languages

11:1 The Sounds of our *English* Words are commonly like those of String Musick, short and transient, that rise and perish upon a single touch; those of other Languages are like the Notes of Wind Instruments, sweet and swelling, and lengthen'd out into variety of Modulation.
Joseph Addison, 4 August 1711, *The Spectator*, no. 135

11:2 [of the 'genius' of different languages] It is certain the light talkative Humour of the *French* has not a little infected their Tongue, as might be shown by many Instances; as the Genius of the *Italians*, which is so much addicted to Musick and Ceremony, has moulded all their Words and Phrases to those particular Uses. The Stateliness and Gravity of the *Spaniard* shews it self to Perfection in the Solemnity of their Language; and the blunt honest Humour of the *Germans* sounds better in the Roughness of the *High Dutch* [German], than it would in a Politer Tongue.
Joseph Addison, 4 August 1711, *The Spectator*, no. 135

11:3 The Greeks Had a Word for It.
Zoë Akins, 1930, play title

11:4 The English language has such range, / Such rhymes and half-rhymes, rhythms strange, / And such variety of tone, / It is a music of its own. / With Milton it has organ power / As loud as bells in Redcliffe tower; / It falls like winter crisp and light / On Cowper's Buckinghamshire night. / It can be gentle as a lake, / Where Wordsworth's oars a ripple make / Or rest with Tennyson at ease / In sibilance of summer seas, / Or languorous as lilies grow, / When Dowson's lamp is burning low – / For endless changes can be rung / On church-bells of the English tongue.
John Betjeman, 1966, *High and Low*, Preface

11:5 The fact is that you cannot find an equivalent for things originally written in Hebrew when you come to translate them into another language.
The Bible, Ecclesiasticus, Prologue: 21 (Jerusalem Bible)

11:6 *Belladonna, n.* In Italian a beautiful lady; in English a deadly poison. A striking example of the essential identity of the two tongues.
Ambrose Bierce, 1911, *The Devil's Dictionary*

11:7 *English, n.* A language so haughty and reserved that few writers succeed in getting on terms of familiarity with it.
Ambrose Bierce, 1911, *The Devil's Dictionary* (entry added by E. J. Hopkins for *The Enlarged Devil's Dictionary*, 1967)

11:8 Nothing surprised me more than the free and unembarrassed manner in which the Portuguese peasantry sustain a conversation, and the purity of the language in which they express their thoughts, and yet few of them can read or write; whereas the peasantry of England, whose education is in general much superior, are in their conversation coarse and dull almost to brutality, and absurdly ungrammatical in their language, though the English tongue is upon the whole more simple in its structure than the Portuguese.
George Borrow, 1843, *The Bible in Spain*, Ch. 1

11:9 [on seeing the monument to Sir James Macdonald] Dr Johnson said, the inscription should have been in Latin, as every thing intended to be universal and permanent, should be.

James Boswell, 1785, 'Sunday 5th September', in *The Journal of a Tour to the Hebrides*

11:10 When I have tense relations with my wife, we speak in Arabic. When we talk business, then we speak English. And when our relationship is better, then we talk French.

Boutros Boutros Ghali, 1998, 'They Said It', in the *Daily Post*, 12 November 1998

11:11 Russia is my home . . . and for everything that I have in my soul I am obligated to Russia and its people. And – this is the main thing – obligated to its language.

Joseph Brodsky, 1 October 1992, *New York Times*

11:12 It is not that the French are not profound, but they all express themselves so well that we are led to take their geese for swans.

Van Wyck Brooks, 1958, *From a Writer's Notebook*

11:13 I love the language, that soft bastard Latin, / Which melts like kisses from a female mouth, / And sounds as if it should be writ on satin, / With syllables which breathe of the sweet South, / And gentle liquids gliding all so pat in, / That not a single accent seems uncouth, / Like our harsh northern whistling, grunting guttural, / Which we're obliged to hiss, and spit, and sputter all.

Lord Byron, 1817, *Beppo*, stanza 44

11:14 Our *English* tongue is (I will not say as sacred as the *Hebrew*, or as learned as the *Greeke*,) but as fluent as the *Latine*, as courteous as the *Spanish*, as courtlike as the *French*, and as amorous as the *Italian*, as some Italianated amorous have confessed.

William Camden, 1605, 'The Languages', in *Remaines Concerning Britain*

11:15 Iacke would be a gentleman, if he could speake any French.

William Camden, 1605, 'The Languages', in *Remaines Concerning Britain* [cf. 11:47]

11:16 [after listing some popular etymologies] This merry playing with words too much vsed by some hath occasioned a great and high personage, to say, that as the *Italian* tongue is fit for courting, the *Spanish* for treating, the *French*

for trafficke: so the *English* is most fit for trifling and toying.

William Camden, 1605, 'The Languages', in *Remaines Concerning Britain*

11:17 [The Red Queen] Speak in French when you ca'n't think of the English for a thing – turn out your toes as you walk – and remember who you are!

Lewis Carroll, 1872, *Through the Looking Glass*, Ch. 2

11:18 I speak Spanish to God, Italian to women, French to men, and German to my horse.

Emperor Charles V, 16th century, attributed, in Lord Chesterfield, *Letters to his Son* (1932), IV, p. 1,497

11:19 It may be doubted whether a composite language like the English is not a happier instrument of expression than a homogeneous one like the German. We possess a wonderful richness and variety of modified meanings in our Saxon and Latin quasi-synonymes, which the Germans have not.

Samuel Taylor Coleridge, 19 August 1832, in Henry Nelson Coleridge (ed.), *Specimens of the Table-Talk of the late Samuel Taylor Coleridge* (1835)

11:20 Imagine the Lord talking French! Aside from a few odd words in Hebrew, I took it for granted that God had never spoken anything but the most dignified English.

Clarence Day, 1935, 'Father Interferes', in *Life with Father*

11:21 The *English* Tongue is a Subject not at all less worthy the Labour of such a Society [an English Academy] than the *French*, and capable of a much greater Perfection. The Learned among the *French* will own, That the Comprehensiveness of Expression is a Glory in which the *English* Tongue not only Equals but Excels its Neighbours.

Daniel Defoe, 1697, 'Of Academies', in *An Essay upon Projects*

11:22 Hence we see the monstrosity of claiming a fine or copious language, for any rude or uncultivated, much more for any savage people, or even for a people of mountaineers, or for a nation subsisting chiefly by hunting, or by agriculture and rural life exclusively, or in any way sequestered and monotonous in their habits. It is philosophically impossible that the Gaelic, or the Hebrew, or the Welsh, or the Manx, or the Armoric, could, at any stage, have been languages of compass or general poetic power.

Thomas De Quincey, April 1839, 'The English Language', *Blackwood's Magazine*

11:23 If I write in French, which is the language of my country, rather than in Latin, which is that of my teachers, it is because I hope that those who use only their pure natural reason will be better judges of my opinions than those who believe only in the books of the ancients; and, as for those who unite good sense with study, whom alone I wish to have for my judges, they will not, I feel sure, be so partial to Latin that they will refuse to hear my reasons because I express them in the vulgar tongue.

René Descartes, 1637, *Discourse on Method* (trans. F. E. Sutcliffe), VI

11:24 [Mr Lillyvick, the tax collector] 'What sort of language do you consider French, sir?' 'How do you mean?' asked Nicholas. 'Do you consider it a good language, sir?' said the collector; 'a pretty language, a sensible language?' 'A pretty language, certainly,' replied Nicholas; 'and as it has a name for everything, and admits of elegant conversation about everything, I presume it is a sensible one.' 'I don't know,' said Mr Lillyvick doubtfully. 'Do you call it a cheerful language, now?' 'Yes,' replied Nicholas, 'I should say it was, certainly.' 'It's very much changed since my time, then,' said the collector, 'very much.'

Charles Dickens, 1838–9, *Nicholas Nickleby*, Ch. 16

11:25 [of Mrs Woodcourt] She would tell me about Morgan ap Kerrig until I was quite low-spirited! Sometimes she recited a few verses from Crumlinwallinwer and the Mewlinwillinwodd (if those are the right names, which I dare say they are not), and would become quite fiery with the sentiments they expressed. Though I never knew what they were (being in Welsh), further than that they were highly eulogistic of the lineage of Morgan ap Kerrig.

Charles Dickens, 1852–3, *Bleak House*, Ch. 30

11:26 An Englishman understates, avoids the superlative, checks himself in compliments, alleging that in the French language one cannot speak without lying.

Ralph Waldo Emerson, 1856, *English Traits*, Ch. 7

11:27 'I hear it's the Hebrew in Heaven, sir – Spanish is seldom spoken,' he explained seraphically.

Ronald Firbank, 1926, *Concerning the Eccentricities of Cardinal Pirelli*, Ch. 8

11:28 Latin. Man's natural language. Spoils your style. Useful for reading the inscriptions on public fountains. Beware of quotations in Latin: they always conceal something improper.

Gustave Flaubert, in *Bouvard et Pécuchet avec un choix des scénarios, du Sottisier, L'Album de la Marquise et Le Dictionnaire des idées reçues* (1881) (trans. G. Wall)

11:29 The quiet monotony of the dead languages.

William Hazlitt, 1818, 'On the Ignorance of the Learned', *Edinburgh Magazine*

11:30 JOHNSON: 'The language of the country of which a learned man was a native, is not the language fit for his epitaph, which should be in ancient and permanent language. Consider, sir, how you should feel were you to find, at Rotterdam, an epitaph upon Erasmus in *Dutch*!'
BOSWELL: 'For my own part, I think it would be best to have epitaphs written both in a learned language, and in the language of the country; so that they might have the advantage of being more universally understood, and at the same time be secured of classical stability.'

Samuel Johnson and James Boswell, 1776, in James Boswell, *The Life of Samuel Johnson* (1791), Ch. 39

11:31 Johnson called the East Indians barbarians.
BOSWELL: 'You will except the Chinese, sir?'
JOHNSON: 'No, sir.'
BOSWELL: 'Have they not arts?'
JOHNSON: 'They have pottery.'
BOSWELL: 'What do you say to the written characters of their language?'
JOHNSON: 'Sir, they have not an alphabet. They have not been able to form what all other nations have formed.'
BOSWELL: 'There is more learning in their language than in any other, from the immense number of their characters.'
JOHNSON: 'It is only more difficult from its rudeness; as there is more labour in hewing down a tree with a stone than with an axe.'

Samuel Johnson and James Boswell, 1778, in James Boswell, *The Life of Samuel Johnson* (1791), Ch. 47

11:32 Greek, sir, is like lace; every man gets as much of it as he can.

Samuel Johnson, 1780, in James Boswell, *The Life of Samuel Johnson* (1791), Ch. 51

11:33 A Frenchman must be always talking, whether he knows anything of the matter or not; an Englishman is content to say nothing, when he has nothing to say.

Samuel Johnson, 1780, in James Boswell, *The Life of Samuel Johnson* (1791), Ch. 51

11:34 [on being asked to perform a baptism in English] The baby doesn't understand English and the Devil knows Latin.

Ronald Knox, 1913, quoted in Evelyn Waugh, *Ronald Knox* (1959), Ch. 5

11:35 The great tragedy of the classical languages is to have been born twins.

Geoffrey Madan, 1981, *Geoffrey Madan's Notebooks*, p. 67

11:36 [after translating a love poem from Turkish] Neither do I think our English proper to express such violence of passion, which is very seldom felt amongst us.

Lady Mary Wortley Montagu, 1 April 1717, letter to Alexander Pope, in Isobel Grundy (ed.), *Lady Mary Wortley Montagu: Selected Letters* (1997)

11:37 My book I write for a few men and for a few years. If it had been on a lasting subject I would have entrusted it to a more durable language [than French].

Michel de Montaigne, 1572–80, 'On Vanity', in *The Complete Essays* (trans. M. A. Screech, 1987), III, no. 9

11:38 American is the language in which people say what they mean as Italian is the language in which they say what they feel. English is the language in which what a character means or feels has to be deduced from what he or she says, which may be quite the opposite.

John Mortimer, 26 March 1989, in the *Mail on Sunday*

11:39 I do not think that anie language, be it whatsoever, is better able to utter all arguments, either with more pith, or greater planesse, then our English tung is, if the English utterer be as skilfull in the matter, which he is to utter: as the foren utterer is.

Richard Mulcaster, 1582, *The First Part of the Elementarie*, Ch. 13

11:40 [in answer to the question 'Which of the languages you speak do you consider the most beautiful?'] My head says English, my heart, Russian, my ear, French.

Vladimir Nabokov, 18 August 1964, interview in *Strong Opinions* (1974), p. 49

11:41 When people tell me French is difficult, I show my dimple. / French is simple.

Ogden Nash, 1952, 'What is Bibbidi-bobbidi-boo in Sanskrit?', in *The Private Dining Room*

11:42 Our English tongue of all languages most swarmeth with the single money of monasillables which are the onely scandall of it. Bookes written in them and no other, seeme like Shopkeepers boxes, that containe nothing else, saue halfepence, three-farthings and two pences.

Thomas Nashe, 1594, *Christs Teares ouer Ierusalem*, p. 2

11:43 Yiddish is a household tongue, and God, like other members of the family, is sweetly informal in it.

Cynthia Ozick, 1989, *Metaphor and Memory*

11:44 Arabic is good for flattering men, Turkish for reproving them, and Persian for convincing them.

Proverbial (Persian)

11:45 Arabic is science, Persian is sugar, Hindustani is salt, but Turki is art.

Proverbial (Turkestan)

11:46 The devil himself was learning the Basque language for seven years and then he only learned three words.

Proverbial (Basque)

11:47 Jack would be a gentleman if he could but speak French.

Proverbial [cf. 11:15]

11:48 The Englishman has his intelligence at the end of his fingers, the Frenchman at the end of his tongue.

Proverbial (Russian)

11:49 Arabic is a language, Persian a sweetmeat, Turkish an art.

Proverbial (Persian)

11:50 A hen that crows and a woman who knows Latin never come to a good end.

Proverbial (Spanish)

11:51 Adam and Eve spoke of their love in Persian, and the angel who drove them out of Paradise spoke Turkish.

Proverbial (Persian)

11:52 The reply to a Turkish question should be in Turkish.

Proverbial (Persian)

11:53 Our fathers have, in the process of centuries, provided this realm, its colonies and wide dependencies, with a speech as malleable and pliant as Attic, dignified as Latin, masculine, yet free of Teutonic guttural, capable of being as precise as French, dulcet as Italian, sonorous as Spanish, and captaining all these excellences to its service.

Arthur Quiller-Couch, 1900, *The Oxford Book of English Verse*, Preface

11:54 QUEEN KATHERINE [to Cardinal Wolsey]: Out with it boldy. Truth loves open dealing.

CARDINAL WOLSEY: *Tanta est erga te mentis integritas, Regina serenissima* –

QUEEN KATHERINE: O good my lord, no Latin. / I am not such a truant since my coming / As not to know the language I have lived in. / A strange tongue makes my cause more strange suspicious – / Pray, speak in English. ... The willing'st sin I ever yet committed / May be absolved in English.

William Shakespeare, 1613, *Henry VIII (All Is True)*, III. i. 39

11:55 [Cusins] Other languages are the qualifications of waiters and commercial travellers: Greek is to a man of position what the hallmark is to silver.

George Bernard Shaw, 1905, *Major Barbara*, I

11:56 [Lady Britomart Undershaft] Nobody can say a word against Greek: it stamps a man at once as an educated gentleman.

George Bernard Shaw, 1905, *Major Barbara*, I

11:57 [Cusins] I have tried to make spiritual power by teaching Greek. But the world can never be really touched by a dead language and a dead civilization.

George Bernard Shaw, 1905, *Major Barbara*, III

11:58 FANNY: Your *insouciance* –

TROTTER (*frantic*): Stop talking French to me: it's not a proper language for a young girl.

George Bernard Shaw, 1911, *Fanny's First Play*, I

11:59 THE CHAPLAIN: The Maid has actually declared that the blessed saints Margaret and Catherine, and the holy Archangel Michael, spoke to her in French. That is a vital point.

THE INQUISITOR: You think, doubtless, that they should have spoken in Latin?

CAUCHON: No: he thinks they should have spoken in English.

THE CHAPLAIN: Naturally, my lord.

THE INQUISITOR: Well, as we are all here agreed, I think, that these voices of The Maid are the voices of evil spirits tempting her to her damnation, it would not be very courteous to you, Master de Stogumber, or to the King of England, to assume that English is the devil's native language.

George Bernard Shaw, 1923, *Saint Joan*, scene vi

11:60 SECOND COMEDIAN [suggesting a test for humour]: You could get rid of the linguistic overtones by using Esperanto, but that means evening classes for comedian and audience alike while they're all learning Esperanto.

FIRST COMEDIAN: They might not like the joke any more in Esperanto than they did in English.

N. F. Simpson, 1958, *A Resounding Tinkle*, I, i

11:61 [Alf Garnett] Well, your natives have that. They have *sounds* for things, but it's not language. I mean, a dog barks, but it's not language. I mean, yer Jocks an' yer Irish, they've got that, they've got sounds. Yer Gaelic ... but it's no good to 'em 'cept for talking among themselves. They wanna talk to other people, they've got to learn English.

Johnny Speight, 1972, 'The Bird Fancier', in *Till Death Us Do Part*

11:62 The French are certainly misunderstood: – but whether the fault is theirs, in not sufficiently explaining themselves; or speaking with that exact limitation and precision which one would expect on a point of such importance, and which moreover, is so likely to be contested by us – or whether the fault may not be altogether on our side, in not understanding their language always so critically as to know 'what they would be at' – I shall not decide.

Laurence Sterne, 1765, *The Life and Opinions of Tristram Shandy, Gentleman*, VII, Ch. 18

11:63 The English language is nobody's special property. It is the property of the imagination: it is the property of the language itself.

Derek Walcott, 1988, interview in George Plimpton (ed.), *Writers at Work*

11:64 [on the British Empire] It's good that everything's gone, except their language, / Which is everything.

Derek Walcott, 1981, 'North and South', in *The Fortunate Traveller*

11:65 Viewed freely, the English language is the accretion and growth of every dialect, race, and range of time, and is the culling and composition of all. From this point of view, it stands for Language in the largest sense, and is really the greatest of studies.

Walt Whitman, 1885, 'Slang in America', in the *North American Review*, no. 141

11:66 [on writing *Salome* in French] To me there are only two languages in the world: French and Greek.

Oscar Wilde, c.1892, in Richard Ellmann, *Oscar Wilde* (1987), Ch. 14

11:67 [Cecily, to Miss Prism] I don't like German. It isn't at all a becoming language. I know perfectly well that I look quite plain after my German lesson.

Oscar Wilde, 1895, *The Importance of Being Earnest*, II

11:68 It is vain and foolish to talk of knowing Greek.

Virginia Woolf, 1925, 'On Not Knowing Greek', in *The Common Reader*

11:69 [on his mixed feelings, arriving in Switzerland after a memorable tour of Italy] I feign not; witness that unwelcome shock / That followed the first sound of German speech, / Caught the far-winding barrier Alps among. / In that announcement, greeting seemed to mock / Parting; the casual word had power to reach / My heart, and filled that heart with conflict strong.

William Wordsworth, 1837, 'After Leaving Italy: Continued'

See also: 10:21, 10:29, 15:1, 15:16, 43:10, 49:13, 52:34, 65:9

12 *Bilingualism and Multilingualism*

Being proficient in more than one language

12:1 Even a dog we do know is better company than a man whose language we do not know.
St Augustine, 412–27, *City of God* (trans.), XIX, Ch. 7

12:2 He that travelleth into a country before he hath some entrance into the language, goeth to school, and not to travel.
Francis Bacon, 1625, 'Of Travel', in *Essays*

12:3 They were all filled with the Holy Spirit, and began to speak foreign languages as the Spirit gave them the gift of speech. Now there were devout men living in Jerusalem from every nation under heaven, and at this sound they all assembled, each one bewildered to hear these men speaking his own language.
The Bible, Acts 2:4 (Jerusalem Bible)

12:4 *Linguist, n.* A person more learned in the languages of others than wise in his own.
Ambrose Bierce, 1911, *The Devil's Dictionary* (entry added by E. J. Hopkins for *The Enlarged Devil's Dictionary*, 1967)

12:5 There has never been a time when the ability to communicate with other cultures and in their own languages was more important to our nation's well-being and prosperity.
Tony Blair, 1998, message of greeting to the Central Bureau for Educational Visits and Exchanges 50th Anniversary Review, *A World of Understanding*

12:6 An individual may speak and read a dozen languages, and yet be an exceedingly poor creature, scarcely half a man; and the pursuit of tongues for their own sake, and the mere satisfaction of acquiring them, surely argues an intellect of a very low order; a mind disposed to be satisfied with mean and grovelling things; taking more pleasure in the trumpery casket than in the precious treasure which it contains, in the pursuit of words, than in the acquisition of ideas.
George Borrow, 1851, *Lavengro*, Ch. 13

12:7 The knowledge of the ancient languages is mainly a luxury.
John Bright, 30 November 1886, letter in the *Pall Mall Gazette*

12:8 I think you always feel braver in another language.
Anita Brookner, 7 August 1988, in the *Observer*

12:9 Polyglottism is neither unnatural nor conducive to neurosis.
Anthony Burgess, 1992, *A Mouthful of Air*, I, Ch. 15

12:10 No sooner are the organs of the brain / Quick to receive, and steadfast to retain / Best knowledges, but all's laid out upon / Retrieving of the curse of Babylon, / To make confounded languages restore / A greater drudg'ry than it barr'd before: / And therefore those imported from the East, / Where first they were incurr'd, are held the best, / Although convey'd in worse Arabian pot-hooks / Than gifted tradesmen scratch in sermon notebooks.
Samuel Butler (1612–80), 1670s, 'Satire upon the Imperfection and Abuse of Human Learning', I

12:11 For the more languages a man can speak, / His talent has but sprung the greater leak; / And for the industry h' has spent upon 't, / Must full as much some other way discount.
Samuel Butler (1612–80), 1670s, 'Satire upon the Imperfection and Abuse of Human Learning', I

12:12 Yet he that is but able to express / No sense at all in several languages, / Will pass for learneder than he that's known / To speak the strongest reason in his own.
Samuel Butler (1612–80), 1670s, 'Satire upon the Imperfection and Abuse of Human Learning', I

12:13 [on foreign scholars] Some write in Hebrew, some in Greek, / And some, more wise, in Arabic, / T' avoid the critic, and th' expense / Of difficulter wit and sense; / And seem more learnedish than those / That at a greater charge compose.
Samuel Butler (1612–80), 1670s, 'Miscellaneous Thoughts'

12:14 The various languages you ought to have: one for your mother, which you will subsequently never speak again; one which you only read but never dare to write; one in which you pray but without understanding a single word; one in which you do arithmetic and to which all money matters belong; one in which you write (but no letters); one in which you travel, and in this you can also write your letters.
Elias Canetti, 1973, '1942', in *The Human Province*

12:15 Knowing many languages . . . is a gift I like to see in the courtier.
Baldesar Castiglione, 1528, *The Book of the Courtier* (trans. G. Bull, Penguin 1967), II, p. 147

12:16 Mr Meagles, who never by any accident acquired any knowledge whatever of the language of any country into which he travelled.
Charles Dickens, 1855–7, *Little Dorrit*, I, Ch. 2

12:17 [Mr Meagles] Anything short of speaking the language I shall be delighted to undertake.
Charles Dickens, 1855–7, *Little Dorrit*, I, Ch. 2

12:18 Salvatore spoke all languages, and no language. Or, rather, he had invented for himself a language which used the sinews of the languages to which he had been exposed – and once I thought that his was, not the Adamic language that a happy mankind had spoken, all united by a single tongue from the origin of the world to the Tower of Babel, or one of the languages that arose after the dire event of their division, but precisely the Babelish language of the first day after the divine chastisement, the language of primeval confusion.
Umberto Eco, 1980, *The Name of the Rose* (trans.), Day One, Sext

12:19 We are greatly helped to develop objectiv-

ity of taste if we can appreciate the work of foreign authors, living in the same world as ourselves, and expressing their vision of it in another great language.
T. S. Eliot, 15 April 1942, 'The Classics and the Man of Letters', Lecture to the Classical Association, Cambridge

12:20 No man should travel until he has learned the language of the country he visits. Otherwise he voluntarily makes himself a great baby, – so helpless and so ridiculous.
Ralph Waldo Emerson, 1833, *Journals*

12:21 As many languages as he has, as many friends, as many arts and trades, so many times is he a man.
Ralph Waldo Emerson, 1860, 'Culture', in *The Conduct of Life*

12:22 I rarely read any Latin, Greek, German, Italian, sometimes not a French book, in the original, which I can procure in a good version . . . I should as soon think of swimming across Charles River when I wish to go to Boston, as of reading all my books in originals, when I have them rendered for me in my mother tongue.
Ralph Waldo Emerson, 1860, 'In Praise of Books'

12:23 AIMWELL: Then you understand Latin, Mr Bonniface?
BONNIFACE: Not I, Sir, as the saying is, but he talks it so very fast that I'm sure it must be good.
George Farquhar, 1707, *The Beaux' Stratagem*, III. ii

12:24 [of the learned man] He is expert in all the dead and in most of the living languages; but he can neither speak his own fluently, nor use it correctly.
William Hazlitt, 1818, 'On the Ignorance of the Learned', *Edinburgh Magazine*

12:25 To use two languages familiarly, and without contaminating one by the other, is very difficult; and to use more than two is hardly to be hoped. The praises which some have received for their multiplicity of languages may be sufficient to excite industry, but can hardly generate confidence.
Samuel Johnson, 1761, in James Boswell, *The Life of Samuel Johnson* (1791), Ch. 13

12:26 [on verses written in dead languages] I would have as many of these as possible; I would have verses in every language that there are the means of acquiring.

Samuel Johnson, 1775, in James Boswell, *The Life of Samuel Johnson* (1791), Ch. 32

12:27 The reason why one has to parse and construe and grind at the dead tongues in which certain ideas are expressed, is *not* for the sake of what is called intellectual training – that may be given in other ways – but because only in that tongue is that idea expressed with absolute perfection.

Rudyard Kipling, May 1912, 'The Uses of Reading' (speech at Wellington College), in *A Book of Words*

12:28 It is good to be on your guard against an Englishman who speaks French perfectly; he is very likely to be a card-sharper or an attaché in the diplomatic service.

W. Somerset Maugham, 1938, *The Summing Up*, Ch. 29

12:29 A thousand fantasies / Begin to throng into my memory / Of calling shapes, and beckoning shadows dire, / And airy tongues, that syllable men's names / On sands, and shores, and desert wildernesses.

John Milton, 1634, *Comus, A Mask*, 204

12:30 [advice to her daughter about the education of her grand-daughter] Not to think her selfe Learned when she can read Latin or even Greek. Languages are more properly to be calld Vehicles of Learning than Learning it selfe, as may be observ'd in many Schoolmasters, who thô perhaps critics in Grammar are the most ignorant fellows upon Earth. True knowledge consists in knowing things, not words. I would wish her no farther a Linguist than to enable her to read Books in their originals, that are often corrupted and allwaies injur'd by Translations.

Lady Mary Wortley Montagu, 28 January 1753, letter to Lady Bute, in Isobel Grundy (ed.), *Lady Mary Wortley Montagu: Selected Letters* (1997)

12:31 When I was in Italy, I advised a man who was at pains to learn Italian that if it were merely to be understood, without excelling in any other way, he should simply use the first words which came to his lips, Latin, French, Spanish or Gascon, and stick an Italian ending on them; he would never fail to hit on some local dialect, Tuscan, Roman, Venetian, Piedmontese or Neapolitan: there are so many forms that he was bound to coincide with one of them.

Michel de Montaigne, 1572–80, 'An Apology for Raymond Sebond', in *The Complete Essays* (trans. M. A. Screech, 1987), II, no. 12

12:32 'I wonder if there'll ever be a real international language?' said Freddie. 'There is. English.' 'Hilary is so chauvinistic.' 'What about Esperanto?' said Laura. 'Hilary, do you know Esperanto?' 'Of course.' 'Do you think it – ?' 'How can one tolerate a language where the word for "mother" is "little father"?' 'Is it?' 'The Esperanto for "mother" is *patrono*.' 'Down with Esperanto!' said Laura.

Iris Murdoch, 1975, 'Thursday' (second week), in *A Word Child*

12:33 [Hilary] Nothing humbles human pride more than inability to understand a language. It's a perfect image of spiritual limitation. The cleverest man looks a fool if he can't speak a language properly.

Iris Murdoch, 1975, 'Thursday' (second week), in *A Word Child*

12:34 If you're born in India, you're bilingual. And if you're bilingual, you can't read. Not so well.

Mary Norton, 1952, *The Borrowers*, Ch. 9

12:35 That woman speaks eighteen languages, and can't say No in any of them.

Dorothy Parker, quoted in Alexander Woollcott, 'Our Mrs Parker', in *While Rome Burns* (1934)

12:36 With each newly learned language you acquire a new soul.

Proverbial (Slovakian)

12:37 A man who knows two languages is worth two men.

Proverbial (French)

12:38 With Latin, a nag, and money, you can traverse the world.

Proverbial (Spanish)

12:39 For but a man know French men count of him little, / But low men hold to English and to their own speech yet. / I think there are in all the world no countries / That don't hold to their own speech but England alone. / But men well know it is well for to know both, / For the more that a man knows, the more worth he is.

Robert of Gloucester, c.1300, chronicle (trans. A. C. Baugh)

12:40 [said of the philologist, Immanuel Becker] To be silent in seven languages.

Friedrich Schleiermacher, attributed, early 19th century

12:41 SECOND OUTLAW [offering Valentine the captaincy of their band]: Have you the tongues?

VALENTINE: My youthful travel therein made me happy, / Or else I had been often miserable. . . .

FIRST OUTLAW: And partly seeing you are beautified / With goodly shape, and by your own report / A linguist, and man of such perfection / As we do in our quality much want.

William Shakespeare, 1590–1, *The Two Gentlemen of Verona*, IV. i. 32, 53

12:42 CADE: More than that, he can speak French, and therefore he is a traitor!

STAFFORD: O gross and miserable ignorance!

CADE: Nay, answer if you can: the Frenchmen are our enemies; go to, then, I ask but this – can he that speaks with the tongue of an enemy be a good counsellor or no?

ALL CADE'S FOLLOWERS: No, no – and therefore we'll have his head!

William Shakespeare, 1590–1, *Henry VI, Part 2*, IV. ii. 164

12:43 [Sir Toby, of Sir Andrew] He plays o'th'viol-de-gamboys, and speaks three or four languages word for word without book, and hath all the good gifts of nature.

William Shakespeare, 1601, *Twelfth Night*, I. iii. 23

12:44 Is it not as important for the survival of feeling today for a man to know another living language as it was once important for him to be intimate with the classics and Scripture?

George Steiner, 1967, 'To Civilize our Gentlemen', in *Language and Silence*

12:45 And is it not the duty of the critic to avail himself, in some imperfect measure at least, of another language – if only to experience the defining contours of his own?

George Steiner, 1967, 'F. R. Leavis', in *Language and Silence*

12:46 Languages have been, throughout human history, zones of silence to other men and razor-edges of division.

George Steiner, 1975, *After Babel*, Ch. 2

12:47 I didn't know at first that there were two languages in Canada. I just thought that there was one way to speak to my father and another to talk to my mother.

Louis St Laurent, quoted in Dale C. Thomson, *Louis St Laurent* (1967)

12:48 The modern cheap and fertile press, with all its translations, has done little to bring us nearer to the heroic writers of antiquity. They seem as solitary, and the letter in which they are printed as rare and curious, as ever. It is worth the expense of youthful days and costly hours, if you learn only some words of an ancient language, which are raised out of the trivialness of the street, to be perpetual suggestions and provocations.

Henry Thoreau, 1854, 'Reading', in *Walden*

12:49 [of the Swedes] They have a knack at acquiring languages, with tolerable fluency. This may be reckoned an advantage in some respects; but it prevents the cultivation of their own, and any considerable advance in literary pursuits.

Mary Wollstonecraft, 1796, 'Letter 3', in *A Short Residence in Sweden*

See also: 15:5, 53:20, 57:8, 61:10

13 *Translating and Interpreting*

The task of translation and interpreting

13:1 [Arthur] 'Ford,' he said. 'Yeah?' 'What's this fish doing in my ear?' 'It's translating for you. It's a Babel fish.'
Douglas Adams, 1979, *The Hitch-Hiker's Guide to the Galaxy*, Ch. 6

13:2 *'The Babel fish,'* said *The Hitch Hiker's Guide to the Galaxy* quietly, *'is small, yellow and leech-like, and probably the oddest thing in the Universe. It feeds on brainwave energy received not from its own carrier but from those around it. It absorbs all unconscious mental frequencies from this brainwave energy to nourish itself with. It then excretes into the mind of its carrier a telepathic matrix formed by combining the conscious thought frequencies with nerve signals picked up from the speech centres of the brain which has supplied them. The practical upshot of all this is that if you stick a Babel fish in your ear you can instantly understand anything said to you in any form of language. The speech patterns you actually hear decode the brainwave matrix which has been fed into your mind by your Babel fish.'*
Douglas Adams, 1979, *The Hitch-Hiker's Guide to the Galaxy*, Ch. 6

13:3 Any one who attempts to translate from one tongue into another will know moods of despair when he feels he is wasting his time upon an impossible task but, irrespective of success or failure, the mere attempt can teach a writer much about his own language which he would find it hard to learn elsewhere. Nothing else can more naturally correct our tendency to take our own language for granted.
W. H. Auden, 1948, 'Translating Opera Libretti', in *The Dyer's Hand and other essays*

13:4 *Interpreter, n.* One who enables two persons of different languages to understand each other by repeating to each what it would have been to the interpreter's advantage for the other to have said.
Ambrose Bierce, 1911, *The Devil's Dictionary*

13:5 The original is unfaithful to the translation.
Jorge Luis Borges, 'On a Translation by Henley', in *Obras Completas* (trans. 1974), p. 730

13:6 No problem is as completely concordant with literature and with the modest mystery of literature as is the problem posed by a translation.
Jorge Luis Borges, 1957, 'Las versiones Homéricas', in *Discusión* (trans.)

13:7 Translation is at best an echo.
George Borrow, 1851, *Lavengro*, Ch. 25

13:8 The Northern races, and especially the English, have the advantage of us: their genius is never at a loss for an expression, but coins words or borrows them. The result is that our translations, particularly those made from works of some depth or vigour, are never more than pale and colourless copies of their originals.
Jean-Anthelme Brillat-Savarin, 1825, *The Physiology of Taste* (trans.), Preface

13:9 To know certain authors in translation is not to know them at all. . . . The ultimate value of a translation lies in its power to ease our way into the original.
Anthony Burgess, 1992, *A Mouthful of Air*, I, Ch. 11

13:10 Translations, like wives, are seldom faithful if they are in the least attractive.

Roy Campbell, June/July 1949, in the *Poetry Review*

13:11 [the Red Queen] 'Do you know Languages? What's the French for fiddle-de-dee?' 'Fiddle-de-dee's not English,' Alice replied gravely. 'Who ever said it was?' said the Red Queen. Alice thought she saw a way out of the difficulty, this time. 'If you'll tell me what language "fiddle-de-dee" is, I'll tell you the French for it!' she exclaimed triumphantly. But the Red Queen drew herself up rather stiffly, and said 'Queens never make bargains.'

Lewis Carroll, 1872, *Through the Looking Glass*, Ch. 9

13:12 [Count Lodovico] It is very unusual for someone who is not a practised writer, however erudite he may be, to understand completely the demanding work done by writers, or appreciate their stylistic accomplishments and triumphs and those subtle details characteristic of the writers of the ancient world.

Baldesar Castiglione, 1528, *The Book of the Courtier* (trans. G. Bull, Penguin 1967), I, p. 91

13:13 And whan I saw the fayr & straunge termes therin / I doubted that it sholde not please some gentylmen whiche late blamed me sayeng yt [that] in my translacyons I had ouer curyous termes whiche coude not be vnderstande of comyn peple / and desired me to vse olde and homely termes in my translacyons.

William Caxton, c.1490, prologue to Virgil's *Booke of Eneydos* [original punctuation]

13:14 [on translators of poetry] However much care they take, and however much skill they show, they can never make their translations as good as the original.

Miguel de Cervantes, 1605, *The Adventures of Don Quixote* (trans. J. M. Cohen), I, Ch. 6

13:15 It seems to me that translating from one tongue into another, unless it is from those queens of tongues Greek and Latin, is like viewing Flemish tapestries from the wrong side; for although you see the pictures, they are covered with threads which obscure them so that the smoothness and gloss of the fabric are lost; and translating from easy languages argues no talent or power of words, any more than does transcribing or copying one paper from another. By that I do not mean to imply that this exercise of translation is not praiseworthy, for a man

might be occupied in worse things and less profitable occupations.

Miguel de Cervantes, 1605, *The Adventures of Don Quixote* (trans. J. M. Cohen), II, Ch. 62 [cf. 13:33]

13:16 Such is our pride, our folly, or our fate, / That few, but such as cannot write, translate.

John Denham, 1648, 'To Richard Fanshaw'

13:17 That servile path thou nobly do'st decline, / Of tracing Word by Word, and Line by Line. / A new and nobler way thou do'st pursue, / To make Translations and Translators too: / They but preserve the Ashes, thou the Flame, / True to his Sense, but truer to his Fame.

John Denham, 1648, 'To Richard Fanshaw'

13:18 'Tis true, Composing is the Nobler Part, / But good Translation is no easie Art; / For tho Materials have long since been found, / Yet both your fancy and your hands are bound, / And by improving what was writ Before, / Invention Labours less, but Judgment more.

Wentworth Dillon, 1685, *An Essay on Translated Verse*

13:19 [on word-for-word translation] The Verbal Copier is incumber'd with so many difficulties at once, that he can never disentangle himself from all. He is to consider, at the same time, the thought of his Author, and his words, and to find out the Counterpart to each in another Language; And besides this he is to confine himself to the compass of Numbers, and the Slavery of Rhime. 'Tis much like dancing on Ropes with fetter'd Legs: A man can shun a fall by using Caution, but the gracefulness of Motion is not to be expected: And when we have said the best of it, 'tis but a foolish Task; for no sober man would put himself into a danger for the Applause of scaping without breaking his Neck.

John Dryden, 1683, 'Preface concerning Ovid's Epistles'

13:20 No man is capable of translating Poetry, who, besides a Genius to that Art, is not a Master both of his Authors Language, and of his own: Nor must we understand the Language only of the Poet, but his particular turn of Thoughts and of Expression, which are the Characters that distinguish, and as it were individuate him from all other Writers.

John Dryden, 1683, 'Preface concerning Ovid's Epistles'

13:21 [of good translations] It seems to me, that the true reason, why we have so few versions which are tolerable, is not from the too close pursuing of the Authors Sence, but because there are so few, who have all the Talents, which are requisite for Translation, and that there is so little Praise, and so small Encouragement, for so considerable a part of Learning.

John Dryden, 1683, 'Preface concerning Ovid's Epistles'

13:22 A Translator is to make his Author appear as charming as possibly he can, provided he maintains his Character, and makes him not unlike himself. Translation is a kind of Drawing after the Life, where every one will acknowledge there is a double sort of likeness, a good one and a bad. 'Tis one thing to draw the Out-lines true, the Features like, the Proportions exact, the Colouring it self perhaps tolerable, and another thing to make all these graceful, by the posture, the shadowings, and chiefly by the Spirit which animates the whole. I cannot, without some indignation, look on an ill Copy of an excellent Original.

John Dryden, 1685, 'Preface to Sylvae'

13:23 A good Poet is no more like himself, in a dull Translation, than his Carcass would be to his living Body.

John Dryden, 1685, 'Preface to Sylvae'

13:24 A Man shou'd be a nice Critick in his Mother Tongue, before he attempts to Translate a foreign Language. Neither is it sufficient, that he be able to Judge of Words and Stile; but he must be a Master of them too: He must perfectly understand his Authors Tongue, and absolutely command his own: So that, to be a thorow Translator, he must be a thorow Poet.

John Dryden, 1685, 'Preface to Sylvae'

13:25 [of Virgil] They, who have call'd him the torture of Grammarians, might also have called him the plague of Translatours; for he seems to have studied not to be Translated.

John Dryden, 1685, 'Preface to Sylvae'

13:26 Poetry is what is lost in translation. It is also what is lost in interpretation.

Robert Frost, quoted in Louis Untermeyer, *Robert Frost* (1964), p. 18

13:27 Some day software will translate both written and spoken language so well that the need for any common second language could decline. That day is decades away, though, because flawless machine translation is a very tough problem. . . . Count on English to remain valuable for a long time as a common language of international communication.

Bill Gates, 1998, in the *New York Times*, reported in *Language Today*, March 1998, p. 21

13:28 Say what one will of the inadequacy of translation, it remains one of the most important and valuable concerns in the whole of world affairs.

Goethe, July 1827, letter to Thomas Carlyle

13:29 Nothing will more conduce to the improvement of the scholar in his knowledge of the languages, as well as in taste and morality, than his being obliged to translate choice parts and passages of the most approved classics, both poetry and prose, especially the latter . . . By this practice he will become more intimate with the beauties of the writing and the idioms of the language from which he translates; at the same time, it will form his style, and, by exercising his talent of expression, make him a more perfect master of his mother tongue.

Oliver Goldsmith, 1758–65, 'Cultivation of Taste', in *Essays*, no. 13

13:30 It is by the exercise of the mind alone that a language is learned; but a literal translation, on the opposite page, leaves no exercise for the memory at all.

Oliver Goldsmith, 10 November 1759, 'On Education', in *The Bee*, no. 6

13:31 Translation theory strikes me as a horribly pedantic bore. Translation is an art: it's a marvelous, living art, and any theory that attempts to give rules for this extremely fluid, constantly creative innovative art is doomed.

Douglas R. Hofstadter, 1998, *Language International*, no. 10 (1), p. 36

13:32 I really do feel that genuine translation of text requires understanding of the text, and understanding requires having lived in the world and dealt with the physical world and is not just a question of manipulating words.

Douglas R. Hofstadter, 1998, *Language International*, no. 10 (1), p. 35

13:33 Some hold translations not unlike to be / The wrong side of a Turkish tapestry.

James Howell, 1645, *Epistolae Ho-Elianae: Familiar Letters*, I, no. 6 [cf. 13:15, 25:72]

13:34 A translation is like a reproduction of Rembrandt in black and white.

Johan Huizinga, quoted in *Language Today* (March 1988), p. 20

13:35 The great pest of speech is frequency of translation. No book was ever turned from one language into another, without imparting something of its native idiom; this is the most mischievous and comprehensive innovation; single words may enter by thousands, and the fabrick of the tongue continue the same, but new phraseology changes much at once; it alters not the single stones of the building, but the order of the columns.

Samuel Johnson, 1755, *A Dictionary of the English Language*, Preface

13:36 If an academy should be established for the cultivation of our stile, which I, who can never wish to see dependance multiplied, hope the spirit of *English* liberty will hinder or destroy, let them, instead of compiling grammars and dictionaries, endeavour, with all their influence, to stop the licence of translatours, whose idleness and ignorance, if it be suffered to proceed, will reduce us to babble a dialect of *France*.

Samuel Johnson, 1755, *A Dictionary of the English Language*, Preface

13:37 Words, involving notions, are hard enough to render; it is too much to expect us to translate a sound, and give an elegant version to a jingle.

Charles Lamb, 1833, 'Popular Fallacies – viii', in *The Last Essays of Elia*

13:38 He is translation's thief that addeth more, / As much as he that taketh from the store / Of the first author. Here he maketh blots / That mends; and added beauties are but spots.

Andrew Marvell, 1651, 'To his Worthy Friend Doctor Witty upon his Translation of the *Popular Errors*', 13

13:39 Translation is the paradigm, the exemplar of all writing . . . It is translation that demonstrates most vividly the yearning for transformation that underlies every act involving speech, that supremely human gift.

Harry Mathews, 1980, 'The Dialect of the Tribe', in *Country Cooking and Other Stories*

13:40 For is it not in dede a mervellous bondage, to becom servants to one tung for learning sake, the most of our time, with losse of most time, whereas we maie have the verie same treasur in our own tung, with the gain of most time?

Richard Mulcaster, 1582, *The First Part of the Elementarie*, Ch. 13

13:41 Who has ever examined any translation from any language, without finding signs of what seems carelessness or ignorance?

Max Müller, 1898, 'Literary Recollections II', in *Auld Lang Syne* (3rd edition)

13:42 Translation is a difficult art, and scholars, particularly those who know the language from which, or the language into which, they translate as well as their own, consider a good translation almost impossible.

Max Müller, 1898, 'Literary Recollections II', in *Auld Lang Syne* (3rd edition)

13:43 It is easy enough to translate a text, after it has once been translated; it is easy even to improve in a few places on the translations of the first pioneers. But to translate for the first time an ancient text, badly edited or not yet edited at all, is a totally different thing, and those who undertake it have a right not only to the indulgence, but to the gratitude of all who come after them.

Max Müller, 1898, 'Literary Recollections II', in *Auld Lang Syne* (3rd edition)

13:44 What is translation? On a platter / A poet's pale and glaring head, / A parrot's screech, a monkey's chatter, / And profanation of the dead.

Vladimir Nabokov, 1964, 'On Translating *Eugene Onegin*'

13:45 What is most difficult to render from one language into another is the tempo of its style.

Friedrich Nietzsche, 1886, *Beyond Good and Evil* (trans. W. Kaufmann), p. 28

13:46 French into English has always been a problem. In Paris, the audience had been entranced by the young character juvenile who kept repeating '*Je suis cocu*'; but it's not the biggest joke in English for someone to keep on saying, 'I'm a cuckold,' which is in itself an unfamiliar enough word; and if it be helped out with a more explanatory 'I'm a betrayed husband' it frankly casts a gloom.

Laurence Olivier, 1982, *Confessions of an Actor*, p. 135

13:47 Translators, traitors.

Proverbial (Italian)

13:48 The art of translation lies less in knowing the other language than in knowing your own.

Ned Rorem, 1967, 'Random Notes from a Diary', in *Music from Inside Out*

13:49 'Tis good to have Translations, because

they serve as a Comment, so far as the Judgment of one Man goes.

John Selden, 1689, 'XXIX – Books. Authors', in *Table-Talk*

13:50 The vanity of translation; it were as wise to cast a violet into a crucible that you might discover the formal principle of its colour and odour, as seek to transfuse from one language to another the creations of a poet.

Percy Bysshe Shelley, 1821, *A Defence of Poetry*

13:51 Fitzgerald's book [the translation of the *Odyssey*] is a primer in the vexed craft of translation. Teiresias prophesies to Odysseus that he will suffer a gentle, mysterious end. Here is how Fitzgerald renders this famous passage: *Then a seaborne death / soft as this hand of mist will come upon you / when you are wearied out with rich old age.* 'Soft as this hand of mist' is not a bad motto for translators.

George Steiner, 1967, 'Two Translations', in *Language and Silence*

13:52 There are no translations.

George Steiner, 1967, 'Thomas Mann's *Felix Krull*', in *Language and Silence*

13:53 Great translators – and they are very rare – act as a kind of living mirror. They offer to the original not an equivalence, for there can be none, but a vital counterpoise, an echo, faithful yet autonomous, as we find in the dialogue of human love. An act of translation is an act of love. Where it fails, through immodesty or blurred perception, it traduces. Where it succeeds, it transfigures.

George Steiner, 1967, 'Thomas Mann's *Felix Krull*', in *Language and Silence*

13:54 When we read or hear any language-statement from the past, be it Leviticus or last year's best-seller, we translate. Reader, actor, editor are translators of language out of time.

George Steiner, 1975, *After Babel*, Ch. 1

13:55 We possess civilization because we have learnt to translate out of time.

George Steiner, 1975, *After Babel*, Ch. 1

13:56 The translator imports new and alternative options of being.

George Steiner, 1975, *After Babel*, Ch. 5

13:57 We must not trust the translation whose words are entirely 'unbroken'. As with a seashell, the translator can listen strenuously but mistake the rumour of his own pulse for the beat of the alien sea.

George Steiner, 1975, *After Babel*, Ch. 5

13:58 'A translation is no translation,' he said, 'unless it will give you the music of a poem along with the words of it.'

J. M. Synge, 1907, *The Aran Islands*, III

13:59 BELINDA: Ay, but you know we must return good for evil.

LADY BRUTE: That may be a mistake in the translation.

John Vanbrugh, 1697, *The Provok'd Wife*, I. i

13:60 Humour is the first of the gifts to perish in a foreign tongue.

Virginia Woolf, 1925, 'On Not Knowing Greek', in *The Common Reader*

See also: 1:66, 2:30, 11:5, 12:22, 12:30, 15:9, 27:20, 43:26, 49:29, 57:16, 57:33–4

14 *Teaching and Learning*

Principles and practices of language teaching and learning

14:1 We children beg thee, oh teacher, to teach us to speak because we are ignorant and speak incorrectly. / What do you want to say? / What do we care what we say, provided it is correct speech and useful and not foolish or bad.
Aelfric, c.1000, *Colloquy*, opening lines

14:2 [two of the criteria in the curriculum of Auden's 'Daydream College for Bards'] In addition to English, at least one ancient language, probably Greek or Hebrew, and two modern languages would be required ... Courses in prosody, rhetoric and comparative philology would be required of all students.
W. H. Auden, 1948, 'The Poet and the City', in *The Dyer's Hand and other essays*

14:3 [young Borrow's method of learning Danish] Although I cannot obtain a dictionary or grammar, I can perhaps obtain a Bible in this language, and if I can procure a Bible, I can learn the language, for the Bible in every tongue contains the same thing, and I have only to compare the words of the Danish Bible with those of the English, and, if I persevere, I shall in time acquire the language of the Danes.
George Borrow, 1851, *Lavengro*, Ch. 22

14:4 [Lubijova, giving Petworth a lesson in Slaka] 'There, it is not so complicate,' says Lubijova, 'All you must know is the nouns end in "i", or sometimes two or three, but with many exceptions. We have one spoken language and one book language. Really there are only three cases, but sometimes seven. Mostly it is inflected, but also sometimes not. It is different from country to town, also from region to region, because of our confused history. Voc-abulary is a little bit Latin, a little bit German, a little bit Finn. So really it is quite simple, I think you will speak it very well, soon.
Malcolm Bradbury, 1983, *Rates of Exchange*, III, Sect. 3

14:5 Some primers [of modern languages] still inhabit a dream-world where the words for 'international cooperation' are available but the words for 'yes' and 'no' hard to find.
Anthony Burgess, 1992, *A Mouthful of Air*, I, Ch. 11

14:6 What's a' your jargon o' your schools – / Your Latin names for horns an' stools? / If honest Nature made you fools, / What sairs [serves] your grammars? / Ye'd better taen up spades and shools [shovels], / Or knappin-hammers [stone-breaker hammers].
Robert Burns, 1 April 1785, 'Epistle to J. Lapraik' [cf. 14:34]

14:7 [Tarzan, to D'Arnot] Teach me to speak the language of men.
Edgar Rice Burroughs, 1914, *Tarzan of the Apes*, Ch. 23

14:8 [on Ernest's difficulties with Latin and Greek] The deadness inherent in these defunct languages themselves had never been artificially counteracted by a system of *bona fide* rewards for application.
Samuel Butler (1835–1902), 1903, *The Way Of All Flesh*, Ch. 31

14:9 [Bill Potter, on being told that an anthropologist has been put in charge of a government committee to study the teaching of English] They wouldn't put an *English* specialist in charge of an English enquiry, not bloody likely.

A. S. Byatt, 1996, *Babel Tower*, Ch. 2

14:10 [Alexander, on the English language committee's work] We're writing about teaching language and the language we write about teaching language won't stick to the thing we're writing about.

A. S. Byatt, 1996, *Babel Tower*, Ch. 18

14:11 [Professor Teufelsdröckh] My Teachers ... were hide-bound Pedants, without knowledge of man's nature, or of boy's; or of aught save their lexicons and quarterly account-books. Innumerable dead Vocables (no dead Language, for they themselves knew no Language) they crammed into us, and called it fostering the growth of mind. How can an inanimate, mechanical Gerund-grinder, the like of whom will, in a subsequent century, be manufactured at Nürnberg out of wood and leather, foster the growth of anything; much more of Mind, which grows, not like a vegetable (by having its roots littered with etymological compost) but like a spirit, by mysterious contact of Spirit; Thought kindling itself at the fire of living Thought? How shall *he* give kindling, in whose own inward man there is no live coal, but all is burnt-out to a dead grammatical cinder?

Thomas Carlyle, 1833, *Sartor Resartus*, II, Ch. 3

14:12 To those, who design to acquire the language of a country in the country itself, it may be useful, if I mention the incalculable advantage which I derived from learning all the words, that could possibly be so learnt, with the objects before me, and without the intermediation of the English terms.

Samuel Taylor Coleridge, 1817, *Biographia Literaria*, Ch. 10, note 38

14:13 To a teacher of languages there comes a time when the world is but a place of many words and man appears a mere talking animal not much more wonderful than a parrot.

Joseph Conrad, 1911, *Under Western Eyes*, Prologue

14:14 To learning's second seats we now proceed, / Where humming students gilded primers read; / Or books with letters large and pictures gay, / To make their reading but a kind of play – / 'Reading made Easy,' so the titles tell; / But they who read must first begin to spell; / There

may be profit in these arts, but still / Learning is labour, call it what you will.

George Crabbe, 1810, 'Letter XXIV: Schools', 19, in *The Borough*

14:15 At Mr Wackford Squeers's Academy, Dotheboys Hall, at the delightful village of Dotheboys, near Greta Bridge in Yorkshire, Youth are boarded, clothed, booked, furnished with pocket-money, provided with all necessaries, instructed in all languages living and dead ...

Charles Dickens, 1838–9, *Nicholas Nickleby*, Ch. 3

14:16 [Mr Squeers] We go upon the practical mode of teaching, Nickleby; the regular education system. C-l-e-a-n, clean, verb active, to make bright, to scour. W-i-n, win, d-e-r, der, winder, a casement. When the boy knows this out of the book, he goes and does it.

Charles Dickens, 1838–9, *Nicholas Nickleby*, Ch. 8

14:17 [Miss Mowcher] 'Bob swore!' – as the Englishman said for 'Good night,' when he first learnt French, and thought it so like English. 'Bob swore,' my ducks!

Charles Dickens, 1849–50, *David Copperfield*, Ch. 22

14:18 The Learning of dead Languages is a Yoke, that neither we nor our Forefathers could ever bear, when we were Children. And, I fancy, the Loathsomness of that dry Study comes for want of reasoning previously with them enough about the Nature of Words, and their Dependency on one another, in their own Mother Tongue.

Daniel Duncan, 1731, *A New English Grammar*, p. v

14:19 Whatever pains a master may take to make the learning of the languages agreeable to his pupil, he may depend upon it, it will be at first extremely unpleasant. The rudiments of every language, therefore, must be given as a task, not as an amusement.

Oliver Goldsmith, 10 November 1759, 'On Education', in *The Bee*, no. 6

14:20 Weep not for little Léonie / Abducted by a French Marquis! / Though loss of honour was a wrench / Just think how it's improved her French.

Harry Graham, 1930, 'Compensation', in *More Ruthless Rhymes for Heartless Homes*

14:21 This also is proper to vs Englishmen, that sith ours is a meane [in-between] language, and neither too rough nor too smooth in vtterance, we may with much facilitie learne any other language, beside Hebrue, Gréeke, & Latine, and speake it naturallie, as if we were home-borne in those countries; & yet on the other side it falleth out, I wot not by what other meanes, that few forren nations can rightlie pronounce ours, without some and that great note of imperfection, especiallie the French men, who also seldome write any thing that sauoreth of English trulie.

William Harrison, 1587, *The Description of Britaine*, Ch. 6

14:22 We never do anything well till we cease to think about the manner of doing it. This is the reason why it is so difficult for any but natives to speak a language correctly or idiomatically.

William Hazlitt, 1839, 'On Prejudice', in *Sketches and Essays*

14:23 [of English] I feel powerless in the face of this language, this so-called easy language, which I consider more difficult than any other language I have tried to learn.

Louis Hjelmslev, 1954, 'Nu kom den dansk-engelske ordbog [Now comes the Danish-English dictionary]' (trans.), in *Politiken*, 8 October

14:24 [of the Anoch landlord, Lachlan Macqueen] I praised the propriety of his language, and was answered that I need not wonder, for he had learned it by grammar.

Samuel Johnson, 1773, 'Anoch', in *A Journey to the Western Islands of Scotland*

14:25 Rest to the souls of those fine old Pedagogues; the breed, long since extinct, of the Lilys, and the Linacres: who believing that all learning was contained in the languages which they taught, and despising every other acquirement as superficial and useless, came to their task as to a sport! Passing from infancy to age, they dreamed away all their days as in a grammar-school. Revolving in a perpetual cycle of declensions, conjugations, syntaxes, and prosodies.

Charles Lamb, 1823, 'Old and New Schoolmaster', in *The Essays of Elia*

14:26 Unless we go through the organized compulsory curriculum of a school and college we can't get the legal qualification to enter a profession. In order to be a dentist we must first know what a logarithm is, and in order to be a horse doctor you have to learn Latin. The idea is that any man who has tackled a Latin irregular

verb has no trouble with the inside of a horse.

Stephen Leacock, 1938, 'Recovery after Graduation', in *Here are my Lectures*

14:27 In learning languages, accuracy at first is out of place. A boy who learns all the French irregular verbs out of a list, before he uses French and reads French, will never get beyond a list. He might get a job in a French laundry, but that's all.

Stephen Leacock, 1938, 'Recovery after Graduation', in *Here are my Lectures*

14:28 For one must not ask the letters in the Latin tongue, how one ought to speak German; but one must ask the mother in the house, the children in the lanes and alleys, the common man in the market, concerning this; yea, and look at the *moves* of their mouths while they are talking, and thereafter interpret. They understand you then, and mark that one talks German with them.

Martin Luther, 1530, 'Ein Sendbrieff, von Dolmetschen, und Fürbitte der Heiligen' (trans. S. T. Coleridge)

14:29 The easiest way to give the impression of having a good accent or no foreign accent at all is to hold an unlit pipe in your mouth, to mutter between your teeth and finish all your sentences with the question: 'isn't it?' People will not understand much, but they are accustomed to that and they will get a most excellent impression.

George Mikes, 1946, 'The language', *How to be an Alien*, I

14:30 [on poor methods of teaching Latin and Greek, whereby novices are presented with advanced works on logic and metaphysics] So that they having but newly left those Grammatick flats & shallows where they stuck unreasonably to learn a few words with lamentable construction, and now on the sudden transported under another climat to be tost and turmoild with their unballasted wits in fadomles and unquiet deeps of controversie, do for the most part grow in hatred and contempt of learning, mockt and deluded all this while with ragged notions and babblements, while they expected worthy and delightfull knowledge.

John Milton, 1644, 'Of Education'

14:31 [Edward Wortley Montagu has written that the poet Abraham Cowley excelled through not submitting to the rules of grammar] When

Mr Cowley and other people (for I know several have learn't after the same manner) were in places where they had opertunity of being learn't by word of mouth, I don't see any violent necessity of printed rules, but being where, from the top of the house to the bottom, not a Creature in it understands so much as even good English, without the help of a Dictionary or inspiration I know no way of attaining to any Language. Dispairing of the Last I am forc't to make use of the other.

Lady Mary Wortley Montagu, 26 August 1709, letter to Anne Wortley, in Isobel Grundy (ed.), *Lady Mary Wortley Montagu: Selected Letters* (1997)

14:32 Suddenly my mind woke up. Floods of light came in. I began to learn. I began to want to excel in new ways. I learnt French. I started on Latin. Mr Osmand promised me Greek. An ability to write fluent correct Latin prose began to offer me an escape from (perhaps literally) the prison house, began in time to show me vistas headier and more glorious than any I had ever before known how to dream of. In the beginning was the word. *Amo, amas, amat* was my open sesame, 'Learn these verbs by Friday' the essence of my education; perhaps it is *mutatis mutandis* the essence of any education. I also learnt, of course, my own language, hitherto something of a foreign tongue. I learnt from Mr Osmand how to write the best language in the world accurately and clearly and, ultimately, with a hard careful elegance. I discovered words and words were my salvation. I was not, except in some very broken-down sense of that ambiguous term, a love child. I was a word child.

Iris Murdoch, 1975, 'Thursday' (first week), in *A Word Child*

14:33 [of Monsieur Petit] He is a right Frenchman, and full of their own projects, he having a design to reform the universities, and to institute schools for the learning of all languages, to speak them naturally and not by rule, which I know will come to nothing.

Samuel Pepys, 23 October 1660, *Diary*

14:34 What's all the noisy jargon of the schools, / But idle nonsense of laborious fools, / Who fetter reason with perplexing rules?

John Pomfret, 1699, 'Reason', in *Poems on Several Occasions* [cf. 14:6]

14:35 [on the Lifemanship Correspondence College modern languages department] See our list of French phrases O.K. to bring into conversation. See, on the left of the blackboard, correct French; on the right, French translated into English French, phonetically transcribed, a dialect which our students are taught to cultivate with aristocratic downrightness and amusingly insular don't-care-a-damnmanship.

Stephen Potter, 1952, 'Our College', *One-Upmanship*, I, p. 15

14:36 A foreign language is more easily learned in the kitchen than at school.

Proverbial (German)

14:37 Beat a Chinaman enough, and he will speak Tibetan.

Proverbial (Tibetan)

14:38 [Mortimer, to his wife] But I will never be a truant, love, / Till I have learnt thy language, for thy tongue / Makes Welsh as sweet as ditties highly penned, / Sung by a fair queen in a summer's bower / With ravishing division, to her lute.

William Shakespeare, 1597, *Henry IV, Part 1*, III. i. 202

14:39 MISTRESS QUICKLY [after hearing young William Page being taught Latin pronouns]: You do ill to teach the child such words. He teaches him to hick and to hack [*hic, haec, hoc*], which they'll do fast enough of themselves, and to call 'whorum' [*horum*]. Fie upon you!

EVANS: 'Oman, art thou lunatics? Hast thou no understandings for thy cases, and the numbers of the genders?

William Shakespeare, 1597, *The Merry Wives of Windsor*, IV. i. 59

14:40 [Sir Andrew, reacting to Sir Toby's use of *pourquoi*] What is 'Pourquoi'? Do, or not do? I would I had bestowed that time in the tongues that I have in fencing, dancing, and bear-baiting. O, had I but followed the arts!

William Shakespeare, 1601, *Twelfth Night*, I. iii. 89

14:41 [Caliban] You taught me language; and my profit on't / Is I know how to curse. The red plague rid you, / For learning me your language!

William Shakespeare, 1610–11, *The Tempest*, I. ii. 365

14:42 It is a great mistake to suppose that any one nation has a special gift for acquiring sounds of foreign languages generally.

Henry Sweet, 1877, *A Handbook of Phonetics*, Preface

14:43 As regards ease of learning, all languages are intrinsically on a level – they are all equally easy or equally difficult; that is, of course, if we rigorously eliminate all external considerations, and disregard the special relations between individual languages.

Henry Sweet, 1899, *The Practical Study of Languages*, Ch. 8

14:44 I pointed to every thing and inquired the name of it, which I wrote down in my Journal Book when I was alone, and corrected my bad accent by desiring those of the family to pronounce it often. In this employment a sorrel nag, one of the under-servants, was very ready to assist me.

Jonathan Swift, 1726, 'A Voyage to the Country of the Houyhnhnms', *Gulliver's Travels*, IV, Ch. 3

14:45 The men who speak [in public] easily and with natural fluency, are also they who learn languages easily.

Anthony Trollope, 1863, *Rachel Ray*, Ch. 24

See also: 2:20, 9:6, 9:35, 16:16, 18:23, 23:31, 23:65

15 *Foreigner Talk*

Impressions of foreign languages; speech by and to foreigners

15:1 [of the replacement of *-eth* by *-s*] This has wonderfully multiplied a Letter which was before too frequent in the *English* Tongue, and added to that *hissing* in our Language, which is taken so much notice of by Foreigners; but at the same time, humours our Taciturnity, and eases us of many superfluous Syllables.

Joseph Addison, 4 August 1711, *The Spectator*, no. 135

15:2 [Chorus] People are quick to be censorious / Of those who speak with a foreign accent.

Aeschylus, 458 BC, *The Suppliants* (trans. P. Villacott), 973

15:3 Those who wish to make themselves understood by a foreigner in his own language, should speak with much noise and vociferation, opening their mouths wide. Is it surprising that the English are, in general, the worst linguists in the world, seeing that they pursue a system diametrically opposite?

George Borrow, 1843, *The Bible in Spain*, Ch. 1

15:4 A man is always suspicious of what is saying in an unknown tongue; and, if fear be his passion at the time, he grows more afraid.

James Boswell, 1785, 'Sunday 3rd October', in *The Journal of a Tour to the Hebrides*

15:5 Dr Petworth . . . is, though a linguist, not that kind of linguist who knows many languages. He is competent in some tongues, but mostly dead ones: Old and Middle English, Middle High German, and, if pressed, a little Old Norse, a passable Old Icelandic. But otherwise he possesses no more than that conventional, minimal polyglotism that has, for centuries, taken the English, stammering and nodding, baffled and curious, speaking their own tongue very loudly and slowly in the belief that if spoken like this it will be perfectly understood, into every corner of the world.

Malcolm Bradbury, 1983, *Rates of Exchange*, I, Sect. 4

15:6 [Bruno] 'Course he knows no better, if he's Flench! Flenchmen *never* can speak English so goodly as *us!*'

Lewis Carroll, 1893, *Sylvie and Bruno Concluded*, Ch. 12

15:7 We exchanged many frank words in our respective languages.

Peter Cook, 1961, impersonation of Harold Macmillan in *Beyond the Fringe*

15:8 I don't hold with abroad and think that foreigners speak English when our backs are turned.

Quentin Crisp, 1968, *The Naked Civil Servant*, Ch. 4

15:9 [Mr Lillyvick] 'What's the water in French, sir?' '*L'eau*,' replied Nicholas. 'Ah!' said Mr Lillyvick, shaking his head mournfully. 'I thought as much. Lo, eh? I don't think anything of that language – nothing at all.'

Charles Dickens, 1838–9, *Nicholas Nickleby*, Ch. 16

15:10 'Ill fo manger, you know,' says Mr Jobling, pronouncing that word as if he meant a necessary fixture in an English stable. 'Ill fo manger. That's the French saying, and mangering is as necessary to me as it is to a Frenchman. Or more so.'

Charles Dickens, 1852–3, *Bleak House*, Ch. 20

15:11 [on the way the Plornishes addressed the Italian foreigner, Mr Baptist] They began to accommodate themselves to his level, calling him 'Mr Baptist,' but treating him like a baby, and laughing immoderately at his lively gestures and his childish English – more, because he didn't mind it, and laughed too. They spoke to him in very loud voices, as if he were stone deaf. They constructed sentences, by way of teaching him the language in its purity, such as were addressed by the savages to Captain Cook, or by Friday to Robinson Crusoe. Mrs Plornish was particularly ingenious in this art; and attained so much celebrity for saying, 'Me ope you leg well soon,' that it was considered in the Yard but a very short remove indeed from speaking Italian. Even Mrs Plornish herself began to think that she had a natural call towards that language.

Charles Dickens, 1855–7, *Little Dorrit*, I, Ch. 25

15:12 With an unshaken confidence that the English tongue was somehow the mother tongue of the whole world, only the people were too stupid to know it, Mr Meagles harangued innkeepers in the most voluble manner, entered into loud explanations of the most complicated sort, and utterly renounced replies in the native language of the respondents, on the ground that they were 'all bosh'.

Charles Dickens, 1855–7, *Little Dorrit*, II, Ch. 32

15:13 [of Mme Defarge and Miss Pross] Each spoke in her own language; neither understood the other's words; both were very watchful, and intent to deduce from look and manner, what the unintelligible words meant.

Charles Dickens, 1859, *A Tale of Two Cities*, III, Ch. 14

15:14 Mr. The Englishman was not particularly strong in the French language as a means of oral communication, though he read it very well. It is with languages as with people, – when you only know them by sight, you are apt to mistake them; you must be on speaking terms before you can be said to have established an acquaintance.

Charles Dickens, 1862, *Somebody's Luggage*, Ch. 2

15:15 [Mr Podsnap, enquiring of a foreigner whether he found London 'very rich'] The foreign gentleman found it, without doubt, enormément riche. 'Enormously Rich, We say,' returned Mr. Podsnap, in a condescending manner. 'Our English adverbs do Not terminate in Mong, and We Pronounce the "ch" as if there were a 't' before it. We Say Ritch.'

Charles Dickens, 1864–5, *Our Mutual Friend*, I, Ch. 11

15:16 'Our language,' said Mr. Podsnap, with a

gracious consciousness of being always right, 'is Difficult. Ours is a Copious Language, and Trying to Strangers.'

Charles Dickens, 1864–5, *Our Mutual Friend*, I, Ch. 11

15:17 Fielding . . . was often struck by the liveliness with which the younger generation handled a foreign tongue. They altered the idiom, but they could say whatever they wanted to say quickly.

E. M. Forster, 1924, *A Passage to India*, Ch. 7

15:18 [an Indian reaction to some remarks by Fielding] The line of thought was not alien to them, but the words were too definite and bleak. Unless a sentence paid a few compliments to Justice and Morality in passing, its grammar wounded their ears and paralysed their minds.

E. M. Forster, 1924, *A Passage to India*, Ch. 9

15:19 An Englishman would not speak his native language in a company of foreigners, where he was sure that none understood him; a travelling Hottentot himself would be silent if acquainted only with the language of his country; but a Frenchman shall talk to you whether you understand his language or not; never troubling his head whether you have learned French, still he keeps up the conversation, fixes his eye full in your face, and asks a thousand questions, which he answers himself, for want of a more satisfactory reply.

Oliver Goldsmith, 1760–2, *The Citizen of the World*, Letter 78

15:20 [of the Garamantes] They eat snakes and lizards and other reptiles and speak a language like no other, but squeak like bats.

Herodotus, 5th century BC, in *The Histories* (trans. Aubrey de Sélincourt, 1996), IV, Ch. 183

15:21 Every language always sounds foolish to those who speak another one.

Stephen Leacock, 1938, 'The Two Milords', in *Here are my Lectures*

15:22 When we write in a foreign language, we should not think in English; if we do, our writings will be but translations at best. If one is to write in French, one must use oneself to think in French; and even then, for a good while, our Anglicisms will get uppermost, and betray us in writing, as our native accent does in speaking.

Dean Lockier, in Joseph Spence, *Anecdotes, Observations, and Characters of Books and Men* (1820)

15:23 This whole language business is not at all easy. After spending eight years in this country, the other day I was told by a very kind lady: 'But why do you complain? You really speak a most excellent accent without the slightest English.'

George Mikes, 1946, 'The language', *How to be an Alien*, I

15:24 Life is a foreign language: all men mispronounce it.

Christopher Morley, 1925, *Thunder on the Left*, Ch. 14

15:25 SAYE: You men of Kent.

BUTCHER: What say you of Kent?

SAYE: Nothing but this – 'tis *bona terra, mala gens*.

CADE: *Bonum terrum* – zounds, what's that?

BUTCHER: He speaks French.

FIRST REBEL: No, 'tis Dutch.

SECOND REBEL: No, 'tis Out-talian, I know it well enough.

William Shakespeare, 1590–1, *Henry VI, Part 2*, IV. vii. 51

15:26 [Portia, of her English suitor] He understands not me, nor I him. He hath neither Latin, French, nor Italian, and you will come into the court and swear that I have a poor pennyworth in the English. He is a proper man's picture, but alas, who can converse with a dumb show?

William Shakespeare, 1596–7, *The Merchant of Venice*, I. ii. 65

15:27 [Ford, to the Welsh parson, Evans] I will never mistrust my wife again till thou art able to woo her in good English.

William Shakespeare, 1597, *The Merry Wives of Windsor*, V. v. 132

15:28 SIR JOHN FALSTAFF: 'Tis time I were choked with a piece of toasted cheese.

EVANS: Seese is not good to give putter; your belly is all putter.

SIR JOHN: 'Seese' and 'putter'? Have I lived to stand at the taunt of one that makes fritters of English?

William Shakespeare, 1597, *The Merry Wives of Windsor*, V. v. 137

15:29 [Princess Catherine] *De foot* et *de cown*? O Seigneur Dieu! Ils sont les mots de son mauvais, corruptible, gros, et impudique, et non pour les dames d'honneur d'user. Je ne voudrais prononcer ces mots devant les seigneurs de France pour tout le monde. ['The foot' and 'the gown'? Good Lord! They are words with a horrible sound, . . .

and not for honourable ladies to use. I wouldn't say these words in front of the French lords for the world.]

William Shakespeare, 1599, *Henry V*, III. iv. 48

15:30 CASSIUS: Did Cicero say anything?

CASCA: Ay, he spoke Greek.

CASSIUS: To what effect?

CASCA: Nay, an I tell you that, I'll ne'er look you i'th'face again. But those that understood him smiled at one another, and shook their heads. But for mine own part, it was Greek to me.

William Shakespeare, 1599, *Julius Caesar*, I. ii. 278

15:31 [Cokane] We rarely feel the charm of our own tongue until it reaches our ears under a foreign sky.

George Bernard Shaw, 1892, *Widowers' Houses*, I

15:32 MRS DANGLE [having just met two Italians and a less than adequate interpreter]: Mr Dangle, here are two very civil gentlemen trying to make themselves understood, and I don't know which is the interpreter. [*The Interpreter and Signor Pasticcio speak together.*] . . .

DANGLE: Egad, I think the interpreter is the hardest to be understood of the two!

SNEER: Why, I thought, Dangle, you had been an admirable linguist!

DANGLE: So I am, if they would not talk so damned fast.

Richard Sheridan, 1779, *The Critic*, I. ii

15:33 [of M. Grascour] He would only be known to be a foreigner by the correctness of his language.

Anthony Trollope, 1883, *Mr Scarborough's Family*, Ch. 46

15:34 They spell it Vinci and pronounce it Vinchy; foreigners always spell better than they pronounce.

Mark Twain, 1869, *The Innocents Abroad*, Ch. 19

15:35 [Jim to Huckleberry Finn] 'Why, Huck, doan' de French people talk de same way we does?' [Huck] 'No, Jim; you couldn't understand a word they said – not a single word.' [Jim] 'Well, now, I be ding-busted! How do dat come?' [Huck] '*I* don't know; but it's so. I got some of their jabber out of a book. S'pose a man was to come to you and say *Polly-voo-franzy* – what would you think?' [Jim] 'I wouldn' think nuff'n; I'd take en bust him over de head. Dad is, if he warn't white. I wouldn't 'low no nigger to call me dat.' [Huck] 'Shucks, it ain't calling you anything. It's only saying do you know how to talk French.' [Jim] 'Well, den, why couldn't he *say* it?' [Huck] 'Why, he *is* a-saying it. That's a Frenchman's *way* of saying it.' [Jim] 'Well, it's a blame' ridicklous way, en I doan' want to hear no mo' 'bout it. Dey ain' no sense in it.'

Mark Twain, 1884, *The Adventures of Huckleberry Finn*, Ch. 14

15:36 [Sean Connor] I abhor the ignorant use of Franglais.

Mary Wesley, 1986, *The Vacillations of Poppy Carew*, Ch. 16

15:37 I don't object to foreigners speaking a foreign language; I just wish they'd all speak the same foreign language.

Billy Wilder, 1972, *Avanti*

15:38 Into the face of the young man who sat on the terrace of the hotel Magnifique at Cannes there had crept a look of furtive shame, the shifty, hangdog look which announces that an Englishman is about to talk French.

P. G. Wodehouse, 1935, *The Luck of the Bodkins*, Ch. 1

See also: 31:1

Analysing Language

16 Exposing Language

Terms and techniques for analysing language; linguistics and philology

16:1 [on the observation that the words for 'gin and tonic' throughout the worlds of the Galaxy are very similar, though these worlds had had no contact with each other] What can be made of this fact? It exists in total isolation. As far as any theory of structural linguistics is concerned it is right off the graph, and yet it persists. Old structural linguists get very angry when young structural linguists go on about it. Young structural linguists get deeply excited about it and stay up late at night convinced that they are very close to something of profound importance, and end up becoming old structural linguists before their time, getting very angry with the young ones. Structural linguistics is a bitterly divided and unhappy discipline, and a large number of its practitioners spend too many nights drowning their problems in Ouisghian Zodahs.
Douglas Adams, 1980, *The Restaurant at the End of the Universe*, Ch. 24

16:2 Trying to gain a critical perspective on language by means of language is like trying to cut butter with a knife made of butter.
Robert M. Adams, 1980, 'Authenticity-codes and Sincerity-formulas', in L. Michaels and C. Ricks (eds), *The State of the Language*

16:3 Diction as a whole has the following elements: phoneme, syllable, connective, noun, verb, conjunction, inflection, utterance.
Aristotle, 4th century BC, 'Basic Concepts', in *Poetics* (trans. M. Heath), Ch. 20

16:4 An *utterance* is a composite significant vocalization, part or parts of which are significant in their own right.
Aristotle, 4th century BC, 'Basic Concepts', in *Poetics* (trans. M. Heath), Ch. 20

16:5 The most poetical of all scholastic disciplines is, surely, Philology, the study of language in abstraction from its uses, so that words become, as it were, little lyrics about themselves.
W. H. Auden, 1948, 'Making, Knowing and Judging', in *The Dyer's Hand and other essays*

16:6 [of the scholar] He preserves the discourses of famous men; he is at home with the niceties of parables. He researches into the hidden sense of proverbs; he ponders the obscurities of parables.
The Bible, Ecclesiasticus 39:2 (Jerusalem Bible)

16:7 The study of language will be the ground where science gains its first foothold in the understanding and control of human affairs.
Leonard Bloomfield, 1930, 'Linguistics as a Science', in *Studies in Philology*, no. 27

16:8 The only useful generalizations about language are inductive generalizations.
Leonard Bloomfield, 1933, *Language*, Ch. 1

16:9 The most difficult step in the study of language is the first step.
Leonard Bloomfield, 1933, *Language*, Ch. 2

16:10 The linguist of course is the metaperson par excellence. His business is perpetual feasting on the forbidden fruit, to expose language in all its nakedness.
Dwight Bolinger, 1980, 'Fire in a Wooden Stove: On Being Aware in Language', in L. Michaels and C. Ricks (eds), *The State of the Language*

16:11 With me the pursuit of languages has been always modified by the love of horses. ... I might, otherwise, have become a mere philologist: one of those beings who toil night and day in culling useless words for some *opus magnum* which Murray will never publish, and nobody ever read.

George Borrow, 1851, *Lavengro*, Ch. 13

16:12 We are at the commencement of a philological age, every one studies languages: that is, every one who is fit for nothing else.

George Borrow, 1851, *Lavengro*, Ch. 47

16:13 The linguists, whom one meets everywhere these days, explain that every transaction in our culture – our money and mathematics, our games and gardens, our diet and our sexual activity – is a language; this, of course, is why one meets so many linguists these days.

Malcolm Bradbury, 1983, 'Visiting Slaka: A Few Brief Hints', in *Rates of Exchange*

16:14 [on contemporary linguistic studies] Today's Tower of Babel – a fair term for the many-roomed mansion of language study, in which nobody agrees with anybody else.

Anthony Burgess, 1992, *A Mouthful of Air*, I, Ch. 1

16:15 We tend to think of a language as deliberately architectural – a blueprint grammar, a dictionary-load of bricks.

Anthony Burgess, 1992, *A Mouthful of Air*, I, Ch. 1

16:16 [on the lack of phonetics teaching in schools] For that matter, instruction in the use of the IPA [International Phonetic Alphabet] is considered to be a remote academic luxury unrelated to the pragmatics of the studying of English. This view is probably sinful.

Anthony Burgess, 1992, *A Mouthful of Air*, I, Ch. 7

16:17 Phonetics, phonetics, and again phonetics. There cannot be too much phonetics, an aspect of language teaching wretchedly neglected.

Anthony Burgess, 1992, *A Mouthful of Air*, II, Epilogue

16:18 For all a rhetorician's rules / Teach nothing but to name his tools.

Samuel Butler (1612–80), 1663, *Hudibras*, I, Canto 1, 89

16:19 Syntax is the study of the principles and processes by which sentences are constructed in particular languages. Syntactic investigation of a given language has as its goal the construction of a grammar that can be viewed as a device of some sort for producing the sentences of the language under analysis. More generally,

linguists must be concerned with the problem of determining the fundamental underlying properties of successful grammars.

Noam Chomsky, 1957, *Syntactic Structures*, Ch. 1

16:20 I will consider a *language* to be a set (finite or infinite) of sentences, each finite in length and constructed out of a finite set of elements.

Noam Chomsky, 1957, *Syntactic Structures*, Ch. 2

16:21 The fundamental aim in the linguistic analysis of a language L is to separate the *grammatical* sequences which are the sentences of L from the *ungrammatical* sequences which are not sentences of L and to study the structure of the grammatical sequences. The grammar of L will thus be a device that generates all of the grammatical sequences of L and none of the ungrammatical ones.

Noam Chomsky, 1957, *Syntactic Structures*, Ch. 2

16:22 It is obvious that the set of grammatical sentences cannot be identified with any particular corpus of utterances obtained by the linguist in his field work. Any grammar of a language will *project* the finite and somewhat accidental corpus of observed utterances to a set (presumably infinite) of grammatical utterances.

Noam Chomsky, 1957, *Syntactic Structures*, Ch. 2

16:23 As a simple example of the new form for grammars associated with constituent analysis, consider the following: (i) Sentence → NP + VP [noun phrase + verb phrase].

Noam Chomsky, 1957, *Syntactic Structures*, Ch. 4

16:24 Linguistic theory is concerned primarily with an ideal speaker-listener, in a completely homogeneous speech-community, who knows its language perfectly and is unaffected by such grammatically irrelevant conditions as memory limitations, distractions, shifts of attention and interest, and errors (random or characteristic) in applying his knowledge of the language in actual performance.

Noam Chomsky, 1965, *Aspects of the Theory of Syntax*, Ch. 1

16:25 We thus make a fundamental distinction between *competence* (the speaker-hearer's knowledge of his language) and *performance* (the actual use of language in conerete situations).

Noam Chomsky, 1965, *Aspects of the Theory of Syntax*, Ch. 1

16:26 The object of rhetoric is persuasion, – of logic, conviction, – of grammar, significancy. A fourth term is wanting, the rhematic, or logic of sentences.

Samuel Taylor Coleridge, 23 September 1830, in Henry Nelson Coleridge (ed.), *Specimens of the Table-Talk of the late Samuel Taylor Coleridge* (1835)

16:27 Another sport which wastes unlimited time is comma-hunting. Once start a comma and the whole pack will be off, full cry, especially if they have had a literary training. . . . But comma-hunting is so exciting as to be a little dangerous. When attention is entirely concentrated on punctuation, there is some fear that the conduct of business may suffer, and a proposal get through without being properly obstructed on its demerits. It is therefore wise, when a kill has been made, to move at once for adjournment.

Francis M. Cornford, 1908, *Microcosmographia Academica*, Ch. 8

16:28 Learn'd philologists, who chase / A panting syllable through time and space, / Start it at home, and hunt it in the dark, / To Gaul, to Greece, and into Noah's ark.

William Cowper, 1782, *Retirement*, 691

16:29 An evil spirit seems to preside over all branches of clinical language studies. . . . He tempts all to follow him, in the name of clarity and precision, but all who do find only obscurity and quicksand. His name is Terminology.

David Crystal, 1984, 'Terms, Time and Teeth', in *Linguistic Encounters with Language Handicap*

16:30 We must beware of Humpty Dumpty syndrome. We should never take language apart without the intention and ability to put it back together again.

David Crystal, 1984, 'Terms, Time and Teeth', in *Linguistic Encounters with Language Handicap*

16:31 If we possessed a perfect pedigree of mankind, a genealogical arrangement of the races of man would afford the best classification of the various languages now spoken throughout the world; and if all extinct languages, and all intermediate and slowly changing dialects, were to be included, such an arrangement would be the only possible one.

Charles Darwin, 1859, *The Origin of Species*, Ch. 14

16:32 [Nicholas, of Squeers] He is an odd-looking man . . . What of that? Porson was an odd-looking man, and so was Doctor Johnson; all these bookworms are.

Charles Dickens, 1838–9, *Nicholas Nickleby*, Ch. 4

16:33 [of Mr Curdle] He had . . . proved, that by altering the received mode of punctuation, any one of Shakespeare's plays could be made quite different, and the sense completely changed.

Charles Dickens, 1838–9, *Nicholas Nickleby*, Ch. 24

16:34 She was dry and sandy with working in the graves of deceased languages. None of your living languages for Miss Blimber. They must be dead – stone dead – and then Miss Blimber dug them up like a Ghoul.

Charles Dickens, 1848, *Dombey and Son*, Ch. 11

16:35 [Tony Lumpkin] Let schoolmasters puzzle their brain, / With grammar, and nonsense, and learning, / Good liquor, I stoutly maintain, / Gives genius a better discerning.

Oliver Goldsmith, 1773, *She Stoops to Conquer*, I. ii

16:36 In the study of languages, one can safely assume nothing.

Edward T. Hall, 1959, *The Silent Language*, Ch. 5

16:37 A dogmatiser in the province of philology is almost certain to be a good deal in the clouds.

Fitzedward Hall, 1880, 'English Rational and Irrational', *The Nineteenth Century*, no. 43

16:38 Be his use of his native language ever so irreproachable, a man is not consequently a philologist.

Fitzedward Hall, 1880, 'English Rational and Irrational', *The Nineteenth Century*, no. 43

16:39 [of linguistics] The best instrument yet devised for getting inside the human skin.

A. A. Hill, 1957, attributed in Ward H. Goodenough, 'Cultural Anthropology and Linguistics'

16:40 [Maid, remonstrating with the Professor] Arithmetic leads to Philology, and Philology leads to Crime.

Eugène Ionesco, 1951, *The Lesson* (trans. D. Watson, 1958)

16:41 That the weather clerk really makes the weather probably none but infants believe, but that language is made by compilers of dictionaries and grammars is a conception not confined to the young or ignorant.

H. C. G. von Jagemann, 1899, Address to the Modern Language Association

16:42 Who will consider that no dictionary of a living tongue can ever be perfect, since while it is hastening to publication, some words are budding, and some falling away; that a whole

life cannot be spent upon syntax and etymology, and that even a whole life would not
be sufficient; that he, whose design includes
whatever language can express, must often
speak of what he does not understand.

Samuel Johnson, 1755, *A Dictionary of the English Language*, Preface

16:43 The Sanskrit language, whatever be its
antiquity, is of a wonderful structure; more perfect than the Greek, more copious than the
Latin, and more exquisitely refined than either,
yet bearing to both of them a stronger affinity,
both in the roots of verbs, and in the forms of
grammar, than could possibly have been produced by accident; so strong, indeed, that no
philologer could examine them all three, without believing them to have sprung from some
common source, which, perhaps, no longer
exists.

Sir William Jones, 2 February 1786, 'The Third
Anniversary Discourse, on the Hindus', Presidential
Address to the Bengal Asiatick Society

16:44 Heuristic is concerned with language-
dynamics, while logic is concerned with
language-statics.

Imre Lakatos, 1978, *Philosophical Papers* I, p. 1

16:45 I am sometimes told that there are people
who want a study of literature wholly free from
philology; that is, from the love and knowledge
of words. Perhaps no such people exist. If they
do, they are either crying for the moon or else
resolving on a lifetime of persistent and carefully guarded delusion.

C. S. Lewis, 1960, introduction to *Studies in Words*

16:46 Questions of language are indeed the
most important and central subject of all
humanistic studies.

Bronislaw Malinowski, 1923, 'The Problem of
Meaning in Primitive Languages', supplement to
C. K. Ogden and I. A. Richards, *The Meaning of Meaning*

16:47 And though a linguist should pride himself to have all the tongues that Babel cleft the
world into, yet, if he have not studied the solid
things in them as well as the words and lexicons,
he were nothing so much to be esteem'd a
learned man, as any yeoman or tradesman com-
petently wise in his mother dialect only.

John Milton, 1644, 'Of Education'

16:48 Some philosophers were sitting together
in the temple at Delphi one day. 'Either I am

mistaken,' said Demetrius the grammarian, 'or
your calm happy faces show that you are not
having an important discussion.' One of them,
Herakleon of Megara, retorted: 'Furrowed brows
are for grammarians telling us whether *ballo*
takes two *l*s in the future, researching into the
derivation of the comparatives *keiron* and *beltion*
and of the superlatives *keiriston* and *beltiston*:
philosophical discussions habitually make men
happy and joyful, not frowning and sad.'

Michel de Montaigne, 1572–80, 'On Educating
Children', in *The Complete Essays* (trans. M. A.
Screech, 1987), I, no. 26

16:49 When you hear grammatical terms such
as metonymy, metaphor and allegory do they
not seem to refer to some rare, exotic tongue?
Yet they are categories which apply to the
chatter of your chambermaid.

Michel de Montaigne, 1572–80, 'On the Vanity of
Words', in *The Complete Essays* (trans. M. A.
Screech, 1987), I, no. 51

16:50 When shall I ever have done describing
some commotion and revolution of my
thoughts, no matter what subject they happen
upon, when Diomedes [Didymus] wrote six
thousand books on the sole subject of philology? What can babble produce when the
stammering of an untied tongue smothered the
world under such a dreadful weight of volumes?
So many words about nothing but words! O
Pythagoras! Why couldest thou not conjure
such turbulence? [by imposing a rule of silence]

Michel de Montaigne, 1572–80, 'On Vanity', in *The
Complete Essays* (trans. M. A. Screech, 1987), III,
no. 9

16:51 I was not a philological prodigy. I lacked
that uncanny gift which some people have for
language structure which seems akin to a gift for
music or calculation. I never became concerned
with the metaphysical aspects of language. (I
am not interested in Chomsky. That places me.)
And I never thought of myself as a 'writer' or
tried to become one. I was just a brilliant plodder
with an aptitude for grammar and an adoration
for words.

Iris Murdoch, 1975, 'Thursday' (first week), in *A Word
Child* [cf. 16:19, ff.]

16:52 Language cannot be thrust into a vacuum
and examined as though it were something
existing apart from the people who devised it
and the people who use it. To ignore the human
origin, the human dependence, the human
nexus, is fatal; to underestimate the people–

speech interdependence is dangerous, in that such an underestimation will vitiate everything one writes on the subject of general language and particular aspects or phrases or words.

Eric Partridge, 1963, *The Gentle Art of Lexicography*, Ch. 2

16:53 The workings of language are as far from our awareness as the rationale for egg-laying is from the fly's.

Steven Pinker, 1994, *The Language Instinct*, Ch. 1

16:54 But spectacles have a *function*, and they function only when you put them on, to look through them *at the world*. It is the same with language. That is to say, one shouldn't waste one's life in spectacle-cleaning or in talking about language, or in trying to get a clear view of our language, or of 'our conceptual scheme'. The fundamental thing about human languages is that they can and should be used to describe something; and this something is, somehow, the world.

Karl Popper, 1971, 'Discussion among Karl Popper, Peter Strawson and Geoffrey Warnock', in B. Magee (ed.), *Modern British Philosophy*

16:55 As for the special uses and distinctions of words, they should be a subject of study common to all who give any thought to the meaning of language.

Quintilian, 1st century, *Institutio Oratoria* (trans. H. E. Butler), I, Preface

16:56 The study of words is not the right thing for a man without a memory.

Jean-Jacques Rousseau, 1770, *The Confessions* (trans. J. M. Cohen), VI: 1738

16:57 But what is language [*langue*]? It is not to be confused with human speech [*langage*], of which it is only a definite part, though certainly an essential one. It is both a social product of the faculty of speech and a collection of necessary conventions that have been adopted by a social body to permit individuals to exercise that faculty. . . . Speaking [*parole*], on the contrary, is an individual act.

Ferdinand de Saussure, 1916, *Course in General Linguistics* (trans. W. Baskin), Introduction, Ch. 3

16:58 I call the combination of a concept and a sound-image a *sign* [*signe*] . . . I propose to retain the word *sign* to designate the whole and to replace *concept* and *sound-image* respectively by *signified* [*signifié*] and *signifier* [*signifiant*]. . . .

The bond between the signifier and the signified is arbitrary.

Ferdinand de Saussure, 1916, *Course in General Linguistics* (trans. W. Baskin), I, Ch. 1

16:59 Everything that relates to the static side of our science is synchronic; everything that has to do with evolution is diachronic.

Ferdinand de Saussure, 1916, *Course in General Linguistics* (trans. W. Baskin), I, Ch. 3

16:60 Language is a system of interdependent terms in which the value of each term results solely from the simultaneous presence of the others.

Ferdinand de Saussure, 1916, *Course in General Linguistics* (trans. W. Baskin), II, Ch. 4

16:61 THE GENTLEMAN [impressed by the Note Taker's ability to place accents]: How do you do it, if I may ask?

THE NOTE TAKER: Simply phonetics. The science of speech. Thats my profession: also my hobby. Happy is the man who can make a living by his hobby! You can spot an Irishman or a Yorkshireman by his brogue. *I* can place any man within six miles. I can place him within two miles in London. Sometimes within two streets.

George Bernard Shaw, 1913, *Pygmalion*, I

16:62 PICKERING: I rather fancied myself because I can pronounce twenty-four distinct vowel sounds; but your hundred and thirty beat me. I cant hear a bit of difference between most of them.

HIGGINS: Oh, that comes with practice. You hear no difference at first; but you keep on listening, and presently you find theyre all as different as A from B.

George Bernard Shaw, 1913, *Pygmalion*, II

16:63 [Mrs Pearce, to Higgins] When you get what you call interested in people's accents, you never think or care what may happen to them or you.

George Bernard Shaw, 1913, *Pygmalion*, II

16:64 [Anderson, of linguistic analysis] A lot of chaps pointing out that we don't always mean what we say, even when we manage to say what we mean.

Tom Stoppard, 1977, *Professional Foul*

16:65 [Anderson] I like to collect little curiosities for the language chaps. It's like handing round a bag of liquorice allsorts. They're terribly grateful.

Tom Stoppard, 1977, *Professional Foul*

16:66 Grammar deals with the general facts of language, lexicology with the special facts.

Henry Sweet, 1876, 'Words, Logic and Grammar', *Transactions of the Philological Society*

16:67 [of phonetics] The indispensable foundation of all study of language. [also said elsewhere of phonology]

Henry Sweet, 1877, *A Handbook of Phonetics*, Preface

16:68 The main axiom of living philology is that all study of language must be based on phonetics . . . The second main axiom of living philology is that all study of language, whether theoretical or practical, ought to be based on the spoken language.

Henry Sweet, 1899, *The Practical Study of Languages*, Chs. 2, 7

16:69 Language never deceives, if only we know how to question it aright.

Richard Chenevix Trench, 1851, 'On the History in Words', in *On the Study of Words*, Lecture 4

16:70 But take here a word or two of warning before we advance any further. You cannot, of course, expect to make any original investigations in language; but you can follow safe guides, such as shall lead you by right paths, even as you may follow such as can only lead you astray. Do not fail to keep in mind that perhaps in no region of human knowledge are there such a multitude of unsafe leaders as in this; for indeed this science of words is one which many, professing for it an earnest devotion, have done their best or their worst to bring into discredit, and to make a laughing-stock at once of the foolish and the wise.

Richard Chenevix Trench, 1851, 'The Schoolmaster's Use of Words', in *On the Study of Words*, Lecture 7

16:71 The science of language has large and close analogies in geological science, with its ceaseless evolution, its fossils, and its numberless submerged layers and hidden strata, the infinite go-before of the present.

Walt Whitman, 1885, 'Slang in America', in the *North American Review*, no. 141

16:72 The whole subject of linguistic investigation may be conveniently summed up in the single inquiry, 'Why do we speak as we do?'

William Dwight Whitney, 1867, *Language and the Study of Language*

See also: 1:45, 8:12, 12:4

The nature and functions of speech and speaking

17:1 It is generally better to deal by speech than by letter, and by the mediation of a third than by a man's self.

Francis Bacon, 1597/1625, 'Of Negotiating', in *Essays*

17:2 [on talking to someone dying] Speech becomes sacred near silence everlasting / Oh if I *must* speak, have I words to say?

John Betjeman, 1958, 'Inevitable', in *Collected Poems*

17:3 Be quick to listen, and deliberate in giving an answer. If you understand the matter, give your neighbour an answer; if not, put your hand over your mouth. Both honour and disgrace come from talking; a man's tongue can cause his downfall.

The Bible, Ecclesiasticus 5:11 (Jerusalem Bible)

17:4 *Talk, v. t.* To commit an indiscretion without temptation, from an impulse without purpose.

Ambrose Bierce, 1911, *The Devil's Dictionary* (entry added by E. J. Hopkins for *The Enlarged Devil's Dictionary*, 1967)

17:5 In a symbol there is concealment and yet revelation: here, therefore, by Silence and by Speech acting together, comes a double significance. And if both the Speech be itself high, and the Silence fit and noble, how expressive will their union be!

Thomas Carlyle, 1833, *Sartor Resartus*, III, Ch. 3

17:6 [Scipio, to Berganza] Look to your tongue, for the greatest evils in human life come from it.

Miguel de Cervantes, 1613, 'The Dogs' Colloquy', in *Exemplary Stories* (trans. C. A. Jones)

17:7 [Maskwell, to Lady Touchwood] Oh, who would not lose his Speech, upon condition to have Joys above it?

William Congreve, 1694, *The Double-Dealer*, IV. ii

17:8 [of Lady Dedlock] Words, sobs, and cries, are but air; and air is so shut in and shut out throughout the house in town, that sounds need be uttered trumpet-tongued indeed by my Lady in her chamber, to carry any faint vibration to Sir Leicester's ears; and yet this cry is in the house, going upward from a wild figure on its knees.

Charles Dickens, 1852–3, *Bleak House*, Ch. 29

17:9 A word is dead / When it is said, / Some say. / I say it just / Begins to live / That day.

Emily Dickinson, c.1862–6, *Complete Poems*, no. 1,212

17:10 Speech is one symptom of Affection / And Silence one / The perfectest communication / Is heard of none.

Emily Dickinson, c.1862–6, *Complete Poems*, no. 1,681

17:11 Speech is the telephone network, the nervous system of our society much more than the vehicle for the lyrical outbursts of the individual soul. It is a network of bonds and obligations.

J. R. Firth, 1937, *The Tongues of Men*, Ch. 10

17:12 Human speech is like a cracked kettle on which we tap out tunes that can make bears dance, when we would move the stars.

Gustave Flaubert, 1857, *Madame Bovary* (trans.), I, Ch. 12

17:13 Language is the flower of the mouth. In

language the earth blossoms toward the bloom of the sky.

Martin Heidegger, 1959, 'The Nature of Language', in *On the Way to Language* (trans. P. D. Hertz)

17:14 The essential being of language is Saying as Showing.

Martin Heidegger, 1959, 'The Way to Language', in *On the Way to Language* (trans. P. D. Hertz)

17:15 [on the deaf and dumb son of Croesus] When the city was stormed, a Persian soldier was about to cut Croesus down, not knowing who he was. Croesus saw him coming, but because in his misery he did not care if he lived or died, he made no effort to defend himself. But this dumb son, seeing the danger, was so terrified by the fearful thing that was about to happen that he broke into speech, and cried: 'Do not kill Croesus, fellow!' Those were the first words he ever uttered – and he retained the power of speech for the rest of his life.

Herodotus, 5th century BC, in *The Histories* (trans. Aubrey de Sélincourt, 1996), I, Ch. 85

17:16 All life comes back to the question of our speech – the medium through which we communicate.

Henry James, quoted as an epigraph in C. K. Ogden and I. A. Richards, *The Meaning of Meaning* (1923)

17:17 *Speech* is the only benefit man hath to express his excellencie of mind above other creatures.

Ben Jonson, 1640 (published posthumously), *Timber: or, Discoveries made upon Men and Matter*

17:18 No glasse renders a mans forme, or likenesse, so true as his speech.

Ben Jonson, 1640 (published posthumously), *Timber: or, Discoveries made upon Men and Matter*

17:19 The opposite of talking isn't listening. The opposite of talking is waiting.

Fran Lebowitz, 1981, 'People', in *Social Studies*

17:20 Speech is civilization itself. The word, even the most contradictious word, preserves contact – it is silence which isolates.

Thomas Mann, 1924, *The Magic Mountain* (trans. H. T. Lowe-Porter), Ch. 6

17:21 Speech is the small change of silence.

George Meredith, 1859, *The Ordeal of Richard Feverel*, Ch. 34

17:22 [Laura] 'Oh if I could only get you *talking*!' [Hilary] 'I chatter artlessly in your presence.'

[Laura] 'You do nothing artlessly. You use words as a hiding place.'

Iris Murdoch, 1975, 'Saturday' (first week), in *A Word Child*

17:23 Ten persons who speak make more noise than ten thousand who are silent.

Napoleon I, 1804–15, *Maxims* (trans.)

17:24 Speaking is a beautiful folly: with that man dances over all things.

Friedrich Nietzsche, 1883–92, 'The Convalescent', in *Thus Spake Zarathustra* (trans. W. Kaufmann), III

17:25 There are some who speak well and write badly. For the place and the audience warm them, and draw from their minds more than they think of without that warmth.

Blaise Pascal, 1654–62, *Pensées* (trans. W. F. Trotter), no. 47

17:26 But as our guarded selves in mutual speech / slowly unite in communication, / for dialogue is love and love must reach / past obstacles to perfect consummation, / so question and answer meet in statued pose, / as drums and violins announce the close.

Elias Pater, 1983, 'Classical Dancers', in *Jerusalem Sonnets and Collected Poems*

17:27 One way of looking at speech is to say it is a constant stratagem to cover nakedness.

Harold Pinter, quoted in Robert I. Fitzhenry (ed.), *Barnes and Noble Book of Quotations*

17:28 The echo knows all languages.

Proverbial (Finnish)

17:29 The mouth is the healer and executioner of the body.

Proverbial (Danish)

17:30 Speak little with others, much with yourself.

Proverbial (Estonian)

17:31 Speak that I may see thee.

Proverbial

17:32 Speak, lest tomorrow you be prevented.

Proverbial (Kenyan)

17:33 He who speaks alone cannot go wrong.

Proverbial (Swahili)

17:34 The speaker may forget, but he who is spoken to does not.

Proverbial (Zambian)

17:35 Speech is the messenger of the heart.
Proverbial (Hebrew)

17:36 Who is poor in speech?
Proverbial (Sanskrit)

17:37 Speech must be bold as a lion, soft as a gentle hare, impressive as a serpent, pointed as an arrow, and evenly balanced like a sceptre held in the middle.
Proverbial (Tibetan)

17:38 Speech should float forth freely like a bird in the sky, and be clothed in charming dress like a goddess.
Proverbial (Tibetan)

17:39 The whole end of speech is to be understood.
Proverbial (Chinese)

17:40 Talk if you wish to be known.
Proverbial (Spanish)

17:41 Talking pays no toll.
Proverbial (Irish)

17:42 Talking comes by nature, silence by understanding.
Proverbial

17:43 The ills of man come to him from his tongue.
Proverbial (Arabic)

17:44 Spoken words are like winds, neither caught in a net nor overtaken with greyhounds.
Proverbial (Romanian)

17:45 Speech is a mirror of the soul; as a man speaks, so is he.
Publilius Syrus, 1st century BC, *Moral Sayings* (trans. D. Lyman), no. 1,073

17:46 What, O wise man, is the tongue in the mouth? It is a key to the casket of the intellectual treasurer; so long as the lid remains shut how can any person say whether he be a dealer in gems or in pedlery?
Sadi, 1258, *Gulistan [Rose Garden]* (trans. J. Ross), Introduction

17:47 The articulate voice is more distracting than mere noise.
Seneca, 1st century, *Letters to Lucilius* (trans. E. Phillips Barker), no. 56

17:48 [Mowbray, on being exiled] The language

I have learnt these forty years, / My native English, now I must forgo, / And now my tongue's use is to me no more / Than an unstrìngèd viol or a harp, / Or like a cunning instrument cased up, / Or, being open, put into his hands / That knows no touch to tune the harmony. / Within my mouth you have enjailed my tongue, / Doubly portcullised with my teeth and lips, / And dull unfeeling barren ignorance / Is made my jailer to attend on me.
William Shakespeare, 1595, *Richard II*, I. iii. 153

17:49 Speech is the mirror of action.
Solon, 6th century BC, quoted in Diogenes Laertius' *Lives and Opinions of Eminent Philosophers* (trans. R. D. Hicks)

17:50 The true call of the desert, of the mountains, or the sea, is their silence – free of the networks of dead speech.
Freya Stark, 1948, *Perseus in the Wind*

17:51 There is a Wit for Discourse, and a Wit for Writing.
Richard Steele, 31 August 1709, 'Wit: the Propriety of Words and Thoughts', *The Tatler*, no. 62

17:52 The bitterest tears shed over graves are for words left unsaid and deeds left undone.
Harriet Beecher Stowe, 1865, *Little Foxes*, Ch. 3

17:53 Nature, which gave us two eyes to see, and two ears to hear, has given us but one tongue to speak.
Jonathan Swift, 1707, *A Tritical [trite, commonplace] Essay Upon the Faculties of the Mind*

17:54 [Chorus] Thy speech flickers like a blown-out flame.
Algernon Charles Swinburne, 1865, *Atalanta in Calydon*

17:55 [Althæa] Speech too bears fruit, being worthy; and air blows down / Things poisonous, and high-seated violences, / And with charmed words and songs have men put out / Wild evil, and the fire of tyrannies.
Algernon Charles Swinburne, 1865, *Atalanta in Calydon*

17:56 [on books] It is not enough even to be able to speak the language of that nation by which they are written, for there is a memorable interval between the spoken and the written language, the language heard and the language read. The one is commonly transitory, a sound, a tongue, a dialect merely, almost brutish, and we learn it unconsciously, like the brutes, of our mothers. The other is the maturity and experience of that; if that is our mother tongue, this is our father tongue, a reserved and select expression, too significant to be heard by the ear, which we must be born again in order to speak.

Henry Thoreau, 1854, 'Reading', in *Walden*

17:57 However much we may admire the orator's occasional bursts of eloquence, the noblest written words are commonly as far behind or above the fleeting spoken language as the firmament with its stars is behind the clouds.

Henry Thoreau, 1854, 'Reading', in *Walden*

17:58 When a man is speaking, he cannot be breathing: this is the sacrifice of breath to speech. And when a man is breathing he cannot be speaking: this is the sacrifice of speech to breath. These are the two never-ending immortal offerings of man, whether he is awake or whether he is asleep.

'Kaushitaki Upanishad', 6th century BC, II, Ch. 5, in *The Upanishads* (trans. Juan Mascaró, 1965)

17:59 When consciousness rules speech, with speech we can speak all words.

'Kaushitaki Upanishad', 6th century BC, III, Ch. 6, in *The Upanishads* (trans. Juan Mascaró, 1965)

17:60 It is not speech which we should want to know: we should know the speaker.

'Kaushitaki Upanishad', 6th century BC, III, Ch. 8, in *The Upanishads* (trans. Juan Mascaró, 1965)

See also: 1:36, 2:4, 2:42, 2:131, 10:8, 10:18, 20:4, 21:22–3, 21:41, 21:43, 21:65, 21:76, 21:88, 23:66, 28:20, 29:6, 31:18, 52:6

18 *Pronunciation*

Speech sounds, vocal organs, and the sound of the voice

18:1 I think it would be very proper that some Man of good Sense and sound Judgment should preside over these publick Cries, who should permit none to lift up their Voices in our Streets, that have not tuneable Throats, and are not only able to overcome the Noise of the Croud, and the rattling of Coaches, but also to vend their respective Merchandizes in apt Phrases and in the most distinct and agreeable Sounds.

Joseph Addison, 18 December 1711, 'The Cries of London', *The Spectator*, no. 251

18:2 In the name of every consonant there is a vowel, for the consonants can neither be named nor pronounced without a vowel.

Anonymous Icelandic scholar (the 'first grammarian'), 12th century, *First Grammatical Treatise* (trans. E. Haugen)

18:3 Words are imitations, and we are equipped with a voice that is the most imitative of all our parts.

Aristotle, 4th century BC, *The Art of Rhetoric* (trans. H. C. Lawson-Tancred), Ch. 3, Sect. 1

18:4 [of Milton] He pronounced the letter R (*littera canina*) very hard – a certain sign of a satirical wit.

John Aubrey, 'John Milton', in *Brief Lives* (ed. John Walker, 1813)

18:5 Why didn't Kafka stutter? . . . Stutterers devise elaborate routines to avoid or to ambush and take by surprise troublesome consonants, of which K is one of the most difficult. It's a good job Kafka didn't stutter. With two Ks he might have got started on his name and never seen the end of it. As it is he docks it, curtails it, leaves its end behind much as lizards do when something gets hold of their tail.

Alan Bennett, 1987, 'Kafka at Las Vegas', in the *London Review of Books*, reprinted in *Writing Home* (1994), p. 337

18:6 [concerning the Ephraimite unable to pronounce Shibboleth] A course in phonetics might have saved his life.

Anthony Burgess, 1992, *A Mouthful of Air*, I, Ch. 1 [cf. 51:9]

18:7 [on the vocal organs] If you can bear to examine this apparatus frequently in a mirror you will experience a sense of wonder that it should be able, with the aid of the concept-breeding brain, to create all the languages of the world. The whole structure is so damnably simple.

Anthony Burgess, 1992, *A Mouthful of Air*, I, Ch. 4

18:8 There is no doubt something gross and brash and materialistic about consonants: they are noises made by banging things together, rubbing, hissing, buzzing. Vowels, on the other hand, are pure music – woodwind to the consonantal percussion – and, because they are produced by the creation of space between the tongue and the hard or soft palate, and these spaces are not measured scientifically but arrived at by a sort of acoustic guesswork, they tend to be indefinite and mutable. The history of the sound-changes of a language is mainly a history of its vowels.

Anthony Burgess, 1992, *A Mouthful of Air*, I, Ch. 4

18:9 The occasions upon which the Master used correct pronunciation were when reciting the *Songs* or the *Books* and when practising ritual acts. At all such times he used the correct pronunciation.

Confucius, 5th century BC, *The Analects* (trans. A. Waley), VII, Sect. 17

18:10 You can't be happy with a woman who pronounces both d's in Wednesday.

Peter de Vries, 1981, *Sauce for the Goose*

18:11 [Martin Chuzzlewit, on being greeted by a stranger after arriving in New York] 'The old ship will keep afloat a year or two longer yet, perhaps,' said Martin with a smile, partly occasioned by what the gentleman said, and partly by his manner of saying it, which was odd enough, for he emphasised all the small words and syllables in his discourse, and left the others to take care of themselves: as if he thought the larger parts of speech could be trusted alone, but the little ones required to be constantly looked after.

Charles Dickens, 1843–4, *Martin Chuzzlewit*, Ch. 16

18:12 [Mrs General, on having heard Amy address Mr Dorrit as 'Father'] 'Papa is a preferable mode of address,' observed Mrs General. 'Father is rather vulgar, my dear. The word Papa, besides, gives a pretty form to the lips. Papa, potatoes, poultry, prunes, and prism are all very good words for the lips: especially prunes and prism. You will find it serviceable, in the formation of a demeanour, if you sometimes say to yourself in company – on entering a room, for instance – Papa, potatoes, poultry, prunes and prism, prunes and prism.'

Charles Dickens, 1855–7, *Little Dorrit*, II, Ch. 5

18:13 [Pip] ('You listen to this,' said my sister to me, in a severe parenthesis.)

Charles Dickens, 1861, *Great Expectations*, Ch. 4

18:14 Surely it is part of the meaning of an American to sound like one.

J. R. Firth, 1951, 'Modes of Meaning', in *Essays and Studies*

18:15 One may view the vowels as the necessary coloring or animation of all words, as the breath without which they would not even exist. The real individuality of the word rests on the vowel sound; it affords the finest relationships.

Jacob Grimm, 1819, 'A Survey of the Consonants', in *Germanic Grammar* (trans. W. P. Lehmann), I

18:16 Articulation is the tongue-tied's fighting.

Tony Harrison, 1978, 'On Not Being Milton'

18:17 [Professor, to the Pupil, explaining how sounds are made] Air has to be pitilessly forced out of the lungs and then made to pass gently over the vocal cords, lightly brushing them, so that like harps or leaves beneath the wind, they suddenly start quivering, trembling, vibrating, vibrating, vibrating or hissing, or rustling, or bristling, or whistling, and with a whistle set everything in motion: uvula, tongue, palate, teeth … lips … Finally words come out through the nose, the mouth, the ears, the pores of the skin, bringing in their train all the uprooted organs of speech we've just named, a powerful, majestic swarm, no less than what we improperly call the voice, modulating in song or rising in terrible symphonic wrath, a regular procession, sheaves of assorted blossoms, of sonorous conceits: labials, dentals, plosives, palatals, and the rest, some soft and gentle, some harsh and violent.

Eugène Ionesco, 1951, *The Lesson* (trans. D. Watson, 1958)

18:18 [in relation to Henry Sweet's inability to hear the way his wife pronounced a particular word] It was not the first time, nor was it to be the last, that I found that intelligent men were unaware of the pronunciation of those close to them and deluded themselves that a form they saw written phonetically was low, although it was part of natural educated speech.

Otto Jespersen, 1938, quoted in A. Juul, H. F. Nielsen and J. E. Nielsen (eds), *A Linguist's Life* (1995), p. 63

18:19 To be a good mimic requires great powers; great acuteness of observations, great retention of what is observed, and great pliancy of organs to represent what is observed.

Samuel Johnson, 1771, in James Boswell, *The Life of Samuel Johnson* (1791), Ch. 23

18:20 [on the effect of smoking on Elia's stammer] Only in the use of the Indian weed he might be thought a little excessive. He took it, he would say, as a solvent of speech. Marry – as the friendly vapour ascended, how his prattle would curl up sometimes with it! the ligaments which tongue-tied him, were loosened, and the stammerer proceeded a statist [statesman]!

Charles Lamb, 1833, *The Last Essays of Elia*, Preface

18:21 Never have an operation you cannot spell / Or live in a town you mispronounce.
Roger McGough, 1992, 'Bath – Avon', in *Defying Gravity*

18:22 It's never what you say, but how / You make it sound sincere.
Marya Mannes, 1955–64, 'Controverse', in *But Will It Sell?*

18:23 [on a curriculum for classical languages] First they should begin with the chief and necessary rules of some good Grammar, either that now us'd, or any better: and while this is doing, their speech is to be fashion'd to a distinct and cleer pronuntiation, as neer as may be to the Italian, especially in the vowels. For we Englishmen being farre northerly, doe not open our mouthes in the cold air, wide enough to grace a Southern tongue; but are observ'd by all other nations to speak exceeding close and inward: So that to smatter Latin with an english mouth, is as ill a hearing as law French.
John Milton, 1644, 'Of Education'

18:24 How many ways we have of speaking to our dogs and they of replying to us! We use different languages again, and make different cries, to call birds, pigs, bulls and horses; we change idiom according to each species.
Michel de Montaigne, 1572–80, 'An Apology for Raymond Sebond', in *The Complete Essays* (trans. M. A. Screech, 1987), II, no. 12

18:25 A black, E white, I red, U green, O blue: vowels, / Some day I will tell of the births that may be yours.
Arthur Rimbaud, 1870, *Voyelles* (trans.)

18:26 [Lear, of Cordelia] Her voice was ever soft, / Gentle, and low, an excellent thing in woman.
William Shakespeare, 1605–6, *King Lear*, V. iii. 247

18:27 [Panthea, of Prometheus] I could hear / His voice, whose accents lingered ere they died / Like footsteps of weak melody.
Percy Bysshe Shelley, 1820, *Prometheus Unbound*, II. i

18:28 [Mrs Malaprop's views about what a young woman should know] But above all, Sir Anthony, she should be mistress of orthodoxy, that she might not mis-spell, and mispronounce words so shamefully as girls usually do; and likewise that she might reprehend the true meaning of what she is saying.
Richard Sheridan, 1775, *The Rivals*, I. ii

18:29 What music is more enchanting than the voices of young people, when you can't hear what they say?
Logan Pearsall Smith, 1933, 'Afterthoughts', in *All Trivia*

18:30 The vowel is born out of man's inmost being; it is the channel through which this inner content of the soul streams outwards. The consonant is born out of the comprehension of external nature; the way in which we perceive them with the eyes, all this is built into the form of the consonants.
Rudolf Steiner, 26 August 1923, *A Lecture on Eurythmy* (published 1967)

18:31 Whatever thou hast to say, be it more or less, forget not to utter it in a low soft tone of voice. Silence, and whatever approaches it, weaves dreams of midnight secrecy into the brain.
Laurence Sterne, 1765, *The Life and Opinions of Tristram Shandy, Gentleman*, VIII, Ch. 34

18:32 [on Mrs Wadman's expostulation] Now there are such an infinitude of notes, tunes, cants, chants, airs, looks, and accents with which the word *fiddlestick* may be pronounced in all such causes as this, every one of 'em impressing a sense and meaning as different from the other, as *dirt* from *cleanliness* – That Casuists (for it is an affair of conscience on that score) reckon up no less than fourteen thousand in which you may do either right or wrong.
Laurence Sterne, 1767, *The Life and Opinions of Tristram Shandy, Gentleman*, IX, Ch. 25

18:33 [third girl, on an anticipated male encounter] I shall whisper / Heavenly labials in a world of gutterals. / It will undo him.
Wallace Stevens, 1923, 'The Plot against the Giant', in *Harmonium*

18:34 It isn't what I do, but how I do it. It isn't what I say, but how I say it – And how I look when I do and say it.
Mae West, attributed, mid 20th century

18:35 He spoke with a certain what-is-it in his voice, and I could see that, if not actually disgruntled, he was far from being gruntled.
P. G. Wodehouse, 1938, *The Code of the Woosters*, Ch. 1

See also: 8:13, 8:58, 11:1; 15:1, 16:16–17, 16:61–2, 25:53, 25:64, 57:37, 59:13, 59:28, 64:11–12, 64:22, 64:26–7, 64:30, 64:32, 64:34–5, 64:37, 64:60

19 *Listening*

The nature and functions of listening and hearing

19:1 If you love listening you will learn; if you lend an ear, wisdom will be yours.
The Bible, Ecclesiasticus 6:33 (Jerusalem Bible)

19:2 Listen before you answer; and do not interrupt a speech in the middle.
The Bible, Ecclesiasticus 11:8 (Jerusalem Bible)

19:3 To retort without first listening is folly to work one's own confusion.
The Bible, Proverbs 18:13 (Jerusalem Bible)

19:4 Oh – I listen a lot and talk less. You can't learn anything when you're talking.
Bing Crosby, 1975, interview with Michael Parkinson on BBC television

19:5 Charley verified the adage about little pitchers, I am sure; for she heard of more sayings and doings, in a day, than would have come to my ears in a month.
Charles Dickens, 1852–3, *Bleak House*, Ch. 37

19:6 The hearing ear is always found close to the speaking tongue.
Ralph Waldo Emerson, 1856, 'Race', in *English Traits*

19:7 A bigot is a stone-deaf orator.
Kahlil Gibran, 1926, *Sand and Foam*

19:8 If to talk to oneself when alone is folly, it must be doubly unwise to listen to oneself in the presence of others.
Baltasar Gracián, 1647, *The Art of Worldly Wisdom* (trans. J. Jacobs), p. 141

19:9 The art of conversation is the art of hearing as well as of being heard.
William Hazlitt, 1826, 'On the Conversation of Authors', in *The Plain Speaker*

19:10 Speaking is of itself a listening.
Martin Heidegger, 1959, 'The Way to Language', in *On the Way to Language* (trans. P. D. Hertz)

19:11 It is the province of knowledge to speak and it is the privilege of wisdom to listen.
Oliver Wendell Holmes, senior, 1872, *The Poet at the Breakfast Table*, p. 10

19:12 [Professor, to the Pupil] Sounds, Mademoiselle, should be caught in flight by their wings so that they do not fall on deaf ears.
Eugène Ionesco, 1951, *The Lesson* (trans. D. Watson, 1958)

19:13 [on deaf pupils] They not only speak, write, and understand what is written, but if he that speaks looks towards them, and modifies his organs by distinct and full utterance, they know so well what is spoken, that it is an expression scarcely figurative to say, they hear with the eye.
Samuel Johnson, 1773, 'Inch Kenneth', in *A Journey to the Western Islands of Scotland*

19:14 It is less dishonour to hear imperfectly than to speak imperfectly. The ears are excused: the understanding is not.
Ben Jonson, 1640 (published posthumously), *Timber: or, Discoveries made upon Men and Matter*

19:15 Someone was drawing water and my teacher placed my hand under the spout. As the cool stream gushed over one hand she spelled into the other the word *water*, first slowly, then rapidly. I stood still, my whole attention fixed upon the motions of her fingers. Suddenly I felt a misty consciousness as of something forgotten – a thrill of returning thought; and somehow the mystery of language was revealed to me. I knew then that 'w-a-t-e-r' meant the wonderful cool something that was flowing over my hand. That living word awakened my soul, gave it light, joy, set it free!

Helen Keller, 1902, *The Story of My Life*

19:16 All man's life among men is nothing more than a battle for the ears of others.

Milan Kundera, 1979, *The Book of Laughter and Forgetting*, IV, p. 1

19:17 To listen closely and reply well is the highest perfection we are able to attain in the art of conversation.

Duc de La Rochefoucauld, 1665, *Maxims* (trans. K. Pratt), no. 139

19:18 Accustom yourself to give careful attention to what others are saying, and try your best to enter into the mind of the speaker.

Marcus Aurelius, 2nd century, *Meditations* (trans. M. Staniforth, 1964, Penguin), VI, Sect. 53

19:19 [explaining why the deaf do not learn to talk] It is not simply because they are unable to receive instruction in speech through the ear but rather because of the intimate relationship which exists between the faculty of hearing (the power they are deprived of) and the faculty of speech, which are by their nature closely sutured together. Whenever we talk, we must first talk as it were to ourselves: our speech first sounds in our own ears, then we utter it into the ears of other people.

Michel de Montaigne, 1572–80, 'An Apology for Raymond Sebond', in *The Complete Essays* (trans. M. A. Screech, 1987), II, no. 12

19:20 Words belong half to the speaker, half to the hearer. The latter must prepare himself to receive them according to such motion as they acquire, just as among those who play royal-tennis the one who receives the ball steps backwards or prepares himself, depending on the movements of the server or the form of his stroke.

Michel de Montaigne, 1572–80, 'On Experience', in *The Complete Essays* (trans. M. A. Screech, 1987), III, no. 13

19:21 We only consult the ear because the heart is wanting.

Blaise Pascal, c.1654–62, *Pensées* (trans. W. F. Trotter), no. 30

19:22 Donmanship he [A. Thornton] defines as 'the art of Criticizing without Actually Listening'.

Stephen Potter, 1950, *Lifemanship*, Ch. 6

19:23 It is the ear that troubles the mouth.

Proverbial (Ghanaian)

19:24 The ear is nothing more than a door.

Proverbial (Surinam)

19:25 Ear no hear, heart no leap.

Proverbial (Jamaican)

19:26 Ill hearing makes bad rehearsing.

Proverbial

19:27 A healthy ear can stand hearing sick words.

Proverbial (Senegalese)

19:28 A listener needs more intelligence than a speaker.

Proverbial (Turkish)

19:29 Tellers there are; listeners there are none.

Proverbial (Kenyan)

19:30 From listening comes wisdom, and from speaking repentance.

Proverbial (Italian)

19:31 Let your ear hear what comes out of your mouth.

Proverbial (Turkish)

19:32 He who speaks sows and he who listens harvests.

Proverbial (Silesian)

19:33 Talk is the ears' food.

Proverbial (Jamaican)

19:34 A man who listens because he has nothing to say can hardly be a source of inspiration. The only listening that counts is that of the talker who alternately absorbs and expresses ideas.

Agnes Repplier, 1904, 'The Luxury of Conversation', in *Compromises*

19:35 [Queen Elizabeth] Pitchers have ears.

William Shakespeare, 1592–3, *Richard III*, II. iv. 37

19:36 [Rosaline] A jest's prosperity lies in the

ear / Of him that hears it, never in the tongue /
Of him that makes it.
William Shakespeare, 1593–4, *Love's Labour's Lost*, V.
ii. 847

19:37 [Falstaff] It is the disease of not listening,
the malady of not marking, that I am troubled
withal.
William Shakespeare, 1597, *Henry IV, Part 2*, I. ii. 123

19:38 It is a Secret known but to few, yet of no
small use in the Conduct of Life, that when you
fall into a Man's Conversation, the first thing
you should consider is, whether he has a greater
Inclination to hear you, or that you should hear
him. The latter is the more general Desire, and
I know very able Flatterers that never speak a
word in Praise of the Persons from whom they
obtain daily Favours, but still practise a skilful
Attention to whatever is uttered by those with
whom they converse.
Richard Steele, 26 April 1711, 'The Coffee-house', *The
Spectator*, no. 49

19:39 Walls have tongues, and hedges ears.
Jonathan Swift, 1727, 'A Pastoral Dialogue between
Richmond Lodge and Marble Hill', 8

19:40 A good listener is not someone who has
nothing to say. A good listener is a good talker
with a sore throat.
Katharine Whitehorn, quoted in Herbert V.
Prochnow, *The Public Speaker's Treasure Chest* (1986)

19:41 There's nothing like eavesdropping to
show you that the world outside your head is
different from the world inside your head.
Thornton Wilder, 1954, *The Matchmaker*, III

19:42 [of the ear] Thy functions are ethereal, /
As if within thee dwelt a glancing mind, / Organ
of vision! And a Spirit aerial / Informs the cell
of Hearing, dark and blind; / Intricate labyrinth,
more dread for thought / To enter than oracular
cave; / Strict passage, through which sighs are
brought, / And whispers for the heart, their
slave; / And shrieks, that revel in abuse / Of
shivering flesh; and warbled air, / Whose pierc-
ing sweetness can unloose / the chains of frenzy,
or entice a smile / Into the ambush of despair; /
Hosannas, pealing down the long-drawn aisle, /
And requiems answered by the pulse that beats /
Devoutly, in life's last retreats!
William Wordsworth, 1828, 'On the Power of Sound'

19:43 It is not the hearing that one misses but
the over-hearing.
David Wright, 1970, *Deafness*

19:44 Listening is one of the lesser-known skills
that mistresses offer.
Betty Jane Wylie, 1988, *All in the Family*

See also: 26:27, 30:47, 36:61, 62:5

The nature and functions of reading and books

20:1 To read is to translate, for no two persons' experiences are the same. A bad reader is like a bad translator: he interprets literally when he ought to paraphrase and paraphrases when he ought to interpret literally. In learning to read well, scholarship, valuable as it is, is less important than instinct; some great scholars have been poor translators.

W. H. Auden, 1948, 'Prologue: Reading', in *The Dyer's Hand and other essays*

20:2 Read not to contradict and confute; nor to believe and take for granted; nor to find talk and discourse; but to weigh and consider.

Francis Bacon, 1597/1625, 'Of Studies', in *Essays*

20:3 Some books are to be tasted, others to be swallowed, and some few to be chewed and digested: that is, some books are to be read only in parts; others to be read, but not curiously [carelessly]; and some few to be read wholly and with diligence and attention.

Francis Bacon, 1597/1625, 'Of Studies', in *Essays*

20:4 Reading maketh a full man; conference a ready man; and writing an exact man. And therefore, if a man write little, he had need have a great memory; if he confer little, he had need have a present wit [ready mind]; and if he read little, he had need have much cunning, to seem to know that he doth not.

Francis Bacon, 1597/1625, 'Of Studies', in *Essays* [cf. 1:20]

20:5 [George] Books are on their way out, nowadays, didn't you know that? Words are on their last legs. Words, print and also thought. That's also for the high jump. The sentence, that dignified entity with subject and predicate, is shortly to be made illegal. It probably already is in Torremolinos.

Alan Bennett, 1972, *Getting On*, II

20:6 This is not to pretend that reading is a passive act. On the contrary, it is highly creative, or re-creative; itself an art.

Joyce Cary, 1939, *Mister Johnson*, Preface

20:7 [of books] Silent they are, but, though deprived of sound, / Here all the living languages abound; / Here all that live no more; preserved they lie, / In tombs that open to the curious eye.

George Crabbe, 1781, 'The Library', 64

20:8 Books! Bottled chatter! Things that some other simian has formerly said.

Clarence Day, 1920, *This Simian World*

20:9 To read good books is like holding a conversation with the most eminent minds of past centuries and, more-over, a studied conversation in which these authors reveal to us only the best of their thoughts.

René Descartes, 1637, *Discourse on Method* (trans. F. E. Sutcliffe), I

20:10 [Mr Boffin, of Silas Wegg] A literary man – *with* a wooden leg – and all Print is open to him!

Charles Dickens, 1864–5, *Our Mutual Friend*, I, Ch. 5

20:11 [Mr Boffin] Now, it's too late for me to begin shovelling and sifting at alphabeds and grammar-books. I'm getting to be a old bird, and I want to take it easy. But I want some reading – some fine bold reading. Some splendid book in a gorging Lord-Mayor's-Show of wollumes.

Charles Dickens, 1864–5, *Our Mutual Friend*, I, Ch. 5

20:12 [Mr Boffin] I didn't think this morning there was half so many Scarers in Print. But I'm in for it now!

Charles Dickens, 1864–5, *Our Mutual Friend*, I, Ch. 5

20:13 Readin' is th' nex' thing this side iv goin' to bed f'r restin' th' mind.

Finley Peter Dunne, 1902, 'A Little Essay on Books', in *Observations by Mr Dooley*

20:14 A text is not a 'crystal'. If it were a crystal, the cooperation of the reader would be part of its molecular structure.

Umberto Eco, 1979, *The Role of the Reader*, Introduction

20:15 Do not read, as children do, to amuse yourself, or like the ambitious, for the purpose of instruction. No, read in order to live.

Gustave Flaubert, June 1857, letter to Mlle de Chantepie, in M. Nadeau (ed.), *Les Oeuvres* (trans., 1964)

20:16 Reading is sometimes an ingenious device for avoiding thought.

Sir Arthur Helps, 1847, *Friends in Council*, II, Ch. 1

20:17 [on starting to read, but not finishing, a book] When I take up the end of a web, and find it pack-thread, I do not expect, by looking further, to find embroidery.

Samuel Johnson, 1769, in James Boswell, *The Life of Samuel Johnson* (1791), Ch. 20

20:18 Books are faithful repositories, which may be a while neglected or forgotten; but when they are opened again, will again impart their instruction: memory, once interrupted, is not to be recalled. Written learning is a fixed luminary, which, after the cloud that had hidden it has past away, is again bright in its proper station. Tradition is but a meteor, which, if once it falls, cannot be rekindled.

Samuel Johnson, 1773, 'Ostig in Sky', in *A Journey to the Western Islands of Scotland*

20:19 When a language begins to teem with books, it is tending to refinement; as those who undertake to teach others must have undergone some labour in improving themselves, they set a proportionate value on their own thoughts, and wish to enforce them by efficacious expressions; speech becomes embodied and permanent; different modes and phrases are

compared, and the best obtains an establishment. By degrees one age improves upon another. Exactness is first obtained, and afterwards elegance. But diction, merely vocal, is always in its childhood. As no man leaves his eloquence behind him, the new generations have all to learn. There may possibly be books without a polished language, but there can be no polished language without books.

Samuel Johnson, 1773, 'Ostig in Sky', in *A Journey to the Western Islands of Scotland*

20:20 He then took occasion to enlarge on the advantages of reading, and combated the idle, superficial notion that knowledge enough may be acquired in conversation. 'The foundation,' said he, 'must be laid by reading. General principles must be had from books, which, however, must be brought to the test of real life. In conversation you never get a system. What is said upon a subject is to be gathered from a hundred people. The parts of a truth which a man gets thus, are at such a distance from each other that he never attains to a full view.'

Samuel Johnson, 1775, in James Boswell, *The Life of Samuel Johnson* (1791), Ch. 31

20:21 It is strange that there should be so little reading in the world, and so much writing. People in general do not willingly read, if they can have anything else to amuse them.

Samuel Johnson, 1783, in James Boswell, *The Life of Samuel Johnson* (1791), Ch. 57

20:22 When I am not walking, I am reading; I cannot sit and think. Books think for me.

Charles Lamb, 1833, 'On Books and Reading', in *The Last Essays of Elia*

20:23 What is reading but silent conversation?

Walter Savage Landor, 1824–53, 'Aristoteles and Callisthenes', in *Imaginary Conversations*

20:24 Some people read too much: the bibliobuli . . . who are constantly drunk on books, as other men are drunk on whiskey or religion. They wander through the most diverting and stimulating of worlds in a haze, seeing nothing and hearing nothing.

H. L. Mencken, 1956, 'Minority Report', in *Notebooks*

20:25 [advice about the education of her granddaughter] No Entertainment is so cheap as reading, nor any pleasure so lasting.

Lady Mary Wortley Montagu, 28 January 1753, letter to her daughter, Lady Bute, in Isobel Grundy (ed.), *Lady Mary Wortley Montagu: Selected Letters* (1997)

20:26 [answering a question about whether people are becoming less inclined to write] In reality, people read because they want to write. Anyway, reading is a sort of rewriting.

Jean-Paul Sartre, 1959, interview in Madeleine Chapsal, *Les Écrivains en personne* (trans. J. Matthews, 1960)

20:27 [on someone reading a book to him for the first time] After a moment, I realized: it was the book that was talking. Sentences emerged that frightened me: they were like real centipedes; they swarmed with syllables and letters, span out their diphthongs and made their double consonants hum; fluting, nasal, broken up with sighs and pauses, rich in unknown words, they were in love with themselves and their meanderings and had no time for me: sometimes they disappeared before I could understand them; at others, I had understood in advance and they went on rolling nobly towards their end without sparing me a comma. These words were obviously not meant for me.

Jean-Paul Sartre, 1964, 'Reading', in *Words* (trans. I. Clephane), I

20:28 I came to prefer prefabricated tales to impoverished ones; I became sensitive to the unchanging sequence of words: they would return each time you read them, always the same ones and always in the same order, and I would wait for them.

Jean-Paul Sartre, 1964, 'Reading', in *Words* (trans. I. Clephane), I

20:29 [Dogberry, to Seacoal, a member of the Watch] To be a well-favoured man is the gift of fortune, but to write and read comes by nature.

William Shakespeare, 1598–9, *Much Ado About Nothing*, III. iii. 13

20:30 [Posthumus, to Innogen, before his departure] Thither write, my queen, / And with mine eyes I'll drink the words you send / Though ink be made of gall.

William Shakespeare, 1610–11, *Cymbeline*, I. i. 100

20:31 LORD SUMMERHAYS: Reading is a dangerous amusement, Tarleton. I wish I could persuade your free library people of that.

TARLETON: Why, man, it's the beginning of education.

LORD SUMMERHAYS: On the contrary, it's the end of it. How can you dare teach a man to read until youve taught him everything else first?

George Bernard Shaw, 1910, *Misalliance*, I

20:32 MRS MALAPROP [after hearing Lydia Languish express her views strongly]: There's a little intricate hussy for you!

SIR ANTHONY ABSOLUTE: It is not to be wondered at, ma'am, – all this is the natural consequence of teaching girls to read. Had I a thousand daughters, by Heaven! I'd as soon have them taught the black art as their alphabet!

Richard Sheridan, 1775, *The Rivals*, I. ii

20:33 Reading is seeing by proxy.

Herbert Spencer, 1876–96, *The Principles of Sociology*, Ch. 15

20:34 But reading is not idleness ... it is the passive, receptive side of civilization without which the active and creative world would be meaningless. It is the immortal spirit of the dead realised within the bodies of the living. It is sacramental.

Stephen Spender, 4 January 1980, journal entry

20:35 Reading is to the mind what exercise is to the body.

Richard Steele, 18 March 1710, *The Tatler*, no. 147

20:36 Digressions, incontestably, are the sunshine; – they are the life, the soul of reading.

Laurence Sterne, 1760, *The Life and Opinions of Tristram Shandy, Gentleman*, I, Ch. 22

20:37 Chapters relieve the mind.

Laurence Sterne, 1761, *The Life and Opinions of Tristram Shandy, Gentleman*, IV, Ch. 10

20:38 My first, and greatest, liberty was that of being able to read everything and anything I cared to. I read indiscriminately, and with my eyes hanging out. I could never have dreamt that there were such goings-on in the world between the covers of books, such sand-storms and ice-blasts of words, such slashing of humbug, and humbug too, and staggering peace, such enormous laughter, such and so many blinding bright lights breaking across the just-awaking wits and splashing all over the pages in a million bits and pieces all of which were words, words, words, and each of which was alive forever in its own delight and glory and oddity and light.

Dylan Thomas, 1961, poetic manifesto, *Texas Quarterly*, no. 4, issue 4

20:39 [Algernon, to Jack] Oh! it is absurd to have a hard and fast rule about what one should read and what one shouldn't. More than half of modern culture depends on what one shouldn't read.

William Wordsworth, 1805, *The Prelude*, XIII, 208

Oscar Wilde, 1895, *The Importance of Being Earnest*, I

20:40 [on his youthful reading] In fine, / I was a better judge of thoughts than words, / Misled in estimating words, not only / By common inexperience of youth, / But by the trade in classic niceties, / The dangerous craft, of culling term and phrase / From languages that want the living voice / To carry meaning to the natural heart; / To tell us what is passion, what is truth, / What reason, what simplicity and sense.

William Wordsworth, 1805, *The Prelude*, VI, 105

20:41 How books mislead us, seeking their reward / From judgments of the wealthy Few, who see / By artificial lights; how they debase / The Many for the pleasure of those Few; / Effeminately level down the truth / To certain general notions, for the sake / Of being understood at once, or else / Through want of better knowledge in the heads / That framed them; flattering self-conceit with words, / That, while they most ambitiously set forth / Extrinsic differences, the outward marks / Whereby society has parted man / From man, neglect the universal heart.

William Wordsworth, 1805, *The Prelude*, XIII, 208

See also: 1:20, 6:79, 16:32, 23:45

The nature and functions of writing; techniques of successful writing

21:1 A memorandum is written not to inform the reader but to protect the writer.
Dean Acheson, 8 September 1977, *Wall Street Journal*

21:2 Among all kinds of Writing, there is none in which Authors are more apt to miscarry than in Works of Humour, as there is none in which they are more ambitious to excel.
Joseph Addison, 10 April 1711, *The Spectator*, no. 35

21:3 In general what is written must be easy to read and easy to speak, which is the same.
Aristotle, 4th century BC, *The Art of Rhetoric* (trans. H. C. Lawson-Tancred), Ch. 3, Sect. 5

21:4 He that will write well in any tongue, must follow the counsel of Aristotle, to speak as the common people do, to think as wise men do; and so should every man understand him, and the judgement of wise men allow him.
Roger Ascham, 1545, 'To All Gentlemen and Yeomen of England', in *Toxophilus*

21:5 [Asquith to Oscar Wilde, complaining of a Wilde mannerism] The man who uses italics is like the man who raises his voice in conversation and talks loudly in order to make himself heard.
Herbert Henry Asquith, c.1894, in Richard Ellmann, *Oscar Wilde* (1987), Ch. 16 [cf. 21:92]

21:6 Writing is an artificial activity. It is a lonely and private substitute for conversation.
Brooks Atkinson, 1951, 'June 13', in *Once Around the Sun*

21:7 [Caroline Bingley] It is a rule with me, that a person who can write a long letter, with ease, cannot write ill.
Jane Austen, 1813, *Pride and Prejudice*, Ch. 10

21:8 A phrase is born into the world both good and bad at the same time. The secret lies in a slight, an almost invisible twist. The lever should rest in your hand, getting warm, and you can only turn it once, not twice.
Isaac Babel, 1932, *Guy de Maupassant* (trans.)

21:9 No iron can stab the heart with such force as a full stop put just at the right place.
Isaac Babel, 1932, *Guy de Maupassant* (trans.)

21:10 Writers, like teeth, are divided into incisors and grinders.
Walter Bagehot, 1858, 'The First Edinburgh Reviewers', in *Estimates of Some Englishmen and Scotchmen*

21:11 I am of the firm belief that everybody could write books and I never understand why they don't. After all, everybody speaks. Once the grammar has been learnt it is simply talking on paper and in time learning what not to say.
Beryl Bainbridge, quoted in D. I. Kirkpatrick (ed.), *Contemporary Novelists* (1976)

21:12 The pen is the tongue of the hand – a silent utterer of words for the eye.
Henry Ward Beecher, 1887, *Proverbs from Plymouth Pulpit*

21:13 *Abridgement, n.* A brief summary of some person's literary work, in which those parts that tell against the convictions of the abridger are omitted for want of space.
Ambrose Bierce, 1911, *The Devil's Dictionary* (entry

added by E. J. Hopkins for *The Enlarged Devil's Dictionary*, 1967)

21:14 *Circumlocution, n.* A literary trick whereby the writer who has nothing to say breaks it gently to the reader.
Ambrose Bierce, 1911, *The Devil's Dictionary* (entry added by E. J. Hopkins for *The Enlarged Devil's Dictionary*, 1967)

21:15 *Postscript, n.* The only portion of a lady's letter which you need read, if you are in a hurry.
Ambrose Bierce, 1911, *The Devil's Dictionary* (entry added by E. J. Hopkins for *The Enlarged Devil's Dictionary*, 1967)

21:16 [of the opening of Chapter 19 of Mark Twain's *Huckleberry Finn*] The most beautiful prose paragraph yet written by any American.
Harold Bloom, 1994, *The Western Canon*

21:17 Somebody talked of happy moments for composition; and how a man can write at one time, and not at another. 'Nay,' said Dr Johnson, 'a man may write at any time, if he will set himself *doggedly* to it.'
James Boswell, 1785, 'Monday 16th August', in *The Journal of a Tour to the Hebrides*

21:18 I could see now that a literary education did not fit one for the popular novelist's trade. Once you had started using words like flavicomous or acroamatic, because you liked the sound of them, you were lost.
Anthony Burgess, 1990, *You've Had Your Time*, Ch. 1

21:19 But words are things, and a small drop of ink, / Falling like dew upon a thought, produces / That which makes thousands, perhaps millions, think. / 'Tis strange, the shortest letter which man uses / Instead of speech, may form a lasting link / Of ages. To what straits old Time reduces / Frail man, when paper, even a rag like this, / Survives himself, his tomb, and all that's his.
Lord Byron, 1819–24, *Don Juan*, Canto 3, stanza 88

21:20 Writing has laws of perspective, of light and shade, just as painting does, or music. If you are born knowing them, fine. If not, learn them. Then rearrange the rules to suit yourself.
Truman Capote, 1958, interview in Malcolm Cowley (ed.), *Writers at Work*

21:21 [Count Lodovico] Writing is nothing other than a kind of speech which remains in being after it has been uttered, the represen-

tation, as it were, or rather the very life of our words.
Baldesar Castiglione, 1528, *The Book of the Courtier* (trans. G. Bull, Penguin 1967), I, p. 71

21:22 [Count Lodovico] What is proper in writing is also proper in speaking; and the finest speech resembles the finest writing.
Baldesar Castiglione, 1528, *The Book of the Courtier* (trans. G. Bull, Penguin 1967), I, p. 72

21:23 [Count Lodovico] It is more important to make one's meaning clear in writing than in speaking; because unlike someone listening, the reader is not always present when the author is writing.
Baldesar Castiglione, 1528, *The Book of the Courtier* (trans. G. Bull, Penguin 1967), I, p. 72

21:24 An original writer is not one who imitates nobody; but one whom nobody can imitate.
Vicomte de Chateaubriand, 1802, *Le Génie du Christianisme*, II, Book 1, Ch. 3 (trans.)

21:25 The easiest books are generally the best; for, whatever author is obscure and difficult in his own language, certainly does not think clearly.
Lord Chesterfield, 8 February 1750, letter to his son

21:26 One must regard the hyphen as a blemish to be avoided wherever possible.
Winston Churchill, attributed, mid 20th century, in William Safire's 'Hyphenating Americans', in *On Language* (1980)

21:27 Works of imagination should be written in very plain language; the more purely imaginative they are the more necessary it is to be plain.
Samuel Taylor Coleridge, 31 May 1830, in Henry Nelson Coleridge (ed.), *Specimens of the Table-Talk of the late Samuel Taylor Coleridge* (1835)

21:28 [of a script] What I have crossed out I didn't like. What I haven't crossed out I'm dissatisfied with.
Cecil B. de Mille, attributed, mid 20th century, in L. Halliwell, *The Filmgoer's Book of Quotes* (1978)

21:29 There were half a dozen lions from London – authors, real authors, who had written whole books, and printed them afterwards – and here you might see 'em, walking about, like ordinary men, smiling, and talking – aye, and talking pretty considerable nonsense too, no doubt with the benign intention of rendering themselves intelligible to the common people about them.

Charles Dickens, 1836–7, *The Pickwick Papers*, Ch. 15

21:30 To ladies and gentlemen who are not in the habit of devoting themselves practically to the science of penmanship, writing a letter is no very easy task; it being always considered necessary in such cases for the writer to recline his head on his left arm, so as to place his eyes as nearly as possible on a level with the paper, while glancing sideways at the letters he is constructing, to form with his tongue imaginary characters to correspond. These motions, although unquestionably of the greatest assistance to original composition, retard in some degree the progress of the writer.

Charles Dickens, 1836–7, *The Pickwick Papers*, Ch. 33

21:31 [Sam Weller, after reading aloud his valentine to Mary] ' "Except of me Mary my dear as your walentine and think over what I've said. – My dear Mary I will now conclude." That's all,' said Sam. 'That's rather a sudden pull up, ain't it, Sammy?' inquired Mr Weller. 'Not a bit on it,' said Sam; 'she'll vish there wos more, and that's the great art o' letter writin'.' 'Well,' said Mr Weller, 'there's somethin' in that, and I wish your mother-in-law 'ud only conduct her conwersation on the same gen-teel principle.'

Charles Dickens, 1836–7, *The Pickwick Papers*, Ch. 33

21:32 *Pereant . . . qui ante nos nostra dixerunt.* Confound those who have made our remarks before us.

Aelius Donatus, 4th century, in St Jerome, *Commentary on Ecclesiastes*, I

21:33 Sir, more than kisses, letters mingle Soules; / For, thus friends absent speake.

John Donne, c.1597–8, 'To Sir Henry Wotton', 1

21:34 [what a man should say to himself, after engaging in the 'woman's work' of writing] What's a big, sthrong, able-bodied, two-hundhred-an'-tin-pound, forty-four-acrossth'-chest crather like me doin' here, pokin' these funny hireyoglyphics into a piece iv pa-aper with a little sthick? I guess I'll go out an' shoe a horse.

Finley Peter Dunne, 1902, 'A Little Essay on Books', in *Observations by Mr Dooley*

21:35 In good writing, words become one with things.

Ralph Waldo Emerson, 1831, *Journals*

21:36 You don't write because you want to say something; you write because you've got something to say.

F. Scott Fitzgerald, in *The Crack-Up* (ed. Edmund Wilson, 1945)

21:37 Any one who wishes to become a good writer should endeavour, before he allows himself to be tempted by the more showy qualities, to be direct, simple, brief, vigorous, and lucid.

H. F. Fowler and F. G. Fowler, 1906, *The King's English*, Ch. 1

21:38 Most of my writing consists of an attempt to translate aphorisms into continuous prose.

Northrop Frye, quoted in Richard Kostelanetz, 'The Literature Professors' Literature Professor', *Michigan Quarterly Review* (Fall, 1978)

21:39 Do you see anything good now-a-days, that is not filled with strokes – and dashes? – Sir, a well-placed dash makes half the wit of our writers of modern humour.

Oliver Goldsmith, 1760–2, *The Citizen of the World*, Letter 51

21:40 The first requisite for any writer is to know just what meaning he wants to convey, and it is only by clothing his thoughts in words that he can think at all.

Ernest Gowers, 1954, *The Complete Plain Words*, Prologue

21:41 Writing or printing is like shooting with a rifle; you may hit your reader's mind, or miss it; – but talking is like playing at a mark with the pipe of an engine: if it is within reach, and you have time enough, you can't help hitting it.

Oliver Wendell Holmes, senior, 1858, *The Autocrat of the Breakfast Table*, Ch. 2

21:42 A writer and nothing else: a man alone in a room with the English language, trying to get human feelings right.

John K. Hutchens, 10 September 1961, *New York Herald Tribune*

21:43 A written word is mummified until someone imparts life to it by transposing it mentally into the corresponding spoken word.

Otto Jespersen, 1924, *The Philosophy of Grammar*, Ch. 1

21:44 All the talk about style and form and quality of expression in writing which agitates literary circles is simply highfalutin bunkum, designed to hoodwink people into the belief that writing is much more mysterious than it really is, by those whose living depends on the maintenance of the mystery, and that if the plain man would only take the trouble to say quite plainly what he thinks, good and even easy writing would be the inevitable result.

C. E. M. Joad, 1926, 'How to Write and How to Write Badly', in *The Bookmark*

21:45 Let us, when we sit down to write, take a solemn oath to say exactly what we mean and to say nothing more, to use the simplest words that will serve our purpose, and to use as few of them as we can.

C. E. M. Joad, 1926, 'How to Write and How to Write Badly', in *The Bookmark*

21:46 [quoting a college tutor] Read over your compositions, and where ever you meet with a passage which you think is particularly fine, strike it out.

Samuel Johnson, 1773, in James Boswell, *The Life of Samuel Johnson* (1791)

21:47 Alas! sir, what can a nation that has not letters tell of its original?

Samuel Johnson, 18 September 1773, in James Boswell, *The Journal of a Tour to the Hebrides* (1785)

21:48 Many writers perplexe their Readers, and Hearers with meere *Non-sense*. Their writings need sunshine.

Ben Jonson, 1640 (published posthumously), *Timber: or, Discoveries made upon Men and Matter*

21:49 Our composition must bee more accurate in the beginning and end, then in the midst; and in the end more, then in the beginning; for through the midst the stream beares us.

Ben Jonson, 1640 (published posthumously), *Timber: or, Discoveries made upon Men and Matter*

21:50 Ready writing makes not good writing, but good writing brings on ready writing.

Ben Jonson, 1640 (published posthumously), *Timber: or, Discoveries made upon Men and Matter*

21:51 For a man to write well, there are required three necessaries: to read the best authors, observe the best speakers, and much exercise of his own style.

Ben Jonson, 1640 (published posthumously), *Timber: or, Discoveries made upon Men and Matter*

21:52 [on the time difference between writing and receiving a letter] This confusion of tenses,

this grand solecism of *two presents*, is in a degree common to all postage.

Charles Lamb, 1823, 'Distant Correspondents', in *The Essays of Elia*

21:53 Clear writers, like clear fountains, do not seem so deep as they are; the turbid look the most profound.

Walter Savage Landor, 1824–53, 'Southey and Porson', in *Imaginary Conversations of Literary Men and Statesmen*

21:54 If it sounds like writing, I rewrite it.

Elmore Leonard, 22 April 1985, *Newsweek*

21:55 [of the need for writing] Wise men speak; their words of wisdom / Perish in the ears that hear them, / Do not reach the generations / That, as yet unborn, are waiting / In the great mysterious darkness / Of the speechless days that shall be!

Henry Wadsworth Longfellow, 1855, 'Picture-writing', *The Song of Hiawatha*, Sect. 14

21:56 [on the need for writing] Face to face we speak together, / But we cannot speak when absent, / Cannot send our voices from us / To the friends that dwell afar off; / Cannot send a secret message, / But the beaver learns our secret, / May pervert it, may betray it, / May reveal it unto others.

Henry Wadsworth Longfellow, 1855, 'Picture-writing', *The Song of Hiawatha*, Sect. 14

21:57 The first law of writing, that law to which all other laws are subordinate, is this: that the words employed should be such as to convey to the reader the meaning of the writer.

Lord Macaulay, quoted in Sir Ernest Gowers, *The Complete Plain Words* (1954), Prologue

21:58 [of writing] Wherein lies its charm? Mainly, I believe, in arranging words in patterns, as if they were bricks, or flowers, or lumps of paint.

Rose Macaulay, 1935, 'Writing', in *Personal Pleasures*

21:59 a prophet said i is not / without honour save on his own / planet wait a minute / said mars / i want to write that down / that is one of your best things / archy is it original / it was once i answered truthfully / and may be again

Don Marquis, 1931, 'archy hears from mars', in *archy and mehitabel*

21:60 i never think at all when i write / nobody

can do two things at the same time / and do them both well.

Don Marquis, 1933, 'archy on the radio', in *archy's life of mehitabel*

21:61 It has been said that good prose should resemble the conversation of a well-bred man.

W. Somerset Maugham, 1938, *The Summing Up*, Ch. 12

21:62 [on discovering a fine classical quotation in his reading] I had languished along behind some French words, words so bloodless, so fleshless and so empty of matter that indeed they were nothing but French and nothing but words. At the end of a long and boring road I came upon a paragraph which was high, rich, soaring to the clouds. If I had found a long gentle slope leading up to it, that would have been pardonable: what I came across was a cliff surging up so straight and so steep that I knew I was winging my way to another world after the first half-a-dozen words. That was how I realized what a slough I had been floundering through beforehand, so base and so deep that I did not have the heart to sink back into it.

Michel de Montaigne, 1572–80, 'On Educating Children', in *The Complete Essays* (trans. M. A. Screech, 1987), I, no. 26

21:63 I speak to my writing-paper exactly as I do to the first man I meet.

Michel de Montaigne, 1572–80, 'On the Useful and the Honourable', in *The Complete Essays* (trans. M. A. Screech, 1987), III, no. 1

21:64 Scribbling seems to be one of the symptoms of an age of excess.

Michel de Montaigne, 1572–80, 'On Vanity', in *The Complete Essays* (trans. M. A. Screech, 1987), III, no. 9

21:65 [on the difference between writing and speaking] In writing, you address the average quantity of sense or information in the world; in speaking, you pick your audience, or at least know what they are prepared for, or else previously explain what you think necessary.

James Northcote, 1830, in William Hazlitt, *Conversations of James Northcote*

21:66 Good prose is like a window-pane.

George Orwell, 'Why I Write', in *Collected Essays* (1968), I

21:67 All letters, methinks, should be free and easy as one's discourse, not studied as an oration, nor made up of hard words like a charm.

Dorothy Osborne, September 1653, in G. C. Moore Smith (ed.), *The Letters of Dorothy Osborne to William Temple* (1928)

21:68 [on punctuation marks] The fig-leaves that hide the private parts of literature.

Pablo Picasso, quoted in Anthony Burgess, *A Mouthful of Air* (1992), p. 92

21:69 True ease in writing comes from art, not chance, / As those move easiest who have learn'd to dance. / 'Tis not enough no harshness gives offence, / The sound must seem an Echo to the sense.

Alexander Pope, 1711, 'An Essay on Criticism', 362

21:70 Many writers profess great exactness in punctuation, who never yet made a point.

George Dennison Prentice, 1860, *Prenticeana*

21:71 A letter is half a meeting.

Proverbial (Swahili)

21:72 Who can read and write has four eyes.

Proverbial (Albanian)

21:73 Where paper speaks, beards are silent.

Proverbial (French)

21:74 Write a bad thing in snow, but a good thing in rock.

Proverbial (Estonian)

21:75 The written letter remains, the weak word perishes.

Proverbial (Latin)

21:76 That which is written is binding, but that which is spoken is forgotten.

Proverbial (Amharic)

21:77 God have mercy on the sinner / Who must write with no dinner, / No gravy and no grub, / No pewter and no pub, / No belly and no bowels, / Only consonants and vowels.

John Crowe Ransom, 1955, 'Survey of Literature', in *Poems and Essays*

21:78 The acid test of a good piece of writing, even if it is of violence and cruelty, is that it must make one's ears water.

Bernice Rubens, 3 April 1988, in the *Sunday Times*

21:79 Since I had discovered the world through language, for a long time I mistook language for the world. To exist was to have a registered trade-name somewhere on the infinite Tables of the Word; writing meant engraving new beings on them or – this was my most persistent illusion – catching lively things in the trap of phrases: if I put words together ingeniously, the object would become entangled in the signs, and I would hold it.

Jean-Paul Sartre, 1964, 'Writing', in *Words* (trans. I. Clephane), II

21:80 You write with ease, to show your breeding, / But easy writing's vile hard reading.

Richard Sheridan, 1771, 'Clio's Protest'

21:81 What I like in a good author is not what he says, but what he whispers.

Logan Pearsall Smith, 1933, 'Afterthoughts', in *All Trivia*

21:82 I said there was no Rule in the World to be made for writing Letters, but that of being as near what you speak Face to Face as you can; which is so great a Truth, that I am of Opinion Writing has lost more Mistresses than any one Mistake in the whole Legend of Love.

Richard Steele, 17 June 1709, 'Love-letters', *The Tatler*, no. 30

21:83 Writing, when properly managed, (as you may be sure I think mine is) is but a different name for conversation.

Laurence Sterne, 1760, *The Life and Opinions of Tristram Shandy, Gentleman*, II, Ch. 11

21:84 That of all the several ways of beginning a book which are now in practice throughout the known world, I am confident my own way of doing it is the best – I'm sure it is the most religious – for I begin with writing the first sentence – and trusting to Almighty God for the second.

Laurence Sterne, 1765, *The Life and Opinions of Tristram Shandy, Gentleman*, VIII, Ch. 2

21:85 First I write one sentence: then I write another. That's how I write. And so I go on. But I have a feeling writing ought to be like running through a field.

Lytton Strachey, 1 November 1938, in Virginia Woolf, *A Writer's Diary*

21:86 All writing, even the clumsy kind, exposes in its loops and slants a yearning deeper than

an intention, the soul of the writer flopping on the clothes-peg of his exclamation mark.

Paul Theroux, 1973, *Saint Jack*, Ch. 1

21:87 A written word is the choicest of relics. It is something at once more intimate with us and more universal than any other work of art. It is the work of art nearest to life itself. It may be translated into every language, and not only be read but actually breathed from all human lips; – not to be represented on canvas or in marble only, but be carved out of the breath of life itself. The symbol of an ancient man's thought becomes a modern man's speech.

Henry Thoreau, 1854, 'Reading', in *Walden*

21:88 Every word . . . has *two* existences, as a spoken word and a written; and you have no right to sacrifice one of these, or even to subordinate it wholly, to the other. A word exists as truly for the eye as for the ear; and in a highly advanced state of society, where reading is almost as universal as speaking, quite as much for the one as for the other.

Richard Chenevix Trench, 1851, 'The Schoolmaster's Use of Words', in *On the Study of Words*, Lecture 7

21:89 We must speak to the eyes, if we wish to affect the mind.

Horace Walpole, 1799, 'Maxim of Writing', in J. Pinkerton, *Walpoliana*

21:90 I put the words down and push them a bit.

Evelyn Waugh, quoted in his obituary in the *New York Times*, 11 April 1966

21:91 Writing is . . . waiting for the word that may not be there until next Tuesday.

Richard Wilbur, 13 October 1987, in the *Los Angeles Times*

21:92 [rejoinder to a criticism by Mr Asquith about Wilde's use of italics] Just as the orator marks his good things by a dramatic pause, or by raising and lowering his voice, or by gesture, so the writer marks his epigrams with italics, setting the little gem, so to speak, like a jeweller.

Oscar Wilde, c.1894, in Richard Ellmann, *Oscar Wilde* (1987), Ch. 16 [cf. 21:5]

See also: 2:4, 6:7, 10:16, 17:1, 17:25, 17:51, 17:56–7, 20:4, 23:106, 25:1, 26:5, 27:23, 30:24, 37:7, 38:12, 57:48

22 *Learning to Read and Write*

Literacy; spelling and its reform; writing systems

22:1 I take it you already know / Of tough and bough and cough and dough? / Others may stumble, but not you / On hiccough, thorough, laugh and through?

Anonymous, 'Hints on Pronunciation for Foreigners', in *The Faber Book of Useful Verse* (1981), p. 144

22:2 Though the tough cough and hiccough plough me through, / O'er life's dark lough my course I still pursue.

Anonymous, 'Hints on Pronunciation for Foreigners', in *The Faber Book of Useful Verse* (1981), p. 143

22:3 Among the other books found by Tarzan in his parents' cabin were a primer, some child's readers, numerous picture books, and a great dictionary. All of these he examined, but the pictures caught his fancy most, though the strange little bugs which covered the pages where there were no pictures excited his wonder and deepest thought.

Edgar Rice Burroughs, 1914, *Tarzan of the Apes*, Ch. 7

22:4 [Mr Weller] Wen you're a married man, Samivel, you'll understand a good many things as you don't understand now; but vether it's worth while goin' through so much, to learn so little, as the charity-boy said ven he got to the end of the alphabet, is a matter o' taste.

Charles Dickens, 1836–7, *The Pickwick Papers*, Ch. 27

22:5 'What's your name, sir?' inquired the judge.

'Sam Weller, my lord,' replied that gentleman.

'Do you spell it with a "V" or a "W"?' inquired the judge.

'That depends upon the taste and fancy of the speller, my lord,' replied Sam; 'I never had occasion to spell it more than once or twice in my life, but I spells it with a "V".'

Charles Dickens, 1836–7, *The Pickwick Papers*, Ch. 34

22:6 [Traddles' opinion of shorthand] A perfect and entire command of the mystery of shorthand writing and reading, was about equal in difficulty to the mastery of six languages.

Charles Dickens, 1849–50, *David Copperfield*, Ch. 36

22:7 [David, on reading his first efforts at shorthand] I might as well have copied the Chinese inscriptions on an immense collection of tea-chests, or the golden characters on all the great red and green bottles in the chemist's shops!

Charles Dickens, 1849–50, *David Copperfield*, Ch. 38

22:8 [on alphabet books] 'A was an archer, and shot at a frog.' Of course he was. He was an apple-pie also, and there he is. He was a good many things in his time, was A, and so were most of his friends, except X, who had so little versatility, that I never knew him to get beyond Xerxes or Xantippe – like Y, who was always confined to a Yacht or a Yew Tree; and Z condemned for ever to be a Zebra or a Zany.

Charles Dickens, 1850, *A Christmas Tree*

22:9 [Caddy, of Young Mr Turveydrop] She said, if he were not so anxious about his spelling, and took less pains to make it clear, he would do better; but he put so many unnecessary letters into short words, that they sometimes quite lost their English appearance. 'He does it with the best intention,' observed Caddy, 'but it hasn't the effect he means, poor fellow!'

Charles Dickens, 1852–3, *Bleak House*, Ch. 14

22:10 It must be a strange state to be like Jo! To shuffle through the streets, unfamiliar with the shapes, and in utter darkness as to the meaning, of those mysterious symbols, so abundant over the shops, and at the corners of streets, and on the doors, and in the windows! To see people read, and to see people write, and to see the postmen deliver letters, and not to have the least idea of all that language – to be, to every scrap of it, stone blind and dumb!

Charles Dickens, 1852–3, *Bleak House*, Ch. 16

22:11 [Mr George, to Grandfather Smallweed] 'Don't you read, or get read to?' The old man shakes his head with sharp sly triumph. 'No, no. We have never been readers in our family. It don't pay. Stuff. Idleness. Folly. No, no!'

Charles Dickens, 1852–3, *Bleak House*, Ch. 21

22:12 Writing was a trying business to Charley, who seemed to have no natural power over a pen, but in whose hand every pen appeared to become perversely animated, and to go wrong and crooked, and to stop, and splash, and sidle into corners, like a saddle-donkey. It was very odd, to see what old letters Charley's young hand had made; they, so wrinkled and shrivelled, and tottering; it, so plump and round. Yet Charley was uncommonly expert at other things, and had as nimble little fingers as I ever watched. 'Well, Charley,' said I, looking over a copy of the letter O in which it was represented as square, triangular, pear-shaped, and collapsed in all kinds of ways, 'we are improving. If we only get to make it round, we shall be perfect, Charley.'

Charles Dickens, 1852–3, *Bleak House*, Ch. 31

22:13 [Tony Jobling/Weevle, of Mr Krook] He'll never read. He can make all the letters separately, and he knows most of them separately when he sees them; he has got on that much, under me; but he can't put them together. He's too old to acquire the knack of it now – and too drunk.

Charles Dickens, 1852–3, *Bleak House*, Ch. 32

22:14 [Pip] I struggled through the alphabet as if it had been a bramble-bush; getting considerably worried and scratched by every letter.

Charles Dickens, 1861, *Great Expectations*, Ch. 7

22:15 No one who can read, ever looks at a book, even unopened on a shelf, like one who cannot.

Charles Dickens, 1864–5, *Our Mutual Friend*, I, Ch. 3

22:16 [in support of spelling reform] If, therefore, we would have the benefit of seeing our language more generally known among mankind, we should endeavour to remove all the difficulties, however small, that discourage the learning of it.

Benjamin Franklin, 26 December 1789, letter to Noah Webster, 'On Modern Innovations in the English Language and in Printing', in *Works* (1793)

22:17 This leads me to mention an old error in our mode of printing. We are sensible that when a question is met with in the reading, there is a proper variation to be used in the management of the voice. We have, therefore, a point, called an interrogation, affixed to the question, in order to distinguish it. But this is absurdly placed at its end, so that the reader does not discover it till he finds that he has wrongly modulated his voice, and is therefore obliged to begin again the sentence.

Benjamin Franklin, 26 December 1789, letter to Noah Webster, 'On Modern Innovations in the English Language and in Printing', in *Works* (1793)

22:18 You must write 'advertise' but 'organize', 'improvise' but 'moralize', 'chastise' but 'cauterize'. Why? Well, it would take a long time to explain, and I am not at all sure that I shall. I have a headache as it is, and I hope that by this time you have a headache too. Besides, much better men than I have explained it already in printed books, and it is not for me to cheat them of their royalties, especially as I have only just got the hang of the thing myself.

A. P. Herbert, 1935, *What a Word!* Ch. 6

22:19 [in support of the *-ize* spelling] I dare say that some of you think that Disarmament and Trade are more important than the British 'Z', but that is a very shallow and indolent thought, and I will not have it in the army.

A. P. Herbert, 1935, *What a Word!* Ch. 6

22:20 Yet even Letters are as it were the Banke of words, and restore themselves to an Author, as the pawnes of Language.

Ben Jonson, 1640 (published posthumously), *Timber: or, Discoveries made upon Men and Matter*

22:21 [Pooh] My spelling is Wobbly. It's good

spelling but it Wobbles, and the letters get in the wrong places.
A. A. Milne, 1926, *Winne-the-Pooh*, Ch. 6

22:22 CADE: Dost thou use to write thy name? Or hast thou a mark to thyself like an honest plain-dealing man?

CLERK: Sir, I thank God I have been so well brought up that I can write my name.

ALL CADE'S FOLLOWERS: He hath confessed – away with him!
William Shakespeare, 1590–1, *Henry VI, Part 2*, IV. ii. 101

22:23 [Mrs Brown] All as I've got to say about spellin' is as it's all rubbish, 'ow you does it, so long as any one can make out wot you means, as is a deal more than I can do with most books as comes in my way, as is all fine words and larnin', as I don't believe them as 'rites 'em knows wot they're a-talkin' about.
Arthur Sketchley, 1876, *Mrs Brown on Spelling Bees*, p. 3

22:24 [Mrs Brown] There's many a score as 'ave got on well in this world, and gone to a better, as didn't know a b from a bull's foot, as the sayin is.
Arthur Sketchley, 1876, *Mrs Brown on Spelling Bees*, p. 4

22:25 Convinced as I am of the immense advantage of following up words to their sources, of 'deriving' them, that is, of tracing each little rill to the river from whence it was first drawn, I can conceive no method of so effectually defacing and barbarizing our English tongue, of practically emptying it of all the hoarded wit, wisdom, imagination, and history which it contains, of cutting the vital nerve which connects its present with the past, as the introduction of the scheme of phonetic spelling, which some have lately been zealously advocating among us.
Richard Chenevix Trench, 1851, 'The Schoolmaster's Use of Words', in *On the Study of Words*, Lecture 7

22:26 [objecting to proposals for phonetic spelling] Words are now a nation, grouped into tribes and families, some smaller, some larger; this change would go far to reduce them to a promiscuous and barbarous horde.
Richard Chenevix Trench, 1851, 'The Schoolmaster's Use of Words', in *On the Study of Words*, Lecture 7

22:27 English orthography satisfies all the requirements of the canons of reputability under the law of conspicuous waste. It is archaic, cumbrous, and ineffective; its acquisition consumes much time and effort; failure to acquire it is easy of detection.
Thorstein Veblen, 1899, *The Theory of the Leisure Class*, Ch. 14

22:28 It is a pity that Chaucer, who had geneyus, was so unedicated. He's the wuss speller I know of.
Artemus Ward, 1867, 'At the Tomb of Shakespeare', in *Artemus Ward in London*, Ch. 4

22:29 I once believed that a reformation of our orthography would be unnecessary and impracticable. This opinion was hasty; being the result of a slight examination of the subject. I now believe with Dr. Franklin that such a reformation is practicable and highly necessary.
Noah Webster, 1789, *Dissertations on the English Language, with Notes Historical and Critical*

See also: 4:16, 9:18, 11:31, 14:16, 18:21, 45:97, 47:33, 48:7, 52:41

23 *Grammar*

Grammar, grammars, and points of grammatical usage

23:1 [on describing the restaurant] The major problem is quite simply one of grammar, and the main work to consult in this matter is Dr Dan Streetmentioner's *Time Traveller's Handbook of 1001 Tense Formations*. It will tell you for instance how to describe something that was about to happen to you in the past before you avoided it by time-jumping forward two days in order to avoid it. The event will be described differently according to whether you are talking about it from the standpoint of your own natural time, from a time in the further future, or a time in the further past and is further complicated by the possibility of conducting conversations whilst you are actually travelling from one time to another with the intention of becoming your own mother or father.

Most readers get as far as the Future Semi-Conditionally Modified Subinverted Plagal Past Subjunctive Intentional before giving up: and in fact in later editions of the book all the pages beyond this point have been left blank to save on printing costs.

The *Hitch Hiker's Guide to the Galaxy* skips lightly over this tangle of academic abstraction, pausing only to note that the term 'Future Perfect' has been abandoned since it was discovered not to be.

Douglas Adams, 1980, *The Restaurant at the End of the Universe*, Ch. 15

23:2 Geometry is to sculpture what grammar is to the art of the writer.

Guillaume Apollinaire, 1913, 'Sur la peinture 3', in *Les Peintres cubistes* (trans.)

23:3 I was told that it was right and proper for me as a boy to pay attention to my teachers, so that I should do well at my study of grammar and get on in the world.

St Augustine, 397–8, *Confessions* (trans. R. S. Pine-Coffin), I, Sect. 9

23:4 I am at a loss in what class to place compound verbs, whether in that of thoughtless chance, or of judicious accommodation.

Anselm Bayly, 1772, *A Plain and Complete Grammar with the English Accidence*

23:5 *Die, n.* The singular of 'dice.' We seldom hear the word, because there is a prohibitory proverb, 'Never say die.'

Ambrose Bierce, 1911, *The Devil's Dictionary*

23:6 *Gender, n.* The sex of words.

A masculine wooed a feminine noun, / But his courting didn't suit her, / So he begged a verb his wishes to crown, / But the verb replied, with a frigid frown: / 'What object have I? I'm neuter.'

Ambrose Bierce, 1911, *The Devil's Dictionary* (entry added by E. J. Hopkins for *The Enlarged Devil's Dictionary*, 1967)

23:7 *Grammar, n.* A system of pitfalls thoughtfully prepared for the feet of the self-made man, along the path by which he advances to distinction.

Ambrose Bierce, 1911, *The Devil's Dictionary*

23:8 *Me, pron.* The objectionable case of I. The personal pronoun in English has three cases, the dominative, the objectionable and the oppressive. Each is all three.

Ambrose Bierce, 1911, *The Devil's Dictionary*

23:9 [Yosser Hughes, to two members of the

Department of Employment] 'Malloy on no occasion never said to me "Here y'are, touch for that".' 'That's a double negative,' noted the assistant manager as Yosser made a gesture to indicate the passing of money. 'Yeah, well, there's two of you, isn't there?' retorted Yosser.

Alan Bleasdale, 1983, *Boys from the Blackstuff* (novel, by Keith Miles, based on the TV play), Ch. 5

23:10 Each sentence is an independent linguistic form, not included by virtue of any grammatical construction in any larger linguistic form.

Leonard Bloomfield, 1933, *Language*, Ch. 11

23:11 [a clergyman's advice to Borrow's father] I never yet knew a boy that was induced, either by fair means or foul, to learn Lilly's Latin Grammar by heart, who did not turn out a man, provided he lived long enough.

George Borrow, 1851, *Lavengro*, Ch. 6

23:12 Our landlord was a sensible fellow: he had learnt his grammar, and Dr Johnson justly observed, that 'a man is the better for that as long as he lives'.

James Boswell, 1785, 'Tuesday, 31st August', in *The Journal of a Tour to the Hebrides*

23:13 [of the grammarian] Was it not great? did he not throw on God / (He loves the burthen) – / God's task to make the heavenly period / Perfect the earthen? / Did he not magnify the mind, show clear / Just what it all meant? / He would not discount life, as fools do here, / Paid by instalment. / He ventured neck or nothing – heaven's success / Found, or earth's failure.

Robert Browning, 1855, 'A Grammarian's Funeral'

23:14 [of the grammarian] So, with the throttling hands of death at strife, / Ground he at grammar; / Still, thro' the rattle, parts of speech were rife: / While he could stammer / he settled *Hoti*'s business – let it be! / – Properly based *Oun* – / Gave us the doctrine of the enclitic *De*, / Dead from the waist down.

Robert Browning, 1855, 'A Grammarian's Funeral'

23:15 Grammar has its own fascination and, in a ghostly manner, its own peculiar truth. . . . There is a satisfactory boniness about grammar which the flesh of vocabulary, or lexis, requires before it can become vertebrate and walk the earth.

Anthony Burgess, 1992, *A Mouthful of Air*, I, Ch. 10

23:16 Few are slow / In thinking that their

enemy is beat / (Or beaten if you insist on grammar, though / I never think about it in a heat).

Lord Byron, 1819–24, *Don Juan*, Canto 7, stanza 42

23:17 [of Professor Teufelsdröckh] Of his sentences perhaps not more than nine-tenths stand straight on their legs; the remainder are in quite angular attitudes, buttressed-up by props (of parentheses and dashes), and ever with this or the other tagrag hanging from them; a few even sprawling helplessly on all sides, quite broken-backed and dismembered.

Thomas Carlyle, 1833, *Sartor Resartus*, I, Ch. 4

23:18 Learn well your grammar, / And never stammer.

Lewis Carroll, c.1845, 'Rules and Regulations', in *The Faber Book of Useful Verse* (1981), p. 90

23:19 [on words] Humpty Dumpty began again. 'They've a temper, some of them – particularly verbs: they're the proudest – adjectives you can do anything with, but not verbs – however, *I* can manage the whole lot of them!'

Lewis Carroll, 1872, *Through the Looking Glass*, Ch. 6

23:20 [Lady Muriel] There's nothing a well-regulated child hates so much as regularity. I believe a really healthy boy would thoroughly enjoy Greek grammar – if only he might stand on his head to learn it!

Lewis Carroll, 1889, *Sylvie and Bruno*, Ch. 17

23:21 'What a singular boy!' the Lord Chancellor whispered to himself: but Bruno had caught the words. 'What do it mean to say "a *singular* boy"?' he whispered to Sylvie. 'It means *one* boy,' Sylvie whispered in return. 'And *plural* means two or three.' 'Then I'm welly glad I *is* a singular boy!' Bruno said with great emphasis. 'It would be *horrid* to be two or three boys! P'raps they wouldn't play with me!'

Lewis Carroll, 1893, *Bruno and Sylvie Concluded*, Ch. 22

23:22 Sentences (1) and (2) are equally nonsensical, but any speaker of English will recognize that only the former is grammatical. (1) Colorless green ideas sleep furiously. (2) Furiously sleep ideas green colorless.

Noam Chomsky, 1957, *Syntactic Structures*, Ch. 2

23:23 A grammar of a language purports to be a description of the ideal speaker-hearer's intrinsic competence. If the grammar is, furthermore, perfectly explicit – in other words, if it does not rely on the intelligence of the understanding reader but rather provides an explicit analysis of his contribution – we may (somewhat redundantly) call it a *generative grammar*.

Noam Chomsky, 1965, *Aspects of the Theory of Syntax*, Ch. 1

23:24 Thus I got into my bones the essential structure of the ordinary British sentence – which is a noble thing.

Winston Churchill, 1930, *My Early Life*, Ch. 2

23:25 [marginal comment about a sentence that clumsily avoided a prepositional ending] This is the sort of English up with which I will not put.

Winston Churchill, attributed, mid 20th century, in Ernest Gowers, *Plain Words* (1954), 'Troubles with Prepositions'

23:26 How many false pretenders to erudition have I exposed to shame merely by my knowledge of grammar! How many of the insolent and ignorant, great and powerful, have I pulled down and made little and despicable!

William Cobbett, 1818, 'Syntax, as Relating to Nouns', *A Grammar of the English Language*, Letter 16

23:27 Nouns of number, or multitude, such as Mob, Parliament, Rabble, House of Commons, Regiment, Court of King's Bench, Den of Thieves, and the like.

William Cobbett, 1818, *A Grammar of the English Language*, Letter 17

23:28 A language which, like the English, is almost without cases, is indeed in its very genius unfitted for compounds. If a writer, every time a compounded word suggests itself to him, would seek for some other mode of expressing the same sense, the chances are always greatly in favour of his finding a better word.

Samuel Taylor Coleridge, 1817, *Biographia Literaria*, Ch. 1, note 1

23:29 [reporting a Danish traveller] Grammar is language, and language is grammar.

Samuel Taylor Coleridge, 1817, 'Satyrane's Letters 1', in *Biographia Literaria*, Ch. 22

23:30 [of his primary school teacher] On one occasion when she had been irritating me over some little question of English grammar I bit her arm right through to the bone, an action which I have never for an instant regretted.

Noel Coward, 1937, *Present Indicative*, Ch. 1

23:31 [of a father, concerning school lessons]

And is he well content his son should find / No nourishment to feed his growing mind, / But conjugated verbs and nouns declin'd? / For such is all the mental food purvey'd / By public hacknies in the schooling trade; / Who feed a pupil's intellect with store / Of syntax, truly, but with little more.

William Cowper, 1785, 'Tirocinium, or A Review of Schools', 617

23:32 [on farmers' sons in school] They, much enduring, sit th' allotted hours, / And o'er a grammar waste their sprightly powers.

George Crabbe, 1810, 'Letter XXIV: Schools', 330, in *The Borough*

23:33 Vernacular speech is that which we acquire without any rule, by imitating our nurses. There further springs from this another secondary speech, which the Romans called grammar. . . . Few, however, acquire the use of this speech, because we can only be guided and instructed in it by the expenditure of much time, and by assiduous study.

Dante, c.1304, *De vulgari eloquentia* (trans. A. G. Ferrers Howell), I, Ch. 1

23:34 [Mr Squeers] A horse is a quadruped, and quadruped's Latin for beast, as every body that's gone through the grammar, knows, or else where's the use of having grammars at all?

Charles Dickens, 1838–9, *Nicholas Nickleby*, Ch. 8

23:35 'Is that you?' inquired Peg. 'Ah! It's me, and me's the first person singular, nominative case, agreeing with the verb "it's", and governed by Squeers understood, as a acorn, a hour; but when the h is sounded, the a only is to be used, as a and, a art, a ighway,' replied Mr Squeers, quoting at random from the grammar. 'At least, if it isn't, you don't know any better. And if it is, I've done it accidentally.'

Charles Dickens, 1838–9, *Nicholas Nickleby*, Ch. 57

23:36 Mr. Pecksniff's manner was so bland, and he nodded his head so soothingly, and showed in everything such an affable sense of his own excellence, that anybody would have been, as Mrs. Lupin was, comforted by the mere voice and presence of such a man; and, though he had merely said 'a verb must agree with its nominative case in number and person, my good friend,' . . . must have felt deeply grateful to him for his humanity and wisdom.

Charles Dickens, 1843–4, *Martin Chuzzlewit*, Ch. 3

23:37 [Jonas Chuzzlewit] He wrote a note for

his portmanteau, and sent it by a messenger, who duly brought his luggage back, with a short note from that other piece of luggage, his wife, expressive of her wish to be allowed to come and see him for a moment. To this request he sent for answer, 'she had better;' and one such threatening affirmative being sufficient, in defiance of the English grammar, to express a negative, she kept away.

Charles Dickens, 1843–4, *Martin Chuzzlewit*, Ch. 41

23:38 [Mark Tapley, on being welcomed by Tom Pinch] 'It's a considerable invasion of a man's jollity to be made so partickler welcome, but a Werb is a word as signifies to be, to do, or to suffer (which is all the grammar, and enough too, as ever I wos taught); and if there's a Werb alive, I'm it. For I'm always a-bein', sometimes a-doin', and continually a-sufferin'.'

Charles Dickens, 1843–4, *Martin Chuzzlewit*, Ch. 48

23:39 [Mrs Gamp to Mrs Prig] 'WHO deniges [denies] of it, Betsey?' Mrs. Gamp inquired again. Then Mrs. Gamp, by reversing the question, imparted a deeper and more awful character of solemnity to the same. 'Betsey, who deniges of it?'

Charles Dickens, 1843–4, *Martin Chuzzlewit*, Ch. 49

23:40 [David, on being an imaginary Captain] The Captain never lost dignity, from having his ears boxed with the Latin Grammar. I did; but the Captain was a Captain and a hero, in despite of all the grammars of all the languages in the world, dead or alive.

Charles Dickens, 1849–50, *David Copperfield*, Ch. 4

23:41 Some men rarely revert to their father, but seem, in the bank-books of their remembrance, to have transferred all the stock of filial affection into their mother's name. Mr Bagnet is one of these. Perhaps his exalted appreciation of the merits of the old girl, causes him usually to make the noun-substantive, Goodness, of the feminine gender.

Charles Dickens, 1852–3, *Bleak House*, Ch. 49

23:42 [on the character of Mrs Merdle's instructions from abroad to Mr Merdle] In the grammar of Mrs Merdle's verbs on this momentous subject, there was only one Mood, the Imperative; and that Mood had only one Tense, the Present. Mrs Merdle's verbs were so pressingly presented to Mr Merdle to conjugate, that his sluggish

blood and his long coat-cuffs became quite agitated.

Charles Dickens, 1855–7, *Little Dorrit*, II, Ch. 12

23:43 [Mr Pancks, on Mr Casby] 'Is any gentleman present,' said Mr Pancks, breaking off and looking round, 'acquainted with the English Grammar?'

Bleeding Heart Yard was shy of claiming that acquaintance.

'It's no matter,' said Mr Pancks. 'I merely wish to remark that the task this Proprietor has set me has been, never to leave off conjugating the Imperative Mood Present Tense of the Verb To Keep Always At It. Keep thou always at it. Let him keep always at it. Keep we or do we keep always at it. Keep ye or do ye or you keep always at it. Let them keep always at it. Here is your benevolent Patriarch of a Casby, and there is his golden rule.'

Charles Dickens, 1855–7, *Little Dorrit*, II, Ch. 32

23:44 [Pip, after receiving a mysterious message, 'Don't go home'] When at last I dozed, in sheer exhaustion of mind and body, it became a vast shadowy verb which I had to conjugate, Imperative mood, present tense: Do not thou go home, let him not go home, let us not go home, do not ye or you go home, let not them go home. Then, potentially: I may not and I cannot go home; and I might not, could not, would not, and should not go home; until I felt that I was getting distracted, and rolled over on the pillow, and looked at the staring rounds upon the wall again.

Charles Dickens, 1861, *Great Expectations*, Ch. 55

23:45 [Contarini] I think I was born with a detestation of grammars. Nature seemed to whisper to me the folly of learning words instead of ideas, and my mind would have grown sterile for want of manure if I had not taken its culture into my own hands, and compensated by my own tillage for my tutor's bad husbandry. I therefore in a quiet way read every book that I could get hold of, and studied as little as possible in my instructor's museum of verbiage, whether his specimens appeared in the anatomy of a substantive, or the still more disgusting form of a dissected verb.

Benjamin Disraeli, 1832, *Contarini Fleming*, Ch. 5

23:46 [correcting proofs of his last Parliamentary speech] I will not go down to posterity talking bad grammar.

Benjamin Disraeli, 31 March 1881, in Robert Blake, *Disraeli* (1966), Ch. 32

23:47 [commenting on a line in Jonson] The Preposition in the end of the sentence; a common fault with him, and which I have but lately observ'd in my own writings.
John Dryden, 1672, 'Defence of the Epilogue', appended to *The Conquest of Granada*

23:48 To be loose with grammar is to be loose with the worst woman in the world.
Otis C. Edwards, 10 January 1966, lecture at Nashotah House

23:49 Mrs Garth, like more celebrated educators, had her favourite ancient paths, and in a general wreck of society would have tried to hold her 'Lindley Murray' above the waves.
George Eliot, 1871–2, *Middlemarch*, III, Ch. 24 [cf. 23:82]

23:50 [young Ben] 'I hate grammar. What's the use of it?' 'To teach you to speak and write correctly, so that you can be understood,' said Mrs Garth, with severe precision. 'Should you like to speak as old Job does?'
   'Yes,' said Ben, stoutly; 'it's funnier. He says, "Yo goo" – that's just as good as "You go".'
George Eliot, 1871–2, *Middlemarch*, III, Ch. 24

23:51 Life lies behind us as the quarry from whence we get tiles and copestones for the masonry of to-day. This is the way to learn grammar. Colleges and books only copy the language which the field and the work-yard made.
Ralph Waldo Emerson, 1837, 'The American Scholar'

23:52 The adjective is the banana peel of the parts of speech.
Clifton Fadiman, September 1956, *Reader's Digest*

23:53 The old-fashioned grammarian certainly has much to answer for. He created a false sense of values that still lingers. . . . Too much importance is still attached to grammarians' fetishes and too little to choosing the right words. But we cannot have grammar jettisoned altogether; that would mean chaos.
Ernest Gowers, 1954, *The Complete Plain Words*, Ch. 9

23:54 There is an instinctive mistrust of grammarians in Britain and the United States, and a pride in following one's natural course in writing.
Robert Graves and Alan Hodge, 1944, *The Reader Over Your Shoulder*, Ch. 2

23:55 A poet . . . must master the rules of grammar before he attempts to bend or break them.
Robert Graves, 1961, letter to *The Times*

23:56 Scholars who have made and taught from English grammars were previously and systematically initiated in the Greek and Latin tongues, so that they have, without deigning to notice the difference, taken the rules of the latter and applied them indiscriminately and dogmatically to the former.
William Hazlitt, 15 March 1829, 'English Grammar', in *The Atlas*

23:57 [arguing against traditional grammarians' ascription of six cases to nouns in English] Thus to instance in the present noun – A case, Of a case, To a case, A case, O Case, From a case – they tell you that the word *case* is here its own nominative, genitive, dative, accusative, vocative, and ablative, though the deuce of any case – that is, inflection of the noun – is there in the case. Nevertheless, many a pedagogue would swear till he was black in the face that it is so; and would lie awake many a restless night boiling with rage and vexation that any one should be so lost to shame and reason as to suspect that there is here also a distinction without a difference.
William Hazlitt, 15 March 1829, 'English Grammar', in *The Atlas*

23:58 In the same manner as the cases and genders of nouns, the whole ramification of the [English] verb is constructed, and hung up for the admiration of the credulous upon the ideal model of the Latin and Greek verb, with all its tenses, persons, moods, and participles, whether there be anything more than a mere skeleton of a resemblance to suspend all this learned patch-work upon or not.
William Hazlitt, 15 March 1829, 'English Grammar', in *The Atlas*

23:59 [on particles in phrasal verbs] If we want to make a verb mean something which it does not mean we set a little fellow to trot astern, rather vaguely, like a cheeky dog behind a solid citizen. It may look disorderly and even absurd – but how English!
A. P. Herbert, 1935, *What a Word!* Ch. 6

23:60 In all the long years of my school career no one, to my recollection, attempted to teach me anything about the English language. I spent years upon the grammar of Latin, Greek, and even French, but never an hour upon the rules of English grammar. I believe that things are different now; but in those days the English language was supposed to come to an English gentleman naturally, without effort, like clean-living or an aptitude for ball-games. We picked up the rules of composition casually while we studied chemistry or practised fielding.

A. P. Herbert, 1935, *What a Word!* Ch. 7

23:61 [The Squire, of Tom Brown] I don't care a straw for Greek particles, or the digamma, no more does his mother.

Thomas Hughes, 1857, *Tom Brown's Schooldays*, I, Ch. 4

23:62 I'm glad you like adverbs – I adore them; they are the only qualifications I really much respect.

Henry James, 5 January 1912, letter to Miss M. Bentham Edwards, in Percy Lubbock (ed.), *The Letters of Henry James* (1920)

23:63 The most important single thing in publishing is the English sentence, and the editor who cannot contemplate it again and again with a sense of wonder has not yet gained respect for the complexity of learning.

William Jovanovich, 1964, *Now, Barabbas*

23:64 [Mrs Battle, on cribbage] She could never heartily bring her mouth to pronounce 'go' or 'that's a go'. She called it an ungrammatical game.

Charles Lamb, 1823, 'Mrs. Battle's Opinions on Whist', in *The Essays of Elia*

23:65 [on the need to study grammar books] The fine dream is fading away fast; and the least concern of a teacher in the present day is to inculcate grammar-rules.

Charles Lamb, 1823, 'Old and New Schoolmaster', in *The Essays of Elia*

23:66 Grammar is the art of speaking. / Speaking is explaining one's thoughts by signs which men have invented for this purpose.

Claude Lancelot and Antoine Arnauld, 1660, *Grammaire générale et raisonnée* [the Port-Royal Grammar] (trans. J. Rieux and B. E. Rollin), Introduction

23:67 Gramer, the grounde of al.

William Langland, 1360–87, *The Vision of Piers Plowman* (B text), Passus XV, 365

23:68 When the geography class was done, we learned by heart, out of a little book called Grammar, the statement that 'There are eight parts of speech, the noun, the pronoun, the

adjective, the verb, the adverb, the preposition, the conjunction and the interjection.' It was just a mass of words. We hadn't the least idea of what a part of speech meant.

Stephen Leacock, 1938, 'Recovery after Graduation', in *Here are my Lectures*

23:69 The principal design of a Grammar of any Language is to teach us to express ourselves with propriety in that Language; and to enable us to judge of every phrase and form of construction, whether it be right or not. The plain way of doing this is, to lay down rules, and to illustrate them by examples. But, beside shewing what is right, the matter may be further explained by pointing out what is wrong.

Robert Lowth, 1762, *A Short Introduction to English Grammar*, p. 1

23:70 Grammar is the art of rightly expressing our thoughts by words.

Robert Lowth, 1762, *A Short Introduction to English Grammar*, p. 1

23:71 It's one of those irregular verbs, isn't it? 'I have an independent mind, you are eccentric, he is round the twist'?

Jonathan Lynn and Antony Jay, 1980s, 'The Bishop's Gambit', in *Yes, Prime Minister*

23:72 It is well to remember that grammar is common speech formulated.

W. Somerset Maugham, 1938, *The Summing Up*, Ch. 13

23:73 If the English language had been properly organized . . . then there would be a word which meant both 'he' and 'she', and I could write, 'If John or May comes, heesh will want to play tennis,' which would save a lot of trouble.

A. A. Milne, 1931, *The Christopher Robin Birthday Book*

23:74 Grammar, which can govern even kings.

Molière, 1672, *Les Femmes savantes*, II. vi (trans.)

23:75 [on meeting two college tutors travelling along a road, but separated by some distance] One of my men asked the first of these tutors who was 'that gentleman coming behind him'? . . . 'He is not a gentleman,' he amusingly replied, 'but a grammarian.'

Michel de Montaigne, 1572–80, 'On Educating Children', in *The Complete Essays* (trans. M. A. Screech, 1987), I, no. 26

23:76 [before launching into an etymology] I have never learned any language except by using it and I still do not know what an adjective is nor a subjunctive nor an ablative: yet here I am, turning into a grammarian.

Michel de Montaigne, 1572–80, 'On War-horses', in *The Complete Essays* (trans. M. A. Screech, 1987), I, no. 48

23:77 [on verbs] THE VERBS are of two kinds – active and passive. Active verbs express action; passive verbs express passion. All feminine verbs are irregular and imperative.

Christopher Morley, 1919, 'Syntax for Cynics', in *Mince Pie*

23:78 [on declension] There are three ways of feminine declining, (1) to say No; (2) to say Yes and mean No; (3) to say nothing.

Christopher Morley, 1919, 'Syntax for Cynics', in *Mince Pie*

23:79 A sentence may be defined as a group of words, uttered in sequence, but without logical connection, to express an opinion or an emotion. A number of sentences if emitted without interruption becomes a conversation. A conversation prolonged over an hour or more becomes a gossip. A gossip, when shared by several persons, is known as a secret. A secret is anything known by a large and constantly increasing number of persons.

Christopher Morley, 1919, 'Syntax for Cynics', in *Mince Pie*

23:80 A certain young man never knew / Just when to say *whom* and when *who*; / 'The question of choosing,' / He said, 'is confusing; / I wonder if *which* wouldn't do?'

Christopher Morley, 1919, 'The Unforgivable Syntax', in *Mince Pie*

23:81 'Never leave a passage until you thoroughly understand every word, every case, every detail of the grammar.' A fluffy vague understanding was not good enough for Mr Osmand. Grammar books were my books of prayer. Looking up words in the dictionary was for me an image of goodness. The endless endless task of learning new words was for me an image of life.

Iris Murdoch, 1975, 'Thursday' (first week), in *A Word Child*

23:82 ENGLISH GRAMMAR is the art of speaking and writing the English language with propriety.

Lindley Murray, 1795, *English Grammar*, Ch. 1

23:83 Oh, I'll be friends if you'll be friends, / The foreigner tells the native, / And we'll work

together for our common ends / Like a preposition and a dative.

Ogden Nash, 1935, 'Goody for our Side and your Side too', in *The Primrose Path*

23:84 [on *like* replacing *as*] I guess it is farewell to grammatical compunction, / I guess a preposition is the same as a conjunction, / I guess an adjective is the same as an adverb, / And 'to parse' is a bad verb.

Ogden Nash, 1957, 'Oafishness Sells Good, like an Advertisement Should', in *You Can't Get There From Here*

23:85 Irregularity in grammar seems like the epitome of human eccentricity and quirkiness.

Steven Pinker, 1994, *The Language Instinct*, Ch. 5

23:86 God is more delighted in adverbs than in nouns.

Proverbial (Hebrew)

23:87 Mr. Kaplan had, by supreme concentration, memorized three axioms anent English grammar, and he clung to them as cosmic verities: 'Wrong tanse!,' 'Dobble nagetif!,' and 'Tsplit infinitif!'

Leo Rosten, 1938, 'H*y*m*a*n K*a*p*l*a*n, Samaritan', in *The Return of H*y*m*a*n K*a*p*l*a*n*

23:88 I never made a mistake in grammar but once in my life and as soon as I done it I seen it.

Carl Sandburg, 1936, *The People, Yes*

23:89 I am still studying verbs and the mystery of how they connect nouns. I am more suspicious of adjectives than at any other time in all my born days.

Carl Sandburg, c.1940, quoted in 'Notes for a Preface', in *The Complete Poems of Carl Sandburg* (1966)

23:90 All grammars leak.

Edward Sapir, 1921, *Language*, Ch. 2

23:91 [of the grammatical uniqueness of *whom* as a pronoun] Words of a feather tend to flock together, and if one strays behind, it is likely to incur danger of life.

Edward Sapir, 1921, *Language*, Ch. 7

23:92 [Cade, to Lord Saye] It will be proved to thy face that thou hast men about thee that usually talk of a noun and a verb and such abominable words as no Christian ear can endure to hear.

William Shakespeare, 1590–1, *Henry VI, Part 2*, IV. vii. 35

23:93 [Host, of the parson, Sir Hugh Evans] He gives me the Proverbs and the No-verbs.

William Shakespeare, 1597, *The Merry Wives of Windsor*, III. i. 96

23:94 LUCIAN [explaining why he hasn't visited Lydia recently]: I have been greatly occupied of late. / The minister to whom I act as scribe / In Downing Street was born in Birmingham, / And, like a thoroughbred commercial statesman, / Splits his infinitives, which I, poor slave, / Must reunite, though all the time my heart / Yearns for my gentle coz's company.

    LYDIA: Lucian: there is some other reason. Think! / Since England as a nation every mood / Her scribes with adverbs recklessly have split, / But thine avoidance dates from yestermonth.

George Bernard Shaw, 1909, *The Admirable Bashville; or, Constancy Unrewarded*, II. i [based on *Cashel Byron's Profession*, 1886]

23:95 LIZA: I got my feelings same as anyone else.

    HIGGINS (*to Pickering, reflectively*): You see the difficulty?

    PICKERING: Eh? What difficulty?

    HIGGINS: To get her to talk grammar. The mere pronunciation is easy enough.

    LIZA: I dont want to talk grammar. I want to talk like a lady.

George Bernard Shaw, 1913, *Pygmalion*, II

23:96 [Mrs Malaprop, to Captain Absolute about Miss Languish] Long ago I laid my positive conjunctions on her, never to think on the fellow again; – I have since laid Sir Anthony's preposition before her; but, I am sorry to say, she seems resolved to decline every particle that I enjoin her.

Richard Sheridan, 1775, *The Rivals*, III. iii

23:97 O Grammar-Rules, O now your virtues show; / So children still read you with awful eyes, / As my young dove may, in your precepts wise, / Her grant to me by her own virtue know: / For late, with heart most high, with eyes most low, / I craved the thing which ever she denies; / She, lightning love, displaying Venus' skies, / Lest once should not be heard, twice said, No, No. / Sing then, my Muse, now *Io Paean* sing; / Heavens, envy not at my high triumphing, / But grammar's force with sweet success con-

firm: / For grammar says, – O this, dear Stella, say, – / For grammar says, – to grammar who says nay? – / That in one speech two negatives affirm!

Philip Sidney, *c*.1582, *Astrophel and Stella*, Sonnet 63

23:98 I am the Roman Emperor, and am above grammar.

Emperor Sigismund, 15th century, attributed, after a cleric had criticized his Latin

23:99 [Walter Shandy] I reckon it as one of the greatest calamities which ever befell the republick of letters, That those who have been entrusted with the education of our children, and whose business it was to open their minds, and stock them early with ideas, in order to set the imagination loose upon them, have made so little use of the auxiliary verbs in doing it, as they have done.

Laurence Sterne, 1762, *The Life and Opinions of Tristram Shandy, Gentleman*, V, Ch. 42

23:100 Now, by the right use and application of these [auxiliary verbs], continued my father, in which a child's memory should be exercised, there is no one idea can enter his brain how barren soever, but a magazine of conceptions and conclusions may be drawn forth from it.

Laurence Sterne, 1762, *The Life and Opinions of Tristram Shandy, Gentleman*, V, Ch. 43

23:101 With sixty staring me in the face, I have developed inflammation of the sentence structure and definite hardening of the paragraphs.

James Thurber, 30 June 1955, in the *New York Post*

23:102 I think Grammar difficult, but I am very far from looking upon it as foolish: indeed so far, that I consider it as absolutely necessary in the search after philosophical truth; which, if not the most useful, perhaps, is at least the most pleasing employment of the human mind. And I think it no less necessary in the most important questions concerning religion and civil society.

John Horne Tooke, 1786, *The Diversions of Purley*, p. 13

23:103 Grammar is the logic of speech, even as logic is the grammar of reason.

Richard Chenevix Trench, 1851, 'Introductory Lecture', in *On the Study of Words*

23:104 Not only humble but umble, which I look upon to be the comparative, or, indeed, superlative degree.

Anthony Trollope, 1858, *Doctor Thorne*, Ch. 4

23:105 Whenever the literary German dives into a sentence, that is the last you are going to see of him till he emerges on the other side of his Atlantic with his verb in his mouth.

Mark Twain, 1889, *A Connecticut Yankee in King Arthur's Court*, Ch. 22

23:106 As to the Adjective: when in doubt, strike it out.

Mark Twain, 1894, 'Pudd'nhead Wilson's Calendar', in *Pudd'nhead Wilson*, Ch. 11

23:107 Damn the subjunctive. It brings all our writers to shame.

Mark Twain, *Notebooks* (1935)

23:108 Syntax is a faculty of the soul.

Paul Valéry, 'Literature', in *Odds and Ends* (trans. S. Gilbert, 1970)

23:109 [of earlier grammarians] They all forced English too rigidly into the mould of Latin (a mistake which nearly everyone makes in descriptions of other modern languages too), giving many useless rules about the cases, genders and declensions of nouns, the tenses, moods and conjugations of verbs, the government of nouns and verbs, and other things of that kind, which have no bearing on our language, and which confuse and obscure matters instead of elucidating them.

John Wallis, 1653, *Grammatica linguae anglicanae* (trans. J. A. Kemp), Preface

23:110 In our language, where the situation is quite different from that in Latin, there is no reason at all for introducing a collection of cases, genders, moods and tenses which are artificial and wholly inappropriate, and for which there is no need and no basis in the language itself.

Nevertheless I thought I had better keep the Latin terminology normally used in this Art, even though it is not entirely suited to our language; I do this partly because the meaning of it is well known, and partly also through an unwillingness to make any unnecessary innovations.

John Wallis, 1653, *Grammatica linguae anglicanae* (trans. J. A. Kemp), Preface

23:111 Why care for grammar as long as we are good?

Artemus Ward, 1867, 'Pyrotechny', in *Artemus Ward in London*, Ch. 3

23:112 A writer who can't write in a grammerly manner better shut up shop.

Artemus Ward, 1872, 'Science and Natural History', in *Artemus Ward in London*, Ch. 7

23:113 A Grammar book does not attempt to teach people how they ought to speak, but on the contrary, unless it is a very bad or a very old work, it merely states how, as a matter of fact, certain people do speak at the time at which it is written.

H. C. Wyld, 1925, *Elementary Lessons in English Grammar*, p. 12

See also: 1:46, 2:21, 3:37, 8:1; 8:4, 8:6, 8:9, 8:19, 8:44, 8:47, 8:50, 9:19, 14:11, 14:16, 14:31, 16:19–23, 20:5, 30:54, 49:21, 49:45, 49:104, 51:19, 52:9, 52:11, 52:19, 60:12

Dictionaries and lexicographers

24:1 Though a work of literature can be read in a number of ways, this number is finite and can be arranged in a hierarchical order; some readings are obviously 'truer' than others, some doubtful, some obviously false, and some, like reading a novel backwards, absurd. That is why, for a desert island, one would choose a good dictionary rather than the greatest literary masterpiece imaginable, for, in relation to its readers, a dictionary is absolutely passive and may legitimately be read in an infinite number of ways.

W. H. Auden, 1948, 'Prologue: Reading', in *The Dyer's Hand and other essays*

24:2 *Dictionary, n.* A malevolent literary device for cramping the growth of a language and making it hard and inelastic.

Ambrose Bierce, 1911, *The Devil's Dictionary* (entry added by E. J. Hopkins for *The Enlarged Devil's Dictionary*, 1967)

24:3 *Lexicographer, n.* A pestilent fellow who, under the pretense of recording some particular stage in the development of a language, does what he can to arrest its growth, stiffen its flexibility and mechanize its methods. . . . The natural servility of the human understanding having invested him with judicial power, surrenders its right of reason and submits itself to a chronicle as if it were a statue.

Ambrose Bierce, 1911, *The Devil's Dictionary*

24:4 A word in a dictionary is very much like a car in a mammoth motorshow – full of potential but temporarily inactive.

Anthony Burgess, 1992, *A Mouthful of Air*, I, Ch. 10

24:5 Were I asked what I deemed the greatest and most unmixt benefit, which a wealthy individual, or an association of wealthy individuals, could bestow on their country and on mankind, I should not hesitate to answer, 'a philosophical English dictionary; with the Greek, Latin, German, French, Spanish, and Italian synonymes, and with correspondent indexes'.

Samuel Taylor Coleridge, 1817, *Biographia Literaria*, Ch. 12, note 44

24:6 [Wackford Squeers, describing the death of one of his boys] A candle in his bed-room on the very night he died – the best dictionary sent up for him to lay his head upon.

Charles Dickens, 1838–9, *Nicholas Nickleby*, Ch. 4

24:7 [of Dr Strong] The Doctor's cogitating manner was attributable to his being always engaged in looking out for Greek roots; which, in my innocence and ignorance, I supposed to be a botanical furor on the Doctor's part, especially as he always looked at the ground when he walked about, until I understood that they were roots of words, with a view to a new Dictionary which he had in contemplation. Adams, our head-boy, who had a turn for mathematics, had made a calculation, I was informed, of the time this Dictionary would take in completing, on the Doctor's plan, and at the Doctor's rate of going. He considered that it might be done in one thousand six hundred and forty-nine years, counting from the Doctor's last, or sixty-second, birthday.

Charles Dickens, 1849–50, *David Copperfield*, Ch. 16

24:8 [the Old Soldier] What a useful work a Dictionary is! What a necessary work! The meanings of words! Without Doctor Johnson, or somebody of that sort, we might have been at this present moment calling an Italian-iron a bedstead.

Charles Dickens, 1849–50, *David Copperfield*, Ch. 45

24:9 Neither is a dictionary a bad book to read. There is no cant in it, no excess of explanation, and it is full of suggestion, – the raw material of possible poems and histories.

Ralph Waldo Emerson, 1860, 'In Praise of Books'

24:10 In the United States . . . anyone who is willing to quarrel with the dictionary is regarded as either eccentric or mad.

S. I. Hayakawa, 1939, *Language in Thought and Action*, Ch. 4

24:11 Modern dictionaries are pusillanimous works, preferring feebly to record what has been done than to say what ought to be done.

A. P. Herbert, 1935, *What a Word!*, Ch. 2

24:12 *DULL*. . . . [illustrative sentence, sense 8] To make dictionaries is dull work.

Samuel Johnson, 1755, *A Dictionary of the English Language*

24:13 *LEXICOGRAPHER*. A writer of dictionaries, a harmless drudge.

Samuel Johnson, 1755, *A Dictionary of the English Language*

24:14 When I took the first survey of my undertaking, I found our speech copious without order, and energetick without rules: wherever I turned my view, there was perplexity to be disentangled, and confusion to be regulated; choice was to be made out of boundless variety, without any established principle of selection; adulterations were to be detected, without a settled test of purity; and modes of expression to be rejected or received, without the suffrages of any writers of classical reputation or acknowledged authority.

Samuel Johnson, 1755, *A Dictionary of the English Language*, Preface

24:15 And such is the fate of hapless lexicography, that not only darkness, but light, impedes and distresses it; things may be not only too little, but too much known, to be happily illustrated.

Samuel Johnson, 1755, *A Dictionary of the English Language*, Preface

24:16 The rigour of interpretative lexicography

requires that *the explanation, and the word explained, should be always reciprocal.*

Samuel Johnson, 1755, *A Dictionary of the English Language*, Preface

24:17 I have studiously endeavoured to collect examples and authorities from the writers before the restoration, whose works I regard as *the wells of English undefiled*, as the pure sources of genuine diction.

Samuel Johnson, 1755, *A Dictionary of the English Language*, Preface

24:18 [Johnson] 'By collecting those [words] of your country, you will do a useful thing towards the history of the language.' He bade me also go on with collections which I was making upon the antiquities of Scotland. 'Make a large book – a folio.'

BOSWELL: 'But of what use will it be, sir?'
JOHNSON: 'Never mind the use; do it.'

Samuel Johnson, 1769, in James Boswell, *The Life of Samuel Johnson* (1791), Ch. 20

24:19 [on poetry being easier than lexicography] Composing a dictionary requires books and a desk: you can make a poem walking in the fields, or lying in bed.

Samuel Johnson, 17 August 1773, in James Boswell, *The Journal of a Tour to the Hebrides* (1785)

24:20 Dictionaries are like watches: the worst is better than none, and the best cannot be expected to go quite true.

Samuel Johnson, 21 August 1784, letter to Francesco Sastres

24:21 The circle of the English language has a well-defined centre but no discernible circumference.

J. A. H. Murray, 1888, 'The Vocabulary', in *A New English Dictionary on Historical Principles*, I, 'General Explanations'

24:22 As sheer casual reading-matter, I still find the English dictionary the most interesting book in the language.

Albert Jay Nock, 1943, *Memoirs of a Superfluous Man*

24:23 That old lady who, on borrowing a dictionary from her municipal library, returned it with the comment, 'A very unusual book indeed – but the stories are extremely short, aren't they?'

Eric Partridge, 1963, *The Gentle Art of Lexicography*, Ch. 1

24:24 Lexicography is an art vastly more complex and difficult and arduous than the lay consulters of dictionaries can possibly imagine. Lexicographers, you may be sure, wish it were otherwise.

Eric Partridge, 1963, *The Gentle Art of Lexicography*, Ch. 4

24:25 A dictionary without quotations is like a table of contents without a book.

James Sledd, 1962, 'The Lexicographer's Uneasy Chair', *College English*, no. 23

24:26 The greatest drawback to the use of a dictionary is bulkiness. The mere physical labour of pulling volume after volume of a big dictionary off the shelf and then replacing them is alone enough to deter the student from the attempt to utilize the material stored up in them.

Henry Sweet, 1899, *The Practical Study of Languages*, Ch. 12

24:27 A Dictionary is an historical monument, the history of a nation.

Richard Chenevix Trench, 1857, 'On Some Deficiencies in our English Dictionaries'

24:28 I cannot imagine that Dr. Johnson's reputation will be very lasting. His dictionary is a surprising work for one man – but sufficient examples in foreign countries shew that the task is too much for one man, and that a society should alone pretend to publish a standard dictionary.

Horace Walpole, 1799, 'Dr. Johnson', in J. Pinkerton, *Walpoliana*

See also: 7:44, 8:40, 23:81

Good and Bad Language

Oratory, eloquence, rhetoric, and other forms of good or bad expression

25:1 Great orators who are not also great writers become very indistinct shadows to the generations following them. The spell vanishes with the voice.

Thomas Bailey Aldrich, 1903, 'Leaves from a Notebook', in *Ponkapog Papers*

25:2 Let rhetoric be the power to observe the persuasiveness of which any particular matter admits.

Aristotle, 4th century BC, *The Art of Rhetoric* (trans. H. C. Lawson-Tancred), Ch. 1, Sect. 2

25:3 The genres of rhetoric are three in number, which is the number of the types of audience. For a speech is composed of three factors – the speaker, the subject and the listener – and it is to the last of these that its purpose is related.

Aristotle, 4th century BC, *The Art of Rhetoric* (trans. H. C. Lawson-Tancred), Ch. 1, Sect. 3

25:4 For there are three things that are investigated, and these are dynamics, harmony and rhythm. Experts in these more or less carry off the prizes at the contests, and just as in the case of tragedy actors now have more effect than the poets, so is it also in political contests, through the baseness of the citizenry. However an art has not yet been composed on these aspects.

Aristotle, 4th century BC, *The Art of Rhetoric* (trans. H. C. Lawson-Tancred), Ch. 3, Sect. 1

25:5 *The form of the diction should be neither fully metrical nor completely without rhythm*; the former is unconvincing (as it is thought to be artificial), and at the same time it is distracting; for it makes one expect the recurrence of a similar rhythmic pattern. . . . On the other hand, the rhythmless is unlimited, and the speech should be circumscribed but not by metre; for what is unbounded is unpleasant and unrecognizable.

Aristotle, 4th century BC, *The Art of Rhetoric* (trans. H. C. Lawson-Tancred), Ch. 3, Sect. 8

25:6 In all kinds of speech, either pleasant, grave, severe, or ordinary, it is convenient to speak leisurely, and rather drawlingly than hastily; because hasty speech confounds the memory, and oftentimes, besides the unseemliness, drives a man either to stammering, a nonplus [perplexity], or harping on that which should follow; whereas a slow speech confirmeth the memory, addeth a conceit of wisdom to the hearers, besides a seemliness of speech and countenance.

Francis Bacon, 1626, 'Hints for Civil Conversation'

25:7 The speaking in a perpetual hyperbole is comely in nothing but in love.

Francis Bacon, 1612/25, 'Of Love', in *Essays*

25:8 [of Russell Harty] He had learned then, by the age of twenty, a lesson it took me half a lifetime to learn, namely that there was nothing that could not be said and no one to whom one could not say it.

Alan Bennett, 14 October 1988, 'Russell Harty, 1934–88', address given at St James's, London

25:9 Let your speech be always with grace, seasoned with salt.

The Bible, Colossians 4:6 (Authorised Version of 1611)

25:10 [Moses, to Yahweh] Never in my life have I been a man of eloquence, either before or since

you have spoken to your servant. I am a slow speaker and not able to speak well.
The Bible, Exodus 4:10 (Jerusalem Bible)

25:11 [Yahweh, to Moses about Aaron] You will speak to him and tell him what message to give. I shall help you to speak, and him too, and instruct you what to do. He himself is to speak to the people in your place; he will be your mouthpiece, and you will be as the god inspiring him.
The Bible, Exodus 4:15 (Jerusalem Bible)

25:12 When a man's stomach is full, it is the fruit of his own mouth, it is the yield of his lips that fills him.
The Bible, Proverbs 18:20 (Jerusalem Bible)

25:13 *Address, n.* A formal discourse, usually delivered to a person who has something by a person who wants something that he has.
Ambrose Bierce, 1911, *The Devil's Dictionary* (entry added by E. J. Hopkins for *The Enlarged Devil's Dictionary*, 1967)

25:14 *Eloquence, n.* The art of orally persuading fools that white is the color that it appears to be. It includes the gift of making any color appear white.
Ambrose Bierce, 1911, *The Devil's Dictionary*

25:15 *Eloquence, n.* A method of convincing fools. The art is commonly presented under the visible aspect of a bald-headed little man gesticulating above a glass of water.
Ambrose Bierce, 1911, *The Devil's Dictionary* (entry added by E. J. Hopkins for *The Enlarged Devil's Dictionary*, 1967)

25:16 *Oratory, n.* A conspiracy between speech and action to cheat the understanding. A tyranny tempered by stenography.
Ambrose Bierce, 1911, *The Devil's Dictionary*

25:17 *Persuasion, n.* A species of hypnotism in which the oral suggestion takes the hindering form of argument or appeal.
Ambrose Bierce, 1911, *The Devil's Dictionary* (entry added by E. J. Hopkins for *The Enlarged Devil's Dictionary*, 1967)

25:18 Grace in speech makes speech memorable; lucidity makes it enjoyable to the hearer; and grace and lucidity come only from a knowledge of words and their quality, and a sense, innate or acquired, of the appropriate word in its appropriate place.
Norman Birkett, July 1953, *The Magic of Words*,

Presidential Address to the English Association, p. 14

25:19 The magic of the tongue is the most dangerous of all spells.
Edward Bulwer-Lytton, 1832, *Eugene Aram*, I, Ch. 8

25:20 His speech was a fine sample, on the whole, / Of rhetoric, which the learned call rigmarole.
Lord Byron, 1819–24, *Don Juan*, Canto 1, stanza 174

25:21 [Count Lodovico] It is the words themselves which give an oration its greatness and magnificence, provided the orator employs good judgement and care, knows how to choose those which best express what he means, and how to enhance them, shaping them to his purpose like wax and arranging them in relation to one another so well that their clarity and worth are immediately evident, as if they were paintings hung in a good and natural light.
Baldesar Castiglione, 1528, *The Book of the Courtier* (trans. G. Bull, Penguin 1967), I, p. 77

25:22 *Rem tene; verba sequentur.* Grasp the subject; the words will follow.
Cato the Elder, 2nd century BC, quoted in Pliny (the Elder), *Historia Naturalis*, XV, Sect. 74, and elsewhere

25:23 *Orator vir bonus discendi peritus.* An orator is a good man, skilled in speaking.
Cato the Elder, 2nd century BC, quoted in Quintilian, *Institutio Oratoria*, XII, Part 1

25:24 [Don Quixote's advice to Sancho] Walk leisurely and speak with deliberation; but not so as to seem to be listening to yourself, for all affectation is bad.
Miguel de Cervantes, 1605, *The Adventures of Don Quixote* (trans. J. M. Cohen), II, Ch. 43

25:25 A dog is not considered good because of his barking, and a man is not considered clever because of his ability to talk.
Chuang Tzu, 4th–3rd century BC, *Works*, Ch. 32, Sect. 1

25:26 And adepts in the speaking trade / Keep a cough by them ready made.
Charles Churchill, 1762, 'The Ghost', II, 545

25:27 When you think of other arts, their very choicest aspects are actually those remotest from the understanding and appreciation of the uninitiated, while for orators, on the other hand, it is a major fault to depart from everyday

language and the accepted usage of the community in general.
Cicero, 55 BC, *On the Orator* (*De oratore*, trans. M. Grant), I, Ch. 3

25:28 [Crassus] I can think of nothing more agreeable to the brain and the ear than a speech adorned and embellished with wise thoughts and fine language.
Cicero, 55 BC, *On the Orator* (*De oratore*, trans. M. Grant), I, Ch. 8

25:29 [Antonius] In an orator . . . we demand the acuteness of a logician, the profundity of a philosopher, the diction virtually of a poet, the memory of a lawyer, the voice of a performer in tragic drama, the gestures, you might almost say, of an actor at the very top of his profession. Here, then, are some of the reasons why a first-class orator is one of the rarest things in the world.
Cicero, 55 BC, *On the Orator* (*De oratore*, trans. M. Grant), I, Ch. 27

25:30 Nothing is so unbelievable that oratory cannot make it acceptable.
Cicero, 46 BC, *Paradoxa Stoicorum*

25:31 Eloquence is the language of nature, and cannot be learned in the schools; but rhetoric is the creature of art, which he who feels least will most excel in.
Charles Caleb Colton, 1825, *Lacon: or, Many Things in Few Words*, I, no. 435

25:32 Someone said, Jan Yung is Good, but he is a poor talker. The Master said, What need has he to be a good talker? Those who down others with clap-trap are seldom popular. Whether he is Good, I do not know. But I see no need for him to be a good talker.
Confucius, 5th century BC, *The Analects* (trans. A. Waley), V, Sect. 4

25:33 When a gentleman has spoken, a team of four horses cannot overtake his words.
Confucius, 5th century BC, *The Analects* (trans. A. Waley), XII, Sect. 8

25:34 MIRABELL [of Petulant]: He wants Words.
  WITWOULD: Ay; but I like him for that now; for his want of Words gives me the pleasure very often to explain his meaning.
William Congreve, 1700, *The Way of the World*, I. i

25:35 'Playful – playful warbler,' said Mr. Pecksniff. It may be observed in connexion with his calling his daughter a 'warbler', that she was not at all vocal, but that Mr. Pecksniff was in the frequent habit of using any word that occurred to him as having a good sound, and rounding a sentence well, without much care for its meaning. And he did this so boldly, and in such an imposing manner, that he would sometimes stagger the wisest people with his eloquence, and make them gasp again.
Charles Dickens, 1843–4, *Martin Chuzzlewit*, Ch. 2

25:36 How empty a thing is Rhetorique! (and yet Rhetorique will make absent and remote things present to your understanding).
John Donne, 1622, *Sermon XXVI: Easter Day*, Sect. 3

25:37 Ivry gr-rcat orator ought to be accompanied by an orchesthry or, at worst, a pianist who wud play trills while th' artist was refreshin' himsilf with a glass iv ice wather.
Finley Peter Dunne, 1919, 'On the Gift of Oratory', in *Mr Dooley on Making a Will*

25:38 The eloquent man is he who is no beautiful speaker, but who is inwardly and desperately drunk with a certain belief.
Ralph Waldo Emerson, 1845, *Journals*

25:39 All the great speakers were bad speakers at first.
Ralph Waldo Emerson, 1860, 'Power', in *The Conduct of Life*

25:40 The soul of good expression is an unexpectedness, which, still, keeps to the mark of meaning, and does not betray truth.
John Galsworthy, July 1924, *On Expression*, Presidential Address to the English Association, p. 3

25:41 Persuasion is the resource of the feeble; and the feeble can seldom persuade.
Edward Gibbon, 1776–88, *The Decline and Fall of the Roman Empire*, Ch. 68

25:42 Of all kinds of success, that of an orator is the most pleasing.
Oliver Goldsmith, 17 November 1759, 'Of Eloquence', in *The Bee*, no. 7

25:43 Eloquence has preceded the rules of rhetoric, as languages have been formed before grammar.
Oliver Goldsmith, 17 November 1759, 'Of Eloquence', in *The Bee*, no. 7

25:44 Oratory is dying; a calculating age has stabbed it to the heart with innumerable dagger-thrusts of statistics.
Keith Hancock, 1930, *Australia*, p. 146

25:45 What if one does say the same things, – of course in a little different form each time, – over and over? If he has anything to say worth saying, that is just what he ought to do.
Oliver Wendell Holmes, senior, 1891, *Over the Teacups*, Ch. 1

25:46 [Odysseus, to Euryalus] A man may be quite insignificant to look at but the gods can grace his words with charm: people watch him with delight as he speaks unfalteringly with winning modesty. He stands out in the gathering and is stared at like a god when he passes through the town. Another may be handsome as an immortal, yet quite deficient in the graceful art of speech.
Homer, c.8th century BC, *The Odyssey* (trans. E. V. Rieu and D. C. H. Rieu), VIII, 170

25:47 You will have expressed yourself admirably if a clever setting gives a spice of novelty to a familiar word.
Horace, 19–18 BC, *Ars Poetica* (trans. E. H. Blakeney), 47

25:48 Talking and Eloquence are not the same: to speake, and to speake well, are two things.
Ben Jonson, 1640 (published posthumously), *Timber: or, Discoveries made upon Men and Matter*

25:49 It is a great misfortune not to possess sufficient wit to speak well, nor sufficient judgement to keep silent.
Jean de La Bruyère, 1688, 'De la société et la conversation', in *Les Caractères* (trans.), no. 5, 18

25:50 The most important things must be said simply, for they are spoiled by bombast; whereas trivial things must be described grandly, for they are supported only by aptness of expression, tone and manner.
Jean de La Bruyère, 1688, 'De la société et la conversation', in *Les Caractères* (trans.), no. 5, 77

25:51 We oftener say things because we can say them well, than because they are sound and reasonable.
Walter Savage Landor, 1824–53, 'Marcus Tullius and Quinctus Cicero', in *Imaginary Conversations*

25:52 True eloquence consists in saying all that should be said, and that only.
Duc de La Rochefoucauld, 1665, *Maxims* (trans. K. Pratt), no. 249

25:53 Eloquence lies as much in the tone of the voice, in the eyes, and in the speaker's manner, as in his choice of words.
Duc de La Rochefoucauld, 1665, *Maxims* (trans. K. Pratt), no. 250

25:54 The finest eloquence is that which gets things done and the worst is that which delays them.
David Lloyd George, 18 January 1919, speech at Paris Peace Conference, in *The Times* (20 January)

25:55 If you tie runners together you will deprive them of their speed; in exactly the same way emotion resents being hampered by conjunctions and other appendages of the kind, for it then loses its freedom of motion and the impression it gives of being shot from a catapult.
Longinus (traditional attribution; in fact by an earlier, unknown author), 1st century BC, *On the Sublime* (trans. T. S. Dorsch), Ch. 21

25:56 Though old the thought and oft exprest, / 'Tis his at last who says it best.
James Russell Lowell, 1868, 'For an Autograph', in *Under the Willows and Other Poems*

25:57 The object of oratory alone is not truth but persuasion.
Lord Macaulay, August 1824, 'Essay on Athenian Orators', in *Knight's Quarterly Magazine*

25:58 Both in the senate and when addressing individuals, use language that is seemly but not rhetorical. Be sane and wholesome in your speech.
Marcus Aurelius, 2nd century, *Meditations* (trans. M. Staniforth, 1964, Penguin), VIII, Sect. 30

25:59 Whoever God has given knowledge / and eloquence in speaking, / should not be silent or secretive, / but should willingly show it.
Marie de France, c.1170, *Lais* (trans.), Prologue

25:60 On the Continent public orators try to learn to speak fluently and smoothly; in England they take a special course in Oxonian stuttering.
George Mikes, 1946, 'A warning to beginners', *How to be an Alien*, I

25:61 It seems that it is, rather, the property of Man's wit to act readily and quickly, while the property of the judgement is to be slow and poised. But there is the same measure of oddness in the man who is struck dumb if he has no time to prepare his speech and the man who cannot take advantage and speak better when he does have time.

Michel de Montaigne, 1572–80, 'On a Ready or Hesitant Delivery', in *The Complete Essays* (trans. M. A. Screech, 1987), I, no. 10

25:62 [on verbosity] I cannot find much difference between always handling words badly and knowing nothing save how to handle them well.

Michel de Montaigne, 1572–80, 'Reflections upon Cicero', in *The Complete Essays* (trans. M. A. Screech, 1987), I, no. 40

25:63 Shame on all eloquence which leaves us with a taste for itself not for its substance.

Michel de Montaigne, 1572–80, 'Reflections upon Cicero', in *The Complete Essays* (trans. M. A. Screech, 1987), I, no. 40

25:64 Take the forms of address which stay ringing in our ears – 'My poor Master'; or 'My dear friend'; or 'Dear papa' or 'My darling daughter': if I examine them closely when their repetition grips me, I discover that the grief lies in grammar and phonetics! What affects me are the words and the intonation (just as it is not the preacher's arguments which most often move a congregation but his interjections – like the pitiful cry of a beast being slaughtered for our use).

Michel de Montaigne, 1572–80, 'On Diversion', in *The Complete Essays* (trans. M. A. Screech, 1987), III, no. 4

25:65 As for reading from a prepared script, that is not only a monstrosity but greatly to the disadvantage of those who by nature are capable of achieving anything directly.

Michel de Montaigne, 1572–80, 'On Vanity', in *The Complete Essays* (trans. M. A. Screech, 1987), III, no. 9

25:66 Spontaneous eloquence seems to me a miracle.

Vladimir Nabokov, 5 June 1962, interview, in *Strong Opinions* (1974), p. 4

25:67 A speech is poetry: cadence, rhythm, imagery, sweep . . . and reminds us that words, like children, have the power to make dance the dullest beanbag of a heart.

Peggy Noonan, 1990, *What I Saw at the Revolution*

25:68 Eloquence should persuade gently, not by force or like a tyrant or king.

Blaise Pascal, c.1654–62, *Pensées* (trans. W. F. Trotter), no. 15

25:69 Eloquence. – It requires the pleasant and the real; but the pleasant must itself be drawn from the true.

Blaise Pascal, c.1654–62, *Pensées* (trans. W. F. Trotter), no. 25

25:70 Continuous eloquence wearies.

Blaise Pascal, c.1654–62, *Pensées* (trans. W. F. Trotter), no. 355

25:71 A thing said walks in immortality / if it has been said well.

Pindar, 5th century BC, 'Isthmia 4', *Odes* (trans.)

25:72 Themistocles replied [to Xerxes, who had asked him about the affairs of Greece] that a man's discourse was like to a rich Persian carpet, the beautiful figures and patterns of which can only be shown by spreading and extending it out; when it is contracted and folded up, they are obscure and lost.

Plutarch, 1st century, 'Themistocles', in *Lives* (trans. A. H. Clough) [cf. 13:33]

25:73 He is the best orator who can turn men's ears into eyes.

Proverbial (Arabic)

25:74 When one has read the book of proverbs, no effort is needed to speak well.

Proverbial (Chinese and Mongolian)

25:75 If your pint is full, your sentence is also good.

Proverbial (Romanian)

25:76 He who speaks much must either know a lot or lie a lot.

Proverbial (German)

25:77 He who speaks well has a shield against every blow.

Proverbial (German)

25:78 Whoever speaks sweetly, eats out of a bowl of red lacquer, but he who speaks ill, eats from the chipped cover of a pot of earthenware.

Proverbial (Palaung)

25:79 One ought to speak as evenly as a rape-pod splits.

Proverbial (Tamil)

25:80 Do not speak in a studied way.

Proverbial (Tamil)

25:81 [of the perfect orator] The first essential for such a one is that he should be a good man, and consequently we demand of him not merely the possession of exceptional gifts of speech, but of all the excellences of character as well.

Quintilian, 1st century, *Institutio Oratoria* (trans. H. E. Butler), I, Preface

25:82 Words must be fitted to a Man's Mouth. 'Twas well said of the Fellow that was to make a Speech for my Lord Mayor; he desired to take measure of his Lordship's Mouth.

John Selden, 1689, 'LXXVI – Language', in *Table-Talk*

25:83 [Holofernes, on his own eloquence] This is a gift that I have, simple, simple – a foolish extravagant spirit, full of forms, figures, shapes, objects, ideas, apprehensions, motions, revolutions. These are begot in the ventricle of memory, nourished in the womb of *pia mater*, and delivered upon the mellowing of occasion. But the gift is good in those in whom it is acute, and I am thankful for it.

William Shakespeare, 1593–4, *Love's Labour's Lost*, IV. ii. 66

25:84 [Duke Theseus, of those who find themselves unable to speak well in his presence] Love, therefore, and tongue-tied simplicity / In least speak most, to my capacity.

William Shakespeare, 1594–5, *A Midsummer Night's Dream*, V. i. 104

25:85 [Solanio] Without any slips of prolixity or crossing the plain highway of talk.

William Shakespeare, 1596–7, *The Merchant of Venice*, III. i. 11

25:86 [King Harry, to Princess Catherine] But before God, Kate, I cannot look greenly, nor gasp out my eloquence, nor I have no cunning in protestation – only downright oaths, which I never use till urged, nor never break for urging. . . . For these fellows of infinite tongue, that can rhyme themselves into ladies' favours, they do always reason themselves out again. What! A speaker is but a prater, a rhyme is but a ballad.

William Shakespeare, 1599, *Henry V*, V. ii. 143, 156

25:87 [Antony] I am no orator as Brutus is, / But, as you know me all, a plain blunt man / That love my friend; and that they know full well / That gave me public leave to speak of him. / For I have neither wit, nor words, nor worth, / Action, nor utterance, nor the power of speech, / To stir men's blood. I only speak right on.

William Shakespeare, 1599, *Julius Caesar*, III. ii. 212

25:88 [Celia, of Orlando] O that's a brave man. He writes brave verses, speaks brave words, swears brave oaths, and breaks them bravely, quite traverse, athwart the heart of his lover, as a puny tilter that spurs his horse but on one side breaks his staff, like a noble goose.

William Shakespeare, 1600, *As You Like It*, III. iv. 36

25:89 [Arcite, of Palamon] He has a tongue will tame / Tempests and make the wild rocks wanton.

William Shakespeare and John Fletcher, 1613–14, *The Two Noble Kinsmen*, II. iii. 16

25:90 O let my books be then the eloquence / And dumb presagers of my speaking breast, / Who plead for love, and look for recompense / More than that tongue that more hath more expressed.

William Shakespeare, Sonnet 23, published in 1609

25:91 Be wise as thou art cruel; do not press / My tongue-tied patience with too much disdain, / Lest sorrow lend me words, and words express / The manner of my pity-wanting pain.

William Shakespeare, Sonnet 140, published in 1609

25:92 [Larry] Fine manners and fine words are cheap in Ireland.

George Bernard Shaw, 1904, *John Bull's Other Island*, II

25:93 [Julia] I'll take another opportunity of paying my respects to Mrs. Malaprop, when she shall treat me, as long as she chooses, with her select words so ingeniously misapplied, without being mispronounced.

Richard Sheridan, 1775, *The Rivals*, I. ii

25:94 [Sir Lucius O'Trigger, commenting on Delia's letter] Lucy, your lady is a great mistress of language. Faith, she's quite the queen of the dictionary! – for the devil a word dare refuse coming at her call – though one would think it was quite out of hearing.

Richard Sheridan, 1775, *The Rivals*, II. ii

25:95 [Mrs Malaprop, reacting to Captain Absolute's letter, in which she is said to 'deck her dull chat with hard words which she don't understand'] There, sir, an attack upon my language! what do you think of that? – an aspersion upon my parts of speech! was ever such a brute! Sure, if I reprehend any thing in this world it is the use of my oracular tongue, and a nice derangement of epitaphs!

Richard Sheridan, 1775, *The Rivals*, III. iii

25:96 Persuasion hung upon his lips, and the elements of Logick and Rhetorick were so blended up in him, . . . that NATURE might have stood up and said, – 'This man is eloquent'.

Laurence Sterne, 1760, *The Life and Opinions of Tristram Shandy, Gentleman*, I, Ch. 19

25:97 [of a French barber's hyperbole] All that can be said against the French sublime in this instance of it, is this: that the grandeur is *more* in the *word*; and *less* in the *thing*.

Laurence Sterne, 1768, 'The Wig', in *A Sentimental Journey*

25:98 I have always combined the study of how to live well with the study of how to speak well.

Sylvester II, 985, letter to Abrard, Abbot of Tours (trans.)

25:99 The power of vocal expression which seems naturally to belong to an American is to an ordinary Englishman very marvellous; but in America the talking man is but little esteemed.

Anthony Trollope, 1863, *Rachel Ray*, Ch. 24

25:100 The right word may be effective, but no word was ever as effective as a rightly timed pause.

Mark Twain, in A. B. Paine (ed.), *Speeches* (1923)

25:101 Take eloquence and wring its neck!

Paul Verlaine, *L'Art poétique*, 21

25:102 [of himself] And one, moreover, little graced with power / Of eloquence even in my native speech.

William Wordsworth, 1805, *The Prelude*, X, 149

25:103 [drawing a contrast with very eloquent men] Others, too, / There are among the walks of homely life / Still higher, men for contemplation framed, / Shy, and unpractised in the strife of phrase; / Meek men, whose very souls perhaps would sink / Beneath them, summoned to such intercourse: / Theirs is the language of the heavens, the power, / The thought, the image, and the silent joy: / Words are but under-agents in their souls.

William Wordsworth, 1805, *The Prelude*, XIII, 265

See also: 12:12, 14:45, 17:37, 28:58, 29:14–15, 29:58, 29:101, 47:20, 49:74, 52:37, 52:48, 59:24, 64:1, 64:15

26 *The Art of Conversation*

Conversational topics and strategies

26:1 For parlor use the vague generality is a life-saver.
George Ade, 1901, 'The Wise Piker', in *Forty Modern Fables*

26:2 There is no food more satiating than milk and honey; and just as such foods produce disgust for the palate, so perfumed and gallant words make our ears belch.
Pietro Aretino, 24 November 1537, letter to Gianfrancesco Pocopanno (trans. S. Putnam)

26:3 All men conduct their conversations in metaphors and pertinent and proper nouns.
Aristotle, 4th century BC, *The Art of Rhetoric* (trans. H. C. Lawson-Tancred), Ch. 3, Sect. 2

26:4 He that questioneth much shall learn much and content [please] much, but especially if he apply his questions to the skill of the persons whom he asketh; for he shall give them occasion to please themselves in speaking, and himself shall continually gather knowledge. But let his questions not be troublesome, for that is fit for a poser [interrogator]. And let him be sure to leave other men their turns to speak. Nay, if there be any that would reign and take up all the time, let him find means to take them off and to bring others on, as musicians use to do with those that dance too long galliards.
Francis Bacon, 1597/1625, 'Of Discourse', in *Essays*

26:5 Improvisation is the essence of good talk. Heaven defend us from the talker who doles out things prepared for us! But let heaven not less defend us from the beautifully spontaneous writer who puts his trust in the inspiration of the moment!
Max Beerbohm, 1946, 'Lytton Strachey', in *Mainly On the Air*

26:6 [of the ethnomethodology of Erving Goffman] Fruitful are the ways of our errors, and frightful too: we spend our lives in a twitter of anxiety and potential embarrassment, and there is no such thing as idle conversation.
Alan Bennett, 1981, 'Cold Sweat', reprinted in *Writing Home*, p. 307

26:7 For conversation seek intelligent men.
The Bible, Ecclesiasticus 9:15 (Jerusalem Bible)

26:8 The lips of gossips repeat the words of others; the words of wise men are carefully weighed.
The Bible, Ecclesiasticus 21:25 (Jerusalem Bible)

26:9 In a shaken sieve the rubbish is left behind; so too the defects of a man appear in his talk. The kiln tests the work of the potter; the test of a man is in his conversation. The orchard where the tree grows is judged on the quality of its fruit; similarly a man's words betray what he feels. Do not praise a man before he has spoken, since this is the test of men.
The Bible, Ecclesiasticus 27:4 (Jerusalem Bible)

26:10 When a man has a ready answer he has joy too; how satisfying is the apt reply!
The Bible, Proverbs 15:23 (Jerusalem Bible)

26:11 *Barber, n.* (Lat. *barbarus*, savage, from *barba*, the beard.) A savage whose laceration of your cheek is unobserved in the superior torment of his conversation.

Ambrose Bierce, 1911, *The Devil's Dictionary* (entry added by E. J. Hopkins for *The Enlarged Devil's Dictionary*, 1967)

26:12 *Conversation, n.* A fair for the display of the minor mental commodities, each exhibitor being too intent upon the arrangement of his own wares to observe those of his neighbor.

Ambrose Bierce, 1911, *The Devil's Dictionary*

26:13 *Discussion, n.* A method of confirming others in their errors.

Ambrose Bierce, 1911, *The Devil's Dictionary*

26:14 I was angry with my friend: / I told my wrath, my wrath did end. / I was angry with my foe: / I told it not, my wrath did grow.

William Blake, 1794, 'A Poison Tree', *Songs of Experience*

26:15 Conversation is never easy for the British, who are never keen to express themselves to strangers or, for that matter, anyone, even themselves.

Malcolm Bradbury, 1983, *Rates of Exchange*, V, Sect. 3

26:16 Like other parties of the kind, it was first silent, then talky, then argumentative, then disputatious, then unintelligible, then altogethery, then inarticulate, and then drunk.

Lord Byron, 31 October 1815, letter to Thomas Moore, in L. A. Marchand (ed.), *Byron's Letters and Journals* (1975), IV

26:17 The banalities of a great man pass for wit.

Alexander Chase, 1966, *Perspectives*

26:18 The one special advantage we enjoy over animals is our power to speak with one another, to express our thoughts in words. For this reason it is a peculiarly satisfactory experience for a man to take pleasure in conversation and seek to excel at it.

Cicero, 55 BC, *On the Orator* (*De oratore*, trans. M. Grant), I, Ch. 8

26:19 Too much agreement kills a chat.

Eldridge Cleaver, 1968, 'A Day in Folsom Prison', in *Soul on Ice*

26:20 Talk ought always to run obliquely, not nose to nose with no chance of mental escape.

Frank Moore Colby, 1926, 'Simple Simon', in *The Colby Essays*, no. 5, p. 1

26:21 It will be a beautiful family talk, mean and worried and full of sorrow and spite and excitement. I cannot be asked to miss it in my weak state. I should only fret.

Ivy Compton-Burnett, 1939, *A Family and a Fortune*, Ch. 10

26:22 Master K'ung said, There are three mistakes that are liable to be made when waiting upon a gentleman. To speak before being called upon to do so; this is called forwardness. Not to speak when called upon to do so; this is called secretiveness. To speak without first noting the expression of his face; this is called blindness.

Confucius, 5th century BC, *The Analects* (trans. A. Waley), XVI, Sect. 6

26:23 How often you and I / Had tired the sun with talking and sent him down the sky.

W. J. Cory, 1863, *Heraclitus*

26:24 Words learn'd by rote a parrot may rehearse, / But talking is not always to converse.

William Cowper, 1782, *Conversation*, 7

26:25 As alphabets in ivory employ, / Hour after hour, the yet unletter'd boy, / Sorting and puzzling with a deal of glee / Those seeds of science call'd his A B C; / So language in the mouths of the adult, / Witness its insignificant result, / Too often proves an implement of play, / A toy to sport with and pass time away.

William Cowper, 1782, *Conversation*, 11

26:26 The pipe, with solemn interposing puff, / Makes half a sentence at a time enough; / The dozing sages drop the drowsy strain, / Then pause, and puff – and speak, and pause again.

William Cowper, 1782, *Conversation*, 245

26:27 No pleasure gives the speech, when all would speak, / And all in vain a civil hearer seek.

George Crabbe, 1810, 'Letter X: Clubs and Social Meetings', 93, in *The Borough*

26:28 Is it possible to cultivate the art of conversation when living in the country all the year round?

E. M. Delafield, 1930, *The Diary of a Provincial Lady*, 7 November

26:29 He believed that the art of conversation was dead. His own small talk, at any rate, was bigger than most people's large.

Peter de Vries, 1956, *Comfort Me with Apples*, Ch. 1

26:30 'Well, Mr Meagles, say no more about it, now it's over,' urged a cheerful feminine voice.

'Over!' repeated Mr Meagles, who appeared (though without any ill-nature) to be in that peculiar state of mind in which the last word spoken by anybody else is a new injury.
Charles Dickens, 1855–7, *Little Dorrit*, I, Ch. 2

26:31 Our bore has travelled. He could not possibly be a complete bore without having travelled. He rarely speaks of his travels without introducing, sometimes on his own plan of construction, morsels of the language of the country – which he always translates.
Charles Dickens, 1858, *Our Bore*, in *Reprinted Pieces*

26:32 [on the Lammles' way of talking to each other] In these matrimonial dialogues they never addressed each other, but always some invisible presence that appeared to take a station about midway between them. Perhaps the skeleton in the cupboard comes out to be talked to, on such domestic occasions?
Charles Dickens, 1864–5, *Our Mutual Friend*, III, Ch. 12

26:33 [of being in the city of London] It is my impression that much of its serene and peaceful character is attributable to the absence of customary Talk.
Charles Dickens, 1867–8, *The Uncommercial Traveller*, Ch. 16

26:34 Villagers never swarm; a whisper is unknown among them, and they seem almost as incapable of an under tone as a cow or a stag. Your true rustic turns his back on his interlocutor, throwing a question over his shoulder as if he meant to run away from the answer, and walking a step or two farther off when the interest of a dialogue culminates.
George Eliot, 1859, *Adam Bede*, Ch. 2

26:35 If men would avoid that general language and general manner in which they strive to hide all that is peculiar, and would say only what was uppermost in their own minds, after their own individual manner, every man would be interesting.
Ralph Waldo Emerson, 1827, *Journals*

26:36 Private, accidental, confidential conversation breeds thought. Clubs produce oftener words.
Ralph Waldo Emerson, 1836, *Journals*

26:37 I learn immediately from any speaker how much he has already lived, through the poverty or splendor of his speech.
Ralph Waldo Emerson, 1837, 'The American Scholar'

26:38 Conversation is a game of circles. In conversation we pluck up the *termini* which bound the common of silence on every side.
Ralph Waldo Emerson, 1841, 'Circles', in *Essays*

26:39 I find this law of *one to one* peremptory for conversation, which is the practice and consummation of friendship. ... You shall have very useful and cheering discourse at several times with two several men, but let all three of you come together and you shall not have one new and hearty word. Two may talk and one may hear, but three cannot take part in a conversation of the most sincere and searching sort.
Ralph Waldo Emerson, 1841, 'Friendship', in *Essays*

26:40 We talk sometimes of a great talent for conversation, as if it were a permanent property in some individuals. Conversation is an evanescent relation – no more. A man is reputed to have thought and eloquence; he cannot, for all that, say a word to his cousin or his uncle.
Ralph Waldo Emerson, 1841, 'Friendship', in *Essays*

26:41 The art of conversation, or the qualification for a good companion, is a certain self-control, which now holds the subject, now lets it go, with a respect for the emergencies of the moment.
Ralph Waldo Emerson, 1854, *Journals*

26:42 The best of life is conversation, and the greatest success is confidence, or perfect understanding between sincere people.
Ralph Waldo Emerson, 1860, 'Behavior', in *The Conduct of Life*

26:43 Conversation is an art in which a man has all mankind for his competitors, for it is that which all are practising every day while they live.
Ralph Waldo Emerson, 1860, 'Considerations by the Way', in *The Conduct of Life*

26:44 Put any company of people together with freedom for conversation, and a rapid self-distribution takes place into sets and pairs. ... All conversation is a magnetic experiment.
Ralph Waldo Emerson, 1870, *Society and Solitude*

26:45 Such is the historical importance of 'griping' in this country that a man, to stand on his own feet in a powerfully changing world, must keep himself up by his own gripes.

Erik H. Erikson, 1950, *Childhood and Society*, Ch. 8

26:46 Never contradict. Never explain. Never apologize. (Those are the secrets of a happy life!)

John Fisher, 5 September 1919, letter to *The Times* [cf. 26:60, 32:76]

26:47 [following a disagreement between Fielding and Aziz] A pause in the wrong place, an intonation misunderstood and a whole conversation went awry.

E. M. Forster, 1924, *A Passage to India*, Ch. 31

26:48 An answer is always a form of death.

John Fowles, 1965, *The Magus*, Ch. 75

26:49 When you speak to a man, look on his eyes; when he speaks to you, look on his mouth.

Benjamin Franklin, 1732–57, *Poor Richard's Almanack*

26:50 Where village statesmen talked with looks profound, / And news much older than their ale went round.

Oliver Goldsmith, 1770, *The Deserted Village*, 223

26:51 In conversation, discretion is more important than eloquence.

Baltasar Gracián, 1647, *The Art of Worldly Wisdom* (trans. J. Jacobs), p. 148

26:52 More trouble is caused in the world by indiscreet answers than by indiscreet questions.

Sydney J. Harris, 27 March 1958, *Chicago Daily News* [cf. 26:134, 26:163]

26:53 Who would succeed in the world should be wise in the use of his pronouns. / Utter the You twenty times, where you once utter the I.

John Hay, c.1871, *Distichs*, 13

26:54 Wit is the salt of conversation, not the food.

William Hazlitt, 1819, 'On Wit and Humour', *Lectures on the English Comic Writers*

26:55 A person who talks with equal vivacity on every subject, excites no interest in any. Repose is as necessary in conversation as in a picture.

William Hazlitt, 1823, *Characteristics*

26:56 The soul of conversation is sympathy.

William Hazlitt, 1826, 'On the Conversation of Authors', in *The Plain Speaker*

26:57 And, when you stick on conversation's burrs, / Don't strew your pathway with those dreadful *urs*.

Oliver Wendell Holmes, senior, 1848, 'A Rhymed Lesson'

26:58 This business of conversation is a very serious matter. There are men that it weakens one to talk with an hour more than a day's fasting would do.

Oliver Wendell Holmes, senior, 1858, *The Autocrat of the Breakfast Table*, Ch. 1

26:59 The whole force of conversation depends on how much you can take for granted.

Oliver Wendell Holmes, senior, 1858, *The Autocrat of the Breakfast Table*, Ch. 3

26:60 Never explain – your friends do not need it and your enemies will not believe you anyway.

Elbert Hubbard, 1900s, in *Motto Book* (1927) [cf. 26:46]

26:61 Be yourself and speak your mind today, though it contradict all you have said before.

Elbert Hubbard, 1900s, in *Motto Book* (1927)

26:62 Is so natural to man, that the mouth is the organ both of eating and speaking. The tongue is set flowing by the bottle. Johnson talked best when he dined, – Addison could not talk at all till he drank. Table and conversation interchange their metaphors. We *devour* wit and argument, and *discuss* a turkey and chine [joint of meat]. That man must be very unhappy, or a mere hog at his trough, who is not moved to say something when he dines.

Leigh Hunt, 1851, *Table-Talk*

26:63 The perfection of conversational intercourse is when the breeding of high life is animated by the fervour of genius.

Leigh Hunt, 1851, in *Table-Talk*

26:64 If you are ever at a loss to support a flagging conversation, introduce the subject of eating.

Leigh Hunt, 1851, in *Table-Talk*

26:65 [The Duchess] Most English talk is a quadrille in a sentry box.

Henry James, 1899, *The Awkward Age*, V, Ch. 4

26:66 When two Englishmen meet, their first talk is of the weather.

Samuel Johnson, 1758, *The Idler*, no. 11

26:67 Gossip is the opiate of the oppressed.

Erica Jong, 1973, *Fear of Flying*, Ch. 6

26:68 Encounters with people of so many different kinds and on so many different psychological levels have been for me incomparably more important than fragmentary conversations with celebrities. The finest and most significant conversations of my life were anonymous.

Carl Gustav Jung, 1962, *Memories, Dreams, Reflections*, Ch. 4

26:69 As long as the answer is right, who cares if the question is wrong?

Norton Juster, 1976, *The Phantom Tollbooth*, Ch. 14

26:70 Conversation is not a search after knowledge, but an endeavour at effect.

John Keats, 10–11 May 1817, letter to Benjamin Robert Haydon

26:71 In telegraphic sentences, half nodded to their friends, / They hint a matter's inwardness – and there the matter ends. / And while the Celt is talking from Valencia to Kirkwall, / The English – ah, the English! don't say anything at all.

Rudyard Kipling, 1906, 'The Puzzler'

26:72 A gossip is one who talks to you about others; a bore is one who talks to you about himself; and a brilliant conversationalist is one who talks to you about yourself.

Lisa Kirk, 9 March 1954, *New York Journal-American*

26:73 The success of conversation consists less in being witty than in bringing out wit in others; the man who leaves after talking with you, pleased with himself and his own wit, is perfectly pleased with you.

Jean de La Bruyère, 1688, 'De la société et la conversation', in *Les Caractères* (trans.), no. 5, 16

26:74 Confidence contributes more to conversation than wit.

Duc de La Rochefoucauld, 1665, *Maxims* (trans. K. Pratt), no. 421

26:75 Good communication is stimulating as black coffee, and just as hard to sleep after.

Anne Lindbergh, 1955, 'Argonauta', in *Gift from the Sea*

26:76 It is notorious that we speak no more than half-truths in our ordinary conversation, and even a soliloquy is likely to be affected by the apprehension that walls have ears.

Eric Linklater, 1931, *Juan in America*, II, Part 4

26:77 No one will ever shine in conversation, who thinks of saying fine things: to please, one must say many things indifferent, and many very bad.

Dean Lockier, in Joseph Spence, *Anecdotes, Observations, and Characters of Books and Men* (1820)

26:78 Conversation is like playing tennis with a ball made of Krazy Putty that keeps coming back over the net in a different shape.

David Lodge, 1984, *Small World*, I, Ch. 1

26:79 A single conversation across the table with a wise man is better than ten years' mere study of books.

Henry Wadsworth Longfellow, 1839, *Hyperion*, Ch. 1

26:80 The great pleasure of ignorance is the pleasure of asking questions. The man who has lost this pleasure or exchanged it for the pleasure of dogma, which is the pleasure of answering, is already beginning to stiffen.

Robert Lynd, 'The Pleasures of Ignorance', in *I Was Just Thinking* (1959)

26:81 At a dinner party one should eat wisely but not too well, and talk well but not too wisely.

W. Somerset Maugham, 1896, *A Writer's Notebook* (1949)

26:82 Do you know that conversation is one of the greatest pleasures in life? But it wants leisure.

W. Somerset Maugham, 1921, 'The Fall of Edward Barnard', in *The Trembling of a Leaf*

26:83 It is not enough to possess wit. One must have enough of it to avoid having too much.

André Maurois, 1921, *On Conversation* (trans.)

26:84 The art of dialling has replaced the art of dialogue.

Gita Mehta, 1991, *Karma Cola*, Ch. 8

26:85 We do not talk – we bludgeon one another with facts and theories gleaned from cursory readings of newspapers, magazines and digests.

Henry Miller, 1945, 'The Shadows', in *The Air-Conditioned Nightmare*

26:86 Open talk opens the way to further talk, as wine does or love.

Michel de Montaigne, 1572–80, 'On the Useful and the Honourable', in *The Complete Essays* (trans. M. A. Screech, 1987), III, no. 1

26:87 To my taste the most fruitful and most natural exercise of our minds is conversation. I find the practice of it the most delightful activity in our lives.

Michel de Montaigne, 1572–80, 'On the Art of Conversation', in *The Complete Essays* (trans. M. A. Screech, 1987), III, no. 8

26:88 In conversation the most painful quality is perfect harmony.

Michel de Montaigne, 1572–80, 'On the Art of Conversation', in *The Complete Essays* (trans. M. A. Screech, 1987), III, no. 8

26:89 What a delicate and rare and gracious art is the art of conversation! With what a dexterity and skill the bubble of speech must be maneuvered if mind is to meet and mingle with mind.

Christopher Morley, 1919, 'What Men Live By', in *Mince Pie*

26:90 Talk is so solemn a rite it should be approached with prayer and must be conducted with nicety and forbearance.

Christopher Morley, 1919, 'What Men Live By', in *Mince Pie*

26:91 If we had our way, we would set aside one day a week for talking.

Christopher Morley, 1919, 'What Men Live By', in *Mince Pie*

26:92 Rumors are a kind of exhalation or intellectual perfume thrown off by the news of the day.

Christopher Morley, 1919, 'As to Rumors', in *Mince Pie*

26:93 Another good thing about gossip is that it is within everybody's reach, / And it is much more interesting than any other form of speech.

Ogden Nash, 1938, 'I Have it on Good Authority', in *I'm a Stranger Here Myself*

26:94 A little bit of gossip does me good.

Ogden Nash, 1938, 'This was Told me in Confidence', in *I'm a Stranger Here Myself*

26:95 No pastime such diversion lends / As talking friends over analytically with friends.

Ogden Nash, 1940, 'Hush, Here they Come', in *The Face is Familiar*

26:96 Persons who have something to say like to talk about the arts and politics and economics, / And even the cultural aspects of the comics. / Among persons who have nothing to say the conversational content worsens; / They talk about other persons.

Ogden Nash, 1957, 'Never Mind the Overcoat,

Button up that Lip', in *You Can't Get There From Here*

26:97 [of a remark by Thomas Fuller] The best way of beginning a sentence, if a man should be out and forget his last sentence (which he never was), that then his last refuge is to begin with an Utcunque [however].

Samuel Pepys, 22 January 1661, *Diary*

26:98 In our social relations, the race is not to the swift but to the verbal.

Steven Pinker, 1994, *The Language Instinct*, Ch. 1

26:99 The more the pleasures of the body fade away, the greater to me is the pleasure and charm of conversation.

Plato, 4th century BC, *The Republic* (trans.)

26:100 At ev'ry word a reputation dies.

Alexander Pope, 1714, *The Rape of the Lock*, Canto 3, 16

26:101 Wit in conversation is only a readiness of thought and a facility of expression, or (in the midwives' phrase) a quick conception, and an easy delivery.

Alexander Pope, 1727, *Thoughts on Various Subjects*

26:102 In conversation play, the important thing is to get in early and stay there. There are always some slow or feeble-witted people in any conversation group who will turn their heads towards the *man who gets going first*.

Stephen Potter, 1950, *Lifemanship*, Ch. 1

26:103 No answer is also an answer.

Proverbial (German)

26:104 Without conversation there is no agreement.

Proverbial (Montenegrin)

26:105 Be not too brief in conversation lest you be not understood, nor too diffuse lest you be troublesome.

Proverbial (Portuguese)

26:106 Conversation is a ladder for a journey.

Proverbial (Sinhalese)

26:107 Conversation on a journey is equal to a conveyance.

Proverbial (Tamil)

26:108 A good conversation is better than a good bed.

Proverbial (Oromo)

26:109 Conversation is the food of the ears.
Proverbial (Creole)

26:110 Conversation is like dry meat; its savour abides.
Proverbial (Tanzanian)

26:111 Discourse is a distaff for spinning.
Proverbial (Maltese)

26:112 Who gossips to you will gossip of you.
Proverbial

26:113 Gossip needs no carriage.
Proverbial (Russian)

26:114 Gossiping and lying are brother and sister.
Proverbial (Kenyan)

26:115 Greeting draws talk.
Proverbial (Moorish)

26:116 Empty greetings go barefoot.
Proverbial (Swedish)

26:117 A good question is like one beating a bell.
Proverbial (Chinese)

26:118 'Tis not every question that deserves an answer.
Proverbial

26:119 By saying and contradicting, a thing is carried through the town.
Proverbial (Swedish)

26:120 He who speaks much of others burns his tongue.
Proverbial (German)

26:121 When you speak of the oil-palm no wine-palm should be near. [Don't speak of anyone in the hearing of their relatives.]
Proverbial (Cameroon)

26:122 He who speaks without being answered, how great is his pain?
Proverbial (Swahili)

26:123 One man's speech is only half a speech.
Proverbial (German)

26:124 One story is good till another's told.
Proverbial

26:125 A good tale, ill told, is marred in the telling.
Proverbial

26:126 Fore-talk spares after-talk.
Proverbial (German)

26:127 When you meet men or devils, talk as they do.
Proverbial (Chinese)

26:128 I find it quite remarkable, don't you, how people always take offence when a conversation ceases to be personal?
Frederic Raphael, 1976, 'An Academic Life', in *The Glittering Prizes*

26:129 It is not what we learn in conversation that enriches us. It is the elation that comes of swift contact with tingling currents of thought.
Agnes Repplier, 1904, 'The Luxury of Conversation', in *Compromises*

26:130 When roused by passion, I can sometimes find the right words to say, but in ordinary conversation I can find none, none at all. I find conversation unbearable owing to the very fact that I am obliged to speak.
Jean-Jacques Rousseau, 1770, *The Confessions* (trans. J. M. Cohen), I: 1723–8

26:131 In private conversation there is always another dificulty, which I consider worse, the necessity of always talking. You have to reply each time you are spoken to, and if the conversation fails, to set it going again. This unbearable constraint would be enough in itself to disgust me with society. I can think of no greater torture than to be obliged to talk continually and without a moment for reflection.
Jean-Jacques Rousseau, 1770, *The Confessions* (trans. J. M. Cohen), III: 1731–2

26:132 Nothing so narrows the mind, nothing engenders more nonsense – tales and mischief, gossiping and lies – than for people to be eternally confined in one another's company, in one room, reduced, for lack of anything to do, to the necessity of incessant chatter. When everyone is busy, no one speaks unless he has something to say. But when one is doing nothing it is imperative to talk all the time; and that is the most wearisome and the most dangerous of all forms of constraint.
Jean-Jacques Rousseau, 1770, *The Confessions* (trans. J. M. Cohen), V: 1732–8

26:133 [on his relationship with his wife] A

twelve-year-old affection had no more need of words. We knew one another too well to have anything fresh to say. The only resources left us were trivialities, scandal, and bad puns.

Jean-Jacques Rousseau, 1770, *The Confessions* (trans. J. M. Cohen), IX: 1756

26:134 There aren't any embarrassing questions – just embarrassing answers.

Carl Rowan, 7 December 1963, *New Yorker* [cf. 26:52, 26:163]

26:135 Whoever interrupts the conversation of others to make a display of his fund of knowledge, makes notorious his own stock of ignorance.

Sadi, 1258, *Gulistan [Rose Garden]* (trans. J. Ross), Sect. 8.95

26:136 I can feel a desire to gossip coming over me. I don't want to give in to it; narrative style should always be brief.

Madame de Sévigné, 17 November 1664, 'To Pomponne', in *Selected Letters* (trans. L. Tancock)

26:137 [Biron, of Boyet] This fellow pecks up wit as pigeons peas, / And utters it again when God doth please. / He is wit's pedlar, and retails his wares / At wakes and wassails, meetings, markets, fairs.

William Shakespeare, 1593–4, *Love's Labour's Lost*, V. ii. 315

26:138 [Adriana] If voluble and sharp discourse be marred, / Unkindness blunts it more than marble hard.

William Shakespeare, 1594, *The Comedy of Errors*, II. i. 91

26:139 [Bastard] And when my knightly stomach is sufficed, / Why then I suck my teeth and catechize / My picked men of countries. 'My dear sir,' / Thus leaning on mine elbow I begin, 'I shall beseech you –'. That is Question now; / And then comes Answer like an Absey book. 'O sir,' says Answer, 'at your best command, / At your employment, at your service, sir.' 'No, sir,' says Question, 'I, sweet sir, at yours.' And so, ere Answer knows what Question would, / Saving in dialogue of compliment, / And talking of the Alps and Apennines, / The Pyrenean and the River Po, / It draws towards supper in conclusion so.

William Shakespeare, 1595–6, *King John*, I. i. 191

26:140 Teas, / Where small talk dies in agonies.

Percy Bysshe Shelley, 1819, *Peter Bell the Third*, 204

26:141 I must own, it makes me very melancholy in Company, when I hear a young Man begin a Story; and have often observed, That one of a Quarter of an Hour long in a Man of Five and twenty, gathers Circumstances every Time he tells it, till it grows into a long, *Canterbury* Tale of two Hours by that Time he is Threescore.

Richard Steele, 10 February 1709, 'The Club at the Trumpet', *The Tatler*, no. 132

26:142 I have more than once taken Notice of an indecent License taken in Discourse, wherein the Conversation on one Part is involuntary, and the Effect of some necessary Circumstance. This happens in travelling together in the same hired Coach, sitting near each other in any publick Assembly, or the like.

Richard Steele, 28 August 1711, 'The Coffee-house Again', *The Spectator*, no. 155

26:143 The sound of tireless voices is the price we pay for the right to hear the music of our own opinions.

Adlai Stevenson, 28 August 1952, speech in New York City

26:144 There can be no fairer ambition than to excel in talk; to be affable, gay, ready, clear, and welcome.

Robert Louis Stevenson, 1882, *Talk and Talkers*, Sect. 1

26:145 [Queen] Plain speech is better than much wit.

Algernon Charles Swinburne, 1865, *Chastelard*, II. i

26:146 It is better to ask some of the questions than to know all of the answers.

James Thurber, 1945, 'The Scotty who Knew Too Much', in *The Thurber Carnival*

26:147 For the most of us, if we do not talk of ourselves, or at any rate of the individual circles of which we are the centres, we can talk of nothing. I cannot hold with those who wish to put down the insignificant chatter of the world.

Anthony Trollope, 1860, *Framley Parsonage*, Ch. 10

26:148 When in danger, ponder. When in trouble, delegate. And when in doubt, mumble.

Robert F. Wagner, junior, 17 February 1991, *New York Times*

26:149 Good company and good discourse are the very sinews of virtue.

Izaak Walton, 1653, *The Compleat Angler*, I, Ch. 2

26:150 It is difficult to be emphatic when no one is emphatic on the other side.

Charles Dudley Warner, 1871, 'Thirteenth Week', in *My Summer in a Garden*

26:151 That talk must be very well in hand, and under great headway, that an anecdote thrown in front of will not pitch off the track and wreck.

Charles Dudley Warner, 1873, 'Third Study', in *Backlog Studies*

26:152 Ambrose lived in and for conversation; he rejoiced in the whole intricate art of it.

Evelyn Waugh, 1942, *Put Out More Flags*, Ch. 1

26:153 [Anthony Blanche] Conversation should be like juggling; up go the balls and the plates, up and over, in and out, good solid objects that glitter in the footlights and fall with a bang if you miss them.

Evelyn Waugh, 1945, *Brideshead Revisited*, Ch. 2

26:154 Conversation is imperative if gaps are to be filled, and old age, it is the last gap but one.

Patrick White, 1955, *The Tree of Man*, Ch. 22

26:155 Exercise! . . . the only possible exercise is to talk, not to walk.

Oscar Wilde, c.1874, in Richard Ellmann, *Oscar Wilde* (1987), Ch. 2

26:156 Talk itself is a sort of spiritualised action.

Oscar Wilde, 4 May 1887, 'Should Geniuses Meet?', in *Court and Society Review*, no. 4, p. 148

26:157 [Lord Henry] There is only one thing in the world worse than being talked about, and that is not being talked about.

Oscar Wilde, 1890, *The Picture of Dorian Gray*, Ch. 1

26:158 If one hears bad music, it is one's duty to drown it in conversation.

Oscar Wilde, 1890, *The Picture of Dorian Gray*, Ch. 4

26:159 Learned conversation is either the affectation of the ignorant or the profession of the mentally unemployed.

Oscar Wilde, 1891, 'The Critic as Artist', in *Intentions*

26:160 LORD WINDERMERE: What is the difference between scandal and gossip?

CECIL GRAHAM: Oh! gossip is charming! His-tory is merely gossip. But scandal is gossip made tedious by morality.

Oscar Wilde, 1892, *Lady Windermere's Fan*, III

26:161 MRS ALLONBY: You should certainly know Ernest, Lady Stutfield. It is only fair to tell you beforehand he has got no conversation at all.

LADY STUTFIELD: I adore silent men.

MRS ALLONBY: Oh, Ernest isn't silent. He talks the whole time. But he has got no conversation. What he talks about I don't know. I haven't listened to him for years.

Oscar Wilde, 1893, *A Woman of No Importance*, II

26:162 [Lord Illingworth, to Gerald] Talk to every woman as if you loved her, and to every man as if he bored you, and at the end of your first season you will have the reputation of possessing the most perfect social tact.

Oscar Wilde, 1893, *A Woman of No Importance*, III

26:163 [Mrs Cheveley, to Sir Robert Chiltern] Questions are never indiscreet. Answers sometimes are.

Oscar Wilde, 1895, *An Ideal Husband*, I [cf. 26:52, 26:134]

26:164 [Mrs Cheveley, to Lord Goring] If one could only teach the English how to talk, and the Irish how to listen, society here would be quite civilized.

Oscar Wilde, 1895, *An Ideal Husband*, III

26:165 'What ho!' I said. 'What ho!' said Motty. 'What ho! What ho!' 'What ho! What ho! What ho!' After that it seemed rather difficult to go on with the conversation.

P. G. Wodehouse, 1919, 'Jeeves and the Unbidden Guest', in *My Man Jeeves*

26:166 And for this cause to thee / I speak, unapprehensive of contempt, / The insinuated scoff of coward tongues, / And all that silent language which so soft / In conversation between man and man / Blots from the human countenance all trace / Of beauty and of love.

William Wordsworth, 1805, *The Prelude*, II, 454

See also: 5:79, 9:15, 11:8, 19:2, 19:9, 20:9, 20:20, 21:6, 21:61, 21:83, 23:79, 27:6–8, 27:18–19, 27:32, 34:5, 35:19, 46:4, 48:24, 50:26, 52:3, 52:37, 62:41–2, 64:21, 64:23, 64:58

Topics, knowledge, opinions, and beliefs as expressed by language

27:1 I prefer a noble Sentiment that is depressed with homely Language, infinitely before a vulgar one that is blown up with all the Sound and Energy of Expression.
Joseph Addison, 14 April 1711, 'English Tragedy: Style, Language and Verse', *The Spectator*, no. 39

27:2 Wit, as he defines it, is 'a Propriety of Words and Thoughts adapted to the Subject.' If this be a true Definition of Wit, I am apt to think that *Euclid* was the greatest Wit that ever set Pen to Paper.
Joseph Addison, 11 May 1711, 'True, False and Mixed Wit', *The Spectator*, no. 62 [cf. 2:29]

27:3 AESCHYLUS: Schoolboys have a master to teach them, grown-ups have the poets. We have a duty to see that what we teach them is right and proper.
EURIPEDES: And you think that the right and proper way to teach them is to write your kind of high-flown Olympian language, instead of talking like a human being?
AESCHYLUS: My poor dear fellow, noble themes and noble sentiments must be couched in suitably dignified language. If your characters are demigods, they should talk like demigods.
Aristophanes, 405 BC, *The Frogs* (trans. D. Barrett), II

27:4 Ye know not, what hurt ye do to learning, that cares not for wordes, but for matter.
Roger Ascham, 1582, *The Scholemaster*

27:5 [on reading worthless stories] I have nothing against the words themselves. They are like choice and costly glasses, but they contain the wine of error which had already gone to the heads of the teachers who poured it out for us to drink.
St Augustine, 397–8, *Confessions* (trans. R. S. Pine-Coffin), I, Sect. 16

27:6 On every formal visit a child ought to be of the party, by way of provision for discourse.
Jane Austen, 1811, *Sense and Sensibility*, II, Ch. 6

27:7 The honourablest part of talk is to give the occasion [suggest the topic], and again to moderate and pass to somewhat else, for then a man leads the dance.
Francis Bacon, 1597/1625, 'Of Discourse', in *Essays*

27:8 Speech of touch towards others [relating to individuals] should be sparingly used, for discourse ought to be as a field, without coming home to any man.
Francis Bacon, 1597/1625, 'Of Discourse', in *Essays*

27:9 Here therefore is the first distemper [abuse] of learning, when men study words and not matter.
Francis Bacon, 1605, *The Advancement of Learning*, I

27:10 For as substance of matter is better than beauty of words, so contrariwise vain matter is worse than vain words.
Francis Bacon, 1605, *The Advancement of Learning*, I

27:11 *Prejudice, n.* A vagrant opinion without visible means of support.
Ambrose Bierce, 1911, *The Devil's Dictionary*

27:12 Without deviation, without exception, without any ifs, buts, or whereases, freedom of speech means you shall not do something to people for views they have, express, speak, or write.

Hugo Black, quoted in Irving Dillard (ed.), *One Man's Stand for Freedom* (1963)

27:13 And here's the secret of a hundred creeds, – / Men get opinions as boys learn to spell / By re-iteration chiefly.

Elizabeth Barrett Browning, 1856, *Aurora Leigh*, VI, 5

27:14 If people would dare to speak to one another unreservedly, there would be a good deal less sorrow in the world a hundred years hence.

Samuel Butler (1835–1902), 1903, *The Way of All Flesh*, Ch. 44

27:15 Whate'er the scene, let this advice have weight: – / Adapt your language to your hero's state.

Lord Byron, 1811, *Hints From Horace*, 127

27:16 There is nothing so absurd but some philosopher has said it.

Cicero, 45–44 BC, *De divinatione*, II, Ch. 119

27:17 Ignorance is a blank sheet, on which we may write; but error is a scribbled one, on which we must first erase.

Charles Caleb Colton, 1825, *Lacon: or, Many Things in Few Words*, I, no. 1

27:18 Nonsense, in fact, is a very difficult thing. Not every seventh son of a seventh son (to use Milton's words) is equal to the task of keeping and maintaining a company of decent men in orthodox nonsense for a matter of two hours.

Thomas De Quincey, 1856, revision of *Confessions of an English Opium Eater* (1822), Sect. 14

27:19 Come from what fountain it may, all talk that succeeds to the extent of raising a wish to meet the talker again, must contain *salt*; must be seasoned with some flavouring element pungent enough to neutralise the natural tendencies of all mixed conversation, not vigilantly tended, to lose itself in insipidities and platitudes.

Thomas De Quincey, 1856, revision of *Confessions of an English Opium Eater* (1822), Sect. 14

27:20 A thing well said will be wit in all languages . . . though it may lose something in the translation.

John Dryden, 1668, *An Essay of Dramatic Poesy*

27:21 When you don't like something the words come more readily.

Clement Greenberg, 3 October 1991, *New York Times*

27:22 Knowledge can be communicated, but not wisdom. One can find it, live it, be fortified by it, do wonders through it, but one cannot communicate and teach it.

Herman Hesse, 1923, 'Govinda', in *Siddhartha* (trans. H. Rosner)

27:23 The secret of all good writing is sound judgement. . . . Get the facts in clear perspective and the words will follow naturally.

Horace, 19–18 BC, *Ars Poetica* (trans. E. H. Blakeney), 309

27:24 Facts are ventriloquist's dummies. Sitting on a wise man's knee they may be made to utter words of wisdom; elsewhere they say nothing, or talk nonsense.

Aldous Huxley, 1945, *Time Must Have a Stop*

27:25 I am not yet so lost in lexicography, as to forget that *words are the daughters of earth, and that things are the sons of heaven*. Language is only the instrument of science, and words are but the signs of ideas: I wish, however, that the instrument might be less apt to decay, and that signs might be permanent, like the things which they denote.

Samuel Johnson, 1755, *A Dictionary of the English Language*, Preface [cf. 3:36]

27:26 The test of interesting people is that subject matter doesn't matter.

Louis Kronenberger, 1954, *Company Manners*, Ch. 3

27:27 We would rather speak badly of ourselves than not talk about ourselves at all.

Duc de La Rochefoucauld, 1665, *Maxims* (trans. K. Pratt), no. 138

27:28 The extreme pleasure we take in speaking of ourselves should make us apprehensive that it gives hardly any to those who listen to us.

Duc de La Rochefoucauld, 1665, *Maxims* (trans. K. Pratt), no. 314

27:29 Great people talk about ideas, average people talk about things, and small people talk about wine.

Fran Lebowitz, 1981, 'People', in *Social Studies*

27:30 [on sexuality] As soon as you deal with it explicitly, you are forced to choose between

the language of the nursery, the gutter and the anatomy class.
C. S. Lewis, quoted in Kenneth Tynan, *In Search of C. S. Lewis* (1975), p. 154

27:31 Impropriety is the soul of wit.
W. Somerset Maugham, 1919, *The Moon and Sixpence*

27:32 On my travels, in order to be ever learning something from my meetings with other people (which is one of the best of all schools), I observe the following practice: always to bring those with whom I am talking back to the subjects they know best. . . . For the reverse usually happens, everyone choosing to orate about another's job rather than his own, reckoning to increase his reputation by so doing.
Michel de Montaigne, 1572–80, 'The Doings of Certain Ambassadors', in *The Complete Essays* (trans. M. A. Screech, 1987), I, no. 17

27:33 Nowhere are defects of style more obvious than when the subject-matter itself has little to commend it.
Michel de Montaigne, 1572–80, 'On Vanity', in *The Complete Essays* (trans. M. A. Screech, 1987), III, no. 9

27:34 Subjects choose me . . . I lie in wait like a leopard on a branch-strained metaphor.
Marianne Moore, quoted by Louis Untermeyer in 'Five Famous Poetesses', *Ladies' Home Journal* (May 1964)

27:35 Talking about oneself can also be a means to conceal oneself.
Friedrich Nietzsche, 1886, *Beyond Good and Evil* (trans. W. Kaufmann), p. 169

27:36 The sum of human wisdom is not contained in any one language, and no single language is capable of expressing all forms and degrees of human comprehension.
Ezra Pound, 1934, *The ABC of Reading*, Ch. 1

27:37 There are three hundred and forty-six subjects for elegant conversation.
Proverbial (Chinese)

27:38 Three days' neglect of study leaves one's conversation flavourless.
Proverbial (Chinese)

27:39 The truest jests sound worst in guilty ears.
Proverbial

27:40 Some say what they know and some know what they say.
Proverbial (Spanish)

27:41 It is easier to speak than to say something.
Proverbial (Russian and Ukrainian)

27:42 One who can speak, speaks of the city; one who can't, speaks merely of household affairs.
Proverbial (Chinese)

27:43 Those who can speak well have not always the best things to say.
Proverbial (Chinese)

27:44 Children talk about what they are doing; old people about what they used to do; fools about what they ought to be doing; courageous people about what they want to do; the wise about what is meet to do.
Proverbial (Croatian)

27:45 The tongue will reach a point when skins of flies can be sewn together. [The tongue speaks on so many matters, that it would be impossible to put them all together.]
Proverbial (Sotho)

27:46 Experience is always larger than language.
Adrienne Rich, 1991, interview in *American Poetry Review* (Jan/Feb)

27:47 [Giacomo] I am the master of my speeches, and would undergo what's spoken, I swear.
William Shakespeare, 1610–11, *Cymbeline*, I. iv. 138

27:48 Nothing has yet been said that has not been said before.
Terence, 161 BC, *Eunuchus [The Eunuch]* (trans.), Prologue, 41

27:49 I disapprove of what you say, but I will defend to the death your right to say it.
Voltaire, 18th century, attributed in S. G. Tallentyre, *The Friends of Voltaire* (1906), Ch. 7 [cf. 35:29]

27:50 [on hearing an old woman talk about her dead husband] Is there not / An art, a music, and a strain of words / That shall be life, the acknowledged voice of life, / Shall speak of what is done among the fields, / Done truly there, or felt, of solid good / And real evil, yet be sweet withal, / More grateful, more harmonious than the breath, / The idle breath of softest pipe attuned / To pastoral fancies?
William Wordsworth, c.1800, *The Recluse*, 401

See also: 2:29, 2:37, 25:22, 25:50, 26:96, 26:133, 52:30, 60:13, 65:17

28 *Language Clear and Unclear*

Obscurity, vagueness, imprecision, ambiguity, and other issues of clarity

28:1 Obscurity often brings safety.
Aesop, ?6th century BC, 'The Tree and the Reed', in *Fables*

28:2 I said, 'By the way, Bailey, Mrs Flowers sent you some tea cookies – ' Momma shouted, 'What did you say, Sister? You, Sister, what did you say?' Hot anger was crackling in her voice. . . . [and after being punished] I found that my violation lay in using the phrase 'by the way.' Momma explained that 'Jesus was the Way, the Truth and the Light,' and anyone who says 'by the way' is really saying 'by Jesus', or 'by God' and the Lord's name would not be taken in vain in her house. When Bailey tried to interpret the words with: 'Whitefolks use "by the way" to mean while we're on the subject,' Momma reminded us that 'whitefolks' mouths were most in general loose and their words were an abomination before Christ'.
Maya Angelou, 1969, *I Know Why the Caged Bird Sings*, Ch. 15

28:3 A man sometimes makes a slip, without meaning what he says; and which of us has never sinned by speech?
The Bible, Ecclesiasticus 19:16 (Jerusalem Bible)

28:4 Better a slip on the pavement than a slip of the tongue.
The Bible, Ecclesiasticus 20:18 (Jerusalem Bible)

28:5 It may be that universal history is the history of the different intonations given a handful of metaphors.
Jorge Luis Borges, 1952, 'La esfera de Pascal [The fearful sphere of Pascal]', in *Otras inquisiciones* (trans.)

28:6 Ambiguity is dangerous in utilitarian language, but it provides the harmonics of the complicated music of literature.
Anthony Burgess, 1992, *A Mouthful of Air*, II, Ch. 11

28:7 For talking idly is admir'd, / And speaking nonsense held inspir'd.
Samuel Butler (1612–80), 1670s, 'On a Hypocritical Nonconformist'

28:8 And dullest nonsense has been found / By some to be the solid'st and the most profound.
Samuel Butler (1612–80), 1670s, 'On a Hypocritical Nonconformist'

28:9 I do not mind lying, but I hate inaccuracy.
Samuel Butler (1835–1902), *The Note-Books of Samuel Butler* (1912)

28:10 [Bruno] 'I'm counting the Pigs in the field!' 'How many are there?' I enquired. 'About a thousand and four,' said Bruno. 'You mean "about a thousand",' Sylvie corrected him. 'There's no good saying "*and four*": you *ca'n't* be sure about the four!' 'And you're as wrong as ever!' Bruno exclaimed triumphantly. 'It's just the *four* I *can* be sure about; 'cause they're here, grubbing under the window! It's the *thousand* I isn't pruffickly sure about!'
Lewis Carroll, 1893, *Sylvie and Bruno Concluded*, Ch. 5

28:11 [Mein Herr] 'Which of your teachers do you value the most highly, those whose words are easily understood, or those who puzzle you at every turn?' I feel obliged to admit that we generally admired most the teachers we couldn't quite understand.

Lewis Carroll, 1893, *Sylvie and Bruno Concluded*, Ch. 19

28:12 A man does not know what he is saying until he knows what he is not saying.

G. K. Chesterton, 1936, 'About Impenitence', in *As I was Saying*

28:13 Unusual and new coined words are doubtless an evil; but vagueness, confusion, and imperfect conveyance of our thoughts, are a far greater.

Samuel Taylor Coleridge, 1817, *Biographia Literaria*, Ch. 12

28:14 [on refusing to describe his combat against his 'abiding sickness'] I attempt no description of this combat, knowing the unintelligibility and the repulsiveness of all attempts to communicate the Incommunicable.

Thomas De Quincey, 1856, revision of the Preface to *Confessions of an English Opium Eater* (1822)

28:15 [on the meeting between Pogram and the three literary ladies] Suffice it, that being all four out of their depths, and all unable to swim, they splashed up words in all directions, and floundered about famously.

Charles Dickens, 1843–4, *Martin Chuzzlewit*, Ch. 34

28:16 [David] I had been reading to Peggotty about crocodiles. I must have read very perspicuously, or the poor soul must have been deeply interested, for I remember she had a cloudy impression, after I had done, that they were a sort of vegetable.

Charles Dickens, 1849–50, *David Copperfield*, Ch. 2

28:17 [Guster] announces that Mr and Mrs Chadband have appeared in the Court. The bell at the inner door in the passage immediately thereafter tinkling, she is admonished by Mrs Snagsby, on pain of instant reconsignment to her patron saint, not to omit the ceremony of announcement. Much discomposed in her nerves (which were previously in the best order) by this threat, she so fearfully mutilates that point of state as to announce 'Mr and Mrs Cheeseming, least which, I meantersay, whatsername!' and retires conscience-stricken from the presence.

Charles Dickens, 1852–3, *Bleak House*, Ch. 19

28:18 As long as words a different sense will bear, / And each may be his own interpreter, /

Our airy faith will no foundation find; / The word's a weathercock for every wind.

John Dryden, 1687, 'The Hind and the Panther', I, 462

28:19 [Fedelma] Our words have wings, but fly not where we would.

George Eliot, 1868, 'The Spanish Gypsy'

28:20 Out of the slimy mud of words, out of the sleet and hail of verbal imprecisions, / Approximate thoughts and feelings, words that have taken the place of thoughts and feelings, / There spring the perfect order of speech, and the beauty of incantation.

T. S. Eliot, 1934, *Choruses from 'The Rock'*, no. IX

28:21 Words strain, / Crack and sometimes break, under the burden, / Under the tension, slip, slide, perish, / Decay with imprecision, will not stay in place, / Will not stay still. Shrieking voices / Scolding, mocking, or merely chattering, / Always assail them.

T. S. Eliot, 1944, 'Burnt Norton', Part 5, in *Four Quartets*

28:22 So here I am, in the middle way, having had twenty years – / Twenty years largely wasted, the years of *l'entre deux guerres* – / Trying to learn to use words, and every attempt / Is a wholly new start, and a different kind of failure / Because one has only learnt to get the better of words / For the thing one no longer has to say, or the way in which / One is no longer disposed to say it. And so each venture / Is a new beginning, a raid on the inarticulate / With shabby equipment always deteriorating / In the general mess of imprecision of feeling, / Undisciplined squads of emotion.

T. S. Eliot, 1944, 'East Coker', Part 5, in *Four Quartets*

28:23 I hope / I've done nothing so monosyllabic as to cheat, / A spade is never so merely a spade as the word / Spade would imply.

Christopher Fry, 1950, *Venus Observed*, II. i

28:24 The novel is born from the very fact that we do not understand one another any longer, because unitary, orthodox language has broken down.

Carlos Fuentes, 24 February 1989, in the *Guardian*

28:25 [Pooh-Bah, defending himself] Merely corroborative detail, intended to give artistic verisimilitude to an otherwise bald and unconvincing narrative.

W. S. Gilbert, 1885, *The Mikado*, II

28:26 Names are but noise and smoke, / Obscuring heavenly light.

Goethe, 1808, 'Martha's Garden', in *Faust* (trans. P. Wayne), I

28:27 No one would talk much in society, if he only knew how often he misunderstands others.

Goethe, 1809, *Elective Affinities* (trans.), p. 22

28:28 Since I've become a central banker, I've learned to mumble with great coherence . . . If I seem unduly clear to you, you must have misunderstood what I said.

Alan Greenspan, 1987, speech to Congress, quoted in the *San Francisco Chronicle* (9 June 1995)

28:29 I worry incessantly that I might be too clear.

Alan Greenspan, 25 June 1995, *New York Times*

28:30 Obscurity is the refuge of incompetence.

Robert A. Heinlein, 1961, *Stranger in a Strange Land*, p. 33

28:31 After all, when you come right down to it, how many people speak the same language even when they speak the same language?

Russell Hoban, 1972, *The Lion of Boaz-Jachin and Jachin-Boaz*, Ch. 27

28:32 Nothing can be so clearly and carefully expressed that it cannot be utterly misinterpreted.

Fred W. Householder, 1971, *Linguistic Speculations*, Preface

28:33 Emotion is always new and the word has always served; therein lies the difficulty of expressing emotion.

Victor Hugo, 1866, *Les Travailleurs de la mer* (trans.), III, Book 1, Ch. 2

28:34 Language is by its very nature a communal thing; that is, it expresses never the exact thing but a compromise – that which is common to you, me and everybody.

Thomas Ernest Hulme, 1923, 'Romanticism and Classicism', in *Speculations*

28:35 Some experience of popular lecturing had convinced me that the necessity of making things plain to uninstructed people was one of the very best means of clearing up the obscure corners in one's own mind.

T. H. Huxley, 1894, *Man's Place in Nature* (revised edition), Preface

28:36 Straightforward words / Seem paradoxical.

Lao Tzu, 6th century BC, *Tao Te Ching* (trans. D. C. Lau, 1963), II, Ch. 78

28:37 The only way to escape misrepresentation is never to commit oneself to any critical judgement that makes an impact – that is, never *say anything*.

F. R. Leavis, 1948, *The Great Tradition*, Ch. 1

28:38 And no / Words, only these shapes of things that seem / Ways of knowing what it is I am knowing. / I write these things in books, on pieces of paper / . . . / It is always the same: I cannot read what the words say. / It is always the same: there are signs and I cannot read them.

Archibald MacLeish, 1935, 'The Hamlet of A. MacLeish', in *Poems*

28:39 People who write obscurely are either unskilled in writing or up to mischief.

Peter Medawar, 1984, *Science and Literature in Pluto's Republic*, p. 52

28:40 Can anyone deny that glosses increase doubts and ignorance, when there can be found no book which men toil over in either divinity or the humanities whose difficulties have been exhausted by exegesis?

Michel de Montaigne, 1572–80, 'On Experience', in *The Complete Essays* (trans. M. A. Screech, 1987), III, no. 13

28:41 It is more of a business to interpret the interpretations than to interpret the texts, and there are more books on books than on any other subject: all we do is gloss each other.

Michel de Montaigne, 1572–80, 'On Experience', in *The Complete Essays* (trans. M. A. Screech, 1987), III, no. 13

28:42 PERSPICUITY
Is the fundamental quality of style: a quality so essential in every kind of writing that for the want of it nothing can atone.

Lindley Murray, 1795, *English Grammar*, Appendix [introduction]

28:43 The inflated style is itself a kind of euphemism. A mass of Latin words falls upon the facts like soft snow, blurring the outlines and covering up the details. The great enemy of clear language is insincerity. When there is a gap between one's real and one's declared aims, one turns as it were instinctively to long

words and exhausted idioms, like a cuttlefish squirting out ink.
George Orwell, 1946, 'Politics and the English Language', *Horizon*, no. 13

28:44 The more acute the experience the less articulate its expression.
Harold Pinter, programme note to *The Room* (1957) and *The Dumb Waiter* (1960)

28:45 Which words / Will come through air unbent, / Saying, so to say, only what / they mean?
Peter Porter, 16 July 1982, *Times Literary Supplement*, p. 771

28:46 There is no saying without a double meaning.
Proverbial (Nandi)

28:47 There is as much hold of his word as of a wet eel by the tail.
Proverbial

28:48 Every word has three explanations and three interpretations.
Proverbial (Irish)

28:49 Duplicity lies at the heart of language: only Trappists avoid the trap.
Frederic Raphael, 31 May 1987, in the *Sunday Times*

28:50 GLAND: I would say it's somehow redolent, and full of vitality.
HILDA: Well, I would say it's got about as much life in it as a potted shrimp.
GLAND: Well, I think we're probably both trying to say the same thing in different words.
Henry Reed, 1958, *The Primal Scene, as it were* (radio play), in *Hilda Tablet and Others* (1971), p. 162

28:51 Clarity is the politeness of the man of letters.
Jules Renard, 1892, *Journal* (trans. L. Bogan and E. Roget)

28:52 Without contemplating last and late the true nature of poetry. The drive to connect. The dream of a common language.
Adrienne Rich, 1978, 'Origins and History of Consciousness', in *The Dream of a Common Language*

28:53 What is not clear is not French.
Comte de Rivarol, 1784, *Discours sur l'universalité de la langue française* (trans.)

28:54 What sets men at variance is but the treachery of language, for always they desire the same things.
Antoine de Saint-Exupéry, published in 1948, *The Wisdom of the Sands* (trans. S. Gilbert), Ch. 17

28:55 When I think over what I have said, I envy dumb people.
Seneca, 1st century, 'On a Happy Life', in *Moral Essays* (trans. A. Stewart)

28:56 [Duke Theseus, of Peter Quince's Prologue] His speech was like a tangled chain – nothing impaired, but all disordered.
William Shakespeare, 1594–5, *A Midsummer Night's Dream*, V. i. 123

28:57 [Friar Laurence] Be plain, good son, and homely in thy drift. / Riddling confession finds but riddling shrift.
William Shakespeare, 1594–5, *Romeo and Juliet*, II. ii. 55

28:58 Words calculated to catch everyone may catch no one.
Adlai Stevenson, 21 July 1952, speech to the Democratic National Convention, Chicago

28:59 [Player] We are tied down to a language which makes up in obscurity what it lacks in style.
Tom Stoppard, 1967, *Rosencrantz and Guildenstern Are Dead*, II

28:60 Vague words! but ah, how hard to frame / In matter-moulded forms of speech, / Or ev'n for intellect to reach / Thro' memory that which I became.
Alfred, Lord Tennyson, 1850, *In Memoriam A. H. H.*, Canto 94

28:61 Precision of communication is important, more important than ever, in our era of hair-trigger balances, when a false, or misunderstood word may create as much disaster as a sudden thoughtless act.
James Thurber, 1961, 'Friends, Romans, Countrymen, Lend me your Ear Muffs', in *Lanterns and Lances*

28:62 All erroneous ideas would perish of their own accord if given clear expression.
Vauvenargues, 1746, *Reflections and Maxims* (trans. F. G. Stevens), no. 6

See also: 1:15, 1:76, 2:68, 29:101, 30:27, 49:5

29 *Saying Too Much*

Verbosity, long-windedness, and other forms of excessive speech or writing

29:1 There was nothing wrong with her that a vasectomy of the vocal chords [sic] wouldn't fix.

Lisa Alther, 1976, *Kinflicks*, Ch. 4

29:2 Long and curious [elaborate] speeches are as fit for dispatch as a robe or mantle with a long train is for race.

Francis Bacon, 1612/25, 'Of Dispatch', in *Essays*

29:3 Do not make long-winded speeches in the gathering of elders, and do not repeat yourself at your prayers.

The Bible, Ecclesiasticus 7:14 (Jerusalem Bible)

29:4 A phrase-maker is a terror to his town; a loose talker is detested.

The Bible, Ecclesiasticus 9:18 (Jerusalem Bible)

29:5 Pitiless is the man who is too free with his words; he will not spare you either blows or chains.

The Bible, Ecclesiasticus 13:12 (Jerusalem Bible)

29:6 So is the tongue only a tiny part of the body, but it can proudly claim that it does great things. Think how small a flame can set fire to a huge forest; the tongue is a flame like that. Among all the parts of the body, the tongue is a whole wicked world in itself: it infects the whole body; catching fire itself from hell, it sets fire to the whole wheel of creation. Wild animals and birds, reptiles and fish can all be tamed by man, and often are; but nobody can tame the tongue – it is a pest that will not keep still, full of deadly poison.

The Bible, 2 Timothy 3:5 (Jerusalem Bible)

29:7 [Jesus] In your prayers do not babble as the pagans do, for they think that by using many words they will make themselves heard.

The Bible, Matthew 6:7 (Jerusalem Bible)

29:8 Death and life are in the gift of the tongue; those who indulge it must eat the fruit it yields.

The Bible, Proverbs 18:21 (Jerusalem Bible)

29:9 You see some man too ready of speech? More hope for a fool than for him.

The Bible, Proverbs 29:20 (Jerusalem Bible)

29:10 *Bore, n.* A person who talks when you wish him to listen.

Ambrose Bierce, 1911, *The Devil's Dictionary*

29:11 *Loquacity, n.* A disorder which renders the sufferer unable to curb his tongue when you wish to talk.

Ambrose Bierce, 1911, *The Devil's Dictionary*

29:12 *Monologue, n.* The activity of a tongue that has no ears.

Ambrose Bierce, 1911, *The Devil's Dictionary* (entry added by E. J. Hopkins for *The Enlarged Devil's Dictionary*, 1967)

29:13 *Pleonasm, n.* An army of words escorting a corporal of thought.

Ambrose Bierce, 1911, *The Devil's Dictionary*

29:14 [of an orator] For if the language will but bear the test, / No matter what becomes of all the rest: / The ablest orator, to save a word, / Would throw all sense and reason overboard.

Samuel Butler (1612–80), 1670s, 'Satire upon the Imperfection and Abuse of Human Learning', fragments of an intended second part

29:15 And th' artificial wash of eloquence / Is daub'd in vain upon the clearest sense, / Only to stain the native ingenuity / Of equal brevity and perspicuity, / Whilst all the best and sob'rest things he does / Are when he coughs, or spits, or blows his nose.

Samuel Butler (1612–80), 1670s, 'Satire upon the Imperfection and Abuse of Human Learning', fragments of an intended second part

29:16 Epithets, like pepper, / Give zest to what you write; / And if you strew them sparely, / They whet the appetite: / But if you lay them on too thick, / You spoil the matter quite!

Lewis Carroll, 1869, 'Poeta fit, non nascitur'

29:17 [Sancho Panza] In me the need to talk is a primary impulse, and I can't help saying right off what comes to my tongue.

Miguel de Cervantes, 1605, *The Adventures of Don Quixote* (trans. J. M. Cohen), I, Ch. 30

29:18 So loud each tongue, so empty was each head, / So much they talked, so very little said.

Charles Churchill, 1761, 'The Rosciad', 549

29:19 One never repents of having spoken too little, but often of having spoken too much.

Philippe de Commynes, 1524, *Mémoires*, Ch. 1 [cf. 31:70]

29:20 The Master said, Clever talk and a pretentious manner are seldom found in the Good.

Confucius, 5th century BC, *The Analects* (trans. A. Waley), I, Sect. 3

29:21 [Witwould] I know a Lady that loves talking so incessantly, she won't give an Eccho fair play; she has that everlasting Rotation of Tongue, that an Eccho must wait till she dies, before It can catch her last Words.

William Congreve, 1700, *The Way of the World*, II. i

29:22 A story, in which native humour reigns, / Is often useful, always entertains: / A graver fact, enlisted on your side, / May furnish illustration, well applied; / But sedentary weavers of long tales / Give me the fidgets, and my patience fails.

William Cowper, 1782, *Conversation*, 203

29:23 We talk about the tyranny of words, but we like to tyrannise over them too; we are fond of having a large superfluous establishment of words to wait upon us on great occasions; we think it looks important, and sounds well. As we are not particular about the meaning of our liveries on state occasions, if they be but fine and numerous enough, so, the meaning or necessity of our words is a secondary consideration, if there be but a great parade of them. And as individuals get into trouble by making too great a show of liveries, or as slaves when they are too numerous rise against their masters, so I think I could mention a nation that has got into many great difficulties, and will get into many greater, from maintaining too large a retinue of words.

Charles Dickens, 1849–50, *David Copperfield*, Ch. 52

29:24 When a man has anything of his own to say, and is really in earnest that it should be understood, he does not usually make cavalry regiments of his sentences, and seek abroad for sesquipedalian words.

Charles Dickens, 1858, 'Saxon-English', *Household Words*, no. 18

29:25 Too much Ozone in the air, I am informed and fully believe (though I have no idea what it is), would affect me in a marvellously disagreeable way; why may not too much Talk? I don't see or hear the Ozone; I don't see or hear the Talk. And there is so much Talk; so much too much; such loud cry, and such scant supply of wool; such a deal of fleecing, and so little fleece.

Charles Dickens, 1867–8, *The Uncommercial Traveller*, Ch. 16

29:26 When a man fell into his anecdotage it was a sign for him to retire from the world.

Benjamin Disraeli, 1870, in *Lothair*, Ch. 28

29:27 [a courtier, to Donne] Then, as if he would have sold / His tongue, he prais'd it, and such wonders told / That I was faine to say, If you'had liv'd, Sir, / Time enough to have beene Interpreter / To Babells bricklayers, sure the Tower had stood.

John Donne, 1597, *Satire IV*, 61 [cf. 29:51]

29:28 But far more numerous was the Herd of such / Who think too little and who talk too much.

John Dryden, 1681, *Absalom and Achitophel*, I, 533

29:29 Nothing is more despicable than a professional talker who uses his words as a quack uses his remedies.

François de Fénelon, 1714, 'Letter to the French Academy' (trans.)

29:30 Speeches in our culture are the vacuum that fills a vacuum.

J. Kenneth Galbraith, 1984, speech at the American

University, Washington DC, quoted in *Time* (18 June)

29:31 A barren superfluity of words.
Samuel Garth, 1699, *The Dispensary*, Canto 2, 82

29:32 Is there any place where there is no traffic in empty talk? Is there on this earth one who does not worship himself talking?
Kahlil Gibran, 'Mister Gabber', in *Thoughts and Meditations* (1960)

29:33 You must lie upon the daisies and discourse in novel phrases of your complicated state of mind, / The meaning doesn't matter if it's only idle chatter of a transcendental kind.
W. S. Gilbert, 1881, *Patience*, I

29:34 People do not seem to talk for the sake of expressing their opinions, but to maintain an opinion for the sake of talking.
William Hazlitt, 1821–2, 'On Coffee-house Politicians', in *Table Talk* (ed. William Hazlitt, junior, 1845)

29:35 A sick man that gets talking about himself, a woman that gets talking about her baby, and an author that begins reading out of his own book, never know when to stop.
Oliver Wendell Holmes, senior, 1872, *The Poet at the Breakfast Table*, Ch. 11

29:36 Many people would be more truthful were it not for their uncontrollable desire to talk.
Edgar Watson Howe, 1911, *Country Town Sayings*

29:37 [of Lord Curzon] It does not always pay to have a golden tongue unless one has the ability to hold it.
Paul Johnson, 5 June 1986, in the *Listener*

29:38 Whom the disease of talking still once possesseth, he can never hold his peace.
Ben Jonson, 1640 (published posthumously), *Timber: or, Discoveries made upon Men and Matter*

29:39 Thanne greved hym a goliardeis, a gloton of wordes. [Then a comic versifier angered him, a glutton of words.]
William Langland, 1360–87, *The Vision of Piers Plowman* (B text), Prologue, 139

29:40 You know you haven't stopped talking since I came here? You must have been vaccinated with a phonograph needle.
Groucho Marx, 1933, character in *Duck Soup*, film script by Bert Kalmar *et al.*

29:41 Most people have a furious itch to talk about themselves and are restrained only by the disinclination of others to listen.
W. Somerset Maugham, 1938, *The Summing Up*, Ch. 19

29:42 The capacity of human beings to bore one another seems to be vastly greater than that of any other animals. Some of their most esteemed inventions have no other apparent purpose, for example, the dinner party of more than two, the epic poem, and the science of metaphysics.
H. L. Mencken, 'Minority Report', in *Notebooks* (1956)

29:43 Copiousness of words, however ranged, is always false eloquence, though it will ever impose on some sort of understandings.
Lady Mary Wortley Montagu, 20 July 1754, letter to Lady Bute, in Isobel Grundy (ed.), *Lady Mary Wortley Montagu: Selected Letters* (1997)

29:44 Once you are off, it is hard to cut it short and stop talking. Nothing tells you more about a horse than a pronounced ability to pull up short. I have even known two men who can speak pertinently, who want to stop their gallop but who do not know how to do so. While looking for a way of bringing their hoofs together they amble on like sick men, dragging out trivialities. Old men are particularly vulnerable: they remember the past but forget that they have just told you!
Michel de Montaigne, 1572–80, 'On Liars', in *The Complete Essays* (trans. M. A. Screech, 1987), I, no. 9

29:45 The world is nothing but chatter: I have never met a man who does not say more than he should rather than less. Yet half our life is spent on that; they keep us four or five years learning the meanings of words and stringing them into sentences; four or five more in learning how to arrange them into a long composition, divided into four parts or five; then as many again in plaiting and weaving them into verbal subtleties. Let us leave all that to those who make it their express profession.
Michel de Montaigne, 1572–80, 'On Educating Children', in *The Complete Essays* (trans. M. A. Screech, 1987), I, no. 26

29:46 People whose bodies are too thin pad them out: those whose matter is too slender pad it out too, with words.
Michel de Montaigne, 1572–80, 'On Educating Children', in *The Complete Essays* (trans. M. A. Screech, 1987), I, no. 26

29:47 He bathes daily in a running tap of words.
Brian Moore, 1987, *The Colour of Blood*

29:48 The unluckiest insolvent in the world is the man whose expenditure of speech is too great for his income of ideas.
Christopher Morley, 1923, *Inward Ho!*, Ch. 9

29:49 [of Cicero] He used to ridicule loud speakers, saying that they shouted because they could not speak, like lame men who get on horseback because they cannot walk.
Plutarch, 1st century, 'Cicero', in *Lives* (trans. A. H. Clough)

29:50 Others for *Language* all their care express, / And value books, as women men, for Dress: / Their praise is still, – the Style is excellent! / The Sense, they humbly take upon content. / Words are like leaves; and where they most abound, / Much fruit of sense beneath is rarely found.
Alexander Pope, 1711, 'An Essay on Criticism', 305

29:51 [conversation with a courtier] Thus others' talents having nicely shown, / He came by sure transition to his own: / Till I cry'd out: 'You prove yourself so able, / Pity! you was not Druggerman [interpreter] at Babel; / For had they found a linguist half so good, / I make no question but the Tow'r had stood.'
Alexander Pope, 1733, 'Satire IV', 80, In *Satires of Dr Donne Versified* [cf. 29:27]

29:52 They never taste who always drink / They always talk, who never think.
Matthew Prior, 1740, *Upon this Passage in the Scaligeriana*

29:53 He hath eaten the hen's rump. [Said of a person who is full of talk.]
Proverbial (Italian)

29:54 Loquacity storms the ear, but modesty takes the heart.
Proverbial

29:55 A full purse makes the mouth to speak.
Proverbial

29:56 The drum does not make as much noise as the mouth.
Proverbial (Tsonga)

29:57 He who says what he likes hears what he doesn't like.
Proverbial (Turkish)

29:58 Many speak much that cannot speak well.
Proverbial

29:59 He that speaks lavishly shall hear as knavishly.
Proverbial

29:60 You speak in clusters; you were got in nutting [conceived while gathering nuts].
Proverbial

29:61 He that speaks the thing he shou'd na, hears the things he wa'd na.
Proverbial (Scots)

29:62 When all men speak, no man hears.
Proverbial (Scots)

29:63 To hasten to speak is to hasten death.
Proverbial (Tsonga)

29:64 Where there is least heart there is most speech.
Proverbial (Montenegrin)

29:65 As the sands of the desert are to the weary traveller, so is over-much speech to him who loveth silence.
Proverbial (Oriental)

29:66 Meikle [much] spoken, part spilt [wasted].
Proverbial (Scots)

29:67 Talk much, err much.
Proverbial

29:68 Talk brings on talk.
Proverbial (Irish)

29:69 He talks a stick from every valley. [Said of one who talks much nonsense.]
Proverbial (Syrian)

29:70 A talkative man soon consoles himself.
Proverbial (Spanish)

29:71 As hills of sand to the feet of the traveller, so is the voice of the incessant talker to the ears of the wise.
Proverbial (Arabic)

29:72 Sometimes talking loses what silence has gained.
Proverbial (Spanish)

29:73 Better that the feet slip than the tongue.
Proverbial

29:74 The tongue talks at the head's cost.
Proverbial

29:75 Your tongue runs before your wit.
Proverbial

29:76 His tongue runs on wheels.
Proverbial

29:77 His tongue's na in his pouch.
Proverbial (Scots)

29:78 When the hands and the feet are bound, the tongue runs faster.
Proverbial (German)

29:79 Thirty-two teeth can often not bridle the tongue.
Proverbial (Hungarian)

29:80 A head with a tongue is more costly.
Proverbial (Bulgarian)

29:81 Four horses cannot overtake the tongue.
Proverbial (Chinese)

29:82 The tongue knows no fastening.
Proverbial (Sotho)

29:83 A word and a stone let go cannot be recalled.
Proverbial

29:84 A word flies away like a sparrow and returns to the house like a crow.
Proverbial (German)

29:85 A word which flew out of the mouth like a sparrow cannot be drawn back, even by four horses.
Proverbial (Czech)

29:86 The word that has departed grows on the way.
Proverbial (Norwegian)

29:87 Mony [many] words wa'd hae meikle [have much] drink.
Proverbial (Scots)

29:88 Small cares make many words, great ones are mute.
Proverbial (German)

29:89 Words are like cherries, pick one and ten come.
Proverbial (Italian)

29:90 Behind big words dwells a little soul.
Proverbial (Swiss-German)

29:91 Many words, little sense.
Proverbial (Japanese)

29:92 Whenever I have talked to anyone at too great length, I am like a man who has drunk too much, and ashamed, doesn't know where to put himself.
Jules Renard, December 1893, *Journal* (trans. L. Bogan and E. Roget)

29:93 Adjective salad is delicious, with each element contributing its individual and unique flavor; but a puree of adjective soup tastes yecchy.
William Safire, 1980, 'The Great Permitter', in *On Language*

29:94 An ad lib has its place, but not ad nauseum.
William Safire, 1980, 'Commencement Address', in *On Language*

29:95 Most men make little use of their own speech than to give evidence against their own understanding.
George Savile, 'Of Folly and Fools', in *Political, Moral, and Miscellaneous Thoughts and Reflections* (1750)

29:96 THURIO: Sir, if you spend word for word with me, I shall make your wit bankrupt.
VALENTINE: I know it well, sir. You have an exchequer of words, and, I think, no other treasure to give your followers. For it appears by their bare liveries that they live by your bare words.
William Shakespeare, 1590–1, *The Two Gentlemen of Verona*, II. iv. 39

29:97 [Richard of Gloucester, of Queen Margaret] Why should she live to fill the world with words?
William Shakespeare, 1590–1, *Henry VI, Part 3*, V. v. 43

29:98 [The King, of Armado] A man in all the world's new fashion planted, / That hath a mint of phrases in his brain. / One who the music of his own vain tongue / Doth ravish like enchanting harmony.
William Shakespeare, 1593–4, *Love's Labour's Lost*, I. i. 162

29:99 [Armado] Sweet smoke of rhetoric!
William Shakespeare, 1593–4, *Love's Labour's Lost*, III. i. 61

29:100 [Romeo, of Mercutio] A gentleman, Nurse, that loves to hear himself talk, and will speak more in a minute than he will stand to in a month.
William Shakespeare, 1594–5, *Romeo and Juliet*, II. iii. 138

29:101 [Benedick, of Claudio] He was wont to speak plain and to the purpose, like an honest man and a soldier, and now is he turned orthography. His words are a very fantastical banquet, just so many strange dishes.
William Shakespeare, 1598–9, *Much Ado About Nothing*, II. iii. 18

29:102 [Cassio, on the power of wine] O God, that men should put an enemy in their mouths to steal away their brains!
William Shakespeare, 1603–4, *Othello*, II. iii. 283

29:103 [Antonio, of Gonzalo] Fie, what a spend-thrift is he of his tongue!
William Shakespeare, 1610–11, *The Tempest*, II. i. 25

29:104 Surely human affairs would be far happier if the power in men to be silent were the same as that to speak. But experience more than sufficiently teaches that men govern nothing with more difficulty than their tongues, and can moderate their desires more easily than their words.
Baruch Spinoza, 1677, *Ethics* (trans. A. Boyle), Ch. 3

29:105 [Chorus] But ye, keep ye on earth / Your lips from over-speech, / Loud words and longing are so little worth.
Algernon Charles Swinburne, 1865, *Atalanta in Calydon*

29:106 A bore is a man who, when you ask him how he is, tells you.
Bert Leston Taylor, 1922, *The So-called Human Race*, p. 163

See also: 2:2, 2:9, 2:71, 17:3, 30:8–9, 31:5, 39:22, 41:48

30 *Saying Just Enough*

Brevity, taciturnity, conciseness, and other forms of economy in speech or writing

30:1 [Arthur and Ford encounter a man with a Kill-O-Zap gun] He gestured at the door. 'Out,' he said. People who can supply that amount of fire power don't need to supply verbs as well.
Douglas Adams, 1980, *The Restaurant at the End of the Universe*, Ch. 23

30:2 Modern athletes, heroes, and lovers are none of them expected to use much language, and some evidently cultivate taciturnity on purpose as an accepted signal of manly sincerity.
Robert M. Adams, 1980, 'Authenticity-codes and Sincerity-formulas', in L. Michaels and C. Ricks (eds), *The State of the Language*

30:3 In so far as [things] are said more pithily and antithetically, by so much are they the more popular. And the reason is that understanding is made greater by contrast and swifter through happening in a short space.
Aristotle, 4th century BC, *The Art of Rhetoric* (trans. H. C. Lawson-Tancred), III, Ch. 11

30:4 In dealing with cunning persons, we must ever consider their ends, to interpret their speeches; and it is good to say little to them, and that which they least look for.
Francis Bacon, 1597/1625, 'Of Negotiating', in *Essays*

30:5 Be not rash with thy mouth, and let not thine heart be hasty to utter any thing before God; for God is in heaven, and thou upon earth; therefore let thy words be few.
The Bible, Ecclesiastes 5:2 (Authorized Version of 1611)

30:6 Make scales and weights for your words, and put a door with bolts across your mouth.
The Bible, Ecclesiasticus 28:25 (Jerusalem Bible)

30:7 Speak, young men, if you have to; but twice at most, and then only if questioned. Keep to the point, say much in few words; give the impression of knowing but not wanting to speak.
The Bible, Ecclesiasticus 32:7 (Jerusalem Bible)

30:8 A flood of words is never without its fault; he who has his lips controlled is a prudent man.
The Bible, Proverbs 10:19 (Jerusalem Bible)

30:9 He keeps his life who guards his mouth; he who talks too much is lost.
The Bible, Proverbs 13:3 (Jerusalem Bible)

30:10 He who keeps watch over his mouth and his tongue, preserves himself from disaster.
The Bible, Proverbs 21:23 (Jerusalem Bible)

30:11 If I write four words, I strike out three of them.
Nicolas Boileau, 1665, *Satire 2: A. M. Molière* (trans.)

30:12 For brevity is very good, / When w'are, or are not understood.
Samuel Butler (1612–80), 1663, *Hudibras*, I, Canto 1, 669

30:13 My notes always grow longer if I shorten them. I mean the process of compression makes them more pregnant and they breed new notes. I never try to lengthen them, so I do not know whether they would grow shorter if I did. Perhaps that might be a good way of getting them shorter.
Samuel Butler (1835–1902), *The Note-Books of Samuel Butler* (1912)

30:14 Little said is soon amended.
Miguel de Cervantes, 1605, *The Adventures of Don Quixote* (trans. J. M. Cohen), I, Ch. 3 [cf. 30:37]

30:15 Brevity is the sister of talent.
Anton Chekhov, 11 April 1889, letter to Alexander
Chekhov (trans.), in L. S. Friedland (ed.), *Anton
Chekhov: Letters on the Short Story* (1964) [cf. 30:50]

30:16 Personally I like short words and vulgar
fractions.
Winston Churchill, 10 October 1953, speech in
Margate

30:17 Men are born with two eyes, but with one
tongue, in order that they should see twice as
much as they say.
Charles Caleb Colton, 1825, *Lacon: or, Many Things
in Few Words*, I, no. 112 [cf. 30:58]

30:18 The Master said, In the old days a man
kept a hold on his words, fearing the disgrace
that would ensue should he himself fail to keep
pace with them.
Confucius, 5th century BC, *The Analects* (trans. A.
Waley), IV, Sect. 22

30:19 The Master said, The good man is chary
of speech.
Confucius, 5th century BC, *The Analects* (trans. A.
Waley), XII, Sect. 3

30:20 A tale should be judicious, clear, succinct; / The language plain, and incidents well
link'd; / Tell not as new what ev'rybody knows; /
And, new or old, still hasten to a close.
William Cowper, 1782, *Conversation*, 235

30:21 [Sam Weller] 'Person's a waitin',' said
Sam, epigrammatically.
Charles Dickens, 1836–7, *The Pickwick Papers*, Ch. 15

30:22 'Ah!' repeated Mrs. Gamp; for it was
always a safe sentiment in cases of mourning.
'Ah dear!'
Charles Dickens, 1843–4, *Martin Chuzzlewit*, Ch. 19

30:23 You cannot be absolutely dumb when
you live with a person unless you are an inhab-
itant of the North of England or the State of
Maine.
Ford Madox Ford, 1915, *The Good Soldier*, III, Ch. 4

30:24 It wasn't by accident that the Gettysburg
address was so short. The laws of prose writing
are as immutable as those of flight, of mathematics, of physics.
Ernest Hemingway, 23 July 1945, letter

30:25 Talking is like playing the harp; there is
as much in laying the hand on the strings to
stop their vibrations as in twanging them to
bring out their music.
Oliver Wendell Holmes, senior, 1858, *The Autocrat of
the Breakfast Table*, Ch. 1

30:26 [of poetry] There must be terseness, that
the sense may flow on, unimpeded by words
that burden the ears to weariness.
Horace, 35 BC, 'An Answer to Critics' ('Nempe
incomposito dixi'), in *Satires* (trans. H. W. Wells), I,
no. 10

30:27 *Brevis esse laboro, / Obscurus fio.* I struggle
to be brief, I become obscure.
Horace, 19–18 BC, *Ars Poetica*, 25

30:28 Rule 1: Be cautious, careful, and when in
doubt, keep your mouth shut. Rule 2: When
tempted to say something, take a deep breath
and refer to Rule 1.
Lance Ito, 23 July 1994, *New York Times*

30:29 I have revered always not crude verbosity,
but holy simplicity.
St Jerome, 4th century, letter 'Ad Pammachium'
(trans.)

30:30 In all pointed sentences, some degree of
accuracy must be sacrificed to conciseness.
Samuel Johnson, January 1760, 'On the Bravery of
the British Common Soldier', in the *British Magazine*

30:31 To use words but rarely / Is to be natural.
Lao Tzu, 6th century BC, *Tao Te Ching* (trans. D. C.
Lau, 1963), I, Ch. 23

30:32 We talk little when vanity does not make
us.
Duc de La Rochefoucauld, 1665, *Maxims* (trans. K.
Pratt), no. 137

30:33 It is a pity that intelligent men are so fond
of brevity: by it their reputation is certainly
worth all the more, but we are worth all the
less.
Michel de Montaigne, 1572–80, 'On Educating
Children', in *The Complete Essays* (trans. M. A.
Screech, 1987), I, no. 26

30:34 I have made this [letter] longer than usual,
only because I have not had the time to make
it shorter.
Blaise Pascal, 1657, *Lettres provinciales* (trans.), no. 16

30:35 If thou thinkest twice before thou speak-
est once, thou wilt speak twice the better for it.
William Penn, 1693, *Some Fruits of Solitude*, I, no. 131

30:36 It is a good answer which knows when to stop.
Proverbial (Italian)

30:37 Little said is soon mended, an' a little gear [money] is soon spent.
Proverbial (Scots) [cf. 30:14]

30:38 Think much, speak little, and write less.
Proverbial

30:39 Spare to speak, and spare to speed.
Proverbial

30:40 Keep your tongue on a string.
Proverbial

30:41 Tie up your tongue or she will tie you up.
Proverbial (Irish)

30:42 Give your tongue more holidays than your head.
Proverbial (Scots)

30:43 To the word of this year one replies next. [An offended person is wise to be patient.]
Proverbial (Fulfulde)

30:44 Words must be weighed, not counted.
Proverbial (Polish, Spanish, and Yiddish)

30:45 When you casually meet a man, say three short words; by no means show him all your heart.
Proverbial (Chinese)

30:46 If your words are not pleasing, hold in half of them.
Proverbial (Chinese)

30:47 There was an old owl lived in an oak / The more he heard, the less he spoke; / The less he spoke, the more he heard / O, if men were all like that wise bird!
Punch, 1875, Vol. 68, p. 155

30:48 JULIA [of Proteus]: His little speaking shows his love but small.
    LUCETTA: Fire that's closest kept burns most of all.
William Shakespeare, 1590–1, *The Two Gentlemen of Verona*, I. ii. 29

30:49 [Boy] For Nim, he hath heard that men of few words are the best men, and therefore he scorns to say his prayers, lest a should be thought a coward.
William Shakespeare, 1599, *Henry V*, III. ii. 37

30:50 [Polonius] Therefore, since brevity is the soul of wit, / And tediousness the limbs and outward flourishes, / I will be brief.
William Shakespeare, 1600–1601, *Hamlet*, II. ii. 91 [cf. 30:15]

30:51 [Othello, to Iago] I know thou'rt full of love and honesty, / And weigh'st thy words before thou giv'st them breath.
William Shakespeare, 1603–4, *Othello*, III. iii. 123

30:52 The sovereign'st thing that any man may have / Is little to say, and much to hear and see.
John Skelton, 1499, *The Bouge of Court*, 211

30:53 In composing, as a general rule, run your pen through every other word you have written; you have no idea what vigour it will give your style.
Sydney Smith, 1855, in Lady Holland, *A Memoir of the Reverend Sydney Smith*

30:54 [the first project of the School of Language in the Grand Academy of Lagado] To shorten discourse by cutting polysyllables into one, and leaving out verbs and participles, because in reality all things imaginable are but nouns.
Jonathan Swift, 1726, 'A Voyage to Laputa', *Gulliver's Travels*, III, Ch. 5

30:55 [the second project of the School of Language in the Grand Academy of Lagado] A scheme for entirely abolishing all words whatsoever, . . . urged as a great advantage in point of health as well of brevity. For it is plain that every word we speak is in some degree a diminution of our lungs by corrosion, and consequently contributes to the shortening of our lives.
Jonathan Swift, 1726, 'A Voyage to Laputa', *Gulliver's Travels*, III, Ch. 5

30:56 I always thought I'd like my tombstone to be blank. No epitaph, and no name. Well actually I'd like it to say 'figment'.
Andy Warhol, 1985, *America*

30:57 My efforts to cut out 50,000 words may sometimes result in my adding 75,000.
Thomas Wolfe, 1929, letter to his editor, Maxwell Perkins

30:58 The reason why we have two ears and only one mouth is that we may listen the more and talk the less.
Zeno of Citium, 3rd century, quoted in Diogenes Laertius, *Lives and Opinions of Eminent Philosophers* (trans. R. D. Hicks) [cf. 30:17]

See also: 55:16, 64:64, 65:19

31 *Keeping Quiet*

The nature and functions of silence and pause

31:1 The *English* delight In Silence more than any other *European* Nation, if the Remarks which are made on us by Foreigners are true.
Joseph Addison, 4 August 1711, *The Spectator*, no. 135

31:2 Silence is the virtue of fools.
Francis Bacon, 1623, *De dignitate et augmentis scientiarum*, Antitheta 31

31:3 To every thing there is a season, and a time to every purpose under the heaven: . . . a time to keep silence, and a time to speak . . .
The Bible, Ecclesiastes 3:1, 7 (Authorized Version of 1611)

31:4 There is the rebuke that is untimely, and there is the man who keeps quiet, and he is the shrewd one.
The Bible, Ecclesiasticus 20:1 (Jerusalem Bible)

31:5 There is the man who keeps quiet and is considered wise; another incurs hatred for talking too much. There is the man who keeps quiet, not knowing how to answer; another keeps quiet, because he knows when to speak. A wise man will keep quiet till the right moment; but a garrulous fool will always misjudge it. The man who talks too much will get himself disliked, and the self-appointed oracle will make himself hated.
The Bible, Ecclesiasticus 20:5 (Jerusalem Bible)

31:6 Silences have a climax, when you have got to speak.
Elizabeth Bowen, 1935, *The House in Paris*, Ch. 2

31:7 Language? Tush! / Silence 'tis awe decrees.
Robert Browning, 1889, 'Prologue' to *Asolando*

31:8 Love wants not speech; from silence speech it builds, / Kindness like light speaks in the air it gilds.
Edward Bulwer-Lytton, 1848–9, *King Arthur*, IX, stanza 52

31:9 Silence is not always tact and it is tact that is golden, not silence.
Samuel Butler (1835–1902), *The Note-Books of Samuel Butler* (1912)

31:10 Under all speech that is good for anything there lies a silence that is better. Silence is deep as Eternity; speech is shallow as Time.
Thomas Carlyle, 1830, 'Sir Walter Scott', In *Critical and Miscellaneous Essays*

31:11 Mum's the word.
George Colman (the Younger), 1789, *The Battle of Hexham*, II. i

31:12 When you have nothing to say, say nothing.
Charles Caleb Colton, 1825, *Lacon: or, Many Things in Few Words*, I, no. 183

31:13 The Master said, I would much rather not have to talk. Tzu-kung said, If our Master did not talk, what should we little ones have to hand down about him? The Master said, Heaven does not speak; yet the four seasons run their course thereby, the hundred creatures, each after its kind, are born thereby. Heaven does no speaking!
Confucius, 5th century BC, *The Analects* (trans. A. Waley), XVII, Sect. 19

31:14 Nothing speaks our Griefe so well / As to speake Nothing.

Richard Crashaw, 1631, 'Upon the Death of a Gentleman'

31:15 Is not silence frequently more efficacious than the utmost eloquence? Answer probably yes. Must try to remember this more often than I do.

E. M. Delafield, 1930, *The Diary of a Provincial Lady*, 15 May

31:16 Silence is all we dread. / There's Ransom in a Voice – / But Silence is Infinity.

Emily Dickinson, c.1862–86, *Complete Poems*, no. 1, 251

31:17 The words the happy say / Are paltry melody / But those the silent feel / Are beautiful –.

Emily Dickinson, c.1862–86, *Complete Poems*, no. 1, 750

31:18 Let thy speech be better than silence, or be silent.

Dionysius the Elder, 4th century BC, fragment

31:19 Nothing is often a good thing to say, and always a clever thing to say.

Will Durant, 6 June 1958, *New York World-Telegram & Sun*

31:20 Speech is often barren; but silence also does not necessarily brood over a full nest. Your still fowl, blinking at you without remark, may all the while be sitting on one addled egg; and when it takes to cackling will have nothing to announce but that addled delusion.

George Eliot, 1866, *Felix Holt*, Ch. 15

31:21 Good as is discourse, silence is better, and shames it. The length of the discourse indicates the distance of thought betwixt the speaker and the hearer. If they were at a perfect understanding in any part, no words would be necessary thereon. If at one in all parts, no words would be suffered.

Ralph Waldo Emerson, 1841, 'Circles', in *Essays*

31:22 MISS RICHLAND: There are attractions in modest diffidence, above the force of words. A silent address is the genuine eloquence of sincerity.

CROAKER: Madam, he [Leontine] has forgot to speak any other language; silence is become his mother-tongue.

Oliver Goldsmith, 1768, *The Good-Natured Man*, II. i

31:23 Small griefs find tongues: full casks are ever found / To give (if any, yet) but little sound.

Robert Herrick, 1648, 'Hesperides', 38

31:24 This is a law of fate, that each shall know all others, / That when the silence returns there shall be a language too.

Friedrich Hölderlin, 'Celebration of Peace', in *Friedrich Hölderlin: Poems and Fragments* (trans. M. Hamburger, 1966)

31:25 [Isabel Archer] An Englishman's never so natural as when he's holding his tongue.

Henry James, 1881, *The Portrait of a Lady*, Ch. 10

31:26 No man speaks safely but he that is glad to hold his peace.

Thomas à Kempis, c.1415–24, *The Imitation of Christ* (trans.), I, Ch. 20

31:27 Much speech leads inevitably to silence.

Lao Tzu, 6th century BC, *Tao Te Ching* (trans. D. C. Lau, 1963), I, Ch. 5

31:28 It is never more difficult to speak well than when we are ashamed of keeping silent.

Duc de La Rochefoucauld, 1665, *Maxims* (trans. K. Pratt), no. 556

31:29 Do not the most moving moments of our lives find us all without words?

Marcel Marceau, June 1958, *Reader's Digest*

31:30 There is the silence of age, / Too full of wisdom for the tongue to utter it / In words intelligible to those who have not lived / The great range of life.

Edgar Lee Masters, 1916, 'Silence', in *Songs and Satires*

31:31 Some people mistake weakness for tact. If they are silent when they ought to speak and so feign an agreement they do not feel, they call it being tactful. Cowardice would be a much better name.

Sir Frank Medlicott, July 1958, *Reader's Digest*

31:32 [about A. S. C. Ross] He speaks of the U-habit of silence, and perhaps does not make as much of it as he might. Silence is the only possible U-response to many embarrassing modern situations: the ejaculation of 'cheers' before drinking, for example, or 'it was so nice seeing you', after saying goodbye.

Nancy Mitford, 1956, 'The English Aristocracy', in Nancy Mitford (ed.), *Noblesse Oblige*, p. 43 [cf. 52:32]

31:33 We need a reason to speak, but none to keep silent.
Pierre Nicole, c.1672, *Traité des moyens de conserver la paix avec les hommes* (trans.), Ch. 2, Sect. 1

31:34 Language is the threshold of silence.
Brice Parain, 1942, *Recherches sur la nature et les fonctions du langage* (trans.)

31:35 Do you wish people to believe good of you? Don't speak.
Blaise Pascal, c.1654–62, *Pensées* (trans. W. F. Trotter), no. 44

31:36 Many a time the thing left silent makes for happiness.
Pindar, 5th century BC, 'Isthmia 1', *Odes* (trans.)

31:37 A sage thing is timely silence, and better than any speech.
Plutarch, 1st century, 'The Education of Children', in *Moralia* (trans. M. Hadas)

31:38 A shut mouth catches no flies.
Proverbial

31:39 A wise head makes a close mouth.
Proverbial (French)

31:40 Sweet is the silent mouth.
Proverbial (Irish)

31:41 A close mouth is as good as a priest's blessing any day.
Proverbial (Irish)

31:42 A shut mouth makes no enemies.
Proverbial (Irish)

31:43 Silence seldom doth harm.
Proverbial

31:44 Silence is consent.
Proverbial

31:45 'Tis a good word that can better a good silence.
Proverbial (Dutch)

31:46 Silence is a fence round wisdom.
Proverbial (German)

31:47 With silence one irritates the devil.
Proverbial (Bulgarian)

31:48 He who preserves a wise silence speaks well.
Proverbial (Serbian)

31:49 Silence was never written down.
Proverbial (Spanish)

31:50 Repentance for silence is better than repentance for speaking.
Proverbial (Moorish)

31:51 Silence is in the door of consent.
Proverbial (Moorish)

31:52 Silence is wisdom, when speaking is folly.
Proverbial

31:53 He that is silent gathers stones.
Proverbial

31:54 He who is silent does not say nothing.
Proverbial (Spanish)

31:55 Who speaks sows; who keeps silent reaps.
Proverbial

31:56 Those who know do not speak; those who speak do not know.
Proverbial (Chinese)

31:57 Speech is silver, silence is golden.
Proverbial

31:58 Nature gives speech, but silence teaches understanding.
Proverbial (Danish)

31:59 If speech be one rupee, then silence is two.
Proverbial (Hindi)

31.60 Beware of a man who doesn't talk, and a dog that doesn't bark.
Proverbial (Spanish)

31:61 Keep your tongue within your teeth.
Proverbial

31:62 If you keep your tongue a prisoner, your body may go free.
Proverbial

31:63 Tuck your shirt in between your legs, and your tongue behind your teeth.
Proverbial (Polish)

31:64 The saving of man is the holding of his tongue.
Proverbial (Arabic)

31:65 Nothing is so deserving of a long imprisonment as the tongue.
Proverbial (Arabic)

31:66 The good man carries his heart on his tongue; the prudent man carries his tongue in his heart.
Proverbial (Turkish)

31:67 Padlock your tongue, or it lock you up.
Proverbial (Guiana Creole)

31:68 The best word is the word that remains to be spoken.
Proverbial (Spanish)

31:69 The word which you keep between your lips is your slave, the word spoken out of season is your master.
Proverbial (Arabic)

31:70 I have often regretted my speech, never my silence.
Publilius Syrus, 1st century BC, *Moral Sayings* (trans. D. Lyman), no. 1,070 [cf. 29:19]

31:71 The most precious things in speech are pauses.
Ralph Richardson, attributed, 20th century, in M. J. Cohen (ed.), *The Penguin Thematic Dictionary of Quotations* (1998)

31:72 [Proteus] What, gone without a word? / Ay, so true love should do. It cannot speak, / For truth hath better deeds than words to grace it.
William Shakespeare, 1590–1, *The Two Gentlemen of Verona*, II. ii. 16

31:73 [Graziano] For silence is only commendable / In a neat's [ox's] tongue dried and a maid not vendible [marriageable].
William Shakespeare, 1596–7, *The Merchant of Venice*, I. i. 111

31:74 [Claudio] Silence is the perfectest herald of joy. I were but little happy if I could say how much.
William Shakespeare, 1598–9, *Much Ado About Nothing*, II. i. 287

31:75 [Thersites, of Ajax's strutting about while saying nothing] He's grown a very landfish, languageless, a monster. ... Why, he'll answer nobody. He professes not answering. Speaking is for beggars. He wears his tongue in's arms.
William Shakespeare, 1602, *Troilus and Cressida*, III. iii. 255, 259

31:76 [Countess, to Bertram] Be checked for silence, / But never taxed for speech.
William Shakespeare, 1604–5, *All's Well That Ends Well*, I. i. 64

31:77 [Paulina, to Emilia] The silence often of pure innocence / Persuades when speaking fails.
William Shakespeare, 1610–11, *The Winter's Tale*, II. ii. 44

31:78 [Henry, of Cranmer] He has strangled / His language in his tears.
William Shakespeare, 1613, *Henry VIII (All Is True)*, V. i. 157

31:79 [Ecrasia] Silence is the most perfect expression of scorn.
George Bernard Shaw, 1921, *Back to Methuselah*, V

31:80 People talking without speaking, / People hearing without listening, / People writing songs that voices never shared. / No one dared, / Disturb the sound of silence.
Paul Simon, 1965, 'The Sound of Silence'

31:81 Language can only deal meaningfully with a special, restricted segment of reality. The rest, and it is presumably the much larger part, is silence.
George Steiner, 1967, 'The Retreat from the Word', in *Language and Silence*

31:82 The cruellest lies are often told in silence.
Robert Louis Stevenson, 1881, title essay in *Virginibus Puerisque*, IV

31:83 Silence will save me from being wrong (and foolish), but it will also deprive me of the possibility of being right.
Igor Stravinsky, 1966, 'Contingencies', in *Themes and Episodes*

31:84 [Chorus] But from sharp words and wits men pluck no fruit, / And gathering thorns they shake the tree at root; / For words divide and rend; / But silence is most noble till the end.
Algernon Charles Swinburne, 1865, *Atalanta in Calydon*

31:85 In human intercourse the tragedy begins, not when there is misunderstanding about words, but when silence is not understood.
Henry Thoreau, 1849, 'The Atlantides', in *A Week on the Concord and Merrimack Rivers*

31:86 If we would enjoy the most intimate society with that in each of us which is without, or above, being spoken to, we must not only be silent, but commonly so far apart bodily that we cannot possibly hear each other's voice in any case. Referred to this standard, speech is for the convenience of those who are hard of hearing; but there are many fine things which we cannot say if we have to shout.

Henry Thoreau, 1854, 'Visitors', in *Walden*

31:87 The best thing about animals is that they don't talk much.

Thornton Wilder, 1942, *The Skin of Our Teeth*, 1

See also: 5:81, 17:5, 17:10, 17:20–1, 17:23, 17:42, 18:31, 25:49, 26:38, 36:1, 37:20, 41:8, 41:11, 53:34, 64:2

32 *Friendly Language*

Words of comfort, love, apology, gentleness, praise, and tact

32:1 Do you not know, Prometheus, that words are healers of the sick temper?
Aeschylus, *c.*478 BC, *Prometheus Bound* (trans. David Grene)

32:2 A kindly turn of speech multiplies a man's friends; and a courteous way of speaking invites many a friendly reply.
The Bible, Ecclesiasticus 6:5 (Jerusalem Bible)

32:3 [Jesus] Alas for you when the world speaks well of you!
The Bible, Luke 6:26 (Jerusalem Bible)

32:4 A mild answer turns away wrath: sharp words stir up anger.
The Bible, Proverbs 15:1 (Jerusalem Bible)

32:5 Kindly words are a honeycomb, sweet to the taste, wholesome to the body.
The Bible, Proverbs 16:24 (Jerusalem Bible)

32:6 *Apologize, v. i.* To lay the foundation for a future offence.
Ambrose Bierce, 1911, *The Devil's Dictionary*

32:7 *Commendation, n.* The tribute that we pay to achievements that resemble, but do not equal, our own.
Ambrose Bierce, 1911, *The Devil's Dictionary*

32:8 *Eulogy, n.* Praise of a person who has either the advantages of wealth and power, or the consideration to be dead.
Ambrose Bierce, 1911, *The Devil's Dictionary*

32:9 The words of his mouth were softer than butter, having war in his heart: his words were smoother than oil, and yet they be very swords.
Book of Common Prayer, 1562, *Psalms* 55:22

32:10 The advantage of doing one's praising to oneself is that one can lay it on so thick and exactly in the right places.
Samuel Butler (1835–1902), 1903, *The Way of All Flesh*, Ch. 34

32:11 Diplomacy is the art of saying 'Nice Doggie!' till you can find a rock.
Wynn Catlin, in Roger Kilroy (ed.), *Kiss Me Hardy* (1982)

32:12 Remember, / to keep the tongue locked in the mouth / is to reject love's seasoning: / love-talk enhances love-acts.
Gaius Valerius Catullus, 1st century BC, no. 55 in *The Poems of Catullus* (trans. P. Whigham, Penguin, 1966)

32:13 [to the God of Love] I'll teach him a Receipt to make / Words that weep, and Tears that speak.
Abraham Cowley, 1668, 'The Prophet'

32:14 Words aptly cull'd and meanings well express'd, / Can calm the sorrows of a wounded breast.
George Crabbe, 1783, 'The Village', II, 159

32:15 [Mrs Wilfer, to Bella, who has made a tactful observation about the Boffins] 'Why adopt a circuitous form of speech? It is polite and it is obliging; but why do it? Why not openly say that they are much too kind and too good for *us*? We understand the allusion. Why disguise the phrase?'
Charles Dickens, 1864–5, *Our Mutual Friend*, II, Ch. 8

32:16 Apologies only account for that which they do not alter.
Benjamin Disraeli, 28 July 1871, speech to the House of Commons

32:17 The music that can deepest reach, / And cure all ill, is cordial speech.
Ralph Waldo Emerson, 1860, 'Considerations by the Way', in *The Conduct of Life*

32:18 The gentle and respectful ways of saying 'To hell with you' are being abandoned.
Millicent Hammond Fenwick, attributed, 20th century, in *Chambers Dictionary of Quotations* (1996)

32:19 You can stroke people with words.
F. Scott Fitzgerald, in *The Crack-Up* (ed. Edmund Wilson, 1945)

32:20 There speaks the man of truly noble ways, / Who will not listen to the words of praise. / In modesty averse, and with deaf ears, / He acts as though the others were his peers.
Goethe, 1832, 'On the Lower Peneus', in *Faust* (trans. P. Wayne), II

32:21 Apology is only egotism wrong side out.
Oliver Wendell Holmes, senior, 1860, *The Professor at the Breakfast Table*

32:22 The words that love inspires / Outlive their utterance.
Horace, 19 BC, 'You too shall live' ('Ne forte credas'), in *Odes* (trans. J. O. Sargent), IV, no. 9

32:23 A compliment is something like a kiss through a veil.
Victor Hugo, 1862, 'Saint Denis', in *Les Misérables* (trans.), VIII, Ch. 1

32:24 Give 'em words; / Pour oil into their ears, and send them hence
Ben Jonson, 1606, *Volpone*, I. iv

32:25 [Euphues to Philantus] Fayre words fat few, great promises, without performance, delight for the tyme, but yearke [lash, beat] euer after.
John Lyly, 1580, *Euphues and his England*, last letter

32:26 All really great lovers are articulate, and verbal seduction is the surest road to actual seduction.
Marya Mannes, 1958, *More in Anger*, Ch. 4

32:27 People ask you for criticism, but they only want praise.
W. Somerset Maugham, 1915, *Of Human Bondage*, Ch. 50

32:28 By winning words to conquer willing hearts, / And make persuasion do the work of fear.
John Milton, 1671, *Paradise Regained*, I, 222

32:29 What I do know is that when I hear anyone lingering over the language of these *Essays* I would rather he held his peace: it is not a case of words being extolled but of meaning being devalued.
Michel de Montaigne, 1572–80, 'Reflections upon Cicero', in *The Complete Essays* (trans. M. A. Screech, 1987), I, no. 40

32:30 [of Tommy] She was gallant and intelligent, she tried to coerce me with her words, not with her tears. We did indeed understand each other and this was rare and now that we had given up the sex act I still enjoyed the word act with her, simply the unusual experience of communicating.
Iris Murdoch, 1975, 'Friday' (first week), in *A Word Child*

32:31 Isn't everyone consoled when faced with a trouble or fact he doesn't understand, by a word, some simple word, which tells us nothing and yet calms us?
Luigi Pirandello, 1921, *Six Characters In Search of an Author* (trans. E. Storer), I

32:32 Compliments fly when gentlefolk meet.
Proverbial

32:33 Sweet discourse makes short days and nights.
Proverbial

32:34 An ounce of discretion is worth a pound of wit.
Proverbial

32:35 The virtue of the mouth healeth all it toucheth.
Proverbial

32:36 If a leaf falls from a tree and nobody praises it, the leaf must praise itself.
Proverbial (Nupe)

32:37 Speak fair, and think what you will.
Proverbial

32:38 He that speaks me fair and loves me not, I'll speak him fair, and trust him not.
Proverbial

32:39 His talking is like mixed vegetables. [He speaks softly but not strongly.]
Proverbial (Marathi)

32:40 It is a gude tongue that says nae ill.
Proverbial (Scots)

32:41 A man's beauty is the sweetness of his tongue.
Proverbial (Bosnian)

32:42 Beautify your tongue, you will obtain what you desire.
Proverbial (Moorish)

32:43 A gude word is as soon said as an ill.
Proverbial (Scots)

32:44 A good word never broke a tooth.
Proverbial (Irish)

32:45 A gentle word will make the argument strong.
Proverbial (Welsh)

32:46 A gentle word opens an iron gate.
Proverbial (Bulgarian)

32:47 A word of kindness is better than a fat pie.
Proverbial (Russian)

32:48 A kind word is like a spring day.
Proverbial (Russian)

32:49 A kind word warms for three winters.
Proverbial (Chinese)

32:50 Good words cost naught.
Proverbial (Portuguese)

32:51 Good words cool more than cold water.
Proverbial (Spanish)

32:52 Soft words hurt not the mouth.
Proverbial

32:53 Soft words break no bones.
Proverbial

32:54 Soft words scald not the tongue.
Proverbial (French)

32:55 He who gives fair words feeds you with an empty spoon.
Proverbial

32:56 Soft words are hard arguments.
Proverbial

32:57 Words draw the nails from the heart.
Proverbial (Arabic)

32:58 It is easier to obtain thousands of gold pieces than kind words.
Proverbial (Chinese)

32:59 Golden words open an iron door.
Proverbial (Turkish)

32:60 Good words bring out the lizard from his hole.
Proverbial (Kenyan)

32:61 Of many a shaft, at random sent, / Finds mark the archer little meant! / And many a word, at random spoken, / May soothe or wound a heart that's broken.
Walter Scott, 1813, *The Lord of the Isles*, Canto 5, stanza 18

32:62 [Julia to Lucetta] Didst thou but know the inly touch of love / Thou wouldst as soon go kindle fire with snow / As seek to quench the fire of love with words.
William Shakespeare, 1590–1, *The Two Gentlemen of Verona*, II. vii. 18

32:63 [Valentine] That man that hath a tongue I say is no man / If with his tongue he cannot win a woman.
William Shakespeare, 1590–1, *The Two Gentlemen of Verona*, III. i. 104

32:64 Deep sounds make lesser noise than shallow fords, / And sorrow ebbs, being blown with wind of words.
William Shakespeare, 1593, *The Rape of Lucrece*, 1,329

32:65 [Biron] Honest plain words best pierce the ear of grief.
William Shakespeare, 1593–4, *Love's Labour's Lost*, V. ii. 745

32:66 [Leonato] Men / Can counsel and speak comfort to that grief / Which they themselves not feel, but tasting it / Their counsel turns to passion, which before / Would give preceptial medicine to rage, / Fetter strong madness in a silken thread, / Charm ache with air and agony with words.
William Shakespeare, 1598–9, *Much Ado About Nothing*, V. i. 20

32:67 [Cassius] Antony, / The posture of your blows are yet unknown; / But for your words,

they rob the Hybla bees, / And leave them honeyless.
William Shakespeare, 1599, *Julius Caesar*, V. i. 32

32:68 [Othello] Rude am I in my speech, / And little blessed with the soft phrase of peace.
William Shakespeare, 1603–4, *Othello*, I. iii. 81

32:69 [Hermione] One good deed lying tongueless / Slaughters a thousand waiting upon that. / Our praises are our wages.
William Shakespeare, 1609–10, *The Winter's Tale*, I. ii. 94

32:70 [Gonzalo, to Sebastian] The truth you speak doth lack some gentleness / And time to speak it in. You rub the sore / When you should bring the plaster.
William Shakespeare, 1610–11, *The Tempest*, II. i. 142

32:71 JAILER [of Arcite and Palamon]: They are famed to be a pair of absolute men.
JAILER'S DAUGHTER: By my troth, I think fame but stammers 'em – they stand a grece [step] above the reach of report.
William Shakespeare and John Fletcher, 1613–14, *The Two Noble Kinsmen*, II. i. 26

32:72 [of critics] Unless the bastards have the courage to give you unqualified praise, I say ignore them.
John Steinbeck, 1958, quoted in the introduction to J. Kenneth Galbraith, *The Affluent Society* (1977)

32:73 [Meleager, of Althæa] Womanlike to weave sweet words, and melt / Mutable minds of wise men as with fire.
Algernon Charles Swinburne, 1865, *Atalanta in Calydon*

32:74 To say a compliment well is a high art and few possess it.
Mark Twain, 19 October 1909, letter to John Brisben Walker

32:75 There is nothing you can say in answer to a compliment. I have been complimented myself a great many times, and they always embarrass me – I always feel that they have not said enough.
Mark Twain, 1923, 'Fulton Day, Jamestown', in A. B. Paine (ed.), *Speeches*

32:76 It is a good rule in life never to apologize. The right sort of people do not want apologies, and the wrong sort take a mean advantage of them.
P. G. Wodehouse, 1914, title story in *The Man Upstairs* [cf. 26:46]

32:77 Throughout the world, if it were sought, / Fair words enough a man shall find. / They be good cheap; they cost right naught; / Their substance is but only wind. / But well to say and so to mean – / That sweet accord is seldom seen.
Thomas Wyatt, 1557 (published posthumously), 'Throughout the world if it were sought'

32:78 A good name is seldom got by giving it to one's self.
William Wycherley, 1675, *The Country Wife*, I. i. 40

See also: 1:12, 18:26, 34:10, 34:22, 55:19, 64:25

33 The Language of Flattery

Flattering, smooth, and insincere language

33:1 [Mr Bennet, to Mr Collins] It is happy for you that you possess the talent of flattering with delicacy. May I ask whether these pleasing attentions proceed from the impulse of the moment, or are the result of previous study?
Jane Austen, 1813, *Pride and Prejudice*, Ch. 14

33:2 The arch-flatterer, with whom all the petty flatterers have intelligence [an understanding], is a man's self.
Francis Bacon, 1612/25, 'Of Love', in *Essays*

33:3 The man who flatters his neighbour spreads a net for his feet.
The Bible, Proverbs 29:5 (Jerusalem Bible)

33:4 Beware a tongue that's smoothly hung.
Robert Burns, 1784–6, 'Song – O Leave Novels'

33:5 You know what charm is: a way of getting the answer yes without having asked any clear question.
Albert Camus, 1956, *The Fall* (trans.)

33:6 Every woman is infallibly to be gained by every sort of flattery, and every man by one sort or other.
Lord Chesterfield, 16 March 1752, letter to his son

33:7 I am always of the opinion with the learned, if they speak first.
William Congreve, 1692, *Incognita*

33:8 For the first time I was aware of that layer of blubber which encases an English peer, the sediment of permanent adulation.
Cyril Connolly, 1938, *Enemies of Promise*, Ch. 23

33:9 [to Flattery] O happy child! the glorious day shall shine, / When every ear shall to thy speech incline, / Thy words alluring and thy voice divine: / The sullen pedant and the sprightly wit, / To hear thy soothing eloquence, shall sit; / And both, abjuring Flattery, will agree / That truth inspires, and they must honour thee.
George Crabbe, 1807, *The Birth of Flattery*, 230

33:10 Everyone likes flattery; and when you come to Royalty you should lay it on with a trowel.
Benjamin Disraeli (who attributed the remark to Matthew Arnold), 19th century, quoted in G. W. E. Russell, *Collections and Recollections* (1898), Ch. 23

33:11 Be advised that all flatterers live at the expense of those who listen to them.
Jean de La Fontaine, 1668–94, 'The Crow and the Fox', in *Fables choisies mises en vers* (trans.)

33:12 The habitude of pleasing by flattery makes a language soft; the fear of offending by truth makes it circuitous and conventional.
Walter Savage Landor, 1824–53, 'Demosthenes and Eubulides', in *Imaginary Conversations*

33:13 Flattery is false coin that is only current thanks to our vanity.
Duc de La Rochefoucauld, 1678, *Maxims*, no. 158

33:14 'But do care a bit for flattery, my lady,' said De Craye [to Lady Busshe]. ' 'Tis the finest of the Arts; we might call it moral sculpture. Adepts in it can cut their friends to any shape they like.'
George Meredith, 1879, *The Egoist*, Ch. 36

33:15 He who knows how to flatter also knows how to slander.
Napoleon I, 1804–15, *Maxims* (trans.)

33:16 Our country, south and west of Hatteras, / Abounds in charming feminine flatteras. / Sweet talk is scant by Lake Cayuga, / But in Tennessee, they chatta nougat.
Ogden Nash, 1952, 'Is it True what they Say about Dixie or Is it Just the Way they Say it?', in *The Private Dining Room*

33:17 A man who cannot flatter knows not how to talk.
Proverbial (Sardinian)

33:18 A honey tongue, a heart of gall.
Proverbial (Portuguese and Spanish)

33:19 The too flattering tongue will soon have to lick wounds.
Proverbial (Turkish)

33:20 [Decius, of Caesar] But when I tell him he hates flatterers, / He says he does, being then most flattered.
William Shakespeare, 1599, *Julius Caesar*, II. i. 207

33:21 He that loves to be flattered is worthy o'th' flatterer.
William Shakespeare, 1604, *Timon of Athens*, I. i. 229

33:22 What really flatters a man is that you think him worth flattering.
George Bernard Shaw, 1904, *John Bull's Other Island*, IV

33:23 The World is grown so full of Dissimulation and Compliment, that Mens Words are hardly any Signification of their Thoughts.
Richard Steele, 28 June 1711, *The Spectator*, no. 103

33:24 Flattery is all right – if you don't inhale.
Adlai Stevenson, 1 February 1961, speech

33:25 'Tis an old maxim in the schools, / That flattery's the food of fools; / Yet now and then your men of wit / Will condescend to take a bit.
Jonathan Swift, 1713, *Cadenus and Vanessa*, 758

33:26 This barren verbiage, current among men, / Light coin, the tinsel clink of compliment.
Alfred, Lord Tennyson, 1847, *The Princess*, I, 40

33:27 Yet each man kills the thing he loves, / By each let this be heard, / Some do it with a bitter look, / Some with a flattering word.
Oscar Wilde, 1898, *The Ballad of Reading Gaol*, I, stanza 7

See also: 32:37–8, 32:55, 36:29

34 *Unfriendly Language*

Speaking or writing sharply; sarcasm, ridicule, anger, insult, and slander

34:1 [Jesus] What goes into the mouth does not make a man unclean; it is what comes out of the mouth that makes him unclean.
The Bible, Matthew 15:11 (Jerusalem Bible)

34:2 *Ridicule, n.* Words designed to show that the person of whom they are uttered is devoid of the dignity of character distinguishing him who utters them.
Ambrose Bierce, 1911, *The Devil's Dictionary*

34:3 Sarcasm I now see to be, in general, the language of the devil.
Thomas Carlyle, 1833, *Sartor Resartus*, II, Ch. 4

34:4 It is all too rare today to hear the clear, clean ring of a really original insult.
Jim Richard Carrigan, 28 August 1987, *Time*

34:5 [Berganza, to Scipio] Anyone who wants to keep up a conversation for two hours without lapsing into backbiting has got to be very wise and very careful; because I can see that as far as I am concerned, although I am an animal, I've only got to open my mouth a few times to find words rushing to my tongue like flies to wine, all full of malice and backbiting.
Miguel de Cervantes, 1613, 'The Dogs' Colloquy', in *Exemplary Stories* (trans. C. A. Jones)

34:6 WITWOULD: Sirrah Petulant, thou art an Epitomizer of words.
   PETULANT: Witwould – You are an annihilator of sense.
   WITWOULD: Thou art a retailer of Phrases.
William Congreve, 1700, *The Way of the World*, IV. i

34:7 Though we all disguise our feelings pretty well, / What we mean by 'Very good' is 'Go to hell'.
Noel Coward, 1929, *Bitter Sweet*, I. ii

34:8 [Mr Riderhood, referring to his poor treatment] I should have been worth money at the present time, instead of having a barge-load of bad names chucked at me, and being forced to eat my words, which is a unsatisfying sort of food, wotever a man's appetite!
Charles Dickens, 1864–5, *Our Mutual Friend*, III, Ch. 11

34:9 [of Sir Charles Wood] He has to learn that petulance is not sarcasm, and that insolence is not invective.
Benjamin Disraeli, 16 December 1852, parliamentary speech, in *Hansard*, col. 1,653

34:10 People that talk loud an' offind ye with their insolence are usu'lly shy men thryin' to get over their shyness. 'Tis th' quite, rearved, ca'm spoken man that's mashed on himsilf.
Finley Peter Dunne, 1900, 'Casual Observations', in *Mr Dooley's Philosophy*

34:11 No one can be as calculatedly rude as the British, which amazes Americans, who do not understand studied insult and can only offer abuse as a substitute.
Paul Gallico, 14 January 1962, *New York Times*

34:12 Harsh Words, tho' pertinent, uncouth appear; / None please the Fancy who offend the Ear.
Samuel Garth, 1699, *The Dispensary*, Canto 4, 204

34:13 [Artabanus, accusing Xerxes of slandering the Greeks] Slander is a wicked thing: in a case of slander two parties do wrong and one suffers by it. The slanderer is guilty in that he speaks ill of a man behind his back; and the man who listens to him is guilty in that he takes his word without troubling to find out the truth. The slandered person suffers doubly – from the disparaging words of the one and from the belief of the other that he deserves the disparagement.

Herodotus, 5th century BC, in *The Histories* (trans. Aubrey de Sélincourt, 1996), VII, Ch. 10

34:14 A tart temper never mellows with age, and a sharp tongue is the only edged tool that grows keener with constant use.

Washington Irving, 1819–20, 'Rip Van Winkle', in *The Sketch Book*

34:15 A man, whose business it is to be talked of, is much helped at being attacked.

Samuel Johnson, 1 October 1773, in James Boswell, *The Journal of a Tour to the Hebrides* (1785)

34:16 I hope my tongue in prune juice smothers / If I belittle dogs and mothers.

Ogden Nash, 1949, 'Compliments of a Friend', in *Versus*

34:17 Once a shepherd from Apulia filled these nymphs with sudden panic, and sent them at first fleeing in terror from the spot. However, when they recovered their self-possession, and realized with contempt who was pursuing them, they returned to their choral dancing, matching their steps to the rhythm of the song. The shepherd mocked them, leaping clumsily about in imitation, hurling coarse insults as well, and abusing them in foul language. Nothing silenced him, till finally a tree trunk imprisoned his throat: for he became a wild olive, in the taste of whose fruit one can still recognize the character of the man. In its bitter berries the tree reveals traces of his tongue, and the harshness of his language has passed into the olives.

Ovid, 1st century, *Metamorphoses*, XIV, c.520

34:18 Where argument fails, try abuse.

Proverbial

34:19 Insults and pills must not be chewed.

Proverbial (German)

34:20 There were no ill language were it not ill taken.

Proverbial

34:21 Hanging's stretching; mocking's catching.

Proverbial

34:22 With the mouth one offends, and with the mouth one apologizes.

Proverbial (Tanzanian)

34:23 Scorning is catching.

Proverbial

34:24 Better be ill spoken of by one before all, than by all before one.

Proverbial

34:25 Landlady's talking and dog's barking are the same.

Proverbial (Livonian)

34:26 He that strikes with his tongue must ward with his head.

Proverbial

34:27 One ill word asketh another.

Proverbial

34:28 A hard word is not always a hard heart.

Proverbial (Silesian)

34:29 [King Henry, about the Duke of York] In any case, be not too rough in terms, / For he is fierce and cannot brook hard language.

William Shakespeare, 1590–1, *Henry VI, Part 2*, IV. viii. 44

34:30 [Bastard, reacting to the bold words from one of the citizens of Angers] He speaks plain cannon: fire, and smoke, and bounce; / He gives the bastinado with his tongue; / Our ears are cudgelled; not a word of his / But buffets better than a fist of France. / Zounds! I was never so bethumped with words / Since I first called my brother's father Dad.

William Shakespeare, 1595–6, *King John*, II. i. 463

34:31 [Benedick, of Beatrice] I cannot endure my Lady Tongue.

William Shakespeare, 1598–9, *Much Ado About Nothing*, II. i. 256

34:32 BEATRICE: Foul words is but foul wind, and foul wind is but foul breath, and foul breath is noisome, therefore I will depart unkissed.

BENEDICK: Thou has frighted the word out of his right sense, so forcible is thy wit.

William Shakespeare, 1598–9, *Much Ado About Nothing*, V. ii. 47

34:33 [Sir Toby, advising Sir Andrew how to write a challenge] Go, write it in a martial hand, be curst and brief. It is no matter how witty so it be eloquent and full of invention. Taunt him with the licence of ink. If thou 'thou'st' him some thrice, it shall not be amiss, and as many lies as will lie in thy sheet of paper, although the sheet were big enough for the bed of Ware, in England, set 'em down, go about it. Let there be gall enough in thy ink; though thou write with a goose-pen, no matter. About it.

William Shakespeare, 1601, *Twelfth Night*, III. ii. 40

34:34 [Timon, to the Senators] Speak and be hanged. / For each true word a blister, and each false / Be as cantherizing to the root o'th' tongue, / Consuming it with speaking.

William Shakespeare, 1604, *Timon of Athens*, V. ii. 16

34:35 [Kent, to Oswald] Thou whoreson Z, thou unnecessary letter.

William Shakespeare, 1605–6, *King Lear*, II. ii. 63

34:36 [Alonso, to Gonzalo] You cram these words into mine ears against / The stomach of my sense.

William Shakespeare, 1610–11, *The Tempest*, II. i. 112

34:37 There is no Possibility of succeeding in a Satyrical Way of Writing or Speaking, except a Man throws himself quite out of the Question.

Richard Steele, 25 October 1710, 'Satire', *The Tatler*, no. 242

34:38 [of Arimaze] Never having been able to succeed in the world, he took his revenge by speaking ill of it.

Voltaire, 1747, *Zadig* (trans.), Ch. 4

34:39 Most writers in the course of their careers become thick-skinned and learn to accept vituperation, which in any other profession would be unimaginably offensive, as a healthy counterpoise to unintelligent praise.

Evelyn Waugh, 30 November 1952, in the *New York Times Magazine*

See also: 32:4, 40:12, 40:49, 55:25

Quarrelling, disputing, arguing, and debating

35:1 There is nothing that a New-Englander so nearly worships as an argument.
Henry Ward Beecher, 1887, *Proverbs from Plymouth Pulpit*

35:2 Do not quarrel with a man of quick tongue; do not pile logs on his fire. Do not jest with an ill-mannered man, in case you hear your ancestry insulted.
The Bible, Ecclesiasticus 8:3 (Jerusalem Bible)

35:3 Refuse to be drawn by an arrogant man, for fear he tries to trap you in your words.
The Bible, Ecclesiasticus 8:11 (Jerusalem Bible)

35:4 Tell them in the name of God that there is to be no wrangling about words: all that this ever achieves is the destruction of those who are listening.
The Bible, 2 Timothy 2:14 (Jerusalem Bible)

35:5 *Abuse, n.* The goal of debate.
Ambrose Bierce, 1911, *The Devil's Dictionary* (entry added by E. J. Hopkins for *The Enlarged Devil's Dictionary*, 1967)

35:6 *Harangue, n.* A political speech by an opponent.
Ambrose Bierce, 1911, *The Devil's Dictionary* (entry added by E. J. Hopkins for *The Enlarged Devil's Dictionary*, 1967)

35:7 *Positive, adj.* Mistaken at the top of one's voice.
Ambrose Bierce, 1911, *The Devil's Dictionary*

35:8 For ev'ry why he had a wherefore.
Samuel Butler (1612–80), 1663, *Hudibras*, I, Canto 1, 132

35:9 [Maud, referring to Fergus] He's one of those men who argues by increments of noise – so that as you open your mouth he says another, cleverer, louder thing.
A. S. Byatt, 1990, *Possession*, Ch. 14

35:10 Somebody has to have the last word. If not, every argument could be opposed by another and we'd never be done with it.
Albert Camus, 1956, *The Fall* (trans.)

35:11 Dialectics, a kind of false teeth.
Elias Canetti, 1973, '1970', in *The Human Province*

35:12 Ye pow'rs who rule the tongue, if such there are, / And make colloquial happiness your care, / Preserve me from the thing I dread and hate – / A duel in the form of a debate.
William Cowper, 1782, *Conversation*, 81

35:13 [Mr Pickwick, after being surrounded by a mob of people and joining in with them] 'It's always best on these occasions to do what the mob do.' 'But suppose there are two mobs?' suggested Mr Snodgrass. 'Shout with the largest,' replied Mr Pickwick.
Charles Dickens, 1836–7, *The Pickwick Papers*, Ch. 13

35:14 Our bore is also great in argument. He infinitely enjoys a long humdrum, drowsy interchange of words of dispute about nothing. He considers that it strengthens the mind, consequently, he 'don't see that,' very often. Or, he would be glad to know what you mean by that. Or, he doubts that. Or, he has always understood exactly the reverse of that. Or, he can't admit that. Or, he begs to deny that. Or, surely you don't mean that. And so on.
Charles Dickens, 1858, *Our Bore*, in *Reprinted Pieces*

35:15 [John Willet] Argeyment is a gift of Natur. If Natur has gifted a man with powers of argeyment, a man has a right to make the best of 'em, and has not a right to stand on false delicacy, and deny that he is so gifted; for that is a turning of his back on Natur, a flouting of her, a slighting of her precious caskets, and a proving of one's self to be a swine that isn't worth her scattering pearls before.

Charles Dickens, 1867–8, *Barnaby Rudge*, Ch. 1

35:16 In every age and clime we see, / Two of a trade can ne'er agree.

John Gay, 1729, *Fables*, I, no. 21, 43

35:17 Disagreement may be the shortest cut between two minds.

Kahlil Gibran, 1926, *Sand and Foam*

35:18 In arguing too, the parson owned his skill, / For e'en though vanquished, he could argue still; / While words of learned length, and thundering sound, / Amazed the gazing rustics ranged around; / And still they gazed, and still the wonder grew, / That one small head could carry all he knew.

Oliver Goldsmith, 1770, *The Deserted Village*, 211

35:19 Argument . . . is the death of conversation, if carried on in a spirit of hostility.

William Hazlitt, 1826, 'On the Conversation of Authors', in *The Plain Speaker*

35:20 The two men seemed to agree about everything, but when grown-ups agree they interrupt each other almost as much as if they were quarrelling.

Rudyard Kipling, 1910, 'The Wrong Thing', in *Rewards and Fairies*

35:21 Nation is all but name – a shibboleth – / Where a mistaken accent causes death. / In paradise names only Nature showed, / At Babel names from pride and discord flowed; / And ever since men with a female spite, / First call each other names, and then they fight.

Andrew Marvell, 1669–70, 'The Loyal Scot'

35:22 Argument is often a sieve with which one sifts the truth.

Proverbial (German)

35:23 A quarrel is like buttermilk, once it's out of the churn, the more you shake it, the more sour it grows.

Proverbial (Irish)

35:24 One tale is good till another is told. [Therefore a good judge ought to hear both parties.]

Proverbial

35:25 He'll have the last word though he talk bilk [nothing] for it.

Proverbial

35:26 Bad word and ear-hole never agree.

Proverbial (Jamaican Creole)

35:27 [Justice Credulous, after hearing his wife and daughter argue] A fluent tongue is the only thing a mother don't like her daughter to resemble her in.

Richard Sheridan, 1775, *St Patrick's Day*, I. ii

35:28 [of Uncle Toby's practice of whistling in order to 'answer' any argument] I do therefore, by these presents, strictly order and command, That it be known and distinguished by the name and title of the *Argumentum Fistulatorium* [argument of the pipe-player], and no other; – and that it rank hereafter with the *Argumentum Baculinum* [argument of the stick, i.e., violence] and the *Argumentum ad Crumenam* [argument of the purse], and for ever hereafter be treated of in the same chapter.

Laurence Sterne, 1760, *The Life and Opinions of Tristram Shandy, Gentleman*, I, Ch. 21

35:29 I agree with everything you say but I would attack to the death your right to say it –

Voltaire (the younger).

Tom Stoppard, 1966, *Lord Malquist and Mr Moon*, II [cf. 27:49]

35:30 The chief effect of talk on any subject is to strengthen one's own opinions, and, in fact, one never knows exactly what he does believe until he is warmed into conviction by the heat of attack and defence.

Charles Dudley Warner, 1873, 'Sixth Study', in *Backlog Studies*

35:31 Arguments are to be avoided; they are always vulgar and often convincing.

Oscar Wilde, 1895, *The Importance of Being Earnest*, II

35:32 If two men on the same job agree all the time, then one is useless. If they disagree all the time, then both are useless.

Darryl F. Zanuck, 23 October 1949, 'Sayings of the Week', *Observer*

See also: 39:1, 41:12

Telling the truth, lying, secrets, vows, and other promises

36:1 Nothing is true except that which we do not say.
Jean Anouilh, 1944, *Antigone* (trans.)

36:2 [of his evidence at the Peter Wright–MI5 trial in Melbourne] It contains a misleading impression, not a lie. It was being economical with the truth.
Robert Armstrong, 1986, quoted in 'Sayings of the Year', *Observer* (28 December)

36:3 Truth sits upon the lips of dying men.
Matthew Arnold, 1853–4, 'Sohrab and Rustum', 656

36:4 It is unfortunate, considering that enthusiasm moves the world, that so few enthusiasts can be trusted to speak the truth.
Arthur Balfour, 19 May 1891, letter to Mrs Drew

36:5 It has always been desirable to tell the truth, but seldom if ever necessary to tell the whole truth.
Arthur Balfour, attributed, early 20th century

36:6 A man may say, 'From now on I'm going to speak the truth.' But the truth hears him and runs away and hides before he's even done speaking.
Saul Bellow, 1961, *Herzog* (Fawcett Crest) , p. 331

36:7 Mind you tell no lies, for no good can come of it.
The Bible, Ecclesiasticus 7:13 (Jerusalem Bible)

36:8 Thou shalt not bear false witness against thy neighbour.
The Bible, Exodus 20:16 (Authorized Version of 1611)

36:9 The words of a talebearer are tasty morsels that go right down into the belly.
The Bible, Proverbs 18:8; also 26:22 (Jerusalem Bible)

36:10 The bearer of gossip lets out secrets; have nothing to do with chatterers.
The Bible, Proverbs 20:19 (Jerusalem Bible)

36:11 *Affirm, v. t.* To declare with suspicious gravity when one is not compelled to wholly discredit himself with an oath.
Ambrose Bierce, 1911, *The Devil's Dictionary* (entry added by E. J. Hopkins for *The Enlarged Devil's Dictionary*, 1967)

36:12 *Defame, v. t.* To lie about another. To tell the truth about another.
Ambrose Bierce, 1911, *The Devil's Dictionary*

36:13 *Diplomacy, n.* The patriotic art of lying for one's country.
Ambrose Bierce, 1911, *The Devil's Dictionary*

36:14 *Falsehood, n.* A truth to which the facts are loosely adjusted to an imperfect conformity.
Ambrose Bierce, 1911, *The Devil's Dictionary* (entry added by E. J. Hopkins for *The Enlarged Devil's Dictionary*, 1967)

36:15 *Fib, n.* A lie that has not cut its teeth. An habitual liar's nearest approach to truth: the perigee of his eccentric orbit.
Ambrose Bierce, 1911, *The Devil's Dictionary*

36:16 *Prevaricator, n.* A liar in the caterpillar state.
Ambrose Bierce, 1911, *The Devil's Dictionary*

36:17 *Recollect, v.* To recall with additions something not previously known.
Ambrose Bierce, 1911, *The Devil's Dictionary*

36:18 A truth that's told with bad intent / Beats all the lies you can invent
William Blake, c.1802, 'Auguries of Innocence', 53

36:19 Truth exists; only lies are invented.
Georges Braque, *Le Jour et la nuit: Cahiers 1917–52* (trans.), p. 20

36:20 He said true things, but called them by wrong names.
Robert Browning, 1855, 'Bishop Blougram's Apology', 996, in *Men and Women*

36:21 For he that strains too far a vow / Will break it, like an o'erbent bow.
Samuel Butler (1612–80), 1664, *Hudibras*, II, Canto 2, 273

36:22 Young as he was, his instinct told him that the best liar is he who makes the smallest amount of lying go the longest way.
Samuel Butler (1835–1902), 1903, *The Way of All Flesh*, Ch. 39

36:23 Any fool can tell the truth, but it requires a man of some sense to know how to tell a lie well.
Samuel Butler (1835–1902), *The Note-Books of Samuel Butler* (1912)

36:24 And after all what is a lie? 'Tis but / The truth in masquerade.
Lord Byron, 1819–24, *Don Juan*, Canto 11, stanza 37

36:25 [The Red Queen] Always speak the truth – think before you speak – and write it down afterwards.
Lewis Carroll, 1872, *Through the Looking Glass*, Ch. 9

36:26 [Jeremy] Just the very backside of Truth, – But lying is a figure in speech, that interlards the greatest part of my Conversation.
William Congreve, 1695, *Love for Love*, IV. i

36:27 What, he speaks unseasonable truths sometimes, because he has not wit enough to invent an evasion.
William Congreve, 1700, *The Way of the World*, I. vi

36:28 Propaganda is that branch of the art of lying which consists in nearly deceiving your friends without quite deceiving your enemies.
Francis M. Cornford, 1922 edition of *Microcosmographia Academica*, Preface

36:29 And, of all lies (be that one poet's boast) / The lie that flatters I abhor the most.
William Cowper, 1782, 'Conversation', 87

36:30 Truth disappears with the telling of it.
Lawrence Durrell, 1960, *Clea*, Ch. 2

36:31 Gossip is a sort of smoke that comes from the dirty tobacco-pipes of those who diffuse it: it proves nothing but the bad taste of the smoker.
George Eliot, 1876, *Daniel Deronda*, II, Ch. 13

36:32 Truth has already ceased to be itself if polemically said.
Ralph Waldo Emerson, 1836, *Journals*

36:33 A secret in the Oxford sense: you may tell it to only one person at a time.
Oliver Franks, 30 January 1977, *Sunday Telegraph*

36:34 An exaggeration is a truth that has lost its temper.
Kahlil Gibran, 1926, *Sand and Foam*

36:35 *True* and *False* are attributes of Speech, not of Things. And where Speech is not, there is neither *Truth* nor *Falsehood*.
Thomas Hobbes, 1651, 'Of Speech', in *Leviathan*, I, Ch. 4

36:36 Ears, that unfold to every tale, / Intrusted secrets ill conceal, / And you shall wish, but wish in vain, / To call the fleeting words again.
Horace, 20–13 BC, 'To Lollius [Si bene te novi]', in *Epistles* (trans. P. Francis), I, no. 18

36:37 Conversation is more often likely to be an attempt at deliberate evasion, deliberate confusion, rather than communication. We're all cheats and liars.
James Jones, 1959, interview in *Paris Review* (Winter)

36:38 Calumnies are answered best with silence.
Ben Jonson, 1606, *Volpone*, II. ii

36:39 After all, what was a paradox but a statement of the obvious so as to make it sound untrue?
Ronald Knox, 1918, *A Spiritual Aeneid*

36:40 My word is pure and free of all untruth; it is the word of my father. . . . I will give you my father's words just as I received them; royal griots do not know what lying is.
Mamadou Kouyaté (West African griot), quoted in

V. Edwards and T. J. Sienkewicz, *Oral Cultures Past and Present* (1990), p. 32

36:41 And if, to be sure, sometimes you need to conceal a fact with words, do it in such a way that it does not become known, or, if it does become known, that you have a ready and quick defence.
Niccolò Machiavelli, 1522, 'Advice to Raffaello Girolami when he Went as Ambassador to the Emperor' (trans.)

36:42 White lies are but the gentlemen ushers to black ones.
Frederick Marryat, 1833, *Peter Simple*, Ch. 34

36:43 Lying is an accursed vice. It is only our words which bind us together and make us human. If we realized the horror and weight of lying we would see that it is more worthy of the stake than other crimes.
Michel de Montaigne, 1572–80, 'On Liars', in *The Complete Essays* (trans. M. A. Screech, 1987), I, no. 9

36:44 The best way to keep one's word is not to give it.
Napoleon I, 1804–15, *Maxims* (trans.)

36:45 One of the greatest abilities a person can have, I guess, / Is the ability to say Yes when they mean No and No when they mean Yes.
Ogden Nash, 1940, 'Golly, How Truth will Out!', in *The Face is Familiar*

36:46 To me the truth is something which cannot be told in a few words, and those who simplify the universe only reduce the expansion of its meaning.
Anaïs Nin, Winter 1931–2, *The Diary of Anaïs Nin*

36:47 The greater amount of truth is impulsively uttered; thus the greater amount is spoken, not written.
Edgar Allen Poe, 1844–9, *Marginalia*, Ch. 1

36:48 Lies are essential to humanity. They play perhaps as great a role as the pursuit of pleasure, and are indeed controlled by this pursuit.
Marcel Proust, 1925, 'Albertine disparue', in *A la recherche du temps perdu* (trans.)

36:49 The truth being rather a current which flows from what people say to us, and which we pick up, invisible though it is, than the actual thing they have said.
Marcel Proust, 1921–2, *Cities of the Plain [Sodome et Gomorrhe]* (trans. C. K. Scott-Moncrieff)

36:50 The language of the true is always simple.
Proverbial (Slovakian)

36:51 A lie will go round the world while truth is pulling its boots on.
Proverbial

36:52 One doesn't open one's mouth any wider to tell a lie than to tell the truth.
Proverbial (Walloon)

36:53 A lie has no legs, but a scandal has wings.
Proverbial

36:54 A lie stands upon one leg, but truth upon two.
Proverbial

36:55 Evil that cometh out of thy mouth flieth into thy bosom.
Proverbial

36:56 Promise is a bridge of words, unsafe to walk across.
Proverbial (German)

36:57 Slander sits on the high-road and mocks at all the passers-by.
Proverbial (Greek)

36:58 If slander were to examine itself it would hold its tongue.
Proverbial (Chinese)

36:59 The slanderer kills a thousand times; the assassin but once.
Proverbial (Chinese)

36:60 If you refuse to live with the slanderer, whom are you going to live with?
Proverbial (Hausa)

36:61 Slanderers have the devil in their tongues, but listeners have him in their ears.
Proverbial (Danish)

36:62 Slanders cluster round a widow's door.
Proverbial (Chinese)

36:63 Sit crooked but speak straight.
Proverbial (Turkish)

36:64 What the heart thinketh the tongue speaketh.
Proverbial

36:65 The pen of the tongue should be dipped in the ink of the heart.
Proverbial (Italian)

36:66 Accustom thy tongue to say, 'I know not.'
Proverbial (Hebrew)

36:67 The tongues of men are the pens of truth.
Proverbial (Arabic)

36:68 Wine in, truth out.
Proverbial

36:69 Speak the truth, and shame the devil.
Proverbial

36:70 Where there is whispering there is lying.
Proverbial

36:71 An honest man's word is as good as his bond.
Proverbial

36:72 He who breaks his word will by it be broken.
Proverbial (Bulgarian)

36:73 A word is useful, lies are for adornment.
Proverbial (Swiss-German)

36:74 A true word is not beautiful and a beautiful word is not true.
Proverbial (Japanese)

36:75 The words of the night are coated with butter; as soon as the sun shines they melt away.
Proverbial (Arabic)

36:76 [King Henry, to Suffolk] Hide not thy poison with such sugared words.
William Shakespeare, 1590–1, *Henry VI, Part 2*, III. ii. 45

36:77 QUEEN ELIZABETH: An honest tale speeds best being plainly told.
  KING RICHARD: Then plainly to her tell my loving tale.
  QUEEN ELIZABETH: Plain and not honest is too harsh a style.
William Shakespeare, 1592–3, *Richard III*, IV. iv. 289

36:78 [Rumour] Open your ears; for which of you will stop / The vent of hearing when loud Rumour speaks? . . . Upon my tongues continual slanders ride, / The which in every language

I pronounce, / Stuffing the ears of men with false reports.
William Shakespeare, 1597, *Henry IV, Part 2*, Induction, lines 1–2; 6–8

36:79 [Don Pedro, of Benedick] He hath a heart as sound as a bell, and his tongue in the clapper, for what his heart thinks his tongue speaks.
William Shakespeare, 1598–9, *Much Ado About Nothing*, III. ii. 11 [cf. 36:64]

36:80 DON PEDRO: Officers, what offence have these men done?
  DOGBERRY: Marry, sir, they have committed false report, moreover they have spoken untruths, secondarily they are slanders, sixth and lastly they have belied a lady, thirdly they have verified unjust things, and to conclude, they are lying knaves.
William Shakespeare, 1598–9, *Much Ado About Nothing*, V. i. 208

36:81 [Touchstone, asked to name the degrees of the lie] O sir, we quarrel in print, by the book, as you have books for good manners. I will name you the degrees. The first, the Retort Courteous; the second, the Quip Modest; the third, the Reply Churlish; the fourth, the Reproof Valiant; the fifth, the Countercheck Quarrelsome; the sixth, the Lie with Circumstance; the seventh, the Lie Direct. All these you may avoid but the Lie Direct; and you may avoid that, too, with an 'if'. I knew when seven justices could not take up a quarrel, but when the parties were met themselves, one of them thought but of an 'if', as 'If you said so, then I said so', and they shook hands and swore brothers. Your 'if' is the only peacemaker; much virtue in 'if'.
William Shakespeare, 1600, *As You Like It*, V. iv. 88

36:82 [Iago] Good name in man and woman, dear my lord, / Is the immediate jewel of their souls. / Who steals my purse steals trash; 'tis something, nothing; / 'Twas mine, 'tis his, and has been slave to thousands. / But he that filches from me my good name / Robs me of that which not enriches him / And makes me poor indeed.
William Shakespeare, 1603–4, *Othello*, III. iii. 160

36:83 [Duke] No might nor greatness in mortality / Can censure scape; back-wounding calumny / The whitest virtue strikes. What king so strong / Can tie the gall up in the slanderous tongue?
William Shakespeare, 1604, *Measure for Measure*, III. i. 444

36:84 [Diana] 'Tis not the many oaths that makes the truth, / But the plain single vow that is vowed true.
William Shakespeare, 1604–5, *All's Well That Ends Well*, IV. ii. 22

36:85 [Cornwall, of Kent's plain speaking] This is some fellow / Who, having been praised for bluntness, doth affect / A saucy roughness, and constrains the garb / Quite from his nature. He cannot flatter, he; / An honest mind and plain, he must speak truth.
William Shakespeare, 1605–6, *King Lear*, II. ii. (Oxford) 94

36:86 [Pisanio] Slander, / Whose edge is sharper than the sword, whose tongue / Outvenoms all the worms of Nile, whose breath / Rides on the posting winds and doth belie / All corners of the world.
William Shakespeare, 1610–11, *Cymbeline*, III. iv. 33

36:87 If you want truth to go round the world you must hire an express train to pull it; but if you want a lie to go round the world, it will fly: it is as light as a feather, and a breath will carry it.
Charles Spurgeon, 1859, *Gems from Spurgeon* [cf. 36:51]

36:88 A lie is an abomination unto the Lord, and a very present help in trouble.
Adlai Stevenson, January 1951, speech in Washington

36:89 Win or lose I have told you the truth as I see it. I have said what I meant and meant what I said.
Adlai Stevenson, 10 September 1952, *Time*

36:90 [Gulliver's Houyhnhnm master] He replied that I must needs be mistaken, or that I said the thing which was not, for they have no word in their language to express lying or falsehood.
Jonathan Swift, 1726, 'A Voyage to the Country of the Houyhnhnms', *Gulliver's Travels*, IV, Ch. 3

36:91 Don't lie if you don't have to.
Leo Szilard, 1972, *Science*, no. 176, p. 966

36:92 To be outspoken is easy when you do not wait to speak the complete truth.
Rabindranath Tagore, 1916, *Stray Birds* (trans.), p. 128

36:93 A lie which is all a lie may be met and fought with outright, / But a lie which is part a truth is a harder matter to fight.
Alfred, Lord Tennyson, 1859, 'The Grandmother', stanza 8, 31

36:94 It takes two to speak the truth – one to speak, and another to hear.
Henry Thoreau, 1849, 'Wednesday', in *A Week on the Concord and Merrimack Rivers*

36:95 [on Senator Joseph R. McCarthy] If you think somebody is telling a big lie about you, the only way to answer is with the whole truth.
Harry S. Truman, 1950, quoted in John Hersey, *Aspects of the Presidency* (1980)

36:96 One of the most striking differences between a cat and a lie is that a cat has only nine lives.
Mark Twain, 1894, 'Pudd'nhead Wilson's Calendar', in *Pudd'nhead Wilson*, Ch. 7

36:97 When in doubt, tell the truth.
Mark Twain, 1897, 'Following the Equator', in *Pudd'nhead Wilson's New Calendar*

36:98 Truth is not so threadbare as speech, because fewer people can make use of it.
Vauvenargues, 1746, *Reflections and Maxims* (trans. F. G. Stevens), no. 468

36:99 Lies are the mortar that bind the savage individual man into the social masonry.
H. G. Wells, 1900, *Love and Mrs Lewisham*, Ch. 23

See also: 1:65, 2:123, 11:54, 26:76, 26:114, 28:9, 31:82, 40:34, 41:10, 51:11, 55:1, 55:22, 59:39, 62:62–3

Words

37 Words, Words, Words

Words in general, their nature and function

37:1 Words, those guardians of meaning, are not immortal, are not invulnerable ... Like men, words suffer ... Some can survive, others are incurable.

Arthur Adamov, 1938, *Notebooks*

37:2 INFORMER: Just give me wings.

PEISTHETAERUS: That's exactly what I am doing, by talking to you like this.

INFORMER: How can words give a man wings?

PEISTHETAERUS: Words can give everybody wings.

Aristophanes, 414 BC, *The Birds* (trans. D. Barrett), c.1,440

37:3 Words are man-made things which men use, not persons with a will and consciousness of their own. Whether they make sense or nonsense depends upon whether the speaker uses them correctly or incorrectly.

W. H. Auden, 1948, 'Notes on the Comic', in *The Dyer's Hand and other essays*

37:4 A sentence uttered makes a world appear / Where all things happen as it says they do; / We doubt the speaker, not the tongue we hear: / Words have no words for words that are not true.

W. H. Auden, c.1956, 'Words'

37:5 Words are the tokens current and accepted for conceits, as moneys are for values.

Francis Bacon, 1605, *The Advancement of Learning*, II, Sect. 16

37:6 All words are pegs to hang ideas on.

Henry Ward Beecher, 1887, *Proverbs from Plymouth Pulpit*

37:7 [Petworth, on having his lecture notes examined by Slaka immigration security] The written word, it occurs to him, does not simply have a different *meaning* in a different culture, because of its changed relation to the total vocabulary of that culture; it also has a different *weight* or *status*. So in some cultures – like, for example, Petworth's own – words are expended very freely, readily spoken and fairly easily published; they have a *low* weight on the market. In other cultures – like, for example, this one now – words are traded more selectively and carefully; hence, according to a familiar economic principle, they have a *high* value on the market. In such cultures, text can be trouble, books small bombs. Moreover, it is possible for *low-value words* from one environment to become *high-value words* simply by changing not the words but the *environment* – for instance, by putting them in a bag and taking them somewhere in a plane. Hence environment determines the worth of words.

Malcolm Bradbury, 1983, *Rates of Exchange*, I, Sect. 4

37:8 The whole world is tormented by words / And there is no one who does without words. / But in so far as one is free from words / Does one really understand words.

Buddhist Scriptures, c.850, 'Saraha's *Treasury of Songs*' (trans. E. Conze, 1959), II, Ch. 3, Sect. 6

37:9 Words! / The mason stirs: / Pens are too light. / Take a chisel to write.

Basil Bunting, 1966, *Briggflatts*

37:10 Fumbling for a word is everybody's birthright.

Anthony Burgess, 1992, *A Mouthful of Air*, I, Ch. 11

37:11 Pity the best of words should be but wind!

Robert Burns, September 1788, 'Epistle to Robert Graham, Esq. of Fintry'

37:12 We want words to do more than they can. We try to do with them what comes to very much like trying to mend a watch with a pickaxe or to paint a miniature with a mop; we expect them to help us to grip and dissect that which in ultimate essence is as ungrippable as shadow. Nevertheless there they are; we have got to live with them, and the wise course is to treat them as we do our neighbours, and make the best and not the worst of them. But they are parvenu people as compared with thought and action.

Samuel Butler (1835–1902), *The Note-Books of Samuel Butler* (1912)

37:13 Words are like money; there is nothing so useless, unless when in actual use.

Samuel Butler (1835–1902), *The Note-Books of Samuel Butler* (1912)

37:14 Religion – freedom – vengeance – what you will, / A word's enough to raise mankind to kill.

Lord Byron, 1814, *Lara*, Canto 2, Sect. 8

37:15 But still the heart doth need a language, still / Doth the old instinct bring back the old names.

Samuel Taylor Coleridge, 1800, *The Piccolomini*, II. iv

37:16 [last sentence of the work] He who does not understand words, cannot understand people.

Confucius, 5th century BC, *The Analects* (trans. A. Waley), XX, Sect. 3

37:17 Fluent in all the languages dead or living, the sun comes up with a word of worlds all spinning in a world of words.

Allen Munro Curnow, 1979, 'A Balanced Bait in Handy Pellet Form', in *An Incorrigible Music*

37:18 I've gotta use words when I talk to you.

T. S. Eliot, 1926, 'Fragment of an Agon', in *Sweeney Agonistes*

37:19 I doubt whether from the point of view of *sound* alone, any word is more or less beautiful than another – within its own language, for the question whether some languages are not more beautiful than others is quite another question. The ugly words are the words not fitted for the company in which they find themselves; there are words which are ugly because of rawness or because of antiquation; there are words which

are ugly because of foreignness or ill-breeding (e.g. *television*): but I do not believe that any word well-established in its own language is either beautiful or ugly.

T. S. Eliot, 24 February 1942, lecture at Glasgow University, 'The Music of Poetry'

37:20 Words move, music moves / Only in time; but that which is only living / Can only die. Words, after speech, reach / Into the silence. Only by the form, the pattern, / Can words or music reach / The stillness, as a Chinese jar still / Moves perpetually in its stillness.

T. S. Eliot, 1944, 'Burnt Norton', Part 5, in *Four Quartets*

37:21 Words are signs of natural facts.

Ralph Waldo Emerson, 1836, 'Language', in *Nature*, Ch. 4

37:22 If a people have no word for something, either it does not matter to them or it matters too much to talk about.

Edgar Z. Friedenberg, 1959, 'Adolescence', in *The Vanishing Adolescent*

37:23 So I renounced and sadly see: / Where word breaks off no thing may be.

Stefan George, 1919, *Words*, in *Blätter für die Kunst* (trans. P. Hertz)

37:24 Words are the bugles of social change.

Charles Handy, 1991, *The Age of Unreason*

37:25 The proper force of words lie not in the words themselves, but in their application.

William Hazlitt, 1821, 'On Familiar Style', *Quarterly Review*

37:26 I conceive that words are like money, not the worse for being common, but that it is the stamp of custom alone that gives them circulation or value.

William Hazlitt, 1821, 'On Familiar Style', *Quarterly Review*

37:27 Worry about words, Bobby. Your grandmother is right. For, whatever else you may do, you will be using words always.

A. P. Herbert, 1935, 'Invitation to the War', in *What A Word!*

37:28 Words are really a mask. They rarely express the true meaning; in fact they tend to hide it.

Hermann Hesse, quoted in Miguel Serrano, *C. G. Jung and Hermann Hesse* (trans. F. MacShane, 1966)

37:29 Words form the thread on which we string our experiences.
Aldous Huxley, 1937, *The Olive Tree*

37:30 Words and the meanings of words are not matters merely for the academic amusement of linguists and logisticians, or for the aesthetic delight of poets; they are matters of the profoundest ethical significance to every human being.
Aldous Huxley, 1940, *Words and their Meanings*

37:31 We need words to keep us human. Being human is an accomplishment like playing an instrument. It takes practice.
Michael Ignatieff, 1985, *The Needs of Strangers*, Ch. 4

37:32 You must bring out of each word its practical cash-value, set it at work within the stream of your experience.
William James, 1907, *Pragmatism*, Lecture 2

37:33 Words just say what you want them to; they don't know any better.
A. L. Kennedy, 1990, 'The Role of Notable Silences in Scottish History'

37:34 Words are the living eyes of secrecy.
Velimir Khlebnikov, quoted in George Steiner, *After Babel* (1975), Ch. 3

37:35 Words are, of course, the most powerful drug used by mankind.
Rudyard Kipling, 14 February 1923, speech, in *A Book of Words* [cf. 37:69]

37:36 I am Earth, overtaking all things except words. They alone escape me. Therefore, I lie heavy on their makers.
Rudyard Kipling, 1928, unattributed epigraph to 'Literature', in *A Book of Words*

37:37 I hate false words, and seek with care, difficulty, and moroseness, those that fit the thing.
Walter Savage Landor, 1824–53, 'Bishop Burnet and Humphrey Hardcastle', in *Imaginary Conversations*

37:38 Truthful words are not beautiful; beautiful words are not truthful. Good words are not persuasive; persuasive words are not good.
Lao Tzu, 6th century BC, *Tao Te Ching* (trans. D. C. Lau, 1963), II, Ch. 81

37:39 [comparing with falling rain] Much like words. / But words don't fall exactly; they hang in there / In the heaven of language, immune to gravity / If not to time, entering your mind /

From no direction, travelling no distance at all, / And with rainy persistence tease from the spread earth / So many wonderful scents. And they recur, / Delicious to nose and throat.
Robert Mezey, 1980, 'Words', in L. Michaels and C. Ricks (eds), *The State of the Language*

37:40 Our understanding is conducted solely by means of the word: anyone who falsifies it betrays public society. It is the only tool by which we communicate our wishes and our thoughts; it is our soul's interpreter: if we lack that, we can no longer hold together; we can no longer know each other. When words deceive us, it breaks all intercourse and loosens the bonds of our polity.
Michel de Montaigne, 1572–80, 'On Giving the Lie', in *The Complete Essays* (trans. M. A. Screech, 1987), II, no. 18

37:41 It is interesting that the words which are least used, least written and the least spoken are the very ones which are best known and most widely recognized.
Michel de Montaigne, 1572–80, 'On some Lines of Virgil', in *The Complete Essays* (trans. M. A. Screech, 1987), III, no. 5

37:42 [Ferrante] It's when the thing itself is missing that you have to supply the word.
Henry de Montherlant, 1942, *The Dead Queen*, II. i

37:43 The Vocabulary of a widely-diffused and highly-cultivated living language is not a fixed quantity circumscribed by definite limits. That vast aggregate of words and phrases which constitutes the Vocabulary of English-speaking men presents, to the mind that endeavours to grasp it as a definite whole, the aspect of one of those nebulous masses familiar to the astronomer, in which a clear and unmistakable nucleus shades off on all sides, through zones of decreasing brightness, to a dim marginal film that seems to end nowhere, but to lose itself imperceptibly in the surrounding darkness.
J. A. H. Murray, 1888, 'The Vocabulary', in *A New English Dictionary on Historical Principles*, I, 'General Explanations'

37:44 The death of a word is not an event of which the date can be readily determined.
J. A. H. Murray, 1888, 'The Vocabulary', in *A New English Dictionary on Historical Principles*, I, 'General Explanations'

37:45 The power of words is the most conservative force in our life.

C. K. Ogden and I. A. Richards, 1923, *The Meaning of Meaning*, Ch. 2

37:46 [of the more emotional aspects of modern thought] We shall not be surprised to find a veritable orgy of verbomania.

C. K. Ogden and I. A. Richards, 1923, *The Meaning of Meaning*, Ch. 2

37:47 [Syme] It's a beautiful thing, the destruction of words. Of course the great wastage is in the verbs and adjectives, but there are hundreds of nouns that can be got rid of as well.

George Orwell, 1949, *Nineteen Eighty-Four*, I, Ch. 5

37:48 Words are as beacons to lighten the darkness of our ignorance, but too many of us have been blinded with an excess of light; the excess is ours. Words are a solvent of clotted prejudice, but too many of us have made of them a reinforcement of the insensate atavism of inherited opinions.

Eric Partridge, 1948, 'Words in Vogue: Words of Power', in *Words at War: Words at Peace*

37:49 Now it is not of fools exclusively, but of the greater part of the thinking world, that words are the money.

C. S. Peirce, quoted as an epigraph in Max Black (ed.), *The Importance of Language* (1962)

37:50 [of words] Axes / After whose stroke the wood rings, / And the echoes! / Echoes travelling / Off from the centre like horses.

Sylvia Plath, 1965, 'Words', in *Ariel*

37:51 The escaped word is your master, the kept one your servant.

Proverbial (French)

37:52 A word has caused more than one war.

Proverbial (German)

37:53 A word has a hundred heads.

Proverbial (German)

37:54 One word spoken may last for a lifetime.

Proverbial (Palaung)

37:55 We are masters of the unspoken word, but the spoken word masters us.

Proverbial (Indian)

37:56 A single word creates a debt, a single word releases it.

Proverbial (Malayan)

37:57 Word never finishes in mouth.

Proverbial (Ibo)

37:58 There is nothing one goes to meet with more pleasure than the word.

Proverbial (Rwandan)

37:59 Fair words brok never bane [bone], foul words mony ane [many a one].

Proverbial (Scots)

37:60 Use words like money.

Proverbial (German)

37:61 Words have no boundaries.

Proverbial (Bulgarian)

37:62 Words are like the bees, they have honey and a sting.

Proverbial (Swiss-German)

37:63 Bitter words are medicine; sweet words an epidemic.

Proverbial (Chinese)

37:64 Words are sounds of the heart.

Proverbial (Chinese)

37:65 At the door of the fold, words; within the fold, an account.

Proverbial (Hebrew)

37:66 Words will endure; ways will fall into disuse.

Proverbial (Tamil)

37:67 No word can be judged as to whether it is good or bad, correct or incorrect, beautiful or ugly, or anything else that matters to a writer, in isolation.

I. A. Richards, 1936, 'The Interinanimation of Words', in *The Philosophy of Rhetoric*

37:68 Words not only affect us temporarily; they change us, they socialize or unsocialize us.

David Riesman, 1950, 'Storytellers as Tutors', in *The Lonely Crowd*

37:69 Words must surely be counted among the most powerful drugs man ever invented.

Leo Rosten, attributed, 20th century, in T. Goodman (ed.), *The Forbes Book of Business Quotations* (1997) [cf. 37:35]

37:70 The word . . . is not only a key; it may also be a fetter.

Edward Sapir, 1921, *Language*, Ch. 1

37:71 [Dromio of Ephesus] A man may break a word with you, sir, and words are but wind; /

Ay, and break it in your face, so he break it not behind.
William Shakespeare, 1594, *The Comedy of Errors*, III. i. 76

37:72 [Bolingbroke, after Richard has reduced the period of his exile by four years] How long a time lies in one little word! / Four lagging winters and four wanton springs / End in a word: such is the breath of kings.
William Shakespeare, 1595, *Richard II*, I. iii. 206

37:73 POLONIUS: What do you read, my lord?
  HAMLET: Words, words, words.
William Shakespeare, 1600–1601, *Hamlet*, II. ii. 195

37:74 Words of the world are the life of the world.
Wallace Stevens, quoted in Brendan Gill, *A New York Life* (1990)

37:75 ROSENCRANTZ: What are you playing at?
  GUILDENSTERN: Words, words. They're all we have to go on.
Tom Stoppard, 1967, *Rosencrantz and Guildenstern Are Dead*, I

37:76 For what, after all, is a word, but the enclosure for human use of a certain district, larger or smaller, from the vast outfield of thought or feeling or fact, and in this way a bringing of it under human cultivation, a rescuing of it for human uses? But how extremely unlikely it is that nations, drawing quite independently of one another these lines of enclosure, should draw them in all or most cases exactly in the same direction, neither narrower nor wider; how almost inevitable, on the contrary, that very often the lines should not coincide – and this, even supposing no moral forces at work to disturb the falling of the lines
Richard Chenevix Trench, 1851, 'On the Distinction of Words', in *On the Study of Words*, Lecture 6

37:77 What a wealth of words in almost every language lies inert and unused; and certainly not fewest in our own. How much of what might be as current coin among us, is shut up in the treasure-house of a few classical authors, or is never to be met at all but in the columns of the dictionary, we meanwhile, in the midst of all this riches, condemning ourselves to a voluntary poverty . . . like some workman who, being furnished for an operation that will challenge all his skill with a dozen different tools, each adapted for its own special purpose, should in his indolence and self-conceit persist in using only one; doing coarsely what might have been done finely; or leaving altogether undone that which, with such assistances, was quite within his reach.
Richard Chenevix Trench, 1851, 'On the Distinction of Words', in *On the Study of Words*, Lecture 6

37:78 The source of all names is the word, for it is by the word that all names are spoken. The word is behind all names, even as Brahman is behind the word.
'Brihad-Aranyaka Upanishad', c.800 BC, II, Ch. 23, Sect. 2, in *The Upanishads* (trans. Juan Mascaró, 1965)

37:79 But we live like our names and you would have to be colonial to know the difference, to know the pain of history words contain.
Derek Walcott, 1980, 'The Schooner *Flight*', Part 6, in *The Star-Apple Kingdom*

37:80 One forgets words as one forgets names. One's vocabulary needs constant fertilizing or it will die.
Evelyn Waugh, 25 December 1962, 'Irregular Notes', in M. Davie (ed.), *Diaries*

37:81 All words are spiritual. Nothing is more spiritual than words.
Walt Whitman, quoted in C. K. Ogden and I. A. Richards, *The Meaning of Meaning* (1923), Ch. 2

37:82 [Dorian Gray] It is a sad truth, but we have lost the faculty of giving lovely names to things. Names are everything. I never quarrel with actions. My one quarrel is with words. That is the reason I hate vulgar realism in literature. The man who would call a spade a spade should be compelled to use one. It is the only thing he is fit for.
Oscar Wilde, 1890, *The Picture of Dorian Gray*, Ch. 17

37:83 'Meaning' is one of the words of which one may say that they have odd jobs in our language. . . . What causes most trouble in philosophy is that we are tempted to describe the use of important 'odd-job' words as though they were words with regular functions.
Ludwig Wittgenstein, 1933–4, *The Blue Book*, in *The Blue and Brown Books* (1965), p. 43

37:84 Think of words as instruments characterized by their use, and then think of the use of a hammer, the use of a chisel, the use of a square, of a glue pot, and of the glue.
Ludwig Wittgenstein, 1933–4, *The Blue Book*, in *The Blue and Brown Books* (1965), p. 67

See also: 1:75, 2:3, 5:21, 5:83, 9:25, 18:3, 20:5, 28:22, 48:42, 48:46, 49:8, 49:41

38 *Words Praised*

Words and language praised or celebrated

38:1 Words, when well chosen, have so great a Force in them, that a Description often gives us more lively Ideas than the Sight of Things themselves.

Joseph Addison, 27 June 1712, 'Secondary Pleasures of the Imagination: Consideration Limited to Literature', *The Spectator*, no. 416

38:2 Freshness of words, simplicity of emotions, / If we lost these, would it not be as though / Blindness had stricken Fra Angelico, / Or an actor lost his power of voice and motion?

Anna Akhmatova, 1917, 'Freshness of words . . .', in *White Flock* (trans. D. M. Thomas in *Anna Akhmatova: Selected Poems*, Penguin 1988)

38:3 O there are words that should not be repeated, / And he who speaks them – is a spend-thrift.

Anna Akhmatova, 1917, 'O there are words . . .', in *White Flock* (trans. D. M. Thomas in *Anna Akhmatova: Selected Poems*, Penguin 1988)

38:4 Most of the men and women who use words in public don't care any more which words they are, apart from a feeble hankering after the seemingly stylish. The concept of finding the right words, which used to be a strong influence on that of finding a good word, is being lost. How such people keep awake when they write is beyond me.

Kingsley Amis, 1980, 'Getting it Wrong', in L. Michaels and C. Ricks (eds), *The State of the Language*

38:5 In youth open your mind, And let all learning in; / Words the head does not shape Are worthless, out and in. / Words wit has not salted,

No nearer the heart than the lip, / Are nothing more than wind, A puppy's insolent yelp.

Anonymous, *c.*1500, 'To a Boy', translated from the Irish by Michael O'Donovan; in *Chambers Dictionary of Quotations*

38:6 Words are but the images of matter; and except they have life of reason and invention, to fall in love with them is all one as to fall in love with a picture.

Francis Bacon, 1605, *The Advancement of Learning*, I, Sect. 3

38:7 'Some people', Miss R. said, 'run to conceits or wisdom but I hold to the hard, brown, nutlike word. I might point out that there is enough aesthetic excitement here to satisfy anyone but a damned fool.'

Donald Barthelme, 1968, 'The Indian Uprising', in *Unspeakable Practices, Unnatural Acts*

38:8 What things have we seen, / Done at the Mermaid! heard words that have been / So nimble, and so full of subtil flame, / As if that every one from whence they came, / Had meant to put his whole wit in a jest, / And had resolv'd to live a fool, the rest / Of his dull life.

Francis Beaumont, 1605, 'Letter to Ben Jonson', preface to Jonson's *Volpone*

38:9 Atlantic rollers bursting in my ears, / And pealing church-bells and the puff of trains, / The sight of sailing clouds, the smell of grass – / Were always calling out to me for words. / I caught at them and missed and missed again.

John Betjeman, 1960, *Summoned by Bells*, Ch. 2

38:10 Does not dew relieve the heat? In the same way a word is worth more than a gift. Why

surely, a word is better than a good present; but a generous man is ready with both.
The Bible, Ecclesiasticus 18:16 (Jerusalem Bible)

38:11 Like apples of gold in a silver setting is a word that is aptly spoken.
The Bible, Proverbs 25:11 (Jerusalem Bible)

38:12 *Obsolete, adj.* No longer used by the timid. Said chiefly of words. A word which some lexicographer has marked obsolete is ever thereafter an object of dread and loathing to the fool writer, but if it is a good word and has no exact modern equivalent equally good, it is good enough for the good writer. Indeed, a writer's attitude toward 'obsolete' words is as true a measure of his literary ability as anything except the character of his work.
Ambrose Bierce, 1911, *The Devil's Dictionary*

38:13 [Rousseau] knew / How to make madness beautiful, and cast / O'er erring deeds and thoughts, a heavenly hue / Of words, like sunbeams, dazzling as they past / The eyes, which o'er them shed tears feelingly and fast.
Lord Byron, 1816, *Childe Harold's Pilgrimage*, Canto 1, stanza 77

38:14 [Scipio, to Berganza] Proper words show the propriety of those who speak or write them.
Miguel de Cervantes, 1613, 'The Dogs' Colloquy', in *Exemplary Stories* (trans. C. A. Jones)

38:15 Words, for alas my trade is words, a barren burst of rhymes, / Rubbed by a hundred rhymesters, battered a thousand times, / Take them, you, that smile on strings, those nobler sounds than mine, / The words that never lie, or brag, or flatter, or malign.
G. K. Chesterton, 1915, 'To M. E. W.', in *Poems*

38:16 He who wants to persuade should put his trust not in the right argument, but in the right word. The power of sound has always been greater than the power of sense.
Joseph Conrad, 1912, 'A Familiar Preface', in *A Personal Record*

38:17 [David, having mastered stenography] I wallow in words.
Charles Dickens, 1849–50, *David Copperfield*, Ch. 43

38:18 [John Jarndyce] A word in earnest is as good as a speech.
Charles Dickens, 1852–3, *Bleak House*, Ch. 6

38:19 And every phrase / And sentence that is right (where every word is at home, / Taking its

place to support the others, / The word neither diffident nor ostentatious, / An easy commerce of the old and the new, / The common word exact without vulgarity, / The formal word precise but not pedantic, / The complete consort dancing together) / Every phrase and every sentence is an end and a beginning, / Every poem an epitaph.
T. S. Eliot, 1944, 'Little Gidding', Part 5, in *Four Quartets*

38:20 [Lady Lurewell] Grant me some wild expressions, Heavens, or I shall burst . . . Words, words, or I shall burst!
George Farquhar, 1699, *The Constant Couple*, V. iii

38:21 [of Hamidullah and others, listening to Aziz quoting poetry] It never bored them to hear words, words; they breathed them with the cool night air, never stopping to analyse.
E. M. Forster, 1924, *A Passage to India*, Ch. 1

38:22 [after completing a course of elocution] Something wonderful and new had happened to me, something much more glorious than simply being understood. I had discovered the beauty of speech. Suddenly I had an endless supply of toys: words. Meaningless phatic utterance for its own sake would become my equivalent of a Winnie the Pooh hum, my *music*.
Stephen Fry, 1997, 'Joining in', Sect. 3, in *Moab Is My Washpot*

38:23 For, just when ideas fail, a word at the right time can work wonders for you / And save the situation. / With words you can build a system.
Goethe, 1808, 'Studierzimmer', in *Faust* (trans.), I

38:24 Words – so innocent and powerless as they are, as standing in a dictionary, how potent for good and evil they become, in the hands of one who knows how to combine them!
Nathaniel Hawthorne, 1841–52, *American Notebooks*

38:25 Bone-house: / a skeleton / in the tongue's / old dungeons.
   I push back / through dictions, / Elizabethan canopies, / Norman devices,
   the erotic mayflowers / of Provence / and the ivied latins / of churchmen
   to the scop's / twang, the iron / flash of consonants / cleaving the line.
   In the coffered / riches of grammar / and declensions / I found *ban-hus* [bone-house].
Seamus Heaney, 1975, 'Bone Dreams', in *North*

38:26 I declare a new and ruthless Word War; and I invite all lovers of good words to buckle on their dictionaries and enter the fight, whether on our side or against us.

A. P. Herbert, 1935, 'Invitation to the War', in *What a Word!*

38:27 When I feel inclined to read poetry I take down my dictionary. The poetry of words is quite as beautiful as that of sentences. The author may arrange the gems effectively, but their shape and lustre have been given by the attrition of ages. Bring me the finest simile from the whole range of imaginative writing, and I will show you a single word which conveys a more profound, a more accurate, and a more eloquent analogy.

Oliver Wendell Holmes, senior, 1858, 'The Autocrat's Autobiography', in *The Autocrat of the Breakfast Table*

38:28 Every word fresh from the dictionary brings with it a certain succulence.

Oliver Wendell Holmes, senior, 1858, *The Autocrat of the Breakfast Table*, Ch. 5 [cf. 38:37]

38:29 I am omniverbivorous by nature and training. Passing by such words as are poisonous, I can swallow most others, and chew such as I cannot swallow.

Oliver Wendell Holmes, senior, 1858, *The Autocrat of the Breakfast Table*, Ch. 11

38:30 Winged words.

Homer, *c.*8th century BC, *The Iliad*, I, 201, and elsewhere

38:31 The gift of finding the right and simple word accurately to describe things seen is, at bottom, the same visual power which enables van Eyck to give his portraits their perfect expression.

Johan Huizinga, 1924, *The Waning of the Middle Ages*, Ch. 21

38:32 The Voyce so sweet, the words so faire, / As some soft chime had stroak'd the ayre; / And, though the sound were parted thence, / Still left an Eccho in the sense.

Ben Jonson, 'The Mind', in *Eupheme* (1640)

38:33 A day of dappled seaborne clouds.
The phrase and the day and the scene harmonized in a chord. Words. Was it their colours? He allowed them to glow and fade, hue after hue: sunrise gold, the russet and green of apple orchards, azure of waves, the grey-fringed fleece of clouds. No, it was not their colours: it was the poise and balance of the period itself.

James Joyce, 1916, *Portrait of the Artist as a Young Man*, Ch. 4

38:34 Words that open our eyes to the world are always the easiest to remember.

Ryszard Kapuściński, 1992, 'Daguerreotypes', in *Shah of Shahs*

38:35 I speak to you, companions of revelry, / Drunk like me on words, / Sword-words, poison-words, / Key-words, lockpicker words, / Salt-words, mask and nepenthe.

Primo Levi, 10 February 1981, 'Voices', in *Collected Poems* (trans. R. Feldman, 1988)

38:36 For so long as words, like mortals, call a fatherland their own, / They will be most highly valued where they are best and longest known.

Henry Wadsworth Longfellow, 1846, 'Rhymes' (translation from Friedrich von Logau), in *Poetic Aphorisms*

38:37 Words, those precious gems of queer shapes and gay colours, sharp angles and soft contours, shades of meaning laid one over the other down history, so that for those far back one must delve among the lost and lovely litter that strews the centuries. ... They arrange themselves in the most elegant odd patterns; they sound the strangest sweet euphonious notes; they flute and sing and taber, and disappear, like apparitions, with a curious perfume and a most melodious twang.

Rose Macaulay, 1935, 'Writing', in *Personal Pleasures*

38:38 You cannot throw words like heroism and sacrifice and nobility and honor away without abandoning the qualities they express.

Marya Mannes, 1958, *More in Anger*, Ch. 3

38:39 Words divested of their magic are but dead hieroglyphs.

Henry Miller, 1951, *The Books in My Life*, Ch. 7

38:40 His words, like so many nimble and airy servitors, trip about him at command.

John Milton, 1641–2, *Apology for Smectymnuus*

38:41 I never wanted to be a writer. I loved words, but I was not a word-user, rather a word-watcher, in the way that some people are bird-watchers. I loved languages but I knew by now that I would never speak the languages that I read. I was one for whom the spoken and the written word are themselves different languages.

Iris Murdoch, 1975, 'Friday' (first week), in *A Word Child*

38:42 Seated one day at the dictionary I was pretty weary and also pretty ill at ease, / Because a word I had always liked turned out not to be a word at all, and suddenly I found myself among the v's. / And suddenly among the v's I came across a new word which was a word called *velleity*, / So the new word I found was better than the old word I lost, for which I thank my tutelary deity.

Ogden Nash, 1938, 'Where there's a Will, there's Velleity', in *I'm a Stranger Here Myself*

38:43 Those things for which we find words, are things we have already overcome.

Friedrich Nietzsche, 1888, 'Skirmishes in a War with the Age', in *Twilight of the Idols* (trans. A. M. Ludovici)

38:44 A tiny little word can be a clap of thunder.

Proverbial (French)

38:45 A word spoken at the right moment is like a golden apple on a silver dish.

Proverbial (Silesian)

38:46 [on encountering hard words in his early reading] I did not learn the meanings of these hard, black words until ten or fifteen years later, and, even today, they still remain opaque: they are the leaf-mould of my memory.

Jean-Paul Sartre, 1964, 'Reading', in *Words* (trans. I. Clephane), I

38:47 As a rhetorician, I loved only words: I would raise up cathedrals of words beneath the blue gaze of the word sky. I would build for thousands of years.

Jean-Paul Sartre, 1964, 'Writing', in *Words* (trans. I. Clephane), II

38:48 My father still reads the dictionary every day. He says that your life depends on your power to master words.

Arthur Scargill, 10 January 1982, in the *Sunday Times*

38:49 [Phoebe] 'Tis but a peevish boy. Yet he talks well. / But what care I for words? Yet words do well / When he that speaks them pleases those that hear.

William Shakespeare, 1600, *As You Like It*, III. v. 111

38:50 POMPEY: I have fair meanings, sir.

ANTONY: And fair words to them.

William Shakespeare, 1606, *Antony and Cleopatra*, II. vi. 67

38:51 [Philisides] Art? What can be that art that thou dost mean by thy speech? / What be the fruits of speaking art? What grows by the words? / O much more than words: those words serv'd more me to bless.

Philip Sidney, 1581, 'Second Eclogues', in *The Old Arcadia*

38:52 I cannot love a friend whose love is words.

Sophocles, 5th century BC, *Antigone* (trans. E. Wyckoff)

38:53 In poetry, you must love the words, the ideas and the images and rhythms with all your capacity to love anything at all.

Wallace Stevens, 1957, 'Adagia', in *Opus Posthumous*

38:54 [on Olivia's mother] To her, words are more ardent if a man must struggle to find them, if he says '*amor*' with a trill rather than ordinary 'love'.

Amy Tan, 1995, 'The Ghost Merchant's House', in *The Hundred Secret Senses*, Ch. 4

38:55 All the charm of all the Muses / often flowering in a lonely word.

Alfred, Lord Tennyson, 1882, 'To Virgil', stanza 3

38:56 I fell in love – that is the only expression I can think of – at once, and am still at the mercy of words, though sometimes now, knowing a little of their behaviour very well, I think I can influence them slightly and have even learned to beat them now and then, which they appear to enjoy.

Dylan Thomas, 1961, poetic manifesto, *Texas Quarterly*, no. 4, issue 4

38:57 I do not like writing about words, because then I often use bad and wrong and stale and woolly words. What I like to do is to treat words as a craftsman does his wood or stone or what-have-you, carve, mould, coil, polish and plane them into patterns, sequences, sculptures, fugues of sound expressing some lyrical impulse, some spiritual doubt or conviction, some dimly-realised truth I must try to reach and realise.

Dylan Thomas, 1961, poetic manifesto, *Texas Quarterly*, no. 4, issue 4

38:58 *Abbreviations* are the *wheels* of language, the *wings* of Mercury. And though we might be dragged along without them, it would be with much difficulty, very heavily and tediously.

John Horne Tooke, 1786, *The Diversions of Purley*, I, Ch. 1

38:59 Of two possible words always choose the lesser.

Paul Valéry, early 20th century, 'Advice to the Writer', in *Odds and Ends* (trans. S. Gilbert, 1970)

38:60 Words should be an intense pleasure, just as leather should be to a shoemaker.

Evelyn Waugh, 19 November 1950, *New York Times*

38:61 Words have not merely music as sweet as that of viol and lute, colour as rich and vivid as any that makes lovely for us the canvas of the Venetian or the Spaniard, and plastic form no less sure and certain than that which reveals itself in marble or in bronze but thought and passion and spirituality are theirs also, are theirs indeed alone. If the Greeks had criticized nothing but language, they would still have been the great art-critics of the world.

Oscar Wilde, 1891, 'The Critic as Artist', in *Intentions*

38:62 Twice five years / Or less I might have seen, when first my mind / With conscious pleasure opened to the charm / Of words in tuneful order, found them sweet / For their own *sakes*, a passion, and a power; / And phrases pleased me chosen for delight, / For pomp, or love.

William Wordsworth, 1805, *The Prelude*, V, 552

38:63 Oh, wondrous power of words, by simple faith / Licensed to take the meaning that we love!

William Wordsworth, 1805, *The Prelude*, VII, 119

38:64 [on expressing insight] Smooth task! for words find easy way, inspired / By gratitude, and confidence in truth.

William Wordsworth, 1805, *The Prelude*, XIII, 14

38:65 I have come into my strength, / And words obey my call.

W. B. Yeats, 1910, 'Words'

See also: 14:32, 20:27, 20:38, 25:18, 39:49, 49:82

Words and language criticized or condemned

39:1 There is Nothing in Nature so irksome as general Discourses, especially when they turn chiefly upon Words.

Joseph Addison, 5 January 1712, '*Paradise Lost Examined by the Rules of Epic Poetry: the Fable and Action*', *The Spectator*, no. 267

39:2 [Chorus] What good are the oracles to men? Words, more words, / and the hurt comes on us, endless words / and a seer's techniques have brought us / terror and the truth.

Aeschylus, 458 BC, *Agamemnon* (trans. R. Fagles), 1,134

39:3 Let mortals beware / Of words, for / With words we lie, / Can we say peace / When we mean war, / Foul thoughts speak fair / And promise falsely.

W. H. Auden, 1971, '*United Nations Hymn*'

39:4 The ill and unfit choice of words wonderfully obstructs the understanding.

Francis Bacon, 1620, *Novum Organum*, Aphorism 43

39:5 There is no use indicting words, they are no shoddier than what they peddle.

Samuel Beckett, 1958, *Malone Dies*

39:6 A man in the habit of using improper words will never break himself of it however long he lives.

The Bible, Ecclesiasticus 23:15 (Jerusalem Bible)

39:7 [on Dylan Thomas's poetry] Such a fatigue of adjectives, a drone of alliterations, a huffing of hyphenated words hurdling the meter like tired horses. Such a faded upholstery of tears, stars, bells, bones, flood and blood ... a thud of consonants in tongue, night, dark, dust, seed, wound and wind.

Anatole Broyard, 1974, *Aroused by Books*

39:8 [Professor Teufelsdröckh] What are your Axioms, and Categories, and Systems, and Aphorisms? Words, words. High Air-castles are cunningly built of Words, the Words well bedded also in good Logic-mortar, wherein, however, no Knowledge will come to lodge ... Be not the slave of Words.

Thomas Carlyle, 1833, *Sartor Resartus*, I, Ch. 8

39:9 Words are but empty thanks.

Colley Cibber, 1697, *Woman's Wit*, V

39:10 [on looking for the right book to decode a cipher] The vocabulary of 'Bradshaw' [the railway timetable] is nervous and terse, but limited. The selection of words would hardly lend itself to the sending of general messages.

Arthur Conan Doyle, 1915, *The Valley of Fear*, Ch. 1

39:11 MASKWELL: Guilt is ever at a loss and confusion waits upon it, when Innocence and bold Truth are always ready for expression –

LADY TOUCHWOOD: Not in Love, Words are the weak support of Cold indifference; Love has no Language to be heard.

William Congreve, 1694, *The Double-Dealer*, IV. ii

39:12 *Words* without *Sense* make but dull Musick.

Daniel Defoe, 1697, '*Of Academies*', in *An Essay upon Projects*

39:13 An abstract term is like a box with a false bottom; you may put in it what ideas you please, and take them out again without being observed.

Alexis de Tocqueville, 1835–40, *De la Démocratie en Amérique [Democracy in America]* (trans.), Ch. 16

39:14 [of Mr Crummles' daughter] Language was not powerful enough to describe the infant phenomenon.

Charles Dickens, 1838–9, *Nicholas Nickleby*, Ch. 23

39:15 [advice from a family raven] You are mighty proud about your language; but it seems to me that you don't deserve to have words, if you can't make a better use of 'em.

Charles Dickens, 1858, *From the Raven in the Happy Family*, Sect. 1, in *Reprinted Pieces*

39:16 Language thou art too narrow, and too weake / To ease us now; / great sorrow cannot speake; / If we could sigh out accents, and weepe words, / Griefe weares, and lessens, that tears breath affords.

John Donne, c.1609, 'An Elegy upon the Death of Mistress Boulstred' (also known as *Elegy*, 'Death'), 1

39:17 [Charles] It's strange that words are so inadequate. / Yet, like the asthmatic struggling for breath, / So the lover must struggle for words.

T. S. Eliot, 1958, *The Elder Statesman*, III

39:18 Words are no good . . . words don't ever fit even what they are trying to say.

William Faulkner, 1930, *As I Lay Dying*

39:19 In a culture like ours, language is exclusive, not inclusive. Those on easy terms with words are distrusted. I was always encouraged to believe that cleverness and elegance with words obscured and twisted decent truth: Britain's idea of a golden mean was (and still is) healthy inarticulacy.

Stephen Fry, 1997, 'Joining in', Sect. 3, in *Moab Is My Washpot*

39:20 Words have no language which can utter the secrets of love; and beyond the limits of expression is the expounding of desire.

Hafiz, 14th century, ghazals in the *Divan* (trans. J. H. McCarthy), no. 46

39:21 Articulate words are a harsh clamor and dissonance. When man arrives at his highest perfection, he will again be dumb!

Nathaniel Hawthorne, April 1841, *American Notebooks*

39:22 I hate anything that occupies more space than it is worth. I hate to see a load of bandboxes

go along the street, and I hate to see a parcel of big words without anything in them.

William Hazlitt, 1821, 'On Familiar Style', *Quarterly Review*

39:23 For words are wise mens counters, they do but reckon by them: but they are the mony [money] of fooles, that value them by the authority of an *Aristotle*, a *Cicero*, or a *Thomas*, or any other Doctor whatsoever, if but a man.

Thomas Hobbes, 1651, 'Of Speech', in *Leviathan*, I, Ch. 4

39:24 Words have killed images or are concealing them. A civilization of words is a civilization distraught. Words create confusion. Words are not the word. . . . The fact is that words say nothing, if I may put it that way . . . There are no words for the deepest experience. The more I try to explain myself, the less I understand myself. Of course, not everything is unsayable in words, only the living truth.

Eugène Ionesco, journal entry, quoted in George Steiner, 'The Retreat from the Word', in *Language and Silence* (1967)

39:25 Words, like glass, obscure when they do not aid vision.

Joseph Joubert, 1842, *Pensées* (trans.), Sect. 21, Part 15

39:26 [Stephen, walking to college,] found himself glancing from one casual word to another on his right or left in stolid wonder that they had been so silently emptied of instantaneous sense until every mean shop legend bound his mind like the words of a spell and his soul shrivelled up sighing with age as he walked on in a lane among heaps of dead language.

James Joyce, 1916, *Portrait of the Artist as a Young Man*, Ch. 5

39:27 I fear those big words, Stephen said, which make us so unhappy.

James Joyce, 1922, *Ulysses*, I (p. 29 of 1937 edition)

39:28 Distrust of words is a trait often found among those who create with their eyes.

Arthur Koestler, 1964, 'The Word and the Vision', in *The Act of Creation*, Ch. 7

39:29 Juan wondered if words meant anything at all. Certainly they rarely meant as much as their users thought, and often they were meaningless as a bullfrogs' chorus. Nine-tenths of all words were parrot-noises, not weighed, savoured, and tested, but merely repeated; a token coinage, defaced by long usage; there were whole sentences that lay on the surface of public memory and were paid-out ten thousand times a day – flipped off the tongue, rebounding from the tympanum – without a thought to give them life; and to nine-tenths of this vain nine-tenths no one listened. So that it was doubly vain. A minute disturbance in the air.

Eric Linklater, 1931, *Juan in America*, p. 280

39:30 How strangely do we diminish a thing as soon as we try to express it in words.

Maurice Maeterlinck, 1896, 'Mystic Morality', in *The Treasure of the Humble* (trans. A. Sutro)

39:31 [on expressing feelings of anger about the world] We have a great amount of trouble expressing it because we don't trust words. Our anger is so great we can only blurt and stammer. Our semantic chickens have come home to roost . . . We have come to accept all sorts of semantic inversions, just as George Orwell told us we would.

David Mamet, 1986, 'Semantic Chickens', in *Writing in Restaurants*

39:32 [Sir John] One cut from ven'son to the heart can speak / Stronger than ten quotations from the Greek; / One fat Sir Loin possesses more sublime / Than all the airy castles built by rhyme.

Peter Pindar, 1786, *Bozzy and Piozzi*, II

39:33 All our life is crushed by the weight of words: the weight of the dead.

Luigi Pirandello, 1922, *Henry IV* (trans. E. Storer), II

39:34 The mouth is burnt. [His words are valueless.]

Proverbial (Tsonga)

39:35 All that one suffers from unhappiness comes from the tongue.

Proverbial (Turkish)

39:36 A good word travels far, a bad one farther.

Proverbial (Bulgarian)

39:37 If one word misses the mark, a thousand will do the same.

Proverbial (Chinese)

39:38 The poison of a word is a word.

Proverbial (Swahili)

39:39 Words and feathers are tossed by the wind.

Proverbial (Spanish)

39:40 An ox is bound with ropes and a man with words.

Proverbial (Italian)

39:41 Cloth shrinks, words still more.

Proverbial (Russian)

39:42 How describe the delicate thing that happens when a brilliant insect alights on a flower? Words, with their weight, fall upon the picture like birds of prey.

Jules Renard, September 1893, *Journal* (trans. L. Bogan and E. Roget)

39:43 One of our defects as a nation is a tendency to use what have been called 'weasel words'. When a weasel sucks eggs the meat is sucked out of the egg. If you use a 'weasel word' after another there is nothing left of the other.

Theodore Roosevelt, 31 May 1916, speech in St Louis

39:44 In the faculty of speech man excels the brute; but if thou utterest what is improper, the brute is thy superior.

Sadi, 1258, *Gulistan [Rose Garden]* (trans. J. Ross), Introduction

39:45 Look how you use proud words, / When you let proud words go, it is not easy to call them back, / They wear long boots, hard boots; they walk off proud; they can't hear you calling – / look out how you use proud words.

Carl Sandburg, 1922, 'Primer Lesson', in *Slabs of the Sunburnt West*

39:46 Words may be false and full of art; / Sighs are the natural language of the heart.

Thomas Shadwell, 1675, *Psyche*, III

39:47 DUCHESS OF YORK: Why should calamity be full of words?

QUEEN ELIZABETH: Windy attorneys to their client woes, / Airy recorders of intestate joys, / Poor breathing orators of miseries. / Let them have scope. Though what they will impart / Help nothing else, yet do they ease the heart.

William Shakespeare, 1592–3, *Richard III*, IV. iv. 126

39:48 [King Richard] Conscience is but a word that cowards use, / Devised at first to keep the strong in awe.

William Shakespeare, 1592–3, *Richard III*, V. vi. 39

39:49 [Biron] O, never will I trust to speeches penned, / Nor to the motion of a schoolboy's tongue, / Nor never come in visor to my friend, / Nor woo in rhyme, like a blind harper's song. / Taffeta phrases, silken terms precise, / Three-

piled hyperboles, spruce affectation, / Figures pedantical – these summer flies / Have blown me full of maggot ostentation. / I do forswear them, and I here protest, / By this white glove – how white the hand, God knows! – / Henceforth my wooing mind shall be expressed / In russet yeas, and honest kersey noes.
William Shakespeare, 1593–4, *Love's Labour's Lost*, V. ii. 402

39:50 [Lucrece] This helpless smoke of words doth me no right.
William Shakespeare, 1593, *The Rape of Lucrece*, 1,027

39:51 [Lucrece] Out, idle words, servants to shallow fools, / Unprofitable sounds, weak arbitrators! / Busy yourselves in skill-contending schools, / Debate where leisure serves with dull debaters, / To trembling clients be you mediators.
William Shakespeare, 1593, *The Rape of Lucrece*, 1,016

39:52 [Hotspur, of the perfumed noble who demanded his prisoners] With many holiday and lady terms / He questioned me.
William Shakespeare, 1596–7, *Henry IV, Part 1*, I. iii. 45

39:53 [Falstaff] What is honour? A word. What is that word, honour? Air. A trim reckoning!
William Shakespeare, 1596–7, *Henry IV, Part 1*, V. i. 133

39:54 ROSALIND [asking Celia ten questions at once about Orlando]: Answer me in one word.
CELIA: You must borrow me Gargantua's mouth first, 'tis a word too great for any mouth of this age's size. To say ay and no to these particulars is more than to answer in a catechism.
William Shakespeare, 1600, *As You Like It*, III. ii. 219

39:55 FESTE: A sentence is but a cheveril glove to a good wit, how quickly the wrong side may be turned outward.
VIOLA: Nay, that's certain. They that dally nicely with words may quickly make them wanton.
FESTE: I would therefore my sister had no name, sir.
VIOLA: Why, man?
FESTE: Why, sir, her name's a word, and to dally with that word might make my sister wanton. But indeed, words are very rascals since bonds disgraced them.
VIOLA: Thy reason, man?
FESTE: Troth, sir, I can yield you none without

words, and words are grown so false I am loath to prove reason with them.
William Shakespeare, 1601, *Twelfth Night*, III. i. 11

39:56 [Feste, of Olivia] I am indeed not her fool, but her corrupter of words.
William Shakespeare, 1601, *Twelfth Night*, III. i. 34

39:57 [Ulysses, describing Patroclus' mocking imitations of Agamemnon] And when he speaks / 'Tis like a chime a-mending, with terms unsquared / Which from the tongue of roaring Typhon dropped / Would seem hyperboles.
William Shakespeare, 1602, *Troilus and Cressida*, I. iii. 158

39:58 [Brabanzio] These sentences, to sugar or to gall, / Being strong on both sides, are equivocal. / But words are words. I never yet did hear / That the bruised heart was piercèd through the ear.
William Shakespeare, 1603–4, *Othello*, I. iii. 215

39:59 [Flavius, to Timon] The world is but a word. / Were it all yours to give it in a breath, / How quickly were it gone.
William Shakespeare, 1604, *Timon of Athens*, II. ii. 149

39:60 CARDINAL WOLSEY [to the Lords demanding that he resign]: Where's your commission, lords? Words cannot carry / Authority so weighty.
SUFFOLK: Who dare cross 'em / Bearing the King's will from his mouth expressly?
CARDINAL WOLSEY: Till I find more than will or words to do it – / I mean your malice – know, officious lords, / I dare and must deny it.
William Shakespeare, 1613, *Henry VIII (All Is True)*, III. ii. 234

39:61 Why write I still all one, ever the same, / And keep invention in a noted weed, / That every word doth almost tell my name, / Showing their birth and where they did proceed? . . . So all my best is dressing old words new, / Spending again what is already spent.
William Shakespeare, Sonnet 76, published in 1609

39:62 [Prometheus, to Earth] Words are quick and vain.
Percy Bysshe Shelley, 1820, *Prometheus Unbound*, I

39:63 When the lute is broken, / Sweet tones are remembered not; / When the lips have spoken, / Loved accents are soon forgot.
Percy Bysshe Shelley, 1822, 'Lines: When the Lamp is Shattered'

39:64 But with your Rubarb words you must contend / To grieve me worse.

Philip Sidney, c.1582, *Astrophel and Stella*, Sonnet 14

39:65 The use we make of our monosyllabic sounds is somewhat wasteful and capricious. Some of them are made to bear the weight of many significations, while others are not made use of at all, and lie idle, like bits of unstamped coin, in the treasury of our speech.

Logan Pearsall Smith, 1928, 'Needed Words', Society for Pure English, Tract 31

39:66 [Chorus] What shall be said? for words are thorns to grief.

Algernon Charles Swinburne, 1865, *Atalanta in Calydon*

39:67 [Francisco] A mere tale of a tub, my words are idle, / But to express the sonnet by natural reason.

John Webster, 1612, *The White Devil*, II. i.

39:68 LORD GORING [reacting to Mrs Cheveley's decision to expose Sir Robert]: It would be vile, horrible, infamous.

MRS CHEVELEY: Oh! don't use big words. They mean so little.

Oscar Wilde, 1895, *An Ideal Husband*, III

39:69 People are able to live with only half a heart, to live without real compassion, because they are able to use words that are only forms.

Angus Wilson, 1972, interview in the *Iowa Review*, no. 3

39:70 [to a boy who had visited London] Much I questioned him; / And every word he uttered, on my ears / Fell flatter than a cagèd parrot's note, / That answers unexpectedly awry, / And mocks the prompter's listening.

William Wordsworth, 1805, *The Prelude*, VII, 98

39:71 I might have thrown poor words away / And been content to live.

W. B. Yeats, 1910, 'Words'

See also: 1·24, 2·125, 6·19, 6·85, 31·17, 49·21, 57:35

40 *Words as Weapons*

Words seen as weapons or ammunition

40:1 [of Bailey] Just after our return he had taken to sarcasm, picked it up as one might pick up a stone, and put it snufflike under his lip. The double entendres, the two-pronged sentences, slid over his tongue to dart rapier-like into anything that happened to be in the way. Our customers, though, generally were so straight thinking and speaking that they were never hurt by his attacks. They didn't comprehend them.
Maya Angelou, 1969, *I Know Why the Caged Bird Sings*, Ch. 14

40:2 [Chorus, anticipating the contest between Euripides and Aeschylus] Words are their weapons: watch out, as the armour-clad syllables hurtle, / Helmeted, crested, and plumed, from the lips of the Poet Most High! / Wait for the clash and the din as the metaphors mingle and jumble, / The sparks as the particles fly.
Aristophanes, 405 BC, *The Frogs* (trans. D. Barrett), II

40:3 [of the Thunderer] Huge are the words that he hurls, great compounds with rivets and bolts in, / And epithets hewed out of stone.
Aristophanes, 405 BC, *The Frogs* (trans. D. Barrett), II

40:4 Although we think we govern our words, and prescribe it well, . . . yet certain it is that words, as a Tartar's bow, do shoot back upon the understanding of the wisest, and mightily entangle and pervert the judgment.
Francis Bacon, 1605, *The Advancement of Learning*, II

40:5 A stroke of the whip raises a weal; but a stroke of the tongue breaks bones. Many have fallen by the edge of the sword; but many more have fallen by the tongue.
The Bible, Ecclesiasticus 28:17 (Jerusalem Bible)

40:6 There are some whose thoughtless words pierce like a sword; but the tongue of the wise brings healing.
The Bible, Proverbs 12:18 (Jerusalem Bible)

40:7 *Logomachy, n.* A war in which the weapons are words and the wounds punctures in the swim-bladder of self-esteem.
Ambrose Bierce, 1911, *The Devil's Dictionary*

40:8 A blow with a word strikes deeper than a blow with a sword.
Robert Burton, 1621, *Anatomy of Melancholy*, I, Sect. 2, Memb. 4, Subsect. 4

40:9 A bitter jest, a slander, a calumny, pierceth deeper than any loss, danger, bodily pain, or injury whatsoever.
Robert Burton, 1621, *Anatomy of Melancholy*, I, Sect. 2, Memb. 4, Subsect. 4

40:10 As old knights-errant in their harness fought / As safe as in a castle or redoubt, / Gave one another desperate attacks, / To storm the counterscarps upon their backs; / So disputants advance, and post their arms, / To storm the works of one another's terms; / Fall foul on some extravagant expression, / But ne'er attempt the main design and reason – / So some polemics use to draw their swords / Against the language only and the words; / As he who fought at barriers with Salmasius, / Engag'd with nothing but his style and phrases.
Samuel Butler (1612–80), 1670s, 'Satire upon the Imperfection and Abuse of Human Learning', fragments of an intended second part

40:11 A word carries far – very far – deals

destruction through time as the bullets go flying through space.

Joseph Conrad, 1900, *Lord Jim*, Ch. 15

40:12 Blows are sarcasms turned stupid: wit is a form of force that leaves the limbs at rest.

George Eliot, 1866, *Felix Holt*, Ch. 30

40:13 Speak what you think today in words as hard as cannon balls, and tomorrow speak what tomorrow thinks in hard words again, though it contradict everything you said today.

Ralph Waldo Emerson, 1841, 'Self-reliance', in *Essays*

40:14 [Elliott Carver] Words are the new weapons.

Bruce Feirstein, 1997, screenplay for the James Bond film *Tomorrow Never Dies*

40:15 [Aeneas, to Achilles] Do not let us stand here in the heart of a battle talking like silly boys. We could sling plenty of insults at each other – enough in fact to sink a merchantman. The tongue is glib. With a wide range of words at its command, it can express our thoughts in any style; and as a rule one gets the kind of answer one has asked for.

Homer, *c.*8th century BC, *Iliad* (trans. E. V. Rieu), XX, 248

40:16 In the old days of barbarism, the people fought with hatchets. Civilized men buried the hatchet, and now fight with gossip.

Edgar Watson Howe, 1911, *Country Town Sayings*

40:17 'Vile bug of a coward,' said Lypiatt [to Mr Mercaptan], 'why don't you defend yourself like a man? You can only be dangerous with words.'

Aldous Huxley, 1923, *Antic Hay*, Ch. 18

40:18 It is almost worse for a C.O. not to have expressive written (not spoken) words at his command than not to have men. With luck you can always scratch a few men together out of the hospitals or the Army Service Corps; but if you send in a report that nobody can make head or tail of, because you haven't the words to tell your case, you can lose a thousand men in half an hour. So you *must* get your words, and a working knowledge of the use of words. And words come out of literature – even if you make no other use of it.

Rudyard Kipling, May 1912, 'The Uses of Reading' (speech at Wellington College), in *A Book of Words*

40:19 [on the Elizabethan age and today] And in both ages you can see writers raking the dumps of the English language for words that shall range farther, hit harder, and explode over a wider area than the service-pattern words in common use.

Rudyard Kipling, June 1926, 'Fiction' (speech to the Royal Literary Society), in *A Book of Words*

40:20 [Hiawatha] Big words do not smite like warclubs, / Boastful breath is not a bowstring, / Taunts are not so sharp as arrows, / Deeds are better things than words are, / Actions mightier than boastings!

Henry Wadsworth Longfellow, 1855, 'Hiawatha and the Pearl-feather', *The Song of Hiawatha*, Sect. 9

40:21 All books are either dreams or swords, / You can cut, or you can drug, with words.

Amy Lowell, 1914, 'Sword Blades and Poppy Seeds'

40:22 Sticks and stones are hard on bones. / Aimed with angry art, / Words can sting like anything. / But silence breaks the heart.

Phyllis McGinley, 1954, 'Ballade of Lost Objects', in *The Love Letters of Phyllis McGinley*

40:23 Wit has a deadly aim and it is possible to prick a large pretense with a small pin.

Marya Mannes, 1955–64, 'Controverse', in *But Will It Sell?*

40:24 A candour affected is a dagger concealed.

Marcus Aurelius, 2nd century, *Meditations* (trans. M. Staniforth, 1964, Penguin), XI, Sect. 15

40:25 In our language rhyme is a barrel. A barrel of dynamite. The line is a fuse. The line smoulders to the end and explodes; and the town is blown sky-high in a stanza.

Vladimir Mayakovsky, 1926, 'Conversation with an Inspector of Taxes about Poetry' (trans. D. Obolensky)

40:26 To 'language up' an opponent is . . . to confuse, irritate and depress by the use of foreign words, fictitious or otherwise, either singly or in groups.

Stephen Potter, 1950, *Lifemanship*, Ch. 1

40:27 The greatest war is the war of the mouth.

Proverbial (Tswana)

40:28 A swearer is said to be armed with teeth.

Proverbial (Fijian)

40:29 The tongue's not steel, yet it cuts.

Proverbial

40:30 A kick is better than a tongue-blow.
Proverbial (Breton)

40:31 The tongue has no bones, yet it breaks bones.
Proverbial

40:32 When the wise man makes an arm of his tongue, he makes it a shield and not a sword.
Proverbial (Russian)

40:33 In the tongue there lurks a dragon's den; no blood is seen and yet it murders men.
Proverbial (Chinese)

40:34 [of slander] The third tongue slays three: the speaker, the spoken to, and the spoken of.
Proverbial (Hebrew)

40:35 A word is no arrow, but it can pierce the heart.
Proverbial (Bulgarian)

40:36 Many words hurt more than swords.
Proverbial (Spanish)

40:37 To kill with words is also murder.
Proverbial (German)

40:38 Words leave no scar.
Proverbial (Rwandan)

40:39 Wounds inflicted by the sword heal more easily than those inflicted by the tongue.
Cardinal Richelieu, 1688, *Testament politique* (trans.)

40:40 [Portnoy] My God! The English language is a form of communication! Conversation isn't just crossfire where you shoot and get shot at! Where you've got to duck for your life and aim to kill! Words aren't only bombs and bullets – no, they're little gifts, containing meanings!
Philip Roth, 1969, 'The Most Prevalent Form of Degradation in Erotic Life', in *Portnoy's Complaint* (Vintage), p. 221

40:41 The pen is mightier than the sword, but not the mouth.
Charles Schulz, attributed, 20th century [cf. 6:7]

40:42 [Silvia, to Thario and Valentine] A fine volley of words, gentlemen, and quickly shot off.
William Shakespeare, 1590–1, *The Two Gentlemen of Verona*, II. iv. 32

40:43 [Benedick, of Beatrice] She speaks poniards, and every word stabs. If her breath were

as terrible as her terminations, there were no living near her, she would infect to the North Star.
William Shakespeare, 1598–9, *Much Ado About Nothing*, II. i. 231

40:44 [Benedick, of Beatrice] Shall quips and sentences and these paper bullets of the brain awe a man from the career of his humour?
William Shakespeare, 1598–9, *Much Ado About Nothing*, II. iii. 227

40:45 [Boy] For Pistol, he hath a killing tongue and a quiet sword – by the means whereof a breaks words, and keeps whole weapons.
William Shakespeare, 1599, *Henry V*, III. ii. 34

40:46 [Hamlet, of Gertrude] I will speak daggers to her, but use none. / My tongue and soul in this be hypocrites – / How in my words somever she be shent, / To give them seals never my soul consent.
William Shakespeare, 1600–1601, *Hamlet*, III. ii. 385

40:47 CELIA: Why cousin, why Rosalind – Cupid have mercy, not a word?
  ROSALIND: Not one to throw at a dog.
  CELIA: No, thy words are too precious to be cast away upon curs. Throw some of them at me. Come, lame me with reasons.
William Shakespeare, 1600, *As You Like It*, I. iii. 1 [cf. 64:25]

40:48 BRUTUS [to Coriolanus, who has risen from his place rather than hear himself praised]: Sir, I hope / My words disbenched you not?
  CORIOLANUS: No sir, yet oft / When blows have made me stay I fled from words.
William Shakespeare, 1608, *Coriolanus*, II. ii. 70

40:49 [Queen to Cymbeline, about Innogen] Beseech your majesty / Forbear sharp speeches to her. She's a lady / So tender of rebukes that words are strokes, / And strokes death to her.
William Shakespeare, 1610–11, *Cymbeline*, III. v. 38

40:50 [Prometheus, to Fury] Thy words are like a cloud of wingèd snakes.
Percy Bysshe Shelley, 1820, *Prometheus Unbound*, I

40:51 [of Don Pasquito] But a word stung him like a mosquito.
Edith Sitwell, 1923, 'Tango-Pasodoble', in *Façade*

40:52 My parents kept me from children who

were rough / Who threw words like stones and who wore torn clothes.

Stephen Spender, 1933, 'My Parents Kept me from Children who were Rough'

40:53 In dagger-contests, and the artillery of words, / (For swords are madmen's tongues, and tongues are madmen's swords).

Jonathan Swift, 1692, 'Ode to Dr. William Sancroft'

40:54 [Toxeus] How long will ye whet spears with eloquence, / Fight, and kill beasts dry-

handed with sweet words? / Cease, or talk still and slay thy boars at home.

Algernon Charles Swinburne, 1865, *Atalanta in Calydon*

40:55 [Althæa] Refrain your lips, O brethren, and my son, / Lest words turn snakes and bite you uttering them.

Algernon Charles Swinburne, 1865, *Atalanta in Calydon*

See also: 32:9, 44:8, 53:26

41 *Wise and Foolish Talk*

Words of wisdom or advice; words careless or foolish

41:1 The words of the sages are like goads, like pegs driven deep.
The Bible, Ecclesiastes 12:11 (Jerusalem Bible; Authorized Version, 'The words of the wise . . .')

41:2 Do not ignore the talk of the wise; be conversant with their proverbs.
The Bible, Ecclesiasticus 8:8 (Jerusalem Bible)

41:3 Do not open your heart to every man; or solicit favours from all comers.
The Bible, Ecclesiasticus 8:19 (Jerusalem Bible)

41:4 Work from skilled hands will earn its praise, but a leader of the people must be shrewd of speech.
The Bible, Ecclesiasticus 9:17 (Jerusalem Bible)

41:5 Those who understand sayings have themselves grown wise, and have poured out apt proverbs.
The Bible, Ecclesiasticus 18:29 (Jerusalem Bible)

41:6 Like an arrow stuck in the flesh of a thigh, such is a piece of news inside a fool.
The Bible, Ecclesiasticus 19:12 (Jerusalem Bible)

41:7 A maxim is rejected when coming from a fool, since he does not utter it on the apt occasion.
The Bible, Ecclesiasticus 20:20 (Jerusalem Bible)

41:8 Who scoffs at his neighbour is a fool: the man of discernment holds his tongue.
The Bible, Proverbs 11:12 (Jerusalem Bible)

41:9 The fools' mouth contains a rod of pride; the wise man's lips watch over him.
The Bible, Proverbs 14:3 (Jerusalem Bible)

41:10 Fine words do not become the foolish; false words become a prince still less.
The Bible, Proverbs 17:7 (Jerusalem Bible)

41:11 If a fool can hold his tongue, even he can pass for wise; and pass for clever if he keeps his lips tight shut.
The Bible, Proverbs 17:28 (Jerusalem Bible)

41:12 The lips of the fool draw him into arguments; and his mouth pleads for a beating.
The Bible, Proverbs 18:6 (Jerusalem Bible)

41:13 The mouth of the fool works his own ruin; his lips are a snare for his own life.
The Bible, Proverbs 18:7 (Jerusalem Bible)

41:14 Unreliable as a lame man's legs, so is a proverb in the mouth of fools.
The Bible, Proverbs 26:7 (Jerusalem Bible)

41:15 A thorn branch in a drunkard's hand; such is a proverb in the mouth of fools.
The Bible, Proverbs 26:9 (Jerusalem Bible)

41:16 SCIPIO: In order to know how to be silent in one's mother tongue and speak in Latin one needs to be wise, brother Berganza.
BERGANZA: That is true, because it is as easy to say something stupid in Latin as in the vernacular.
Miguel de Cervantes, 1613, 'The Dogs' Colloquy', in *Exemplary Stories* (trans. C. A. Jones)

41:17 But words once spoke can never be recalled.
Wentworth Dillon, 1680, *The Art of Poetry*, 438 [cf. 29:83]

41:18 The heart of a fool is in his mouth, but the mouth of a wise man is in his heart.
Benjamin Franklin, 1732–57, *Poor Richard's Almanack*

41:19 There is always time to add a word, never to withdraw one.
Baltasar Gracián, 1647, *The Art of Worldly Wisdom* (trans. J. Jacobs), p. 160

41:20 Nobody talks much that doesn't say unwise things – things he did not mean to say; as no person plays much without striking a false note sometimes.
Oliver Wendell Holmes, senior, 1860, *The Professor at the Breakfast Table*, Ch. 1

41:21 [to Boswell] My dear friend, clear your *mind* of cant. You may *talk* as other people do: you may say to a man, 'Sir, I am your most humble servant.' You are *not* his most humble servant. . . . You tell a man, 'I am sorry you had such bad weather the last day of your journey, and were so much wet.' You don't care sixpence whether he is wet or dry. You may *talk* in this manner; it is a mode of talking in society; but don't *think* foolishly.
Samuel Johnson, 1783, in James Boswell, *The Life of Samuel Johnson* (1791), Ch. 57

41:22 I have loved badly, loved the great / Too soon, withdrawn my words too late; / And eaten in an echoing hall / Alone and from a chipped plate / The words that I withdrew too late.
Edna St Vincent Millay, 1939, 'Theme and Variations', in *Huntsman, What Quarry?*

41:23 Any man may speak truly: few men can speak ordinately, wisely, adequately.
Michel de Montaigne, 1572–80, 'On the Art of Conversation', in *The Complete Essays* (trans. M. A. Screech, 1987), III, no. 8

41:24 It is easy to utter what has been kept silent, but impossible to recall what has been uttered.
Plutarch, 1st century, 'The Education of Children', in *Moralia* (trans. M. Hadas)

41:25 Give advice to all; but be security for none.
Proverbial

41:26 If you wish good advice, consult an old man.
Proverbial

41:27 The dumbness in the eyes of animals is more touching than the speech of men, but the dumbness in the speech of men is more agonizing than the eyes of animals.
Proverbial (Hindustani)

41:28 A wise man who knows proverbs reconciles difficulties.
Proverbial (Yoruba)

41:29 A fool may ask more questions in an hour, than a wise man can answer in seven years.
Proverbial

41:30 One may say what one has kept silent, but not keep silent what one has said.
Proverbial (Swiss)

41:31 He is a fool who speaks and listens to himself.
Proverbial (Turkish)

41:32 Among the walnuts only the empty one speaks.
Proverbial (Moorish)

41:33 For empty speech there is plenty of room.
Proverbial (Serbian)

41:34 Let not your tongue cut your throat.
Proverbial

41:35 A person ties a knot with his tongue that cannot be loosed by his teeth.
Proverbial (Irish)

41:36 One's tongue has often broken his nose.
Proverbial (Irish)

41:37 Dip your tongue in wisdom, then give counsel.
Proverbial (Bulgarian)

41:38 The tongue of the wise is in his heart, the heart of the fool is in his mouth.
Proverbial (Arabic)

41:39 A word is enough for the wise.
Proverbial (Latin, Italian, and French)

41:40 A word is medicine to the wise.
Proverbial (Telugu)

41:41 A wise man hears one word and understands two.
Proverbial (Yiddish)

41:42 Few words sufficeth to a wise man.
Proverbial

41:43 Old words are wise words.
Proverbial (Basque)

41:44 Hold fast to the words of your ancestors.
Proverbial (Maori)

41:45 The words of a chief are built in an enclosure. [The words of a chief are carefully remembered.]
Proverbial (Sotho)

41:46 [Julia, of Proteus] His words are bonds, his oaths are oracles.
William Shakespeare, 1590–1, *The Two Gentlemen of Verona*, II. vii. 75

41:47 [John of Gaunt] O, but they say the tongues of dying men / Enforce attention, like deep harmony. / Where words are scarce they are seldom spent in vain, / For they breathe truth that breathe their words in pain.
William Shakespeare, 1595, *Richard II*, II. i. 5

41:48 [Lorenzo, of Lancelot Gobbo] O dear discretion, how his words are suited! The fool hath planted in his memory / An army of good words, and I do know / A many fools that stand in better place, / Garnished like him, that for a tricksy word / Defy the matter.
William Shakespeare, 1596–7, *The Merchant of Venice*, III. v. 60

41:49 A fool and his words are soon parted.
William Shenstone, 1764, 'On Reserve'

41:50 Man does not live by words alone, despite the fact that sometimes he has to eat them.
Adlai Stevenson, 5 September 1952, speech in Denver, Colorado, in *Speeches* (1952)

41:51 [Meleager] Peace, and be wise; no gods love idle speech.
Algernon Charles Swinburne, 1865, *Atalanta in Calydon*

41:52 Error flies from mouth to mouth, from pen to pen, and to destroy it takes ages.
Voltaire, 1764, 'Assassin', in *Philosophical Dictionary* (trans.)

See also: 9:8, 26:8, 29:19, 29:57, 29:61, 29:95, 29:102, 31:2, 31:52, 39:23, 40:6, 62:7, 62:46, 62:48, 62:61

42 *Slang*

Slang and fashionable language

42:1 Dialect tempered with slang is an admirable medium of communication between persons who have nothing to say and persons who would not care for anything properly said.
Thomas Bailey Aldrich, 1903, 'Leaves from a Notebook', in *Ponkapog Papers*

42:2 [of Bailey] He had made friends during that youth-shattering summer with a group of slick street boys. His language had changed. He was forever dropping slangy terms into his sentences like dumplings in a pot.
Maya Angelou, 1969, *I Know Why the Caged Bird Sings*, Ch. 33

42:3 There is something suspect (and potentially ridiculous) about those in the vanguard of slang.
Alan Bennett, 1981, 'Cold Sweat', reprinted in *Writing Home*, p. 309

42:4 *Slang, n.* The grunt of the human hog (*Pignoramus intolerabilis*) with an audible memory. The speech of one who utters with his tongue what he thinks with his ear, and feels the pride of a creator in accomplishing the feat of a parrot. A means (under Providence) of setting up as a wit without a capital of sense.
Ambrose Bierce, 1911, *The Devil's Dictionary*

42:5 [of slang] 'Dustbin language'.
Robert Burchfield, 1985, *The English Language*, Ch. 7

42:6 The word 'slang' is vague and its etymology obscure. It suggests the slinging of odd stones or dollops of mud at the windows of the stately home of linguistic decorum.
Anthony Burgess, 1992, *A Mouthful of Air*, II, Ch. 7

42:7 All slang is metaphor, and all metaphor is poetry.
G. K. Chesterton, 1901, 'Defence of Slang', in *The Defendant*

42:8 Mom said, 'Oh you *kids*! I guess I'm just not in the loop.' Being 'in the loop' is this year's big expression. Only three more weeks remain before the phrase becomes obsolete, like an Apple Lisa computer. Language is such a technology.
Douglas Coupland, 1995, 'Monday', in *Microserfs*, Ch. 4

42:9 [of Little Swills] Being asked what he thinks of the proceedings, characterizes them (his strength lying in a slangular direction) as 'a rummy start'.
Charles Dickens, 1852–3, *Bleak House*, Ch. 11

42:10 [of Lady Dedlock] She is discussed by her dear friends with all the genteelest slang in vogue, with the last new word, the last new manner, the last new drawl, and the perfection of polite indifference.
Charles Dickens, 1852–3, *Bleak House*, Ch. 58

42:11 [Fred Vincey] All choice of words is slang. It marks a class.
George Eliot, 1871–2, *Middlemarch*, I, Ch. 11

42:12 [Fred Vincey] Correct English is the slang of prigs who write history and essays. And the strongest slang of all is the slang of poets.
George Eliot, 1871–2, *Middlemarch*, I, Ch. 11

42:13 Slang is vigorous and apt. Probably most of our vital words were once slang.
John Galsworthy, 1927, *Castles in Spain and Other Screeds*

42:14 His slang . . . was always a little out of date, as though he had studied in a dictionary of popular usage, but not in the latest edition.
Graham Greene, 1966, *The Comedians*, I, Ch. 1

42:15 [on American slang] It is one part 'natural growth' and nine parts a nervous disorder. It is St. Vitus's Talk.
A. P. Herbert, 1935, *What a Word!*, Ch. 2

42:16 [referring to a definition of slang as 'language which has taken its coat off'] I think of it, reluctantly, as language which is always taking its trousers off (and vaguely prancing in the street).
A. P. Herbert, 1935, *What a Word!*, Ch. 2

42:17 Most of us are bower birds of language. We pick up the brightest new slang, Broadway, Yiddish, Cockney, and from other fertile sources of new language, to decorate our discourse with for a while. It becomes tarnished from overuse, and we drop it and pick up something else.
Philip Howard, 1978, contribution to 'Language: U and non-U, double-U, E and non-E', in Richard Buckle (ed.), *U and Non-U Revisited*, p. 43

42:18 Slang is a linguistic luxury, it is a sport, and, like any other sport, something that belongs essentially to the young.
Otto Jespersen, 1946, 'Slang', in *Mankind, Nation and Individual*, Ch. 8

42:19 Slang is a poor-man's poetry.
John C. Moore, 1962, *You English Words*

42:20 Slang, the acme and quintessence of spoken and informal language.
Eric Partridge, 1940, 'Slang', Society for Pure English, Tract 55

42:21 Some people worry that slang will somehow 'corrupt' the language. We should be so lucky. Most slang lexicons are preciously guarded by their subcultures as membership badges.
Steven Pinker, 1994, *The Language Instinct*, Ch. 12

42:22 Slang is a language that rolls up its sleeves, spits on its hands and goes to work.
Carl Sandburg, 13 February 1959, *New York Times*, p. 21

42:23 [Biron, of Armado] A man of fire-new words, fashion's own knight.
William Shakespeare, 1593–4, *Love's Labour's Lost*, I. i. 175

42:24 [Mercutio] The pox of such antic, lisping, affecting phantasims [fantastic beings], these new tuners of accent! 'By Jesu, a very good blade, a very tall man, a very good whore.' Why is this not a lamentable thing, grandsire, that we should be thus afflicted with these strange flies, these fashion-mongers, these 'pardon-me's', who stand so much on the new form that they cannot sit at ease on the old bench?
William Shakespeare, 1594–5, *Romeo and Juliet*, II. iii. 26

42:25 A Man who has been out of Town but one half Year, has lost the Language, and must have some Friend to stand by him, and keep him in Countenance for talking common Sense.
Richard Steele, 5 May 1709, 'Things are Come to this Pass', *The Tatler*, no. 12

42:26 [Lily Dale] I fancy I do like slang. I think it's awfully jolly to talk about about things being jolly. Only that I was afraid of your nerves I should have called him stunning. It's so slow, you know, to use nothing but words out of a dictionary.
Anthony Trollope, 1862, *The Small House at Allington*, Ch. 2

42:27 There is one fact about slang that is quite certain – its fugacious and ephemeral nature. Freshness is of its very essence; slang terms are the mayflies of language; by the time they get themselves recorded in a dictionary, they are already museum specimens.
J. M. Wattie, March 1930, *The Grammarian and His Material* (The English Association, London), Pamphlet 75, p. 12

42:28 Slang, profoundly considered is the lawless germinal element, below all words and sentences, and behind all poetry, and proves a certain freedom and perennial rankness and protestantism in speech.
Walt Whitman, 1885, 'Slang in America', in the *North American Review*, no. 141

42:29 Slang . . . is the wholesome fermentation or eructation of those processes eternally active in language, by which froth and specks are thrown up, mostly to pass away; though occasionally to settle and permanently crystallize.
Walt Whitman, 1885, 'Slang in America', in the *North American Review*, no. 141

See also: 7:63, 11:65, 44:11, 44:18, 52:46, 57:21

Swearing, cursing, obscenity, and other exclamatory language

43:1 Some guy hit my fender the other day, and I said unto him, 'Be fruitful and multiply.' But not in those words.

Woody Allen, quoted in B. Adler and J. Feinman, *Woody Allen: Crown Prince of American Humor* (1976), Ch. 2

43:2 Many little cuss words, bother, dash and blow, / And other little wuss words, can send us down below.

Anonymous, 'Nursery Rules from Nannies', in *The Faber Book of Useful Verse* (1981), p. 91

43:3 In holy anger, and pious grief, / He solemnly cursed that rascally thief! / He cursed him at board, he cursed him in bed; / From the sole of his foot to the crown of his head; / He cursed him in sleeping, that every night / He should dream of the devil, and wake in a fright.

R. H. Barham, 1840, 'The Jackdaw of Rheims', in *The Ingoldsby Legends*, First Series

43:4 The English, in truth, do add here and there some other words when speaking; but it is obvious that 'God-damn' is the foundation of their language.

Pierre Augustin de Beaumarchais, 1784, *Le Mariage de Figaro* (trans.), III. v

43:5 Thou shalt not take the name of the Lord thy God in vain; for the Lord will not hold him guiltless that taketh his name in vain.

The Bible, Exodus 20:7 (Authorized Version of 1611)

43:6 [Jesus] Do not swear at all, either by heaven, since that is God's throne; or by the earth, since that is his footstool; or by Jerusalem, since that is the city of the great king. Do not swear by your own head either, since you cannot turn a single hair white or black. All you need say is 'Yes' if you mean yes, 'No' if you mean no; anything more than this comes from the evil one.

The Bible, Matthew 5:34 (Jerusalem Bible)

43:7 Oaths are but words, and words but wind: / Too feeble implements to bind.

Samuel Butler (1612–80), 1664, *Hudibras*, II, Canto 2, 107

43:8 [on the evil of swearing] How copious is our language lately grown, / To make blaspheming wit, and a jargon! / And yet how expressive and significant, / In *damme* at once to curse, and swear and rant!

Samuel Butler (1612–80), 1670s, 'Satire upon the Licentious Age of Charles II'

43:9 [on blasphemy] For what can any language more enrich, / Than to pay souls for vitiating speech

Samuel Butler (1612–80), 1670s, 'Satire upon the Licentious Age of Charles II'

43:10 She liked the English and the Hebrew tongue / And said there was analogy between 'em; / She proved it somehow out of sacred song, / But I must leave the proofs to those who've seen 'em. / But this I heard her say, and can't be wrong, / And all may think which way their judgements lean 'em, / ' 'Tis strange, the Hebrew noun which means "I am", / The English always use to govern damn.'

Lord Byron, 1819–24, *Don Juan*, Canto 1, stanza 14

43:11 And yet the British damme's rather Attic. / Your Continental oaths are but incontinent / And turn on things which no aristocratic / Spirit would name, and therefore even I won't anent [concerning] / This subject quote, as it would be schismatic / In politesse and have a sound affronting in't. / But damme's quite ethereal, though too daring, / Platonic blasphemy, the soul of swearing.

Lord Byron, 1819–24, *Don Juan*, Canto 11, stanza 43

43:12 'G–d damn!' – those syllables intense, – / Nucleus of England's native eloquence.

Lord Byron, 1823, *The Island*, Canto 3, Sect. 5

43:13 Oaths terminate, as Paul observes, all strife – / Some men have surely then a peaceful life!

William Cowper, 1782, *Conversation*, 55

43:14 It's hard to put two words together in creole without swearing. Words are spat out from the mouth like live squibs, not pronounced with elocution.

David Dabydeen, 1990, 'On Not Being Milton: Nigger Talk in England Today', in L. Michaels and C. Ricks (eds), *The State of the Language*

43:15 There is nothing so Impertinent, so Sensless and Foolish, as our vulgar way of Discourse, when mix'd with Oaths and Curses.

Daniel Defoe, 1697, 'Of Academies', in *An Essay upon Projects*

43:16 *Swearing*, that Lewdness of the Tongue, that Scum and Excrement of the Mouth, is of all Vices the most foolish and sensless; it makes a man's Conversation *unpleasant*, his Discourse *fruitless*, and his Language *Nonsense*.

Daniel Defoe, 1697, 'Of Academies', in *An Essay upon Projects*

43:17 [Mr Peggotty] swore a dreadful oath that he would be 'Gormed' if he didn't cut and run for good, if it [his generosity] was ever mentioned again. It appeared, in answer to my inquiries, that nobody had the least idea of the etymology of this terrible verb passive to be gormed; but that they all regarded it as constituting a most solemn imprecation.

Charles Dickens, 1849–50, *David Copperfield*, Ch. 3

43:18 Immodest words admit of no defence, / For want of decency is want of sense.

Wentworth Dillon, 1684, *Essay on Translated Verse*, 113

43:19 Swearin' belongs to some thrades, – like printin', bricklayin' an' plumbin'. It is no help at all, at all to tailors, shoemakers, hair-dressers, dintists or authors. A surgeon needs it but a doctor niver.

Finley Peter Dunne, 1902, 'Swearing', in *Observations by Mr Dooley*

43:20 Sojers mus' swear. They'se no way out iv it. It's as much th' equipment iv a sojer as catridges.

Finley Peter Dunne, 1902, 'Swearing', in *Observations by Mr Dooley*

43:21 [of swearing] It's a kind iv a first aid to th' injured. It seems to deaden th' pain.

Finley Peter Dunne, 1902, 'Swearing', in *Observations by Mr Dooley*

43:22 [on not swearing too much] Put a little pro-fanity by f'r rainy days, says I. Ye won't miss it an' at th' end iv th' year whin ye renew ye'er lease ye'll be surprised to find out how much ye have on hand.

Finley Peter Dunne, 1902, 'Swearing', in *Observations by Mr Dooley*

43:23 They ain't too much pro-fanity in th' wurruld . . . Th' govermint ought to presarve it an' prevint annywan fr'm swearin' more thin was niciss'ry f'r to support life.

Finley Peter Dunne, 1902, 'Swearing', in *Observations by Mr Dooley*

43:24 Th' best thing about a little judicyous swearin' is that it keeps th' temper. 'Twas intinded as a compromise between runnin' away an' fightin'. Befure it was invinted they was on'y th' two ways out iv an argymint.

Finley Peter Dunne, 1902, 'Swearing', in *Observations by Mr Dooley*

43:25 No one is ever capable of swearing properly in any language other than their own.

Ben Elton, 1989, 'Love among the Radicals', in *Stark*

43:26 My English text is chaste, and all licentious passages are left in the obscurity of a learned language.

Edward Gibbon, 1796, *Memoirs of my Life*, Ch. 8 [altered to 'decent obscurity' in a parody in the *Anti-Jacobin* the following year]

43:27 CAPTAIN: Bad language or abuse, / I never, never use, / Whatever the emergency; / Though 'Bother it' I may / Occasionally say, / I never use a big, big D——
   ALL: What, never?
   CAPTAIN: No, never!
   ALL: What *never*?
   CAPTAIN: Well, hardly ever!

ALL: Hardly ever swears a big, big D—— / Then give three cheers, and one cheer more, / For the well-bred Captain of the *Pinafore*!

W. S. Gilbert, 1878, *HMS Pinafore*

43:28 Ethelberta breathed a sort of exclamation, not right out, but stealthily, like a parson's damn.

Thomas Hardy, 1876, *The Hand of Ethelberta*, Ch. 26

43:29 The English (it must be owned) are rather a foul-mouthed nation.

William Hazlitt, 1822, 'On Criticism', in *Table Talk* (ed. William Hazlitt, junior, 1845), II

43:30 [The Oracle's response to Glaucus, who had asked if he should perjure himself to rob the Milesians of their property] Today, indeed, Glaucus, son of Epicydes, it is more profitable / To prevail by false-swearing and rob them of their money. / Swear if you will; for death awaits even the true-swearer. / Yet an oath has a son, nameless, without hands or feet, / But swift to pursue until he has seized and destroyed / Utterly the race and house of the perjured one. / The children of him who keeps his oath are happier hereafter.

Herodotus, 5th century BC, in *The Histories* (trans. Aubrey de Sélincourt, 1996), VI, Ch. 86

43:31 All pro athletes are bilingual. They speak English and profanity.

Gordie Howe, quoted in the *Toronto Star* (27 May 1975)

43:32 Out of the same mouth proceedeth blessing and cursing. My brethren, these things ought not so to be. Doth a fountain send forth at the same place sweet water and bitter?

James, The Bible, James 3:10 (Authorized Version of 1611)

43:33 Swear not, neither by heaven, neither by the earth, neither by any other oath: but let your yea be yea; and your nay, nay.

James, The Bible, James 5:12 (Authorized Version of 1611) [cf. 43:6]

43:34 Ordinary men . . . / Put up a barrage of common sense to baulk / Intimacy but by mistake interpolate / Swear-words like roses in their talk.

Louis MacNeice, 1940, 'Conversation'

43:35 [referring to a saying of Androclides] Cheat boys with dice, and men with oaths.

Plutarch, 1st century, 'Lysander', in *Lives* (trans. A. H. Clough)

43:36 He speaks bear-garden [uses rude language].

Proverbial

43:37 [Suffolk] Could curses kill, as doth the mandrake's groan. / I would invent as bitter searching terms, / As curst, as harsh, and horrible to hear, / Delivered strongly through my fixed teeth, / With full as many signs of deadly hate, / As lean-faced envy in her loathsome cave. / My tongue should stumble in mine earnest words.

William Shakespeare, 1590–1, *Henry VI, Part 2*, III. ii. 314

43:38 HOTSPUR: Come, Kate, I'll have your song too.

LADY PERCY: Not mine, in good sooth.

HOTSPUR: Not yours, in good sooth! Heart, you swear like a comfit-maker's wife: 'Not you, in good sooth!' and 'As true as I live!' and / 'As God shall mend me!' and 'As sure as day!'; / And giv'st such sarcenet surety for thy oaths / As if thou never walks't further than Finsbury. / Swear me, Kate, like a lady as thou art, / A good mouth-filling oath, and leave 'in sooth' / And such protest of pepper gingerbread / To velvet-guards and Sunday citizens.

William Shakespeare, 1596–7, *Henry IV, Part 1*, III. i. 243

43:39 [Mistress Quickly] I pray thee, go to the casement and see if you can see my master, Master Doctor Caius, coming. If he do, i'faith, and find anybody in the house, here will be an old abusing of God's patience and the King's English.

William Shakespeare, 1597, *The Merry Wives of Windsor*, I. iv. 2

43:40 SIR TOBY: So soon as ever thou seest him, draw, and as thou drawest, swear horrible, for it comes to pass oft that a terrible oath, with a swaggering accent sharply twanged off, gives manhood more approbation than ever proof itself would have earned him. Away.

SIR ANDREW: Nay, let me alone for swearing.

William Shakespeare, 1601, *Twelfth Night*, III. iv. 174

43:41 [Isabella] That in the captain's but a choleric word, / Which in the soldier is flat blasphemy.

William Shakespeare, 1604, *Measure for Measure*, II. ii. 134

43:42 [Cloten, after gaming] I had a hundrd pound on't, and then a whoreson jackanapes

must take me up for swearing, as if I borrowed mine oaths of him, and might not spend them at my pleasure.
William Shakespeare, 1610–11, *Cymbeline*, II. i. 2

43:43 [Cloten] When a gentleman is disposed to swear it is not for any standers-by to curtail his oaths.
William Shakespeare, 1610–11, *Cymbeline*, II. i. 10

43:44 [Captain La Hire] If ever I utter an oath again may my soul be blasted to eternal damnation!
George Bernard Shaw, 1923, *Saint Joan*, scene ii

43:45 ACRES: A commander in our militia, a great scholar, I assure you, says that there is no meaning in the common oaths, and that nothing but their antiquity makes them respectable; because, he says, the ancients would never stick to an oath or two, but would say, by Jove! or by Bacchus! or by Mars! or by Venus! or by Pallas, according to the sentiment: so that to swear with propriety, says my little major, the oath should be an echo to the sense; and this we call the *oath referential*, or *sentimental swearing* – ha! ha! 'tis genteel, isn't it.
ABSOLUTE: Very genteel, and very new, indeed! – and I dare say will supplant all other figures of imprecation.
ACRES: Ay, ay, the best terms will grow obsolete. – Damns have had their day.
Richard Sheridan, 1775, *The Rivals*, II. i

43:46 Curses are like young chickens, they always come home to roost.
Robert Southey, 1810, motto for *The Curse of Kehama*

43:47 [on hearing the curses of Ernulphus] Our armies swore terribly in *Flanders*, cried my uncle *Toby*, – but nothing to this.
Laurence Sterne, 1761, *The Life and Opinions of Tristram Shandy, Gentleman*, III, Ch. 11

43:48 [advice on how to curse reluctant mules without sin] Now I see no sin in saying, *bou, bou, bou, bou, bou*, a hundred times together; nor is there any turpitude in pronouncing the syllable *ger, ger, ger, ger, ger*, were it from our matins to our vespers: Therefore, my dear daughter, continued the abbess of Andoüillets – I will say *bou*, and thou shalt say *ger*; and then alternately, as there is no more sin in *fou* than in *bou* – Thou shalt say *fou* – and I will come in (like fa, sol, la, re, mi, ut, at our complines) with *ter*. [*bouger* 'move' (cf. *bougre*, 'bugger'), *foutre* 'fuck']
Laurence Sterne, 1765, *The Life and Opinions of Tristram Shandy, Gentleman*, VII, Ch. 25

43:49 Grant me, O ye powers which touch the tongue with eloquence in distress! – whatever is my *cast*, grant me but decent words to exclaim in, and I will give my nature way. / But as these were not to be had in France, I resolved to take every evil just as it befel me, without any exclamation at all.
Laurence Sterne, 1768, 'The Bidet', in *A Sentimental Journey*

43:50 A foreign swear-word is practically inoffensive except to the person who has learnt it early in life and knows its social limits.
Paul Theroux, 1973, *Saint Jack*, Ch. 12

43:51 When angry, count four; when very angry, swear.
Mark Twain, 1894, 'Pudd'nhead Wilson's Calendar', in *Pudd'nhead Wilson*, Ch. 10

43:52 Let us swear while we may, for in heaven it will not be allowed.
Mark Twain, *Notebooks* (1935)

See also: 14:41, 27:30, 32:18, 53:10

Clichés, platitudes, euphemisms, and other worn-out expressions

44:1 He was full of cliché, but then a cliché is not a cliché if you have never heard it before; and our ordinary reader clearly had not and so was ready to greet each one with the same ecstasy it must have produced when it was first coined. For Cliché is but pauperized Ecstasy.
Chinua Achebe, 1987, *Anthills of the Savannah*, Ch. 1

44:2 Worn, threadbare, filed down, words have become the carcass of words, phantom words; everyone drearily chews and regurgitates the sound of them between their jaws.
Arthur Adamov, quoted in George Steiner, 'The Retreat from the Word', in *Language and Silence* (1967)

44:3 A platitude is simply a truth repeated until people get tired of hearing it.
Stanley Baldwin, 29 May 1924, parliamentary speech, in *Hansard*

44:4 *Euphemism, n.* A figure of speech in which the speaker or writer makes his expression a good deal softer than the facts would warrant him in doing.
Ambrose Bierce, 1911, *The Devil's Dictionary* (entry added by E. J. Hopkins for *The Enlarged Devil's Dictionary*, 1967)

44:5 *Platitude, n.* The fundamental element and special glory of popular literature. A thought that snores in words that smoke. The wisdom of a million fools in the diction of a dullard. A fossil sentiment in artificial rock. A moral without the fable. All that is mortal of a departed truth. A demi-tasse of milk-and-morality. The Pope's-nose of a featherless peacock. A jelly-fish withering on the shore of the sea of thought.

The cackle surviving the egg. A desiccated epigram.
Ambrose Bierce, 1911, *The Devil's Dictionary*

44:6 Until we learn the use of living words we shall continue to be waxworks inhabited by gramophones.
Walter de la Mare, 12 May 1929, 'Sayings of the Week', in the *Observer*

44:7 Where in this small-talking world can I find / A longitude with no platitude?
Christopher Fry, 1949, *The Lady's not for Burning*, III

44:8 It is a cliché that most clichés are true, but then like most clichés, that cliché is untrue. / Sticks and stones may break my bones, but words will always hurt me.
Stephen Fry, 1997, 'Joining in', Sect. 4, in *Moab Is My Washpot*

44:9 Let's have some new clichés.
Samuel Goldwyn, 24 October 1948, 'Sayings of the Week', in the *Observer*

44:10 Words, like clothes, get old-fashioned, or mean and ridiculous, when they have been for some time laid aside.
William Hazlitt, 1821, 'On Familiar Style', *Quarterly Review*

44:11 [on the overuse of fashionable slang] They are the blank cheques of intellectual bankruptcy; – you may fill them up with what idea you like; it makes no difference, for there are no funds in the treasury upon which they are drawn. Colleges and good-for-nothing smoking-clubs are the places where these conversational fungi spring up most luxuriantly.

Oliver Wendell Holmes, senior, 1858, *The Autocrat of the Breakfast Table*, Ch. 11

44:12 [on the proper use of a cant word] It adds piquancy to conversation, as a mushroom does to a sauce. But it is no better than a toadstool, odious to the sense and poisonous to the intellect, when it spawns itself all over the talk of men and youths capable of talking, as it sometimes does.

Oliver Wendell Holmes, senior, 1858, *The Autocrat of the Breakfast Table*, Ch. 11

44:13 Any euphemism ceases to be euphemistic after a time and the true meaning begins to show through. It's a losing game, but we keep on trying.

Joseph Wood Krutch, 1964, title essay in *If You Don't Mind My Saying So*

44:14 It is always easier to draw on the storehouse of memory than to find something original to say.

Michel de Montaigne, 1572–80, 'On Liars', in *The Complete Essays* (trans. M. A. Screech, 1987), I, no. 9

44:15 [of words] Years later I / Encounter them on the road – / Words dry and riderless, / The indefatigable hoof-taps.

Sylvia Plath, 1965, 'Words', in *Ariel*

44:16 The only way to speak of a cliché is with a cliché.

Christopher Ricks, 1980, 'Clichés', in L. Michaels and C. Ricks (eds), *The State of the Language*

44:17 The truths of the past are the clichés of the present.

Ned Rorem, 1967, 'Listening and Hearing', in *Music from Inside Out*

44:18 LADY BRITOMART: Charles: if you must drivel, drivel like a grown-up man and not like a schoolboy.

LOMAX (*out of countenance*): Well, drivel is drivel, don't you know, whatever a man's age.

LADY BRITOMART: In good society in England, Charles, men drivel at all ages by repeating silly formulas with an air of wisdom. Schoolboys make their own formulas out of slang, like you. When they reach your age, and get political private secretaryships and things of that sort, they drop slang and get their formulas out of The Spectator or The Times. You had better confine yourself to The Times. You will find that there is a certain amount of tosh about The Times; but at least its language is reputable.

George Bernard Shaw, 1905, *Major Barbara*, III

44:19 [The Bishop] A man is like a phonograph with half-a-dozen records. You soon get tired of them all; and yet you have to sit at table whilst he reels them off to every new visitor.

George Bernard Shaw, 1908, *Getting Married*, I

44:20 Shall we for ever make new books, as apothecaries make new mixtures, by pouring only out of one vessel into another?

Laurence Sterne, 1762, *The Life and Opinions of Tristram Shandy, Gentleman*, V, Ch. 1

44:21 Man is a creature who lives not upon bread alone, but principally by catchwords.

Robert Louis Stevenson, 1881, title essay in *Virginibus Puerisque*, II

44:22 Is there anything more terrible than a 'call'? It affords an occasion for the exchange of the most threadbare commonplaces. Calls and the theatre are the two great centres for the propagation of platitudes.

Miguel de Unamuno, 1924, 'Large and Small Towns', in *Essays and Soliloquies* (trans.)

44:23 [Mrs Cheveley, to Sir Robert Chiltern] In modern life nothing produces such an effect as a good platitude.

Oscar Wilde, 1895, *An Ideal Husband*, I

See also: 48:61, 59:26

Names and nicknames of people, places, or animals

45:1 Ford Prefect's original name is only pronuncible in an obscure Betelgeusian dialect, now virtually extinct since the Great Collapsing Hrung Disaster of Gal. / Sid. / Year 03758 which wiped out all the old Praxibetel communities on Betelgeuse Seven . . . Because Ford never learned to say his original name, his father eventually died of shame, which is still a terminal disease in some parts of the Galaxy. The other kids at school nicknamed him Ix, which in the language of Betelgeuse Five translates as 'boy who is not able satisfactorily to explain what a Hrung is, nor why it should choose to collapse on Betelgeuse Seven.'
Douglas Adams, 1979, *The Hitch-Hiker's Guide to the Galaxy*, Ch. 5

45:2 Never play cards with any man named 'Doc'.
Nelson Algren, 20th century, attributed in the foreword to H. E. F. Donohue, *Conversations with Nelson Algren* (1964)

45:3 No one on the docks has just one name. Everybody has a nickname too, or the name is shortened, or lengthened, or something is added that recalls a tale, a fight, a woman.
Jorge Amado, 1984, 'Iemanjá', in *Mar Morto [Sea of Death]* (trans.)

45:4 His name was Shadow, short for Shadow That Comes in Sight, an old Indian name, Apache or Cheyenne. I very much approved of this. You don't want dogs called Spot or Pooch. You don't want dogs called Nigel or Keith. The names of dogs should salute the mystical drama of the animal life. *Shadow* – that's a *good* name.
Martin Amis, 1984, *Money* (Penguin), p. 286

45:5 [on being called Mary instead of Margaret] Every person I knew had a hellish horror of being 'called out of his name.' It was a dangerous practice to call a Negro anything that could be loosely construed as insulting because of the centuries of their having been called niggers, jigs, blackbirds, crows, boots and spooks.
Maya Angelou, 1969, *I Know Why the Caged Bird Sings*, Ch. 16

45:6 My name has gotten to be a household word – at least in certain households. I think there are now people who know my name, but don't know what I do. I'm famous for being famous.
John Ashbery, 1985, interview in *PN Review*, no. 46

45:7 Like a line of poetry, a Proper Name is untranslatable.
W. H. Auden, 1948, 'Making, Knowing and Judging', in *The Dyer's Hand and other essays*

45:8 In a brothel, both / The ladies and gentlemen / Have nicknames only.
W. H. Auden, 1964, postscript to 'The Cave of Making', in *Thanksgiving for a Habitat*

45:9 [Mrs Elton] One has no great hopes from Birmingham. I always say there is something direful in the sound.
Jane Austen, 1816, *Emma*, Ch. 36

45:10 I have fallen in love with American names, / The sharp, gaunt names that never get fat, / The snakeskin-titles of mining-claims, / The plumed war-bonnet of Medicine Hat, / Tucson and Deadwood and Lost Mule Flat.
Stephen Benét, 1927, 'American Names'

45:11 When a woman is always called by her Christian name, it is generally a sign that she is loved and lovable. If a man, on the other hand, gets to be known, without any reason for the distinction, by his Christian name, it is generally a sure sign that he is sympathetic, but blind to his own interests.

Walter Besant and James Rice, 1876, *The Golden Butterfly*, Ch. 14

45:12 Bournemouth is one of the few English towns one can safely call 'her'.

John Betjeman, 1949, 'Bournemouth', radio talk, collected in *First and Last Loves* (1952)

45:13 [Abigail] Pay no attention to this ill-tempered man Nabal for his nature is like his name; 'Brute' is his name and brutish his character.

The Bible, 1 Samuel 25:25 (Jerusalem Bible) [*nabal* = 'fool' in Hebrew]

45:14 'I have no name: / I am but two days old.' / What shall I call thee? / 'I happy am, / Joy is my name.' / Sweet joy befall thee!

William Blake, 1789, 'Infant Joy', in *Songs of Innocence*

45:15 [Jasper's name for Borrow, after the latter's rapid progress in Romani] Lav-engro, which in the language of the gorgios meaneth Word Master.

George Borrow, 1851, *Lavengro*, Ch. 17

45:16 [Galy Gay, to Fairchild] Don't take action because of a name! A name is an uncertain thing, you can't count on it!

Bertolt Brecht, 1927, *A Man's a Man*, scene 10

45:17 This flower she stopped at, finger on lip, / Stooped over, in doubt, as settling its claim; / Till she gave me, with pride to make no slip, / Its soft meandering Spanish name: / What a name! Was it love or praise? / Speech half-asleep or song half-awake? / I must learn Spanish, one of these days, / Only for that slow sweet name's sake.

Robert Browning, 1845, 'The Flower's Name', in *Garden Fancies*

45:18 [Constance] A thing's shadow or a name's mere echo / Suffices those who miss the name and thing.

Robert Browning, 1855, *In a Balcony*

45:19 The glory and the nothing of a name.

Lord Byron, 1816, 'Churchill's Grave'

45:20 [of Cossack names] Achilles' self was not more grim and gory / Than thousands of this new and polished nation, / Whose names want nothing but – pronunciation.

Lord Byron, 1819–24, *Don Juan*, Canto 7, stanza 14

45:21 O Beer! O Hodgson, Guinness, Allsopp, Bass! / Names that should be on every infant's tongue!

C. S. Calverley, 1861, 'Beer'

45:22 [Professor Teufelsdröckh] For indeed, . . . there is much, nay almost all, in Names. The Name is the earliest Garment you wrap round the earth-visiting ME; to which it thenceforth cleaves, more tenaciously (for there are Names that have lasted nigh thirty centuries) than the very skin. . . . Names? Could I unfold the influence of Names, which are the most important of all Clothings, I were a second greater Trismegistus. Not only all common Speech, but Science, Poetry itself is no other, if thou consider it, than a right *Naming*.

Thomas Carlyle, 1833, *Sartor Resartus*, II, Ch. 1

45:23 [About the insects in Alice's home] 'What's the use of their having names,' the Gnat said, 'if they wo'n't answer to them?'

Lewis Carroll, 1872, *Through the Looking Glass*, Ch. 3

45:24 '*Must* a name mean something?' Alice asked doubtfully. 'Of course it must,' Humpty said with a short laugh: '*my* name means the shape I am – and a good handsome shape it is, too. With a name like yours, you might be any shape, almost.'

Lewis Carroll, 1872, *Through the Looking Glass*, Ch. 6

45:25 [Narrator, to Bruno] 'What's your name, little one?' I began, in as soft a voice as I could manage. And, by the way, why is it we always begin by asking little children their names? Is it because we fancy a name will help to make them a little bigger? You never thought of asking a real large man his name, now, did you?

Lewis Carroll, 1889, *Sylvie and Bruno*, Ch. 14

45:26 In the case of Smith, the name is so poetical that it must be an arduous and heroic matter for the man to live up to it . . . Yet our novelists call their hero 'Aylmer Valence', which means nothing, or 'Vernon Raymond', which means nothing, when it is in their power to give him this sacred name of Smith – this name of iron and flame . . . If you think the name of 'Smith' prosaic, it is not because you are practical and sensible; it is because you are too much affected with literary refinements. The name shouts poetry at you.

G. K. Chesterton, 1905, *Heretics*, Ch. 3

45:27 Said Jerome K. Jerome to Ford Madox Ford, / There's something, old boy, that I've always abhorred: / When people address me and call me 'Jerome', / Are they being standoffish, or too much at home?' / Said Ford, 'I agree; / It's the same thing with me.'

William Cole, 'Mutual Problem', in *The Oxford Book of American Light Verse* (1979)

45:28 From your unlucky name may quips and puns / Be made by these upbraiding Goths and Huns.

George Crabbe, 1810, 'Letter V: Elections', 55, in *The Borough*

45:29 [Sam Weller, on Job Trotter's first name] And a wery good name it is – only one I know, that ain't got a nickname to it.

Charles Dickens, 1836–7, *The Pickwick Papers*, Ch. 16

45:30 [Mr Bumble] We name our fondlings in alphabetical order.

Charles Dickens, 1837–8, *Oliver Twist*, Ch. 2

45:31 [Mrs Wititterly, to her page] 'Leave the room, Alphonse.' The page left it, but it ever an Alphonse carried plain Bill in his face and figure, that page was the boy.

Charles Dickens, 1838–9, *Nicholas Nickleby*, Ch. 21

45:32 [Aunt Betsy, of Peggotty] 'It's a most extraordinary world,' observed my aunt, rubbing her nose; 'how that woman ever got into it with that name, is unaccountable to me. It would be much more easy to be born a Jackson, or something of that sort, one would think.'

Charles Dickens, 1849–50, *David Copperfield*, Ch. 35

45:33 [David, on appointing a housekeeper] Her name was Paragon. Her nature was represented to us, when we engaged her, as being feebly expressed in her name.

Charles Dickens, 1849–50, *David Copperfield*, Ch. 44

45:34 [Jo, the crossing-sweeper] Name, Jo. Nothing else that he knows on. Don't know that everybody has two names. Never heerd of sich a think. Don't know that Jo is short for a longer name. Thinks it long enough for *him*. He don't find no fault with it. Spell it? No. *He* can't spell it.

Charles Dickens, 1852–3, *Bleak House*, Ch. 11

45:35 [Caddy] Young Mr Turveydrop's name is Prince; I wish it wasn't, because it sounds like a dog, but of course he didn't christen himself. Old Mr Turveydrop had him christened Prince, in remembrance of the Prince Regent.

Charles Dickens, 1852–3, *Bleak House*, Ch. 14

45:36 Reginald Wilfer is a name with rather a grand sound, suggesting on first acquaintance brasses in country churches, scrolls in stained-glass windows, and generally the De Wilfers who came over with the Conqueror. For, it is a remarkable fact in genealogy that no De Anyones ever came over with Anybody else.

Charles Dickens, 1864–5, *Our Mutual Friend*, I, Ch. 4

45:37 [of Wilfer] He was shy, and unwilling to own to the name of Reginald, as being too aspiring and self-assertive a name. In his signature he used only the initial R., and imparted what it really stood for, to none but chosen friends, under the seal of confidence. Out of this, the facetious habit had arisen in the neighbourhood surrounding Mincing Lane of making Christian names for him out of adjectives and participles beginning with R. Some of these were more or less appropriate: as Rusty, Retiring, Ruddy, Round, Ripe, Ridiculous, Ruminative; others derived their point from their want of application: as Raging, Rattling, Roaring, Raffish.

Charles Dickens, 1864–5, *Our Mutual Friend*, I, Ch. 4

45:38 The office door was opened by the dismal boy, whose appropriate name was Blight.

Charles Dickens, 1864–5, *Our Mutual Friend*, I, Ch. 8

45:39 The Secretary, working in the Dismal Swamp betimes next morning, was informed that a youth waited in the hall who gave the name of Sloppy. The footman who communicated this intelligence made a decent pause before uttering the name, to express that it was forced on his reluctance by the youth in question, and that if the youth had had the good sense and good taste to inherit some other name it would have spared the feelings of him the bearer.

Charles Dickens, 1864–5, *Our Mutual Friend*, II, Ch. 9

45:40 [Pleasant Riderhood] Show her a Christening, and she saw a little heathen personage having a quite superfluous name bestowed upon it, inasmuch as it would be commonly addressed by some abusive epithet.

Charles Dickens, 1864–5, *Our Mutual Friend*, II, Ch. 12

45:41 How easy it is to call rogue and villain, and that wittily! But how hard to make a man appear a fool, a blockhead, or a knave, without using any of those opprobrious terms! To spare the grossness of the names, and to do the thing yet more severely, is to draw a full face, and to make the nose and cheeks stand out, and yet not to employ any depth of shadowing.

John Dryden, 1693, 'The Art of Satire', in *A Discourse Concerning the Original and Progress of Satire*

45:42 As a matter of racial pride we want to be called *blacks*. Which has replaced the term *Afro-American*. Which replaced *Negroes*. Which replaced *colored people*. Which replaced *darkies*. Which replaced *blacks*.

Jules Feiffer, quoted in William Safire, *Language Maven Strikes Again* (1990)

45:43 Some word that teems with hidden meaning – like Basingstoke.

W. S. Gilbert, 1887, *Ruddigore*, II

45:44 One reason I try to get people to call me Newt is to break down barriers. It's a whole lot easier for someone to say, 'Newt, you've got a spot on your tie,' than it is to say 'Congressman'.

Newt Gingrich, attributed, 1979

45:45 [on Sam Goldwyn changing his name] A self-made man may prefer a self-made name.

Learned Hand, quoted in Bosley Crowther, *Lion's Share* (1957), Ch. 7

45:46 Nicknames, for the most part, govern the world.

William Hazlitt, 1818, 'On Nicknames', *Scot's Magazine*

45:47 A nickname is the heaviest stone that the devil can throw at a man.

William Hazlitt, 1818, 'On Nicknames', *Scot's Magazine*

45:48 Of all eloquence a nickname is the most concise; of all arguments the most unanswerable.

William Hazlitt, 1818, 'On Nicknames', *Scot's Magazine*

45:49 Nicknames are the talismans and spells that collect and set in motion all the combustible part of men's passions and prejudices.

William Hazlitt, 1818, 'On Nicknames', *Scot's Magazine*

45:50 [of Cleisthenes] He changed the names of the Dorian tribes, in order to make a distinction between the Argive and the Sicyonian; moreover, the distinction was a highly invidious one, and designed to make fools of the Sicyonians, for the names he chose were derived from the words 'donkey' and 'pig' and 'swine', with only the endings changed. This applied to all the tribes except his own, which he named the Archelai – 'rulers of the people' – after his own royal office; the others he named Hyatae – 'pig-men', Oneatae – 'donkey-men', and Choereatae – 'swine-men'. These names continued to be used in Sicyon, not only during Cleisthenes' reign but for sixty years after his death; then the matter was discussed, and the tribes were renamed Hylles, Pamphyli, and Dymanatae.

Herodotus, 5th century BC, in *The Histories* (trans. Aubrey de Sélincourt, 1996), V, Ch. 68

45:51 [of Samuel Francis Smith] Fate tried to conceal him by calling him Smith.

Oliver Wendell Holmes, senior, 1858, 'The Boys'

45:52 [from Odysseus' account of how he blinded the Cyclops] My name is Nobody. That is what I am called by my mother and father and by all my friends. . . . [Cyclops] O my friends, it's Nobody's treachery, not violence that is doing me to death. [Other Cyclops] 'Well then,' came the immediate reply, 'if you are alone and nobody is assaulting you, you must be sick' . . . And off they went, while I laughed to myself at the way in which my cunning notion of a false name had taken them in.

Homer, *c*.8th century BC, *The Odyssey* (trans. E. V. Rieu and D. C. H. Rieu), IX, 365, 408, 414

45:53 Nothing is more common than to mistake surnames, when we hear them carelessly uttered for the first time. To prevent this, he [Johnson] used not only to pronounce them slowly and distinctly, but to take the trouble of spelling them, – a practice which I have often followed, and which I wish were general.

Samuel Johnson, 1783, in James Boswell, *The Life of Samuel Johnson* (1791), Ch. 56

45:54 The ultimate indignity is to be given a bedpan by a stranger who calls you by your first name.

Maggie Kuhn, 20 August 1978, *Observer*

45:55 Nicknames and whippings, when they are once laid on, no one has discovered how to take off.

Walter Savage Landor, 1824–53, 'Peter Leopold and President du Paty', in *Imaginary Conversations*

45:56 The way that can be spoken of / Is not the constant way; / The name that can be named / Is not the constant name. / The nameless was the beginning of heaven and earth; / The named was the mother of the myriad creatures.

Lao Tzu, 6th century BC, *Tao Te Ching* (trans. D. C. Lau, 1963), I, Ch. 1

45:57 The way is for ever nameless.

Lao Tzu, 6th century BC, *Tao Te Ching* (trans. D. C. Lau, 1963), I, Ch. 32

45:58 Marrying left your maiden name disused.

Philip Larkin, 1955, 'Maiden Name'

45:59 Great names abase, instead of elevating, those who do not know how to bear them.

Duc de La Rochefoucauld, 1665, *Maxims* (trans. K. Pratt), no. 94

45:60 The name of a man is a numbing blow from which he never recovers.

Marshall McLuhan, 1964, *Understanding Media*, Ch. 2

45:61 Mandalay has its name; the falling cadence of the lovely word has gathered about itself the chiaroscuro of romance.

W. Somerset Maugham, 1930, *The Gentleman in the Parlour*

45:62 They say that it is a good thing to have a good name (meaning renown and reputation); but it is also a real advantage to have a fine one which is easy to pronounce and remember, since kings and the great can then recognize us more easily and less wilfully forget us. Even where our servants are concerned we usually summon for a job those whose names come most readily to our tongue.

Michel de Montaigne, 1572–80, 'On Names', in *The Complete Essays* (trans. M. A. Screech, 1987), I, no. 46

45:63 In this country American means white. Everybody else has to hyphenate.

Toni Morrison, 29 January 1992, *Guardian*

45:64 [Hilary] We always called each other by endearments or else by our names, never by nicknames. I think Crystal's name meant a lot to her, Crystal Burde. It had been a talisman, a sort of strange consoling thing of beauty in her life: a significant fragment of a splendour past or to come. My name, I felt, derived from hers

by some sort of linguistic law, and it was she alone who beautified it.

Iris Murdoch, 1975, 'Saturday' (first week), in *A Word Child*

45:65 How sweet the name of Jesus sounds / In a believer's ear!

John Newton, 18th century, 'The Name of Jesus'

45:66 [of Mrs Parsons] 'Mrs' was a word somewhat discountenanced by the Party – you were supposed to call everyone comrade.

George Orwell, 1949, *Nineteen Eighty-Four*, I, Ch. 2

45:67 Titles are but nick-names, and every nick-name is a title.

Thomas Paine, 1791, *The Rights of Man* (ed. P. S. Foner, 1945), p. 286

45:68 He that hath an ill name, is half hanged.

Proverbial (Spanish)

45:69 A good name is better than riches.

Proverbial (Spanish)

45:70 Take away my good name, and take away my life.

Proverbial

45:71 He who owns the boat should give it a name.

Proverbial (Norwegian)

45:72 There was an old man of St Omer / Who objected, 'This town's a misnomer; / You've no right to translate / And beatificate / A simple digamma in Homer.'

Arthur Quiller-Couch, 1941, 'A Limerick', in *Chanticlere* (Michaelmas)

45:73 'Is your maid called Florence?' 'Her name is Florinda.' 'What an extraordinary name to give a maid!' 'I did not give it to her; she arrived in my service already christened.' 'What I mean is,' said Mrs Riversedge, 'that when I get maids with unsuitable names I call them Jane; they soon get used to it.' 'An excellent plan,' said the aunt of Clovis coldly; 'unfortunately I have got used to being called Jane myself. It happens to be my name.'

Saki, 1911, 'The Secret Sin of Septimus Brope', in *The Chronicles of Clovis*

45:74 [Juliet] 'Tis but thy name that is my enemy. / Thou art thyself, though not a Montague. / What's Montague? It is not hand, nor foot, / Nor arm, nor face, nor any other part / Belonging to a man. O, be some other name! /

What's in a name? That which we call a rose /
By any other word would smell as sweet.
William Shakespeare, 1594–5, *Romeo and Juliet*, II. i.
80 [First Quarto text: '. . . By any other name . . .']

45:75 [Bastard, having just been made a knight]
And if his name be George I'll call him Peter, /
For new-made honour doth forget men's
names.
William Shakespeare, 1595–6, *King John*, I. i. 186

45:76 [Falstaff] Thou hast the most unsavoury
similes, and art indeed the most comparative,
rascalliest sweet young Prince. But Hal, I prithee
trouble me no more with vanity. I would to God
thou and I knew where a commodity of good
names were to be bought.
William Shakespeare, 1596–7, *Henry IV, Part 1*, I. ii. 79

45:77 [Ford, thinking his wife is unfaithful] I
shall not only receive this villainous wrong, but
stand under the adoption of abominable terms,
and by him that does me this wrong. Terms!
Names! 'Amaimon' sounds well, 'Lucifer' well,
'Barbason' well; yet they are devil's additions,
the names of fiends. But 'cuckold', 'wittol'!
'Cuckold' – the devil himself hath not such a
name.
William Shakespeare, 1597, *The Merry Wives of
Windsor*, II. ii. 283

45:78 [Cassius, to Brutus] Brutus and Caesar:
what should be in that 'Caesar'? / Why should
that name be sounded more than yours? / Write
them together: yours is as fair a name. / Sound
them: it doth become the mouth as well, /
Weigh them: it is as heavy.
William Shakespeare, 1599, *Julius Caesar*, I. ii. 143

45:79 JAQUES: Rosalind is your love's name?
ORLANDO: Yes, just.
JAQUES: I do not like her name.
ORLANDO: There was no thought of pleasing
you when she was christened.
William Shakespeare, 1600, *As You Like It*, III. ii. 258

45:80 [Prometheus, to Panthea] Names are
there, Nature's sacred watchwords.
Percy Bysshe Shelley, 1820, *Prometheus Unbound*, I

45:81 [Mrs Credulous, to her husband about her
daughter's behaviour] Lauretta! ay, you would
have her called so; but for my part I never knew
any good come of giving girls these heathen
Christian names: if you had called her Deborah,
or Tabitha, or Ruth, or Rebecca, or Joan, nothing

of this had ever happened; but I always knew
Lauretta was a runaway name.
Richard Sheridan, 1775, *St Patrick's Day*, II. iii

45:82 And last of all an Admiral came, / A terrible
man with a terrible name, – / A name which
you all know by sight very well; / But which no
one can speak, and no one can spell.
Robert Southey, 1813, 'The March to Moscow',
stanza 8

45:83 Okie use' ta mean you was from Okla-
homa. Now it means you're a dirty son-of-a-
bitch. Okie means you're scum. Don't mean
nothing itself, it's the way they say it.
John Steinbeck, 1939, *The Grapes of Wrath*, Ch. 18

45:84 [Tristram's father, on the choice of Christian names] His opinion . . . was, That there was
a strange kind of magick bias, which good or bad
names, as he called them, irresistibly impress'd
upon our characters and conduct.
Laurence Sterne, 1760, *The Life and Opinions of
Tristram Shandy, Gentleman*, I, Ch. 19

45:85 When once a vile name was wrongfully
or injudiciously given, 'twas not like the case of
a man's character, which, when wrong'd, might
hereafter be clear'd; . . . But the injury of this,
he [Tristram's father] would say, could never be
undone; – nay, he doubted even whether an act
of parliament could reach it.
Laurence Sterne, 1760, *The Life and Opinions of
Tristram Shandy, Gentleman*, I, Ch. 19

45:86 [of Tristram's father] There were still
numbers of names which hung so equally in the
balance before him, that they were absolutely
indifferent to him. *Jack, Dick,* and *Tom* were of
this class: These my father call'd neutral names;
– affirming of them, without a satyr, That there
had been as many knaves and fools, at least, as
wise and good men, since the world began, who
had indifferently borne them; – so that, like
equal forces acting against each other in contrary directions, he thought they mutually
destroyed each others effects.
Laurence Sterne, 1760, *The Life and Opinions of
Tristram Shandy, Gentleman*, I, Ch. 19

45:87 Three things I never lends – my 'oss, my
wife, and my name.
R. S. Surtees, 1845, *Hillingdon Hall*, Ch. 33

45:88 Our names are the light that glows on

the sea waves at night and then dies without leaving its signature.

Rabindranath Tagore, 1916, *Stray Birds* (trans.), p. 229

45:89 'For God, for Country and for Yale,' the outstanding single anti-climax in the English language.

James Thurber, 11 June 1951, *Time*

45:90 [Jack Bannister] See this place, Laku. It's marked as a town of some five thousand inhabitants, fifty miles north of Jacksonburg. Well, there never has been such a place. Laku is the Ishmaelite for 'I don't know.' When the boundary commission were trying to get through to the Sudan in 1898 they made a camp there and asked one of their boys the name of the hill, so as to record it in their log. He said 'Laku,' and they've copied it from map to map ever since.

Evelyn Waugh, 1938, *Scoop*, II, Ch. 1, Sect. 12

45:91 'It's giving girls names like that [Euphemia],' said Buggins, 'that nine times out of ten makes 'em go wrong. It unsettles 'em. If ever I was to have a girl, if ever I was to have a dozen girls, I'd call 'em all Jane.'

H. G. Wells, 1905, *Kipps*, I, Ch. 6

45:92 Once they heard someone call for 'Snooks'. 'I always thought that name was invented by novelists,' said Miss Winchelsea. 'Fancy! Snooks. I wonder which is Mr Snooks?' Finally they picked out a stout and resolute little man in a large check suit. 'If he isn't Snooks, he ought to be,' said Miss Winchelsea.

H. G. Wells, 1913, 'Miss Winchelsea's Heart', in *Tales of Life and Adventure*

45:93 [on learning that a life jacket was to be named after her] I've been in Who's Who and I know what's that, but it's the first time I ever made the dictionary.

Mae West, attributed, mid 20th century

45:94 What a relief most people have in speaking of a man not by his true and formal name,

with a 'Mister' to it, but by some odd or homely appellative.

Walt Whitman, 1885, 'Slang in America', in the *North American Review*, no. 141

45:95 JACK: I think Jack, for instance, a charming name.

GWENDOLEN: Jack? . . . No, there is very little music in the name Jack, if any at all, indeed. It does not thrill. It produces absolutely no vibrations . . . I have known several Jacks, and they all, without exception, were more than usually plain. Besides, Jack is a notorious domesticity for John! And I pity any woman who is married to a man called John. She would probably never be allowed to know the entrancing pleasure of a single moment's solitude. The only really safe name is Ernest.

Oscar Wilde, 1895, *The Importance of Being Earnest*, I

45:96 [Cecily, to Algernon] I pity any poor married woman whose husband is not called Ernest.

Oscar Wilde, 1895, *The Importance of Being Earnest*, II

45:97 [of double-barrelled names] There are a great many hyphens left in America. For my part, I think the most un-American thing in the world is a hyphen.

Woodrow Wilson, 9 September 1919, speech at St Paul, Minnesota

45:98 I call him Jordan and it will do. He has no other name before or after. What was there to call him, fished as he was from the stinking Thames? A child can't be called Thames, no and not Nile either, for all his likeness to Moses. But I wanted to give him a river name, a name not bound to anything, just as the waters aren't bound to anything.

Jeanette Winterson, 1989, *Sexing the Cherry*

45:99 LILL: My massage was marvellous. I feel really relaxed. And my masseur, Harold –

VICTORIA: You can't have a masseur called Harold. It's like having a member of the Royal Family called Ena.

Victoria Wood, 1989, *Victoria Wood* television series

See also: 39:55

46 Words and Expressions

Individual words and expressions praised or condemned

46:1 It can hardly be a coincidence that no language on earth has ever produced the expression 'as pretty as an airport'.
Douglas Adams, 1988, *The Long Dark Tea-Time of the Soul*, Ch. 1

46:2 Polyester . . . the most valuable word to come out of the 70s, the one that defined tacky for all time.
Anonymous, 21 March 1991, *New York Times*, editorial

46:3 Philistinism! – We have not the expression in English. Perhaps we have not the word because we have so much of the thing.
Matthew Arnold, 1865, 'Heinrich Heine', in *Essays in Criticism*

46:4 What a polite game tennis is. The chief word in it seems to be 'sorry' and admiration of each other's play crosses the net as frequently as the ball.
J. M. Barrie, attributed, c. early 20th century, in Colin Jarman, *The Guinness Dictionary of Sports Quotations* (1990)

46:5 Natural rights is simple nonsense: natural and imprescriptable rights, rhetorical nonsense – nonsense upon stilts.
Jeremy Bentham, 'Anarchical Fallacies', in J. Bowring (ed.), *Works* (1838–43), II

46:6 *Horrid, adj.* In English hideous, frightful, appalling. In Young-womanese, mildly objectionable.
Ambrose Bierce, 1911, *The Devil's Dictionary* (entry added by E. J. Hopkins for *The Enlarged Devil's Dictionary*, 1967)

46:7 I found myself growing increasingly irritated with the notion of a British novel, which was really an irritation with the word British, a grey, unsatisfactory, bad-weather kind of word, a piece of linguistic compromise.
Bill Buford, 1994, editorial, *Granta*, no. 43

46:8 *Alone!* – that worn-out word, / So idly spoken, and so coldly heard; / Yet all that poets sing, and grief hath known, / Of hopes laid waste, knells in that word, ALONE!
Edward Bulwer-Lytton, 1846, *The New Timon*, II, stanza 6

46:9 I have no idea what genius is, but so far as I can form any conception about it, I should say it was a stupid word which cannot be too soon abandoned to scientific and literary *claqueurs*.
Samuel Butler (1835–1902), 1903, *The Way Of All Flesh*, Ch. 22

46:10 But still her lips refused to send – 'Farewell!' / For in that word – that fatal word – howe'er / We promise, hope, believe – there breathes despair.
Lord Byron, 1814, *The Corsair*, Sect. 15

46:11 Of all the horrid, hideous notes of woe, / Sadder than owl-songs or the midnight blast / Is that portentous phrase, 'I told you so'.
Lord Byron, 1819–24, *Don Juan*, Canto 14, stanza 50

46:12 All present life is but an interjection, / An 'oh!' or 'ah!' of joy or misery / Or a 'ha, ha!' or 'bah!' a yawn or 'pooh!' / Of which perhaps the latter is most true.
Lord Byron, 1819–24, *Don Juan*, Canto 15, stanza 1

46:13 Of all the words in all languages I know, the greatest concentration is in the English word I.

Elias Canetti, 1973, '1943', in *The Human Province*

46:14 [Humpty Dumpty] Well, '*slithy*' means 'lithe and slimy.' 'Lithe' is the same as 'active.' You see it's like a portmanteau – there are two meanings packed up in one word.

Lewis Carroll, 1872, *Through the Looking Glass*, Ch. 6

46:15 'No,' he resumed – and *why* is it, I pause to ask, that, in taking up the broken thread of a dialogue, one *always* begins with this cheerless monosyllable? I have come to the conclusion that the object in view is the same as that of the schoolboy, when the sum he is working has got into a hopeless muddle, and when in despair he takes the sponge, washes it all out, and begins again. Just in the same way the bewildered orator, by the simple process of denying *everything* that has been hitherto asserted, makes a clean sweep of the whole discussion, and can 'start fair' with a fresh theory.

Lewis Carroll, 1893, *Sylvie and Bruno Concluded*, Ch. 10

46:16 [Bruno, reacting to Sylvie's use of the word *nubble*] 'Nubbly's such a grumbly word to say – when one person's got her head on another person's shoulder. When she talks like that,' he exclaimed to me, 'the talking goes down bofe sides of my face – all the way to my chin – and it *does* tickle so! It's enough to make a beard grow, that it is!'

Lewis Carroll, 1893, *Sylvie and Bruno Concluded*, Ch. 14

46:17 The only sort of four-letter words I use are 'good', 'love', 'warm' and 'kind'.

Catherine Cookson, interview in John Mortimer, *In Character* (1983)

46:18 There must be something very comprehensive in this phrase of 'Never mind,' for we do not recollect to have ever witnessed a quarrel in the street, at a theatre, public room, or elsewhere, in which it has not been the standard reply to all belligerent inquiries . . . It is observable, too, that there would appear to be some hidden taunt in this universal 'Never mind,' which rouses more indignation in the bosom of the individual addressed, than the most lavish abuse could possibly awaken.

Charles Dickens, 1836–7, *The Pickwick Papers*, Ch. 24

46:19 There are few words which perform such various duties as this word 'fix.' It is the Caleb Quotem of the American vocabulary. [Caleb Quotem = 'jack-of-all-trades', from the character in George Colman's *The Review, or Wags of Windsor*, 1808]

Charles Dickens, 1842, *American Notes*, Ch. 10

46:20 [Martin, to Captain Kedgick, on being told he has to receive a visit from local citizens] 'Powers above!' cried Martin, 'I couldn't do that, my good fellow!' 'I reckon you *must* then,' said the Captain. 'Must is not a pleasant word, Captain,' urged Martin. 'Well! I didn't fix the mother language, and I can't unfix it,' said the Captain coolly: 'else I'd make it pleasant. You must re-ceive. That's all.'

Charles Dickens, 1843–4, *Martin Chuzzlewit*, Ch. 22

46:21 [replying to Monsieur Rigaud's request for confirmation that he (Rigaud) was a gentleman] 'ALTRO!' returned John Baptist, closing his eyes and giving his head a most vehement toss. The word being, according to its Genoese emphasis, a confirmation, a contradiction, an assertion, a denial, a taunt, a compliment, a joke, and fifty other things, became in the present instance, with a significance beyond all power of written expression, our familiar English 'I believe you!'

Charles Dickens, 1855–7, *Little Dorrit*, I, Ch. 1

46:22 [Old Orlick to Pip] 'I'm jiggered if I don't see you home!' This penalty of being jiggered was a favourite suppositious case of his. He attached no definite meaning to the word that I am aware of, but used it, like his own pretended Christian name, to affront mankind, and convey an idea of something savagely damaging.

Charles Dickens, 1861, *Great Expectations*, Ch. 17

46:23 [Gaffer Hexam to another boatman] I have been swallowing too much of that word, Pardner. I am no pardner of yours.

Charles Dickens, 1864–5, *Our Mutual Friend*, I, Ch. 1

46:24 [Eugene] If there is a word in the dictionary under any letter from A to Z that I abominate, it is energy. It is such a conventional superstition, such parrot gabble!

Charles Dickens, 1864–5, *Our Mutual Friend*, I, Ch. 3

46:25 [Silas Wegg, to Mr Boffin] 'The collection of ballads will in future be reserved for private study, with the object of making poetry tributary' – Wegg was so proud of having found this word, that he said it again, with a capital letter – 'Tributary to friendship.'

Charles Dickens, 1864–5, *Our Mutual Friend*, I, Ch. 15

46:26 [Riderhood, on being told he 'shall sign a statement'] 'Shall' is summ'at of a hard word, Captain, . . . When you say a man 'shall' sign this and that and t'other, Captain, you order him about in a grand sort of a way.
Charles Dickens, 1864–5, *Our Mutual Friend*, II, Ch. 12

46:27 [Mr Pinto] English is an expressive language . . . but not difficult to master. Its range is limited. It consists, as far as I can observe, of four words: 'nice', 'jolly', 'charming', and 'bore'; and some grammarians add 'fond'.
Benjamin Disraeli, 1870, *Lothair*, Ch. 28

46:28 [a man in a field, responding to the author's request for help] 'Goo' arternoon,' he called.
'You'd think, with its meteorological history, that the English language could have thought up a another greeting, wouldn't you?' said Larry. 'It's perfectly preposterous to say "good afternoon" on a day whose climatic conditions could make even Noah worry.'
Gerald Durrell, 1979, 'The Picnic', in *The Picnic and Suchlike Pandemonium*

46:29 I'll give you a definite maybe.
Samuel Goldwyn, attributed, 20th century, in A. Scott Berg, *Goldwyn* (1989)

46:30 In two words: im – possible.
Samuel Goldwyn, attributed, 20th century, in Alva Johnston, *The Great Goldwyn* (1937)

46:31 Of all the words of tongue and pen, / The saddest are, 'It might have been,' / More sad are these we daily see: 'It is, but hadn't ought to be.'
Bret Harte, 1871, 'Mrs Judge Jenkins' [cf. 46:66]

46:32 Summer afternoon – summer afternoon: to me these have always been the two most beautiful words in the English language.
Henry James, quoted in Edith Wharton, *A Backward Glance* (1934), Ch. 10

46:33 [on Boswell using the word 'terrible' to describe a possible delay in Johnson's journey] Don't, Sir, accustom yourself to use big words for little matters.
Samuel Johnson, 6 August 1763, in James Boswell, *The Life of Samuel Johnson* (1791), Ch. 15

46:34 Duty then is the sublimest word in our language. Do your duty in all things. You cannot do more. You should never wish to do less.
Robert E. Lee, c.1860s, inscription beneath his bust in the Hall of Fame, New York University

46:35 [of England] If you live here long enough, you will find out to your greatest amazement that the adjective *nice* is not the only adjective the language possesses, in spite of the fact that in the first three years you do not need to learn or use any other adjectives.
George Mikes, 1946, 'The language', *How to be an Alien*, I

46:36 [Quentin] The word 'now' is like a bomb through the window, and it ticks.
Arthur Miller, 1964, *After the Fall*, I

46:37 'Good', then, if we mean by it that quality which we assert to belong to a thing, when we say that the thing is good, is incapable of any definition, in the most important sense of the word.
G. E. Moore, 1903, *Principia Ethica*, Ch. 1

46:38 Beware of the conversationalist who adds 'in other words'. He is merely starting afresh.
Robert Morley, 6 December 1964, in the *Observer*

46:39 [Hilary] Goodness is a foreign language.
Iris Murdoch, 1975, 'Thursday' (second week), in *A Word Child*

46:40 [on being told that there was no word in English for French *sensibilité*] Yes we have. Humbug.
Viscount Palmerston, attributed, mid 19th century

46:41 Widow. The word consumes itself.
Sylvia Plath, 1971, 'Widow'

46:42 'But' is a fence over which few venture.
Proverbial (German)

46:43 Bad is called good when worse happens.
Proverbial (Norwegian)

46:44 'If' and 'and' spills mony a gude charter.
Proverbial (Scots)

46:45 Must is a king's word.
Proverbial

46:46 Wishers and woulders are never good householders.
Proverbial

46:47 'Take', 'have', and 'keep' are pleasant words.

Proverbial

46:48 'Yes' and 'No' are small words but produce great things.

Proverbial (German)

46:49 Tram-conductors in Prague salute passengers as they alight by saying 'We have been honoured by your presence.' In London the abbreviated version of this courtesy is 'Push-off.'

Punch, 25 January 1922, 'Charivaria', p. 61

46:50 *Trink* is a panomphaean word. It speaks oracles, that is to say, in all languages.

François Rabelais, 1532, *Pantagruel*, V, Ch. 46

46:51 [Teddy Robinson, to a shop bear] 'Why do you keep saying "actually"?' 'It's only a way of making dull things sound more interesting,' said the shop bear.

Joan G. Robinson, 1956, *Dear Teddy Robinson*, Ch. 1

46:52 [Costard, having received some 'remuneration' from Armado] Now will I look to his remuneration. Remuneration – O, that's the Latin word for three-farthings. Three-farthings – remuneration. 'What's the price of this inkle [linen tape]?' 'One penny.' 'No, I'll give you a remuneration.' Why, it carries it! Remuneration! Why, it is a fairer name than French crown! I will never buy and sell out of this word.

William Shakespeare, 1593–4, *Love's Labour's Lost*, III. i. 133

46:53 COSTARD: Go to, thou hast it *ad dunghill*, at the fingers' ends, as they say.

HOLOFERNES: O, I smell false Latin – 'dunghill' for *unguem*.

William Shakespeare, 1593–4, *Love's Labour's Lost*, V. i. 73

46:54 ARMADO: Sir, it is the King's most sweet pleasure and affection to congratulate the Princess at her pavilion in the posteriors of this day, which the rude multitude call the afternoon.

HOLOFERNES: The posterior of the day, most generous sir, is liable, congruent, and measurable for the afternoon. The word is well culled, choice, sweet, and apt, I do assure you, sir, I do assure.

William Shakespeare, 1593–4, *Love's Labour's Lost*, V. i. 82

46:55 [Duchess of York, to King Henry] An if I were thy nurse, thy tongue to teach, / 'Pardon' should be the first word of thy speech. / I never longed to hear a word till now. / Say 'Pardon', King. Let pity teach thee how. / The word is short, but not so short as sweet; / No word like 'Pardon' for kings' mouths so meet.

William Shakespeare, 1595 *Richard II*, V. iii. 111

46:56 BARDOLPH: Sir, pardon, a soldier is better accommodated than with a wife.

SHALLOW: It is well said, in faith, sir, and it is well said indeed, too. 'Better accommodated' – it is good; yea, indeed is it. Good phrases are surely, and ever were, very commendable. 'Accommodated' – it comes of *accommodo*. Very good, a good phrase.

BARDOLPH: Pardon, sir, I have heard the word – 'phrase' call you it? – By this day, I know not the phrase; but I will maintain the word with my sword to be a soldier-like word, and a word of exceeding good command, by heaven.

William Shakespeare, 1597, *Henry IV, Part 2*, III. ii. 65

46:57 [Polonius] 'To the celestial and my soul's idol, the most beautified Ophelia' – that's an ill phrase, a vile phrase, 'beautified' is a vile phrase.

William Shakespeare, 1600–1601, *Hamlet*, II. ii. 110

46:58 MESSENGER [after giving Cleopatra some good news of Antony]: But yet, madam –

CLEOPATRA: I do not like 'But yet'; it does allay / The good precedence. Fie upon 'But yet'. / 'But yet' is as a jailer to bring forth / Some monstrous malefactor.

William Shakespeare, 1606, *Antony and Cleopatra*, II. v. 49

46:59 ADAM: Make me a beautiful word for doing things tomorrow, for that surely is a great and blessed invention.

THE SERPENT: Procrastination.

EVE: That is a sweet word. I wish I had a serpent's tongue.

THE SERPENT: That may come too. Everything is possible.

George Bernard Shaw, 1921, *Back to Methuselah*, I

46:60 [Captain Absolute, to Faulkland's stammered 'but – but –', after receiving a forgiving letter from Julia] Confound your buts! you never hear anything that would make another man bless himself, but you immediately damn it with a but!

Richard Sheridan, 1775, *The Rivals*, IV. iii

46:61 Forgive! How many will say 'forgive,' and

find / A sort of absolution in the sound / To hate a little longer.

Alfred, Lord Tennyson, 1857, 'Sea Dreams'

46:62 Mr Salter's side of the conversation was limited to expressions of assent. When Lord Copper was right, he said, 'Definitely, Lord Copper'; when he was wrong, 'Up to a point.'

Evelyn Waugh, 1938, *Scoop*, I, Ch. 1, Sect. 3

46:63 The word 'revolution' is a word for which you kill, for which you die, for which you send the labouring masses to their deaths; but which does not contain any content.

Simone Weil, 1955, *Oppression and Liberty* (trans. A. Wills and J. Petrie, 1958)

46:64 [Wisehammer] You have to be careful with words that begin with 'in'. It can turn everything upside down. Injustice. Most of that word is taken up with justice, but the 'in' twists it inside out and makes it the ugliest word in the English language.

Timberlake Wertenbaker, 1988, *Our Country's Good*, I. x

46:65 [Wisehammer] Words with two L's are the worst. Lonely, loveless.

Timberlake Wertenbaker, 1988, *Our Country's Good*, I. x

46:66 For of all sad words of tongue or pen, / The saddest are these: 'It might have been!'

John Greenleaf Whittier, 1854, *Maud Muller* [cf. 46:31]

46:67 MRS ALLONBY: Horrid word 'health'.

LORD ILLINGWORTH: Silliest word in our language.

Oscar Wilde, 1893, *A Woman of No Importance*, I

46:68 There's more in words than I can teach: Yet listen, Child! – I would not preach; / But only give some plain directions / To guide your speech and your affections. / Say not you *love* a roasted fowl, / But you may love a screaming owl. ... And you may love the strawberry-flower, / And love the strawberry in its bower; / But when the fruit, so often praised / For beauty, to your lip is raised, / Say not you *love* the delicate treat, / But *like* it, enjoy it, and thankfully eat.

William Wordsworth, 1832, 'Loving and Liking: Irregular Verses Addressed to a Child (by my Sister)'

See also: 7:19, 38:38, 41:21, 42:26, 48:66

Style, Genre and Variety

The nature of style in language

47:1 As the character is, such is the speech.
Aelius Aristides, 2nd century, *To Plato: In Defence of Rhetoric* (trans.), II, 392

47:2 [of style] It is not sufficient to have a grasp of what one should say, but one must also say these things in the way that one should, and this makes a great contribution to the character that the speech projects.
Aristotle, 4th century BC, *The Art of Rhetoric* (trans. H. C. Lawson-Tancred), Ch. 3, Sect. 1

47:3 Let us lay it down that the *virtue of style is to be clear* (since a speech is a kind of indication; if it does not indicate clearly it will not be performing its function), and to be neither mean nor above the prestige of the subject, but appropriate (the poetic style is doubtless not mean, but it is inappropriate to a speech).
Aristotle, 4th century BC, *The Art of Rhetoric* (trans. H. C. Lawson-Tancred), Ch. 3, Sect. 2

47:4 It is the main *nouns* and *verbs* that make the style clear, and this is made not mean but ornate by the other words, . . . for an unusual replacement for a word makes the style seem the more lofty. Men in fact are 'affected in the same way by style as by foreigners and compatriots. So the discourse must be made to sound exotic; for men are admirers of what is distant, and what is admired is pleasant.
Aristotle, 4th century BC, *The Art of Rhetoric* (trans. H. C. Lawson-Tancred), Ch. 3, Sect. 2

47:5 Style will have *propriety*, if it should be *emotive* and *characterful* and *proportional to the subject-matter*.
Aristotle, 4th century BC, *The Art of Rhetoric* (trans. H. C. Lawson-Tancred), Ch. 3, Sect. 7

47:6 People think that I can teach them style. What stuff it all is! Have something to say, and say it as clearly as you can. That is the only secret of style.
Matthew Arnold, 1898, quoted in G. W. E. Russell, *Collections and Recollections*, Ch. 13

47:7 *Ces choses sont hors de l'homme, le style est l'homme même.* These things [subject matter] are external to the man; style is the man.
Comte de Buffon, 25 August 1753, *Discours sur le style*, to the French Academy

47:8 A man's style in any art should be like his dress – it should attract as little attention as possible. I never knew a writer yet who took the smallest pains with his style and was at the same time readable.
Samuel Butler (1835–1902), *The Note-Books of Samuel Butler* (1912)

47:9 [Count Lodovico] 'Let me ask you: what does the genius of language consist in?'
'In carefully observing its properties,' answered Federico, 'in adopting the same meanings, and using the same style and rhythms, as all the best writers.'
Baldesar Castiglione, 1528, *The Book of the Courtier* (trans. G. Bull, Penguin 1967), I, p. 84

47:10 Style is the dress of thoughts; and let them be ever so just, if your style is homely, coarse, and vulgar, they will appear to as much disadvantage, and be as ill received as your person, though ever so well proportioned, would, if dressed in rags, dirt, and tatters.
Lord Chesterfield, 24 November 1749, letter to his son [cf. 47:44]

47:11 Style is the perfection of a point of view.

Richard Eberhart, 1965, 'Meditation Two', in *Selected Poems 1930–1965*

47:12 The great master of a language should be the great servant of it.

T. S. Eliot, 4 July 1950, lecture at the Italian Institute, London, 'A Talk on Dante', in John Hayward (ed.), *T. S. Eliot: Selected Prose* (1953)

47:13 The great writer finds style as the mystic finds God, in his own soul.

Havelock Ellis, 1923, *The Dance of Life*, Ch. 4

47:14 Use what language you will, you can never say anything but what you are.

Ralph Waldo Emerson, 1860, 'Worship', in *The Conduct of Life*

47:15 Style is life! It is the very life-blood of thought!

Gustave Flaubert, 7 September 1853, letter to Louise Colet, in M. Nadeau (ed.), *Correspondence 1853–6* (trans., 1964)

47:16 We used to say that a passage of good style began with a fresh, usual word, and continued with fresh, usual words to the end; there was nothing more to it.

Ford Madox Ford, 1924, *Joseph Conrad, a Personal Remembrance*, III

47:17 Style is the image of character.

Edward Gibbon, 1796, *Memoirs of my Life*, Ch. 1

47:18 To me, style is just the outside of content, and content the inside of style, like the outside and inside of the human body – both go together, they can't be separated.

Jean-Luc Godard, 1967, introduction to Richard Roud, *Jean-Luc Godard*

47:19 If any man wish to write a clear style, let him be first clear in his thoughts; and if any would write in a noble style, let him first possess a noble soul.

Goethe, 14 April 1824, in Johann Peter Eckermann's *Conversations with Goethe* (trans.)

47:20 True eloquence does not consist, as the rhetoricians assure us, in saying great things in a sublime style, but in a simple style: for there is, properly speaking, no such thing as a sublime style; the sublimity lies only in the things.

Oliver Goldsmith, 17 November 1759, 'Of Eloquence', in *The Bee*, no. 7

47:21 A writer's style is according to his temperament, & my impression is that if he has anything to say which is of value, & words to say it with, the style will come of itself.

Thomas Hardy, 11 October 1887, letter to George Bainton

47:22 I might say that what amateurs call a style is usually only the unavoidable awkwardness in first trying to make something that has not heretofore been made.

Ernest Hemingway, interview in *Writers at Work: Second Series* (1963)

47:23 A man's style should be like his dress. It should be as unobtrusive and should attract as little attention as possible.

C. E. M. Joad, 1926, 'How to Write and How to Write Badly', in *The Bookmark*

47:24 A strict and succinct style is that, where you can take away nothing without losse, and that losse to be manifest.

Ben Jonson, 1640 (published posthumously), *Timber: or, Discoveries made upon Men and Matter*

47:25 Our style should be like a skeine of silke to be carried, and found by the right thred, not ravel'd and perplex'd; then all is a knot, a heape.

Ben Jonson, 1640 (published posthumously), *Timber: or, Discoveries made upon Men and Matter*

47:26 Wee say it is a fleshy style, when there is much *Periphrasis*, and circuit of words; and when with more then enough, it growes fat and corpulent; . . . It hath blood, and juyce, when the words are proper and apt, their sound sweet, and the Phrase neat and pick'd. . . . But where there is Redundancy, both the blood and juyce are faulty, and vitious. . . . Juyce in Language is somewhat lesse then blood; for if the words be but becomming, and signifying , and the sense gentle, there is Juyce: but where that wanteth, the Language is thinne, flagging, poore, starv'd; scarce covering the bone, and shewes like stones in a sack.

Ben Jonson, 1640 (published posthumously), *Timber: or, Discoveries made upon Men and Matter*

47:27 A good style should show no sign of effort. What is written should seem a happy accident.

W. Somerset Maugham, 1938, *The Summing Up*, Ch. 13

47:28 Style is the hallmark of a temperament stamped upon the material at hand.

André Maurois, 1960, *The Art of Writing* (trans.)

47:29 When we see a natural style, we are quite

surprised and delighted, for we expected to see an author and we find a man.

Blaise Pascal, c.1654–62, *Pensées* (trans. W. F. Trotter), no. 29

47:30 Meanings change amazingly. When people get accustomed to horrors, these form the foundation for good style.

Boris Pasternak, 1931, *Safe Conduct* (trans. Beatrice Scott), Ch. 2

47:31 Man is hidden behind his tongue.

Proverbial (Arabic)

47:32 A man is in his words.

Proverbial (Kru)

47:33 [The fictitious novelist Anthony Chivers, dictating to Miss Brookes] Punctuation, Miss Brookes, is the soul of style. . . . Please don't interrupt, Miss Brookes. I've got the thing well started now; I don't wish the thread to be broken. Par quotes oh exclamation mark Sir Henry dash is it you query quotes par quotes yes comma it is I full-stop quotes – um – par her eyes swooped into his par – um par quotes oh comma quotes she said comma quotes Sir Henry.

Punch, 1 February 1922, 'The Broken Thread', p. 87

47:34 Essentially style resembles good manners. It comes of endeavouring to understand others, of thinking for them rather than yourself – of thinking, that is, with the heart as well as the head.

Arthur Quiller-Couch, 1916, *The Art of Writing*

47:35 The uniqueness of each person's language is as unalienable as DNA and far more easily recognized and publicly asserted.

Randolph Quirk, 1990, 'Language and Concepts of Identity', *European Review*, no. 6, p. 291

47:36 Man is who he is, not how he expresses himself.

Antoine de Saint-Exupéry, published in 1948, *Citadelle* (trans.)

47:37 Effectiveness of assertion is the alpha and omega of style.

George Bernard Shaw, 1921, *Man and Superman*, Preface

47:38 Style is a magic wand, and turns everything to gold that it touches.

Logan Pearsall Smith, 1931, *Afterthoughts*, Ch. 5

47:39 The web, then, or the pattern; a web at once sensuous and logical, an elegant and pregnant texture: that is style, that is the foundation of the art of literature.

Robert Louis Stevenson, 1885, 'On Some Technical Elements of Style in Literature', in *The Art of Writing* (1905)

47:40 Proper words in proper places, make the true definition of style.

Jonathan Swift, 9 January 1720, 'Letter to a Young Clergyman Lately Entered into Holy Orders'

47:41 Style, like the human body, is specially beautiful when the veins are not prominent and the bones cannot be counted.

Tacitus, c.81, *A Dialogue on Oratory* (trans. A. J. Church and W. J. Brodribb), Sect. 21

47:42 It is the man determines what is said, not the words.

Henry Thoreau, 11 July 1840, *Journal*

47:43 As for style of writing – if one has anything to say, it drops from him simply and directly, as a stone falls to the ground.

Henry Thoreau, 18 August 1857, letter to Daniel Ricketson

47:44 Style is the dress of thought; a modest dress, / Neat, but not gaudy, will true critics please.

Samuel Wesley, 1700, *An Epistle to a Friend concerning Poetry* [cf. 47:10]

47:45 He most honors my style who learns under it to destroy the teacher.

Walt Whitman, 1855, 'Song of Myself ', in *Leaves of Grass*, Sect. 47

47:46 Properly speaking, there is no such thing as Style; there are merely styles, that is all.

Oscar Wilde, c.1888, in Richard Ellmann, *Oscar Wilde* (1987), Ch. 11

See also: 8:52, 49:29, 59:41

The use of language in literature and criticism

48:1 I have woven for them a great shroud / Out of the poor words I overheard them speak.
Anna Akhmatova, 1940, 'Epilogue II', in *Requiem* (trans. D. M. Thomas in *Anna Akhmatova: Selected Poems*, Penguin 1988)

48:2 Writers, poets especially, have an odd relation to the public because their medium, language, is not, like the paint of the painter or the notes of the composer, reserved for their use but is the common property of the linguistic group to which they belong.
W. H. Auden, 1948, 'Prologue: Writing', in *The Dyer's Hand and other essays*

48:3 However esoteric a poem may be, the fact that all its words have meanings which can be looked up in a dictionary makes it testify to the existence of other people . . . a purely private verbal world is not possible.
W. H. Auden, 1948, 'Prologue: Writing', in *The Dyer's Hand and other essays*

48:4 A poet is, before anything else, a person who is passionately in love with language.
W. H. Auden, 9 October 1960, *New York Times*

48:5 The art of the critic in a nutshell: to coin slogans without betraying ideas.
Walter Benjamin, 1920s, 'Chinese Curios', in *One-way Street* (trans. 1979)

48:6 I'm not good at precise, coherent argument. But plays are suited to incoherent argument, put into the mouths of fallible people.
Alan Bennett, 24 November 1991, *Sunday Times*

48:7 *Fly-Speck, n.* The prototype of punctuation. It is observed by Garvinus that the systems of punctuation in use by the various literary nations depended originally upon the social habits and general diet of the flies infesting the several countries. These creatures, which have always been distinguished for a neighborly and companionable familiarity with authors, liberally or niggardly embellish the manuscripts in process of growth under the pen, according to their bodily habit, bringing out the sense of the work by a species of interpretation superior to, and independent of, the writer's powers.
Ambrose Bierce, 1911, *The Devil's Dictionary*

48:8 Literature, by the way, may be defined as the aesthetic exploitation of language.
Anthony Burgess, 1992, *A Mouthful of Air*, II, Ch. 11

48:9 [Frederica's view of the novel] A novel . . . is made of a long thread of language, like knitting, thicker and thinner in patches. It is made in the head and has to be remade in the head by whoever reads it, who will always remake it differently.
A. S. Byatt, 1996, *Babel Tower*, Ch. 7

48:10 The great rule of the artist . . . is to forget half of himself in favour of communicable expression. This inevitably involves sacrifices. And this quest for an intelligible language whose function is to mask the immensity of his fate, leads him to say not what he pleases but only what he must.
Albert Camus, 1943, 'Intelligence and the Scaffold', in *Selected Essays and Notebooks* (trans. P. Thody, 1970)

48:11 Fragments of a real 'Church Liturgy' and 'Body of Homilies,' strangely disguised from the common eye, are to be found weltering in that huge froth-ocean of Printed Speech we loosely call Literature! Books are our Church too.

Thomas Carlyle, 1840, 'The Hero as a Man of Letters', in *On Heroes, Hero-Worship, and the Heroic in History*, Lecture 5

48:12 'The day must come – if the world lasts long enough – ' said Arthur, 'when every possible tune will have been composed – every possible pun perpetrated – . . . and, worse than that, every possible *book* written! For the number of *words* is finite.' 'It'll make very little difference to the *authors*,' I suggested. 'Instead of saying *"what* book shall I write?" an author will ask himself *"which* book shall I write?" A mere verbal distinction!'

Lewis Carroll, 1893, *Sylvie and Bruno Concluded*, Ch. 9

48:13 Literature is the art of writing something that will be read twice; journalism what will be grasped at once.

Cyril Connolly, 1938, *Enemies of Promise*, Ch. 3

48:14 My task which I am trying to achieve is by the power of the written word, to make you hear, to make you feel – it is, before all, to make you *see*. That – and no more, and it is everything.

Joseph Conrad, 1897, *The Nigger of the Narcissus*, Preface

48:15 [talking about his poetry] I speak of the brokenness of the language which reflects the brokenness and suffering of its original users. Its potential as a naturally tragic language is there in its brokenness and rawness, which is like the rawness of a wound. If one has learnt and used Queen's English for some years, the return to creole is painful, almost nauseous, for the language is uncomfortably raw. One has to shed one's protective sheath of abstracts and let the tongue move freely in blood again.

David Dabydeen, 1990, 'On Not Being Milton: Nigger Talk in England Today', in L. Michaels and C. Ricks (eds), *The State of the Language*

48:16 Books, we are told, propose to *instruct* or to *amuse*. Indeed! . . . The true antithesis to knowledge, in this case, is not *pleasure*, but *power*. All that is literature seeks to communicate power; all that is not literature, to communicate knowledge.

Thomas De Quincey, 1823, 'Letters to a Young Man whose Education has been Neglected', no. 3, in the *London Magazine* (Jan–Jul)

48:17 [Mortimer, on the Dust Contractor's

daughter] She was secretly engaged to that popular character whom the novelists and versifiers call Another.

Charles Dickens, 1864–5, *Our Mutual Friend*, I, Ch. 2

48:18 [Mortimer] We must now return, as the novelists say, and as we all wish they wouldn't, to the man from Somewhere.

Charles Dickens, 1864–5, *Our Mutual Friend*, I, Ch. 2

48:19 There is no longer any such thing as fiction or nonfiction; there's only narrative.

E. L. Doctorow, 27 January 1988, *New York Times Book Review*

48:20 And he, who servilely creeps after sense / Is safe, but ne'er will reach an excellence.

John Dryden, 1669, *Tyrannic Love*, Prologue

48:21 [of a writer] His business is communication through language; when he is an imaginative writer, he is engaged in the most difficult form of communication, where precision is of the utmost importance, a precision which cannot be given beforehand but has to be found in every new phrase.

T. S. Eliot, 15 April 1942, lecture to the Classical Association, Cambridge, 'The Classics and the Man of Letters'

48:22 Since our concern was speech, and speech impelled us / To purify the dialect of the tribe / And urge the mind to aftersight and foresight / Let me disclose the gifts reserved for age.

T. S. Eliot, 1944, 'Little Gidding', Part 2, in *Four Quartets* [cf. 48:34]

48:23 To pass on to posterity one's own language, more highly developed, more refined, and more precise than it was before one wrote it, that is the highest possible achievement of the poet as poet.

T. S. Eliot, 4 July 1950, lecture at the Italian Institute, London, 'A Talk on Dante'

48:24 Good dialogue is character . . . The art of writing true dramatic dialogue is an austere art, denying itself all licence, grudging every sentence devoted to the mere machinery of the play, suppressing all jokes and epigrams severed from character, relying for fun and pathos on the fun and tears of life. From start to finish, good dialogue is hand-made, like good lace; clear, of fine texture, furthering with each thread the harmony and strength of a design to which all must be subordinated.

John Galsworthy, July 1924, *On Expression*, Presidential Address to the English Association, p. 15

48:25 There are certain words in every language particularly adapted to the poetical expression; some from the image or idea they convey to the imagination, and some from the effect they have upon the ear.

Oliver Goldsmith, 1758–65, 'Poetry Distinguished from Other Writing', in *Essays*, no. 15

48:26 A poem must be kept *and used*, like a meerschaum, or a violin. A poem is just as porous as the meerschaum; – the more porous it is, the better. I mean to say that a genuine poem is capable of absorbing an indefinite amount of the essence of our own humanity, – its tenderness, its heroism, its regrets, its aspirations, so as to be gradually stained through with a divine secondary colour derived from ourselves.

Oliver Wendell Holmes, senior, 1858, *The Autocrat of the Breakfast Table*, Ch. 5

48:27 [advice to aspiring poets] Here's a book full of words; one can choose as he fancies, / As a painter his tint, as a workman his tool; / Just think! all the poems, and plays and romances / Were drawn out of this, like the fish from a pool!

Oliver Wendell Holmes, senior, 'A Familiar Letter to Several Correspondents', in *The Faber Book of Useful Verse* (1981), p. 157 [cf. 49:58]

48:28 I have always suspected that the reading is right which requires many words to prove it wrong, and the emendation wrong which cannot without so much labour appear to be right.

Samuel Johnson, 1765, *Preface to Shakespeare*

48:29 I love anecdotes. I fancy mankind may come, in time, to write all aphoristically, except in narrative; grow weary of preparation, and connection, and illustration, and all those arts by which a big book is made. If a man is to wait till he weaves anecdotes into a system, we may be long in getting them, and get but a few, in comparison of what we might get.

Samuel Johnson, 16 August 1773, in James Boswell, *The Journal of a Tour to the Hebrides* (1785)

48:30 There are nine and sixty ways of con-

structing tribal lays, / And every single one of them is right!

Rudyard Kipling, 1895, 'In the Neolithic Age'

48:31 The magic of Literature lies in the words, and not in any man.

Rudyard Kipling, May 1906, 'Literature' (speech at a Royal Academy dinner), in *A Book of Words*

48:32 I own that I am disposed to say grace upon twenty other occasions in the course of the day besides my dinner . . . Why have we none for books, those spiritual repasts – a grace before Milton – a grace before Shakespeare – a devotional exercise proper to be said before reading the Fairy Queen?

Charles Lamb, 1823, 'Grace before Meat', in *The Essays of Elia*

48:33 When I read Shakespeare I am struck with wonder / That such trivial people should muse and thunder / In such lovely language.

D. H. Lawrence, 1929, 'When I Read Shakespeare'

48:34 [of Edgar Allen Poe] To purify the language of the tribe.

Stéphane Mallarmé, 1893, *Poésies, hommages et tombeaux* [cf. 48:22]

48:35 having something / to say is the thing being sincere / counts for more than forms of expression.

Don Marquis, 1933, 'the stuff of literature', in *archy's life of mehitabel*

48:36 Words have weight, sound and appearance; it is only by considering these that you can write a sentence that is good to look at and good to listen to.

W. Somerset Maugham, 1938, *The Summing Up*, Ch. 13

48:37 The thing that makes poetry different from all of the other arts . . . [is] you're using language, which is what you use for everything else – telling lies and selling socks, advertising, and conducting law. Whereas we don't write little concerts or paint little pictures.

W. S. Merwin, 30 September 1994, quoted in the *Washington Post*

48:38 The curse of Scottish literature is the lack of a whole language, which finally means the lack of a whole mind.

Edwin Muir, 1936, *Scott and Scotland*, Introduction

48:39 One thing that literature would be greatly the better for / Would be a more

restricted employment by authors of simile and metaphor.
Ogden Nash, 1935, 'Very Like a Whale', in *The Primrose Path*

48:40 [on contemporary writing] Prose consists less and less of *words* chosen for the sake of their meaning, and more and more of *phrases* tacked together like the sections of a prefabricated henhouse.
George Orwell, 1946, 'Politics and the English Language', *Horizon,* no. 13

48:41 Modern writing at its worst does not consist in picking out words for the sake of their meaning and inventing images in order to make the meaning clearer. It consists in gumming together long strips of words which have already been set in order by someone else, and making the results presentable by sheer humbug.
George Orwell, 1946, 'Politics and the English Language', *Horizon,* no. 13

48:42 A word is not the same with one writer as with another. One tears it from his guts. The other pulls it out of his overcoat pocket.
Charles Péguy, 1943, 'The Honest People', in *Basic Verities* (trans. A. and J. Green)

48:43 Mere elegance of language can produce at best but an empty renown.
Petrarch, 1367–72, *Letter to Posterity* (trans.)

48:44 Objectivity and again objectivity, and expression: no hindside-before-ness, no straddled adjectives (as 'addled mosses dank'), no Tennysonianness of speech; nothing – nothing that you couldn't, in some circumstance, in the stress of some emotion, actually say.
Ezra Pound, January 1915, letter to Harriet Monroe, in D. D. Paige (ed.), *The Selected Letters of Ezra Pound* (1950), p. 48

48:45 Great literature is simply language charged with meaning to the utmost possible degree.
Ezra Pound, 1931, *How to Read*, II

48:46 We are governed by words, the laws are graven in words, and literature is the sole means of keeping those words living and accurate.
Ezra Pound, writing of *Ulysses,* quoted in George Steiner, 'The Retreat from the Word', in *Language and Silence* (1967)

48:47 Language is the medium of literature as marble or bronze or clay are the materials of the sculptor.
Edward Sapir, 1921, *Language,* Ch. 11

48:48 [Gower's prologue] By you being pardoned, we commit no crime / To use one language in each sev'ral clime / Where our scene seems to live.
William Shakespeare and George Wilkins, 1608–9, *Pericles, Prince of Tyre,* scene xviii, 5

48:49 [Puff] I am, sir, a practitioner in panegyric, or, to speak more plainly, a professor of the art of puffing, at your service – or anybody else's.
Richard Sheridan, 1779, *The Critic,* I. ii

48:50 [Mr Puff] Puffing is of various sorts; the principal are, the puff direct, the puff preliminary, the puff collateral, the puff collusive, and the puff oblique, or puff by implication. These all assume, as circumstances require, the various forms of Letter to the Editor, Occasional Anecdote, Impartial Critique, Observation from Correspondent, or Advertisement from the Party.
Richard Sheridan, 1779, *The Critic,* I. ii

48:51 BEEFEATER [a character in Puff's play]: Perdition catch my soul, but I do love thee.
SNEER: Haven't I heard that line before?
PUFF: No, I fancy not. – Where, pray?
DANGLE: Yes, I think there is something like it in Othello.
PUFF: Gad! now you put me in mind on't, I believe there is – but that's of no consequence; all that can be said is, that two people happened to hit upon the same thought – and Shakespeare made use of it first, that's all.
Richard Sheridan, 1779, *The Critic,* I. ii

48:52 For every word has its marrow in the English tongue for order and for delight.
Christopher Smart, 1758–63, *Jubilate Agno,* fragment B, 595

48:53 There is one thing that matters – to set a chime of words tinkling in the minds of a few fastidious people.
Logan Pearsall Smith, 9 March 1946, reported in Cyril Connolly's obituary, *New Statesman*

48:54 The arts babblative and scribblative.
Robert Southey, 1829, *Colloquies on the Progress and Prospects of Society,* X, Part 2

48:55 Remarks are not literature.
Gertrude Stein, 1933, *Autobiography of Alice B. Toklas,* Ch. 7

48:56 'Tis an undercraft [underhand trick] of authors to keep up a good understanding amongst words, as politicians do amongst men – not knowing how near they may be under a necessity of placing them to each other.

Laurence Sterne, 1765, *The Life and Opinions of Tristram Shandy, Gentleman*, VII, Ch. 19

48:57 Phonetics alone can breathe life into the dead mass of letters which constitute a written language: it alone can bring the rustic dialogues of our novels before every intelligent reader as living realities, and make us realize the living power and beauty of the ancient classical languages in prose and verse.

Henry Sweet, 1882–4, 'The Practical Study of Language', *Transactions of the Philological Society*

48:58 Traditional criticism has regarded the aesthetic approach towards literature as apart from the functional approach towards the way of words; languages themselves intensify the differences which appear in literature, but languages and literatures are not two different phenomena, but the same phenomenon.

Dylan Thomas, 1935, review of R. D. Jameson, *A Comparison of Literatures*, in *Adelphi* no. 11 (1)

48:59 Critics search for ages for the wrong word, which, to give them credit, they eventually find.

Peter Ustinov, February 1952, BBC radio broadcast

48:60 *'Language*, man!' roared Parsons; 'why, it's LITERATURE!'

H. G. Wells, 1910, *The History of Mr Polly*, Ch. 1, Part 3

48:61 Literature is the orchestration of platitudes.

Thornton Wilder, 12 January 1953, in *Time*

48:62 The principal object, then, proposed in these Poems, was to choose incidents and situations from common life, and to relate or describe them throughout, as far as was possible, in a selection of language really used by men, and, at the same time, to throw over them a certain colouring of imagination, whereby ordinary things should be presented to the mind in an unusual aspect.

William Wordsworth, 1800, *Lyrical Ballads*, Preface

48:63 The language, too, of these men has been adopted (purified indeed from what appear to be its real defects, from all lasting and rational causes of dislike or disgust), because such men hourly communicate with the best objects from which the best part of language is originally derived; and because, from their rank in society and the sameness and narrow circle of their intercourse, being less under the influence of social vanity, they convey their feelings and notions in simple and unelaborated expressions. Accordingly, such a language, arising out of repeated experience and regular feelings, is a more permanent, and a far more philosophical language, than that which is frequently substituted for it by Poets, who think that they are conferring honour upon themselves and their art in proportion as they separate themselves from the sympathies of men, and indulge in arbitrary and capricious habits of expression, in order to furnish food for fickle tastes and fickle appetites of their own creation.

William Wordsworth, 1800, *Lyrical Ballads*, Preface

48:64 Visionary power / Attends the motions of the viewless winds, / Embodied in the mystery of words: / There, darkness makes abode, and all the host / Of shadowy things work endless changes, – there, / In a mansion like their proper home, / Even forms and substances are circumfused / By that transparent veil with light divine, / And, through the turnings intricate of verse, / Present themselves as objects recognised, / In flashes, and with glory not their own.

William Wordsworth, 1805, *The Prelude*, V, 595

48:65 There are who think that strong affection, love / Known by whatever name, is falsely deemed / A gift, to use a term which they would use, / Of vulgar nature; that its growth requires / Retirement, leisure, language purified / By manners studied and elaborate; / That whoso feels such passion in its strength / Must live within the very light and air / Of courteous usages refined by art.

William Wordsworth, 1805, *The Prelude*, XIII, 186

48:66 I was impelled to write this Sonnet by the disgusting frequency with which the word *artistical*, imported with other impertinences from the German, is employed by writers of the present day: for artistical let them substitute artificial, and the poetry written on this system, both at home and abroad, will be for the most part much better characterised.

William Wordsworth, 1842, author's note in *Miscellaneous Sonnets*

See also: 9:4, 28:6, 32:27, 49:97, 49:106–7, 59:33

The distinctive language of poetry; the differences between poetry and prose

49:1 I am . . . very much offended when I see a Play in Rhyme; which is as absurd in *English*, as a Tragedy of *Hexameters* would have been in Greek or *Latin*.

Joseph Addison, 14 April 1711, 'English Tragedy: Style, Language and Verse', *The Spectator*, no. 39

49:2 It is one of the great Beauties of Poetry, to make hard Things intelligible, and to deliver what is abstruse of it self in such easy Language as may be understood by ordinary Readers.

Joseph Addison, 9 February 1712, 'Defects in the Fable, Characters, Sentiments and Language of *Paradise Lost*', *The Spectator*, no. 297

49:3 Poetry is music written for the human voice.

Maya Angelou, 15 September 1989, 'The Power of the Word' (radio talk)

49:4 We speak iambics in conversation with each other very often, but rarely dactylic hexameters – and only when we depart from the normal conversational tone.

Aristotle, 4th century BC, 'Tragedy', in *Poetics* (trans. M. Heath), Ch. 4

49:5 The most important quality in diction is clarity, provided there is no loss of dignity.

Aristotle, 4th century BC, 'Qualities of Poetic Style', in *Poetics* (trans. M. Heath), Ch. 22

49:6 Poetry, in fact, bears the same kind of relation to Prose, using prose simply in the sense of all those uses of words that are not poetry, that algebra bears to arithmetic.

W. H. Auden and J. Garrett, 1935, *The Poet's Tongue*, Introduction

49:7 The poet is the father of his poem; its mother is a language: one could list poems as race horses are listed – *out of L by P*.

W. H. Auden, 1948, 'Prologue: Writing', in *The Dyer's Hand and other essays*

49:8 A poet has to woo, not only his own Muse but also Dame Philology, and, for the beginner, the latter is the more important. As a rule, the sign that a beginner has a genuine original talent is that he is more interested in playing with words than in saying something original; his attitude is that of the old lady, quoted by E. M. Forster – 'How can I know what I think till I see what I say?' It is only later, when he has wooed and won Dame Philology, that he can give his entire devotion to his Muse.

W. H. Auden, 1948, 'Prologue: Writing', in *The Dyer's Hand and other essays* [cf. 2:141]

49:9 There are some poets, Kipling for example, whose relation to language reminds one of a drill sergeant: the words are taught to wash behind their ears, stand properly at attention and execute complicated maneuvers, but at the cost of never being allowed to think for themselves. There are others, Swinburne, for example, who remind one more of Svengali: under their hypnotic suggestion, an extraordinary performance is put on, not by raw recruits, but by feeble-minded schoolchildren.

W. H. Auden, 1948, 'Prologue: Writing', in *The Dyer's Hand and other essays*

49:10 If speech can never become music, neither can it ever become algebra. Even in the most 'prosy' language, in informative and technical prose, there is a personal element because language is a personal creation . . . A purely poetic language would be unlearnable, a purely prosaic not worth learning.

W. H. Auden, 1948, 'Prologue: Writing', in *The Dyer's Hand and other essays*

49:11 Unrhymed, unrhythmical, the chatter goes: / Yet no one hears his own remarks as prose.

W. H. Auden, c.1963, 'At the Party'

49:12 A dance is a measured pace, as a verse is a measured speech.

Francis Bacon, 1605, *The Advancement of Learning*, II, Sect. 16

49:13 By its very looseness, by its way of evoking rather than defining, suggesting rather than saying, English is a magnificent vehicle for emotional poetry.

Max Beerbohm, 1920, 'On Speaking French', in *And Even Now*

49:14 Prose is when all the lines except the last go on to the end. Poetry is when some of them fall short of it.

Jeremy Bentham, attributed, c. early 19th century, in M. S-J. Packe, *The Life of John Stuart Mill* (1954), I, Ch. 2

49:15 [of poetry] The right words in the right order.

Alexander Blok, quoted in D. Burg and G. Feifer, *Solzhenitsyn* (1973)

49:16 Whether one is treating a light or an exalted subject, let the sense and the rhyme always agree.

Nicolas Boileau, 1674, *L'Art poétique*, Canto 1, 27

49:17 They used language concentrating emotion, detail and image until they arrived at a form of dew-like steel.

Richard Brautigan, 1978, 'On Japanese Poets', in *June 30th–June 30th*

49:18 [of Samuel Daniel] Well-languag'd Danyel: Brooke, whose polisht lines / Are fittest to accomplish high designes.

William Browne, 1616, *Britannia's Pastorals*, II, Song 2

49:19 Language is arbitrary, conventional, and has been so from the beginning; only the poet can invent a Golden Age of iconic language in which thing and word enjoyed a blissful marriage. . . . A definition of poetry as 'conventional language trying to be iconic' is worth arguing about.

Anthony Burgess, 1992, *A Mouthful of Air*, I, Ch. 1

49:20 Some rhyme a neibor's name to lash; / Some rhyme (vain thought!) for needfu' cash; / Some rhyme to court the countra clash [gossip], / An' raise a din; / For me, an aim I never fash; / I rhyme for fun.

Robert Burns, 1786, 'Epistle to James Smith', stanza 5

49:21 Who ever did a language so enrich, / To scorn all little particles of speech? / For tho' they make the sense clear, yet they're found / To be a scurvy hind'rance to the sound.

Samuel Butler (1612–80), 1660s, 'On the British Princes: a Palinodie'

49:22 For rhyme the rudder is of verses, / With which like ships they steer their courses.

Samuel Butler (1612–80), 1663, *Hudibras*, I, Canto 1, 457

49:23 But those that write in rhyme still make / The one verse for the other's sake; / For one for sense, and one for rhyme, / I think's sufficient at one time.

Samuel Butler (1612–80), 1664, *Hudibras*, II, Canto 1, 27

49:24 Reason ne'er was hand and glove / With rhyme, but always leant less to improving / The sound than sense.

Lord Byron, 1819–24, *Don Juan*, Canto 9, stanza 74

49:25 I have nothing to say / and I am saying it and that is / poetry.

John Cage, 1961, 'Lecture on Nothing'

49:26 I must mention again it was gorgeous weather, / Rhymes are so scarce in this world of ours.

C. S. Calverley, 'Lovers, and a Reflection', in *Complete Works* (1901)

49:27 Poets paint with words, painters speak with works.

Annibale Carracci, attributed, c. late 16th century, in G. P. Bellori, *Vite* (1672)

49:28 Apt Alliteration's artful aid.

Charles Churchill, 1763, 'The Prophecy of Famine', 86

49:29 In poetry, in which every line, every phrase, may pass the ordeal of deliberation and deliberate choice, it is possible, and barely possible, to attain that ultimatum which I have ventured to propose as the infallible test of a blameless style; its *untranslatableness* in words of the same language without injury to the meaning.

Samuel Taylor Coleridge, 1817, *Biographia Literaria*, Ch. 22

49:30 [of John Donne] Rhyme's sturdy cripple, fancy's maze and clue, / Wit's forge and fire-blast, meaning's press and screw.

Samuel Taylor Coleridge, 1818, 'On Donne's Poetry'

49:31 Prose = words in their best order; poetry = the best words in the best order.

Samuel Taylor Coleridge, 12 July 1827, in Henry Nelson Coleridge (ed.), *Specimens of the Table-Talk of the late Samuel Taylor Coleridge* (1835) [cf. 59:4]

49:32 Poetry is certainly something more than good sense, but it must be good sense at all events; just as a palace is more than a house, but it must be a house, at least.

Samuel Taylor Coleridge, 9 May 1830, in Henry Nelson Coleridge (ed.), *Specimens of the Table-Talk of the late Samuel Taylor Coleridge* (1835)

49:33 MRS MILLAMANT [of her correspondence]: They serve one to pin up one's Hair.

WITWOULD: Madam, do you pin up your hair with all your letters?

MRS MILLAMANT: Only with those in Verse, Mr. Witwould. I never pin up my Hair with Prose. I fancy ones Hair wou'd not curl if it were pinn'd up with Prose.

William Congreve, 1700, *The Way of the World*, II. i

49:34 [Mr Weller] Poetry's unnat'ral; no man ever talked poetry 'cept a beadle on boxin' day, or Warren's blackin' or Rowland's oil, or some o' them low fellows; never you let yourself down to talk poetry, my boy.

Charles Dickens, 1836–7, *The Pickwick Papers*, Ch. 33

49:35 [Silas Wegg, responding to Mr Boffin's question whether reading poetry to him would be more expensive than reading prose] For when a person comes to grind off poetry night after night, it is but right he should expect to be paid for its weakening effect on his mind.

Charles Dickens, 1864–5, *Our Mutual Friend*, I, Ch. 5

49:36 They shut me up in prose – / As when a little girl / They put me in the closet – / Because they liked me 'still'.

Emily Dickinson, c.1862–86, *Complete Poems*, no. 613

49:37 [on Og's inabilities] Rhyme is the Rock on which thou art to wreck, / 'Tis fatal to thy Fame and to thy Neck.

John Dryden, 1681, *Absalom and Achitophel*, II, 486

49:38 And this unpolished rugged verse I chose / As fittest for discourse and nearest prose.

John Dryden, 1682, *Religio Laici*, 453

49:39 Wit will shine / Through the harsh cadence of a rugged line.

John Dryden, 1684, 'To the Memory of Mr Oldham'

49:40 The music of poetry, then, must be a music latent in the common speech of its time. And that means also that it must be latent in the common speech of the poet's *place*.

T. S. Eliot, 24 February 1942, lecture at Glasgow University, 'The Music of Poetry', in John Hayward (ed.), *T. S. Eliot: Selected Prose* (1953)

49:41 [on the associations between words] Not all words, obviously, are equally rich and well-connected: it is part of the business of the poet to dispose the richer among the poorer, at the right points, and we cannot afford to load a poem too heavily with the former – for it is only at certain moments that a word can be made to insinuate the whole history of a language and a civilization.

T. S. Eliot, 24 February 1942, lecture at Glasgow University, 'The Music of Poetry', in John Hayward (ed.), *T. S. Eliot: Selected Prose* (1953)

49:42 Prose was born yesterday – that is what we must tell ourselves. Poetry is pre-eminently the medium of past literatures. All the metrical combinations have been tried; but nothing like this can be said of prose.

Gustave Flaubert, 24 April 1852, letter to Louise Colet, in M. Nadeau (ed.), *Les Oeuvres* (trans., 1964)

49:43 O friend unseen, unborn, unknown, / Student of our sweet English tongue, / Read out my words at night, alone: / I was a poet, I was young.

James Elroy Flecker, 1910, 'To a Poet a Thousand Years Hence'

49:44 We all write poems; it is simply that poets are the ones who write in words.

John Fowles, 1969, *The French Lieutenant's Woman*, Ch. 19

49:45 A sentence is a sound in itself on which sounds called words may be strung.

Robert Frost, 22 February 1914, letter to John Bartlett

49:46 Writing free verse is like playing tennis with the net down.

Robert Frost, 17 May 1935, speech at Milton Academy, Massachusetts

49:47 What do I mean by a phrase? A clutch of words that gives you a clutch at the heart.

Robert Frost, 16 November 1960, interview in the *Saturday Evening Post*

49:48 Poetry is the language in which man explores his own amazement.

Christopher Fry, 3 April 1950, *Time*

49:49 As soon as war is declared, it is impossible to hold back the poets. Rhyme is still the most effective drum.

Jean Giraudoux, 1935, *La Guerre de Troi n'aura pas lieu* (trans.), II. iv

49:50 [on poetry] It is a species of painting with words, in which the figures are happily conceived, ingeniously arranged, affectingly expressed, and recommended with all the warmth and harmony of colouring.

Oliver Goldsmith, 1758–65, 'Poetry Distinguished from Other Writing', in *Essays*, no. 15

49:51 In every incipient language the poet and the prose writer are very distinct in their qualifications: the poet ever proceeds first; treading unbeaten paths, enriching his native funds, and employed in new adventures. The other follows with more cautious steps, and though slow in his motions, treasures up every useful or pleasing discovery. But when once all the extent and the force of the language is known, the poet then seems to rest from his labour, and is at length overtaken by his assiduous pursuer.

Oliver Goldsmith, 1760–2, *The Citizen of the World*, Letter 40

49:52 [on writing novels to support his writing of poetry] Prose books are the show dogs I breed and sell to support my cat.

Robert Graves, 13 July 1958, *New York Times*

49:53 The language of the age is never the language of poetry, except among the French, whose verse, where the thought or image does not support it, differs in nothing from prose.

Thomas Gray, 8 April 1742, letter to Richard West, in H. W. Starr (ed.), *Correspondence of Thomas Gray* (1971), I

49:54 Poetry proper is never merely a higher mode (*melos*) of everyday language. It is rather the reverse: everyday language is a forgotten and therefore used up poem, from which there hardly resounds a call any longer.

Martin Heidegger, *Language*, quoted in Bruce Chatwin, *The Songlines* (1988)

49:55 Rhythm and rhyme and the harmonies of musical language, the play of fancy, the fire of imagination, the flashes of passion, so hide the nakedness of a heart laid open, that hardly any confession, transfigured in the luminous halo of poetry, is reproached as self-exposure.

Oliver Wendell Holmes, senior, 1858, *The Autocrat of the Breakfast Table*, Ch. 3

49:56 When you write in prose you say what you mean. When you write in rhyme you say what you must.

Oliver Wendell Holmes, senior, 1891, *Over the Teacups*, Ch. 4

49:57 [advice to aspiring poets] Perhaps you will answer all needful conditions / For winning the laurels to which you aspire, / By docking the tails of the two prepositions / I' the style o' the bard you so greatly admire.

Oliver Wendell Holmes, senior, 'A Familiar Letter to Several Correspondents', in *The Faber Book of Useful Verse* (1981), p. 157

49:58 [advice to aspiring poets] Don't mind if the index of sense is at zero, / Use words that run smoothly, whatever they mean; / Leander and Lilian and Lillibullero / Are much the same thing in the rhyming machine.

Oliver Wendell Holmes, senior, 'A Familiar Letter to Several Correspondents', in *The Faber Book of Useful Verse* (1981), p. 157 [cf. 48:27]

49:59 The poetical language of an age should be the current language heightened, to any degree heightened and unlike itself, but not (I mean normally: passing freaks and graces are another thing) an obsolete one.

Gerard Manley Hopkins, 1879, letter to Robert Bridges

49:60 Even when poetry has a meaning, as it usually has, it may be inadvisable to draw it out. 'Poetry gives most pleasure', said Coleridge, 'when only generally and not perfectly understood'; and perfect understanding will sometimes almost extinguish pleasure.

A. E. Housman, 1933, Leslie Stephen Lecture at Cambridge on 'The Name and Nature of Poetry'

49:61 Your words / Like bits of beetles and spiders / Retched out by owls. Fluorescent, / Blue-black, splintered. Bat-skulls. One day, I thought, / I shall understand this tomb-Egyptian, / This talking in tongues to a moon-mushroom.

Ted Hughes, 1998, 'Moonwalk', in *Birthday Letters*

49:62 Your words, / Faces reversed from the light, / Holding in their entrails.
Ted Hughes, 1998, 'The Tender Place', in *Birthday Letters*

49:63 A poem is at once the most primitive and most sophisticated use of language, but my emphasis is on the former.
Stanley Kunitz, 1985, 'The Wisdom of the Body', in *Next-to-Last Things*

49:64 Prose on certain occasions can bear a great deal of poetry: on the other hand, poetry sinks and swoons under a moderate weight of prose.
Walter Savage Landor, 1824–53, 'Archdeacon Hare and Walter Landor', in *Imaginary Conversations*

49:65 Poetry can communicate the actual quality of experience with a subtlety and precision unapproachable by any other means.
F. R. Leavis, 1932, *New Bearings in English Poetry*, Ch. 2

49:66 [of the chiming bells of Bruges] and I thought how like these chimes / Are the poet's airy rhymes, / All his rhymes and roundelays, / His conceits, and songs, and ditties, / From the belfry of his brain, / Scattered downward, though in vain, / On the roofs and stones of cities!
Henry Wadsworth Longfellow, 1846, 'Carillon', in *The Belfry of Bruges*

49:67 [of Dante] Whose words, like coloured garnet-shirls in lava, / Betray the heat in which they were engendered.
Henry Wadsworth Longfellow, 1884, *Michael Angelo*, I, Sect. 1

49:68 [of words] Sometimes they trap me / Stop me in my tracks.
Thinking my way through / Towards a promising idea
When I am distracted / By a sound. A spelling crackles.
Roger McGough, 1992, 'Word Trap', in *Defying Gravity*

49:69 A poem should be wordless / As the flight of birds.
Archibald MacLeish, 1926, 'Ars Poetica'

49:70 A poem should not mean / But be.
Archibald MacLeish, 1926, 'Ars Poetica'

49:71 Poets . . . are literal-minded men who will squeeze a word till it hurts.
Archibald MacLeish, June 1972, 'Apologia', in *Harvard Law Review*

49:72 Poetry is an expression, through human language restored to its essential rhythm, of the mysteriousness of existence.
Stéphane Mallarmé, 27 June 1884, letter to M. Léo d'Orfer (trans.)

49:73 The major words of poetry are the major words of the common spelling books. They are for prose also.
Josephine Miles, 1980, 'Values in Language: or, Where have Goodness, Truth, and Beauty Gone?', in L. Michaels and C. Ricks (eds), *The State of the Language*

49:74 If we may be forgiven the antithesis, we should say that eloquence is *heard*, poetry is *overheard*.
John Stuart Mill, 1859, 'Thoughts on Poetry and its Varieties', in *Dissertations and Discussions*, I

49:75 [of *Paradise Lost*] The measure is English heroic verse without rhyme . . . rhyme being no necessary adjunct or true ornament of poem or good verse, in longer works especially, but the invention of a barbarous age, to set off wretched matter with lame metre.
John Milton, 1668, 'The Verse', *Paradise Lost*, Preface

49:76 The troublesome and modern bondage of rhyming.
John Milton, 1668, 'The Verse', *Paradise Lost*, Preface

49:77 M. JOURDAIN: What? When I say, 'Nicole, bring me my slippers and give me my nightcap', that's prose?
PHILOSOPHY TEACHER: Yes, sir.
M. JOURDAIN: Gracious me! I've been talking prose for more than forty years without knowing it.
Molière, 1670, *Le Bourgeois Gentilhomme* (trans.), II. iv

49:78 Just as the voice of the trumpet rings out clearer and stronger for being forced through a narrow tube so too a saying leaps forth much more vigorously when compressed into the rhythms of poetry, striking me then with a livelier shock.
Michel de Montaigne, 1572–80, 'On Educating Children', in *The Complete Essays* (trans. M. A. Screech, 1987), I, no. 26

49:79 Poetry is the original language of the gods.
Michel de Montaigne, 1572–80, 'On Vanity', in *The Complete Essays* (trans. M. A. Screech, 1987), III, no. 9

49:80 I am governed by the pull of the sentence as the pull of a fabric is governed by gravity.
Marianne Moore, quoted in Louis Untermeyer, 'Five Famous Poetesses', in *Ladies' Home Journal* (May 1964)

49:81 I would be inclined to define a good poem of any length as a concentrate of good prose, with or without the addition of recurrent rhythm and rhyme. The magic of prosody may improve upon what we call prose by bringing out the full flavor of meaning, but in plain prose there are also certain rhythmic patterns, the music of precise phrasing, the beat of thought rendered by recurrent peculiarities of idiom and intonation. As in today's scientific classifications, there is a lot of overlapping in our concept of poetry and prose today. The bamboo bridge between them is the metaphor.
Vladimir Nabokov, January 1964, interview, in *Strong Opinions* (1974), p. 44

49:82 Poets are always in search of the right word, the adjective that is inevitable, / Because an ill-chosen adjective induces levity in the reader, and no poet wishes to be levitable.
Ogden Nash, 1962, 'A Strange Casement of the Poetic Apothecary', in *Everyone but Thee and Me*

49:83 [of the Chaos beheld by Dullness] How hints, like spawn, scarce quick in embryo lie, / How new-born nonsense first is taught to cry, / Maggots half-form'd in rhyme exactly meet, / And learn to crawl upon poetic feet. / Here one poor word an hundred clenches [puns] makes, / And ductile Dulness new mæanders takes.
Alexander Pope, 1728, *The Dunciad*, I, 59

49:84 Poetry must be *as well written as prose*.
Ezra Pound, January 1915, letter to Harriet Monroe, in D. D. Paige (ed.), *The Selected Letters of Ezra Pound* (1950), p. 48

49:85 The true poet is most easily distinguished from the false when he trusts himself to the simplest expression and writes without adjectives.
Ezra Pound, quoted in Patricia C. Willis (ed.), *The Complete Poems of Marianne Moore* (1986)

49:86 Use no word that under stress of emotion you could not actually say.
Ezra Pound, quoted in Patricia C. Willis (ed.), *The Complete Poems of Marianne Moore* (1986)

49:87 [on poetic motivation] The ache to utter and see in word / The silhouette of a brooding soul.
Carl Sandburg, 1904, *In Reckless Ecstasy*

49:88 Only rhythm brings about a poetic short-circuit and transforms the copper into gold, the words into life.
Léopold Senghor, 1956, *Ethiopiques*, Postface

49:89 [Benedick, on being in love] Marry, I cannot show it in rhyme. I have tried. I can find out no rhyme to 'lady' but 'baby', an innocent rhyme; for 'scorn' 'horn', a hard rhyme; for 'school' 'fool', a babbling rhyme. Very ominous endings. No, I was not born under a rhyming planet, nor I cannot woo in festival terms.
William Shakespeare, 1598–9, *Much Ado About Nothing*, V. ii. 34

49:90 But oh! the dialogues, where jest and mock / Is held up like a rest at shittle-cock; / Or else, like bells, eternally they chime, / They sigh in simile, and die in rhyme.
John Sheffield, 1682, *Essay on Poetry*

49:91 Poetry therefore, is an art of *imitation* . . . a representing, counterfeiting, or figuring forth to speak metaphorically. A speaking picture, with this end: to teach and delight.
Philip Sidney, 1595, *The Defence of Poetry*

49:92 It has to be living, to learn the speech of the place, / It has to face the man of the time.
Wallace Stevens, 1942, 'Of Modern Poetry', in *Parts of a World*

49:93 [to Lady Flora] Turn your face, / Nor look with that too-earnest eye – / The rhymes are dazzled from their place / And order'd words asunder fly.
Alfred, Lord Tennyson, 1842, *The Day-dream*, Prologue

49:94 Poets have got to enjoy themselves sometimes, and the twistings and convolutions of words, the inventions and contrivances, are all part of the joy that is part of the painful, voluntary work.
Dylan Thomas, 1961, poetic manifesto, *Texas Quarterly*, no. 4, issue 4

49:95 Out of us all / That make rhymes, / Will

you choose / Sometimes – / As the winds use / A crack in a wall / Or a drain, / Their joy or their pain / To whistle through – / Choose me / You English words?

Edward Thomas, 1915, 'Words'

49:96 Among the forests / Of metal the one human / Sound was the lament of / The poet for deciduous language.

R. S. Thomas, 1972, 'Postscript'

49:97 We are beginning to see / now it is matter is the scaffolding / of spirit; that the poem emerges / from morphemes and phonemes.

R. S. Thomas, 1978, 'Emerging', in *Frequencies*

49:98 The poet from afar has taken speech, / Speech takes the poet far. A poet's speech begins a great way off. / A poet is carried away by the speech.

Marina Tsvetayeva, 'The Poet' (trans. E. Feinstein, 1971)

49:99 The poem – that prolonged hesitation between sound and sense.

Paul Valéry, 1943, *Tel quel* (trans.)

49:100 Poetry is to prose as dancing is to walking.

John Wain, 13 January 1976, BBC radio broadcast

49:101 A poet's pleasure is to withhold a little of his meaning, to intensify by mystification.

E. B. White, 1942, 'Poetry', in *One Man's Meat*

49:102 Do I contradict myself ? / Very well then I contradict myself, / (I am large, I contain multitudes.)

Walt Whitman, 1855, 'Song of Myself ', in *Leaves of Grass*, Sect. 51

49:103 I too am not a bit tamed. I too am untranslatable, / I sound my barbaric yawp over the roofs of the world.

Walt Whitman, 1855, 'Song of Myself ', in *Leaves of Grass*, Sect. 52

49:104 Poetry is idealized grammar.

Oscar Wilde, c.1883, in Richard Ellmann, *Oscar Wilde* (1987), Ch. 8

49:105 The poet gives us his essence, but prose takes the mould of the body and mind entire.

Virginia Woolf, 'Reading', in *The Captain's Death Bed* (published 1950)

49:106 The Reader will find that personifications of abstract ideas rarely occur in these volumes, and are utterly rejected as an ordinary device to elevate the style and raise it above prose.

William Wordsworth, 1800, *Lyrical Ballads*, Preface

49:107 There will also be found in these volumes little of what is usually called poetic diction; as much pains has been taken to avoid it as is ordinarily taken to produce it; this has been done for the reason already alleged, to bring my language near to the language of men.

William Wordsworth, 1800, *Lyrical Ballads*, Preface

49:108 There neither is, nor can be, any *essential* difference between the language of prose and metrical composition.

William Wordsworth, 1800, *Lyrical Ballads*, Preface

See also: 1:16–17, 5:26–7, 7:34, 21:69, 24:19, 38:53, 39:7, 40:25, 42:7, 42:12, 48:62–3, 50:23, 58:2

50   *Metaphors and Similes*

The use of images in speech and writing

50:1 Allegories, when well chosen, are like so many Tracks of Light in a Discourse, that make every thing about them clear and beautiful. A noble Metaphor, when it is placed to an Advantage, casts a kind of Glory round it, and darts a Lustre through a whole Sentence.
Joseph Addison, 3 July 1712, 'Appeal to the Imagination in Writing on Abstract Subjects by Allusion to the Natural World: Imagination Liable to Cause Pain as well as Pleasure', *The Spectator*, no. 421

50:2 A metaphor is the application of a noun which properly applies to something else. The transfer may be from genus to species, from species to genus, from species to species, or by analogy.
Aristotle, 4th century BC, 'Classification of Nouns', in *Poetics* (trans. M. Heath), Ch. 21

50:3 The successful use of metaphor is a matter of perceiving similarities.
Aristotle, 4th century BC, 'Qualities of Poetic Style', in *Poetics* (trans. M. Heath), Ch. 22

50:4 *Metaphor* pre-eminently involves *clarity*, *pleasantness* and *unfamiliarity*, and it cannot be drawn from any other source.
Aristotle, 4th century BC, *The Art of Rhetoric* (trans. H. C. Lawson-Tancred), Ch. 3, Sect. 2

50:5 Scratch the simplest expressions, and you will find the metaphor. Written words are handage, inkage, and paperage; it is only by metaphor, or substitution and transposition of ideas, that we can call them language.
Samuel Butler (1835–1902), 1890, lecture in London on 'Thought and Language'

50:6 [Count Lodovico, of the ideal Courtier] I would like him to use certain words in a metaphorical sense, whenever it is appropriate, putting them to novel use like a gardener grafting a branch on to a healthier trunk, and so increasing their attractiveness and beauty, so that what is said or written makes us seem to experience things at first hand and greatly increases our enjoyment.
Baldesar Castiglione, 1528, *The Book of the Courtier* (trans. G. Bull, Penguin 1967), I, p. 78

50:7 As anyone who has ever forked out for a quarter-pound of mixed metaphors will testify, once a bastion falls, the flood-gates open and before you know where you are you're up to the neck in wrung withers.
Alan Coren, 16 February 1972, *Punch*

50:8 For all of us, grave or light, get our thoughts entangled in metaphors, and act fatally on the strength of them.
George Eliot, mid 19th century, quoted as an epigraph in Max Black (ed.), *The Importance of Language* (1962)

50:9 The world is emblematic. Parts of speech are metaphors because the whole of nature is a metaphor of the human mind.
Ralph Waldo Emerson, 1836, 'Language', in *Nature*, Ch. 4

50:10 I love metaphor the way some people love junk food.
William H. Gass, 1977, interview in *Paris Review* (Summer)

50:11 The metaphor is a shorter simile, or rather

a kind of magical coat, by which the same idea assumes a thousand different appearances.
Oliver Goldsmith, 1758–65, 'Poetry Distinguished from Other Writing', in *Essays*, no. 16

50:12 I sought out quaint words, and trim invention; / My thoughts began to burnish, sprout, and swell, / Curling with metaphors a plain intention, / Decking the sense, as if it were to sell.
George Herbert, 'Jordan (1)', in *The Temple* (1633)

50:13 All language is, in some sort, a collection of faded metaphors.
Jean Paul, early 19th century, in *On the Study of Words* (trans. Richard Chenevix Trench, 1851), Lecture 2

50:14 As to metaphorical expression, that is a great excellence in style, when it is used with propriety, for it gives you two ideas for one; conveys the meaning more luminously, and generally with a perception of delight.
Samuel Johnson, 1777, in James Boswell, *The Life of Samuel Johnson* (1791), Ch. 41

50:15 He who would increase the meaning and decrease the meaningless verbiage in his own speech and writing, must do two things. He must become conscious of the fossilized metaphors in his words; and he must freely use new metaphors, which he creates for himself.
C. S. Lewis, 1939, 'Bluspels and Flalansferes', in *Rehabilitations and Other Essays*

50:16 Figurative language is a natural source of grandeur, and metaphors contribute to sublimity.
Longinus (traditional attribution; in fact by an earlier, unknown author), 1st century BC, *On the Sublime* (trans. T. S. Dorsch), Ch. 32

50:17 I love metaphor. It provides two loaves where there seems to be one. Sometimes it throws in a load of fish.
Bernard Malamud, 1975, interview in *Paris Review* (Spring)

50:18 The metaphor is perhaps one of man's most fruitful potentialities. Its efficacy verges on magic, and it seems a tool for creation which

God forgot inside one of His creatures when He made him.
José Ortega y Gasset, 1925, *The Dehumanization of Art* (trans.)

50:19 Half the wrong conclusions at which mankind arrive are reached by the abuse of metaphors, and by mistaking general resemblance of imaginary similarity for real identity.
Viscount Palmerston, 1 September 1839, letter to Henry Bulwer

50:20 One Simile, that solitary shines / In the dry desert of a thousand lines, / Or lengthen'd Thought that gleams through many a page, / Has sanctify'd whole poems for an age.
Alexander Pope, 1737, 'The First Epistle of The Second Book of Horace', 111

50:21 No simile ever yet ran on all fours.
Proverbial (Latin)

50:22 DUKE SENIOR: But what said Jaques? Did he not moralize this spectacle? [the death of a deer]
FIRST LORD: O yes, into a thousand similes.
William Shakespeare, 1600, *As You Like It*, II. i. 43

50:23 Figures of speech, which poets think so fine, / (Art's needless varnish to make Nature shine) / All are but paint upon a beauteous face, / And in descriptions only claim a place.
John Sheffield, 1682, *Essay on Poetry*

50:24 [of metaphors] There is nothing more dishonest in an historian, than the use of one.
Laurence Sterne, 1761, *The Life and Opinions of Tristram Shandy, Gentleman*, III, Ch. 23

50:25 The highest stretch of improvement a single word is capable of, is a high metaphor.
Laurence Sterne, 1762, *The Life and Opinions of Tristram Shandy, Gentleman*, V, Ch. 42

50:26 The pleasure which the mind derives from the perception of similitude in dissimilitude . . . is the great spring of the activity of our minds, and their chief feeder . . . it is the life of our ordinary conversation.
William Wordsworth, 1800, *Lyrical Ballads*, Preface

See also: 2:16, 2:34, 26:3, 42:7, 49:81, 58:10, 63:3, 63:13

51 *Accents and Dialects*

Regional ways of talking, in pronunciation, grammar, vocabulary, and style

51:1 [Standard English is] that kind of English which is the official language of the entire English-speaking world, and is also the language of all educated English-speaking people. What I mean by Standard English has nothing to do with the way people pronounce: Standard English is a language, not an accent, and it is as easily recognizable as Standard English when it is written down as when it is spoken. It is, in fact, the only form of English to be at all widely written nowadays.
David Abercrombie, 1965, 'RP and Local Accent', in *Studies in Phonetics and Linguistics*

51:2 Adams never learned to talk German well, but the same might be said of his English, if he could believe Englishmen. He learned not to annoy himself on this account.
Henry Adams, 1907, 'Berlin', in *The Education Of Henry Adams*, Ch. 5

51:3 In the classroom we all learned past participles, but in the streets and in our homes Blacks learned to drop *s*'s from plurals and suffixes from past-tense verbs. We were alert to the gap separating the written word from the colloquial. We learned to slide out of one language and into another without being conscious of the effort. At school, in a given situation, we might respond with 'That's not unusual.' But in the street, meeting the same situation, we easily said, 'It be's like that sometimes.'
Maya Angelou, 1969, *I Know Why the Caged Bird Sings*, Ch. 29

51:4 English and French spoken; Australian understood.
Anonymous, 1990s, shop notice in Turkey (and elsewhere)

51:5 [to Louis MacNeice] For Grammar we both inherited / good mongrel barbarian English.
W. H. Auden, 1964, 'The Cave of Making', in *Thanksgiving for a Habitat*

51:6 I haven't been abroad in so long that I almost speak English without an accent now.
Robert Benchley, 1938, *After 1903 – What?*

51:7 I think anyone not brought up in the North finds it hard to get dialect pronunciation exactly right.
Alan Bennett, 1972, Production Diary of *A Day Out*, reprinted in *Writing Home* (1994), p. 262

51:8 [of Liverpudlians] The accent doesn't help. There is a rising inflection in it, particularly at the end of a sentence, that gives even the most formal exchange a built-in air of grievance. They all have the chat, and it laces every casual encounter, everybody wanting to do you their little verbal dance.
Alan Bennett, 1985, Production Diary of *The Insurance Man*, reprinted in *Writing Home* (1994), p. 289

51:9 [Gileadite challenge to an Ephraimite fugitive] 'Are you an Ephraimite?' If he answered 'No', they said, 'Then say Shibboleth'. He would say 'Sibboleth', since he could not pronounce the word correctly. Thereupon they seized and slaughtered him by the fords of the Jordan.
The Bible, Judges 12:6 (Jerusalem Bible) [cf. 18:6]

51:10 I have heard the Gallegans say that in no two villages is [their language] spoken in one and the same manner, and that very frequently they do not understand each other. The worst of this language is, that everybody on first hear-

ing it thinks that nothing is more easy than to understand it, as words are continually occurring which he has heard before; but these merely serve to bewilder and puzzle him, causing him to misunderstand everything that is said; whereas, if he were totally ignorant of the tongue, he would occasionally give a shrewd guess at what was meant.
George Borrow, 1843, *The Bible in Spain*, Ch. 25

51:11 The English are polite by telling lies. The Americans are polite by telling the truth.
Malcolm Bradbury, 1965, *Stepping Westward*, II, Sect. 5

51:12 Lee Mellon didn't have any Southern accent. 'You don't have much of a Southern accent,' I said.
'That's right, Jesse. I read a lot of Nietzsche, Schopenhauer and Kant when I was a kid,' Lee Mellon said.
I guess in some strange way that was supposed to get rid of a Southern accent. Lee Mellon thought so, anyway. I couldn't argue because I had never tried a Southern accent against the German philosophers.
Richard Brautigan, 1964, 'Augustus Mellon, CSA', in *A Confederate General from Big Sur*

51:13 A language may be termed a dialect that waves a national flag.
Anthony Burgess, 1992, *A Mouthful of Air*, I, Ch. 14

51:14 In days when mankind were but callans [boys] / At grammar, logic, an' sic talents, / They took nae pains their speech to balance, / Or rules to gie; / But spak their thoughts in plain, braid lallans [Lowland Scots], / Like you or me.
Robert Burns, May 1785, 'Epistle to William Simson'

51:15 Nature hath given man five instruments for the pronouncing of all letters, the lips, the teeth, the tongue, the palate, and throate . . . but some among vs do pronounce more fully, some flatly, some broadly, and no few mincingly, offending in defect, excesse, or change of letters, which is rather to be imputed to the persons and their education, than to the language. Whenas generally wee pronounce by the confession of strangers, as sweetely, smoothly, and moderately, as any of the Northerne Nations of the world, who are noted to soupe [utter forcibly] their words out of the throat with fat and full spirits.
William Camden, 1605, 'The Languages', in *Remaines Concerning Britain*

51:16 Nay all speech, even the commonest speech, has something of song in it: not a parish in the world but has its parish-accent: – the rhythm or *tune* to which the people there *sing* what they have to say! Accent is a kind of chanting; all men have accent of their own, – though they only *notice* that of others. Observe too how all passionate language does of itself become musical, – with a finer music than the mere accent; the speech of a man even in zealous anger becomes a chant, a song.
Thomas Carlyle, 1840, 'The Hero as Poet', in *On Heroes, Hero-Worship, and the Heroic in History*, Lecture 3

51:17 [of an American] When the slow-maturing anecdote is ripest, / He'll dictate it like a Board of Trade Report, / And because he has no time to call a typist, / He calls her a Stenographer for short.
G. K. Chesterton, 1927, 'A Ballad of Abbreviations', in *New Poems*

51:18 Anterior to cultivation, the lingua communis of every country, as Dante has well observed, exists every where in parts, and no where as a whole.
Samuel Taylor Coleridge, 1817, *Biographia Literaria*, Ch. 17 [cf. 51:19]

51:19 If, therefore, the speech of the same people varies . . . successively in course of time, and cannot in any wise stand still, the speech of people living apart and removed from one another must needs vary in different ways, since they are not rendered stable either by nature or by intercourse, but arise according to men's inclinations and local fitness. Hence were set in motion the inventors of the art of grammar, which is nothing else but a kind of unchangeable identity of speech in different times and places.
Dante, c.1304, *De vulgari eloquentia* (trans. A. G. Ferrers Howell), I, Ch. 9

51:20 Whenever an Englishman would cry 'All right!' an American cries 'Go ahead!' which is somewhat expressive of the national character of the two countries.
Charles Dickens, 1842, *American Notes*, Ch. 9

51:21 'Pray, sir!' said Mrs. Hominy, 'where do you hail from?' 'I am afraid I am dull of comprehension,' answered Martin, 'being extremely tired; but upon my word I don't understand you.' Mrs. Hominy shook her head with a melancholy smile that said, not inexpressively,

'They corrupt even the language in that old country!' and added then, as coming down a step or two to meet his low capacity, 'Where was you rose?' 'Oh!' said Martin, 'I was born in Kent.'

Charles Dickens, 1843–4, *Martin Chuzzlewit*, Ch. 22

51:22 'Then there's the sea; and the boats and ships; and the fishermen; and the beach; and Am to play with –'. Peggotty meant her nephew Ham, mentioned in my first chapter; but she spoke of him as a morsel of English Grammar.

Charles Dickens, 1849–50, *David Copperfield*, Ch. 2

51:23 An Englishman appears resarved because he can't talk.

Finley Peter Dunne, 1900, 'Casual Observations', in *Mr Dooley's Philosophy*

51:24 [of using Anglo-Saxon and Latin words] Mixture is a secret of the English island; and, in their dialect, the male principle is the Saxon, the female, the Latin; and they are combined in every discourse.

Ralph Waldo Emerson, 1856, *English Traits*, Ch. 14

51:25 The father spoke with a strong Midland accent, using words of dialect by no means disagreeable to the son's ear – for dialect is a very different thing from the bestial jargon which on the lips of the London vulgar passes for English.

George Gissing, 1892, *Born in Exile*, VII, Ch. 3

51:26 English is a vernacular of vernaculars.

Robert Graves and Alan Hodge, 1944, *The Reader Over Your Shoulder*, Ch. 1

51:27 Her occasional pretty and picturesque use of dialect words – those terrible marks of the beast to the truly genteel.

Thomas Hardy, 1886, *The Mayor of Casterbridge*, Ch. 20

51:28 Mrs Durbeyfield habitually spoke the dialect; her daughter, who had passed the Sixth Standard in the National School under a London-trained mistress, spoke two languages; the dialect at home, more or less; ordinary English abroad and to persons of quality.

Thomas Hardy, 1891, *Tess of the D'Urbervilles*, Ch. 3

51:29 The English don't raise their voices, Arthur, although they may have other vulgarities.

Lillian Hellman, 1973, 'Arthur W. A. Cowan', in *Pentimento*

51:30 I decided that Europeans and Americans are like men and women: they understand each other worse, and it matters less, than either of them suppose.

Randall Jarrell, *Pictures from an Institution*, IV, Ch. 10

51:31 In literate nations, though the pronunciation, and sometimes the words of common speech may differ, as now in England, compared with the south of Scotland, yet there is a written diction, which pervades all dialects, and is understood in every province. But where the whole language is colloquial, he that has only one part, never gets the rest, as he cannot get it but by change of residence.

Samuel Johnson, 1773, 'Ostig in Sky', in *A Journey to the Western Islands of Scotland*

51:32 The conversation of the Scots grows every day less unpleasing to the English; their peculiarities wear fast away; their dialect is likely to become in half a century provincial and rustick, even to themselves. The great, the learned, the ambitious, and the vain, all cultivate the English phrase and the English pronunciation.

Samuel Johnson, 1773, 'Inch Kenneth', in *A Journey to the Western Islands of Scotland*

51:33 The American I have heard up to the present is a tongue as distinct from English as Patagonian.

Rudyard Kipling, 1889, *From Sea to Sea*

51:34 The accent of one's birthplace lives on in our mind and in our heart as it does in our speech.

Duc de La Rochefoucauld, 1678, *Maxims*, no. 342

51:35 The Englishman claims many birthrights, not the least of which is his right to speak his own language as, subject to the good-will of his friends, it pleases him to do; perhaps next in importance must be ranked his right to think whatever he pleases of any style of speech that is different from his own.

Arthur Lloyd James, 1926, 'Broadcast English', BBC pamphlet

51:36 [on BBC announcers] If I were the dictator of the English language I should choose the educated Scottish person, or perhaps President Roosevelt, as an international standard for the whole of the English speaking world.

Arthur Lloyd James, 1939, 'The Voice of Britain', in *The Listener* (2 March)

51:37 *Standard English* A widely used term that resists easy definition but is used as if most educated people nonetheless know precisely what it refers to.

Tom McArthur, 1992, 'Standard English', in *The Oxford Companion to the English Language*, p. 982

51:38 In pronunciation, among other things, my French is corrupted by home-grown barbarisms; I have never known a man from our part of the world who did not obviously reek of dialect and who did not offend pure French ears.

Michel de Montaigne, 1572–80, 'On Presumption', in *The Complete Essays* (trans. M. A. Screech, 1987), II, no. 17

51:39 All good young Englishmen go to Oxford or Cambridge and they all write and publish books before their graduation, / And I often wondered how they did it until I realized that they have to do it because their genteel accents are so developed that they can no longer understand each other's spoken words so the written word is their only means of intercommunication.

Ogden Nash, 1938, 'England Expects', in *I'm a Stranger Here Myself*

51:40 In a Lancashire cotton-town you could probably go for months on end without once hearing an 'educated' accent, whereas there can hardly be a town in the South of England where you could throw a brick without hitting the niece of a bishop.

George Orwell, 1937, *The Road to Wigan Pier*, Ch. 7

51:41 The preservation of the English language in its purity throughout the United States is an object deserving the attention of every American, who is a friend to the literature and science of his country.

John Pickering, 1816, *A Vocabulary, or Collection of Words and Phrases which have been supposed to be Peculiar to the United States of America*

51:42 It is slightly annoying to the English to be told that their English accent is 'perfect' or 'sweet' or 'cute', since the Englishman rightly believes that he alone has no accent whatever.

Stephen Potter, 1952, 'Behaviour', in *One-Upmanship*, II, p. 157

51:43 The potatoes would be dug, washed, cooked and eaten by the Ulsterman while the Munsterman would be saying 'potato'.

Proverbial (Irish)

51:44 Our maker [poet] therfore at these days shall not follow *Piers plowman* nor *Gower* nor *Lydgate* nor yet *Chaucer*, for their language is now out of vse with vs: neither shall he take the termes of Northern-men, such as they vse in dayly talke, whether they be noble men or gentle-men, or of their best clarkes, all is a matter: nor in effect any speach vsed beyond the river of Trent, though no man can deny but that theirs is the purer English Saxon at this day, yet it is not so Courtly nor so currant as our Southerne English is, no more is the far Westerne mans speach.

George Puttenham, 1589, 'Of Language', in *The Arte of English Poesie*, III

51:45 English, no longer an English language, now grows from many roots.

Salman Rushdie, 3 July 1982, *The Times*

51:46 ORLANDO [meeting the disguised Rosalind in the forest]: Your accent is something finer than you could purchase in so removed a dwelling.

ROSALIND: I have been told so of many; but indeed an old religious uncle of mine taught me to speak, who was in his youth an inland man.

William Shakespeare, 1600, *As You Like It*, III. ii. 331

51:47 [Kent, disguised] If but as well I other accents borrow / That can my speech diffuse, my good intent / May carry through itself to that full issue / For which I razed my likeness.

William Shakespeare, 1605–6, *King Lear*, I. iv. 1

51:48 [Straker's view of Malone's American accent] A joke thoughtfully provided by Providence expressly for the amusement of the British race.

George Bernard Shaw, 1905, *Man and Superman*, IV

51:49 England and America are two countries divided by a common language [also: separated by the same language].

George Bernard Shaw, 20th century, attributed in *Reader's Digest* (November 1942)

51:50 [on the effects of the spread of English around the world] It would be ironic if the answer to Babel were pidgin and not Pentecost.

George Steiner, 1975, *After Babel*, Ch. 6

51:51 Even though his tongue acquire the Southern knack, he will have a strong Scots accent of the mind.

Robert Louis Stevenson, 1887, 'The Foreigner at Home', in *Memories and Portraits*, Ch. 1

51:52 [Huckleberry Finn to Tom Sawyer] 'What's the name of the gal?' 'It ain't a gal at all – it's a girl.' 'It's all the same, I reckon; some says gal, some says girl – both's right, like enough.'

Mark Twain, 1876, *The Adventures of Tom Sawyer*, Ch. 26

51:53 When I speak my native tongue in its utmost purity in England, an Englishman can't understand me at all.

Mark Twain, 1882, *The Stolen White Elephant*

51:54 There is no such thing as the Queen's English. The property has gone into the hands of a joint stock company and we own the bulk of the shares.

Mark Twain, 1894, 'Following the Equator', in *Pudd'nhead Wilson's New Calendar*

51:55 I have traveled more than anyone else, and I have noticed that even the angels speak English with an accent.

Mark Twain, 1894, 'Following the Equator', in *Pudd'nhead Wilson's New Calendar*

51:56 As an independent nation, our honor requires us to have a system of our own, in language as well as government. Great Britain, whose children we are, should no longer be *our* standard; for the taste of her writers is already corrupted, and her language on the decline. But if it were not so, she is at too great a distance to be our model, and to instruct us in the principles of our own tongue.

Noah Webster, 1789, *Dissertations on the English Language, with Notes Historical and Critical*

51:57 The English vocabulary is now federated rather than centralized. No one person's English is all English, but each English speaker is to some extent 'multilingual' within English.

Edmund Weiner, 1990, 'The Federation of English', in L. Michaels and C. Ricks (eds), *The State of the Language*

51:58 My Irish accent was one of the many things I forgot at Oxford.

Oscar Wilde, c.1874, in Richard Ellmann, *Oscar Wilde* (1987), Ch. 2

51:59 We have really everything in common with America nowadays, except, of course, language.

Oscar Wilde, c.1881–2, in Richard Ellmann, *Oscar Wilde* (1987), Ch. 6

51:60 The amount of pleasure one gets out of dialect is a matter entirely of temperament. To say 'mither' instead of 'mother' seems to many the acme of romance. There are others who are not quite so ready to believe in the pathos of provincialisms.

Oscar Wilde, 6 June 1885, '*As You Like It* at Coombe House', in *Dramatic Review*

See also: 7:18, 10:32, 11:38, 14:29, 15:2; 15:23, 16:61, 18:6, 25:99, 35:1, 42:1, 52:15, 52:41, 52:45

Language in society; social class and politeness

52:1 [Momma] She didn't cotton to the idea that whitefolks could be talked to at all without risking one's life. And certainly they couldn't be spoken to insolently. In fact, even in their absence they could not be spoken of too harshly unless we used the sobriquet 'They'.

Maya Angelou, 1969, *I Know Why the Caged Bird Sings*, Ch. 7

52:2 The educated speak common and general things, while the uneducated speak from what they know, and things nearer to the mass mind.

Aristotle, 4th century BC, *The Art of Rhetoric* (trans. H. C. Lawson-Tancred), Ch. 2, Sect. 22

52:3 Men prominent in life are mostly hard to converse with. They lack small-talk, and at the same time one doesn't like to confront them with their own great themes.

Max Beerbohm, 1946, 'T. Fenning Dodworth', in *Mainly On the Air*

52:4 The rich man speaks and everyone stops talking; and then they praise his discourse to the skies. The poor man speaks and people say, 'Who is this?'; and if he staggers they push him down.

The Bible, Ecclesiasticus 13:23 (Jerusalem Bible)

52:5 [Count Lodovico] Our courtier, therefore, will be judged to be perfect and will show grace in everything, and especially in his speech, if he shuns affectation.

Baldesar Castiglione, 1528, *The Book of the Courtier* (trans. G. Bull, Penguin 1967), I, p. 70

52:6 Tzu-lu said, If the prince of Wei were waiting for you to come and administer his country for him, what would be your first measure? The Master said, It would certainly be to correct language. Tzu-lu said, Can I have heard you aright? Surely what you say has nothing to do with the matter. Why should language be corrected? The Master said, Yu! How boorish you are! A gentleman, when things he does not understand are mentioned, should maintain an attitude of reserve. If language is incorrrect, then what is said does not concord with what was meant; and if what is said does not concord with what was meant, what is to be done cannot be effected. If what is to be done cannot be effected, then rites and music will not flourish. If rites and music do not flourish, then mutilations and lesser punishments will go astray. And if mutilations and lesser punishments go astray, then the people have nowhere to put hand or foot. Therefore the gentleman uses only such language as is proper for speech, and only speaks of what it would be proper to carry into effect. The gentleman, in what he says, leaves nothing to mere chance.

Confucius, 5th century BC, *The Analects* (trans. A. Waley), XIII, Sect. 3

52:7 [Mr Omer, the undertaker] It's one of the drawbacks of our line of business. When a party's ill, we *can't ask* how the party is.

Charles Dickens, 1849–50, *David Copperfield*, Ch. 30

52:8 [Pip, of Joe] Whenever he subsided into affection, he called me Pip, and whenever he relapsed into politeness he called me Sir.

Charles Dickens, 1861, *Great Expectations*, Ch. 27

52:9 [Tope, of Mr Jasper] 'He has been took a little poorly.' 'Say "taken", Tope – to the Dean,' the younger rook interposes in a low tone with this touch of correction, as who should say: 'You may offer bad grammar to the laity, or the humbler clergy, not to the Dean.'

Charles Dickens, 1870, *The Mystery of Edwin Drood*, Ch. 2

52:10 Now if any ask me, whence it is that our conversation is so much refin'd? I must freely, and without flattery, ascribe it to the Court: and, in it, particularly to the King; whose example gives a law to it.

John Dryden, 1672, 'Defence of the Epilogue', appended to *The Conquest of Granada*

52:11 [of Mrs Turton] She had learned the lingo, but only to speak to her servants, so she knew none of the politer forms, and of the verbs only the imperative mood.

E. M. Forster, 1924, *A Passage to India*, Ch. 7

52:12 [Lord Chancellor] When you're lying awake with a dismal headache, and repose is taboo'd by anxiety, / I conceive you may use any language you choose to indulge in, without impropriety.

W. S. Gilbert, 1882, *Iolanthe*, II

52:13 Mrs Hinks still spoke the laundress tongue, unmitigated and inimitable.

George Gissing, 1891, *New Grub Street*, Ch. 8

52:14 Language as a class-indicator was never black and white, but, like most things, muddy grey. Some U people always talked non-U.

Philip Howard, 1978, contribution to 'Language: U and non-U, double-U, E and non-E', in Richard Buckle (ed.), *U and Non-U Revisited*, p. 30 [cf. 52:32]

52:15 [Mr Bojanus] When the revolution comes, Mr Gumbril . . . it won't be the owning of a little money that'll get a man into trouble. It'll be his class-habits, Mr Gumbril, his class-speech, his class-education. It'll be Shibboleth all over again, Mr Gumbril; mark my words. The Red Guards will stop people in the street and ask them to say some such word as 'towel'.

Aldous Huxley, 1923, *Antic Hay*, Ch. 3 [cf. 51:9]

52:16 It sometimes happens that by conquest, intermixture, or gradual refinement, the cultivated parts of a country change their language.

Samuel Johnson, 1773, 'The Highlands', in *A Journey to the Western Islands of Scotland*

52:17 Educated people do indeed speak the same languages; cultivated ones need not speak at all.

Louis Kronenberger, 1964, 'Overture', in *The Cart and the Horse*, Ch. 1

52:18 [Henry Higgins] An Englishman's way of speaking absolutely classifies him. / The moment he talks he makes some other Englishman despise him. / One common language I'm afraid we'll never get. / Oh, why can't the English learn to set / A good example to people whose English is painful to your ears? / The Scotch and the Irish leave you close to tears. / There even are places where English completely disappears. / In America, they haven't used it for years!

Alan J. Lerner, *My Fair Lady* (1956), based on George Bernard Shaw, *Pygmalion* (1913) [cf. 52:41]

52:19 A good foundation in the General Principles of Grammar is in the first place necessary for all those who are initiated in a learned education.

Robert Lowth, 1762, *A Short Introduction to English Grammar*, Preface

52:20 For there is no other way to guard yourself against flattery than by making men understand that telling you the truth will not offend you; but when each man is able to tell you the truth you lose their respect. Therefore, a wise prince should take a third course, choosing wise men for his state and giving only those free rein to speak the truth to him, and only on such matters as he inquires about and not on others. But he should ask them about everything and should hear their opinions, and afterwards he should deliberate by himself in his own way; and with these counsels and with each of his advisers he should conduct himself in such a manner that all will realize that the more freely they speak the more they will be acceptable to him.

Niccolò Machiavelli, 1532, 'On How to Avoid Flatterers', in *The Prince* (trans. P. Bonandella and M. Musa), Ch. 23

52:21 A gentleman need not know Latin, but he should at least have forgotten it.

Brander Matthews, early 20th century, advice to Dr Joseph Shipley

52:22 The language of the two social extremes is similar. I find it to consist in an instinctively lavish use of vowels and adjectives.

George Meredith, 1859, *The Ordeal of Richard Feverel*, Ch. 34

52:23 [Lady Camper] Vulgar phrases have to be endured, except when our intimates are guilty, and then we are not merely offended, we are compromised by them.

George Meredith, 1877, *The Case of General Ople and Lady Camper*, Ch. 4

52:24 [when the hoped-for Socialism comes] And then perhaps this misery of class-prejudice will fade away, and we of the sinking middle class – the private schoolmaster, the half-starved free-lance journalist, the colonel's spinster daughter with £75 a year, the jobless Cambridge graduate, the ship's officer without a ship, the clerks, the civil servants, the commercial travellers and the thrice-bankrupt drapers in the country towns – may sink without further struggles into the working class where we belong, and probably when we get there it will not be so dreadful as we feared, for, after all, we have nothing to lose but our aitches.

George Orwell, 1937, *The Road to Wigan Pier*, Ch. 13 [last sentence of the book]

52:25 Most of their discourse was about hunting, in a dialect I understand very little.

Samuel Pepys, 22 November 1663, *Diary*

52:26 [of a courtier] This thing has travell'd, speaks each language too, / And knows what's fit for every state to do; / Of whose best phrase and courtly accent join'd, / He forms one tongue, exotic and refin'd.

Alexander Pope, 1733, 'Satire IV', 46, in *Satires of Dr Donne Versified*

52:27 [conversation with a courtier] 'What *Speech* esteem you most?' 'The *King's*,' said I. / 'But the best *words?*' – 'O Sir, the *Dictionary*.'

Alexander Pope, 1733, 'Satire IV', 68, in *Satires of Dr Donne Versified*

52:28 I was beginning to learn the exact value of the language, spoken or mute, of aristocratic affability, an affability that is happy to shed balm upon the sense of inferiority of those to whom it is directed, though not to the point of dispelling that inferiority, for in that case it would no longer have any *raison d'être*.

Marcel Proust, 1921–2, *Cities of the Plain [Sodome et Gomorrhe]* (trans. C. K. Scott-Moncrieff)

52:29 People who never have had money, speak like the flowers of the pumpkin; people who never have been poor, have words as sweet as jaggery [sugar].

Proverbial (Palaung)

52:30 Servants talk about People; Gentlefolk discuss Things.

Proverbial

52:31 [recommending southern English as a desirable standard] Ye shall therefore take the vsuall speach of the Court, and that of London and the shires lying about London within lx. [sixty] myles, and not much aboue.

George Puttenham, 1589, 'Of Language', in *The Arte of English Poesie*, III

52:32 [speaking of the 1950s] It is solely by its language that the upper class is clearly marked off from the others.

Alan S. C. Ross, 1956, 'U and non-U: an Essay in Sociological Linguistics', in Nancy Mitford (ed.), *Noblesse Oblige* [cf. 31:32]

52:33 In England today – just as much as in the England of many years ago – the question 'Can a non-U speaker become a U-speaker?' is one noticeably of paramount importance for many Englishmen (and for some of their wives). The answer is that an adult can never attain complete success.

Alan S. C. Ross, 1956, 'U and non-U: an Essay in Sociological Linguistics', in Nancy Mitford (ed.), *Noblesse Oblige*

52:34 Among European languages, English is, surely, the one most suited to the study of linguistic class-distinction.

Alan S. C. Ross, 1956, 'U and non-U: an Essay in Sociological Linguistics', in Nancy Mitford (ed.), *Noblesse Oblige*

52:35 [of Mme d'Houdetot] I carried the familiarity that I had assumed in my intoxication to the extent of addressing her in the second person singular, but in such a delicate way that she certainly could not have been hurt by it.

Jean-Jacques Rousseau, 1770, *The Confessions* (trans. J. M. Cohen), IX: 1757

52:36 English is a stretch language; one size fits all.

William Safire, 1980, 'The Great Permitter', in *On Language*

52:37 Eloquence is a republican art, as conversation is an aristocratic one.

George Santayana, 1921, *Character and Opinion in the United States*, Ch. 1

52:38 [Warwick, to King Henry, about Prince Harry's taking up again with Falstaff *et al.*] The Prince but studies his companions, / Like a strange tongue, wherein, to gain the language, / 'Tis needful that the most immodest word / Be looked upon and learnt, which once attained, / Your highness knows, comes to no further use / But to be known and hated.

William Shakespeare, 1597, *Henry IV, Part 2*, IV. iii. 68

52:39 HAMLET: The concernancy, sir? Why do we wrap the gentleman in our more rawer breath?

OSRIC: Sir?

HORATIO: Is't not possible to understand in another tongue? You will to't, sir, rarely.

HAMLET: What imports the nomination of this gentleman?

OSRIC: Of Laertes?

HORATIO (*aside to Hamlet*): His purse is empty already; all's golden words are spent.

William Shakespeare, 1600–1601, *Hamlet*, from the Second Quarto addition to the First Folio at V. ii. 107

52:40 Titles distinguish the mediocre, embarrass the superior, and are disgraced by the inferior.

George Bernard Shaw, 1903, 'Maxims for Revolutionists: Titles', in *Man and Superman*

52:41 The English have no respect for their language, and will not teach their children to speak it. They spell it so abominably that no man can teach himself what it sounds like. It is impossible for an Englishman to open his mouth without making some other Englishman hate or despise him.

George Bernard Shaw, 1913, *Pygmalion*, Preface [cf. 52:18]

52:42 [The Note Taker (Higgins)] You see this creature with her kerbstone English: the English that will keep her in the gutter to the end of her days. Well, sir, in three months I could pass that girl off as a duchess at an ambassador's garden party. I could even get her a place as lady's maid or shop assistant, which requires better English. Thats the sort of thing I do for commercial millionaires. And on the profits of it I do genuine scientific work in phonetics, and a little as a poet on Miltonic lines.

George Bernard Shaw, 1913, *Pygmalion*, I

52:43 [Higgins] You have no idea how fright-

fully interesting it is to take a human being and change her into a quite different human being by creating a new speech for her. It's filling up the deepest gulf that separates class from class and soul from soul.

George Bernard Shaw, 1913, *Pygmalion*, III

52:44 [Mr Puff, about the language in his play] I am not for making slavish distinctions, and giving all the fine language to the upper sort of people.

Richard Sheridan, 1779, *The Critic*, III. i

52:45 Standard English, like Standard French, is now a class-dialect more than a local dialect: it is the language of the educated all over Great Britain. . . . The best speakers of Standard English are those whose pronunciation, and language generally, least betray their locality.

Henry Sweet, 1908, *The Sounds of English*, pp. 7, 8

52:46 [of Mrs Rawdon Crawley] This young woman had got up the genteel *jargon* so well, that a native could not speak it better; and it was only from her French being so good, that you could know she was not a born woman of fashion.

William Makepeace Thackeray, 1847–8, *Vanity Fair*, Ch. 29

52:47 Where shall we look for standard English, but to the words of a standard man?

Henry Thoreau, 1849, 'Sunday', in *A Week on the Concord and Merrimack Rivers*

52:48 There are a class of men, – or rather more than a class, a section of mankind, – to whom a power of easy expression by means of spoken words comes naturally. English country gentlemen, highly educated as they are, undaunted as they usually are, self-confident as they in truth are at the bottom, are clearly not in this section.

Anthony Trollope, 1863, *Rachel Ray*, Ch. 24

52:49 It is very vulgar to talk like a dentist when one isn't a dentist. It produces a false impression.

Oscar Wilde, 1895, *The Importance of Being Earnest*, I

See also: 11:15, 11:47, 11:56, 12:15, 23:95, 25:24, 25:33, 26:22, 31:32, 42:11, 51:39, 51:46, 62:13

Opinions and attitudes about male and female speech

53:1 Women like silent men. They think they're listening.

Marcel Achard, 4 November 1956, *Quote*

53:2 [Dion] As men / Do walk a mile, women should talk an hour / After supper. 'Tis their exercise.

Francis Beaumont and John Fletcher, 1609, *Philaster*, II. iv

53:3 As in all the churches of the saints, women are to remain quiet at meetings since they have no permission to speak; they must keep in the background as the Law itself lays it down. If they have any questions to ask, they should ask their husbands at home: it does not seem right for a woman to raise her voice at meetings.

The Bible, 1 Corinthians 14:34 (Jerusalem Bible)

53:4 As climbing up a sandhill is for elderly feet, such is a garrulous wife for a quiet husband.

The Bible, Ecclesiasticus 25:20 (Jerusalem Bible)

53:5 I have but one simile, and that's a blunder, / For wordless woman, which is silent thunder.

Lord Byron, 1819–24, *Don Juan*, Canto 6, stanza 57

53:6 As to the effect of the anti-eloquent and allusive language of sisterhood on the evolution of the English language toward the end of the century, I leave the reader to draw his own conclusions. Please observe, from the above sentence, that the English language does indeed assume everybody to be male unless they are proved to be otherwise; and this kind of usage is, simply, silly, because it does not adequately reflect social reality, which is the very least one can expect language to do.

Angela Carter, 1980, 'The Language of Sisterhood', in L. Michaels and C. Ricks (eds), *The State of the Language*

53:7 But though we find it written that the woman spoke first, it is, however, reasonable for us to suppose that the man spoke first; and it is unseemly to think that so excellent an act of the human race proceeded even earlier from woman than from man.

Dante, c.1304, *De vulgari eloquentia* (trans. A. G. Ferrers Howell), I, Ch. 4

53:8 Mr and Mrs Snagsby are not only one bone and one flesh, but, to the neighbours' thinking, one voice too. That voice, appearing to proceed from Mrs Snagsby alone, is heard in Cook's Court very often. Mr Snagsby, otherwise than as he finds expression through these dulcet tones, is rarely heard.

Charles Dickens, 1852–3, *Bleak House*, Ch. 10

53:9 A woman's sinse iv humor is in her husband's name.

Finley Peter Dunne, 1900, 'Casual Observations', in *Mr Dooley's Philosophy*

53:10 Women can't swear. They have th' feelin' but not th' means.

Finley Peter Dunne, 1902, 'Swearing', in *Observations by Mr Dooley*

53:11 Half the sorrows of women would be averted if they could repress the speech they know to be useless; nay, the speech they have resolved not to make.

George Eliot, 1866, *Felix Holt*, Ch. 2

53:12 They had started speaking of 'women and children' – that phrase that exempts the male from sanity when it has been repeated a few times.

E. M. Forster, 1924, *A Passage to India*, Ch. 20

53:13 [Bathsheba] It is difficult for a woman to define her feelings in language which is chiefly made by men to express theirs.

Thomas Hardy, 1874, *Far from the Madding Crowd*, Ch. 51

53:14 The two camps were then united, and Amazons and Scythians lived together, every man keeping as his wife the woman whose favours he had first enjoyed. The men could not learn the women's language, but the women succeeded in picking up the men's.

Herodotus, 5th century BC, in *The Histories* (trans. Aubrey de Sélincourt, 1996), IV, Ch. 114

53:15 Women speak because they wish to speak, whereas a man speaks only when driven to speech by something outside himself – like, for instance, he can't find any clean socks.

Jean Kerr, 1960, 'How to Talk to a Man', in *The Snake Has All the Lines*

53:16 Men speak the truth as they understand it, and women as they think men would like to understand it.

Rudyard Kipling, 1888, 'Bitters Neat', in *Plain Tales from the Hills*

53:17 Unlike women, words don't talk.

Claude Lévi-Strauss, quoted in George Steiner, 'Orpheus with his Myths: Claude Lévi-Strauss', in *Language and Silence* (1967)

53:18 Fatigue makes women talk more and men less.

C. S. Lewis, 1942, *The Screwtape Letters*, p. 30

53:19 Men are less measured in their expressions than women, but when women once take to strong expressions they are much worse.

Lord Melbourne, mid 19th century, in Viscount Esher, *The Girlhood of Queen Victoria* (1912), II, p. 210

53:20 [when asked if he would teach his daughters foreign languages] One tongue is sufficient for a woman.

John Milton, attributed, 17th century [cf. 53:25]

53:21 Women have been known to have good sound teeth extracted so as to rearrange them in a better order or in the hope of making their voices softer or fuller.

Michel de Montaigne, 1572–80, 'That the Taste of Good and Evil Things Depends in Large Part on the

Opinion we Have of them', in *The Complete Essays* (trans. M. A. Screech, 1987), I, no. 14

53:22 The feminine language consists of words placed one after another with extreme rapidity, with intervals for matinees. The purpose of this language is (1) to conceal, and (2) to induce, thought.

Christopher Morley, 1919, 'Syntax for Cynics', in *Mince Pie*

53:23 The nightingale will run out of songs before a woman runs out of conversation.

Proverbial (Spanish)

53:24 Ten measures of garrulity came down from heaven, says the Talmud, and the woman took nine of them.

Proverbial (Hebrew)

53:25 One tongue is enough for a woman.

Proverbial [cf. 53:20]

53:26 A woman's sword is her tongue and she does not let it rust.

Proverbial (Chinese)

53:27 Even a fifty-tongued man cannot equal a single-tongued woman at abusing.

Proverbial (Singhalese)

53:28 A man never knows how to say goodbye; a woman never knows when to say it.

Helen Rowland, 1909, *Reflections of a Bachelor Girl*

53:29 SPEED [part of a list of suggested vices in the woman Lance loves]: '*Item*, she doth talk in her sleep.'

LANCE: It's no matter for that, so she sleep not in her talk.

SPEED: '*Item*, she is slow in words.'

LANCE: O villain, that set this down among her vices! To be slow in words is a woman's only virtue. I pray thee out with't, and place it for her chief virtue.

William Shakespeare, 1590–1, *The Two Gentlemen of Verona*, III. i. 322

53:30 [Slender] Mistress Anne Page? She has brown hair, and speaks small like a woman?

William Shakespeare, 1597, *The Merry Wives of Windsor*, I. i. 43

53:31 [Viola, disguised as a man, to Orsino] We men may say more, swear more, but indeed / Our shows are more than will; for still we prove / Much in our vows, but little in our love.

William Shakespeare, 1601, *Twelfth Night*, II. iv. 116

53:32 [Innogen to Pisanio] O, / Men's vows are women's traitors.
William Shakespeare, 1610–11, *Cymbeline*, III. iv. 54

53:33 [Loveless, to Amanda] Will you then make no difference, Amanda, between the language of our sex and yours? There is a modesty restrains your tongues, which makes you speak by halves when you commend; but roving flattery gives a loose to ours, which makes us still speak double what we think.
Richard Sheridan, 1777, *A Trip to Scarborough*, II. i

53:34 Silence makes a woman beautiful.
Sophocles, 5th century BC, *Ajax*, 293

53:35 You see in no Place of Conversation the Perfection of Speech so much as in an accomplished Woman.
Richard Steele, 31 August 1709, 'Wit: the Propriety of Words and Thoughts', *The Tatler*, no. 62

53:36 A Woman seldom writes her Mind but in her Postscript.
Richard Steele, 31 May 1711, *The Spectator*, no. 79

53:37 If the Choice had been left to me, I would rather have trusted the Refinement of our Language, as far as it relates to Sound, to the Judgment of the Women, than of illiterate Court-Fops, half-witted-Poets, and University-Boys.
Jonathan Swift, 1712, 'A Proposal for Correcting, Improving and Ascertaining the English Tongue'

53:38 Now, though I would by no means give Ladies the Trouble of advising us in the Reformation of our Language; yet I cannot help thinking, that since they have been left out of all Meetings, except Parties at Play, or where worse Designs are carried on, our Conversation hath very much degenerated.
Jonathan Swift, 1712, 'A Proposal for Correcting, Improving and Ascertaining the English Tongue'

53:39 I always say that if you want a speech made you should ask a man, but if you want something done you should ask a woman.
Margaret Thatcher, 26 July 1982, at the AGM of the Townswomen's Guild

53:40 Women are a decorative sex. They never have anything to say, but they say it charmingly.
Oscar Wilde, 1891, *The Picture of Dorian Gray*, Ch. 4

53:41 The experience . . . of the woman writer is completely schizophrenic. One is always torn between two approaches: on the one hand, to use a language that is not ours . . . and on the other, the battle one fights to break all this up, in order to do something else through and in language.
Monique Wittig, quoted in Jean-François Josselin, *Le Nouvel Observateur* (1973)

See also: 2:114, 6:20, 6:54, 18:26, 21:34, 23:78, 29:21, 45:11

Academic language, and jargon in general

54:1 The difference between the man who uses language scientifically and the man who uses it emotively is not that the one produces sentences which are incapable of arousing emotion, and the other sentences which have no sense, but that the one is primarily concerned with the expression of true propositions, the other with the creation of a work of art.
A. J. Ayer, 1936, *Language, Truth and Logic*, Ch. 1

54:2 What is it about sociology that instantly bogs us down in fens of jargon?
Russell Wayne Baker, 15 December 1990, *New York Times*

54:3 Ours is the age of substitutes: instead of language, we have jargon; instead of principles, slogans; and, instead of genuine ideas, Bright Ideas.
Eric Bentley, 1954, *The Dramatic Event*

54:4 Oversimplification is now a common term of reproach in academic discussions; everyone is against oversimplification. But there is no parallel term nearly as frequently used to describe the opposite phenomenon, which surely occurs as often, if not more so.
Bennett M. Berger, 1990, *Authors of Their Own Lives*, Introduction

54:5 [describing Dr Petworth] He is an expert on real, imaginary and symbolic exchanges among skin-bound organisms working on the linguistic interface, which is what linguists call you and me.
Malcolm Bradbury, 1983, *Rates of Exchange*, I, Sect. 4

54:6 So, when men argue, the great'st part / O' th' contest falls on terms of art, / Until the fustian stuff be spent, / And then they fall to th' argument.
Samuel Butler (1612–80), 1663, *Hudibras*, I, Canto 3, 1,363

54:7 For nonsense has the amplest privileges, / And more than all the strongest sense obliges, / That furnishes the schools with terms of art, / The mysteries of science to impart; / Supplies all seminaries with recruits / Of endless controversies and disputes; / For learned nonsense has a deeper sound / Than easy sense, and goes for more profound.
Samuel Butler (1612–80), 1670s, 'Satire upon the Imperfection and Abuse of Human Learning', fragments of an intended second part

54:8 I am tempted to say of metaphysicians what Scaliger used to say of the Basques: they are said to understand one another, but I don't believe a word of it.
Nicolas-Sébastien Chamfort, 1796, *Maximes et pensées* (trans.), Ch. 7

54:9 And let a scholar all Earth's volumes carry, / He will be but a walking dictionary.
George Chapman, 1609, *The Tears of Peace*, 530

54:10 The exact kind of language we employ in philosophical analyses of abstract truth is one thing, and the language used in attempts to popularize the subject is another.
Cicero, *c*.45–44 BC, *On Duties [De officiis]* (trans. M. Grant), II, Ch. 10

54:11 A philosopher's ordinary language and admissions, in general conversation or writings *ad populum*, are as his watch compared with his astronomical timepiece. He sets the former by the town clock, not because he believes it right, but because his neighbours and his cook go by it.

Samuel Taylor Coleridge, 1 September 1832, in Henry Nelson Coleridge (ed.), *Specimens of the Table-Talk of the late Samuel Taylor Coleridge* (1835)

54:12 [after discussing the style of various essayists] I have called this style the Mandarin style, since it is beloved by literary pundits, by those who would make the written word as unlike as possible to the spoken one. It is the style of those writers whose tendency is to make their language convey more than they mean or more than they feel, it is the style of most artists and all humbugs, and one which is always menaced by a puritan opposition.

Cyril Connolly, 1938, *Enemies of Promise*, Ch. 20

54:13 [on being a mere scholar, as distinguished from a man of polite learning] A mere book-case, a bundle of letters, a head stuffed with the jargon of languages, a man that understands every body but is understood by no body.

Daniel Defoe, 1728–9, *The Complete English Gentleman*, Ch. 5

54:14 For insight into human affairs I turn to stories and poems rather than to sociology. This is the result of my upbringing and background. I am not able to make use of the wisdom of the sociologists because I do not speak their language.

Freeman J. Dyson, 1979, *Disturbing the Universe*, Ch. 1

54:15 Sociology is a new science concerning itself not with esoteric matters outside the comprehension of the layman, as the older sciences do, but with the ordinary affairs of ordinary people. This seems to engender in those who write about it a feeling that the lack of any abstruseness in their subject matter demands a compensatory abstruseness in their language.

Ernest Gowers, 1965, 'Sociologese', in H. F. Fowler, *A Dictionary of Modern English Usage* (2nd edition)

54:16 [Stephen, of the dean] The language in which we are speaking is his before it is mine. How different are the words *home*, *Christ*, *ale*, *master*, on his lips and on mine! I cannot speak or write these words without unrest of spirit. His language, so familiar and so foreign, will always be for me an acquired speech. I have not made or accepted its words. My voice holds them at bay. My soul frets in the shadow of his language.

James Joyce, 1916, *Portrait of the Artist as a Young Man*, Ch. 5

54:17 [My Lady, on being frightened by the long words in a medical report] So she made Sir John write to *The Times* to command the Chancellor of the Exchequer for the time being to put a tax on long words –

A light tax on words over three syllables, which are necessary evils, like rats, but, like them, must be kept down judiciously.

A heavy tax on words over four syllables, as *heterodoxy* . . .

And on words over five syllables (of which I hope no one will wish to see any examples), a totally prohibitory tax.

And a similar prohibitory tax on words derived from three or more languages at once; words derived from two languages having become so common that there was no more hope of rooting out them than of rooting out peth-winds [convolvulus]. [The Bill falls through, due to Irish and Scots opposition.]

Charles Kingsley, 1863, *The Water-Babies*, Ch. 4

54:18 Sociology is the science of talk, and there is only one law in sociology. Bad talk drives out good.

Frank H. Knight, quoted in Paul A. Samuelson, *The Samuelson Sampler* (1973)

54:19 [Pooh] I am a Bear of Very Little Brain, and long words Bother me.

A. A. Milne, 1926, *Winne-the-Pooh*, Ch. 4

54:20 Don't appear so scholarly, pray. Humanize your talk, and speak to be understood. Do you think a Greek name gives more weight to your reasons?

Molière, 1663, *The Critique of the School for Wives* (trans. D. M. Frame), scene vi

54:21 Once you have the cap and gown all you need do is open your mouth. Whatever nonsense you talk becomes wisdom and all the rubbish, good sense.

Molière, 1673, *The Imaginary Invalid* (trans. J. Wood), III

54:22 [of jargon] It is a therapeutic source of amusement and rage, just as long as you can assure yourself that others are to blame, and that this deplorable linguistic malady is quite beyond your own responsibility and control, like a disease that strikes only the uncleanly.

Walter Nash, 1993, *Jargon: Its Uses and Abuses*, Ch. 1

54:23 Just as bad money drives the good beyond our reach, / So has the jargon of the hippie, the huckster and the bureaucrat debased the sterling of our once lucid speech. / What's worse, it has induced the amnesia by which I am faced; / I can't recall the original phraseology which the jargon has replaced.

Ogden Nash, 1972, 'What do you Want, A Meaningful Dialogue, or a Satisfactory Talk?', in *The Old Dog Barks Backwards*

54:24 Bad writers, and especially scientific, political and sociological writers, are nearly always haunted by the notion that Latin or Greek words are grander than Saxon ones.

George Orwell, 1946, 'Politics and the English Language', *Horizon,* no. 13

54:25 In certain kinds of writing, particularly in art criticism and literary criticism, it is normal to come across long passages which are almost completely lacking in meaning.

George Orwell, 1946, 'Politics and the English Language', *Horizon,* no. 13

54:26 [on appealing to wise men for explanations] Yet this solution but once more affords / New change of terms, and scaffolding of words.

Matthew Prior, 1718, 'Knowledge', in *Solomon on the Vanity of the World,* I, p. 478

54:27 [reacting to a report on the teaching of English which condemned this style of writing] Bear up, brave clerklets, though the lights of learning / Your quaint commercial English sadly shocks, / And even bosses are agreed in spurning / Your 'inst.' and 'ult.' and 'prox.' / I like the pleasant jargon: I should miss it / If firms no more (*'per pro.'* before their name) / Should 'thanks me for past favours and solicit / Continuance of the same.'

Punch, 1 March 1922, 'Commercialisms', p. 176

54:28 Whenever men with book learning used big words in dealing with him, he came out the loser. It startled him just to hear those words. Obviously they were just a cover for robbery. But they sounded nice.

Graciliano Ramos, 1938, 'Contas', in *Vidas secas [Barren Lives]* (trans., 1965)

54:29 [on the Armory Show] There is no reason why people should not call themselves Cubists, or Octagonists, Parallelopipedonists, or Knights of the Isosceles Triangle, or Brothers of the Cosine, if they so desire; as expressing anything serious and permanent, one term is as fatuous as another.

Theodore Roosevelt, 9 March 1913, 'A Layman's Views of an Art Exhibition', in the *Outlook*

54:30 The cold metal of economic theory is in Marx's pages immersed in such a wealth of steaming phrases as to acquire a temperature not naturally its own.

Joseph Schumpeter, 1942, *Capitalism, Socialism, and Democracy,* p. 21

54:31 MOTE: They [Holofernes and Nathaniel] have been at a great feast of languages and stolen the scraps.

COSTARD: O, they have lived long on the alms-basket of words. I marvel thy master hath not eaten thee for a word, for thou art not so long by the head as *honorificabilitudinitatibus.*

William Shakespeare, 1593–4, *Love's Labour's Lost,* V. i. 36

54:32 HOLOFERNES: *Via,* goodman Dull! Thou hast spoken no word all this while.

DULL: Nor understood none neither, sir.

William Shakespeare, 1593–4, *Love's Labour's Lost,* V. i. 142

54:33 Of all the cants which are canted in this canting world, – though the cant of hypocrites may be the worst, – the cant of criticism is the most tormenting!

Laurence Sterne, 1761, *The Life and Opinions of Tristram Shandy, Gentleman,* III, Ch. 12

54:34 I hate set dissertations, – and above all things in the world, 'tis one of the silliest things in one of them, to darken your hypothesis by placing a number of tall, opake words, one before another, in a right line, betwixt your own and your readers conception, – when in all likelihood, if you had looked about, you might have seen something standing, or hanging up, which would have cleared the point at once.

Laurence Sterne, 1761, *The Life and Opinions of Tristram Shandy, Gentleman,* III, Ch. 20

54:35 A classic lecture, rich in sentiment, / With scraps of thundrous Epic lilted out / By violet-hooded Doctors, elegies / And quoted odes, and jewels five-words-long, / That on the stretch'd forefinger of all Time / Sparkle for ever.

Alfred, Lord Tennyson, 1847, *The Princess,* I, 352

54:36 It is a safe rule to apply that, when a mathematical or philosophical author writes with a misty profundity, he is talking nonsense.

A. N. Whitehead, 1911, *Introduction to Mathematics*

See also: 8:25, 16:29, 50:24, 58:3

The jargon of politics, diplomacy, the civil service, and public administration

55:1 No professional diplomatists worried about falsehoods. Words were with them forms of expression which varied with individuals, but falsehood was more or less necessary to all. The worst liars were the candid. What diplomatists wanted to know was the motive that lay beyond the expression.

Henry Adams, 1907, 'Foes Or Friends', *The Education Of Henry Adams*, Ch. 9

55:2 [of the Reagan administration] America has just passed through an eight-year coma in which slogans were confused with solutions and rhetoric passed for reality.

Lloyd Bentsen, junior, 21 July 1988, speech accepting the Democratic nomination for Vice President

55:3 [of the student of politics] He must also be on his guard against the old words, for the words persist when the reality that lay behind them has changed.

Aneurin Bevan, 1952, *In Place of Fear*

55:4 [Dixie Dean, to the assistant manager of the Fraud Section] 'Now, what's the score?' 'Routine,' said the man. 'Merely administrative routine.' 'I can use big words, too,' boasted the other, leaning forward to enunciate with great clarity. 'Elastoplast!'

Alan Bleasdale, 1983, *Boys from the Blackstuff* (novel based on the TV play, by Keith Miles), Ch. 3

55:5 [clerk, to Dixie Dean] 'Name?' 'Y'already know it. Y've used it y'self.' 'Name?' 'And so did he.' 'Name?' insisted the girl. 'Are y' sure this isn't a trick question?' As the girl repeated the question yet again, Dixie asked it in unison with her, providing the answer as well. He asked the succeeding questions in unison as well, chant-

ing them like a litany, and interleaving the answers. Eventually, she asked a question out of the usual sequence. He sounded betrayed. 'You changed the order! That's not fair!'

Alan Bleasdale, 1983, *Boys from the Blackstuff* (novel based on the TV play, by Keith Miles), Ch. 3

55:6 Tell stories scandalous and false / I' th' proper language of cabals, / Where all a subtle statesman says / Is half in words and half in face.

Samuel Butler (1612–80), 1678, *Hudibras*, III, Canto 2, 1,487

55:7 [on electioneering methods] The proser who, upon the strength / Of his one vote, has tales of three hours' length; / This sorry rogue you bear, yet with surprise / Start at his oaths, and sicken at his lies.

George Crabbe, 1810, 'Letter V: Elections', 39, in *The Borough*

55:8 [of speech-making in the House of Commons] The music of the parliamentary bagpipes.

Charles Dickens, 1849–50, *David Copperfield*, Ch. 48

55:9 [Mr Boythorn] As to Corporations, Parishes, Vestry-Boards, and similar gatherings of jolter-headed clods, who assemble to exchange such speeches that, by Heaven! they ought to be worked in quicksilver mines for the short remainder of their miserable existence, if it were only to prevent their detestable English from contaminating a language spoken in the presence of the Sun.

Charles Dickens, 1852–3, *Bleak House*, Ch. 13

55:10 The Circumlocution Office was (as everybody knows without being told) the most important Department under government. No public business of any kind could possibly be done at any time without the acquiescence of the Circumlocution Office. Its finger was in the largest public pie, and in the smallest public tart. It was equally impossible to do the plainest right, and to undo the plainest wrong, without the express authority of the Circumlocution Office. If another Gunpowder Plot had been discovered half an hour before the lighting of the match, nobody would have been justified in saving the Parliament until there had been half a score of boards, half a bushel of minutes, several sacks of official memoranda, and a family-vault-full of ungrammatical correspondence, on the part of the Circumlocution Office.

Charles Dickens, 1855–7, *Little Dorrit*, I, Ch. 10

55:11 [Mr Clennam, on raising a question with Mr Barnacle of the Circumlocution Office] 'Am I correctly informed?'

It being one of the principles of the Circumlocution Office never, on any account whatever, to give a straightforward answer, Mr Barnacle said 'Possibly.'

Charles Dickens, 1855–7, *Little Dorrit*, I, Ch. 10

55:12 [of MPs] Our honourable friend is triumphantly returned to serve in the next Parliament. He is the honourable member for Verbosity – the best represented place in England.

Charles Dickens, 1858, *Our Honourable Friend*, in *Reprinted Pieces*

55:13 Why, why, above all, in either house of Parliament must the English language be set to music – bad and conventional beyond any parallel on earth.

Charles Dickens, 1858, *A Few Conventionalities*, in *Reprinted Pieces*

55:14 Finality is not the language of politics.

Benjamin Disraeli, 28 February 1859, parliamentary speech, in *Hansard*, col. 998

55:15 I used to think I was poor. Then they told me I wasn't poor, I was needy. They told me it was self-defeating to think of myself as needy, I was deprived. Then they told me underprivileged was over-used, I was disadvantaged. I still don't have a dime. But I have a great vocabulary.

Jules Feiffer, 1956, cartoon caption

55:16 Making every allowance for the customs of a House where Bills can still, it seems, be

talked out, and members are obliged to speak lest other members should speak in place of them, there is still a rich margin of need for that considered brevity which, if not the soul of wit, is at least an aid to good and vigorous English, and a guarantee against sleep.

John Galsworthy, July 1924, *On Expression*, Presidential Address to the English Association, p. 13 [cf. 30:50]

55:17 Where there is official censorship it is a sign that speech is serious. Where there is none, it is pretty certain that the official spokesmen have all the loud-speakers.

Paul Goodman, 1960, *Growing Up Absurd*, Ch. 2

55:18 [of Charles James Fox] All bills this favoured statesman frames, / And clothes with tapestries of rhetoric / Disguising their real web of commonplace.

Thomas Hardy, 1910, *The Dynasts*, I. i

55:19 Conferences at the top level are always courteous. Name-calling is left to the foreign ministers.

W. Averell Harriman, 1 August 1955, US broadcast news summaries

55:20 Diplomacy – lying in state.

Oliver Herford, in Laurence J. Peter, *Peter's Quotations* (1977)

55:21 The politician is trained in the art of inexactitude. His words tend to be blunt or rounded, because if they have a cutting edge they may later return to wound him.

Edward R. Murrow, attributed, mid 20th century

55:22 Political language . . . is designed to make lies sound truthful and murder respectable, and to give an appearance of solidity to pure wind.

George Orwell, 1946, 'Politics and the English Language', *Horizon*, no. 13

55:23 If an ambassador says yes, it means perhaps; if he says perhaps, it means no; if he ever said no, he would cease to be an ambassador.

K. M. Panikkar, mid 20th century, in Ved Bhushan (ed.), *New Light's Dictionary of Quotations*

55:24 Diplomats write Notes, because they wouldn't have the nerve to tell the same thing to each other's face.

Will Rogers, 1949, *The Autobiography of Will Rogers*, Ch. 12

55:25 When political ammunition runs low,

inevitably the rusty artillery of abuse is wheeled into action.

Adlai Stevenson, 22 September 1952, speech in New York City

55:26 A diplomat is a person who can tell you to go to hell in such a way that you actually look forward to the trip.

Caskie Stinnett, 1960, *Out of the Red*

55:27 Revolutions are always verbose.

Leon Trotsky, 1930, *History of the Russian Revolution*, XI, Ch. 12

55:28 Diplomacy is the lowest form of politeness because it misquotes the greatest number of people. A nation, like an individual, if it has anything to say, should simply say it.

E. B. White, 1944, 'Compost', in *One Man's Meat*

55:29 [on listening to orators in law courts and parliament] Words follow words, sense seems to follow sense: / What memory and what logic! till the strain / Transcendent, superhuman as it seemed, / Grows tedious even in a young man's ear.

William Wordsworth, 1805, *The Prelude*, VII, 508

55:30 An ambassador is an honest man sent to lie abroad for the commonwealth.

Sir Henry Wotton, 1604, witticism written in the autograph album of Christopher Fleckmore

See also: 8:8

Legal terms, personalities, and procedures

56:1 The first to plead is adjudged to be right; in comes his opponent, then the trial begins.
The Bible, Proverbs 18:17 (Jerusalem Bible)

56:2 *Oath, n.* In law, a solemn appeal to the Deity, made binding upon the conscience by a penalty for perjury.
Ambrose Bierce, 1911, *The Devil's Dictionary*

56:3 Others believe no voice t'an organ / So sweet as lawyer's in his bar-gown, / Until with subtle cobweb-cheats / They're catch'd in knotted law like nets: / In which, when once they are imbrangled, / The more they stir the more they're tangled.
Samuel Butler (1612–80), 1664, *Hudibras*, II, Canto 3, 15

56:4 [Don Quixote, on getting a letter copied] Do not give it to a lawyer's clerk to write, for they use a legal hand that Satan himself will not understand.
Miguel de Cervantes, 1605, *The Adventures of Don Quixote* (trans. J. M. Cohen), I, Ch. 25

56:5 Closely related to legal ability is the gift of eloquence, which is a more elaborate art and wields an even greater power to attract goodwill.
Cicero, 45–44 BC, *On Duties [De officiis]*, (trans. M. Grant), II, Ch. 19

56:6 'Here's a subpœna for you, Mr Weller,' said Jackson. 'What's that in English?' inquired Sam.
Charles Dickens, 1836–7, *The Pickwick Papers*, Ch. 31

56:7 [on members of the High Court of Chancery] Tripping one another up on slippery precedents, groping knee-deep in technicalities, running their goat-hair and horse-hair warded heads against walls of words.
Charles Dickens, 1852–3, *Bleak House*, Ch. 1

56:8 [Mr Guppy] Being in the law, I have learnt the habit of not committing myself in writing.
Charles Dickens, 1852–3, *Bleak House*, Ch. 29

56:9 I know you lawyers can, with ease, / Twist words and meanings as you please; / That language, by your skill made pliant, / Will bend to favour ev'ry client.
John Gay, 1729, 'The Dog and the Fox', in *Fables*

56:10 You're an attorney. It's your duty to lie, conceal and distort everything, and slander everybody.
Jean Giraudoux, 1945, *The Madwoman of Chaillot*, II

56:11 A verbal contract isn't worth the paper it is written on.
Sam Goldwyn, in Alva Johnson, *The Great Goldwyn* (1937), Ch. 1

56:12 The peculiarities of legal English are often used as a stick to beat the official with.
Ernest Gowers, 1954, *The Complete Plain Words*, Ch. 2

56:13 There is something monstrous in commands couched in invented and unfamiliar language; an alien master is the worst of all. The language of the law must not be foreign to the ears of those who are to obey it.
Learned Hand, 11 May 1929, speech in Washington DC

56:14 [on addressing a legal committee] You must not argue there, as if you were arguing in the schools; close reasoning will not fix their attention – you must say the same thing over and over again, in different words. If you say it but once, they miss it in a moment of inattention. It is unjust, sir, to censure lawyers for multiplying words when they argue; it is often *necessary* for them to multiply words.

Samuel Johnson, 1781, in James Boswell, *The Life of Samuel Johnson* (1791), Ch. 53

56:15 [said about a fellow lawyer] He can compress the most words into the smallest idea of any man I ever met.

Abraham Lincoln, attributed by Tuli Kupferberg in *Juris Doctor* (Oct/Nov 1978) [cf. 64:16]

56:16 The law is a profession of words.

David Mellinkoff, 1963, *The Language of the Law*, Preface

56:17 Why is it that our tongue, so simple for other purposes, becomes obscure and unintelligible in wills and contracts?

Michel de Montaigne, 1572–80, 'On Experience', in *The Complete Essays* (trans. M. A. Screech, 1987), III, no. 13

56:18 DEFENCE COUNSEL [referring to Mr Groomkirby's reluctance to take the oath]: I understand that if the oath is administered there is a strong possibility of prevarication, m'lord.

JUDGE: You mean he's a liar?

DEFENCE COUNSEL: Only when on oath, m'lord. I am told he looks on the oath in the light of a challenge, m'lord.

N. F. Simpson, 1959, *One Way Pendulum*, II

56:19 Let all the laws be clear, uniform, and precise; to interpret laws is almost always to corrupt them.

Voltaire, 1764, *Philosophical Dictionary* (trans.)

See also: 55:29

57 The Language of Religion

Talking to or about God, and other forms of religious language

57:1 [on having heard a good sermon] I could heartily wish that more of our Country-Clergy would follow this Example; and instead of wasting their Spirits in laborious Compositions of their own, would endeavour after a handsome Elocution, and all those other Talents that are proper to enforce what has been penned by greater Masters. This would not only be more easy to themselves, but more edifying to the People.
Joseph Addison, 2 July 1711, 'Sir Roger's Household in the Country', *The Spectator*, no. 106

57:2 *Verbum infans*, the Word without a word, not able to speak a word.
Lancelot Andrewes, 1618, *Of the Nativity*, Sermon 12

57:3 Those of us who are Anglicans know well that the language of the Book of Common Prayer, its extraordinary beauties of sound and rhythm, can all too easily tempt us to delight in the sheer sound without thinking what the words mean or whether we mean them. In the General Confession, for example, what a delight to the tongue and ear it is to recite 'We do earnestly repent and are heartily sorry for these our misdoings; the remembrance of them is grievous unto us; the burden of them is intolerable.' Is it really intolerable? Not very often.
W. H. Auden, 1968, *Secondary Worlds*

57:4 I think too of services caught by chance, sitting on winter afternoons in the nave of Ely or Lincoln and hearing from the (so-called) loudspeaker a dry, reedy, unfleshed voice taking evensong. And one was grateful that the voice was without feeling – no more emotion than from an announcer giving the times of the departure of trains: the words themselves so powerful that they do not need feeling injected into them, any more than poetry does.
Alan Bennett, 12 May 1990, 'Comfortable Words', address to the Prayer Book Society, Blackburn, reprinted in *Writing Home* (1994), p. 354

57:5 Anybody with the gift of tongues speaks to God, but not to other people; because nobody understands him when he talks in the spirit about mysterious things. On the other hand, the man who prophesies does talk to other people, to their improvement, their encouragement and their consolation. The one with the gift of tongues talks for his own benefit, but the man who prophesies does so for the benefit of the community. While I should like you all to have the gift of tongues, I would much rather you could prophesy, since the man who prophesies is of greater importance than the man with the gift of tongues, unless of course the latter offers an interpretation so that the church may get some benefit.
The Bible, 1 Corinthians 14:1 (Jerusalem Bible)

57:6 Think of a musical instrument, a flute or a harp; if one note on it cannot be distinguished from another, how can you tell what tune is being played? Or if no one can be sure which call the trumpet has sounded, who will be ready for the attack? It is the same with you: if your tongue does not produce intelligible speech, how can anyone know what you are saying? You will be talking to the air. There are any number of different languages in the world, and not one of them is meaningless, but if I am ignorant of what the sounds mean, I am a savage to the man who is speaking, and he is a savage to me.

The Bible, 1 Corinthians 14:7 (Jerusalem Bible)

57:7 I thank God that I have a greater gift of tongues than all of you, but when I am in the presence of the community I would rather say five words that mean something than ten thousand words in a tongue.

The Bible, 1 Corinthians 14:18 (Jerusalem Bible)

57:8 You are not being sent to a nation that speaks a difficult foreign language; you are being sent to the House of Israel. Not to big nations that speak difficult foreign languages, and whose words you would not understand – if I sent you to them, they would listen to you; but the House of Israel will not listen to you because it will not listen to me.

The Bible, Ezekiel 2:5 (Jerusalem Bible)

57:9 In the beginning was the Word, and the Word was with God, and the Word was God.

The Bible, John 1:1 (Authorized Version of 1611)

57:10 Man does not live on bread alone, but on every word that comes from the mouth of God.

The Bible, Matthew 4:4 (Jerusalem Bible)

57:11 Now your word is a lamp to my feet, a light on my path.

The Bible, Psalms 119:105 (Jerusalem Bible)

57:12 Both read the Bible day and night, / But thou read'st black where I read white.

William Blake, 1810, The Everlasting Gospel, alpha

57:13 It is expedient that Baptism be administered in the vulgar tongue.

Book of Common Prayer, 1562, 'Public Baptism of Infants', Introduction

57:14 It is a thing plainly repugnant to the Word of God, and the custom of the Primitive Church, to have publick Prayer in the Church, or to minister the Sacraments in a tongue not understanded of the people.

Book of Common Prayer, 1562, Articles of Religion, no. 24

57:15 The Lord Buddha has said: in the language of angels, / of serpents, of fairies, / in the speech of the demons, / the talk of the humans, / in them all I've expounded / the dharma's deep teachings, / and in any tongue / that a being may grasp them.

Buddhist Scriptures, c. 18th century, 'The Buddha's

Law among the Birds [Bya Chos]' (trans. E. Conze, 1959), II, Ch. 1, Sect. 5

57:16 Communications between God and man must always be either above words or below them; for with words come in translations, and all the interminable questions therewith connected.

Samuel Butler (1835–1902), The Note-Books of Samuel Butler (1912)

57:17 Our version of the Bible is to be loved and prized for this, as for a thousand other things, – that it has preserved a purity of meaning to many terms of natural objects. Without this holdfast, our vitiated imaginations would refine away language to mere abstractions.

Samuel Taylor Coleridge, 24 June 1827, in Henry Nelson Coleridge (ed.), Specimens of the Table-Talk of the late Samuel Taylor Coleridge (1835)

57:18 Sermons remain one of the last forms of public discourse where it is culturally forbidden to talk back.

Harvey Cox, 1966, The Secular City, Ch. 10

57:19 [on the preacher's effect on wicked spirits] Again he sounded, and we heard the cry / Of the word-wounded, as about to die.

George Crabbe, 1810, 'Letter IV: Sects and Professions in Religion', 518, in The Borough

57:20 [on the members of the Vestry] Transported beyond grammar by its kindled ire, it spoke in unknown tongues, and vented unintelligible bellowings, more like an ancient oracle than the modern oracle it is admitted on all hands to be.

Charles Dickens, 1858, Our Vestry in Reprinted Pieces

57:21 All slangs and twangs are objectionable everywhere, but the slang and twang of the conventicle [religious meeting] – as bad in its way as that of the House of Commons, and nothing worse can be said of it – should be studiously avoided.

Charles Dickens, 1867–8, The Uncommercial Traveller, Ch. 4

57:22 My God, my God, thou art a direct God, may I not say a literal God . . . [but also] a figurative, a metaphorical God too: a God in whose words there is such a height of figures, such voyages, such peregrinations to fetch remote and precious metaphors, such extensions, such spreadings, such curtains of allegories, such third heavens of hyperboles, so harmonious elocutions, so retired and so reserved expressions, so commanding persuasions, so persuading commandments, such sinews even in thy milk, and such things in thy words, as all profane authors seem of the seed of the serpent that creeps; thou art the dove that flies.

John Donne, 1624, 'The Language of God', in *Devotions Upon Emergent Occasions*, Expostulation 19

57:23 [of the clergy] They are commonly the first corrupters of Eloquence, and the last reform'd from vicious Oratory.

John Dryden, 1672, 'Defence of the Epilogue', appended to *The Conquest of Granada*

57:24 And prayer is more / Than an order of words, the conscious occupation / Of the praying mind, or the sound of the voice praying. / And what the dead have no speech for, when living / They can tell you, being dead: the communication / Of the dead is tongued with fire beyond the language of the living.

T. S. Eliot, 1944, 'Little Gidding', Part 1, in *Four Quartets*

57:25 Go into one of our cool churches, and begin to count the words that might be spared, and in most places the entire sermon will go.

Ralph Waldo Emerson, 1834, *Journals*

57:26 God, to me, it seems, / is a verb / not a noun, / proper or improper.

R. Buckminster Fuller, 1940, in *No More Secondhand God* (1963)

57:27 [on oratory in preaching] Common sense is seldom swayed by fine tones, musical periods, just attitudes, or the display of a white handkerchief: oratorical behaviour, except in very able hands indeed, generally sinks into awkward and paltry affectation.

Oliver Goldsmith, 1758–65, 'On the English Clergy and Popular Preachers', in *Essays*, no. 4

57:28 *Car le mot, c'est le Verbe, et le Verbe c'est Dieu.* For the word is the Verb, and the Verb is God.

Victor Hugo, 1856, *Les Contemplations*, I, Ch. 8

57:29 It is now universally confessed, that men pray as they speak on other occasions, according to the general measure of their abilities and attainments.

Samuel Johnson, 1773, 'Ostig in Sky', in *A Journey to the Western Islands of Scotland*

57:30 When suave politeness, tempering bigot zeal, / Corrected *I believe* to *One does feel*.

Ronald Knox, 1913, 'Absolute and Abitofhell'

57:31 [on a Quakers' meeting] For a man to refrain even from good words, and to hold his peace, it is commendable; but for a multitude, it is great mastery.

Charles Lamb, 1823, 'A Quakers' Meeting', in *The Essays of Elia*

57:32 The English Bible, a book which, if everything else in our language should perish, would alone suffice to show the whole extent of its beauty and power.

Lord Macaulay, 1843, 'On John Dryden', in *Critical and Historical Essays*

57:33 [on translations of the Bible] How silly they are who think they have made it accessible to the vulgar simply by translating it into the vulgar tongues. When people fail to understand everything they read is it only the fault of the words! I would go further. By bringing Scripture that little bit nearer they actually push it further away.

Michel de Montaigne, 1572–80, 'On Prayer', in *The Complete Essays* (trans. M. A. Screech, 1987), I, no. 56

57:34 [on translating the Bible] I also believe that the liberty everyone takes of broadcasting so religious and so vital a text into all sorts of languages is less useful than dangerous. Jews, Mahometans and virtually all the others have reverently espoused the tongue in which their mysteries were first conceived; any changes or alterations are forbidden; not, it seems, without reason. Can we be sure that in the Basque country or in in Brittany there are enough good judges, men adequate enough to establish the right translation in their languages? . . . When it is a case of preaching or speaking our translations can be vague, free, variable and partial: that is not at all the same thing.

Michel de Montaigne, 1572–80, 'On Prayer', in *The Complete Essays* (trans. M. A. Screech, 1987), I, no. 56

57:35 [of God] To those who know thee not, no words can paint! / And those who know thee know all words are faint!

Hannah More, 1801, 'Sensibility', in *Sacred Dramas*

57:36 No writer, sacred or profane, ever uses the words 'he' or 'him' of the soul. It is always 'she' or 'her'; so universal is the intuitive knowledge that the soul, with regard to God who is her life, is feminine.

Coventry Patmore, 1896, 'Aurea Dicta' no. 21, in *The Rod, the Root, and the Flower*

57:37 The Tone in preaching does much in working upon the people's Affections. If a Man should make Love in an ordinary Tone, his Mistress would not regard him; and therefore he must whine. If a Man should cry Fire, or Murder, in an ordinary Voice, nobody would come out to help him.

John Selden, 1689, 'CXI – Preaching', in *Table-Talk*

57:38 Preachers say, Do as I say, not as I do.

John Selden, 1689, 'CXI – Preaching', in *Table-Talk*

57:39 LIZA: Is the Professor coming?

MRS HIGGINS: Certainly not. He cant behave himself in church. He makes remarks out loud all the time on the clergyman's pronunciation.

George Bernard Shaw, 1913, *Pygmalion*, V

57:40 Preaching has become a by-word for a long and dull conversation of any kind; and whoever wishes to imply, in any piece of writing, the absence of everything agreeable and inviting, calls it a sermon.

Sydney Smith, 1855, In Lady Holland, *A Memoir of the Reverend Sydney Smith*

57:41 Of such deep learning little had he need, / Ne yet of Latin, ne of Greek that breed / Doubts 'mongst divines, and difference of texts, / From when arise diversity of sects, / And hateful heresies.

Edmund Spenser, 1591, *Prosopopoia*, 385

57:42 Poetry is the natural language of all religions.

Mme de Staël, 1810, *De l'Allemagne* (trans.)

57:43 Aunt Polly had family worship; it began with a prayer built from the ground up of solid courses of scriptural quotations, welded together with a thin mortar of originality.

Mark Twain, 1876, *The Adventures of Tom Sawyer*, Ch. 4

57:44 The lower wisdom is in the four sacred *Vedas*, and in the six kinds of knowledge that help to know, to sing, and to use the *Vedas*: definition and grammar, pronunciation and poetry, ritual and the signs of heaven. But the

higher wisdom is that which leads to the Eternal.

Mundaka Upanishad, 6th century BC, Ch. 1, in *The Upanishads* (trans. Juan Mascaró, 1965)

57:45 This Atman is the eternal Word OM. Its three sounds, A, U, and M, are the first three states of consciousness, and these three states are the three sounds. The first sound A is the first state of waking consciousness, common to all men. It is found in the words *Apti*, 'attaining', and *Adimatvam*, 'being first'. Who knows this attains in truth all his desires, and in all things becomes first. The second sound U is the second state of dreaming consciousness. It is found in the words *Utkarsha*, 'uprising', and *Ubhayatvam*, 'bothness'. Who knows this raises the tradition of knowledge and attains equilibrium. In his family is never born any one who knows not Brahman. The third sound M is the third state of sleeping consciousness. It is found in the words *Miti*, 'measure', and in the root *Mi*, 'to end', that gives *Apiti*, 'final end'. Who knows this measures all with his mind and attains the final End. The word OM as one sound is the fourth state of supreme consciousness. It is beyond the senses and is the end of evolution. It is non-duality and love. He goes with his self to the supreme Self who knows this, who knows this.

Mandukya Upanishad, 6th century BC, in *The Upanishads* (trans. Juan Mascaró, 1965)

57:46 Preach not because you have to say something, but because you have something to say.

Richard Whately, 1854, *Apophthegms*

57:47 Nor did the Pulpit's oratory fail / To achieve its higher triumph. Not unfelt / Were its admonishments, nor lightly heard / The awful truths delivered thence by tongues / Endowed with various power to search the soul; / Yet ostentation, domineering, oft / Poured forth harangues, how sadly out of place! – / There have I seen a comely bachelor, / Fresh from a toilette of two hours, ascend / His rostrum, with seraphic glance look up, / And, in a tone elaborately low / Beginning, lead his voice through many a maze / A minuet course; and, winding up his mouth, / From time to time, into an orifice / Most delicate, a lurking eyelet, small, / And only not invisible, again / Open it out, diffusing thence a smile / Of rapt irradiation, exquisite.

William Wordsworth, 1805, *The Prelude*, VII, 544

57:48 [Buddha, to Monkey, who has discovered

he has been given blank copies of the Scriptures by the monks] Scriptures ought not to be given on too easy terms or received gratis. ... No wonder they gave you blank copies when they saw you did not intend to make any payment at all. As a matter of fact, it is such blank scrolls as these that are the true scriptures. But I quite see that the people of China are too foolish and ignorant to believe this, so there is nothing for it but to give them copies with some writing on.

Wu Ch'êng-ên, 16th century, *Monkey* (trans. Arthur Waley, 1942), Ch. 28

See also: 6:15, 11:34, 28:2; 29:3, 29:7, 43:9, 45:40, 45:65, 48:32, 64:49

The language used in science and technology

58:1 Science and technology multiply around us. To an increasing extent they dictate the languages in which we speak and think. Either we use those languages, or we remain mute.

J. G. Ballard, 1974, *Crash*

58:2 When it comes to atoms, language can be used only as in poetry. The poet, too, is not nearly so concerned with describing facts as with creating images.

Niels Bohr, quoted in J. Bronowski, *The Ascent of Man* (1975), p. 340

58:3 Science in the modern world has many uses; its chief use, however, is to provide long words to cover the errors of the rich.

G. K. Chesterton, 1905, *Heretics*, Ch. 13

58:4 Do you wish to learn science easily? Then begin by learning your own language.

Étienne de Condillac, 1746, *Essai sur l'origine des connaissances humaines* (trans.)

58:5 We used to think that if we knew one, we knew two, because one and one are two. We are finding that we must learn a great deal more about 'and'.

Arthur Eddington, early 20th century, in A. L. Mackay (ed.), *Dictionary of Scientific Quotations*

58:6 If you want to find out anything from the theoretical physicists about the methods they use, I advise you to stick closely to one principle: Don't listen to their words, fix your attention on their deeds.

Albert Einstein, 1949, *The World as I See It* (trans. A. Harris)

58:7 Science [is] knowledge of the truth of Propositions and how things are called.

Thomas Hobbes, 1650, *Human Nature*, Ch. 6

58:8 Seeing then that *truth* consisteth in the right ordering of names in our affirmations, a man that seeketh precise *truth*, had need to remember what every name he uses stands for; and to place it accordingly; or else he will find himselfe entangled in words, as a bird in lime twiggs; the more he struggles, the more belimed. And therefore In Geometry, (which is the onely Science that it hath pleased God hitherto to bestow on mankind,) men begin at settling the significations of their words; which settling of significations, they call *Definitions*; and place them in the beginning of their reckoning.

Thomas Hobbes, 1651, 'Of Speech', in *Leviathan*, I, Ch. 4

58:9 Specialized meaninglessness has come to be regarded, in certain circles, as a kind of hall mark of true science.

Aldous Huxley, 1937, 'Beliefs', in *Ends and Means*

58:10 Science is all metaphor.

Timothy Leary, 24 September 1980, interview in *Contemporary Authors*, no. 107

58:11 Don't ask *what are* questions, ask *what do* questions, don't ask *why* questions, ask *how* questions.

Karl Popper, quoted by Bernard Levin in the *Sunday Times*, 16 April 1989

58:12 Ordinary language is totally unsuited for expressing what physics really asserts, since the words of everyday life are not sufficiently abstract. Only mathematics and mathematical logic can say as little as the physicist means to say.

Bertrand Russell, 1931, *The Scientific Outlook*

58:13 Mathematics may be defined as the subject in which we never know what we are talking about, nor whether what we are saying is true.

Bertrand Russell, 1917, 'Mathematics and the Metaphysicians', in *Mysticism and Logic*, Ch. 4

58:14 Scientific controversies constantly resolve themselves into differences about the meaning of words.

Arthur Schuster, quoted as an epigraph in C. K. Ogden and I. A. Richards, *The Meaning of Meaning* (1923)

58:15 The task of word-creation has been almost completely left to the very men who are in many ways least fitted to fulfil it, to the men of science, who have evolved a special system of nomenclature of their own.

Logan Pearsall Smith, 1928, 'Needed Words', Society for Pure English, Tract 31

58:16 The chasm between the languages of words and of mathematics grows constantly wider. Standing on either rim are men who, in respect of each other, are illiterate. There is as great a sum of illiteracy in not knowing the basic concepts of calculus or spherical geometry as there is in not knowing grammar.

George Steiner, 1967, 'The Retreat from the Word', in *Language and Silence*

58:17 Prayers for the condemned man will be offered on an adding machine. Numbers constitute the only universal language.

Nathanael West, 1933, *Miss Lonelyhearts*

58:18 The simplicities of natural laws arise through the complexities of the languages we use for their expression.

Eugene Wigner, 1959, *Communications on Pure and Applied Mathematics*, no. 13

See also: 36:91, 54:36

59 *The Language of the Media*

Communication in the press, advertising, radio, and television

59:1 The great Art in writing Advertisements, is the finding out a proper Method to catch the Reader's Eye; without which a good Thing may pass over unobserved, or be lost among Commissions of Bankrupt.
Joseph Addison, 13 September 1710, 'Advertisements', *The Tatler*, no. 224

59:2 It is another great Imperfection in our *London* Cries, that there is no just Time nor Measure observed in them. Our News should indeed be published in a very quick Time, because it is a Commodity that will not keep cold. It should not however be cried with the same Precipitation as *Fire*.
Joseph Addison, 18 December 1711, 'The Cries of London', *The Spectator*, no. 251

59:3 [said to reporters of Senator Barry Goldwater's presidential nomination campaign in 1964] Don't report what he says, report what he means.
Anonymous, quoted in Robert MacNeil, *The Right Place at the Right Time* (1982)

59:4 Good prose is the selection of the best words; poetry is the best words in the best order; and journalese is any old words in any old order.
Anonymous, quoted by Adam Brewer, 21 August 1987, in a letter to *The Times* [cf. 49:31]

59:5 Early to bed and early to rise ain't never no good if you don't advertise.
American slogan

59:6 [of a newspaper] It was a hostile broth of black print.
Saul Bellow, 1961, *Herzog* (Fawcett Crest) , p. 47

59:7 Journalists say a thing that they know isn't true, in the hope that if they keep saying it long enough it will be true.
Arnold Bennett, 1918, *The Title*, II

59:8 [advice from Dr Johnson on writing travel descriptions] We should see how a thing might be covered in words, so as to induce people to come and survey it.
James Boswell, 1785, 'Wednesday, 18th August', in *The Journal of a Tour to the Hebrides*

59:9 Never forget that if you don't hit a newspaper reader between the eyes with your first sentence, there is no need of writing a second one.
Arthur Brisbane, c.1900, quoted in Oliver Carlson, *Brisbane: A Candid Biography* (1937), Ch. 5

59:10 Common phrases are, as it were, so stereotyped now by conventional use, that it is really much easier to write on the ordinary politics of the day in the common newspaper style, than it is to make a good pair of shoes.
Samuel Taylor Coleridge, 21 April 1832, in Henry Nelson Coleridge (ed.), *Specimens of the Table-Talk of the late Samuel Taylor Coleridge* (1835)

59:11 I sing of NEWS, and all those vapid sheets / The rattling hawker vends through gaping streets; / Whate'er their name, whate'er the time they fly, / Damp from the press, to charm the reader's eye.
George Crabbe, 1785, 'The Newspaper', 49

59:12 [on newspaper articles] Their careless authors only strive to join / As many words, as make an even line; / As many lines, as fill a row complete; / As many rows, as furnish up a sheet /

From side to side, with ready types they run, /
The measure's ended, and the work is done.
George Crabbe, 1785, 'The Newspaper', 219

59:13 'For I ain't, you must know,' said Betty,
'much of a hand at reading writing-hand,
though I can read my Bible and most print. And
I do love a newspaper. You mightn't think it,
but Sloppy is a beautiful reader of a newspaper.
He do the Police in different voices.'
Charles Dickens, 1864–5, *Our Mutual Friend*, I, Ch. 16

59:14 They used to say a man's life was a closed
book. So it is but it's an open newspaper.
Finley Peter Dunne, 1902, 'Newspaper Publicity', in
Observations by Mr Dooley

59:15 When journalese was at its rifest the Min-
istry of Health was established – possibly a
coincidence.
John Galsworthy, July 1924, *On Expression*,
Presidential Address to the English Association, p. 12

59:16 The life of the journalist is poor, nasty,
brutish and short. So is his style.
Stella Gibbons, 1932, *Cold Comfort Farm*, Foreword

59:17 [satirizing the style of *Time* magazine]
Backward ran sentences until reeled the mind.
Wolcott Gibbs, 28 November 1936, *New Yorker*

59:18 When he [man] ceased any longer to
heed the words of the seers and prophets,
Science lovingly brought forth the Radio
Commentator.
Jean Giraudoux, 1933, *The Enchanted* (trans.), III

59:19 [Bat Masquerier] 'I always tell My people
there's a limit to the size of the lettering,' he
said. 'Overdo that and the ret'na doesn't take it
in. Advertisin' is the most delicate of all the
sciences.'
Rudyard Kipling, 1913, 'The Village that Voted the
Earth was Flat'

59:20 [Ollyett] He spoke and wrote trade-
English – a toothsome amalgam of American-
isms and epigrams.
Rudyard Kipling, 1913, 'The Village that Voted the
Earth was Flat'

59:21 Journalists write because they have nothing to say, and have something to say because
they write.
Karl Kraus, 1909, 'In Hollow Heads', in *Half-truths
and One-and-a-half Truths* (trans., 1976)

59:22 Newspapers always excite curiosity. No

one ever lays one down without a feeling of
disappointment.
Charles Lamb, 1833, 'On Books and Reading', in *The
Last Essays of Elia*

59:23 [the problem facing BBC announcers] To
translate into terms of spoken language –
human, warm, lively, colourful, hesitant – the
dead bones of a script that has been carved out
on a typewriter by somebody brought up to
regard language as a thing of letters, who has
never understood the relation between the
printed language and the spoken language.
Arthur Lloyd James, 1939, 'The Voice of Britain', in
The Listener (2 March)

59:24 Today it is not the classroom nor the
classics which are the models of eloquence, but
the ad agencies.
Marshall McLuhan, 1951, 'Plain Talk', in *The
Mechanical Bride*

59:25 The medium is the message.
Marshall McLuhan, 1964, *Understanding Media*, Ch. 1

59:26 The art of newspaper paragraphing is to
stroke a platitude until it purrs like an epigram.
Don Marquis, in E. Anthony, *O Rare Don Marquis*
(1962), p. 354

59:27 A reporter is always concerned with
tomorrow. There's nothing tangible of yesterday. All I can say I've done is agitate the air ten
or fifteen minutes and then boom – it's gone.
Edward R. Murrow, 31 December 1955, US broadcast
news summaries

59:28 I believe that the BBC, in spite of the
stupidity of its foreign propaganda and the
unbearable voices of its announcers, is very
truthful.
George Orwell, 15 April 1941, in the *Partisan Review*

59:29 There is something very noticeable about
radio-programme phrases. They seem, most of
them, to have a very short life.
Eric Partridge, 1948, 'Those Radio Catch-phrases', in
Words at War: Words at Peace

59:30 The printing-press is the mother of errors.
Proverbial (Italian)

59:31 Good words sell bad wares.
Proverbial (German)

59:32 Words make the market and gold pays.
Proverbial (Italian)

59:33 [on Pinter's early radio plays] Words, isolated in the velvet of radio, took on a jewelled particularity. Television has quite the opposite effect: words are drowned in the visual soup in which they are obliged to be served.

Frederic Raphael, 1980, 'The Language of Television', in L. Michaels and C. Ricks (eds), *The State of the Language*

59:34 In America journalism is apt to be regarded as an extension of history: in Britain, as an extension of conversation.

Anthony Sampson, 1965, *The Anatomy of Britain Today*, Ch. 9

59:35 Those who prefer their English sloppy have only themselves to thank if the advertisement writer uses his mastery of vocabulary and syntax to mislead their weak minds.

Dorothy L. Sayers, 19 November 1937, 'The Psychology of Advertising', in *The Spectator*

59:36 [Puff] Even the auctioneers now – the auctioneers, I say – though the rogues have lately got some credit for their language – not an article of the merit theirs: take them out of their pulpits, and they are as dull as catalogues! – No, sir; 'twas I first enriched their style – 'twas I first taught them to crowd their advertisements with panegyrical superlatives, each epithet rising above the other, like the bidders in their own auction rooms! From me they learned to inlay their phraseology with variegated chips of exotic metaphor.

Richard Sheridan, 1779, *The Critic*, I. ii

59:37 The Press is at once the eye and the ear and the tongue of the people. It is the visible speech, if not the voice, of the democracy. It is the phonograph of the world.

William Stead, 1886, 'Government by Journalism', in *Contemporary Review* (May)

59:38 My Contemporaries the Novelists [journalists] have, for the better spinning out Paragraphs, and working down to the End of the Columns, a most happy Art in Saying and Unsaying, giving Hints of Intelligence, and Interpretations of indifferent Actions, to the great Disturbance of the Brains of ordinary Readers. This Way of going on in the Words and making no Progress in the Sense, is more particularly the Excellence of my most ingenious and renowned Fellow-Labourer, the *Post-Man* [a Whig newspaper]; and it is to this Talent in him that I impute the Loss of my Upholsterer's Intellects.

Richard Steele, 29 May 1710, 'The Dangers of Reading Newspapers', *The Tatler*, no. 178

59:39 What is the difference between unethical and ethical advertising? Unethical advertising uses falsehoods to deceive the public; ethical advertising uses truth to deceive the public.

Vilhjalmur Stefansson, *Discovery* (1964)

59:40 Definition of a slogan: a form of words for which memorability has been *bought*.

Richard Usbourne, 1964, in a letter to his editors

59:41 [Mr Salter, of Boot] 'He's supposed to have a particularly high-class style: "Feather-footed through the plashy fen passes the questing vole"... would that be it?' 'Yes,' said the Managing Editor. 'That must be good style. At least it doesn't sound like anything else to me.'

Evelyn Waugh, 1938, *Scoop*, I, Ch. 1, Sect. 4

59:42 News is what a chap who doesn't care much about anything wants to read. And it's only news until he's read it. After that it's dead.

Evelyn Waugh, 1938, *Scoop*, I, Ch. 5, Sect. 1

59:43 Discourse was deemed Man's noblest attribute, / And written words the glory of his hand; / Then followed Printing with enlarged command / For thought – dominion vast and absolute / For spreading truth, and making love expand. / Now prose and verse sunk into disrepute / Must lacquey a dumb Art that best can suit / The taste of this once-intellectual Land. / A backward movement surely have we here, / From manhood, – back to childhood; for the age – / Back towards caverned life's first rude career. / Avaunt this vile abuse of pictured page! / Must eyes be all in all, the tongue and ear / Nothing? Heaven keep us from a lower stage!

William Wordsworth, 1846, 'Illustrated Books and Newspapers'

59:44 Rock journalism is people who can't write interviewing people who can't talk for people who can't read.

Frank Zappa, quoted in Linda Botts, *Loose Talk* (1980), p. 177

See also: 18:1, 36:28, 48:13

60 *The Performing Arts*

The language of theatre, cinema, and mime

60:1 If there are cat-calls . . . you are sure at least that the audience is still there.
Caryl Brahms and S. J. Simon, 1986, *Six Curtains for Stroganova*, Ch. 13

60:2 Dubbing, like murder, is a craft; one can deplore the end while admiring the means.
Anthony Burgess, 1980, 'Dubbing', in L. Michaels and C. Ricks (eds), *The State of the Language*

60:3 For nature form'd at first the inward man, / And actors copy nature – when they can. / She bids the beating heart with rapture bound, / Raised to the stars, or levell'd with the ground; / And for expression's aid, 'tis said, or sung, / She gave our mind's interpreter – the tongue, / Who, worn with use, of late would fain dispense / (At least in theatres) with common sense; / O'erwhelm with sound the boxes, gallery, pit, / And raise a laugh with anything – but wit.
Lord Byron, 1811, *Hints From Horace*, 151

60:4 A preoccupation with words for their own sake is fatal to good film-making. It's not what films are for.
Raymond Chandler, 7 November 1951, to Dale Warren, quoted in *Chambers Dictionary of Quotations* (1996)

60:5 I mean, the question actors most often get asked is how they can bear saying the same things over and over again night after night, but God knows the answer to *that* is, don't we all *anyway*; might as well get paid for it.
Elaine Dundy, 1958, *The Dud Avocado*, Ch. 9

60:6 If Elizabeth hadn't encouraged Sir Humphrey Gilbert and Sir Walter Raleigh to explore the New World, I'd have been born speaking Spanish instead of speaking (unrecognizably, to be sure) the tongue that Shakespeare spoke. Well, that's of importance to nobody but me. What's important to half the world is that thanks to Elizabeth, Shakespeare was free to speak the tongue that Shakespeare spoke, as an actor/playwright on a public stage. She was the first English monarch who loved the theatre and encouraged it instead of ordering sheriffs to hound the players out of town.
Helene Hanff, 1985, *Q's Legacy*, Ch. 4 [cf. 7:74]

60:7 Words can be deceitful, but pantomime necessarily is simple, clear and direct.
Marcel Marceau, March 1958, *Theatre Arts*

60:8 Words can keep people apart; mime can be a bridge between them.
Marcel Marceau, attributed, late 20th century

60:9 I had now a Shakespeare-trained intellect, and had come to terms with the verse-speaking problem by reaching the truth behind the text *through* the verse – never ignoring it, never singing it (natural speech is essential), but working in harmony with the inherent fabric, rhythm, beat, with full awareness of all the poetic values and nuances.
Laurence Olivier, 1982, *Confessions of an Actor*, p. 165

60:10 [Hamlet, to the players] Speak the speech, I pray you, as I pronounced it to you – trippingly on the tongue; but if you mouth it, as many of your players do, I had as lief the town-crier had spoke my lines.
William Shakespeare, 1600–1601, *Hamlet*, III. ii. 1

60:11 [Hamlet, to the players] Suit the action to the word, the word to the action.

Shakespeare, 1600–1601, *Hamlet*, III. ii. 17

60:12 And how did *Garrick* speak the soliloquy last night? – Oh, against all rule, my Lord, – most ungrammatically! betwixt the substantive and the adjective, which should agree together in *number*, *case* and *gender*, he made a breach thus, – stopping, as if the point wanted settling; – and betwixt the nominative case, which your lordship knows should govern the verb, he suspended his voice in the epilogue a dozen times, three seconds and three fifths by a stop-watch, my Lord, each time. – Admirable grammarian!

Laurence Sterne, 1761, *The Life and Opinions of Tristram Shandy, Gentleman*, III, Ch. 12

60:13 You can pick out actors by the glazed look that comes into their eyes when the conversation wanders away from themselves.

Michael Wilding, attributed, mid 20th century

61 The Musical World

Language in relation to music, opera, and song

61:1 Nothing is capable of being well set to Musick, that is not Nonsense.
Joseph Addison, 21 March 1711, 'The Italian Opera', *The Spectator*, no. 18

61:2 It oftentimes happened likewise, that the finest Notes in the Air fell upon the most insignificant Words in the Sentence. I have known the Word *And* pursued through the whole Gamut [range of notes], have been entertained with many a melodious *The*, and have heard the most beautiful Graces Quavers and Divisions [descants] bestowed upon *Then, For,* and *From*; to the eternal Honour of our *English* Particles.
Joseph Addison, 21 March 1711, 'The Italian Opera', *The Spectator*, no. 18

61:3 I do not mind what language an opera is sung in so long as it is a language I don't understand.
Edward Appleton, 28 August 1955, *Observer*

61:4 Today, what is not worth being said is sung.
Pierre Augustin de Beaumarchais, 1775, *Le Barbier de Séville* (trans.), I. ii

61:5 Let the singing singers / With vocal voices, most vociferous, / In sweet vociferation, out-vociferize / Even sound itself.
Henry Carey, 1734, *Chrononhotonthologos*, I. i

61:6 [of an Irish acquaintance] I remember on one occasion, when she was asked to sing the English version of the touching melody 'The Red-Haired Man's Wife', she replied, 'I will sing it for you; but the English words and the air are like a quarrelling man and wife; the Irish melts into the tune, but the English doesn't.'
William Carleton, 1830, *Traits and Stories of the Irish Peasantry*, Introduction

61:7 Many people apparently don't trust their reactions to art or to music unless there's a verbal *explanation* for it. In music the only thing that matters is whether you *feel* it or not.
Ornette Coleman, 1959, sleeve-note to *Change of the Century*

61:8 The whole problem can be stated quite simply by asking, 'Is there a meaning to music?' My answer would be 'Yes'. And 'Can you state in so many words what the meaning is?' My answer to that would be 'No'.
Aaron Copland, 1939, *What to Listen for in Music*

61:9 Admirable, but what language was he singing in?
Frederick Delius (after a recital of his own songs), in Sir Thomas Beecham, *A Mingled Chime* (1944), Ch. 19

61:10 [the Misses Noriss] They sang in all languages – except their own. German, French, Italian, Spanish, Portuguese, Swiss; but nothing native; nothing so low as native. For, in this respect, languages are like many other travellers; ordinary and commonplace enough at home, but specially genteel abroad.
Charles Dickens, 1843–4, *Martin Chuzzlewit*, Ch. 17

61:11 Playing bop is like playing Scrabble with all the vowels missing.
Duke Ellington, 10 August 1954, *Look*

61:12 [replying to Mozart, who had advised him not to go to England because he could not speak the language] But all the world understands my language.

Franz Joseph Haydn, 1790, in Ian Crofton and Donald Fraser, *A Dictionary of Musical Quotations* (1985)

61:13 I have sat through an Italian Opera, till, for sheer pain, and inexplicable anguish, I have rushed out into the noisiest places of the crowded streets, to solace myself with sounds, which I was not obliged to follow, and get rid of the distracting torment of endless, fruitless, barren attention!

Charles Lamb, 1823, 'A Chapter on Ears', in *The Essays of Elia*

61:14 Music-hall songs provide the dull with wit, just as proverbs provide them with wisdom.

W. Somerset Maugham, 1892, *A Writer's Notebook* (1949)

61:15 As every nation has a particular accent and tone in discourse, so as the tone of one not to agree with or please the other, no more can the fashion of singing to words, for that the better the words are set, the more they take in of the ordinary tone of the country whose language the song speaks, so that a song well composed by an Englishman must be better to an Englishman than it can be to a stranger, or than if set by a stranger in foreign words.

Samuel Pepys, 7 April 1667 (Easter Day), *Diary*

61:16 I know two kinds of audience only – one coughing and one not coughing.

Artur Schnabel, 1934, *My Life and Music* (trans., 1970), II, Ch. 10

61:17 [of the stage] There, Farce is Comedy; bombast called strong; / Soft words, with nothing in them, make a song.

Edmund Waller, 17th century, 'To Mr Creech, on his Translation of Lucretius'

61:18 An unalterable and unquestioned law of the musical world required that the German text of French operas sung by Swedish artists should be translated into Italian for the clearer understanding of English-speaking audiences.

Edith Wharton, 1920, *The Age of Innocence*, I, Ch. 1

61:19 [Lady Bracknell, about the music for a concert] French songs I cannot possibly allow. People always seem to think that they are improper, and either look shocked, which is vulgar, or laugh, which is worse. But German sounds a thoroughly respectable language, and indeed, I believe is so.

Oscar Wilde, 1895, *The Importance of Being Earnest*, I

See also: 51:16

62 *Proverbial Wisdom*

Proverbs, maxims, epigrams, and other succinct expressions

62:1 Among the Ibo the art of conversation is regarded very highly, and proverbs are the palm-oil with which words are eaten.
Chinua Achebe, 1958, *Things Fall Apart*, Ch. 1

62:2 The people's voice the Voice of God we call; and what are proverbs but the people's voice? Coined first and current made by common choice? Then sure they must have weight and truth withal.
Anonymous, 1659, preface to J. Howell, *Proverbs*

62:3 *The maxim, then, is a declaration, but not indeed about particulars*, such as what sort of a man Iphicrates is, but general, nor about all cases, as that the straight is opposite to the curved, but of things in connection with which actions are done, and things that are to be chosen or avoided for action.
Aristotle, 4th century BC, *The Art of Rhetoric* (trans. H. C. Lawson-Tancred), Ch. 2, Sect. 21

62:4 The use of maxims suits the older age, and in connection with things of which one has experience, so that it is improper for one of the wrong age to use maxims, as also with story-telling, and if they are about things of which one is inexperienced, then the effect is foolish and uneducated. And there is a sufficient proof in that peasants are particularly maxim-prone and readily cite them.
Aristotle, 4th century BC, *The Art of Rhetoric* (trans. H. C. Lawson-Tancred), Ch. 2, Sect. 21

62:5 Listen willingly to any discourse coming from God; do not let shrewd proverbs escape you.
The Bible, Ecclesiasticus 6:35 (Jerusalem Bible)

62:6 Inventing proverbs is weary work.
The Bible, Ecclesiasticus 13:26 (Jerusalem Bible)

62:7 If a cultured man hears a wise saying, he praises it and caps it with another; if an imbecile hears it, he laughs at it, and tosses it behind his back.
The Bible, Ecclesiasticus 20:15 (Jerusalem Bible)

62:8 *Epigram, n.* A short sharp saying, commonly in rhyme, characterized by a vivacious acidity of thought calculated to make him of whom it is written wish it had been an epitaph instead.
Ambrose Bierce, 1911, *The Devil's Dictionary* (entry added by E. J. Hopkins for *The Enlarged Devil's Dictionary*, 1967)

62:9 *Epitaph, n.* A monumental inscription designed to remind the deceased of what he might have been if he had had the will and opportunity.
Ambrose Bierce, 1911, *The Devil's Dictionary* (entry added by E. J. Hopkins for *The Enlarged Devil's Dictionary*, 1967)

62:10 *Saw, n.* A trite popular saying, or proverb. (Figurative and colloquial.) So called because it makes its way into a wooden head.
Ambrose Bierce, 1911, *The Devil's Dictionary*

62:11 [Don Quixote, to Sancho] You must not interlard your conversation with the great number of proverbs you usually do; for though proverbs are maxims in brief, you often drag them in by the hair, and they seem more like nonsense.
Miguel de Cervantes, 1605, *The Adventures of Don Quixote* (trans. J. M. Cohen), II, Ch. 43

62:12 [Don Quixote, to Sancho] I do not find fault with a proverb aptly introduced, but to load and string on proverbs higgledy-piggledy makes your speech mean and vulgar.
Miguel de Cervantes, 1605, *The Adventures of Don Quixote* (trans. J. M. Cohen), II, Ch. 43

62:13 A man of fashion never has recourse to proverbs and vulgar aphorisms.
Lord Chesterfield, attributed, mid 18th century

62:14 What is an Epigram? a dwarfish whole, / Its body brevity, and wit its soul.
Samuel Taylor Coleridge, 1809, 'Epigram'

62:15 A man of maxims only is like a Cyclops with one eye, and that eye placed in the back of his head.
Samuel Taylor Coleridge, 24 June 1827, in Henry Nelson Coleridge (ed.), *Specimens of the Table-Talk of the late Samuel Taylor Coleridge* (1835)

62:16 Aphorisms give you more for your time and money than any other literary form. Only the poem comes near to it, but then most good poems either start off from an aphorism or arrive at one ... Aphorisms and epigrams are the corner-stones of literary art.
Louis Dudek, 1994, *Notebooks 1960–1994*

62:17 [Mrs Gibson] 'In short, mamma, one may steal a horse, but another must not look over the hedge,' said Cynthia   'Be quiet, child! All proverbs are vulgar, and I do believe that is the vulgarest of all.'
Mrs Gaskell, 1865, *Wives and Daughters*, Ch. 28

62:18 The epigram has been compared to a scorpion, because as the sting of the scorpion lieth in the tail, the force of the epigram is in the conclusion.
Lilius Gyraldus, 1545, *De poetica historia* (trans.), Ch. 10

62:19 To adopt a motto is, so to say, to choose a text for the sermon of one's life.
Johan Huizinga, 1924, *The Waning of the Middle Ages*, Ch. 18

62:20 One cannot dictate an aphorism to a typist. It would take far too long
Karl Kraus, 1909, 'Riddles', in *Half-truths and One-and-a-half Truths* (trans., 1976)

62:21 An aphorism never coincides with the truth: it is either a half-truth or one-and-a-half truths.
Karl Kraus, 1909, 'Riddles', in *Half-truths and One-and-a-half Truths* (trans., 1976)

62:22 The excellence and efficacy of a *bon mot* depend frequently so much on the occasion on which it is spoken, on the particular manner of the speaker, on the person of whom it is applied, the previous introduction, and a thousand minute particulars which cannot be easily enumerated, that it is always dangerous to detach a witty saying from the group to which it belongs, and to see it before the eye of the spectator, divested of those concomitant circumstances, which gave it animation, mellowness, and relief.
Edmond Malone, 1786, in footnote added to the 3rd edition of James Boswell, *The Journal of a Tour to the Hebrides*, 'Sunday, 15th August'

62:23 There are aphorisms that, like airplanes, stay up only while they are in motion.
Vladimir Nabokov, 1952, *The Gift* (trans.), Ch. 1

62:24 If, with the literate, I am / Impelled to try an epigram, / I never seek to take the credit; / We all assume that Oscar said it.
Dorothy Parker, 1937, 'Oscar Wilde', in *Not So Deep as a Well*

62:25 Psychologically, a catch-phrase often plays the part of a cigarette or a pipe in times of fear or nervousness, in periods of stress or distress. In a world momentarily or temporarily strange or bewildering or hostile or dangerous it serves the ordinary person, you and me and the other fellow, much as a floating spar does a shipwrecked mariner or as, to a lonely traveller, a known face glimpsed in a foreign land.
Eric Partridge, 1948, 'Those Radio Catch-phrases', in *Words at War: Words at Peace*

62:26 He who reads many epitaphs, loses his memory.
Proverbial (Latin)

62:27 A good maxim is never out of season.
Proverbial

62:28 A proverb is the half-way house to a thought.
Proverbial

62:29 A good saying is a good thing, and a proverb sometimes fits into a fancy better than a foot into a shoe.
Proverbial

62:30 Don't quote your proverb till you bring your ship into port.
Proverbial (Scottish Gaelic)

62:31 A proverb does not tell a lie; an empty pipe does not burn.
Proverbial (Estonian)

62:32 A proverb never lies; it is only its meaning which deceives.
Proverbial (German)

62:33 A good proverb does not strike one in the brow, but full in the eye.
Proverbial (Russian)

62:34 A beautiful proverb in the memory is like a golden piece in the money-chest.
Proverbial (Swiss-German)

62:35 A proverb characterizes nations, but must first dwell amongst them.
Proverbial (Swiss-German)

62:36 A proverb is shorter than a bird's beak.
Proverbial (Swiss-German)

62:37 In a proverb you buy with your ears a good lesson at the cheapest price.
Proverbial (Swiss-German)

62:38 A proverb is to speech what salt is to food.
Proverbial (Arabic)

62:39 The proverb is the leaf that they use to eat a word.
Proverbial (Ibo)

62:40 Proverb or parable is the broth of speech.
Proverbial (Ibo)

62:41 A proverb is the horse of conversation; when the conversation droops, a proverb revives it.
Proverbial (Yoruba)

62:42 Proverbs in conversation – torches in darkness.
Proverbial (Basque)

62:43 All the good sense of the world runs into proverbs.
Proverbial

62:44 Proverbs are the children of experience.
Proverbial

62:45 Proverbs are the wisdom of the streets.
Proverbial

62:46 Proverbs lie on the lips of fools.
Proverbial

62:47 The proverbs of a nation are the great book out of which it is easy to read its character.
Proverbial

62:48 The wise make proverbs and fools repeat them.
Proverbial

62:49 Old proverbs are the children of truth.
Proverbial (Welsh)

62:50 Proverbs are like butterflies, some are caught, others fly away.
Proverbial (German)

62:51 Death and proverbs love brevity.
Proverbial (German)

62:52 There are many blunt proverbs, but they have good meanings.
Proverbial (German)

62:53 Proverbs bear age, and he who would do well may view himself in them as in a looking-glass.
Proverbial (Italian)

62:54 Proverbs are salt-pits from which you may extract salt and sprinkle it where you will.
Proverbial (Latin)

62:55 Proverbs are the coins of the people.
Proverbial (Russian)

62:56 Proverbs are little gospels.
Proverbial (Spanish)

62:57 Proverbs are short sentences drawn from long experience.
Proverbial (Spanish)

62:58 In proverbs the conscience of the people sits in judgement.
Proverbial (Swiss-German)

62:59 What flowers are to gardens, spices to food, gems to a garment, and stars to heaven, such are proverbs interwoven in speech.
Proverbial (Hebrew)

62:60 Who does not heed proverbs will not avoid mistakes.
Proverbial (Turkish)

62:61 Solomon made a book of proverbs, but a book of proverbs never made a Solomon.
Proverbial

62:62 It may be true what some men say; it must be true what all men say.
Proverbial (Scottish)

62:63 Old sayings contain no lies.
Proverbial (Basque)

62:64 The truest sayings are paradoxical.
Proverbial (Taoism)

62:65 A proverb is one man's wit and all men's wisdom.
Lord John Russell, 1835, in R. J. Mackintosh, *Sir James Mackintosh*, II, Ch. 7

62:66 The Proverbs of several nations were much studied by Bishop *Andrews*, and the reason he gave was, Because by them he knew the minds of several Nations, which is a brave thing; as we count him a wise man, that knows the minds and insides of men, which is done by knowing what is habitual to them. Proverbs are habitual to a Nation, being transmitted from Father to Son.
John Selden, 1689, 'CXIX – Proverbs', in *Table-Talk*

62:67 [Leonato] Patch grief with proverbs.
William Shakespeare, 1598–9, *Much Ado About Nothing*, V. i. 17

62:68 The proverbist knows nothing of the two sides of a question. He knows only the roundness of answers.
Karl Shapiro, 1964, *The Bourgeois Poet*, Ch. 1

62:69 A short saying oft contains much wisdom.
Sophocles, 5th century BC, *Aletes* (trans. M. H. Morgan), 99

62:70 A man may appear learned, without talking Sentences [maxims]; as in his ordinary Gesture he discovers he can Dance, tho' he does not cut Capers.
Richard Steele, 5 March 1711, 'Mr Spectator Says More of Himself ', *The Spectator*, no. 4

62:71 Try to imagine a famous witty saying that is not immediately clear.
James Thurber, 11 March 1954, letter to Malcolm Cowley

62:72 But an epitaph is not a proud writing shut up for the studious: it is exposed to all – to the wise and the most ignorant; it is condescending, perspicuous, and lovingly solicits regard; its story and admonitions are brief, that the thoughtless, the busy, and indolent, may not be deterred, nor the impatient tired: the stooping old man cons the engraven record like a second horn-book; – the child is proud that he can read it; – and the stranger is introduced through its mediation to the company of a friend: it is concerning all, and for all: – in the churchyard it is open to the day; the sun looks down upon the stone, and the rains of heaven beat against it.
William Wordsworth, 22 February 1810, 'Essay upon Epitaphs' in *The Friend*

62:73 The first requisite, then, in an Epitaph is, that it should speak, in a tone which shall sink into the heart, the general language of humanity as connected with the subject of death . . . and of life.
William Wordsworth, 22 February 1810, 'Essay upon Epitaphs', in *The Friend*

See also: 16:6, 25:74, 41:5, 41:7, 41:14–15, 41:28

63 *Playing with Language*

Puns, jokes, anagrams, wit, and other kinds of language play

63:1 There is no kind of false Wit which has been so recommended by the Practice of all Ages, as that which consists in a Jingle of Words, and is comprehended under the general Name of *Punning*.

Joseph Addison, 10 May 1711, 'False Wit: Punning', *The Spectator*, no. 61

63:2 [of a pun] I shall here define it to be a Conceit arising from the use of two Words that agree in the Sound, but differ in the Sense. The only way therefore to try a Piece of Wit, is to translate it into a different Language: If it bears the Test you may pronounce it true; but if it vanishes in the Experiment you may conclude it to have been a Punn.

Joseph Addison, 10 May 1711, 'False Wit: Punning', *The Spectator*, no. 61

63:3 Every Resemblance of Ideas is not that which we call Wit, unless it be such an one that gives *Delight* and *Surprize* to the Reader.

Joseph Addison, 11 May 1711, 'True, False and Mixed Wit', *The Spectator*, no. 62

63:4 [Marguerite and Louise] We spent tedious hours teaching ourselves the Tut language. You (Yak oh you) know (kack nug oh wug) what (wack hash a tut). Since all the other children spoke Pig Latin, we were superior because Tut was hard to speak and even harder to understand.

Maya Angelou, 1969, *I Know Why the Caged Bird Sings*, Ch. 20

63:5 My little dears, who learn to read, pray early learn to shun / That very silly thing indeed which people call a pun.

Anonymous, 'Address to Children', in *The World of Wit and Humour* (1893)

63:6 [on *Yipe!* and *Wow!*] I personally associate such exclamations with 'zeebs' – a species I lack space to describe, but one of the characteristics of which is compulsive and inappropriate response cries. Enthusiasts for hi-fi, they frequently lapse into the accents of *The Goon Show*.

Alan Bennett, 1981, 'Cold Sweat', reprinted in *Writing Home*, p. 309

63:7 *Pun, n.* A form of wit, to which wise men stoop and fools aspire.

Ambrose Bierce, 1911, *The Devil's Dictionary* (entry added by E. J. Hopkins for *The Enlarged Devil's Dictionary*, 1967)

63:8 [on Johnson's aversion to puns] For my own part, I think no innocent species of wit or pleasantry should be suppressed, and that a good pun may be admitted among the smaller excellences of lively conversation.

James Boswell, 1791, *The Life of Samuel Johnson*, Ch. 61

63:9 For nonsense being neither false nor true, / A little wit to any thing may screw.

Samuel Butler (1612–80), 1670s, 'Satire upon the Imperfection and Abuse of Human Learning', fragments of an intended second part

63:10 For daring nonsense seldom fails to hit, / Like scatter'd shot, and pass with some for wit.

Samuel Butler (1612–80), 1670s, 'On Modern Critics'

63:11 A pun will sometimes facilitate explanation, as thus; – the Understanding is that which *stands under* the phenomenon, and gives it objectivity. You know *what* a thing is by it.

Samuel Taylor Coleridge, 13 March 1827, in Henry

Nelson Coleridge (ed.), *Specimens of the Table-Talk of the late Samuel Taylor Coleridge* (1835)

63:12 A man who could make so vile a pun would not scruple to pick a pocket.

John Dennis, 1781, *The Gentleman's Magazine*, p. 324

63:13 [the Genius of Despair and Suicide] A joke, without any figure of speech, is the death of me.

Charles Dickens, 1838–9, *Nicholas Nickleby*, Ch. 6

63:14 [Mr Weller] Puns may be wery good things or they may be wery bad 'uns, and a female may be none the better or she may be none the wurse for making of 'em.

Charles Dickens, 1867–8, *Master Humphrey's Clock*, Ch. 3

63:15 Some people have an unconquerable love of riddles. They may have the chance of listening to plain sense, or to such wisdom as explains life; but no, they must go and work their brains over a riddle, just because they do not understand what it means.

Isak Dinesen, 1934, 'The Deluge at Norderney', in *Seven Gothic Tales*

63:16 The lowest and most groveling kind of Wit, which we call clenches [puns].

John Dryden, 1672, 'Defence of the Epilogue', appended to *The Conquest of Granada*

63:17 Thy genius calls thee not to purchase fame / In keen iambics, but mild anagram: / Leave writing plays, and choose for thy command / Some peaceful province in Acrostic Land. / There thou mayest wings display and altars raise, / And torture one poor word ten thousand ways.

John Dryden, 1678, *MacFlecknoe*, 203

63:18 A difference of taste in jokes is a great strain on the affections.

George Eliot, 1876, *Daniel Deronda*, II, Ch. 15

63:19 Life and language are alike sacred. Homicide and *verbicide* – that is, violent treatment of a word with fatal results to its legitimate meaning, which is its life – are alike forbidden. Manslaughter, which is the meaning of the one, is the same as man's laughter, which is the end of the other. A pun is *primâ facie* an insult to the person you are talking with.

Oliver Wendell Holmes, senior, 1858, *The Autocrat of the Breakfast Table*, Ch. 1

63:20 People that make puns are like wanton boys that put coppers on the railroad tracks. They amuse themselves and other children, but their little trick may upset a freight train of conversation for the sake of a battered witticism.

Oliver Wendell Holmes, senior, 1858, *The Autocrat of the Breakfast Table*, Ch. 1

63:21 A pun hath a hearty kind of present ear-kissing smack with it; you can no more transmit it in its pristine flavour, than you can send a kiss. – Have you not tried in some instances to palm off a yesterday's pun upon a gentleman, and has it answered? Not but it was new to his hearing, but it did not seem to come new from you. It did not hitch in. It was like picking up at a village ale-house a two-days-old newspaper. You have not seen it before, but you resent the stale thing as an affront. This sort of merchandise above all requires a quick return. A pun, and its recognitory laugh, must be co-instantaneous. The one is the brisk lightning, the other the fierce thunder. A moment's interval, and the link is snapped. A pun is reflected from a friend's face as from a mirror. Who would consult his sweet visnomy, if the polished surface were two or three minutes (not to speak of twelve-months . . .) in giving back its copy?

Charles Lamb, 1823, 'Distant Correspondents', in *The Essays of Elia*

63:22 A pun is not bound by the laws which limit nicer wit. It is a pistol let off at the ear; not a feather to tickle the intellect.

Charles Lamb, 1833, 'Popular Fallacies – ix', in *The Last Essays of Elia*

63:23 Who has not at one time or other been at a party of professors (himself perhaps an old offender in that line), where, after ringing a round of the most ingenious conceits, every man contributing his shot, and some there the most expert shooters of the day; after making a poor *word* run the gauntlet till it is ready to drop; after hunting and winding it through all the possible ambages of similar sounds; after squeezing and hauling, and tugging at it, till the very milk of it will not yield a drop further, – suddenly some obscure, unthought-of fellow in a corner, who was never 'prentice to the trade, whom the company for very pity passed over, as we do by a known poor man when a money-subscription is going round, no one calling upon him for his quota – has all at once come out with something so whimsical, yet so pertinent; so brazen in its pretensions, yet so impossible to be denied; so exquisitely good, and so deplorably bad, at the same time, – that it has proved a Robin Hood's shot; any thing ulterior to that is despaired of; and the party breaks up, unanimously voting it to be the very worst (that is, best) pun of the evening.

Charles Lamb, 1833, 'Popular Fallacies – ix', in *The Last Essays of Elia*

63:24 The last breath I drew in he wished might be through a pipe and exhaled in a pun.

Charles Lamb, 9 January 1834, quoted in W. Toynbee (ed.), *Diaries of William Charles Macready 1833–1851* (1912)

63:25 There's a hell of a distance between wise-cracking and wit. Wit has truth in it; wise-cracking is simply callisthenics with words.

Dorothy Parker, 1956, in *Paris Review*, p. 81

63:26 The goodness of the true pun is in the direct ratio of its intolerability.

Edgar Allan Poe, 1844–9, *Marginalia*, Ch. 1

63:27 [King Richard, reacting to Gaunt's punning on his own name] Can sick men play so nicely with their names?

William Shakespeare, 1595, *Richard II*, II. i. 84

63:28 SECOND LORD DUMAINE [choosing an interpreter for the nonsense-language to be used to Paroles]: But what linsey-woolsey [wool and flax = medley of nonsense] hast thou to speak to us again?

INTERPRETER: E'en such as you speak to me.

SECOND LORD DUMAINE: He must think us some band of strangers i'th'adversary's entertainment. Now he hath a smack of all neighbouring languages, therefore we must every one be a man of his own fancy. Not to know what we speak one to another, so we seem to know, is to know straight our purpose: choughs' language, gabble enough and good enough.

William Shakespeare, 1604–5, *All's Well That Ends Well*, IV. i. 11

63:29 Pun-provoking thyme.

William Shenstone, 1737, *The Schoolmistress*, stanza 11

63:30 [Mrs Paradock] I don't mind good, solid, practical puns. I don't mind a pun in real life that means something. In fact I like to see somebody using his boot as a hammer, for instance. That's a practical pun.

N. F. Simpson, 1958, *A Resounding Tinkle*, II

63:31 *Dennis* the critick [John Dennis, 1657–1734] could not detest and abhor a pun, or the insinuation of a pun, more cordially than my father.

Laurence Sterne, 1760, *The Life and Opinions of Tristram Shandy, Gentleman*, II, Ch. 12

63:32 Every poet knows the pun is Pierian, that it springs from the same soil as the Muse . . . a matching and shifting of vowels and consonants, an adroit assonance sometimes derided as jackassonance.

Louis Untermeyer, 1965, *Bygones*

See also: 9:1, 61:11, 61:14

64 Personalities

Linguistically distinctive characters in fact and fiction

64:1 [of Winston Churchill] He still had his glorious sense of words drawn from the special reservoir from which Lincoln also drew, fed by Shakespeare and those Tudor critics who wrote the first Prayer Book of Edward VI and their Jacobean successors who translated the Bible.

Dean Acheson, 1961, *Sketches from Life of Men I Have Known*

64:2 [of himself] He never labored so hard to learn a language as he did to hold his tongue and it affected him for life.

Henry Adams, 1907, 'Diplomacy', in *The Education Of Henry Adams*, Ch. 8

64:3 [Daddy] His voice rang like a metal dipper hitting a bucket and he spoke English. Proper English, like the school principal, and even better. Our father sprinkled *ers* and even *errers* in his sentences as liberally as he gave out his twisted-mouth smiles. His lips pulled not down, like Uncle Willie's, but to the side, and his head lay on one side or the other, but never straight on the end of his neck. He had the air of a man who did not believe what he heard or what he himself was saying.

Maya Angelou, 1969, *I Know Why the Caged Bird Sings*, Ch. 9

64:4 Uncle Tommy, who was gruff and chewed his words like Grandfather, was my favorite. He strung ordinary sentences together and they came out sounding either like the most profane curses or like comical poetry.

Maya Angelou, 1969, *I Know Why the Caged Bird Sings*, Ch. 10

64:5 Herbert Asquith's clarity is a great liability because he has nothing to say.

Arthur Balfour, attributed by George Will in *Newsweek* (9 September 1991)

64:6 Mr Lloyd George spoke for 17 minutes, in which period he was detected only once in the use of an argument.

Arnold Bennett, 1921, *Things That Have Interested Me*

64:7 [of Winston Churchill] He has devoted the best years of his life to preparing his impromptu speeches.

Earl of Birkenhead, attributed, early 20th century

64:8 [referring to a remark by Lord Pembroke] 'Dr Johnson's sayings would not appear so extraordinary, were it not for his *bow-wow way*' ... While therefore Doctor Johnson's sayings are read, let his manner be taken along with them.

James Boswell, 1785, *The Journal of a Tour to the Hebrides*, Introduction

64:9 Dr Johnson did not practice the art of accommodating himself to different sorts of people ... Pliability of address I conceive to be inconsistent with that majestick power of mind which he possesses, and which produces such noble effects. A lofty oak will not bend like a supple willow.

James Boswell, 1785, 'Tuesday 5th October', in *The Journal of a Tour to the Hebrides*

64:10 The brethren o' the Commerce-chaumer / May mourn their loss wi' doolfu' clamour; / He was a dictionar and grammar / Among them a'; / I fear they'll now mak mony a stammer; / Willie's awa!

Robert Burns, 13 May 1787, 'Burlesque Lament for the Absence of William Creech, Publisher'

64:11 '*H*advantageous' breathes Arrius heavily / when he means 'advantageous', / intending 'artificial' he labours '*h*artificial', / convinced he is speaking impeccably while / he blows his 'h's about most '*h*artificially'. / One understands that his mother – his uncle – / his family, in fact, on the distaff side / spoke so. / Fortunately he was posted to Syria / and our ears grew accustomed to normal speech again, / unapprehensive for a while of such words / until suddenly the grotesque news reaches us / that the Ionian Sea has become / since the advent of Arrius / no longer Ionian / but (inevitably) *H*ionian.

Gaius Valerius Catullus, 1st century BC, no. 84, in *The Poems of Catullus* (trans. P. Whigham, Penguin, 1966)

64:12 [of the Prioress] And Frenssh she spak ful faire and fetisly, / After the scole of Stratford atte Bowe, / For Frenssh of Parys was to hire unknowe.

Geoffrey Chaucer, *c*.1392, General Prologue, 122, in *The Canterbury Tales*

64:13 [of the Friar] Somewhat he lipsed, for his wantownesse, / To make his Englissh sweete upon his tonge. [He lisped a little, out of affectation, / To sweeten his English on his tongue]

Geoffrey Chaucer, *c*.1392, General Prologue, 264, in *The Canterbury Tales*

64:14 [of the Pardoner] He moste preche and affile his tonge / To wynne silver, as he ful wel koude. [He would preach and polish his tongue / To make money, as well he knew how]

Geoffrey Chaucer, *c*.1392, General Prologue, 712, in *The Canterbury Tales*

64:15 [of Lord Charles Beresford] He is one of those orators of whom it was well said, 'Before they get up, they do not know what they are going to say; when they are speaking, they do not know what they are saying; and when they have sat down, they do not know what they have said.'

Winston Churchill, 20 December 1912, parliamentary speech in *Hansard*, col. 1,893

64:16 Ramsay MacDonald could squeeze less thought into more words than anyone else I know.

Winston Churchill, attributed by Philip Howard in Richard Buckle (ed.), *U and Non-U Revisited* (1978), p. 47 [cf. 56:15]

64:17 [of himself] A draftsman of words.

E. E. Cummings, quoted in the *New York Times* (30 October 1963)

64:18 [of Winston Churchill] In private conversation he tries on speeches like a man trying on ties in his bedroom, to see how he would look in them.

Lionel Curtis, 1912, letter to Nancy Astor

64:19 [of Dylan Thomas] Now we lament one / Who danced on a plume of words, / Sang with a fountain's panache, / Dazzled like slate roofs in sun / After rain, was flighty as birds / And alone as a mountain ash.

C. Day-Lewis, 1953, 'In Memory of Dylan Thomas'

64:20 Mr Pickwick expressed a strong desire to recollect a song which he had heard in his infancy, and the attempt proving abortive, sought to stimulate his memory with more glasses of punch, which appeared to have quite a contrary effect; for, from forgetting the words of the song, he began to forget how to articulate any words at all; and finally, after rising to his legs to address the company in an eloquent speech, he fell into the barrow, and fast asleep, simultaneously.

Charles Dickens, 1836–7, *The Pickwick Papers*, Ch. 19

64:21 [of Mr Pickwick] 'And such a man to speak,' said Mr Muzzle. 'How his ideas flow, don't they?' 'Wonderful,' replied Sam; 'they come's a pouring out, knocking each other's heads so fast, that they seems to stun one another; you hardly know what he's arter, do you?' 'That's the great merit of his style of speaking,' rejoined Mr Muzzle.

Charles Dickens, 1836–7, *The Pickwick Papers*, Ch. 25

64:22 [of a remark by Ralph Nickleby] If an iron door could be supposed to quarrel with its hinges, and to make a firm resolution to open with slow obstinacy, and grind them to powder in the process, it would emit a pleasanter sound in so doing than did these words in the rough and bitter voice in which they were uttered by Ralph.

Charles Dickens, 1838–9, *Nicholas Nickleby*, Ch. 10

64:23 [of Miss Knag] Every now and then, she was accustomed, in the torrent of her discourse, to introduce a loud, shrill, clear 'hem!' the import and meaning of which, was variously interpreted by her acquaintance; some holding that Miss Knag dealt in exaggeration, and introduced the monosyllable, when any fresh invention was in course of coinage in her brain; others, that when she wanted a word, she threw it in to gain time, and prevent anybody else from striking into the conversation.

Charles Dickens, 1838–9, *Nicholas Nickleby*, Ch. 17

64:24 [Mr Scadder] He was a gaunt man in a huge straw hat, and a coat of green stuff. The weather being hot, he had no cravat, and wore his shirt collar wide open; so that every time he spoke something was seen to twitch and jerk up in his throat, like the little hammers in a harpsichord when the notes are struck. Perhaps it was the Truth feebly endeavouring to leap to his lips. If so, it never reached them.

Charles Dickens, 1843–4, *Martin Chuzzlewit*, Ch. 21

64:25 [of Mr Chillip] He was the meekest of his sex, the mildest of little men . . . It is nothing to say that he hadn't a word to throw at a dog. He couldn't have *thrown* a word at a mad dog. He might have offered him one gently, or half a one, or a fragment of one; for he spoke as slowly as he walked; but he wouldn't have been rude to him, and he couldn't have been quick with him, for any earthly consideration.

Charles Dickens, 1849–50, *David Copperfield*, Ch. 1 [cf. 40:47]

64:26 'I couldn't azackly' – that was always the substitute for exactly, in Peggotty's militia of words.

Charles Dickens, 1849–50, *David Copperfield*, Ch. 3

64:27 [of Littimer] He had not a pliant face, he had rather a stiff neck, rather a tight smooth head with short hair clinging to it at the sides, a soft way of speaking, with a peculiar habit of whispering the letter S so distinctly, that he seemed to use it oftener than any other man; but every peculiarity that he had he made respectable.

Charles Dickens, 1849–50, *David Copperfield*, Ch. 21

64:28 [Littimer, on being asked if Mr Steerforth was well] 'Thank you, sir, Mr. Steerforth is tolerably well.' Another of his characteristics. No use of superlatives. A cool calm medium always.

Charles Dickens, 1849–50, *David Copperfield*, Ch. 21

64:29 [of Conversation Kenge] He appeared to enjoy beyond everything the sound of his own voice. I couldn't wonder at that, for it was mellow and full, and gave great importance to every word he uttered. He listened to himself with obvious satisfaction, and sometimes gently beat time to his own music with his head, or rounded a sentence with his hand.

Charles Dickens, 1852–3, *Bleak House*, Ch. 3

64:30 [of Mrs Pardiggle] Always speaking in the same demonstrative, loud, hard tone, so that

her voice impressed my fancy as if it had a sort of spectacles on too.

Charles Dickens, 1852–3, *Bleak House*, Ch. 8

64:31 [Mr Jarndyce, of Lawrence Boythorn] He was then [at school] the loudest boy in the world, and he is now the loudest man. . . . His language is as sounding as his voice. He is always in extremes; perpetually in the superlative degree.

Charles Dickens, 1852–3, *Bleak House*, Ch. 9

64:32 [of Lawrence Boythorn] There was a sterling quality in this laugh, and in his vigorous healthy voice, and in the roundness and fulness with which he uttered every word he spoke, and in the very fury of his superlatives, which seemed to go off like blank cannons and hurt nothing.

Charles Dickens, 1852–3, *Bleak House*, Ch. 9

64:33 Under this provocation, Mr Smallweed's favourite adjective of disparagement [Brimstone] is so close to his tongue, that he begins the words 'my dear friend' with the monosyllable 'Brim'; thus converting the possessive pronoun into Brimmy, and appearing to have an impediment in his speech.

Charles Dickens, 1852–3, *Bleak House*, Ch. 27

64:34 Mr Vholes, after glancing at the official cat who is patiently watching a mouse's hole, fixes his charmed gaze again on his young client, and proceeds in his buttoned-up half-audible voice, as if there were an unclean spirit in him that will neither come out nor speak out.

Charles Dickens, 1852–3, *Bleak House*, Ch. 39

64:35 [of Sir Leicester Dedlock] His voice was rich and mellow; and he had so long been thoroughly persuaded of the weight and import to mankind of any word he said, that his words really had come to sound as if there were something in them.

Charles Dickens, 1852–3, *Bleak House*, Ch. 56

64:36 In facetious homage to the smallness of his talk, and the jerky nature of his manners, Fledgeby's familiars had agreed to confer upon him (behind his back) the honorary title of Fascination Fledgeby.

Charles Dickens, 1864–5, *Our Mutual Friend*, II, Ch. 4

64:37 [of Bradley Headstone] Grinding his words slowly out, as though they came from a rusty mill.

Charles Dickens, 1864–5, *Our Mutual Friend*, II, Ch. 11

64:38 [of Gladstone] A sophistical rhetorician, inebriated with the exuberance of his own verbosity.

Benjamin Disraeli, 29 July 1878, *The Times*

64:39 [Lawrence Durrell, referring to Gerald's *My Family and Other Animals*] 'I wouldn't mind being lampooned in decent prose,' Larry pointed out, blowing his nose vigorously, 'but to be lampooned in bad English is unbearable.'

Gerald Durrell, 1969, 'Conversation', in *Birds, Beasts and Relatives*

64:40 I discovered another of Ursula's charms, and that was her grim, determined, unremitting battle with the English language. Where other people meekly speak their mother tongue in the way that it is taught them, Ursula adopted a more militant and Boadicea-like approach. She seized the English language by the scruff of the neck, shook it thoroughly, turned it inside out, and forced words and phrases to do her bidding, making them express things they were never meant to express.

Gerald Durrell, 1971, *Fillets of Plaice*, Ch. 6

64:41 [of Aneurin Bevan] The only man I knew who could make a curse sound like a caress.

Michael Foot, 1962, *Aneurin Bevan 1897–1945*, I

64:42 [of Mr Wyvern] His voice was very deep, and all his words were weighed in the utterance. This deliberation at times led to peculiarities of emphasis in single words. Probably he was a man of philological crotchets; he said, for instance, 'pro-spect'.

George Gissing, 1886, *Demos*, Ch. 1

64:43 [of Charles Lamb] His sayings are generally like women's letters; all the pith is in the postscript.

William Hazlitt, 1826–7, *Conversations of James Northcote*

64:44 [on I. A. Richards] A gifted glassblower of language.

John Hersey, 18 July 1988, *New Yorker*

64:45 'Here's an end to any civilized conversation,' Mr Mercaptan complained, hissing on the *c*, labiating lingeringly on the *v* of 'civilized' and giving the first two *i*'s their fullest value. The word, in his mouth, seemed to take on a special and a richer significance.

Aldous Huxley, 1923, *Antic Hay*, Ch. 4

64:46 It was an oddity of Mrs Lowder's that her face in speech was like a lighted window at night, but that silence immediately drew the curtain.

Henry James, 1902, *The Wings of a Dove*, II, Ch. 2

64:47 The devil mostly speaks a language called Bellsybabble which he makes up himself as he goes along but when he is very angry he can speak quite bad French very well though some who have heard him say that he has a strong Dublin accent.

James Joyce, 1936, *The Cat and the Devil*

64:48 [on Winston Churchill] He mobilized the English language and sent it into battle.

John F. Kennedy, 9 April 1963, speech conferring honorary US citizenship on Churchill [cf. 64:55]

64:49 [of an impressive Quaker] He seemed not to speak, but to be spoken from.

Charles Lamb, 1823, 'A Quakers' Meeting', in *The Essays of Elia*

64:50 [of John Foster Dulles' conversational style] Thoughts die and are buried in the silences between sentences.

Anne Lindbergh, 1980, *War Within and Without*

64:51 Walt Whitman, who laid end to end words never seen in each other's company before outside of a dictionary, and Herman Melville who split the atom of the traditional novel in the effort to make whaling a universal metaphor.

David Lodge, 1975, *Changing Places*, Ch. 5

64:52 [of Chaucer] Off our language he was the lodesterre [lodestar].

John Lydgate, 1431–9, *The Fall of Princes*, Prologue, 252

64:53 Mr Robert Montgomery's genius [is] far too free and aspiring to be shackled by the rules of syntax . . . readers must take such grammar as they can get and be thankful.

Lord Macaulay, April 1830, 'Robert Montgomery', in the *Edinburgh Review*

64:54 [of Ruskin] He was one of the few Englishmen I knew who, instead of tumbling out their sentences like so many portmanteaux, bags, rugs, and hat-boxes from an open railway van, seemed to take a real delight in building up their sentences, even in familiar conversation, so as to make each deliverance a work of art.

Max Müller, 1898, 'Literary Recollections III', in *Auld Lang Syne* (3rd edition)

64:55 [of Winston Churchill] He mobilized the English language and sent it into battle to steady his fellow countrymen and hearten those Europeans upon whom the long dark night of tyranny had descended.
Edward R. Murrow, 30 November 1954, broadcast discussion [cf. 64:48]

64:56 Poor Knight! he really had two periods, the first – a dull man writing broken English, the second – a broken man writing dull English.
Vladimir Nabokov, 1941, *The Real Life of Sebastian Knight*, Ch. 1

64:57 [of David Lloyd George] An American author has written a *Short History of the International Language Movement*. The report that a Short History of the International Bad Language Movement is promised from the pen of a gifted Prime Minister has not yet been confirmed.
Punch, 29 March 1922, 'Charivaria', p. 241

64:58 [of Macaulay] He has occasional flashes of silence, that make his conversation perfectly delightful.
Sydney Smith, 1855, in Lady Holland, *A Memoir of the Reverend Sydney Smith*, I, Ch. 11

64:59 [Reverend Mr Veal] Whenever he spoke (which he did almost always), he took care to produce the very finest and longest words of which the vocabulary gave him the use; rightly judging, that it was as cheap to employ a hand

some, large, and sonorous epithet, as to use a little stingy one.
William Makepeace Thackeray, 1847–8, *Vanity Fair*, Ch. 56

64:60 [on Margaret Thatcher] I cannot bring myself to vote for a woman who has been voice-trained to speak to me as though my dog has just died.
Keith Waterhouse, attributed, 1978

64:61 [on Stephen Spender] To watch him fumbling with our rich and delicate English language is like seeing a Sèvres vase in the hands of a chimpanzee.
Evelyn Waugh, quoted by Eric Pace in the *New York Times* (18 July 1955)

64:62 [of Rousseau] Whatever he speaks, he pronounces as an oracle.
John Wesley, 3 February 1770, entry in his *Journal*

64:63 I have horrible nightmares of Sir Almwroth Wright's limp sentences wandering through the arid desert of his mind looking for dropped punctuation marks.
Rebecca West, 17 October 1913, 'Lynch Law: The Tragedy of Ignorance', in the *Clarion*

64:64 [on his wife, Katharine S. White] She would write 8 or 10 words, then draw her gun and shoot them down.
E. B. White, 1979, *Onward and Upward in the Garden*

See also: 23:36, 26:161, 52:46, 56:15

Postscript

The use and abuse of quotations

65:1 The surest way to make a monkey of a man is to quote him.
Robert Benchley, 1936, *My Ten Years in a Quandary*

65:2 *Quotation, n.* The act of repeating erroneously the words of another. The words erroneously repeated.
Ambrose Bierce, 1911, *The Devil's Dictionary*

65:3 If you try to give an on-the-one-hand-or-the-other-hand answer, only one of the hands tends to get quoted.
Alan Blinder, 23 June 1995, 'On Economic Forecasting', in the *Wall Street Journal*

65:4 [on quotation] It gives a kind of papery vitality and independence to, precisely, cultural clichés cut free from the web of language that gives them precise meaning.
A. S. Byatt, 1996, *Babel Tower*, Ch. 14

65:5 That sentences in Authors, like haires in an horse-taile, concurre in one roote of beauty and strength, but being pluckt out one by one, serve onely for springes and snares.
John Donne, 1590s, 'News from the Very Countery'

65:6 [Sir Hugo, to Daniel] Much quotation of any sort, even in English, is bad. It tends to choke ordinary remark.
George Eliot, 1876, *Daniel Deronda*, Ch. 16

65:7 I hate quotations. Tell me what you know.
Ralph Waldo Emerson, 1849, *Journals*

65:8 Next to the originator of a good sentence is the first quoter of it.
Ralph Waldo Emerson, 1875, 'Quotation and Originality', in *Letters and Social Aims*

65:9 [about quotations] No Greek; as much Latin as you like; and never French under any circumstances. No English poet unless he has completed his century.
Charles James Fox, attributed, 18th century, in Benjamin Disraeli, *Endymion* (1880), Ch. 76

65:10 Every quotation contributes something to the stability or enlargement of the language.
Samuel Johnson, 1755, *A Dictionary of the English Language*, Preface

65:11 [on quotation being censured as pedantry] No, sir, it is a good thing; there is a community of mind in it. Classical quotation is the *parole* of literary men all over the world.
Samuel Johnson, 1781, in James Boswell, *The Life of Samuel Johnson* (1791), Ch. 54

65:12 He that has but ever so little examined the citations of writers cannot doubt how little credit the quotations deserve, where the originals are wanting; and consequently how much less quotations of quotations can be relied on.
John Locke, 1690, *An Essay Concerning Humane Understanding*, III, Ch. 16

65:13 A book that furnishes no quotations is, *me judice*, no book – it is a plaything.
Thomas Love Peacock, 1831, *Crotchet Castle*, Ch. 9

65:14 Misquotation is, in fact, the pride and privilege of the learned. A widely-read man never quotes accurately, for the rather obvious reason that he has read too widely.
Hesketh Pearson, 1934, *Common Misquotations*, Introduction

65:15 Nor suffers Horace more in wrong Translations / By Wits, than Critics in as wrong Quotations.

Alexander Pope, 1711, 'An Essay on Criticism', 663

65:16 He who fills his head with other people's words will find no place where he may put his own.

Proverbial (Moorish)

65:17 Seek not to know who said something, but take note of what has been said.

Thomas à Kempis, c.1415–24, *The Imitation of Christ*, I, Ch. 5

65:18 In the dying world I come from, quotation is a national vice. No one would think of making an after-dinner speech without the help of poetry. It used to be classics, now it's lyric verse.

Evelyn Waugh, 1948, *The Loved One*, Ch. 9

65:19 Don't quote Latin; say what you have to say, and then sit down.

Arthur Wellesley, Duke of Wellington, attributed, early 19th century, advice to a new MP

65:20 Some, for *renown*, on scraps of learning doat, / And think they grow immortal as they *quote*.

Edward Young, 1725, 'Satire 1', in *The Love of Fame, the Universal Passion*

See also: 21:62, 55:28

Index of Authors

Index of Sources

Titles of books, plays, large poetic works, independent essays, periodicals, and newspapers are in italics; titles of individual poems, journal articles, and contributory essays are in quotes; untitled items are in roman without quotes. The order of the index is letter-by-letter.

Index of Key Words, Phrases, and Concepts

This index is a guide to the key words, phrases, and concepts specifically related to language which are found in the quotations (or their associated context); incidental comments, observations, and descriptions which happen to be part of the quotations are not indexed.

Short expressions which have achieved status as a widely recognized quotation are indexed as wholes; longer expressions of this kind are broken down into their constituent phrases or key words. When expressions are indexed as wholes, any archaic or dialect spellings and constructions are left unchanged; otherwise they are modernized.

The alphabetical arrangement of the index is word-by-word.

Words, word-elements, and phrases used as citations from an individual language are given in italics, and placed after any equivalent words in roman.

The word 'language(s)' is not indexed as a headword (apart from in a few established quotations); quotations which contain this word are indexed using its associated words.

carving,
– in Latin or Greek 7:70
– of a thought (by words) 2:124
– scripts out on a typewriter 59:23
– words 38:57
– words out of the breath of life 21:87
Casby, Mr (in Dickens) 23:43
Casca (in Shakespeare, *Julius Caesar*) 15:30
case,
– as part of soliloquy 60:12
– in Latin misunderstood 14:39
– in Slaka 14:4
– nominative 23:35–6
– not useful for English 23:28, 23:57, 23:109–10
– of personal pronouns 23:8
casket,
– analogy with language learning 12:6
– key to the (of the tongue) 17:46
casks, analogy with speech 31:23
Cassio (in Shakespeare, *Othello*) 29:102
Cassius (in Shakespeare, *Julius Caesar*) 15:30,
    32:67, 45:78
casting,
– violets into a crucible (analogy with transla-
    tion) 13:50
– words upon curs 40:47
castles, built by rhyme 39:32
casual,
– picking up of rules of composition 23:60
– reading-matter (of the dictionary) 24:22
– words 11:69, 39:26
cat,
– prose books sold to support the 49:52
– talking French grammar 4:5
cat with nine lives, analogy with lying 36:96
cat-calls, proving existence of audience 60:1
catalogues, dull as (of auctioneers) 59:36
catching,
– everyone/no one through words 28:58
– lively things in the trap of phrases 21:79
– mocking is 34:21
– no flies with a shut mouth 31:38
– scorning is 34:23
– the reader's eye 59:1
catch-phrases, analogies for 62:25
catchwords, men living principally by 44:21
catechism, answering in a 39:54
catechizing, picked men of countries 26:139
categories, as words 39:8
caterpillar, state (of a liar) 36:16
cathedrals, of words 38:47
Catherine, Princess (in Shakespeare, *Henry V*)
    15:29
Cauchon (in Shaw) 11:59
caught,
– at words and missed 38:9
– in flight (of sounds) 19:12
cause [= goal], made more strange by a strange
    tongue 11:54

cause [= reason]
– of change in a language 7:45
– of dislike and disgust in language 48:63
– of war by words 37:52
– registered by speech 1:29
cautious, lyricism 8:8
cavalry, regiments of sentences 29:24
cave, oracular 19:42
ceaseless, flaming thought of men 7:42
ceasing,
– to complain/think 2:88
– to heed words of seers and prophets 59:18
Cecily (in Wilde) 11:67, 45:96
celebrities, conversations with 26:68
Celia (in Shakespeare, *As You Like It*) 2:114,
    25:88, 39:54, 40:47
cell, of hearing informed by a spirit aerial 19:42
Celts, talking from Valencia to Kirkwall 26:71
cement, of words 4:8
censor, of words 8:61
censoriousness, of foreign accents 15:2
censorship, official 55:17
censure,
– of lawyers for multiplying words 56:14
– of writers and translators 8:26
centipedes, analogy with sentences 20:27
centrality, of language questions in humanistics
    16:46
centralization, of vocabulary 51:57
centre, well-defined (of English) 24:21
centres, for the propagation of platitudes 44:22
centuple, use/meaning of words 5:28
century, quoting poets after a 65:9
ceremony,
– analogy with words 8:27
– Italian addiction to 11:2
– languages breaking free without 7:5
– of announcement 28:17
Chadband, Mr and Mrs (in Dickens) 28:17
chains, not spared by one too free with words
    29:5
challenge,
– of language diversity 10:9
– writing a 34:33
chambermaid, chatter of the (applying terms to
    the) 16:49
chance,
– not giving true ease in writing 21:69
– nothing left to (in speaking) 52:6
– of listening to plain sense 63:15
– thoughtless (of compound verbs) 23:4
change,
– causes of (in a language) 7:45
– continuous in living languages 7:40
– cycles of linguistic 7:6
– daily (in English) 7:70
– endless (in English) 11:4
– in dialects 16:31
– in English 7:38, 7:66

falsehood,
– absent without speech 36:35
– as truth 36:14
– Bierce's definition of 36:14
– diplomats not worried about 55:1
– injected into language 1:65
– no word to express 36:90
– to deceive the public (in ads) 59:39
falsifying, of words betrays society 37:40
falsity,
– of promises 39:3
– of sentences 5:3, 5:5
– of some readings 24:1
Falstaff (in Shakespeare, *Henry IV*) 4:23, 19:37, 39:53, 45:76
Falstaff (in Shakespeare, *The Merry Wives of Windsor*) 15:28
fame,
– but stammers them 32:71
– pretence to (by using old words) 7:57
– purchased in iambics vs. anagrams 63:17
– rhyme fatal to 49:37
– true to (in translations) 13:17
familiar,
– facts in discourse 2:34
– language 54:16
– words given a spice of novelty 25:47
familiarity,
– difficult to use two languages with 12:25
– in address 52:35
– of flies with authors 48:7
– of words in Gallegan 51:10 with English 11:7
– with words (not helping understanding) 5:41
families, of words 22:26
family talk, characteristics of 26:21
family-vault-full, of correspondence 55:10
famous,
– preserving discourses of the 16:6
– witty sayings are immediately clear 62:71
famous for being famous 45:6
fanatical, phantasims 8:58
fancies,
– in usage exposed 8:26
– that broke through language and escaped 2:8
fancy,
– maze and clue of 49:30
– of the speller 21:30
– of writers 8:24
– proverb fitting into a 62:29
– voice impressing the 64:30
– words not pleasing the 34:12
fancy, vs. *imagination* 5:86
Fanny (in Shaw) 11:58
fantastic,
– tawdry lining words 2:11
– words (if too new or old) 7:58
fantastical, banquet (of words) 29:101
far, words travelling 39:36

farewell, to grammatical compunction 23:84
farewell, as a fatal word 46:10
farmers, sons in school 23:32
fascination, of grammar 23:15
Fascination Fledgeby (in Dickens) 64:36
fashion,
– analogy with words 7:58
– language is purely a species of 8:14
– men of (not using proverbs or aphorisms) 62:13
– of singing to words 61:15
– powerful movements of (in language) 8:65
– words in 7:36
– worn-out poetical 5:26
fashionable,
– conversation 4:7
– slang overused 44:11
fashioning, speech to a clear pronunciation 18:23
fast,
– Latin spoken very 12:23
– running of the tongue 29:78
– talking 15:32
fastening, tongue knows no 29:82
fasting,
– good words don't fill the 6:42
– less weakening than talking 26:58
fat, style 47:26
fatal,
– acting on the strength of metaphors 50:8
– for film-makers to be preoccupied with words 60:4
– to ignore the human origins of language 16:52
– to one's fame and neck (of rhyme) 49:37
– word (*farewell*) 46:10
fate,
– masked through language 18:10
– of hapless lexicography 24:15
– tried to conceal him by calling him *Smith* 45:51
father,
– dialect associated with a 9:4
– did not give words to his child 9:14
– language used to one's 12:47
  learning wisdom from one's 9:8
– of a poem is the poet 49:7
– viewing school lessons 23:31
– words of my 36:40
father, vs. *papa* as mode of address 18:12
father tongue, vs. mother tongue 17:56
fatherland, of words 38:36
fatigue,
– effect of (on speech of women vs. men) 53:18
– of adjectives 39:7
fatuousness, of terms in modern art 54:29
Faulkland (in Sheridan) 46:60
fault,
– common (of end-placed preposition) 23:47
– found with proverbs 62:12
– in a flood of words 30:8
– in style 47:26
– of the mind (not tongue slips) 2:102

Hiawatha (in Longfellow) 40:20
hidden,
– meaning in words 45:43
– sense of proverbs 16:6
– taunt in *never mind* 46:18
hide not thy poison with such sugared words
   36:76
hide-bound, pedants 14:11
hideous, notes of woe 46:11
hiding,
– all that is peculiar (in language) 26:35
– behind the tongue 47:31
– private parts of literature (of punctuation)
   21:68
– secrets not from eyes/ears 4:14
– the truth 36:6
– true meaning (of words) 37:28
hiding place, of words 17:22
hierarchy, of ways of reading literature 24:1
hieroglyphics, poked into paper with a stick
   21:34
hieroglyphs, dead (of words) 38:39
Higgins, Henry (in Lerner) 52:18
Higgins, Henry (in Shaw) 16:62–3, 23:95, 52:43
Higgins, Mrs (in Shaw) 57:39
higgledy-piggledy, proverbs 62:12
High Court of Chancery 56:7
high,
– art of complimenting 32:74
– designs (polished lines accomplishing) 49:18
– esteem (of words) 8:36
– metaphors 50:25
– mode of everyday language (of poetry) 49:54
– paragraph 21:62
– speech 17:5
– words and deeds (distance between) 6:81
high-class, style 59:41
high-flown language 27:3
high-official, method of shaking hands 4:27
high-road, sitting on the (of slander) 36:57
highest,
– achievement of the poet 48:23
– perfection of conversation 19:17
highfalutin bunkum, talked about writing
   21:44
highly-cultivated, language (of English) 37:43
highway
– of thought and speech 8:2
– of talk 25:85
Hilary (in Murdoch) 12:32–3, 17:22, 46:39
Hilda (in Reed) 28:50
hills, indignant (preserving old names) 10:34
him, used for *he* 8:9
hindrance,
– particles as a scurvy 49:21
– to sciences (of language) 1:7
hindside-before-ness, not in poetry 48:44
Hindustani, is salt 11:45
Hinks, Mrs (in Gissing) 52:13

hints,
– at matter's inwardness (from telegraphic sentences) 26:71
– scarce quick in embryo lie 49:83
– to writers to stop at periods 2:74
hippie, jargon of the 54:23
hissing,
– in accents 11:13
– in English 15:1
– of consonants 18:8
– on *c* 64:45
– vocal cords 18:17
historians, metaphors dishonest in 50:24
historical monument (of a dictionary) 24:27
history,
– dictionaries as raw material of 24:9
– journalism as an extension of 59:34
– language as the archives of 1:17
– merely gossip 26:160
– metaphors in universal 28:5
– of a language insinuated by words 49:41
– of a language through collecting words 24:18
– of a nation (in a dictionary) 24:27
– of different intonations 28:5
– of language 3:18
– of sound-changes 18:8
– pain of (in words) 37:79
– prigs writing 42:12
hit, achieved by daring nonsense 63:10
Hitch-Hiker's Guide to the Galaxy, The 13:2, 23:1
hitting,
– newspaper readers with a first sentence 59:9
– of words 40:19
– reader's mind 21:41
hoard, worthless (of antipathies about English)
   8:32
hodgepodge, English as a 7:62
Hodgson, name on every infant's tongue 45:21
hog, slang as the grunt of the human 42:4
hold,
– fast (to ancestors' words) 41:44
– *Lindley Murray* above the waves 23:49
– of one's word 28:47
– on to words 30:18
– one's golden tongue 29:37
– one's peace 29:38, 31:26
– one's peace (of Quakers) 57:31
– the subject 26:41
– the tongue 31:25, 31:64, 41:8, 41:11, 64:2
– the tongue (of slander) 36:58
– unlit pipe in the mouth 14:29
hold back, poets impossible in wartime 49:49
hold in,
– words 30:46
– entrails (of words) 49:62
hold with, abroad 15:8
holiday, and lady terms 39:52
holidays, more for the tongue than the head
   30:42

noun *(cont.)*
– God is a verb not a 57:26
– masculine wooed a feminine 23:6
– phrases 16:23
nouns,
– all imaginable things are (at Lagado) 30:54
– as glasses of wine 4:2
– declining of 23:31
– forming participle passives 8:22
– getting rid of 37:47
– give less delight to God than adverbs 23:86
– Hebrew 43:10
– in conversations 26:3
– in diction 16:3
– in English having six cases 23:57
– in English treated as Latin 23:109
– in style 47:4
– inflection of 23:57
– knowing how to decline 7:21
– lack of 4:2
– less than verbs in importance 6:4
– men who talk of 23:92
– metaphors as the application of 50:2
– of multitude 23:27
– of number 23:27
– of the intellect 5:28
– pertinent and proper 26:3
– Slaka endings of 14:4
– verbs connecting to 23:89
nourished in the womb of *pia mater* (of elo-
    quence) 25:83
nourishment, for growing minds 23:31
novel [= new],
– phrases in discourse 29:33
– use of words 50:6
novelists,
– calling a character Another 48:17
– inventing names 45:92
– naming heroes 45:26
– style of 48:18
– trade of popular 21:18
novels,
– analogy with knitting 48:9
– born from not understanding each other
    28:24
– irritation with the notion of British 46:7
– made in the head 48:9
– made of a long thread of language 48:9
– read backwards 24:1
– splitting the atom of traditional 64:51
– writing 49:52
novelty,
– spice of (for familiar words) 25:47
– words repeated for 7:36
now, like a bomb through a window 46:36
nuances, poetic (awareness of) 60:9
nubble, as a child word 46:16
nuclear war, survivors' effect on English
    7:26

nucleus of England's native eloquence 43:12
number [= frequency],
– of Chinese characters 11:31
– of words is finite 48:12
number [= grammar],
– as part of soliloquy 60:12
– agreement 23:36
– in Latin misunderstood 14:39
– nouns of 23:27
numbers [= metre], compass of 13:19
numbers [= numerals],
– analogy with words 2:22
– only universal language 58:17
numbing, blow (of a person's name) 45:60
nursed, and petted melancholy 9:35
nursery, language of the 27:30
nurses,
– imitated to acquire the vernacular 23:33
– of children must speak correctly 9:31
– teaching one's tongue 46:55
nutlike, word 38:7

O,
– blue colour of 18:25
– represented by various shapes 22:12
oak will not bend like a supple willow 64:9
oath,
– Bierce's definition of 56:2
– swearing a dreadful 43:17
– taking the 56:18
– to say what one means 21:45
oaths,
– are but words 43:7
– are oracles 41:46
– binding upon the conscience 56:2
– borrowing and spending 43:42
– cheat with 43:35
– Continental 43:11
– curtailed by standers-by 43:43
– discourse mixed with 43:15
– discrediting oneself with 36:11
– downright 25.06
– given closer than before (of kissing) 4:22
– have nameless sons 43:30
– keeping one's 43:30
– many (do not make the truth) 36:84
– meaning in the common 43:45
– mouth-filling 43:3
– not swearing by any 43:33
– of prosers 55:7
– referential 43:45
– should be an echo to the sense 43:45
– terminate all strife 43:13
– terrible 43:40
– uttering 43:44
obeying,
– language of the law 56:13
– my call (of words) 38:65
– rules of grammar 8:7